ARTE DEL PUEBLO

The Outdoor Public Art of San Antonio

BY FREDERICK R. PRESTON
& CARMEN TAFOLLA

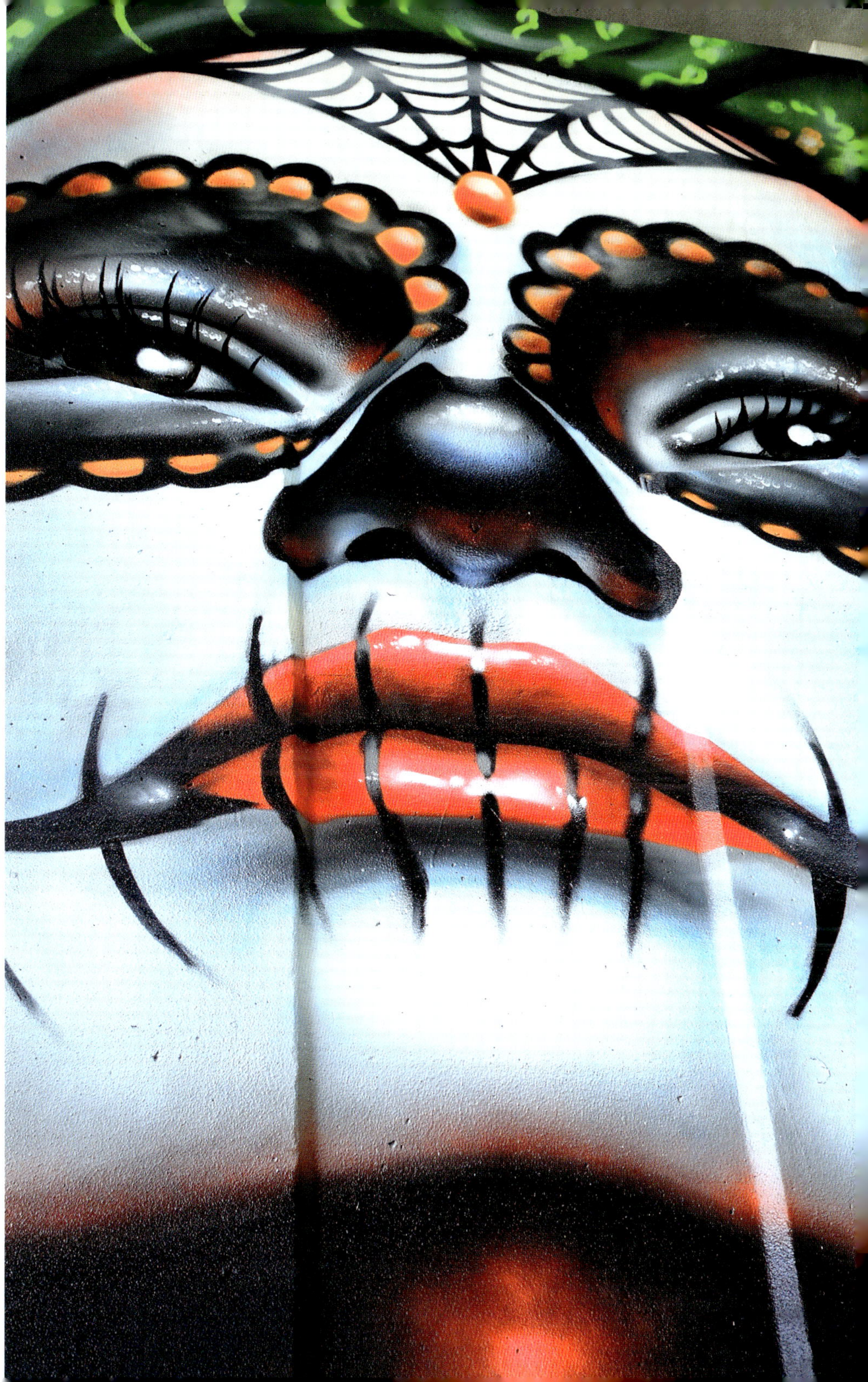

Untitled, 2018. Paul Garson. Aerosol painting.
St. Mary's Street and IH 35.

Other Schiffer Books by Frederick R. Preston
Historic Doorways of San Antonio, ISBN 978-0-7643-3167-1

Other Schiffer Books on Related Subjects
Outsider Art of the South, Kathy Moses, ISBN 978-0-7643-0729-4

Library of Congress Control Number: 2022931737

Interior Designed by Lori Butanis
Cover design by Molly Shields

Front cover: *Poder del Muralismo: Cuentos son Artes*, 2016. Gerardo Quetzatl García, Cardee Garcia, Mary Agnes Rodríguez, and Juan Miguel Ramos. Community member Joleen García blesses the mural with copal. South Brazos Street.

Back cover: *The Saga*, 2014. Xavier de Richemont. A 7,000-square-foot video art projection onto San Fernando Cathedral combines digital art mapping, choreographed music, and narrative storytelling.

Type set in Frankling Gothic

Bernice Appelin-Williams's photo, courtesy of Ramin Samandari
Jesse Treviño's photo, courtesy of City of San Antonio Department of Arts & Culture
Sebastián's photo, courtesy of Joel Salcido
Excerpt from "Homesteaders," courtesy of Rosemary Catacalos
Excerpts from "San Antonio Is a Young Yanaguana Woman," "River Music," and "Fragile Flames," courtesy of Wings Press

ISBN: 978-0-7643-6468-6
Printed in India

Published by Schiffer Publishing, Ltd.
4880 Lower Valley Road
Atglen, PA 19310
Phone: (610) 593-1777; Fax: (610) 593-2002
Email: Info@schifferbooks.com
Web: www.schifferbooks.com

Twenty-Five Windows & a Frame, 2018. Daniel Muñoz. Magik Theater, Alamo Street.

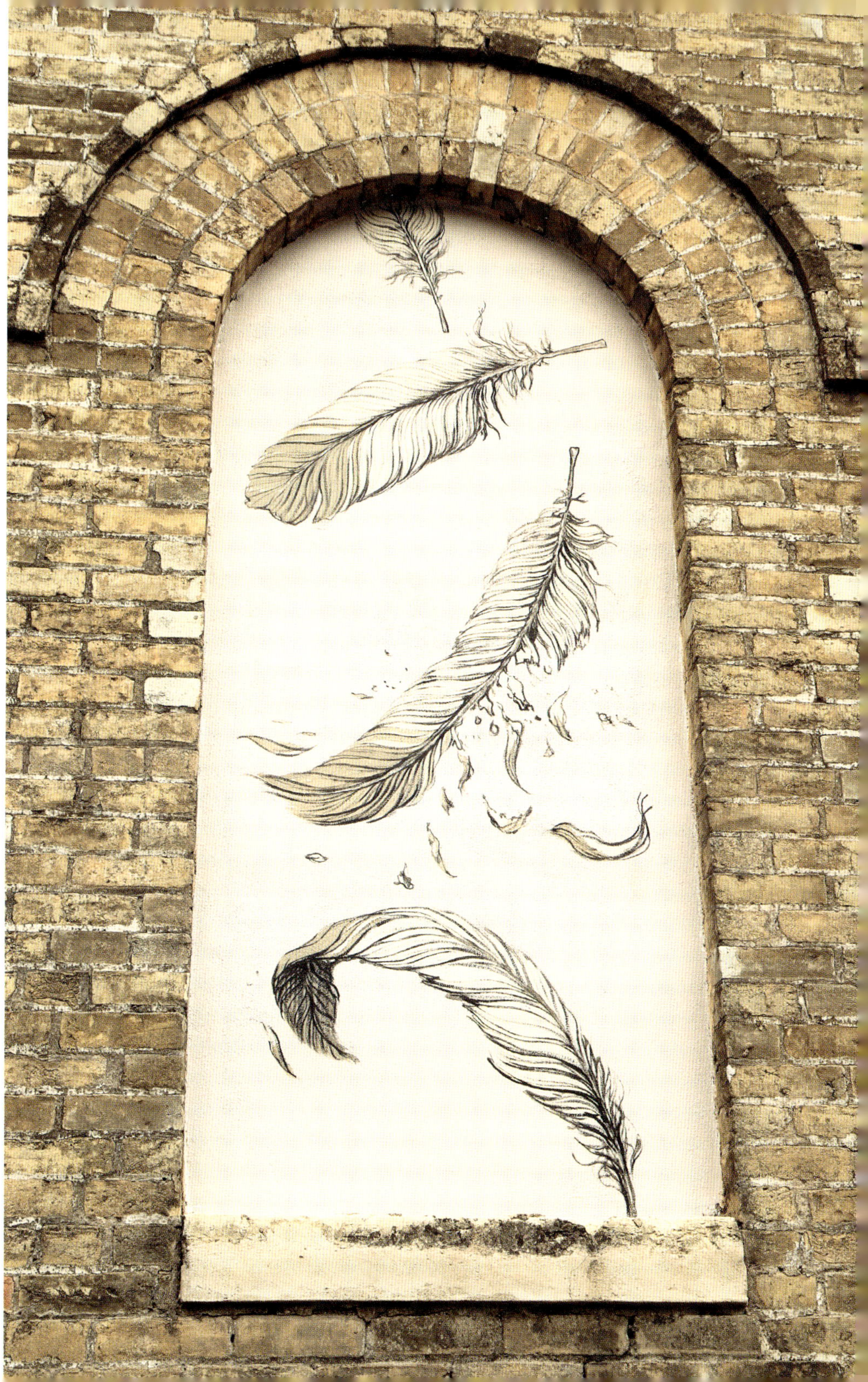

SCHIFFER PUBLISHING®

4880 Lower Valley Road • Atglen, PA 19310

DEDICATION

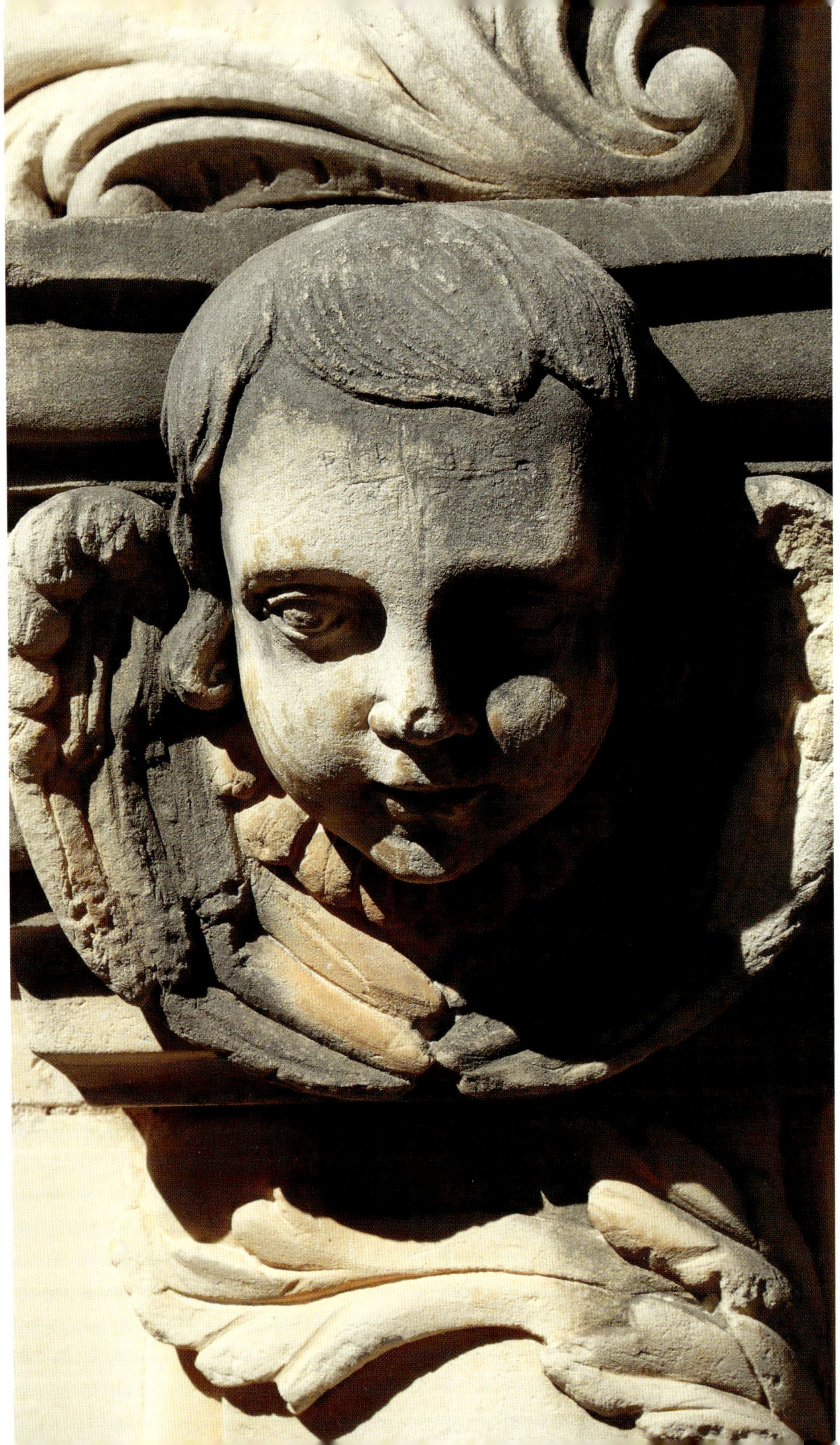

To all the generations of artists here,
past and present:
the first artists of this region
who painted onto rock,
etched into flint, and carved into wood
at the San Antonio River, the Medina, the Gault Site,
and the pre-Mission dwellings
twelve to twenty thousand years ago
and to all those who have migrated here since,
crossing borders with courage
and expanding the cultural richness of humanity

—F.P. & C.T.

Angelito, ca. 1768.
Artist unknown.
Mission San José.

OPPOSITE PAGE
Citlali (Stargazer), 2022.
Pedro Reyes. River Walk
Public Art Garden.

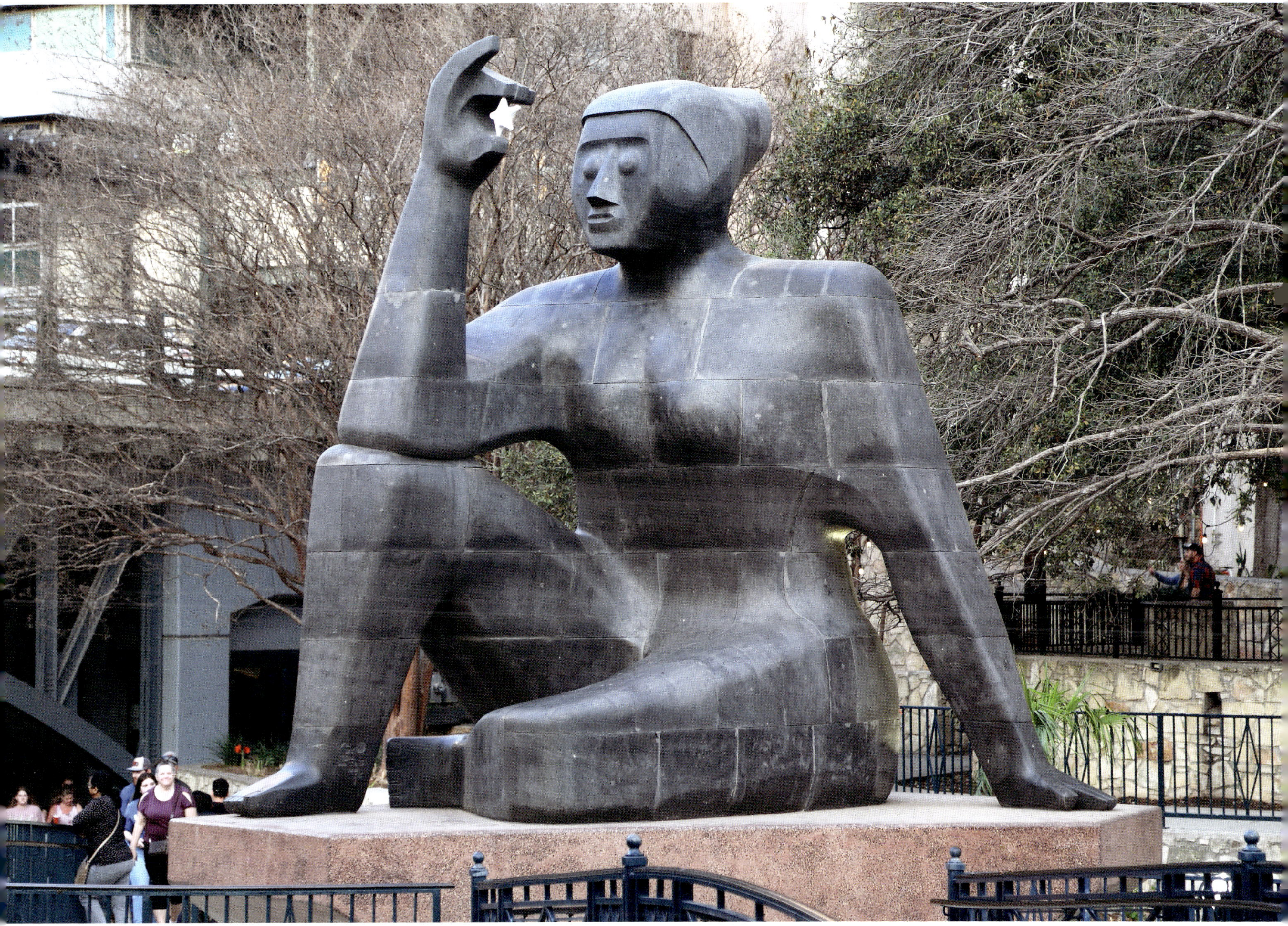

CONTENTS

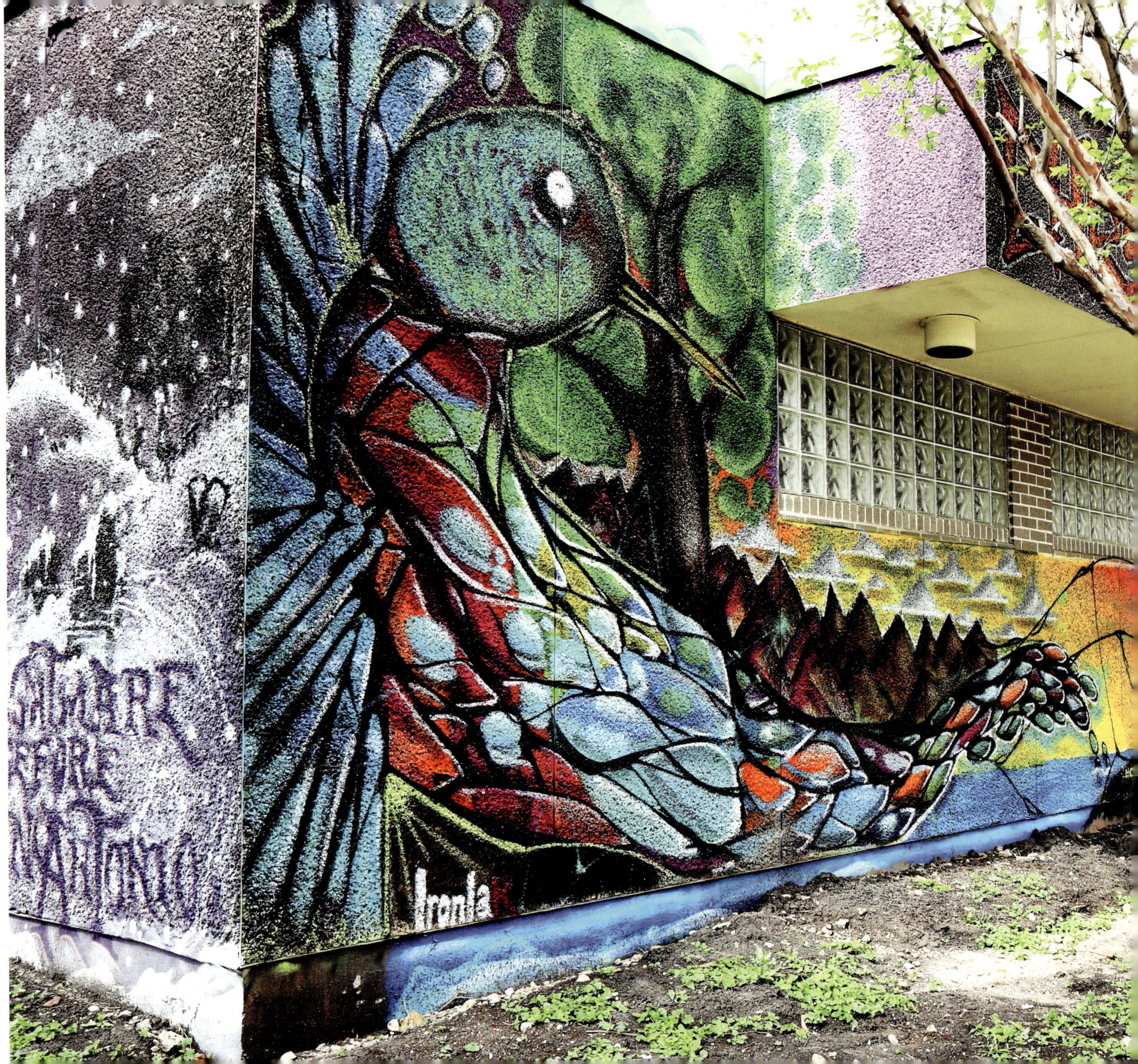

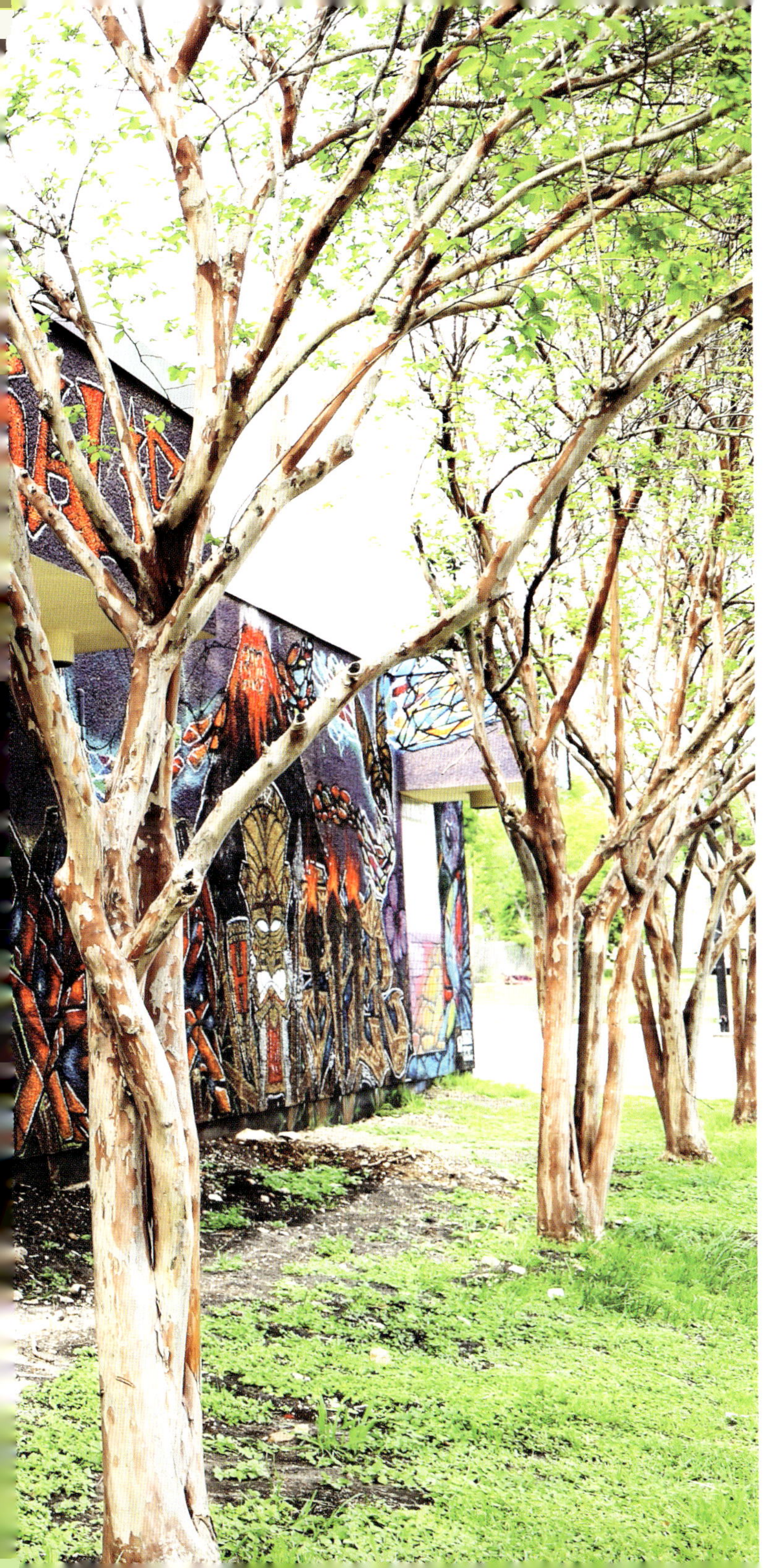

Phoenix, 2016.
Hyper and Trubz.
Chrysalis Ministries,
San Pedro Avenue.

FOREWORD

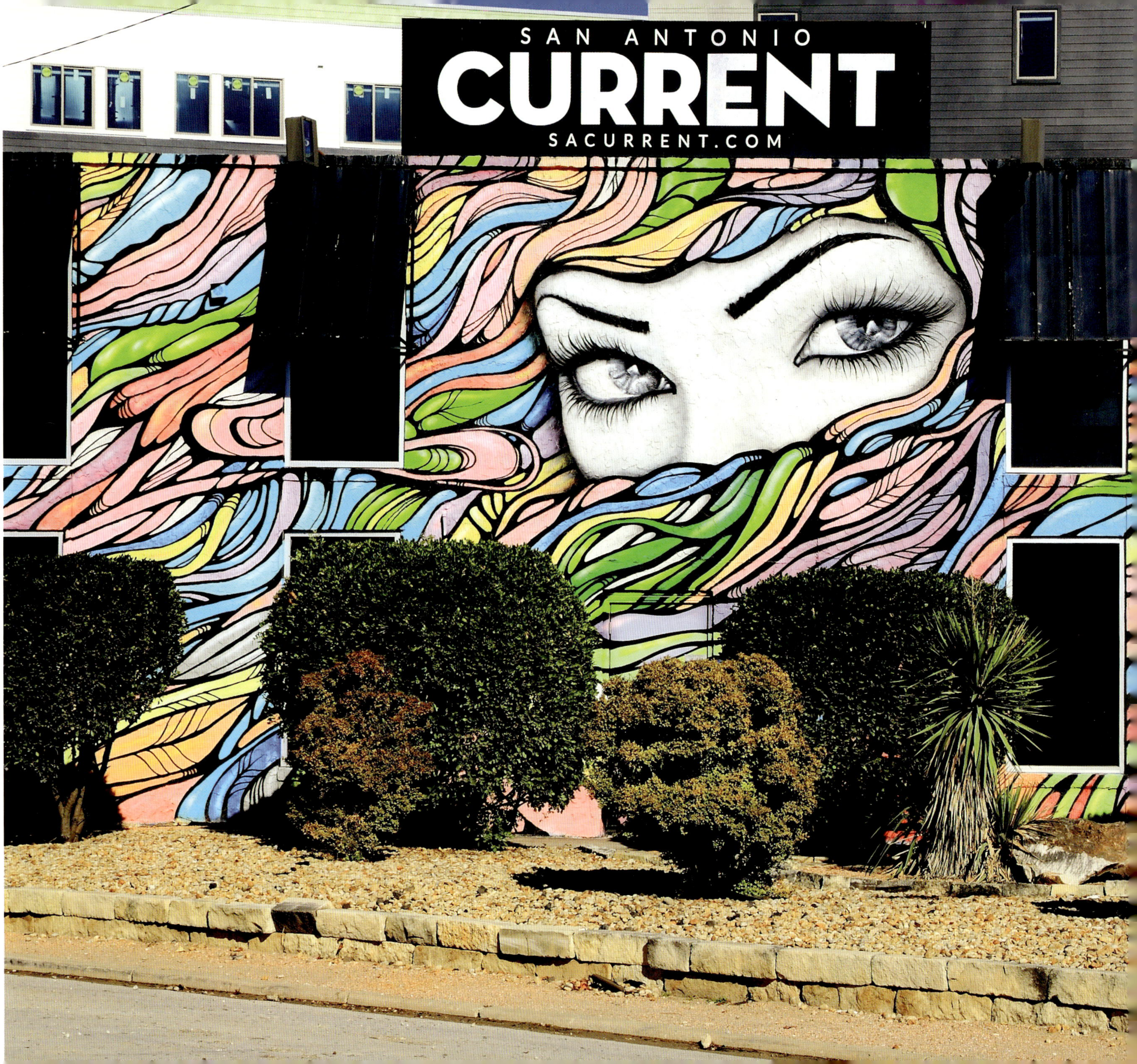

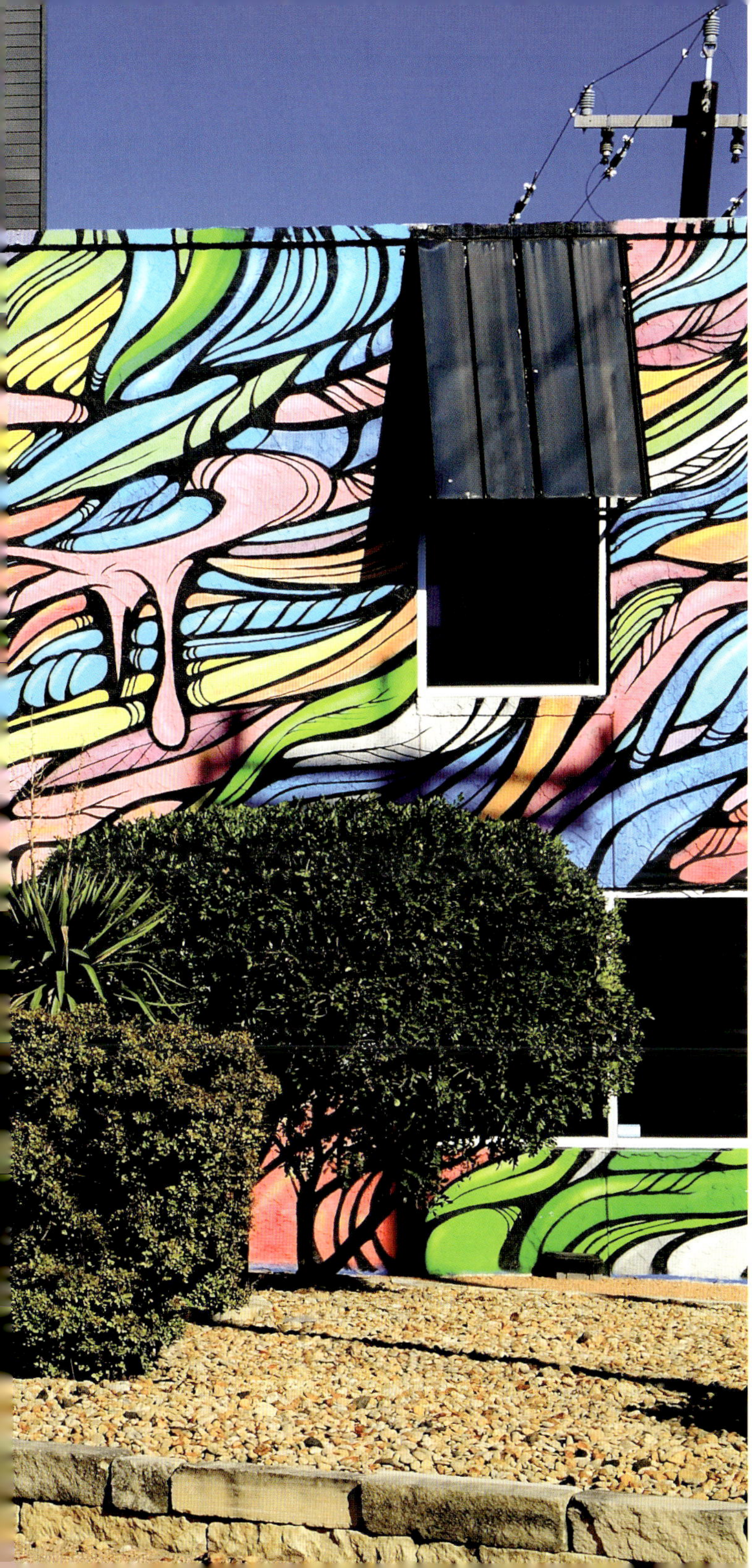

Untitled, 2016. Los Otros. San Antonio Current Office, N. St. Mary's Street. Aerosol painting.

Scientists tell us it is at the confluence of separate streams that we find the mixture of life, a convergence of species to create a new, fertile ecosystem. In short, the spark of life. It is no wonder, then, that volumes have been written about the unique art and cultural heritage of San Antonio de Bejar.

Our great city of San Antonio has been called the crossroads, where America's railroads met, then our highway system, even where the nations of North and Central America continue to meet. At this spot on the map—the confluence—is where cultures, both native and from all over the world, have met for centuries, brought here by the convergence of waterways in South Texas: Salado, Leon, Cibolo, Medina, and the San Antonio River, all fed in part by the Edwards Aquifer.

Public art is the soul of community made manifest—our struggles, our dreams, our losses, and our triumphs. And it's the joining of diverse peoples throughout time in San Antonio that makes our public art unique and critically important to all the world. There is no doubt that public art —from the iconic *La Antorcha de la Amistad* by Sebastián to lesser-known works such as the *Justicia* mural on Buena Vista Law Office—played a big role in helping make our city an internationally renowned cultural destination. Visitors, and even San Antonio residents, learn the stories of our history and culture through the arts.

But the arts in San Antonio mean so much more than that. They are an essential element of our children's education, in many ways just as important as reading, writing, and arithmetic. Exposure to the arts is fundamental to the healthy development of our children's minds and spirits and is key to unlocking their understanding of our city's history and dynamic present, thereby freeing their own potential in the future.

This is precisely why we will continue to ensure that all people, regardless of age or circumstance, have meaningful access to our stories through public art.

This book captures the heart and soul of San Antonio through the moving photography of Dr. Frederick Preston and the captivating poetry of Dr. Carmen Tafolla. May it inspire you and be enjoyed as a testament to the artists past and present who have breathed inspiration here and told the story of our confluence of cultures.

—Ron Nirenberg, mayor, City of San Antonio

ACKNOWLEDGMENTS

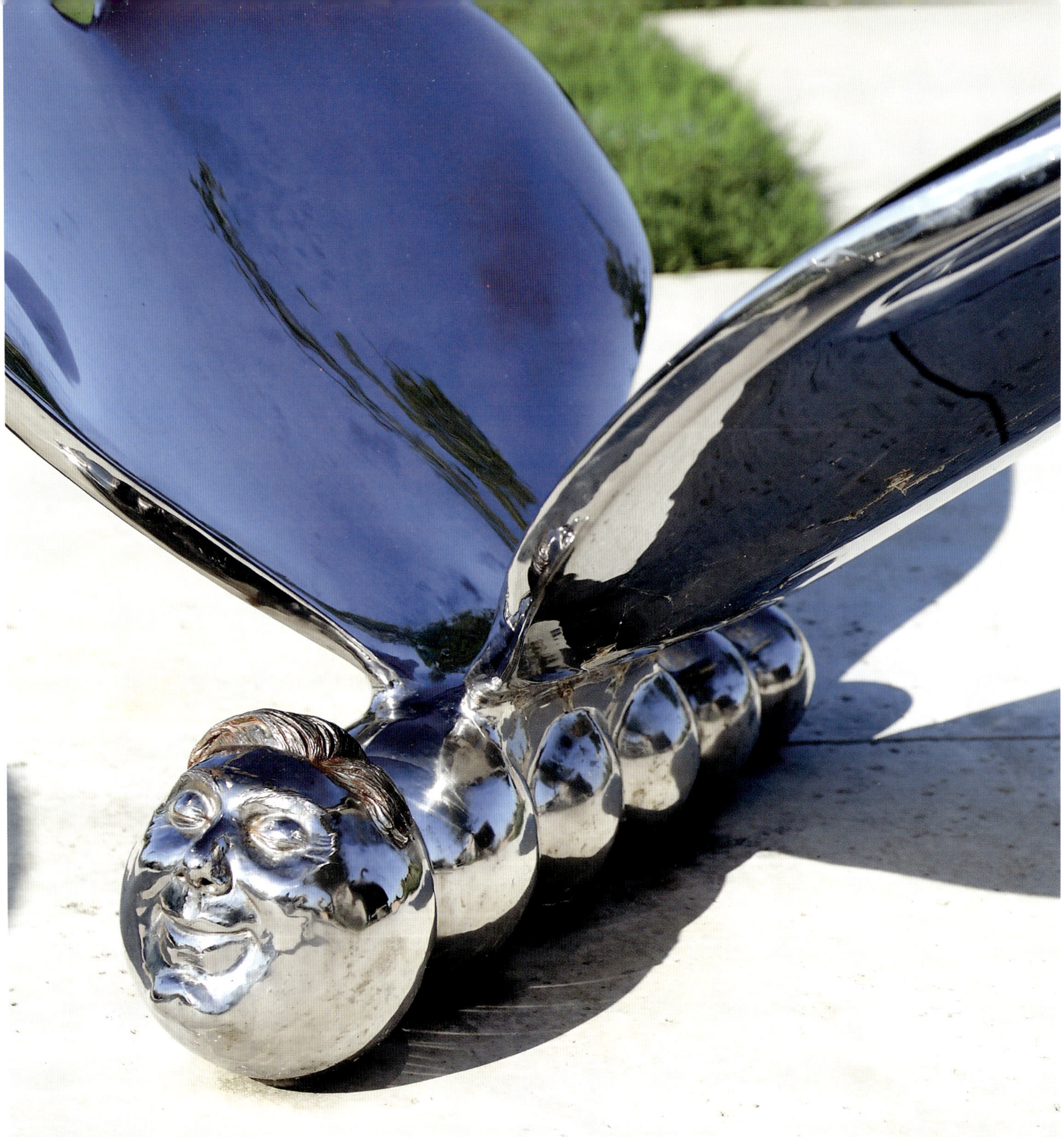

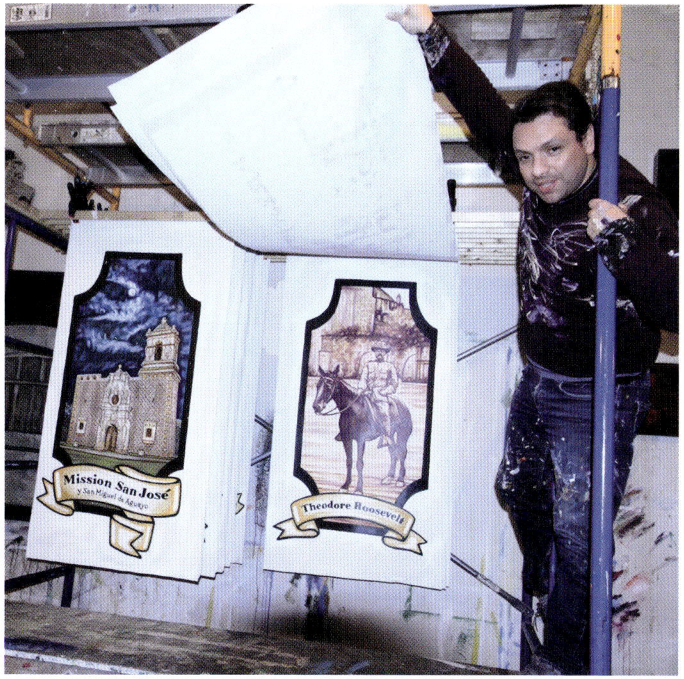

LEFT
Brooks Butterfly, 2018. Brad Oldham and Christy Coltrin. Greenline Park.

ABOVE
Artwork for *Windows to Our Heritage*, 2018. David Blancas. Blancas reviews designs for Mission San José and Teddy Roosevelt in preparation for installation along the World Heritage Mural Trail.

The authors owe deepest gratitude to the artists, arts administrators, museums, and cultural arts organizations of San Antonio for their support of all arts—traditional, cutting-edge experimental, and fusion—from a broad diversity of the city's residents and visitors. We also would like to give a shout-out to the many arts-supporting organizations: Carver Community Center, Esperanza Peace and Justice Center, Guadalupe Cultural Arts Center, Avenida Guadalupe Association, San Antonio Museum of Art, DoSeum Children's Museum, Centro Cultural Aztlán, San Antonio River Foundation, Briscoe Museum of Western Art, Witte Museum, and McNay Art Institute. Thanks also to the universities, schools, and colleges in the greater San Antonio Metropolitan Area, Main Plaza Conservancy, Essex Modern City Art Project, San Antonio Street Art Initiative, Blue Star Arts Complex, San Anto Cultural Arts, the Pearl, Urban-15, San Antonio Botanical Garden, Galeria Eva, and many more, as well as the ever-active Department of Arts & Culture of the City of San Antonio. We appreciate the enthusiastic support of Debbie Racca-Sittre, Sarah Farwell, Jimmy LeFlore, Krystal Jones, and too many more to name.

Also, deepest gratitude to our photo review panel: Lisa Schmidt, Tony Cantú, Joanna Foster, Tonia Fite, Joe Edwards, Evelyn Brown, Letty Tijerina, Lenore Donatt; to our text editors Sally Andrade and Jen Yañez-Alaniz; to our contact detective, Margaret Kanyusik, who provided numerous key contacts; to Alexandra Klein and David Hernández for heroic technical assistance; and to the very special support of artists "Shek," David Blancas, Adriana García, Oscar Alvarado, and Paul Garson, as well as Colleen Swain (WHO San Antonio), Cassandra Parker-Norwicki (Carver Community Cultural Center), Aissatou Sidime (San Antonio Ethnic Art Society), Kris Feldman (Essex Modern City Art Project), Kathy Armstrong (Luminaria), and Kelly O'Connor (Linda Pace Foundation).

Thanks to Rosemary Catacalos for allowing us to quote from her iconic poem "Homesteaders" (in *Again for the First Time*, Tooth of Time Books, 1984; 30th-Anniversary Edition, Wings Press, 2013) and to Wings Press for allowing us to reprint sections of Carmen Tafolla's poems "San Antonio Is a Young Yanaguana Woman," "River Music," and "Fragile Flames" (in *This River Here*, Wings Press, 2014.)

Also, gratitude to Joel Salcido for allowing us to use his amazing photo of Sebastián, to Ramin Samandari for the great artist photo of Bernice Appelin-Williams, and to Laura Nikas and Jen Yañez-Alaniz for the author photos. And to Cheryl Weber, Schiffer Publishing, and all of our many helpers unnamed, *gracias*. It takes a village to birth a book.

INTRODUCTION

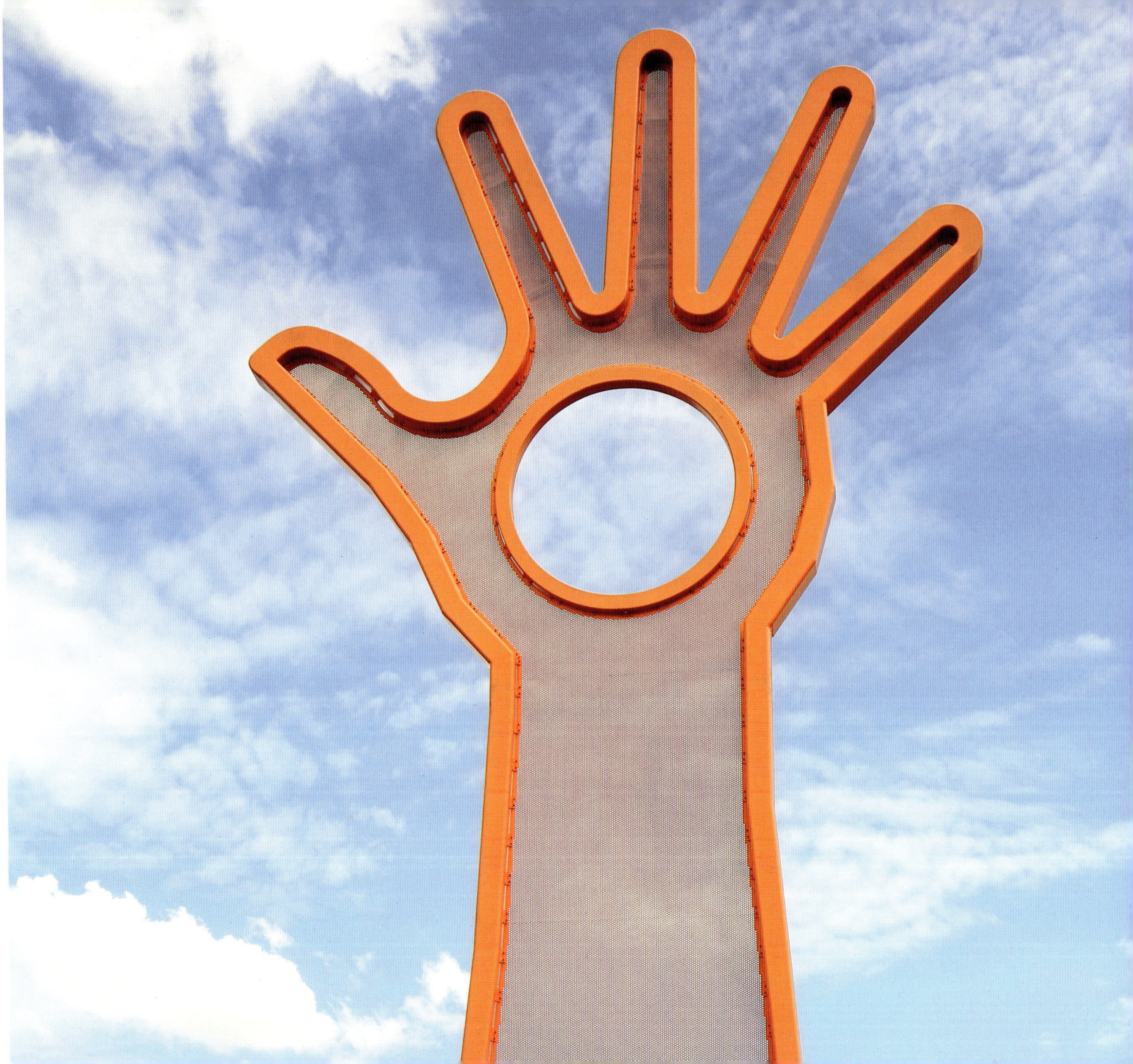

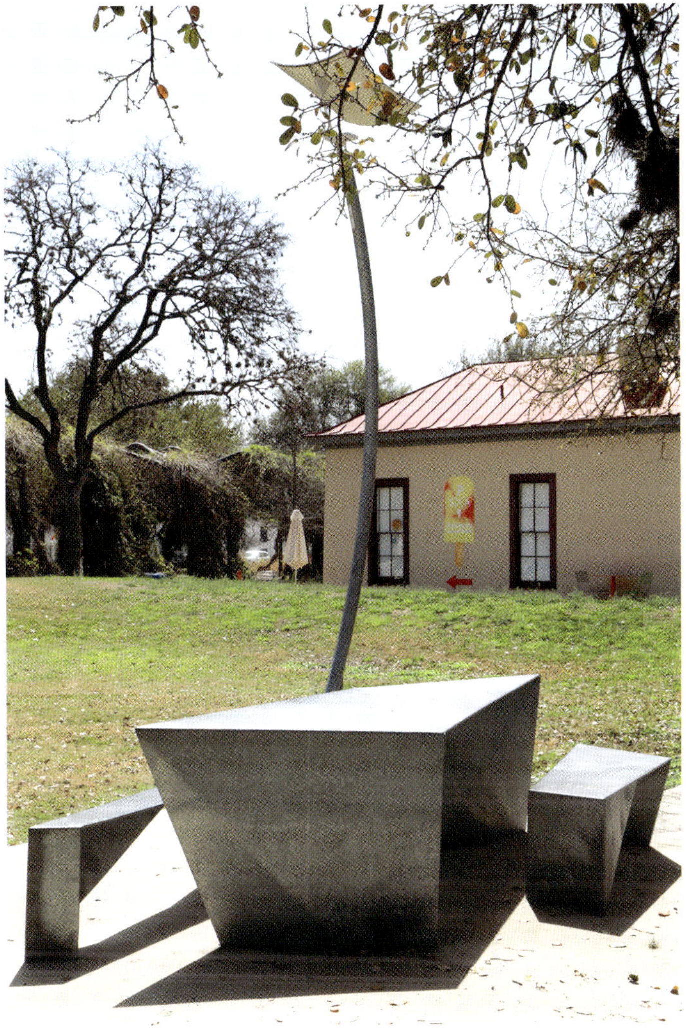

LEFT
Open Hand, Open Mind, Open Heart, 2015. Douglas Kornfeld. Pittman-Sullivan Park.

ABOVE
Kite Table, 2015. Stuart Allen. This table in Hemisfair Park teaches visitors how to build a kite.

San Antonio has long been considered one of America's unique cities. An attractive multicultural crossroads, its history begins with the many Indigenous nations that have lived in this area for thousands of years.[1] The city combines a rich history with the dynamic potential that crossroads bring, and this is reflected in its public art. From the natural beauty of its winding downtown river to the powerful presence of its three-hundred-year-old missions (a UNESCO World Heritage Site and the largest concentration of Spanish colonial missions in North America[2]), this sprawling metropolis exemplifies all the excitement of a city whose hospitals, parks, playgrounds, and corner stores are draped in public art.

Why is art so important in the life of a community? Art shares with us our history, affirms our experiences and passions, helps us understand our identities and values, and, most importantly, gives voice to those stirrings inside our hearts and those longings inside our dreams. Art helps us understand who we are, what we feel, and why we matter.

And why have the authors chosen to focus on *outdoor* public art in this book? Because, like the *muralismo*[3] of the Mexican Revolution (for which San Antonio served as capital in exile), accessibility to *all* is crucial to an art that belongs to the pueblo. That this art is accessible to everyone at no cost is a stride for social and economic justice. And it holds the potential to impact the entire community. Outdoor art becomes a doorway for developing broad-based arts appreciation throughout a city and provides an almost unlimited arts canvas. It offers expanded opportunities to nurture the diverse talents of emerging young artists, seasoned natives, and international artists who find new challenges in this venue. Removing boundaries and obstacles, outdoor art opens up a city full of raw materials to a variety of artists from every part of the world. And as many artists who move here have noted, the lower cost of living and art production enables many to work in studios spacious enough to accommodate metal, stone, and ceramic sculpture. In short, here they can afford to create their artistic visions.

Visitors often comment that despite being the seventh-largest city in the nation, San Antonio feels and acts like a small-town neighborhood. This is neither a myth nor an illusion. It is real. The friendliness and personalism that characterize this city come from a sense of community and a sense of family that is easily reflected in its use of a collaborative model to expand its public arts presence. Many of the city's outdoor art projects involve a joint sponsorship by city, county, and grassroots nonprofits, such as San Anto Cultural Arts,[4] the San Antonio River Authority / San Antonio River Foundation,[5] Luminaria,[6] and the Esperanza Peace and Justice Center.[7] This team approach demonstrates the desire of city and community leaders and representatives to showcase a diversity of artist communities, backgrounds, genres, and styles.

The surge of public art that began here, at a less well-funded pace, in the 1960s and '70s was often initiated and funded by the community and by community cultural organizations. But it gained momentum in 2011 with the city's support and initiation of a formal public art program. The City of San Antonio's Public Art Collection holds over five hundred artworks, more than half of these accessible outdoors. "Public art supports the development, growth, health, and very fabric of what makes San Antonio a top place to live, work, and visit," commented San Antonio Department of Arts & Culture executive director Debbie Racca-Sittre. "The collaborative process of our Public Art

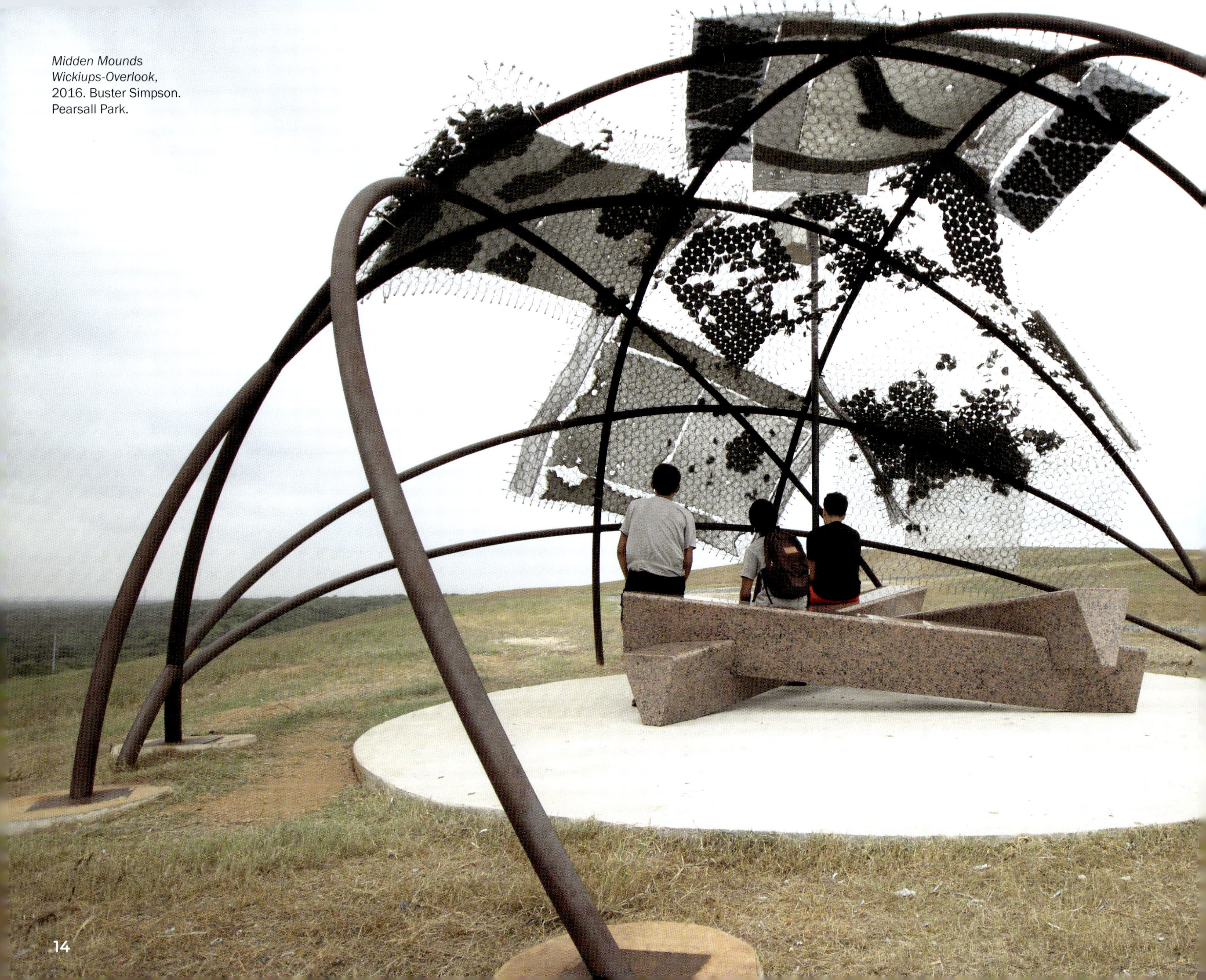

Midden Mounds Wickiups-Overlook, 2016. Buster Simpson. Pearsall Park.

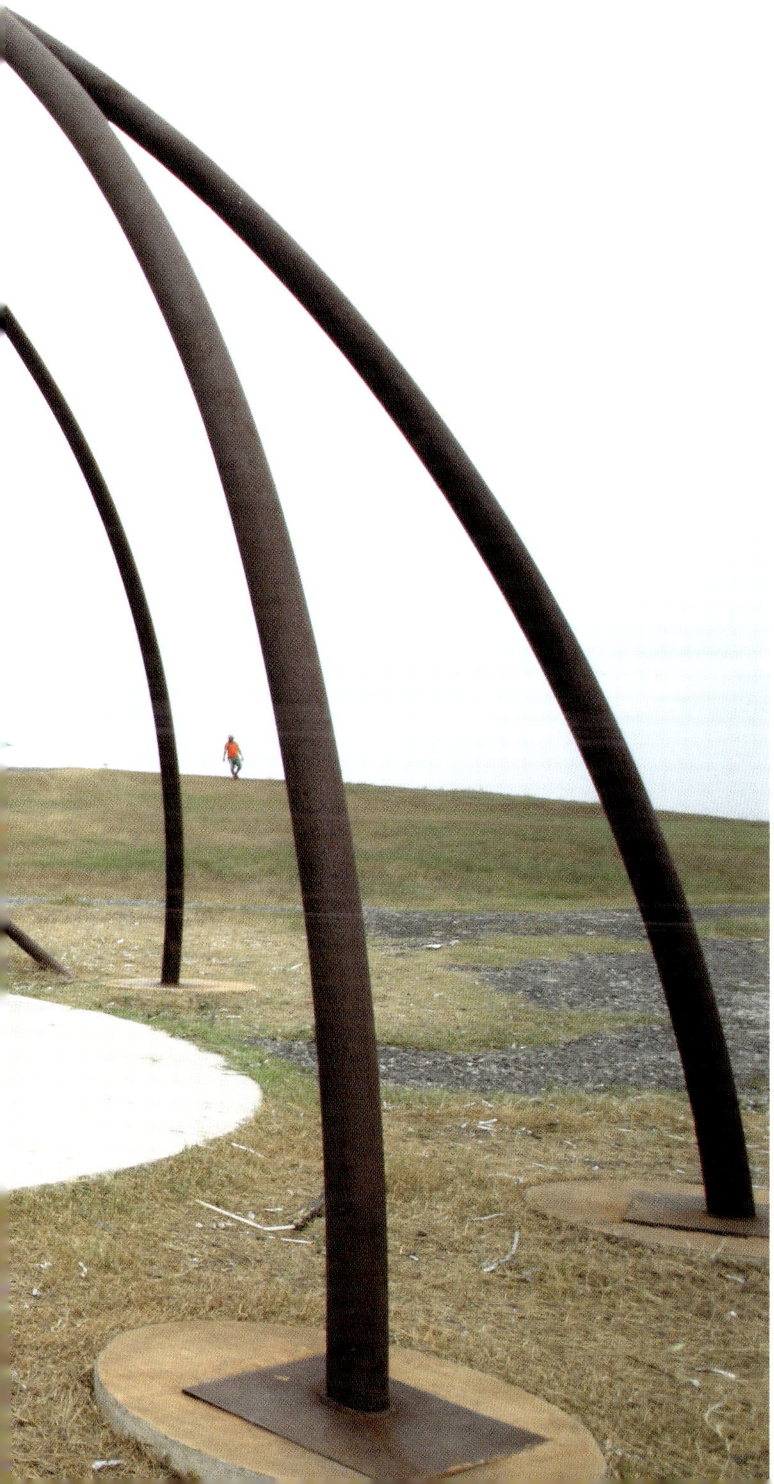

Program allows us to tell our story and history in an authentic and unique way that lasts for generations, while also building toward a brighter future by enhancing the city's identity, character, accessibility, and connectivity."

Perhaps especially unique to San Antonio are the artistic collaborations that reflect an immersive community engagement. One such collaboration is the Árbol de la Vida (page 42), which combines the work of laypeople and professional artists in the more than seven hundred separate sculptures hanging from the Tree of Life that represent the community's experiences and memories. Few cities have such a complete interactive experience that involves a broader community throughout the entire process, from the birth of the ideas to the hands-on production.

Many art projects here welcome all—young students, beginners, and internationally recognized grand masters—working side by side to create murals, Chalk-It-Up artworks on sidewalks, and MujerArtes' ceramic *talleres*. Community inclusion aids equal representation and a more socially just perspective. MujerArtes, a community women's art cooperative, sprouted organically as a process of the Esperanza Peace and Justice Center in 1995 to focus on women's empowerment in the arts.[8] Esperanza director Graciela Sánchez explained, "So much of the art being featured was from men. And the women asked, 'Where are WE?'" Today's MujerArtes Cooperativa is a vibrant art collective run by and expressing the concerns of community women, on issues spanning community health, historical preservation, COVID-19 education, gender representation, and more.

Another example of community collaboration is the *La Peregrina* (page 28, 131) community library school bus, created jointly by a church congregation, a local artist, and fifty children from diverse immigrant and nonimmigrant communities who collaborated in the painting of a bus dedicated to the migrant experience.

In like manner, local artists frequently form alliances to produce group art initiatives such as Birds of a Feather[9] and the San Antonio Street Art Initiative.[10] As a significant example, the World Heritage Mural Trail has filled the South Side routes to the San Antonio Missions with a series of murals that create a visual reflection of heritage, collaborative effort, and celebration. And an entire community is involved in artistic dialogue through the mural creations and events at Essex.[11]

The city has commissioned and funded such functional public art projects as the Yanaguana Gardens (Hemisfair Park) and the Midden Mound Wickiups (Pearsall Park, this page and page 55). Atop the mounds of a repurposed landfill site sit Pearsall Park's artfully crafted sculptures honoring the shape and spirit of early Indigenous shelters. These wickiup structures are topped by the sculpted interpretation of woven Indian blankets and solar panels to power nighttime lighting. Visitors can sit overlooking the city, Lackland Air Force Base, and Leon Creek with a 360-degree view, in a pleasant breeze and under the cool shade of the wickiups. Here they can contemplate this historical overlay—a landfill converted into our own cultural midden, an artistic commentary on ecology and consumption. Or they can simply absorb the sounds of birds from miles around and the timelessness of gathering in natural landscapes.

Another collaborative effort, the San Pedro Creek Culture Park, wove together artists, community members, and a cohort of government agencies from the greater San Antonio area to turn a drainage ditch into a beautiful and exciting culture park (see pages 48-50, 88-89, and 91). Carrie Brown, public art curator

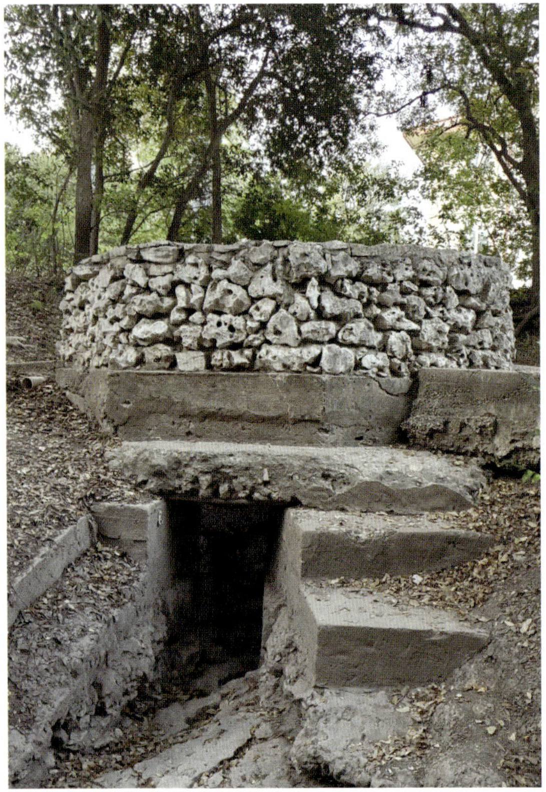

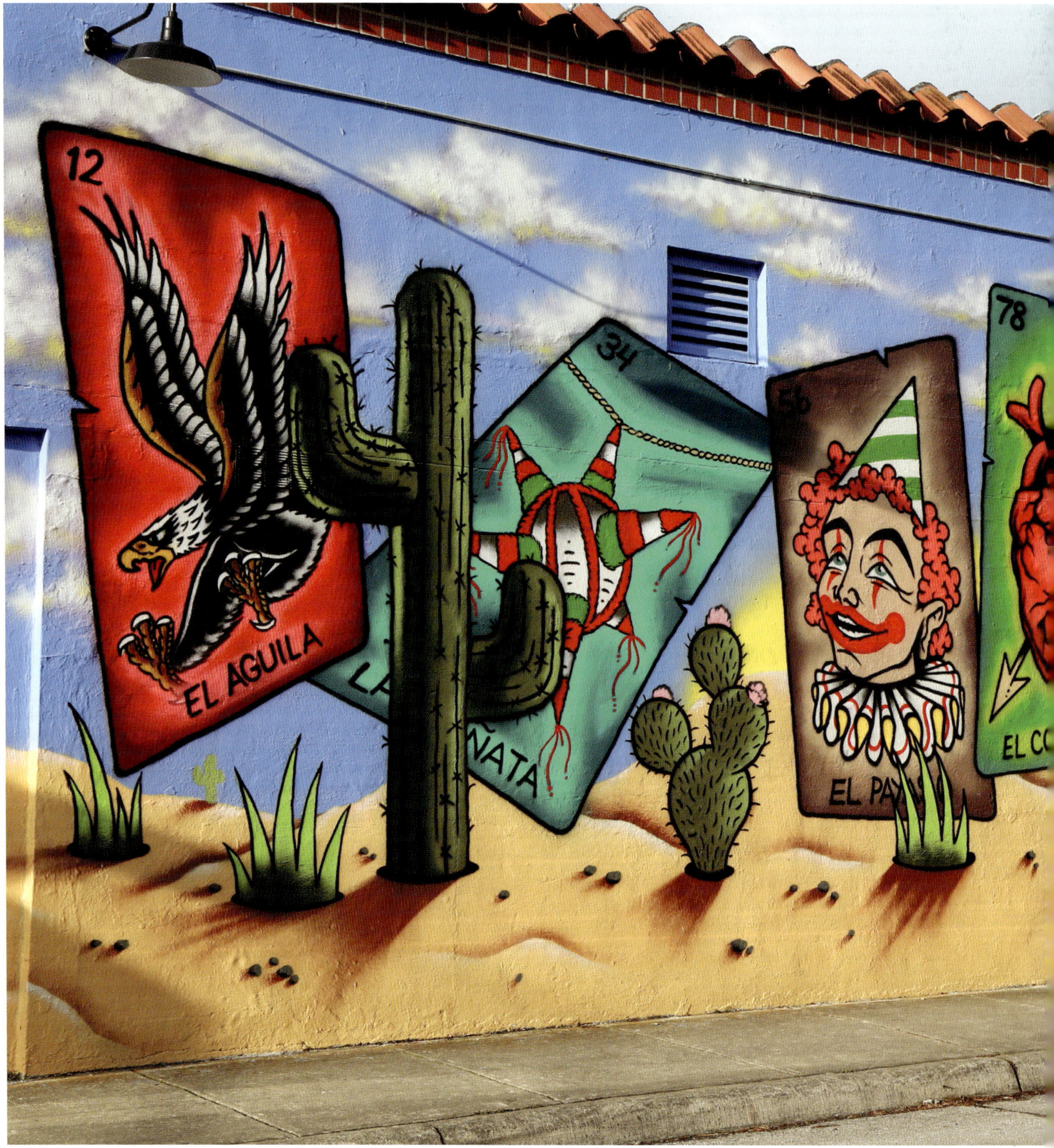

ABOVE
Blue Hole. University of the Incarnate Word campus. A natural spring once sprouted 20 feet into the air and is part of San Antonio's origin story among Indigenous peoples. The Blue Hole still serves as artistic inspiration to the city's native and nonnative peoples.

RIGHT
Lotería Cards, 2019. Kelly Edwards and Slokeone. N. St. Mary's Street.

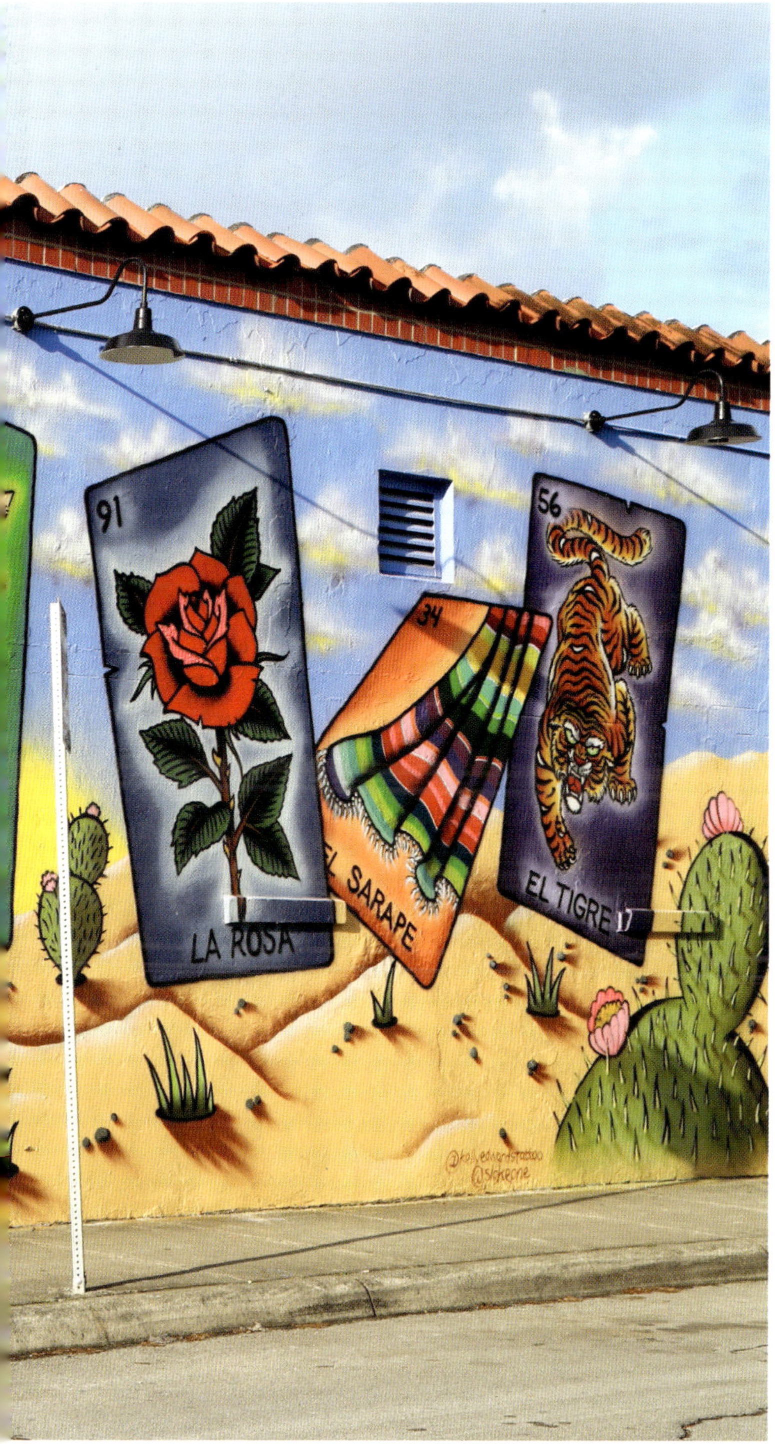

for the Culture Park, described the process: "The seamless connections from San Pedro Creek Culture Park to the many nearby cultural institutions represent a vital connection between our city's rich history and its vibrant future. We achieve this through an inclusive process that embraces artistic vision and presents a variety of artwork types and engagement strategies that provide multiple ways to experience the park."

The reader will also find examples here of art on apartments, condos, low-income housing projects, and other residential complexes. By adding art to housing, the residential power of the town is enhanced.

At least three different cultural-environmental factors have heavily influenced San Antonio artists. First and foremost is the city's central lifeblood, its waterways. As State Poet Laureate 2013 Rosemary Catacalos has so eloquently stated, "They came for the water / . . . sank hand and tool into / soil where the bubble of springs / gave off hope . . . the song of the water."[12] Indigenous creation stories recount the tale of a blue panther, a water bird, and the sprouting up of water at the springs now marked by the Blue Hole. This blue spring, which once sprouted 20 feet into the air, is part of San Antonio's origin story and still serves as inspiration to San Antonio's native and nonnative peoples alike. "The Blue Panther of the Yanaguana" creation story[13] symbolizes the power and strength of the water that gave birth to the native peoples here and became what is today known as the San Antonio River. Today's *PanterAzul* (page 120) smirks a playful smile as children clamber up to play in the Yanaguana Gardens in the heart of San Antonio. From the Blue Hole to its eighteenth-century aqueducts to its captivating River Walk, San Antonio has for many millennia been a gathering place by these inspiring Yanaguana spirit waters. For centuries, artists sought to capture the river's essence, and today's artists continue the quest in works such as Alex Rubio's mural of Yanaguana (page 52), Mary Agnes Rodríguez's *Sacred Water / Agua es Vida* bus stop (page 20), and Oscar Alvarado's mosaic bench sculpture at Elmendorf Lake (page 31).

Another major influence that had an impact on this region's art derives from its ranching and *vaquero* legacy. This region marked the starting point for massive cattle drives from San Antonio to Kansas City. Local music, Tejano hats and boots, and folklore have been influenced greatly by this cowboy heritage. The giant sculpted boots (page 65) by Bob "Daddy-O" Wade that landmark North Star Mall reflect this echo of past and present. Cowboy culture originated with native Indians and Spanish-speaking *vaqueros* whose Spanish and Indian words and cattle-wrangling techniques were later adopted by the English speakers, both white and black, who joined the Trail Drives as fellow *vaqueros*. Such defining cowboy terminology as rodeo, lasso, lariat, mustang, and hundreds more were "loan words" from the Spanish of the original *vaqueros*. The sculpture *Camino de Galvez* (page 64) exemplifies the courage and persistence of these trail drivers.

The third and probably largest cultural-historical influence on this city's public art comes from its strong Mexicotejano roots. Intermingled with the original Indigenous residents,[14] the Mexicotejanos have formed the cultural heart of this city for the last three hundred years. The uniquely Mexican American dimension they created is still evident in the city's food, folklore, festivities, language, courtesy, and artistic traditions, including Fiesta, Día de los Muertos, Luminaria, La Gran Tamalada, and Charreada,[15] all of which continue to have an impact on the region's art scene.

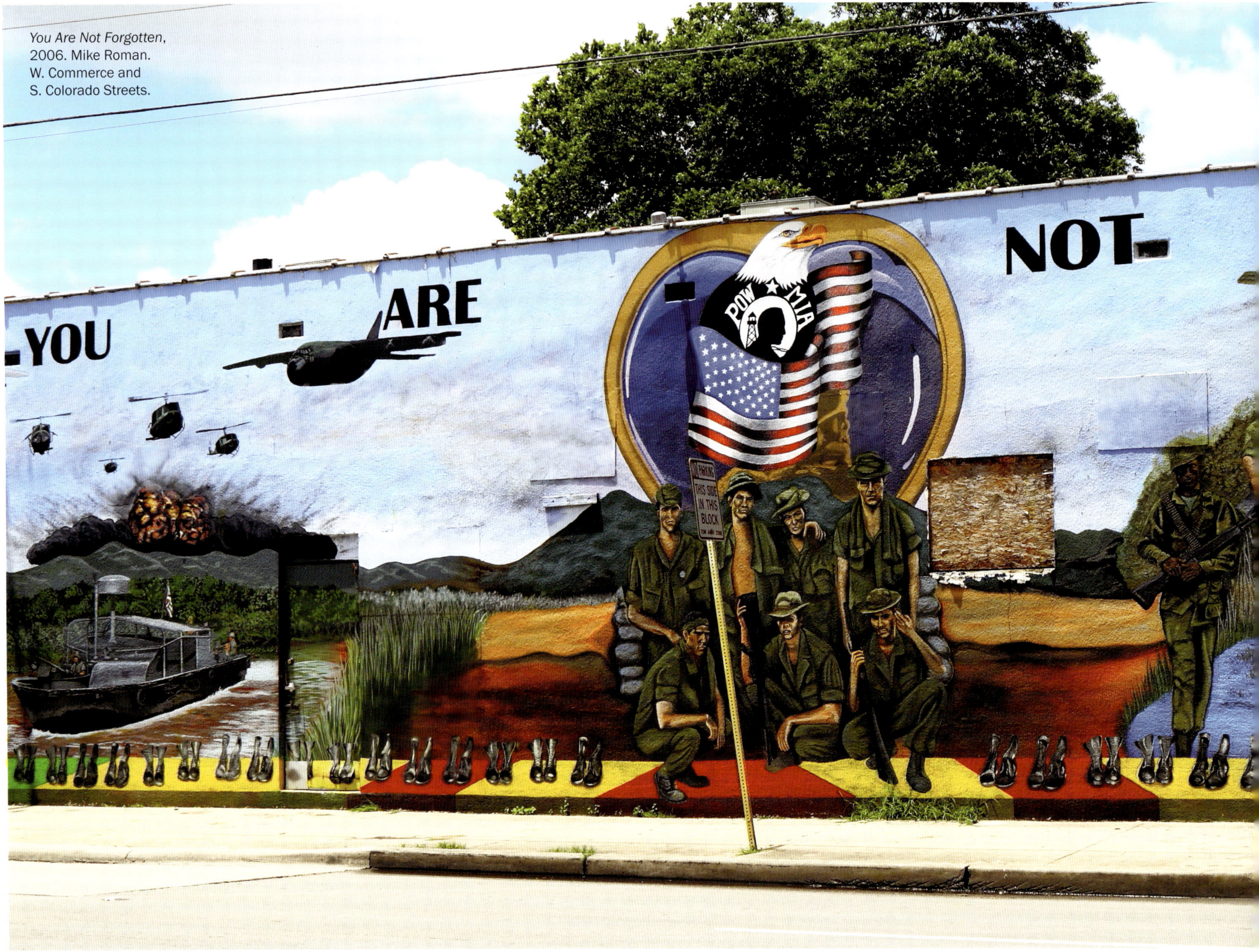

You Are Not Forgotten, 2006. Mike Roman. W. Commerce and S. Colorado Streets.

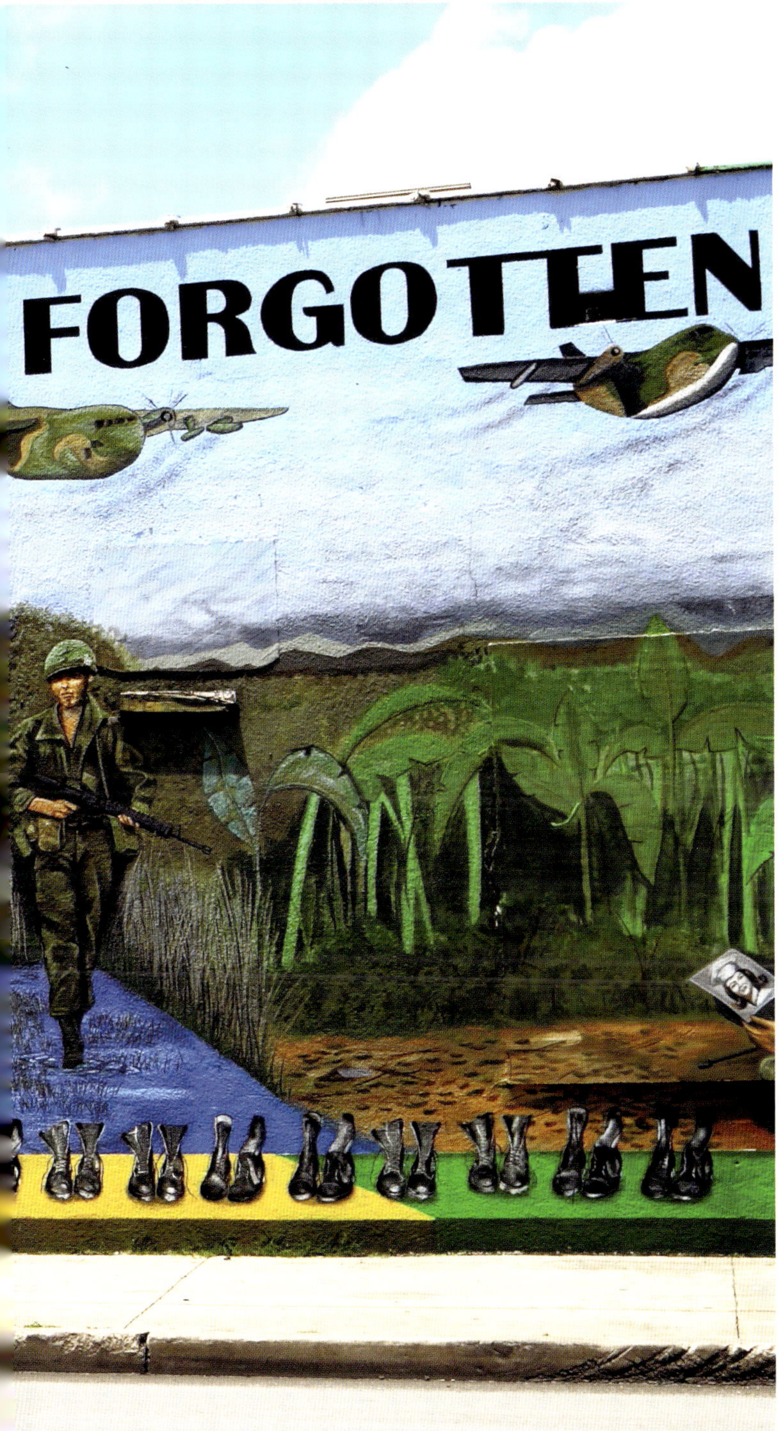

Mexican social and political influence heightened during the Mexican Revolution (1910–1920), as concepts and ideals from the revolution wove themselves into San Antonio's culture. Most notable among these was a desire for *justicia*, justice for individuals of all economic and racial backgrounds (page 105). The concept of *muralismo* was born and developed in Mexico during this time period and became one of the world's great art movements. Mexican *muralismo* is now credited as the inspiration for muralists and street artists throughout the world. *Muralismo* expressed the belief that art should be accessible to all and visible to all who travel down a city's streets. It also emphasized revaluing the beauty of the common people and of their lives and history. Muralists flourished in Mexico during and since the Mexican Revolution, bringing social commentaries to the people through large, publicly visible works, most notably embodied in the works of Diego Rivera, José Clemente Orozco, and David Alfaro Siqueiros. Two of Mexico's most revered muralists, Juan O'Gorman and Carlos Mérida, brought their world-respected skills to San Antonio's 1968 world's fair, Hemisfair, to create two permanent and iconic murals, both named *Confluence of Civilizations in the Americas* (pages 51 and 74).

The community's bonds with Mexico—which had by 1829 not only outlawed slavery but also elected its first of two Black presidents)—influenced the city's early opposition to slavery, and partially explains why, when the rest of Texas enthusiastically chose to secede from the Union in 1861, the city of San Antonio barely passed the vote. This, along with a multicultural bonding woven into the city's fabric, may also explain why almost a hundred years later, the first peacefully desegregated lunch counter in the South occurred in the downtown Woolworth's in 1960.

San Antonio's Mexican American neighborhoods were catalyzed by the Chicano movement, which began in the 1960s, and its renaissance of Mexican art forms. The painting of community murals flourished, first on the city's West Side and then spreading south, east, and downtown.[16] These elements combined with symbols and values of native Indigenous cultures to give a rich and complex depth to San Antonio's art scene (see page 108, mural, and page 56, sculpture).

Other significant influences (military, railroads, healthcare, higher education, ethnic immigrations and festivities, etc.) could be added to this summary, but the art represented here gives a taste of their impact. The city's military heritage dates back to pre-Columbian intertribal warfare and the 1718 Spanish military Presidio and continues through various battles for many of Texas's independence movements[17] (among them the 1836 Battle of the Alamo) and the arrival of figures such as Teddy Roosevelt and Geronimo to Ft. Sam Houston. San Antonio's armed-service role expanded in the twentieth century from birthplace of American military aviation in 1910 to the home of five military bases. Soon after, it began to be called Military City USA, not only for the many recruits and trainees stationed here, but also for the many soldiers and airmen who, after traveling the world, returned to make San Antonio their home. More than 400,000 residents of this city have a family member in the military.

A number of San Antonio's murals and sculptures—most notably *Tribute to Freedom* by George Schroeder, *Nightwatch* by Jonas Perkins (in front of the Tobin Center), and San Anto Cultural Arts' mural *You Are Not Forgotten*—pay homage to San Antonio's military service members and veterans.

In a city filled with the innovations of rasquachismo, where a plastic kiddie pool can be reshaped into a grotto in the front yard, and where cultural and linguistic innovations can

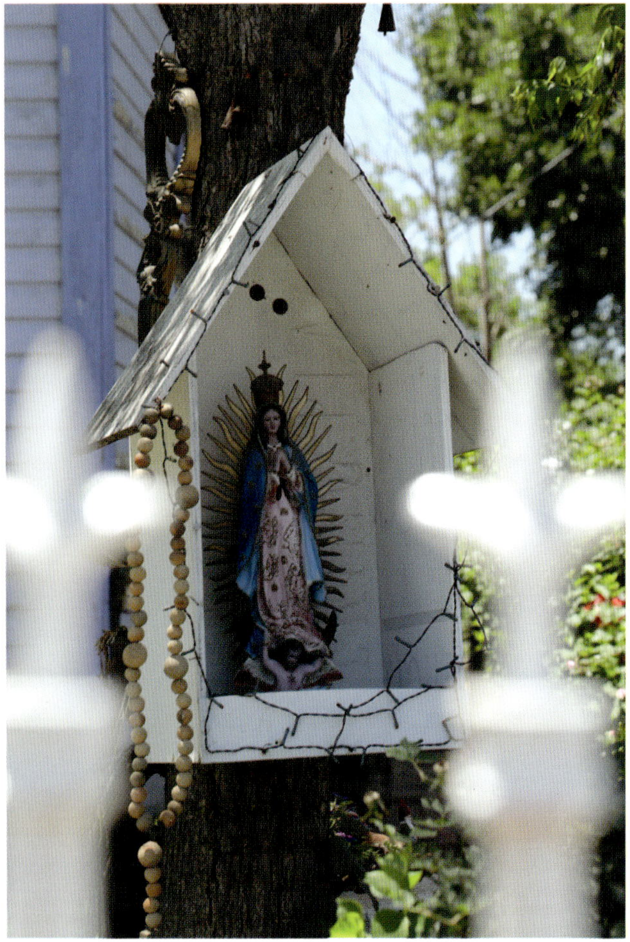

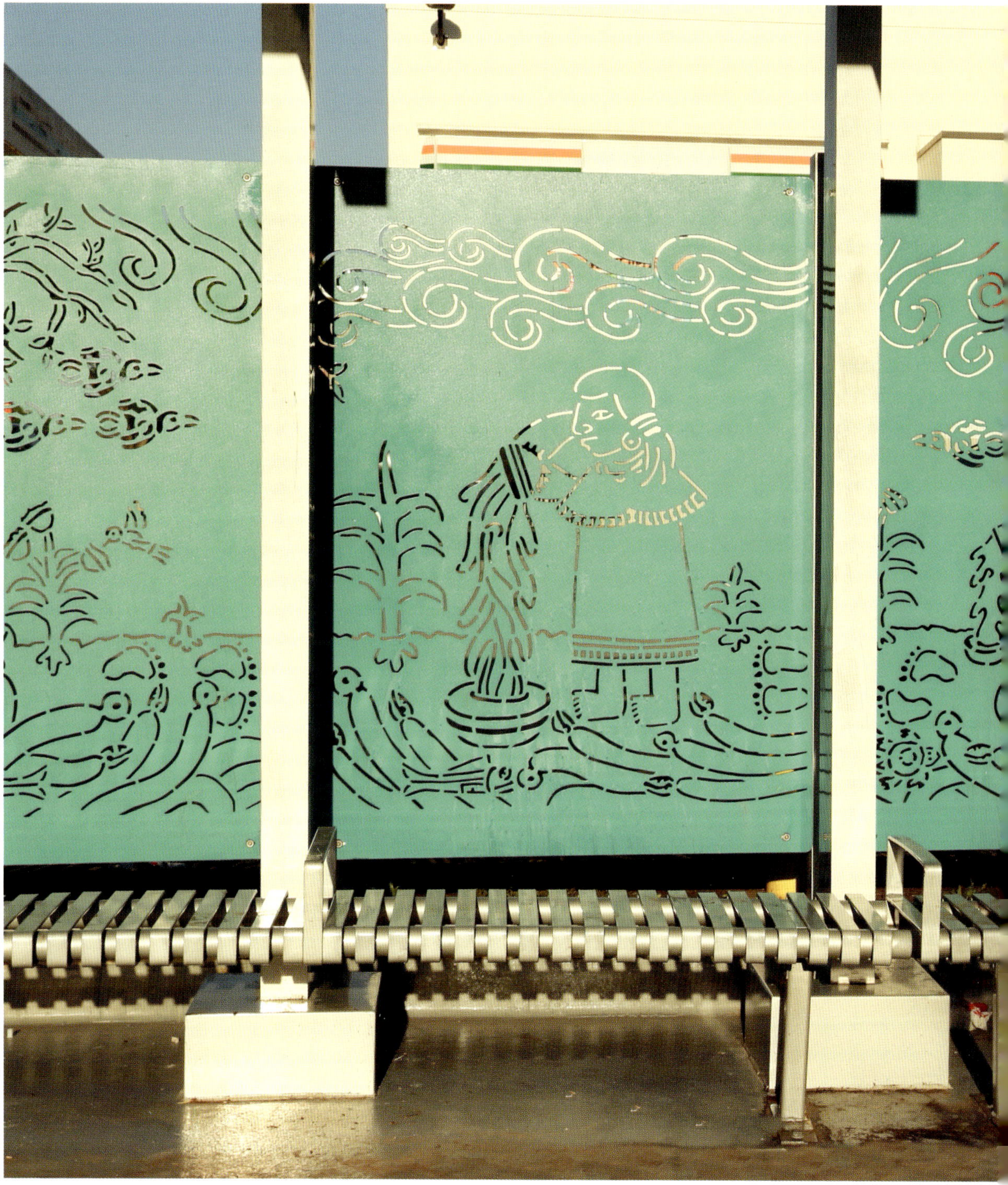

ABOVE
Nicho a la Virgen. Familia Luna. 217 N. Cíbolo. Home altar built in fulfillment of a promesa.

RIGHT
Sacred Water / Agua es Vida, 2018. Mary Agnes Rodríguez. Bus stop at N. Zarzamora Street and Culebra Road.

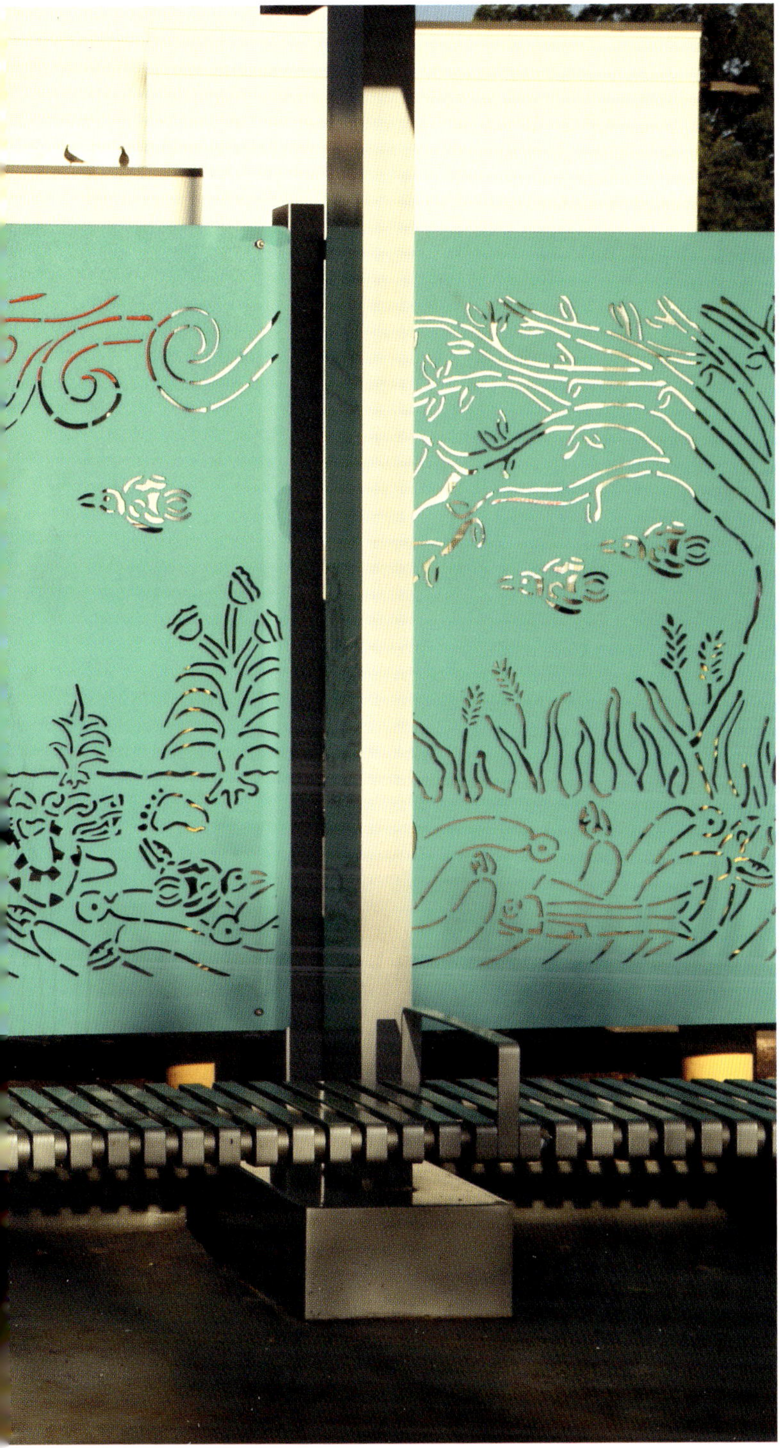

create the West Side Sound, a Tex-Mex inter-language, or low-cholesterol quinoa tamales, it's not surprising to find a public art that is broad in its diversity and bold in its passion for innovation. The centuries-long tradition of religious *altares*[18] in front yards, businesses, and front porches blends with the practicality of homemade materials to create a Chicano aesthetic of beauty, affirmation, and sharing with community.

The authors view this collection as a visual story of the people of this place, reflecting the history, culture, and spirit of a great American city. Fred's photographs, taken over the 2016–2022 period, and Carmen's narrative, weaving these photographs together, aim to bring the dreams, passions, and pueblo of these art pieces to life. Their goal is to enable the reader to feel the heartbeat of this city's dynamic present, as well as to hear the echo of its past. The book samples from a huge diversity of themes, styles, techniques (mural, sculpture, aerosol, mixed media, and digital), and professional levels, from the academically trained to the budding high school student.

Featuring seven sections, the book samples a beautiful array of art across the San Antonio metropolitan landscape. The first section serves as a photographic sample to introduce the reader to the spirit and diversity of San Antonio's public art. The second section explores San Antonio history through examples of local art pieces. The third deals with art that graces the river and waterways. The fourth tours West Side Barrio initiatives, which exploded with murals that bloom from *washaterias* and healing herb *yerberías* and now spread throughout town. In the fifth, one can see public art's reach into unexpected and creative canvases of highways and elevators, parks and planters. And in the sixth, the authors explore the excitement of street art, festivals, group art, and temporary installations. Section VII features the works and words of eleven San Antonio artists across a range of styles and genres. A resource list of the artists represented here and tour suggestions for seeing these works of art in person, plus notes and glossary, are included for further exploration of the significance of these works.

Selecting from artwork publicly visible during the 2016–2022 period, this book includes about three hundred photographs and represents more than 230 artists. Except for practical considerations of weight and cost, this book could have easily included twice as many. With a nod to the heritage of artists that preceded us and a focused eye on artists currently producing in this city, this collection is a glimpse of this city's song of artistic expression. If the reader (whether native, visitor, or scholar of the humanities) finds that this book whets their appetite enough to hungrily plot a route to tour some of their favorite pieces in person, there are several suggested self-tours at the back of this book. So many more artists, not included here, helped build this tradition of *aprecio* and *respeto* for the pueblo's arts. San Antonio's public art goes back for millennia, but this focus on the fruition of today is a small way to honor those who came before us and to bless those who are yet to come.

Con cariño y arte,
Fred Preston & Carmen Tafolla

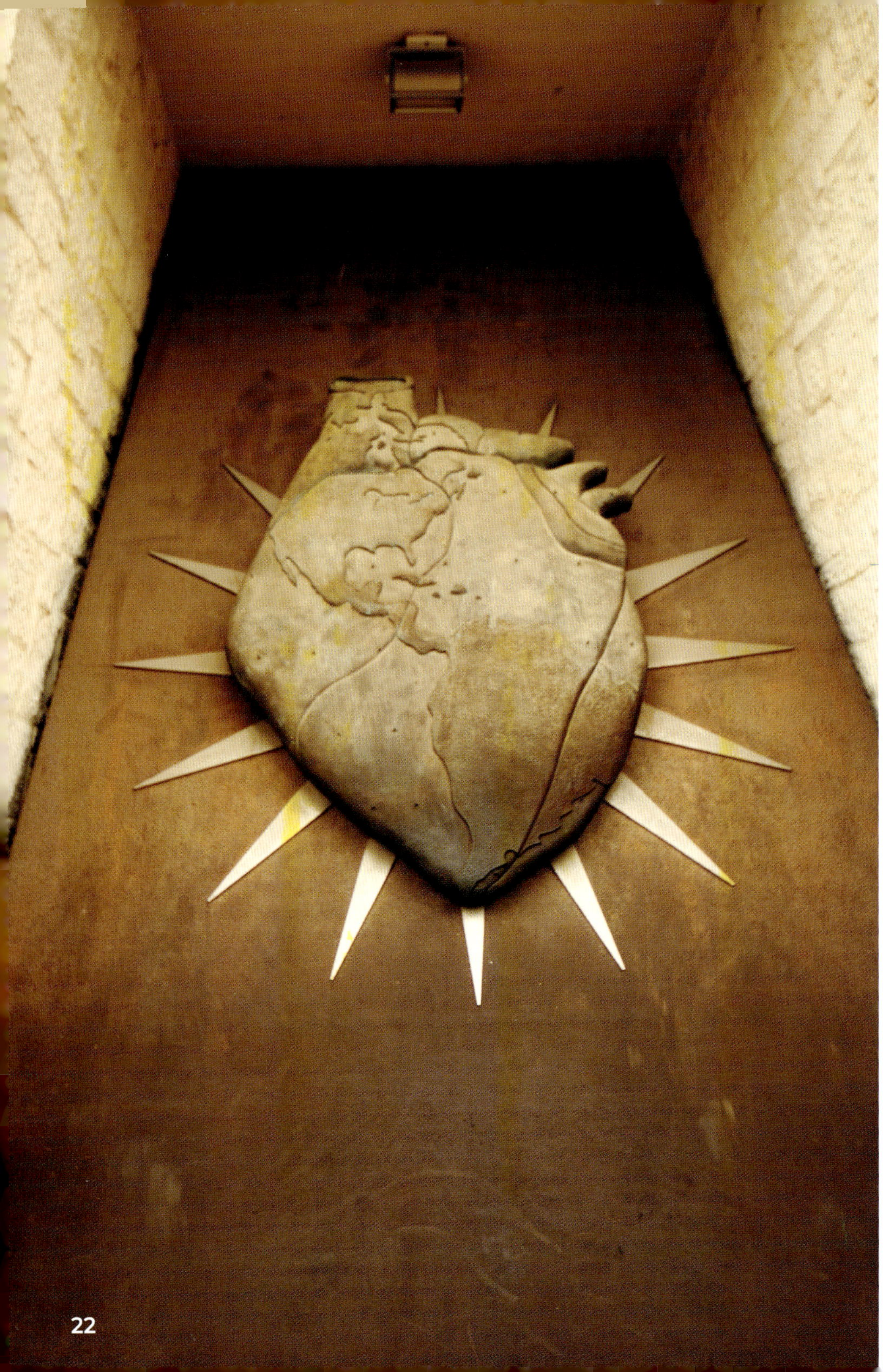

San Antonio de mi corazón,
tu corazón es arte.

Corazón, 2004. Benito Huerta. A ceramic heart with the Americas mapped on it hangs in the Henry B. Gonzalez Convention Center.

Translation:
San Antonio of my heart,
your heart is art.

NOTES

1. The American Indians of Texas-Spanish Colonial Missions, the Comecrudo, and other Coahuiltecan tribes trace their origins to this area. The state archeologist and the UTSA Center for Archaeological Research are analyzing the exact age of a structure discovered in San Antonio that dates from the Late Archaic period, spanning from 3000 to 1000 BCE; some archeological research dates human settlement in south-central Texas to ten thousand to twelve thousand years ago, and the central Texas Gault site has provided evidence of almost continuous human occupation for at least 16,000 years, including incised stone art pieces from this pre-Clovis era 16,000–20,000 years ago, some of the oldest examples of art in the Western Hemisphere (Thomas J. Williams, Michael B. Collins, Kathleen Rodrigues, et al. "Evidence of an Early Projectile Point Technology in North America at the Gault Site, Texas, USA," *Science Advances* 4.7 [2018]: eaar5954). According to Betty Bueche, Bexar County facilities manager, "There is a cultural continuum from the occupation of the Native American groups, to the arrival of the Spaniards, to modern day" (mysanantonio.com/new/local_news/article/Oldest-structure-in-San-Antonio-gets much-older-2472992.php).

2. The five San Antonio Missions were established between 1718 and 1755 by Franciscan friars and populated by the native Indigenous tribes of Texas. As the largest concentration of Spanish colonial missions in North America, they were named a World Heritage Site in 2015 by the United Nations Educational, Scientific and Cultural Organization (UNESCO).

3. *Muralismo* is the term describing an outpouring of public wall paintings created during the Mexican Revolution (1910–1920) and thereafter. Artists focused on the history and symbols of Mexican, Aztec, and pre-Columbian Indigenous cultures, as well as on the struggles of working people and on an egalitarian philosophy that art should be available to all, regardless of socioeconomic class. Muralists often adopted a populist approach even in their fees. For example, Diego Rivera sometimes insisted that he be paid for his world-renowned murals by the meter, like a common bricklayer. San Antonio was highly influenced by the Mexican Revolution, since more than 100,000 exiles from the revolution immigrated to San Antonio, which served as capitol in exile, at one point in 1917 having five ex-presidents and twenty-eight former cabinet members residing here. The impact of the Mexican Revolution on San Antonio's Mexican American culture was such that many Chicano-based organizations, such as the **CCAO (Community Cultural Arts Organization)**, would often select heroes of the Mexican Revolution (Zapata, La Adelita, et al.) to build a sense of pride and heritage in their community. For CCAO, this numbered more than 1,800 high school and middle-school students who became involved in the many murals they created. Information collected via conversations with Juan Hernandez, May 2021.

4. Founded in 1993 by Manny Castillo, Cruz Ortiz, and Juan Miguel Ramos, **San Anto Cultural Arts** cultivates, promotes, and preserves traditional and contemporary Chicano, Latino, and Native American arts and culture through multidisciplinary programming. One of its ongoing initiatives is the development of murals (sixty-one, to date, installed throughout the city's barrios) involving the community in their creation and more than three thousand young people in painting murals.

5. The Texas Legislature created the **San Antonio River Authority** (SARA) in 1937 to address flood control. It was reorganized in the 1960s for basin stream monitoring and surveillance, as well as improvement of urban parks and recreation, and several neighboring counties were added to Bexar County. SARA works in collaboration with numerous public arts supporters, including the **San Pedro Creek Culture Park** project. In 2017, the International River Foundation awarded the Thiess International Riverprize Award, the world's foremost award in river basin management, to the San Antonio River. The **San Antonio River Foundation** is the organization that works alongside SARA to manage and fund the art along the river.

6. The **Luminaria Contemporary Festival** was initially launched in 2008, and its public presentations took place throughout downtown featuring regional artists of varied media. An annual event, the festival moved to Hemisfair Park in 2011 and continues to be a major community event celebrating all the arts in San Antonio and features both regional and international artists.

7. A group of Chicana activists and supporters founded the **Esperanza Peace and Justice Center** in 1980, seeking to bring together diverse movements for peace and justice in San Antonio and around the world. For the last thirty years, Esperanza has emerged as a unique institution, galvanizing a multiracial/bilingual cultural-arts and social-change community headed by Latinas, a significant number of whom are lesbians, and focused on a broad variety of community issues and needs for all underserved populations.

8. **MujerArtes Colectiva** was created in 1995 in response to what seemed to be a flood of commissioned artworks by predominantly male artists. It focuses on themes of women's and community empowerment. The artists' ceramic *talleres* educate and bring recognition to talented women from all levels of professional experience, many of whom would not have had access to art education or production. They are affiliated with the Esperanza Peace and Justice Center and located in the heart of the city's West Side.

9. ***Birds of a Feather*** was a collaborative and permanent mural art exhibit at the Blue Star Arts Complex in 2018 headed by artist Robert Tatum and featuring more than twenty-seven artists, each bringing their own interpretation to the theme Birds of a Feather.

10. In 2019 artist David "Shek" Vega founded the nonprofit **San Antonio Street Art Initiative**, which debuted its projects with the transformation of a parking lot under an overpass into what they dubbed the "Largest Outdoor Gallery in Texas." Dozens of artists took part in painting murals on the concrete supports.

11. A testament to how art can build community, the **Essex Art Project** was initially created in 2017 as a monthly event to display art, engage the local street art community, and provide a venue for creative dialogue. The 8 acres with multiple buildings and walls had previously been a semideserted wasteland of pallets and known for its massive fires. When considering community, the developers Jake Harris and Anton Bayer realized it had very little to do with buildings and a lot to do with people connecting. Their monthly events feature both local and national street artists, and an ongoing canvas for the installation of new murals, new ideas, and a dialogue through art about our community's hopes, concerns, and visions of who we hope to become.

12. Excerpted from the poem "Homesteaders" by RoseMary Catacalos. The poem appears in *Again for the First Time* (Santa Fe, NM: Tooth of Time Books, 1984; 30th-Anniversary Edition: San Antonio, TX: Wings Press, 2013).

13. The Payaya creation story tells of a Blue Hole, a blue panther who lived there, and an anhinga water bird. As the panther tried to pounce on the anhinga, the bird took flight, dropping water droplets from her wings and seeding the native peoples to grow here. The panther symbolized the strength of the Spirit Waters that gave birth to the shootings springs and the Yanaguana River (now known as the San Antonio River), which provided life and sustenance to the peoples here.

14. Historically, various tribes of Native Americans lived in different regions of Texas, the most well known including the Tonkawa, Caddo, Karankawa, Coahuiltecan, Comanche, and Lipán Apache. Research in the Bexar County Spanish Archives by county archivist Richard G. Santos uncovered a report by the chairman of the Standing Committee on Indian Affairs for the Republic of Texas in 1837, stating that all Texan Indian "People called Lipan, Karankawa, and Tonkawa your committee considers a part of the Mexican Nation and no longer to be considered as a different People from that Nation. They occupy the Western part of Texas." This policy move declaring that Indians were to be considered a part of the Mexican people in essence stripped them of their legal ethnic heritage and simplified anti-Mexican and anti-Indian discrimination. First published by Richard G. Santos in *San Antonio Express-News*, May 31, 1970, reprinted by Center for Public School Ethnic Studies and other sources at various times.

15. La Charreada is a culturally based festivity celebrating the many equestrian skills of early *mexicotejano vaqueros* (cowboys) and the ranching culture that developed these skills in charros, both male and female.

16. In Section IV of this book, "El Corazón del West Side: Heart, Art & Muralismo," one sees still the symbols and social concerns of the Mexican Revolution reflected in West Side murals—a revaluing of the beauty of the barrio residents, a decrying of oppression and classism, a focus on community education in people's history, and an emphasis on concepts of feminism and equality.

17. Texas independence movements included numerous attempts by residents in the Spanish and later Mexican state of Tejas to break away from both the Kingdom of Spain and later the Republic of Mexico. These included the 1804 Rebellion, the Casas Revolt of 1810, the Republic of Fredonia (1826), and the Texian Rebellion, led by Sam Houston in 1835–1836. The latter established an independent Republic of Texas for nine years until it was annexed by the United States in 1845, resulting in the US-Mexican War of 1846–1848 and, in 1848, in Mexico ceding almost one-third of its territory to the US, including Texas, New Mexico, Arizona, California, Colorado, and parts of Utah and Nevada.

18. Altares are religious altars containing a statue of the Virgin or a favorite saint, many of them homemade, innovated with roses, recycled materials, or rasquachismo and occupying places of prominence in the front yard or the kitchen. When built into a small, boxed enclosure, they are called *nichos*.

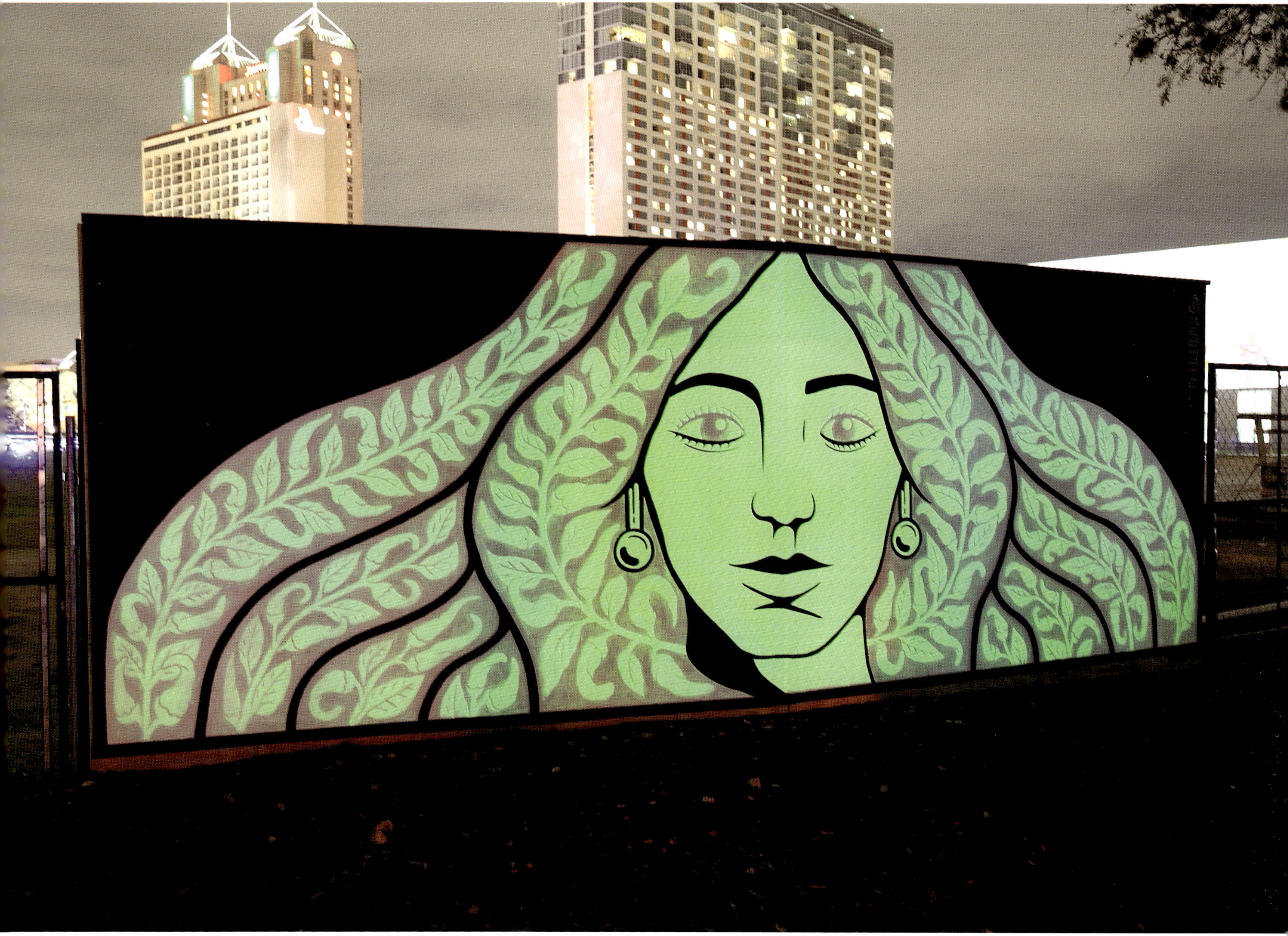

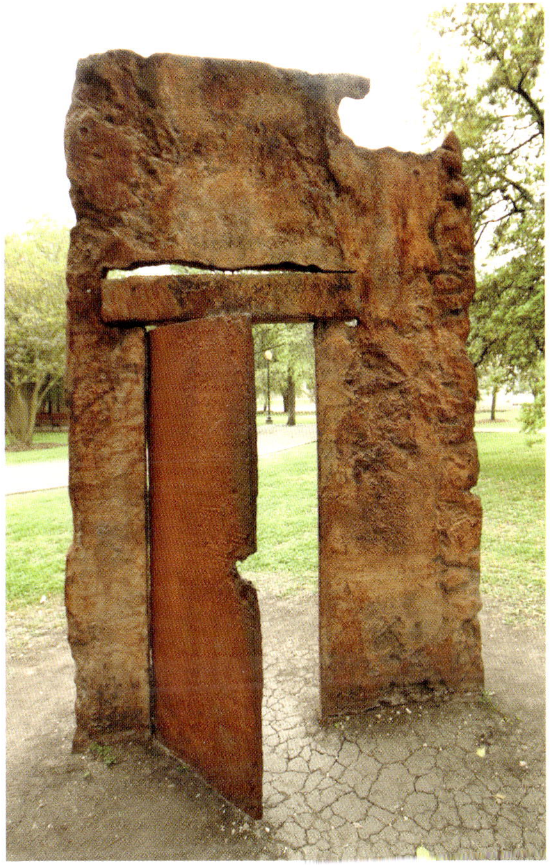

I. THE SOUL OF PUBLIC ART IN SAN ANTONIO

LEFT
Chili Queen, 2017. Maria López and Javier de Riba ("Reskate"). For Luminaria, Hemisfair Park.

ABOVE
My Home Is Your Home, 1992. Diana Calvillo de Chapa. Hemisfair Park.

Art reaches deep into the flutter of our soul
captures the song of our origins and our futures
paints the meaning of our everyday lives
here and now.

The Grotto, 2009. Carlos Cortés. River Walk near Camden and Newell Streets. A three-story "Trabajo Rústico" sculpted structure. River Walk near Camden and Newell Streets.

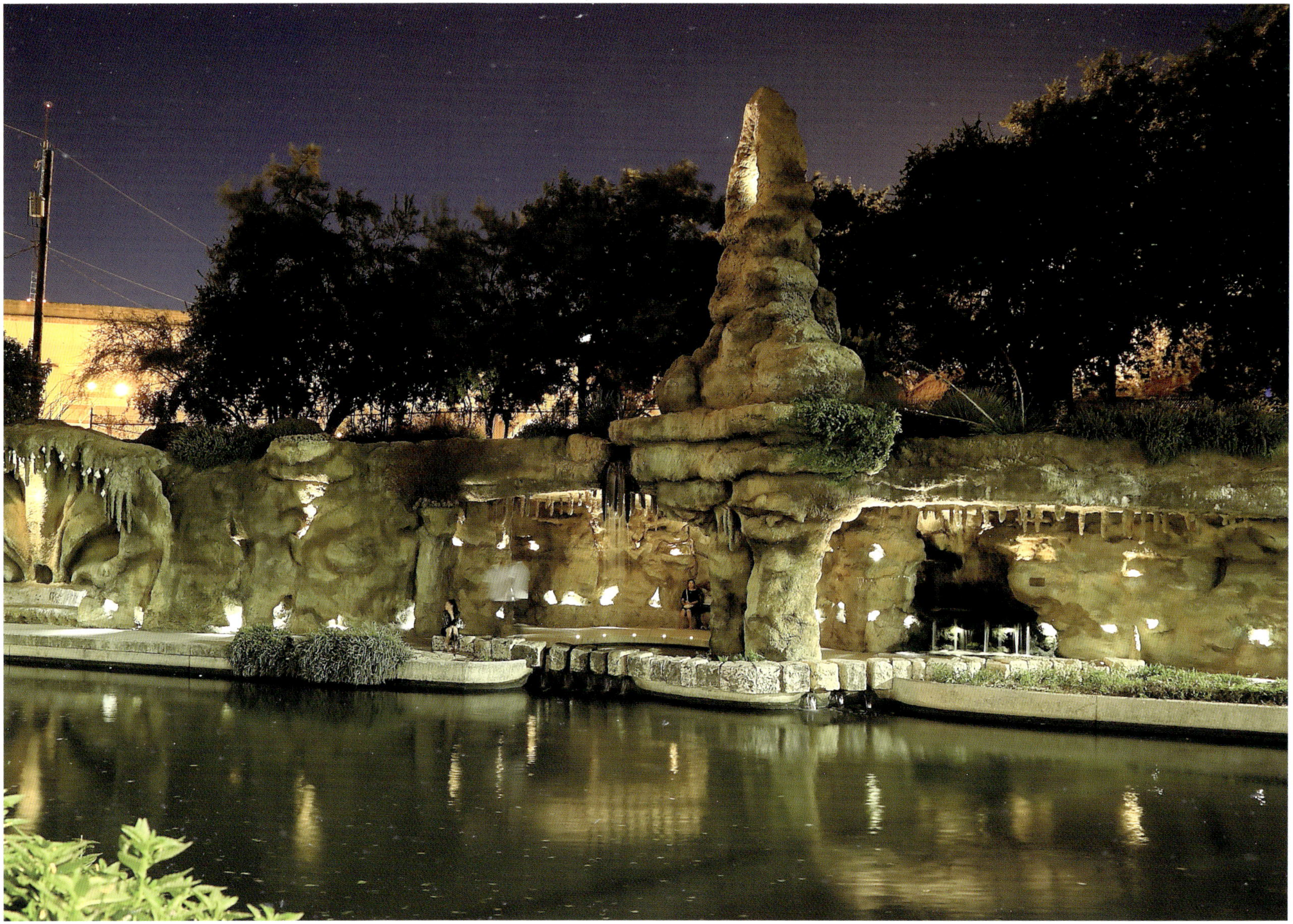

Art fills our lungs with the wind of passion
and at the same time steals our breath away
makes time stop
and eternity flourish.

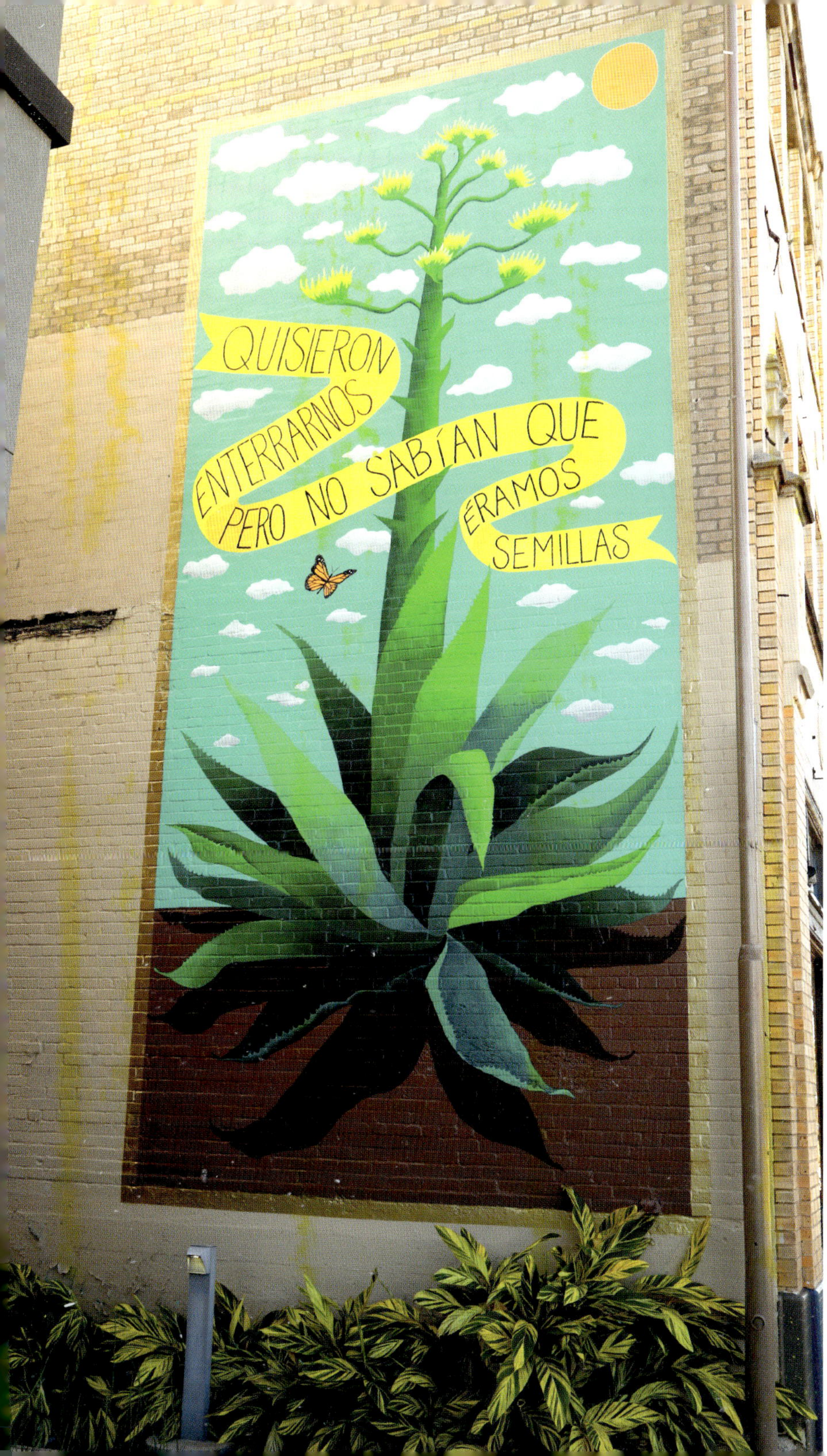

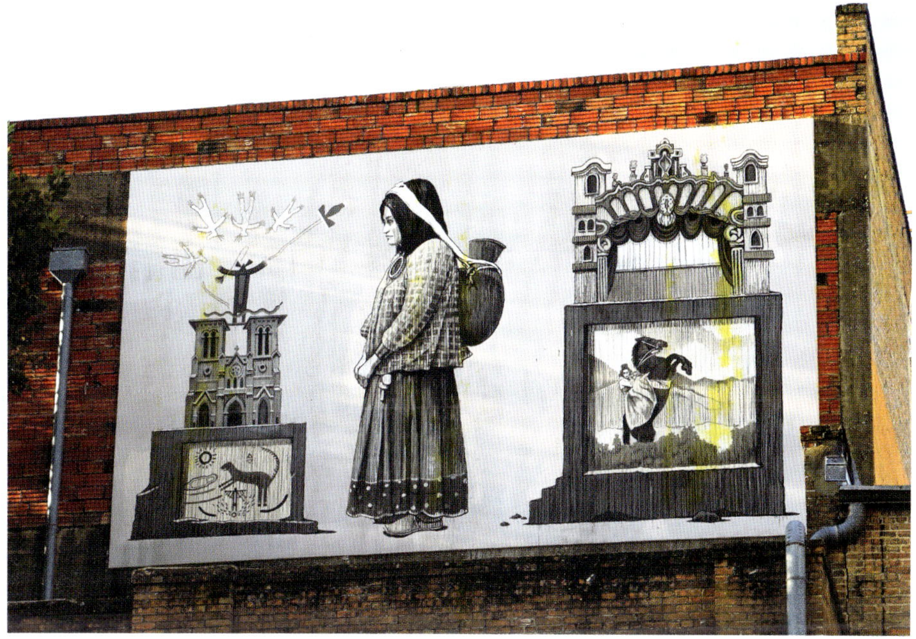

But el arte del pueblo,
the art that is for the public and of the public,
owned by la gente and singing its daily song,
is unbound, unlimited, and glows with
the rhythm of our lives.

LEFT
Quisieron enterrarnos. Pero no sabían que eramos semillas, 2002. Hailey Marmolejo. Translation: They tried to bury us. But they did not know we were seeds. Broadway near IH 35.

ABOVE
Twenty-Five Windows & a Frame, 2018. Daniel Muñoz. Magik Theater.

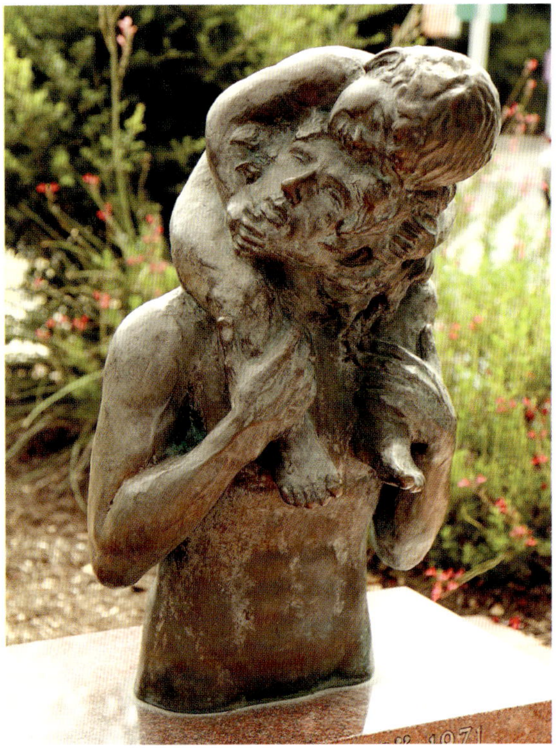

This is the art that truly marks this earth
with its own beautiful scar
beats with the pulse of our planet's own heart
with its people's own passions and dreams.

ABOVE
First Born, 2017. Victor Salmones. The DoSeum: San Antonio Children's Museum.

RIGHT
La Peregrina—Mobile Library, 2020. Regina Moya

OPPOSITE PAGE
Glorieta, 2006. Anne Wallace. Bronze and natural tree trunk slices. Brackenridge Park.

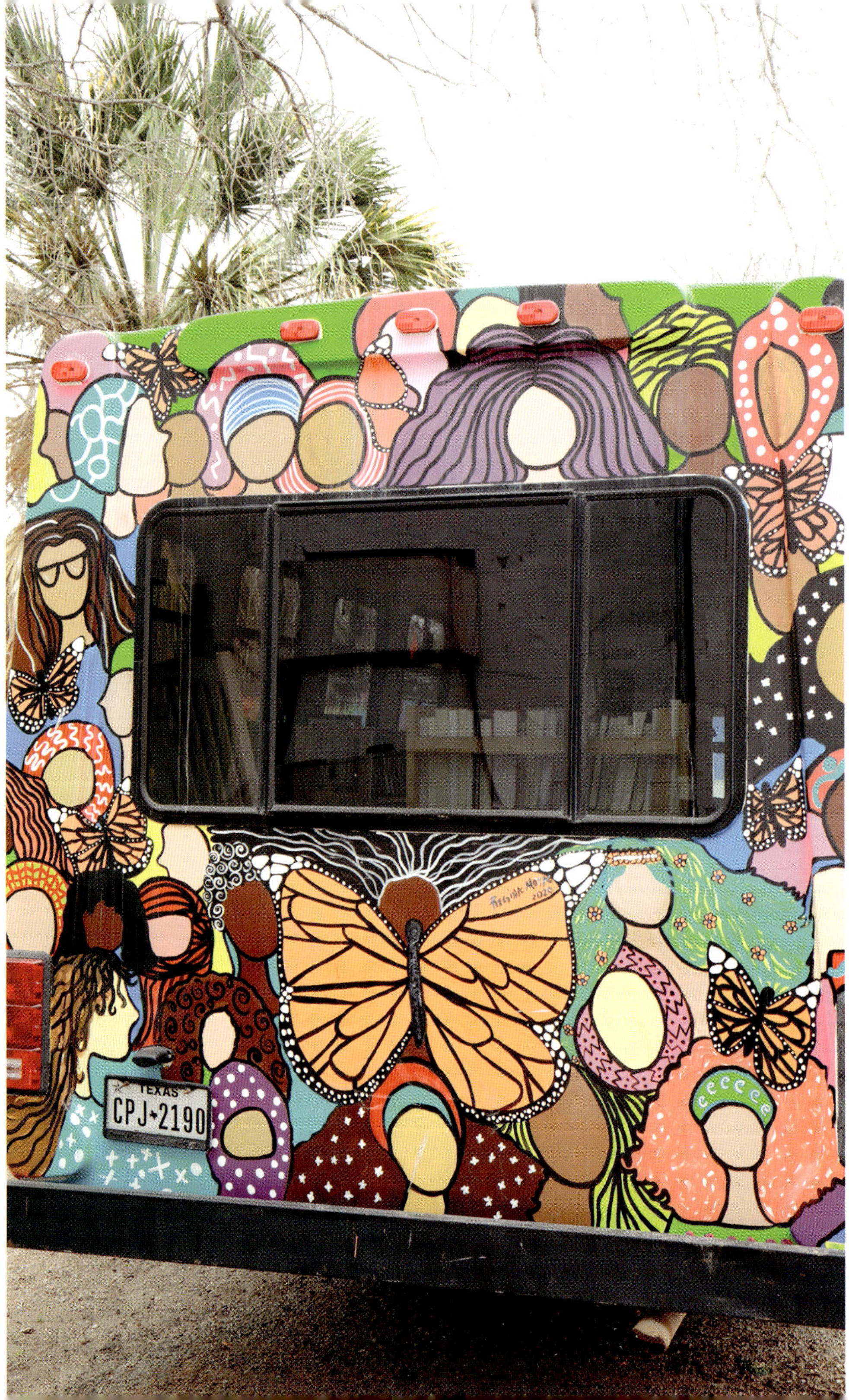

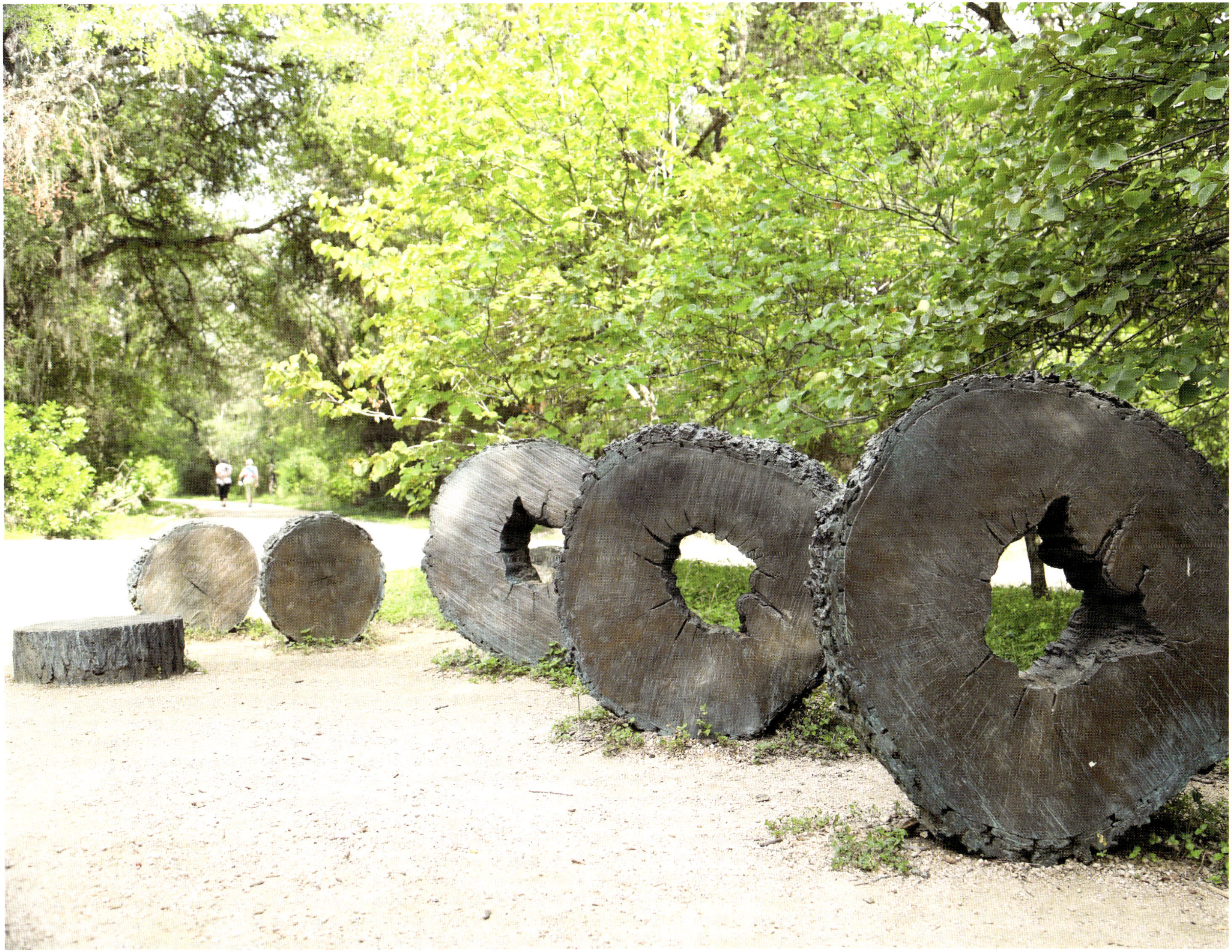

Pulling us into its deep-breathed beauty,
the enchanting song of rippling water,
the pulsing heart of life drawn here,
to this river, OUR river,

it inspires a pueblo in tune with art
breathing art
blooming art
free to all
part of us all

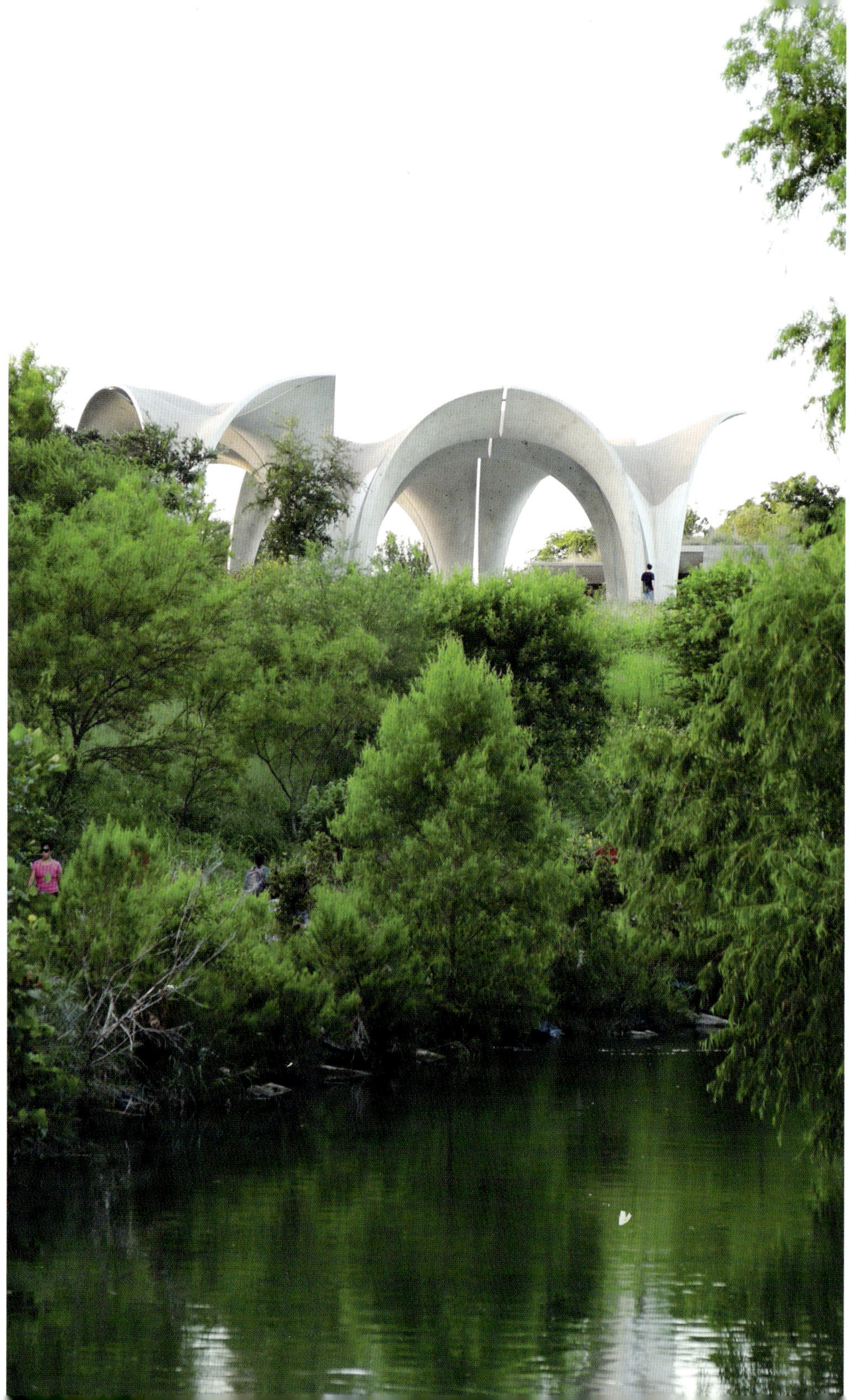

Untitled, 2018. Andrew Kudless, Matsys Studio. Confluence Park.

OPPOSITE PAGE
Mosaic Bench, 2016. Oscar Alvarado. Elmendorf Park.

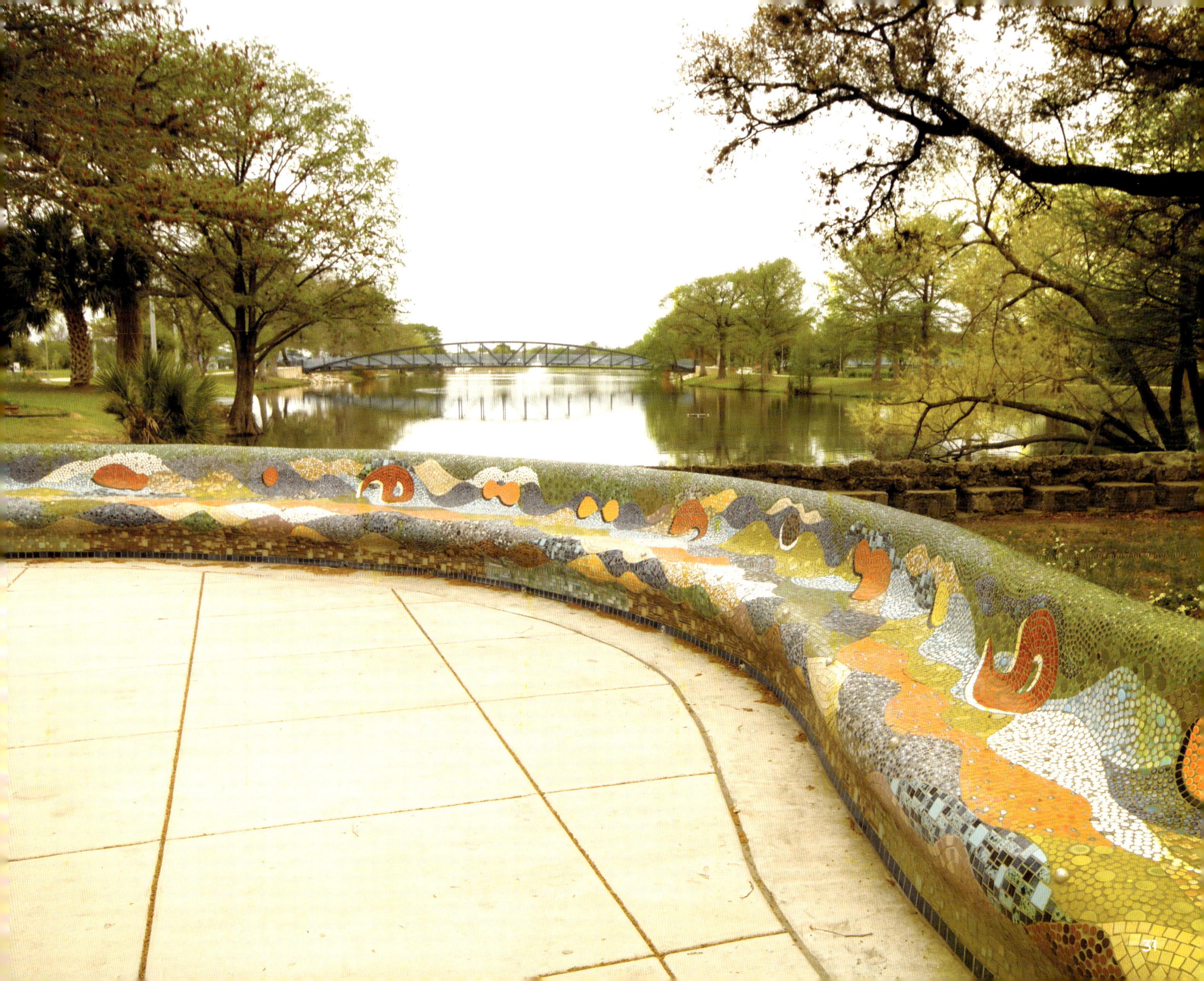

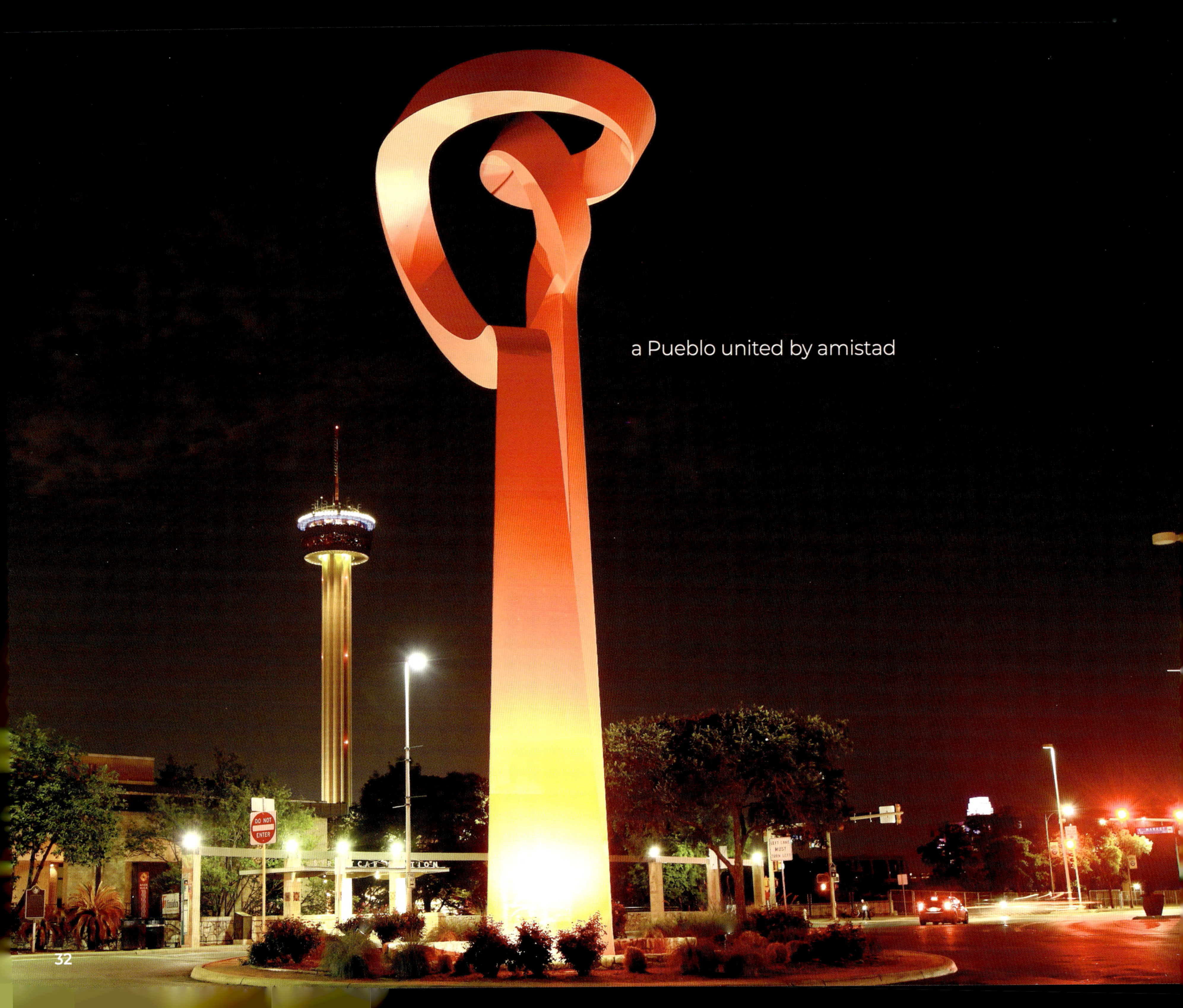

a Pueblo united by amistad

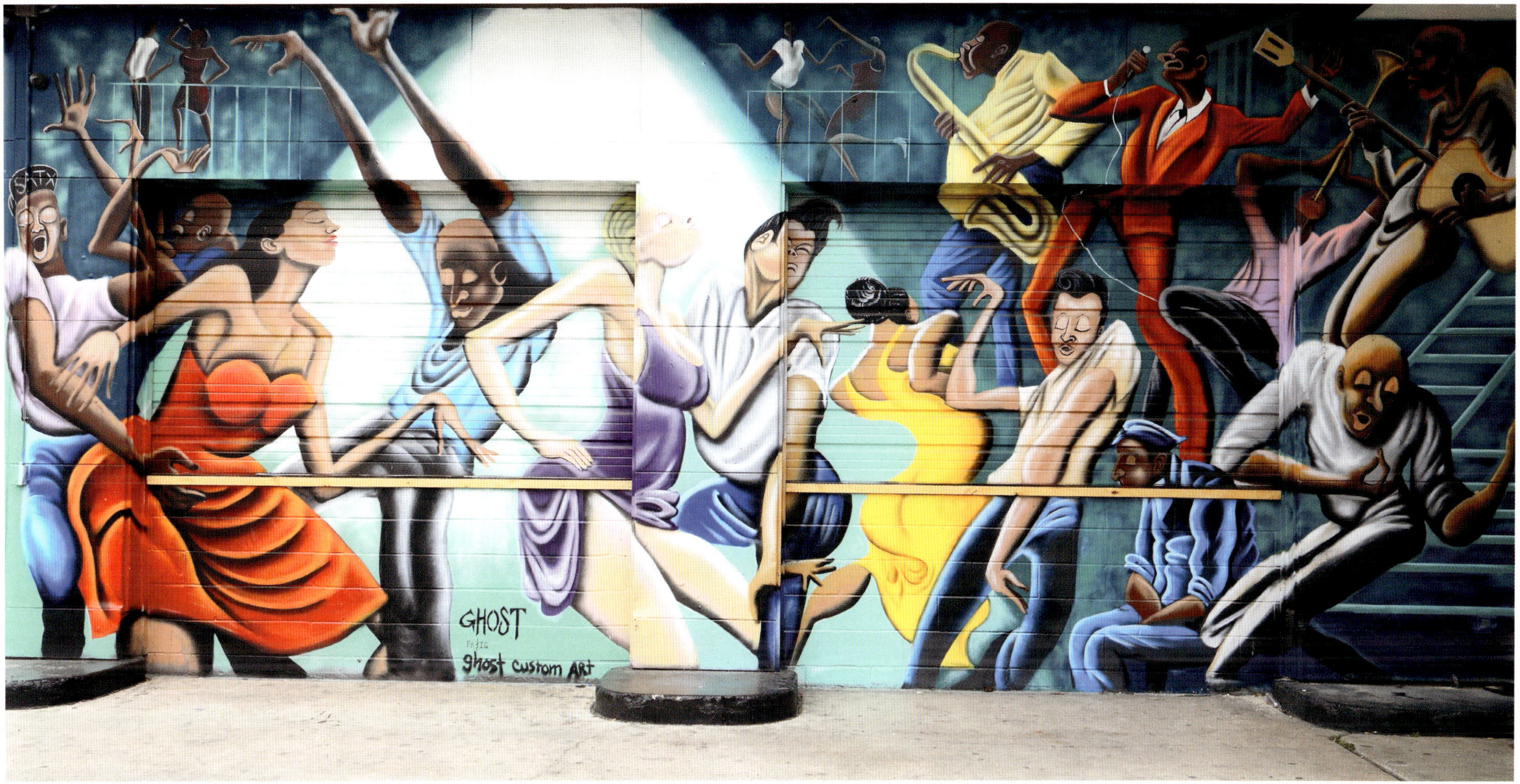

and by a festive and stubborn survival.

OPPOSITE PAGE
Torch of Friendship / Antorcha de la Amistad, 2011. Sebastián. Alamo and Commerce Streets.

THIS PAGE
The East Side Bar, 2020. Gerardo "Ghost" Cázares. New Braunfels and Hays Streets.

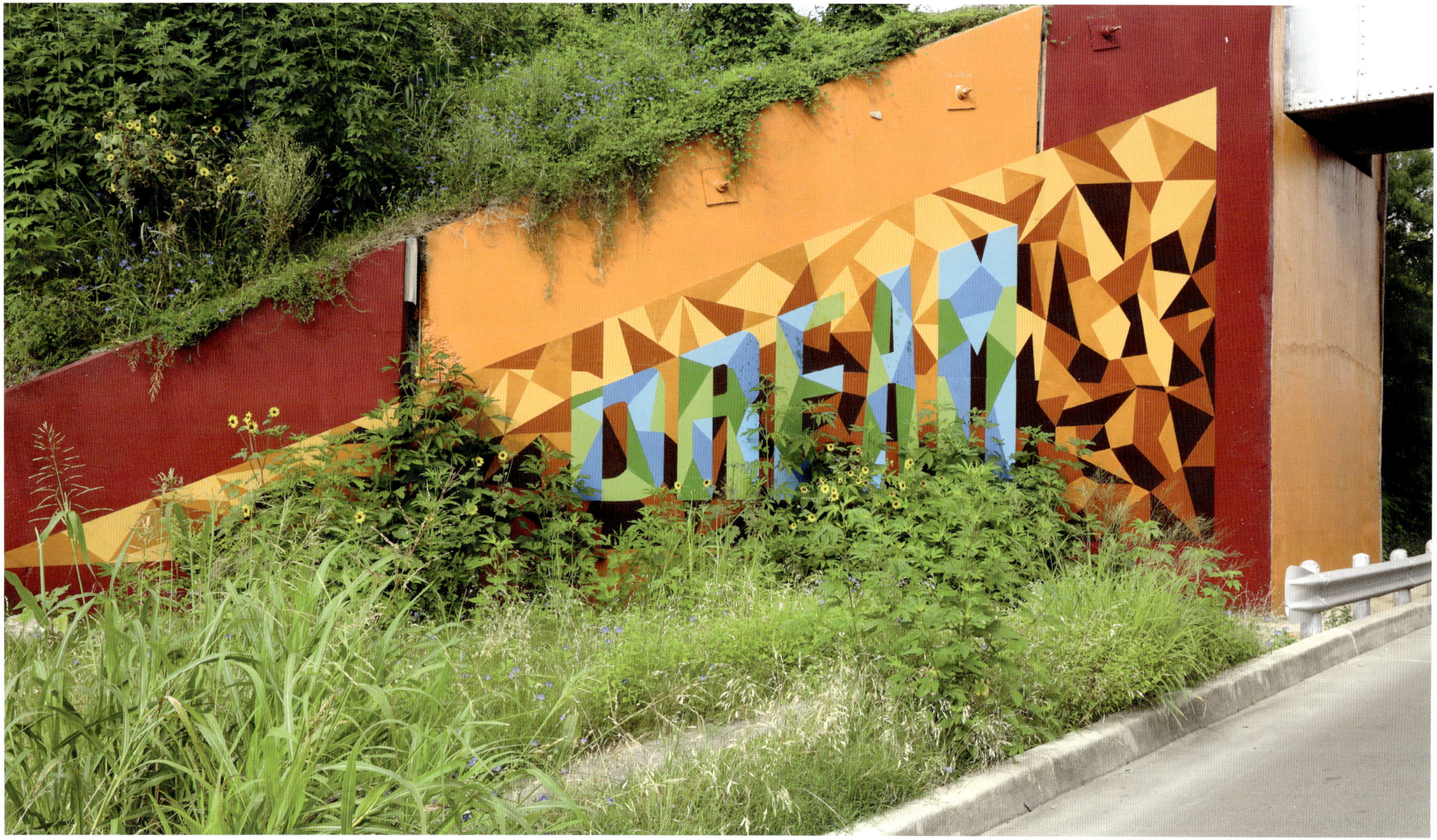

So Art is born that claims its place,

Dream, 2016. Los Otros. Railroad Overpass, South Side.

OPPOSITE PAGE
Roots Chair, 2015. Attie Jonker. The DoSeum: San Antonio Children's Museum, on Broadway.

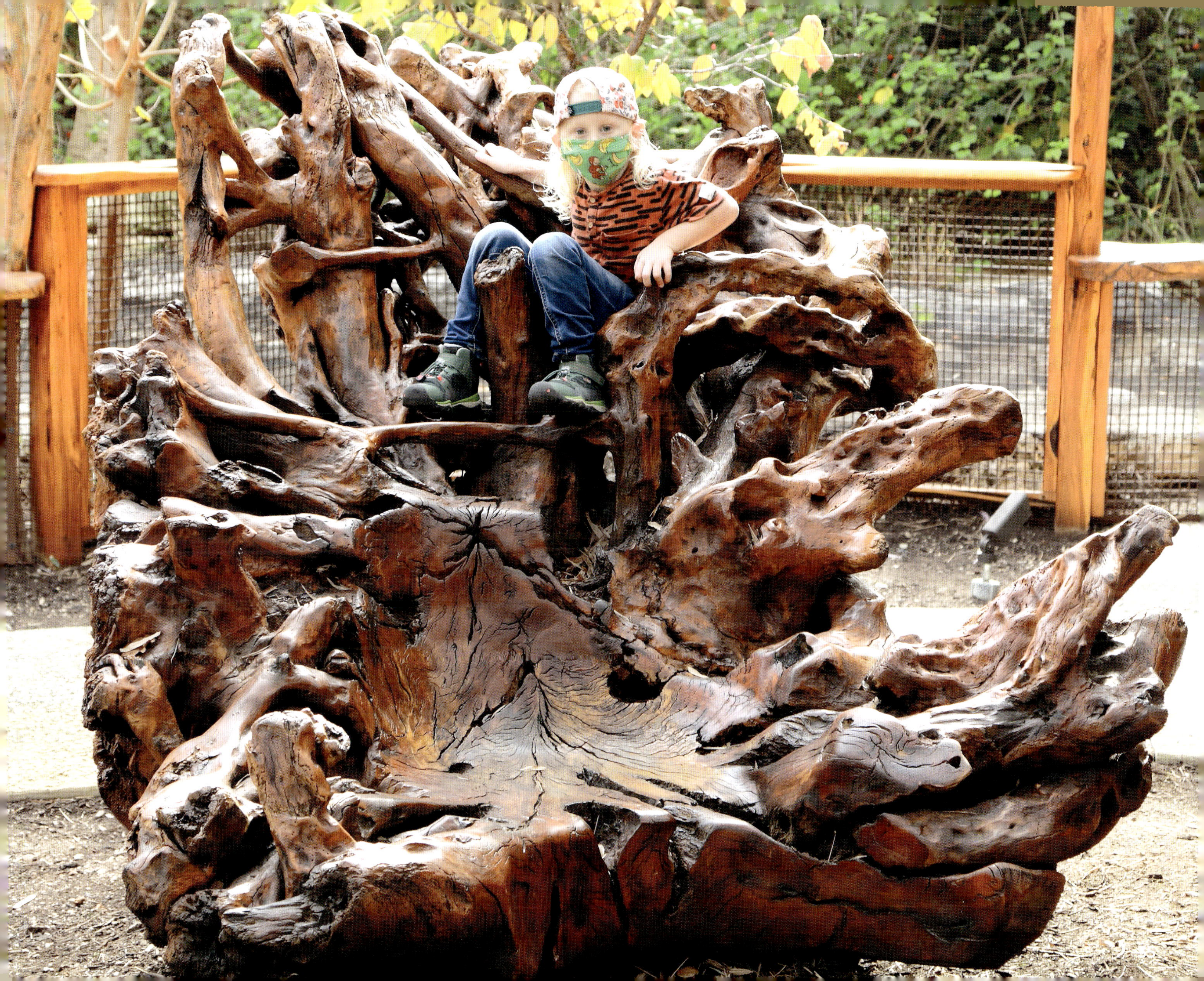

SA Is Amor, 2020. Martha Martínez. Best Western Hotel, 220 Broadway. The traditional *papel picado* cut-paper design overlays the background of this gleeful celebration of bicultural bilingualism. *SA Is Amor* is the bilingual Tex-Mex rendition of "San Antonio Is Love."

OPPOSITE PAGE
LEFT
Vessel, 2006. Roger Colombik. San Antonio Botanical Garden.

CENTER
The Dance of Unwitting Resistance, 2019. Danville Chadbourne.

RIGHT
Golden Age, 2013. Anne Wallace. A tribute to the prairie, its wheels are made from side roll irrigator parts. Hardberger Park.

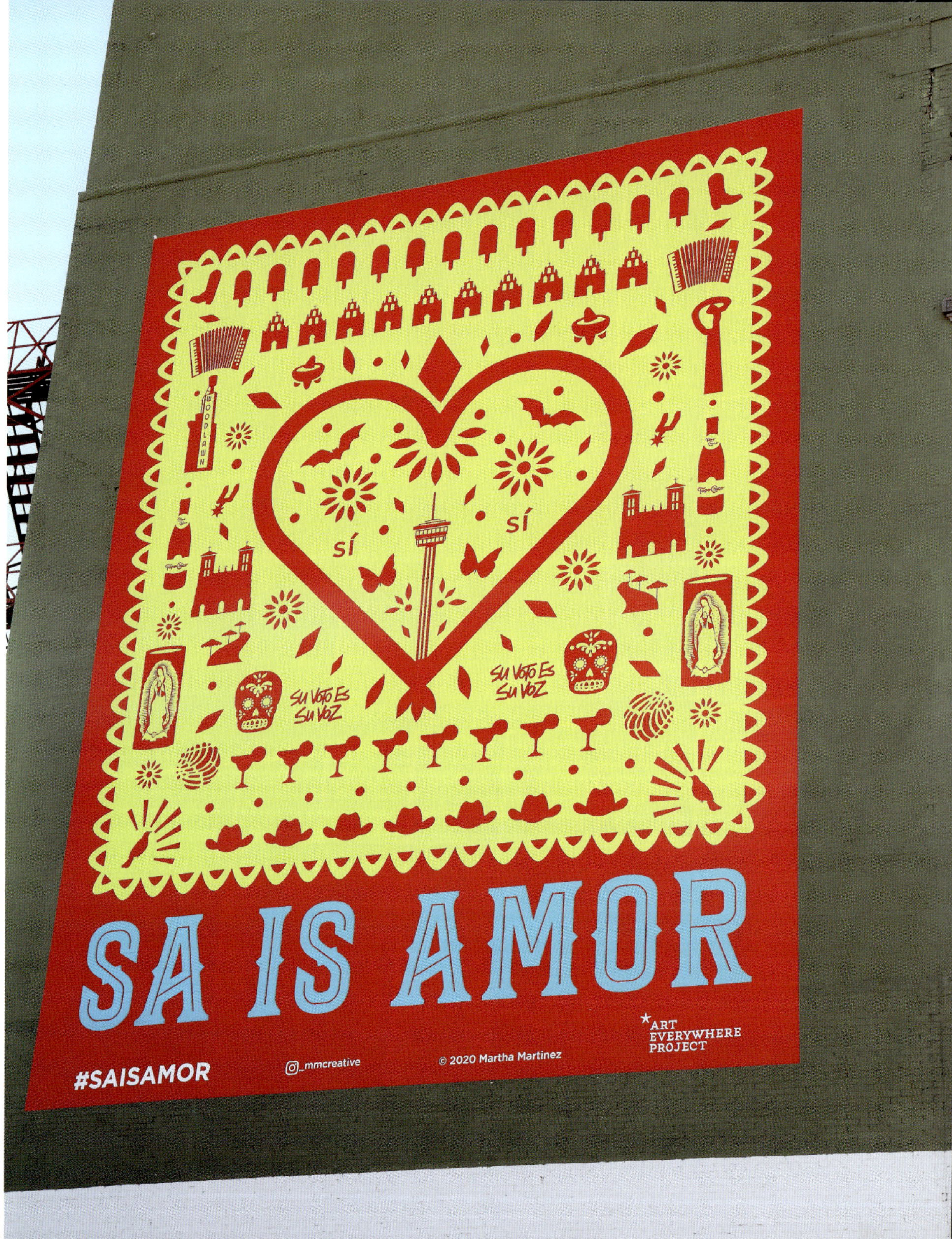

that marks our existence here
in every language of the heart.

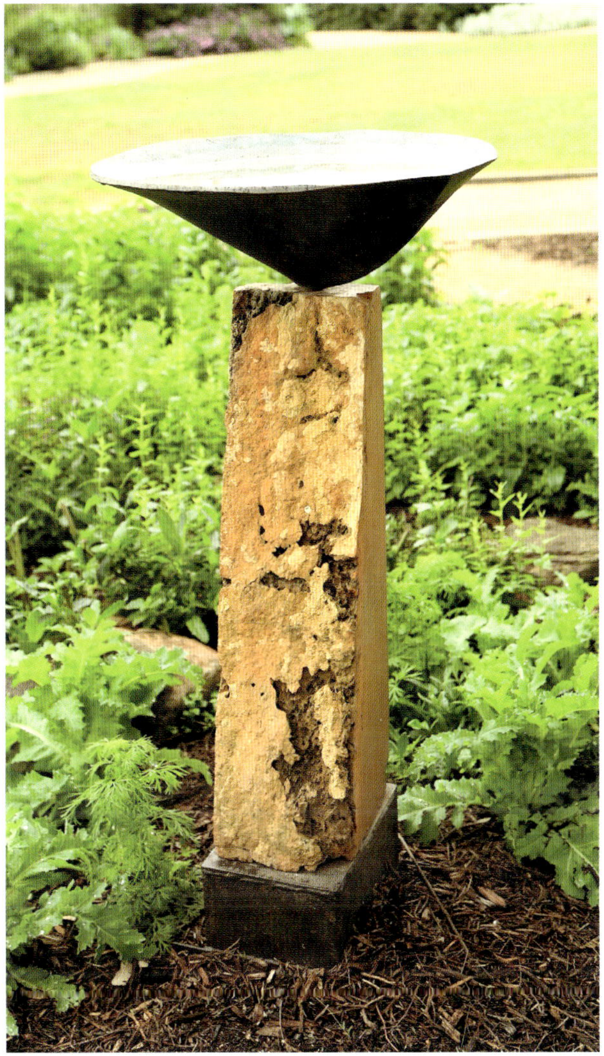

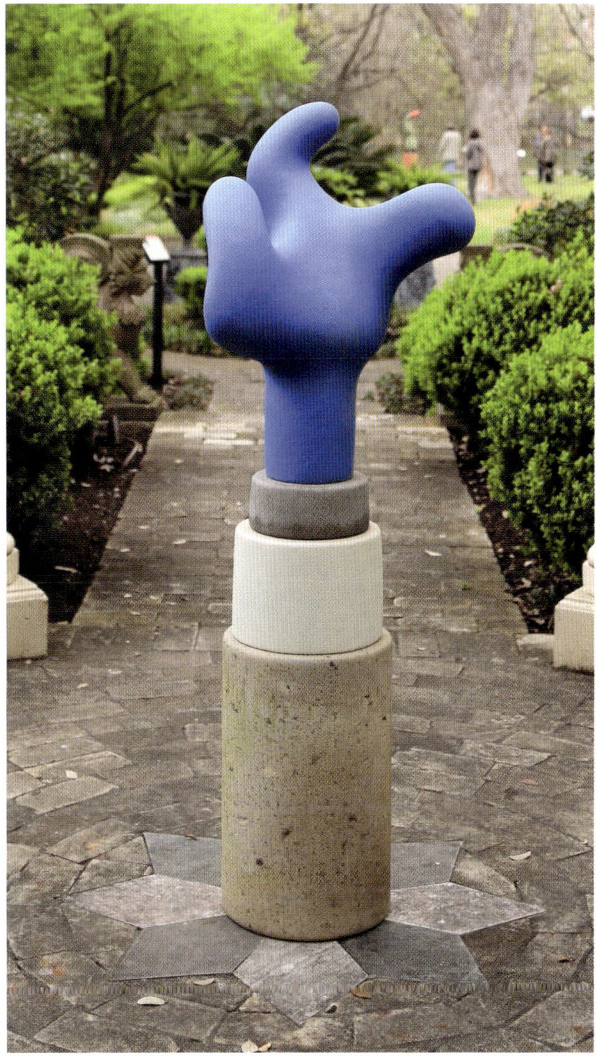

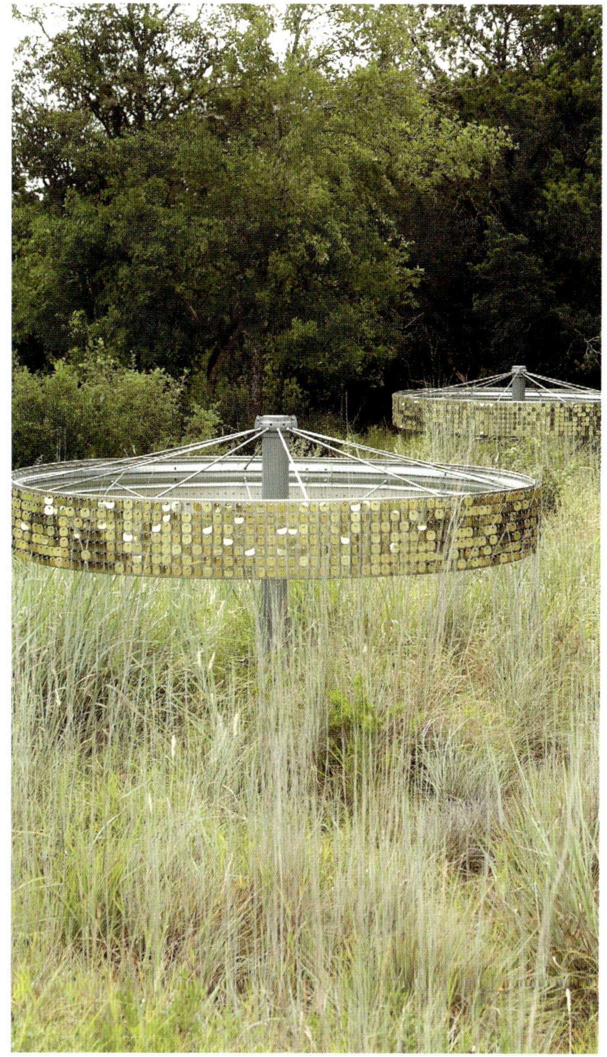

Art that shines and shape-shifts
from its form to its theme
from its making to its makers
to those who drink it in and find survival
in the cool quench of meaning,
the affirmation of having existed

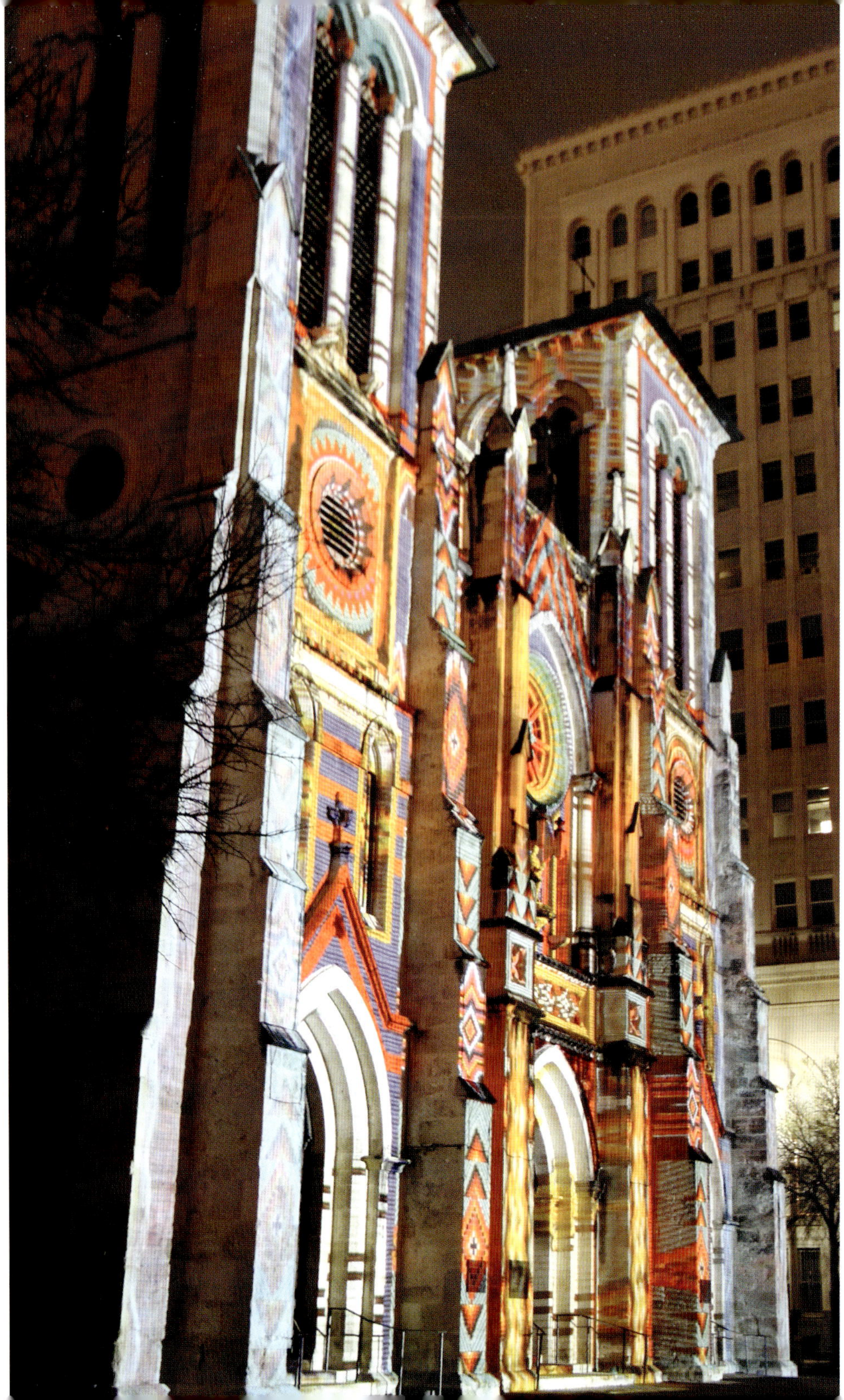

The Saga, 2014. Xavier de Richemont (France). San Fernando Cathedral, Main Plaza.

OPPOSITE PAGE
Cultura y Revolución, 2004. Raúl Valdez. 1013 S. Trinity Street.

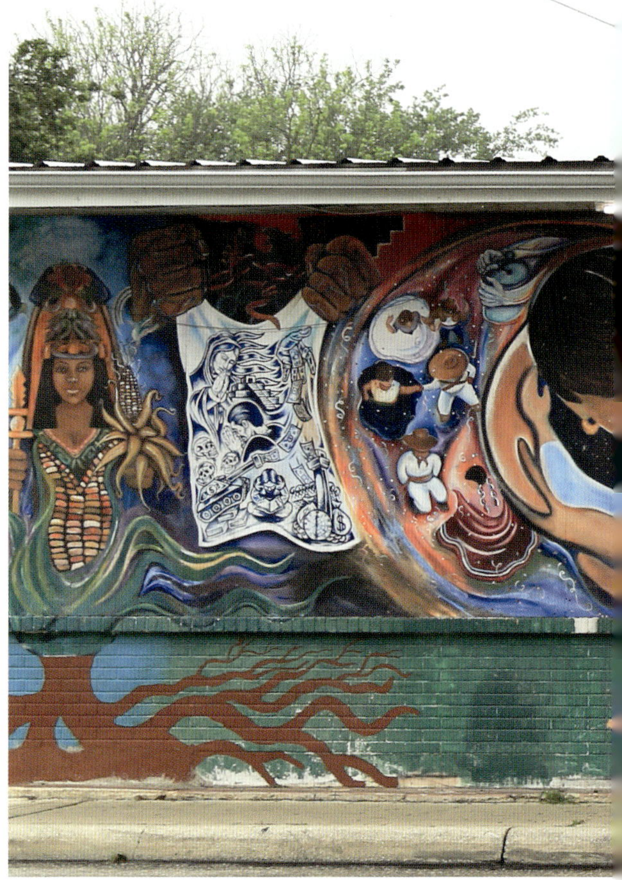

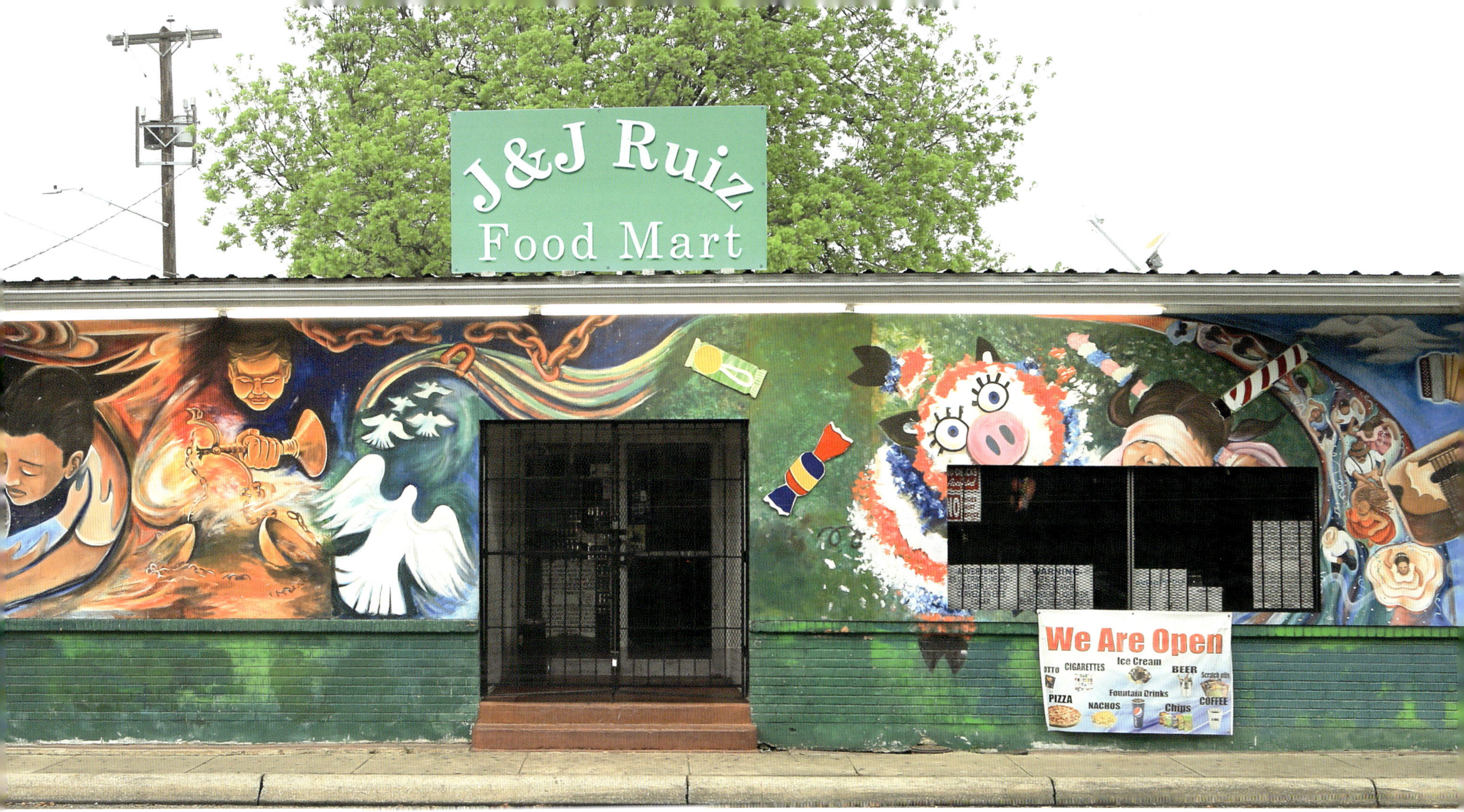

and left our mark
in the public space of our plazas and our parks
our patios and our playgrounds
the walls of stores and of schools,
of hospitals, highways, missions, and homes.

It is immersed in the essence of our lives
And it was created for us.

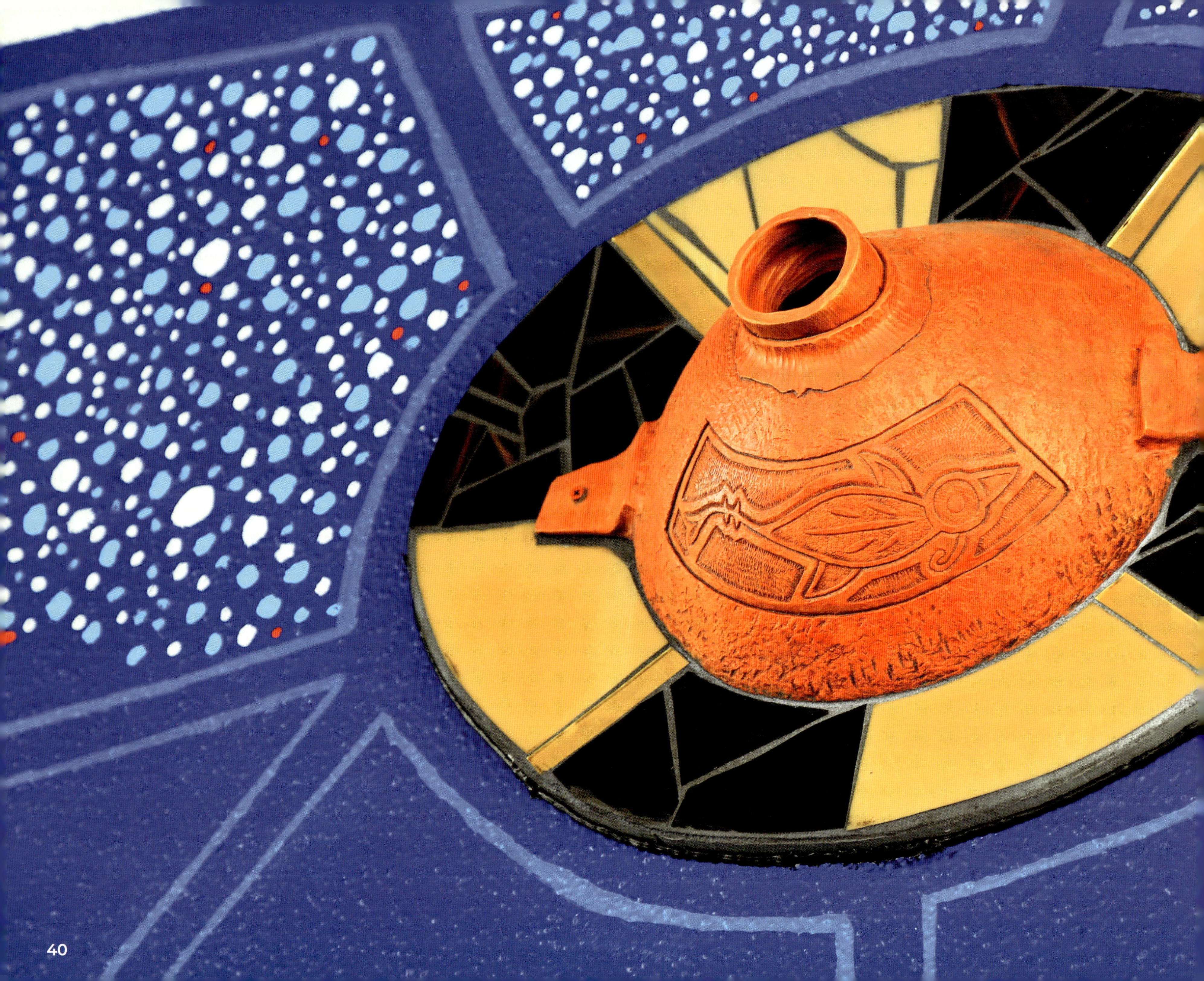

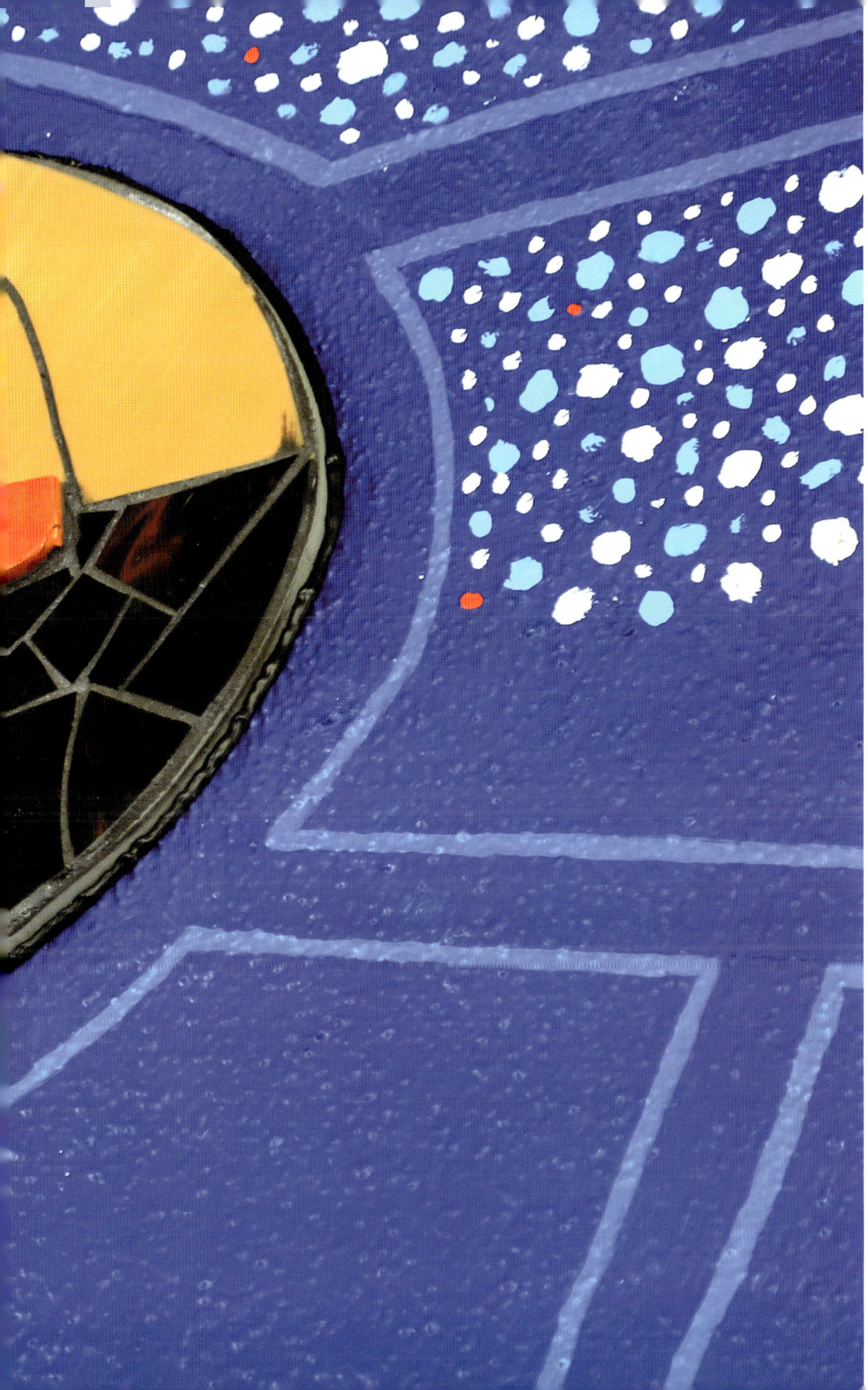

It is the public process of creation,
concepts universal and not bound by deed or title
but owned by the community by the pueblo.

Where I End & You Begin, 2017. Jason E. González Martínez. World Heritage Mural Trail (WHMT), Mission Parkway at SW Military Drive.

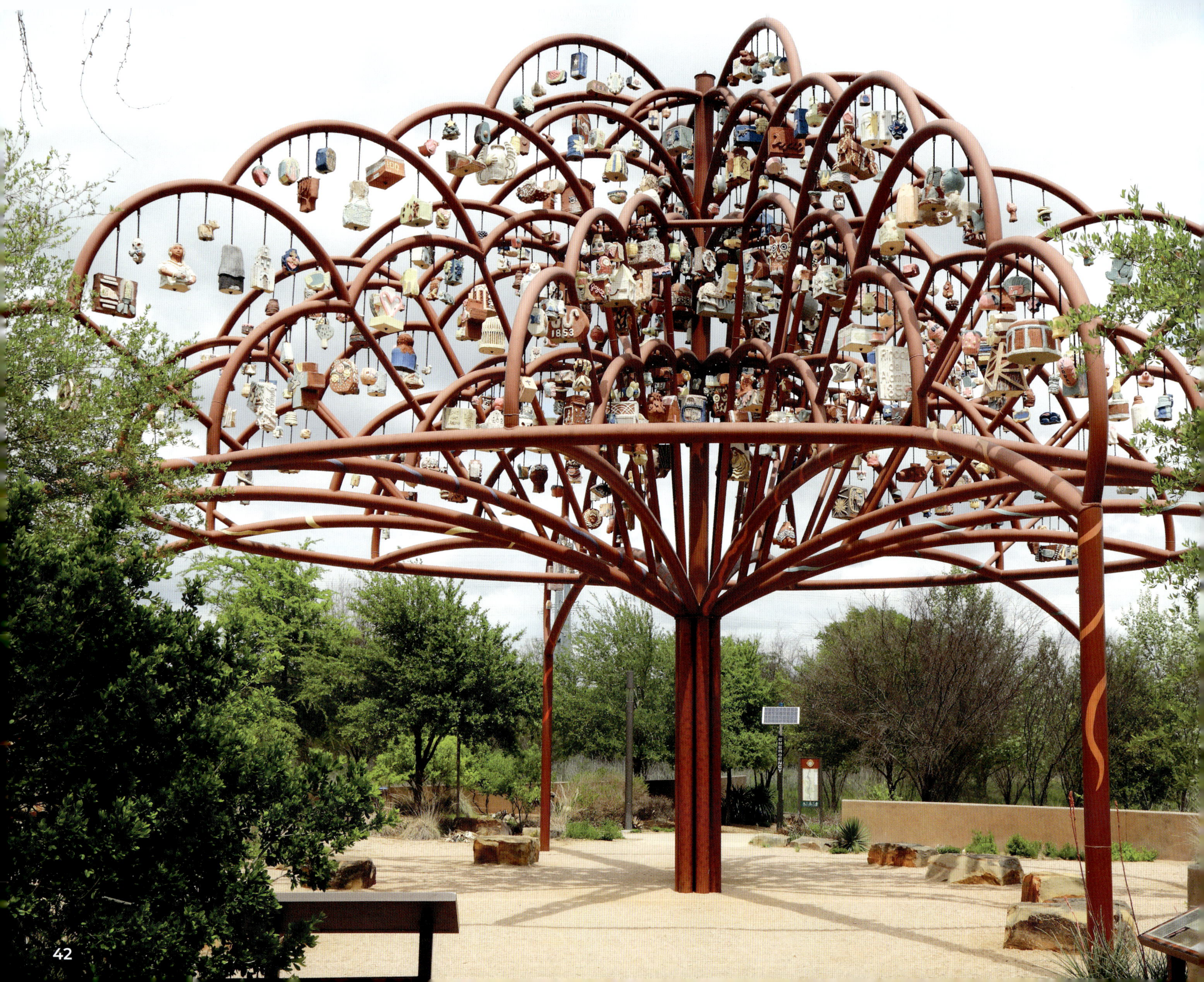

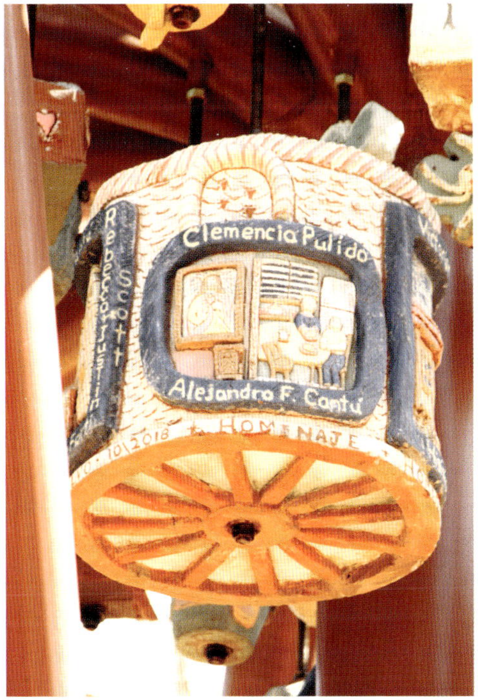

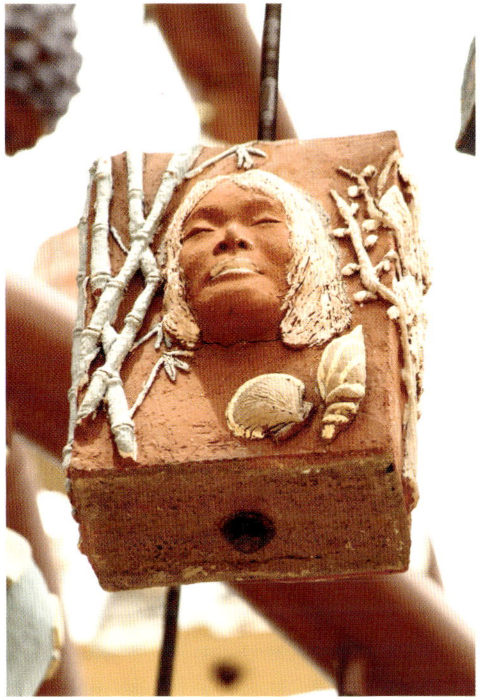

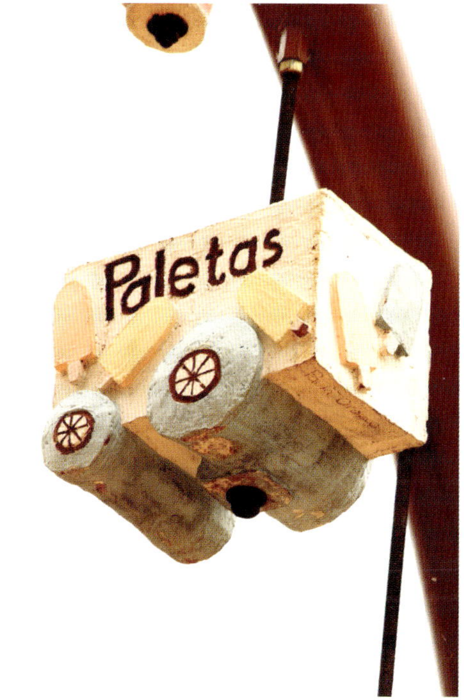

OPPOSITE PAGE
Árbol de la Vida: Memorias y Voces de la Tierra (Tree of Life: Memories and Voices of the Earth), 2019. Margarita Cabrera and community artists. Mission Reach, Mission Espada.

THIS PAGE
Three of the more than seven hundred individual pieces on the *Arbol de la Vida* by Cabrera and community artists

An Immersive Community Engagement,
Cocreation with all the generations who have come before us
and all the peoples who will come after.
A Tree of Life that captures the moments and the messages of our lives—
the paleta wagon that made us run, squealing with delight
the family celebration that made us laugh
the ghost of an ancestor shining through the bones of our dreams
the heirlooms of spirit that help us survive.

Cocreators we are all, a community building a monument,
Adding a leaf to this tree of life, this shade of nurturance.

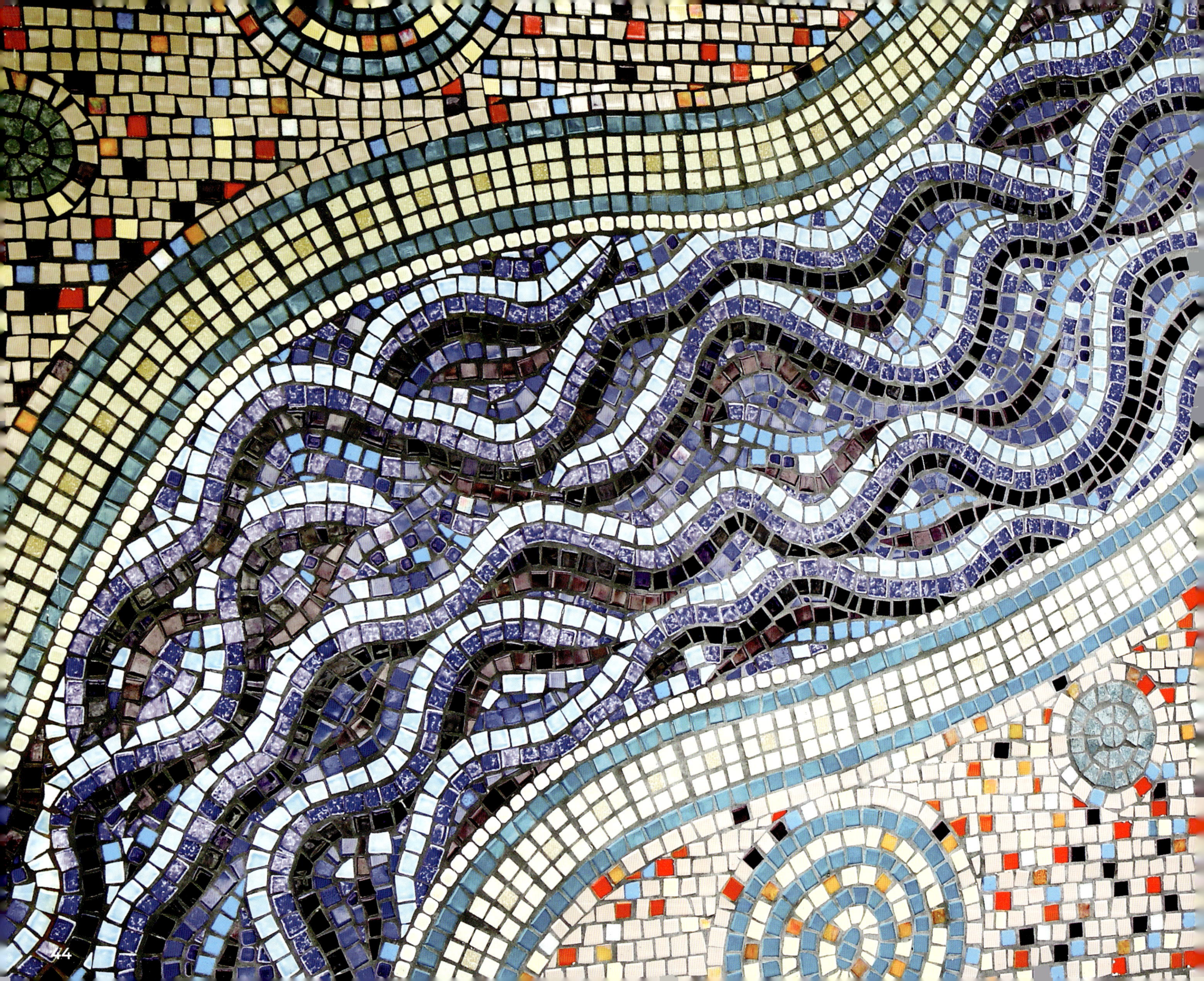

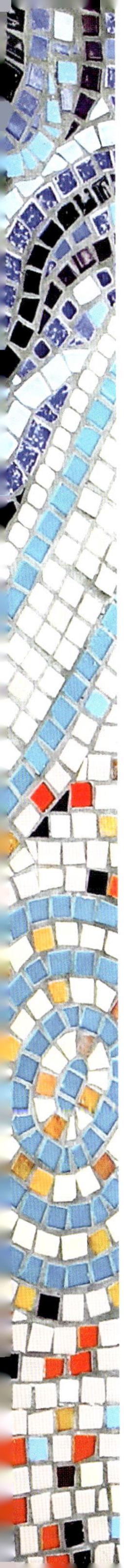

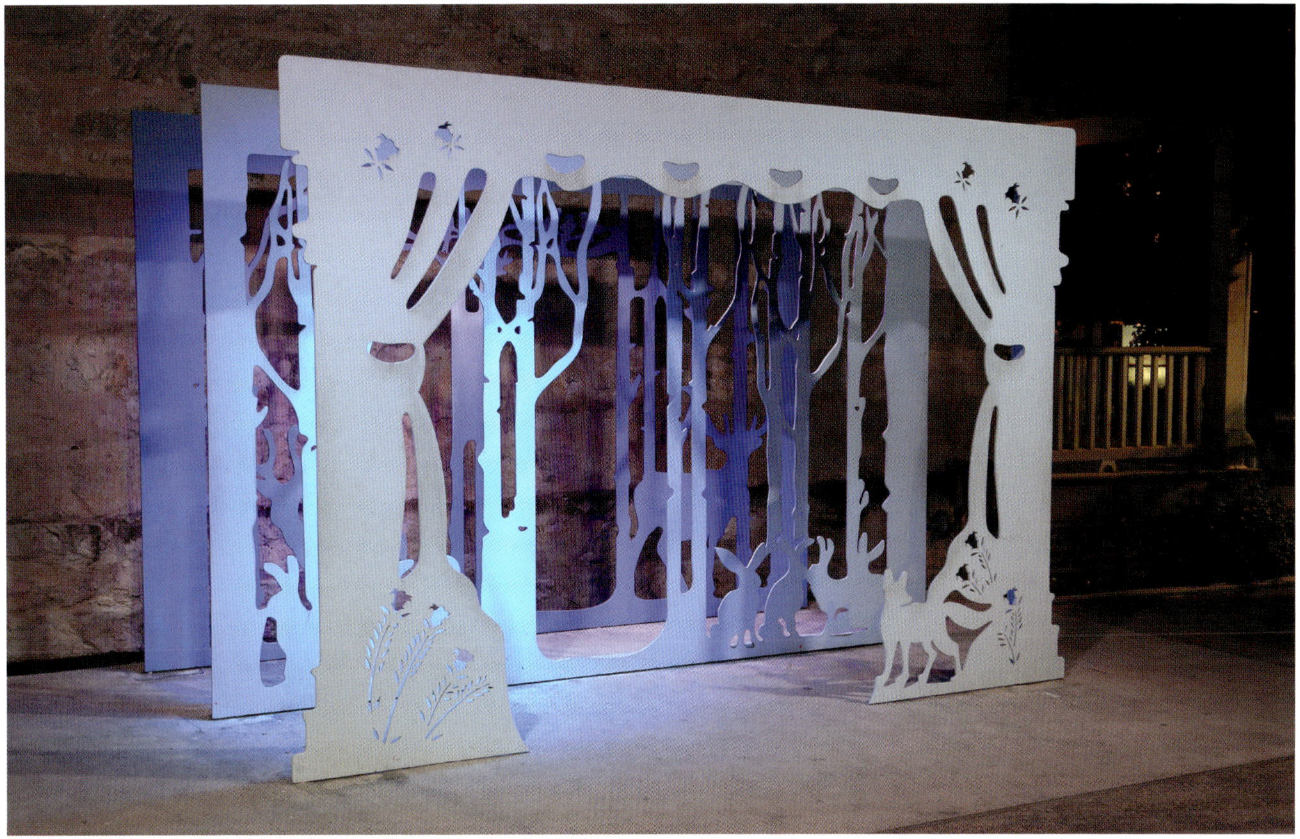

OPPOSITE PAGE
Detail from Mosaic Wall along River Walk, 2002. Oscar Alvarado.

THIS PAGE
Sideshow, 2015. Jennifer Khoshbin. Hemisfair Park, Yanaguana Garden.

This public expression
of the meaning of our lives,
this song of our sweat
and rainbow of our voices,
like the magic spring of Yanaguana,
is fed by our love of it. It blossoms
through our enchanted eyes. And we
blossom through its reflection.
Its impact—
        our lives enriched.

Whispers, 2015.
Arne Quinze.
Mission Reach.

OPPOSITE PAGE
Humans of San Antonio, 2019.
Michael Cirlos.
Broadway-Peacock Alley. Wheat paste photo on paper, 100 feet wide.

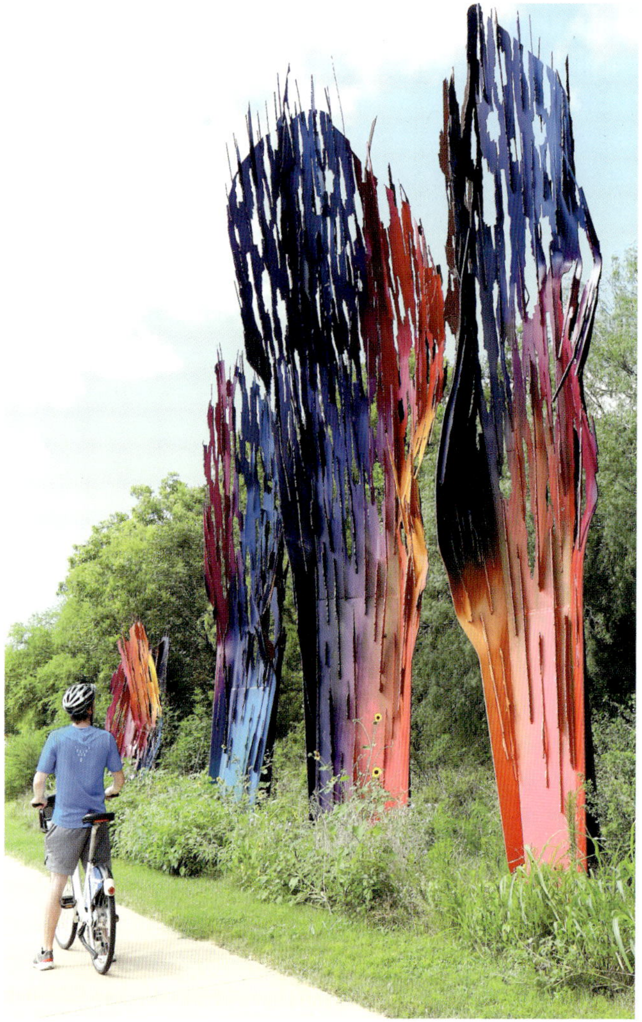

The artists, like prophets,
are see-ers,
capturing what is truly before us
So that we may fully live it, absorb it,
see it. Breathe it.

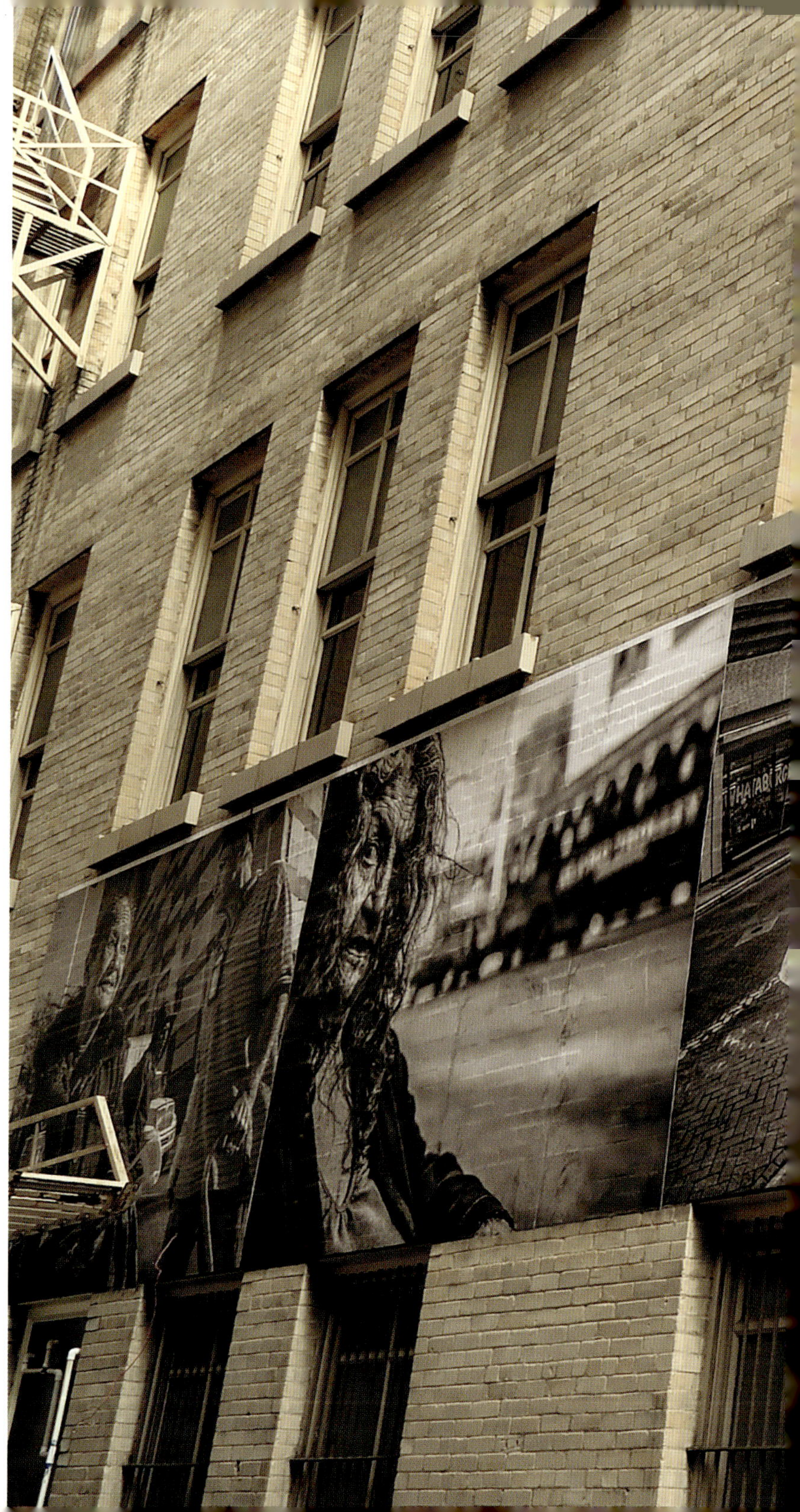

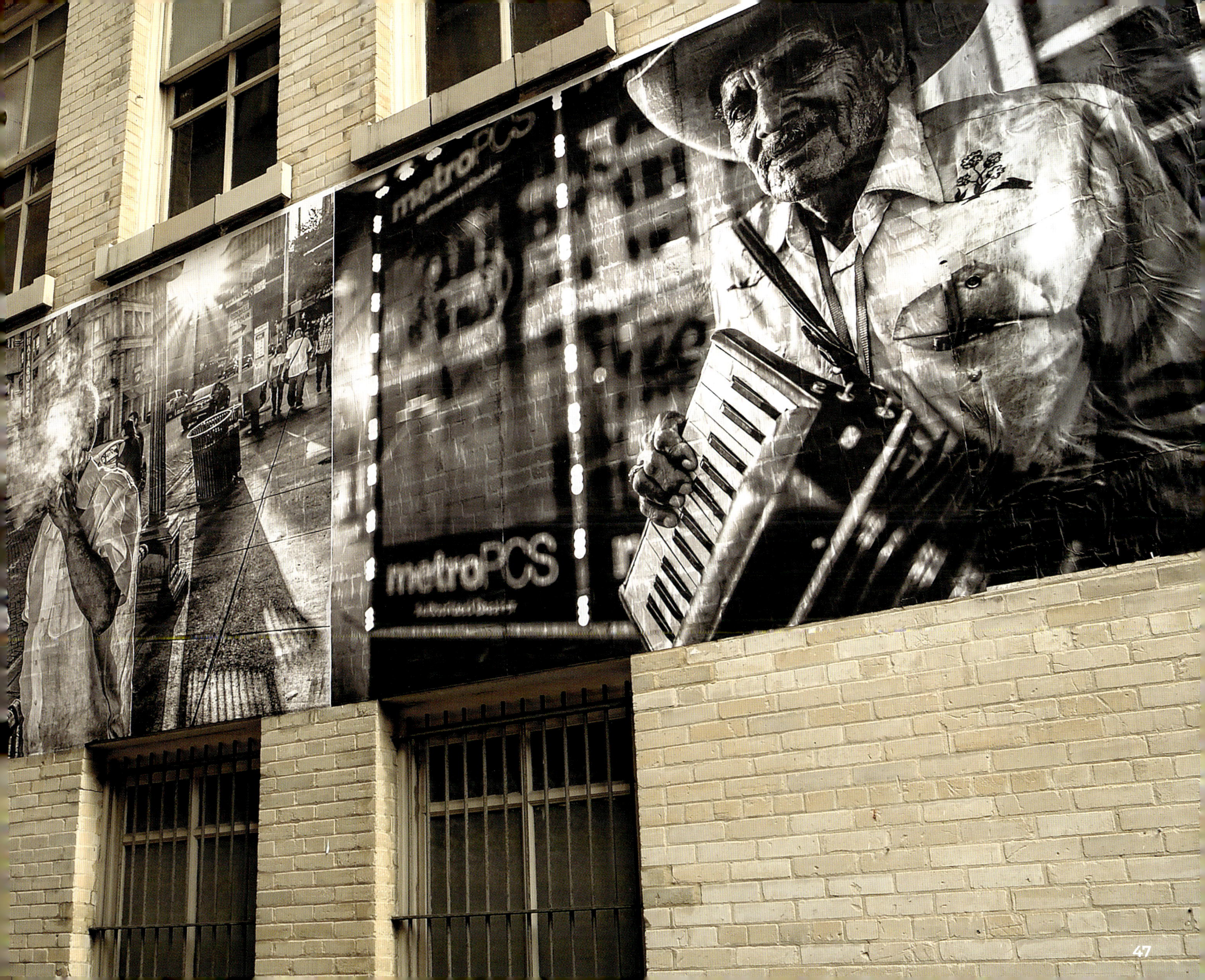
metroPCS
metroPCS

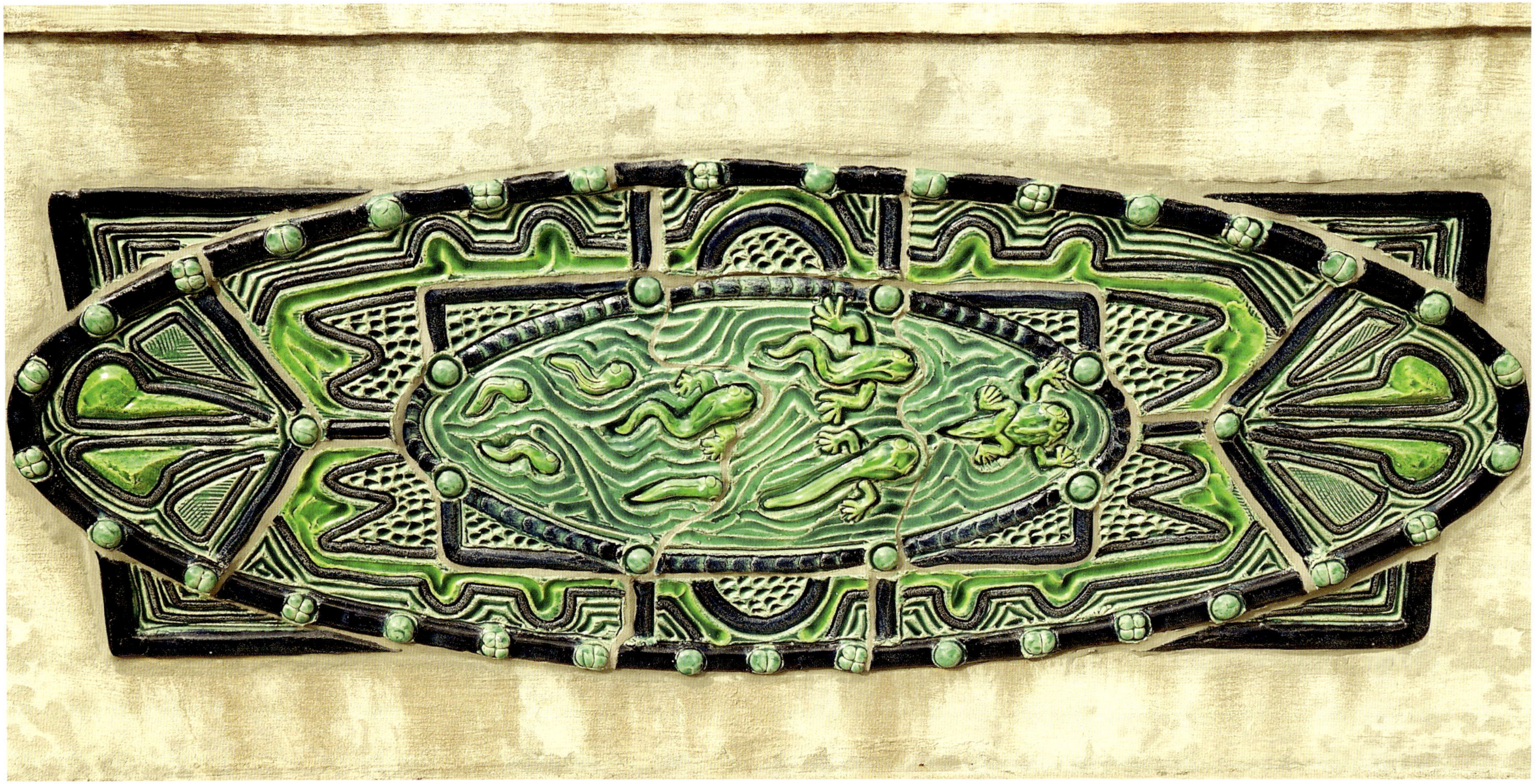

ABOVE
Life Cycle of the Gulf Coast Toad, 2011. Diana Kersey. E. Mulberry bridge at Brackenridge Park.

BOTTOM LEFT
Red Arch, 2018. Katie Pell. San Pedro Creek Culture Park.

BOTTOM RIGHT
Where I End & You Begin, 2017. Jason E. González. Mission Parkway and SW Military Drive.

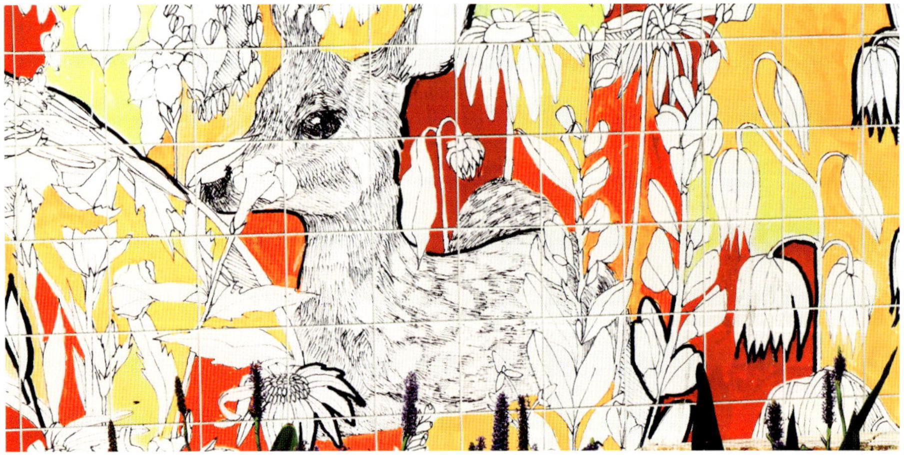

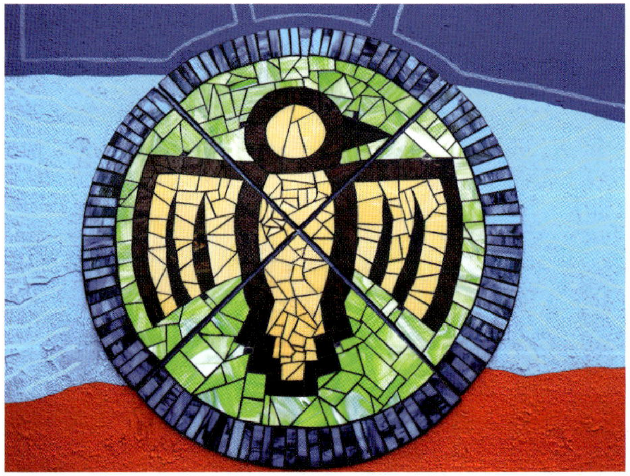

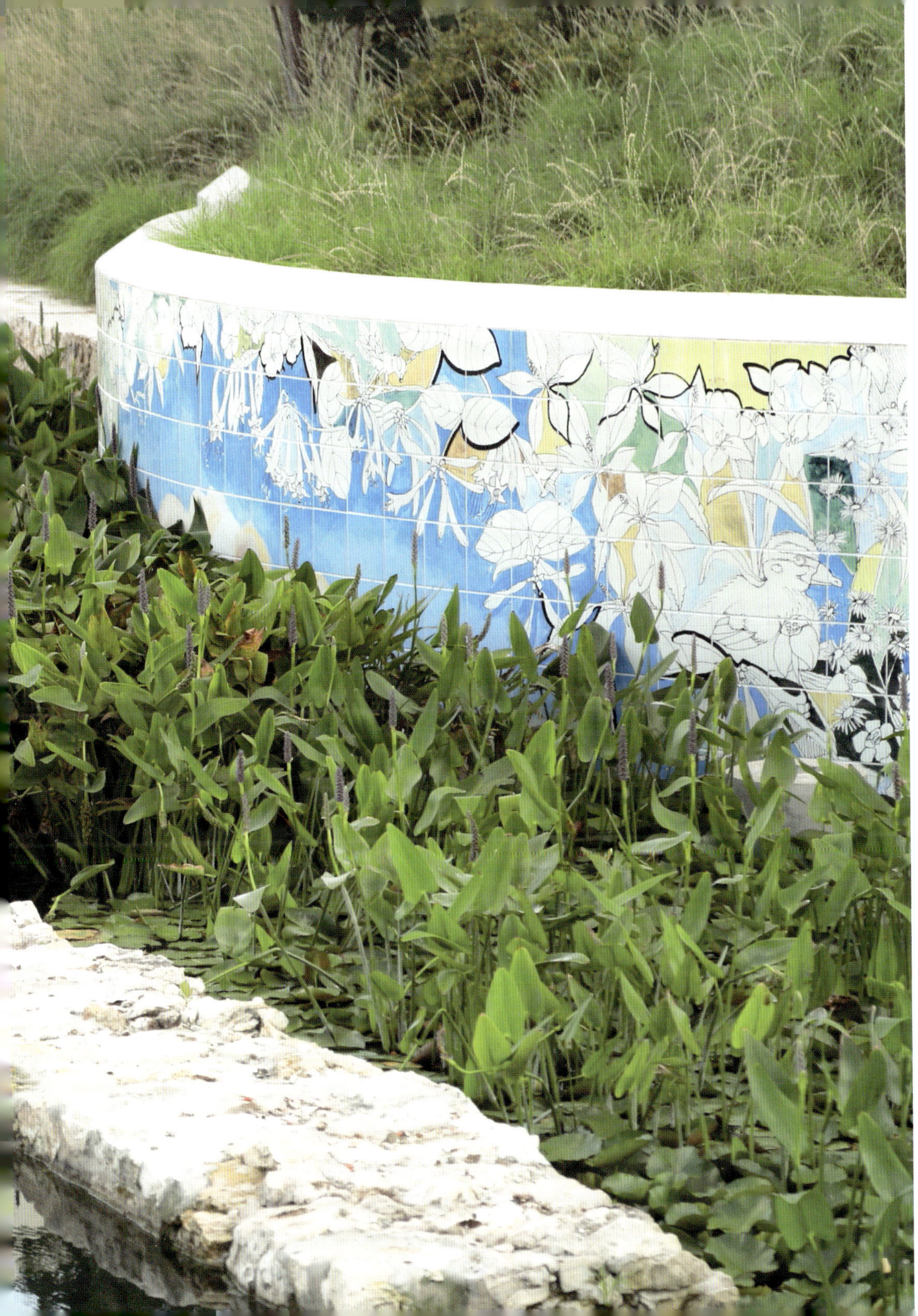

II. TELLING OUR STORY

AFFIRMING OUR HERITAGE

From the beginning of time
the turtles and the birds
the fish and the four-footed creatures
came, drank, found rest
and a shade of coolness here,

Blue Arch.
Katie Pell.
San Pedro Creek.

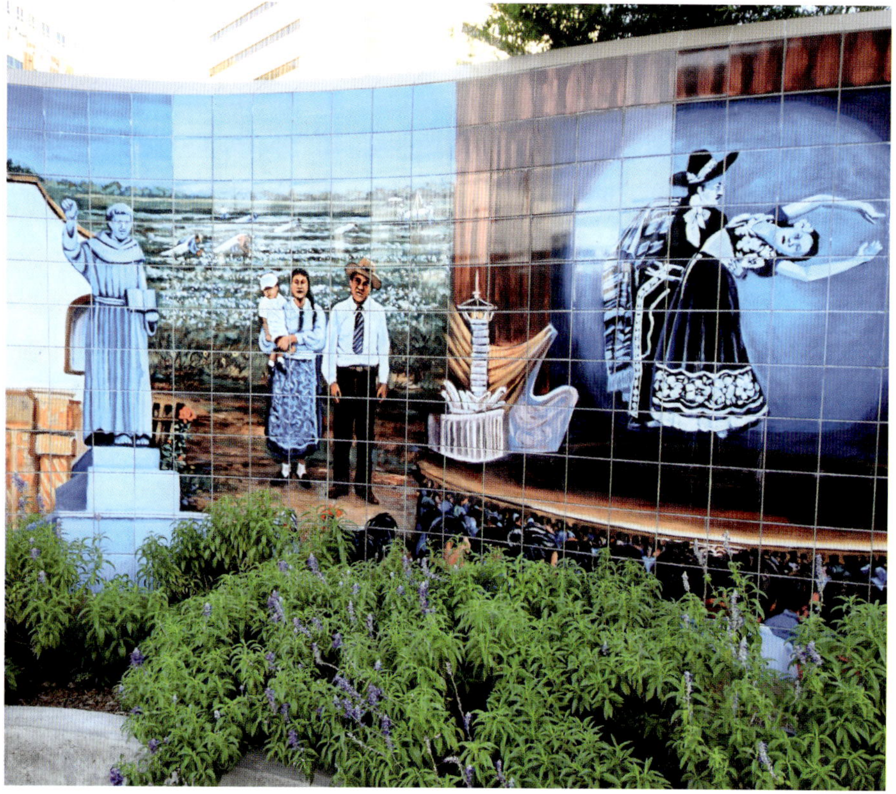

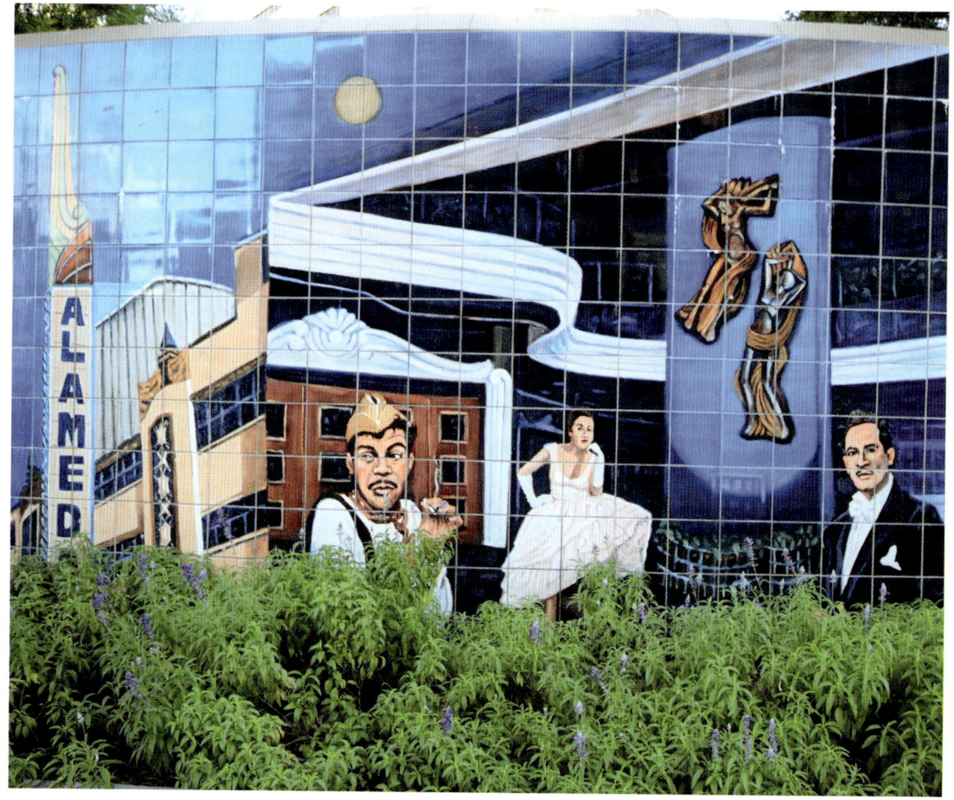

as do we today, all forms of life,
still seeking out this beauty that belongs to
all of us gathered here to create what is
San Antonio, un pueblo de Arte.
Un Arte del pueblo.

Some come here thinking we began with the world's fair.
Some come believing this all started with the Battle of the Alamo.
Some come claiming we were founded by Spaniards three hundred years ago.
But our story precedes that by thousands of years.

ABOVE LEFT AND RIGHT *Beautiful Memories of the Alameda Theatre & Times Passed*, 2018. Joe López. San Pedro Creek.

OPPOSITE PAGE *Confluence of Civilizations in the Americas*, 1968. Juan O'Gorman. Lila Cockrell Theater, Henry B. González Convention Center.

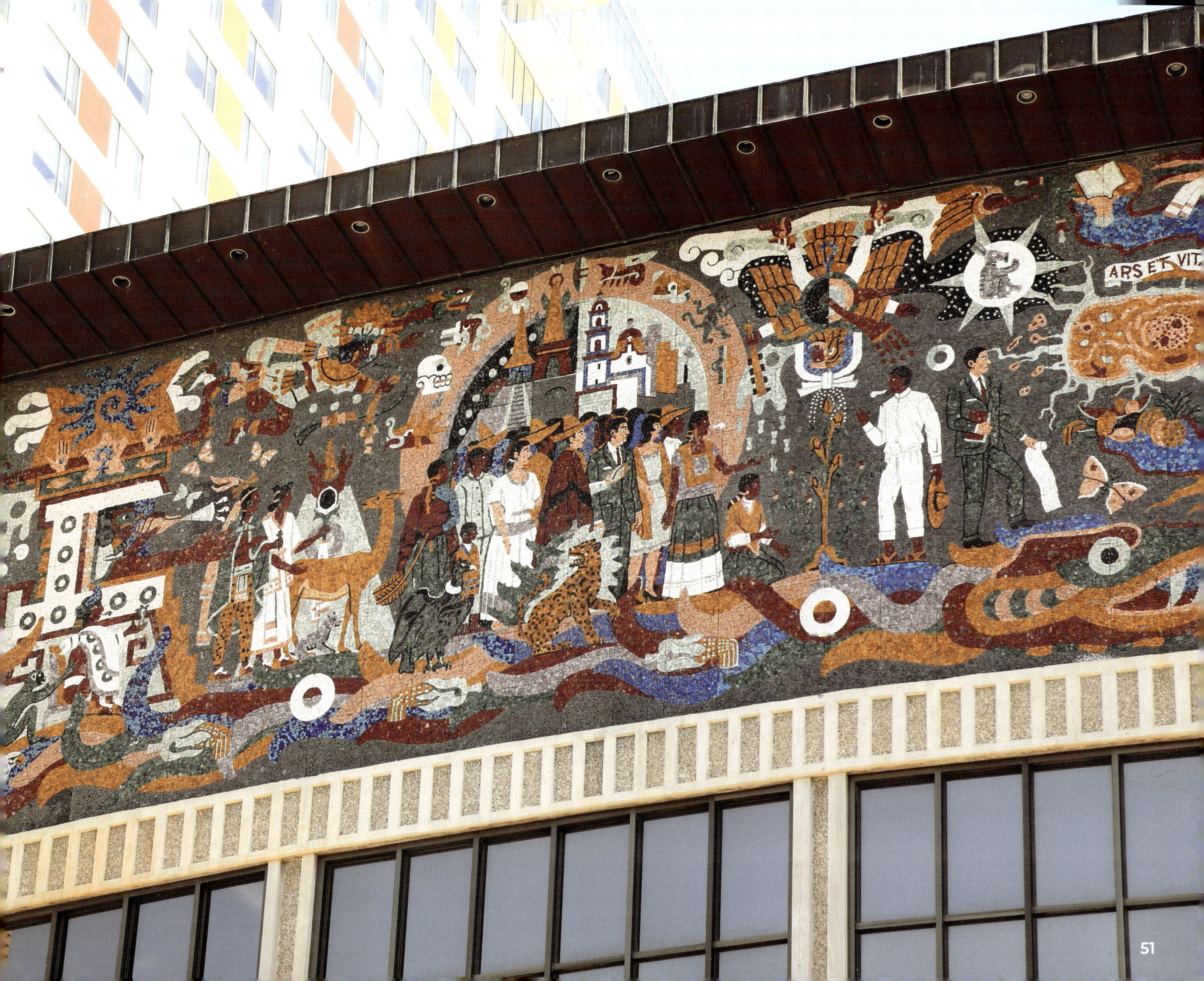
ARS ET VIT

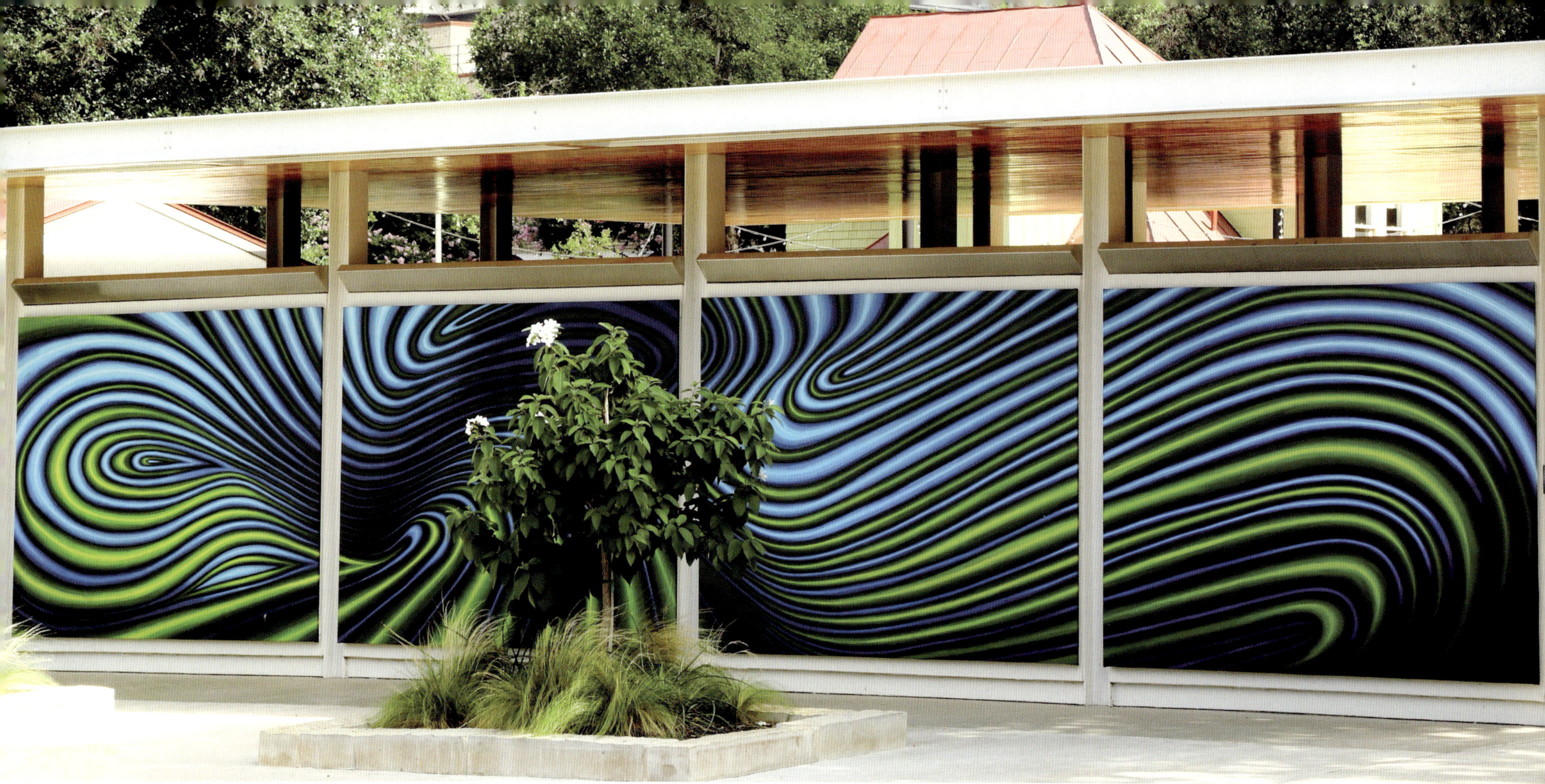

Our history sprouts from this Yanaguana spring
shooting 20 feet into the turquoise sky.
A sacred place, a joyous abundance,
the Blue Hole fed us, for millennia.

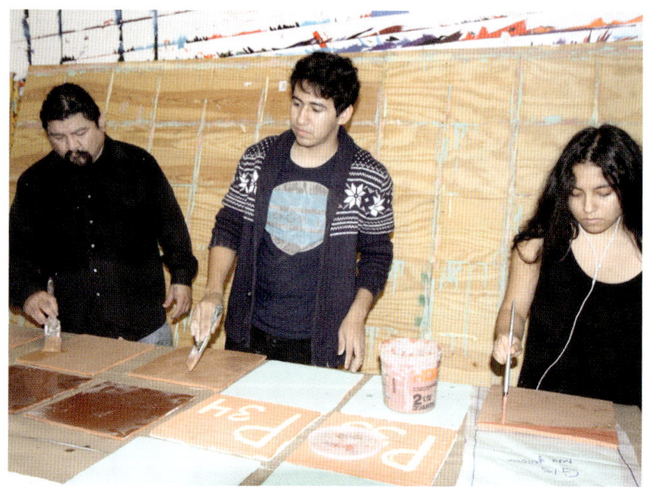

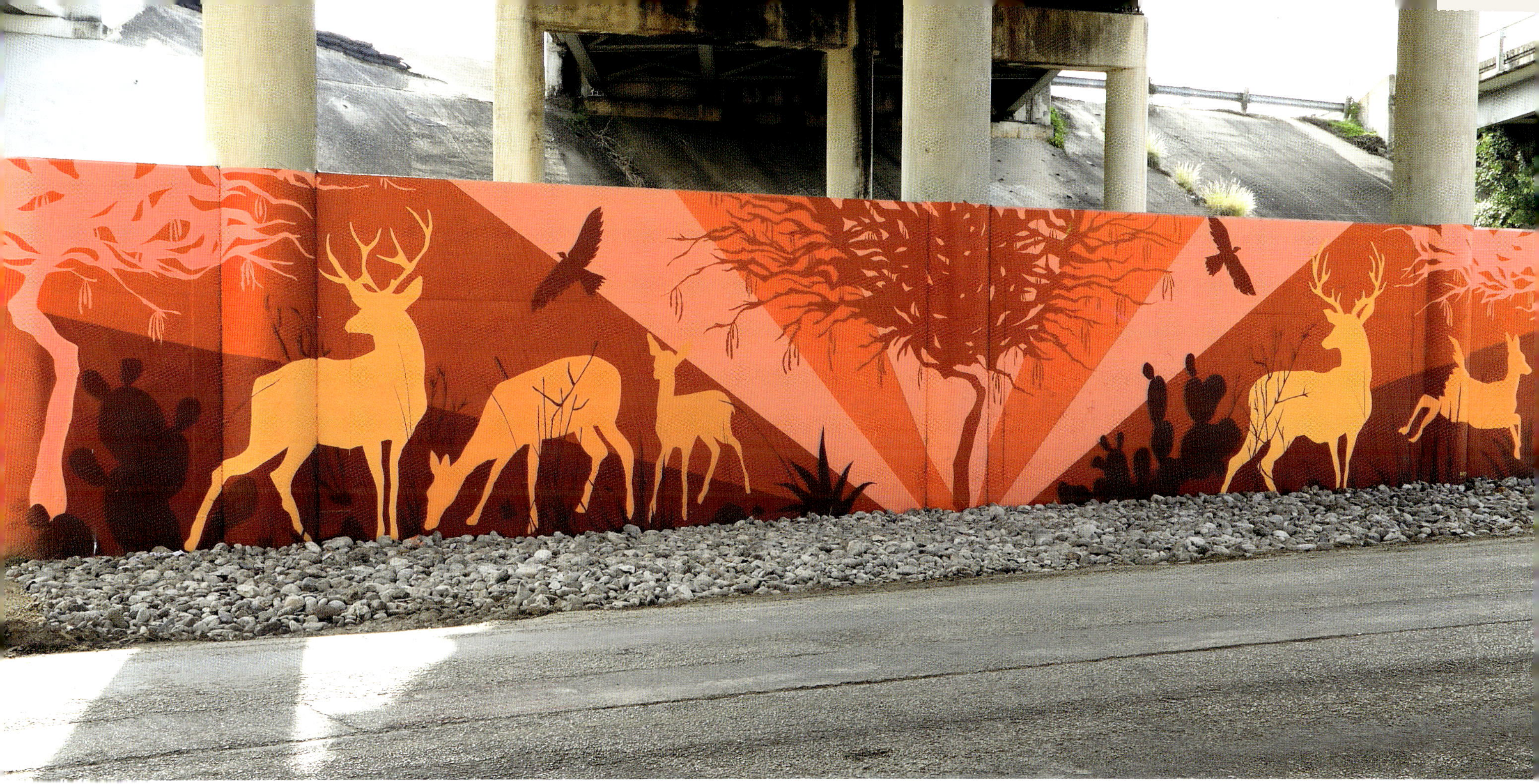

OPPOSITE PAGE
TOP
Yanaguana, 2015. Alex Rubio and Blue Star Contemporary Art Museum's MOSAIC student artists. Yanaguana Garden.

BOTTOM
Alex Rubio cocreating art with students at Blue Star Arts Complex, 2015

THIS PAGE
Fall, 2017. Chris Montoya. World Heritage Mural Trail (WHMT), Villamain Road.

First nations flourished here thousands of years ago
on venison and black bass, pecan and mesquite bean.
The Payaya, Coahuilteca, Lipán Apache,
Comanche, Comecrudo, and more.
And more.

Ramón Vásquez y Sánchez, Tap Pilam Coahuiltecan elder, blessing the mural *Winter*, 2017. Cristina Sosa Noriega. WHMT.

OPPOSITE PAGE *Midden Mounds Wickiups-Encampment*, 2016. Buster Simpson. Pearsall Park. Built over the modern middens of a landfill, these midden mounds are sculpted wickiups covered by Indian "blankets" made of colorful woven wire mesh and geometric Hexcel.

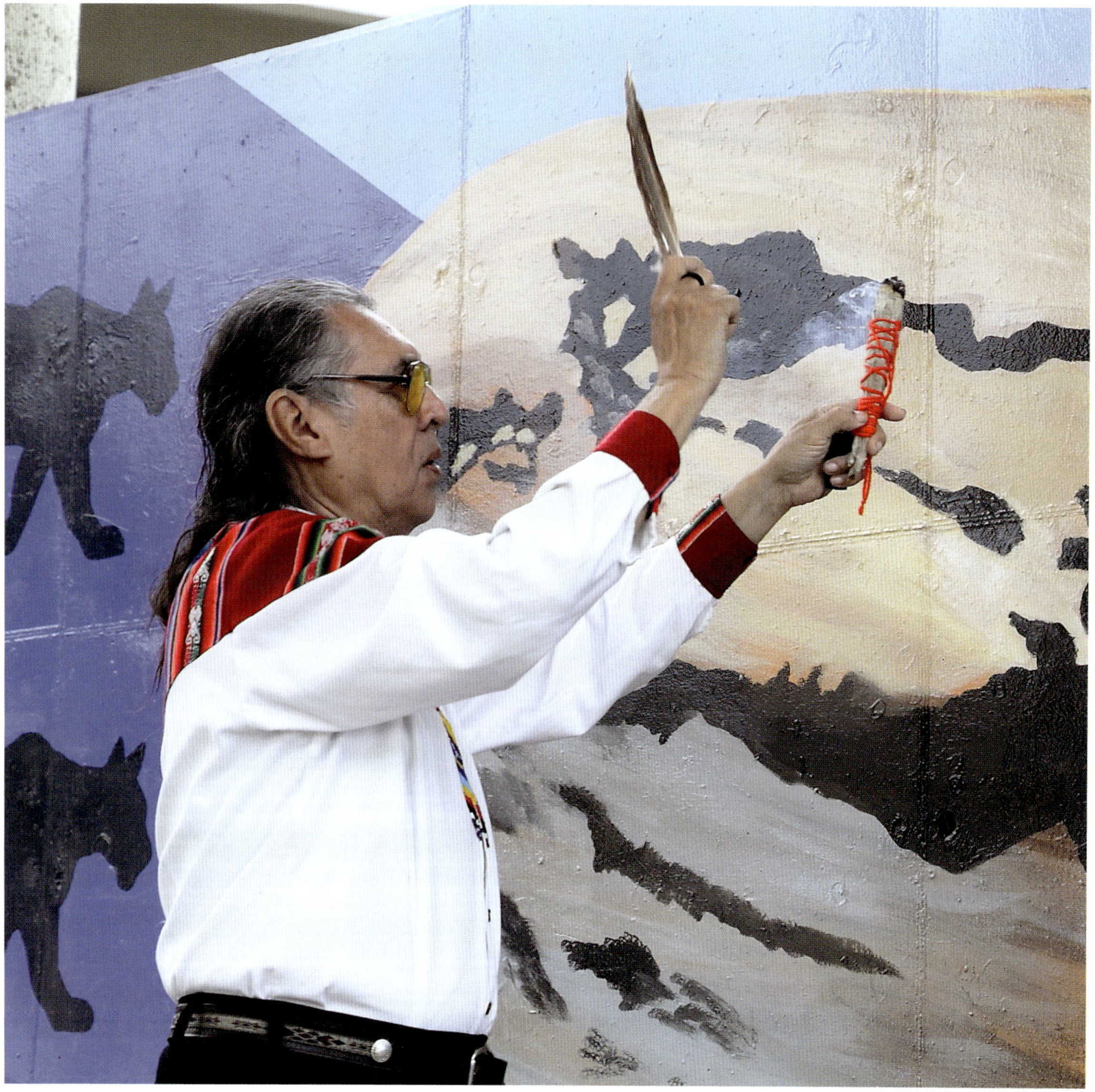

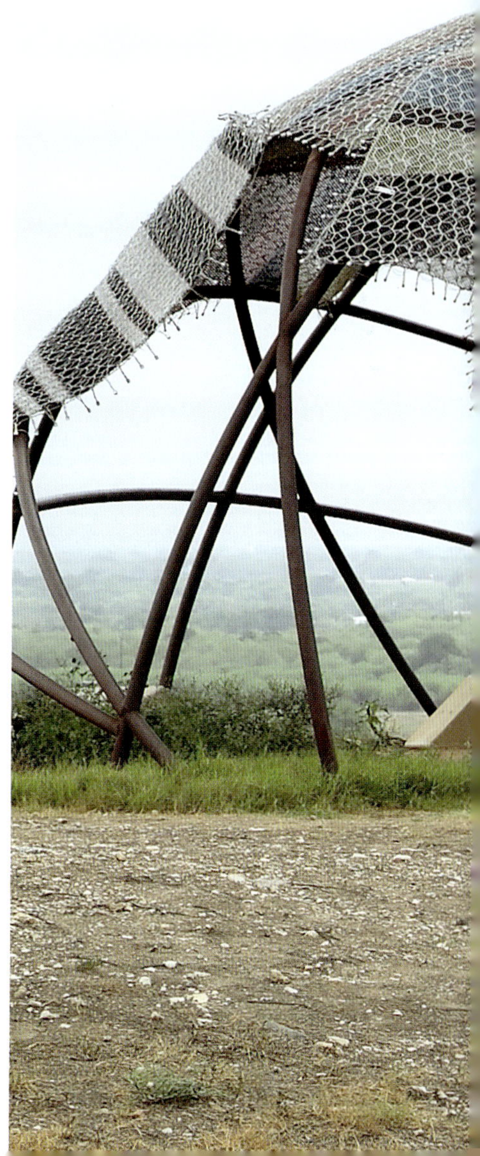

Our art reflects our history. It is a human voice
crying out to let its story be heard—
the sacred copal smoke of its memories,
the graceful dance of deer in its dreams,
its concrete pain, its struggles, its rumbling power.

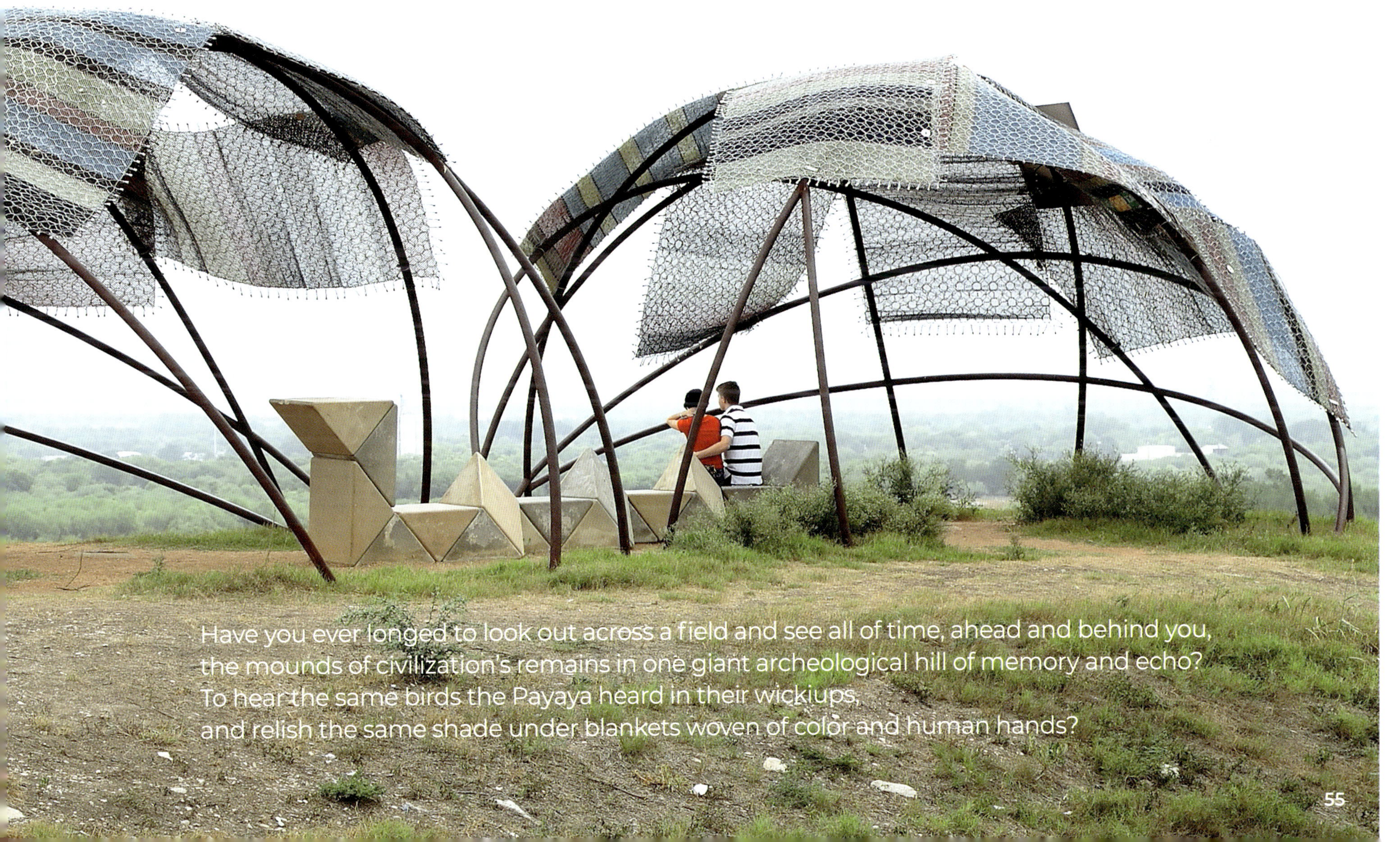

Have you ever longed to look out across a field and see all of time, ahead and behind you,
the mounds of civilization's remains in one giant archeological hill of memory and echo?
To hear the same birds the Payaya heard in their wickiups,
and relish the same shade under blankets woven of color and human hands?

Najo Jam, 2021. Carlos Cortés and Doroteo Garza. Comanche Park.

OPPOSITE PAGE *The Founders Monument*, 2019. Armando García Hinojosa. Bexar County Courthouse Complex.

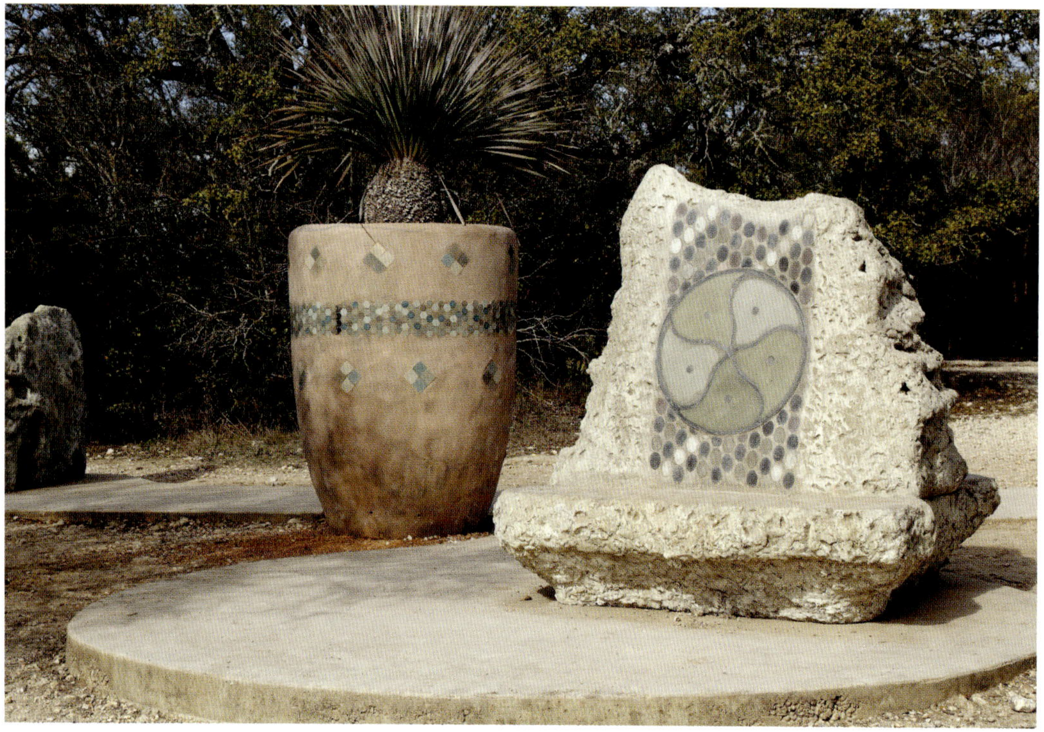

Then look. For we are here.
Not disappeared, or conquered. Not ignored.
Not fragments of the past, but breathing right beside you.
For these first nations have left their mark, their legends and values,
their art designs, their words and songs, and us, their people.
Their genes, singing in our blood. Their dreams, in our children.

It's a beautiful place for a mission,
said the priest in 1718.
And the Indians who'd befriended him
set out to build its walls,
to carve its stone, and paint the native colors on
San Antonio de Valero, then San José, Espada,
San Juan Capistrano, and Concepción.

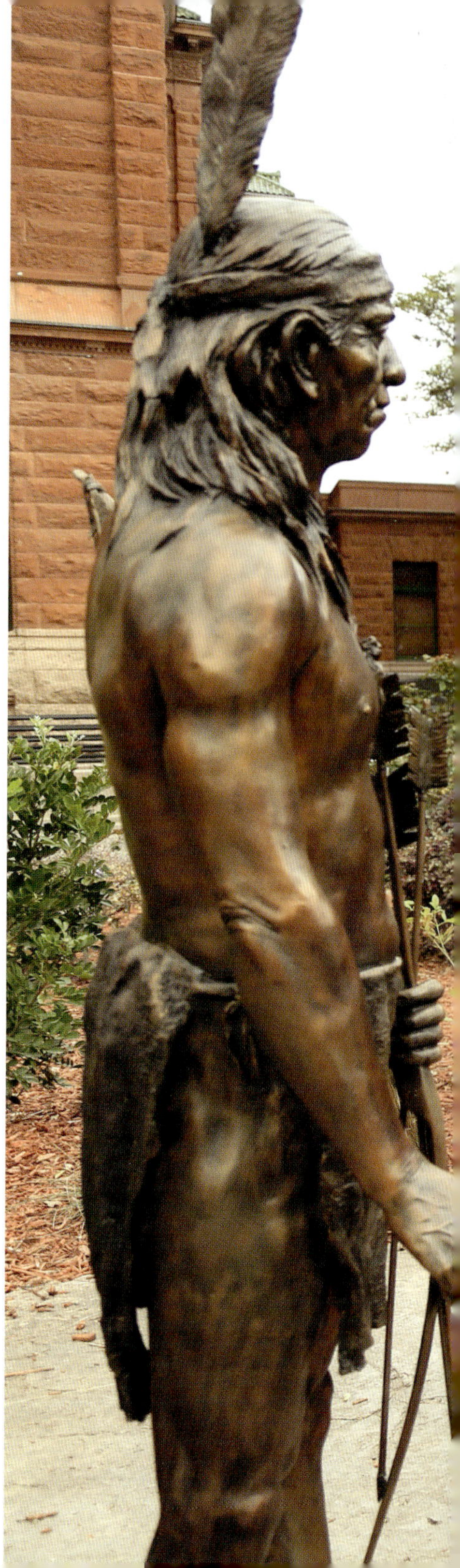

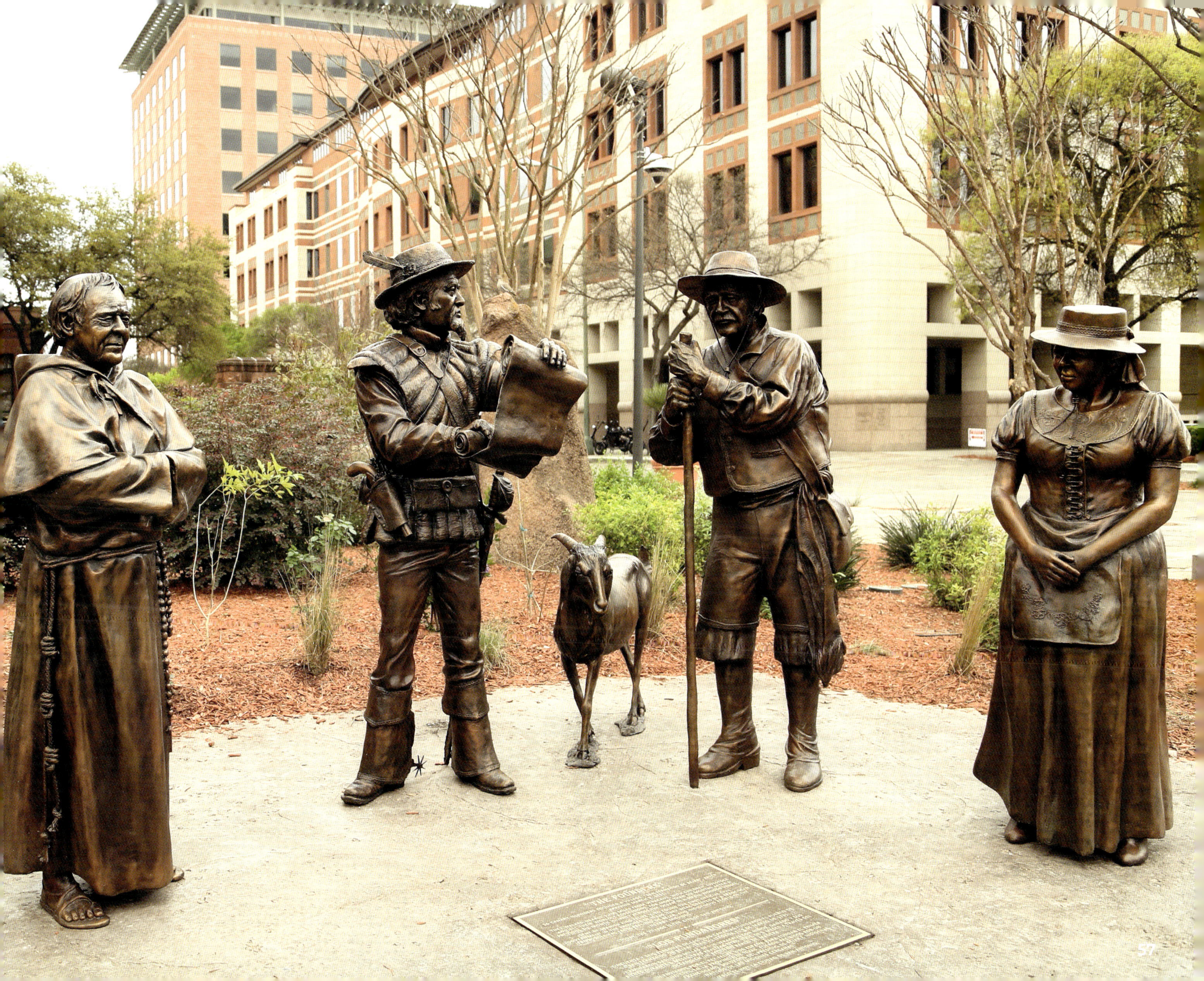

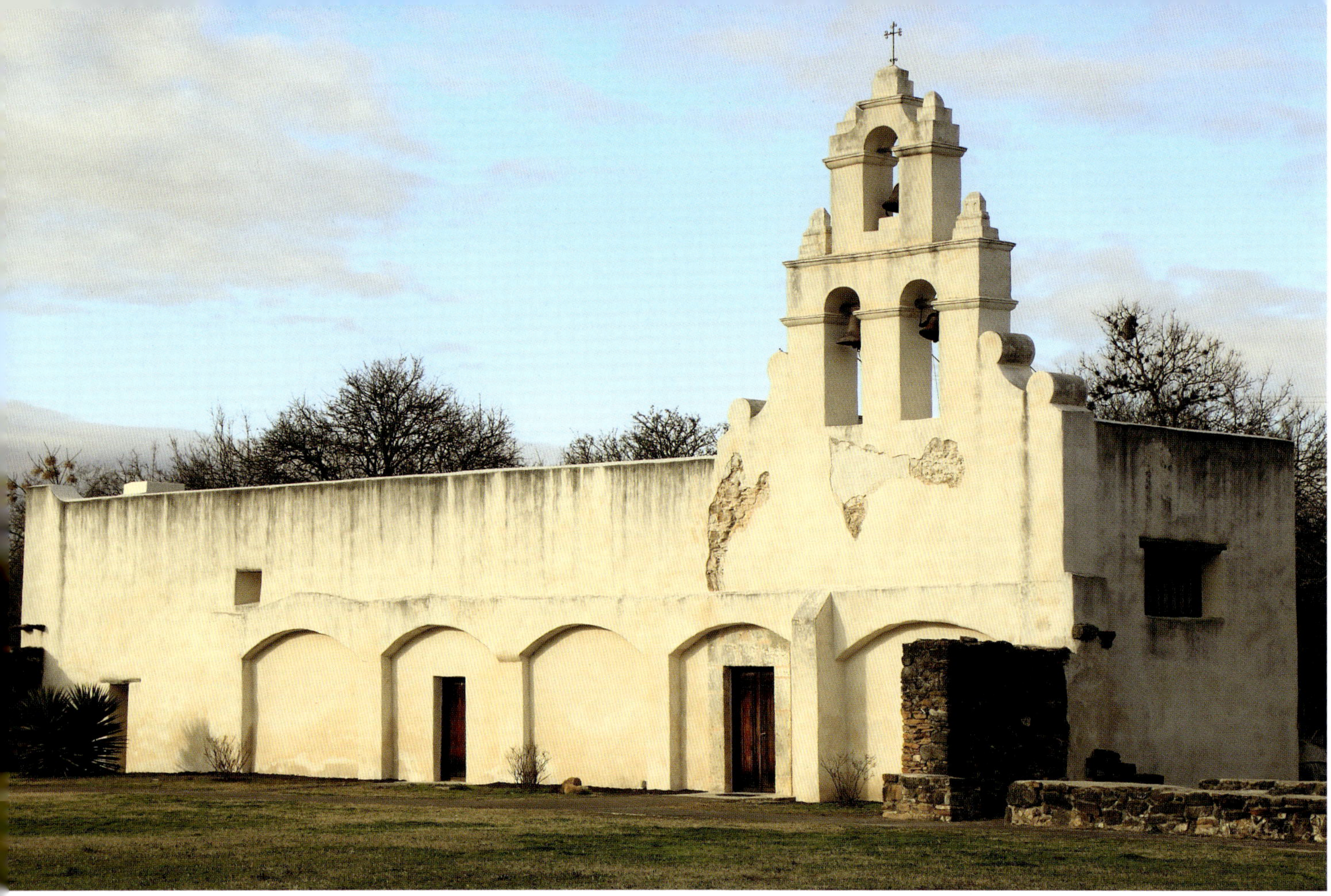

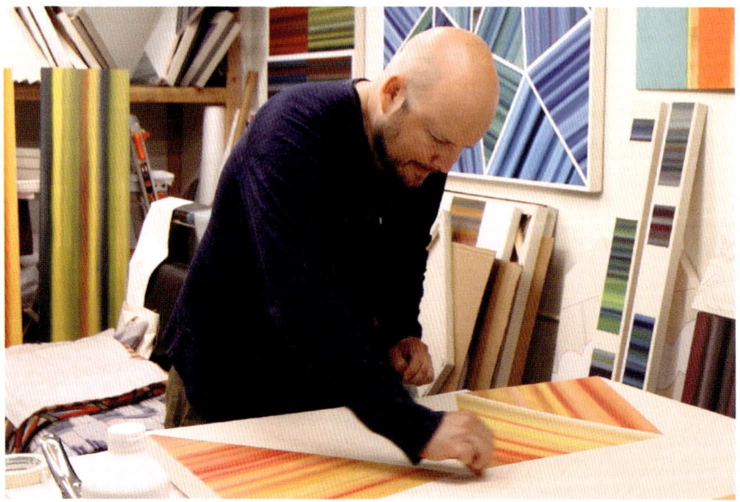

ABOVE
Mission San Juan Capistrano, built in 1756 by Indigenous peoples and Franciscan friars

RIGHT
Louis Vega Treviño in his studio

OPPOSITE PAGE
Mission San Juan light display, 2018. Louis Vega Treviño.

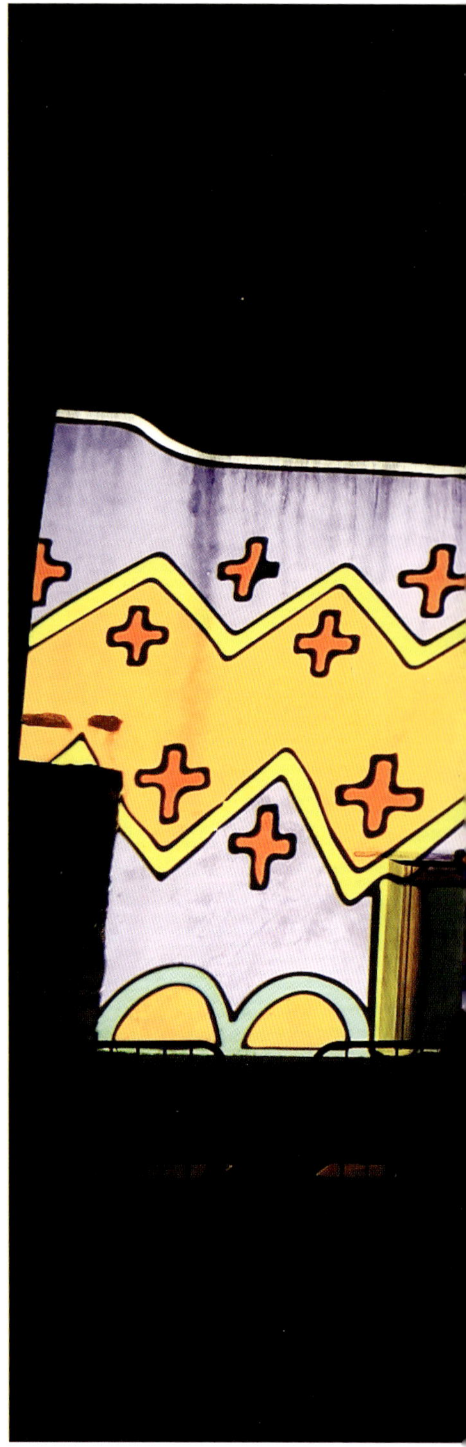

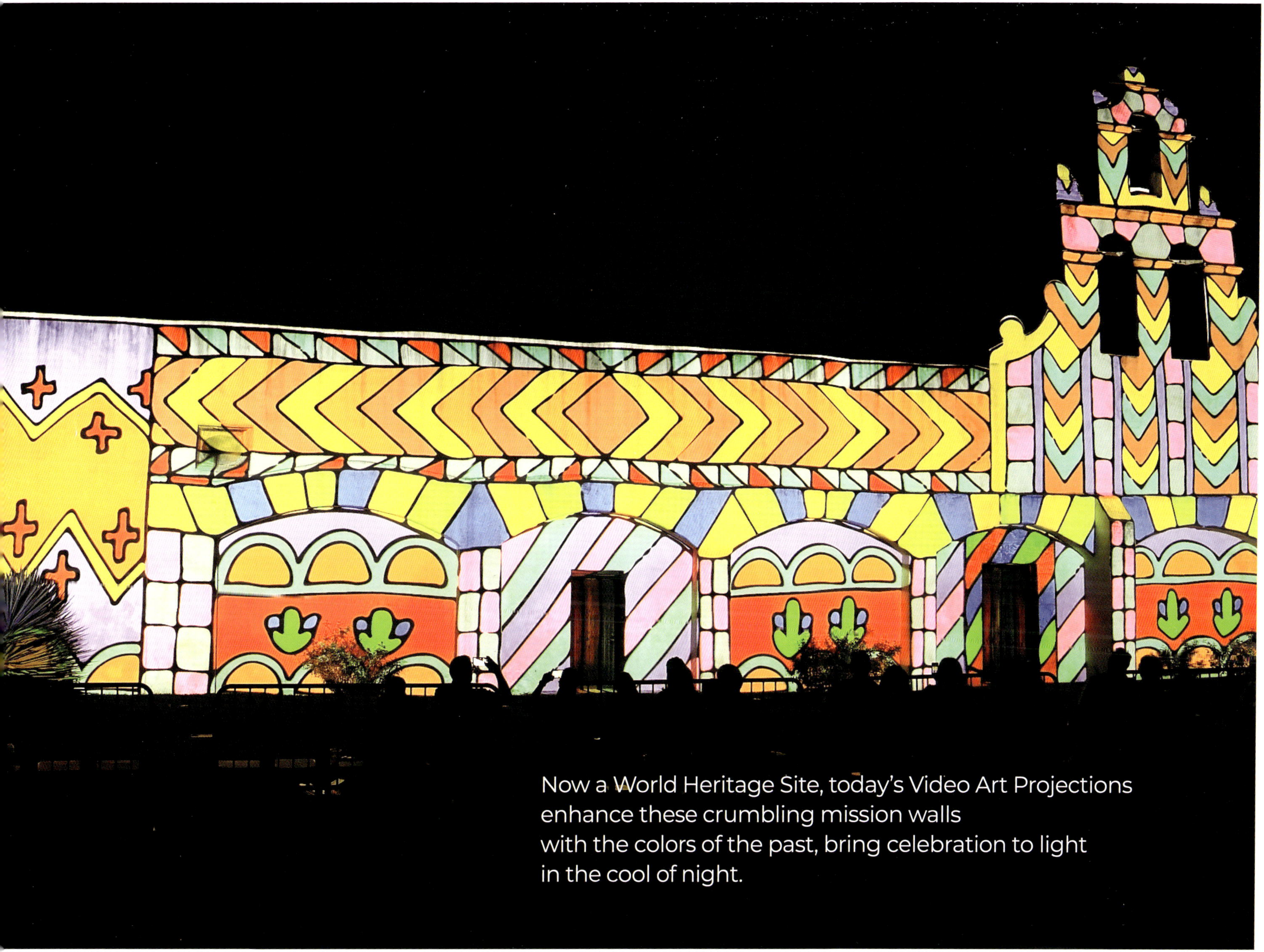

Now a World Heritage Site, today's Video Art Projections
enhance these crumbling mission walls
with the colors of the past, bring celebration to light
in the cool of night.

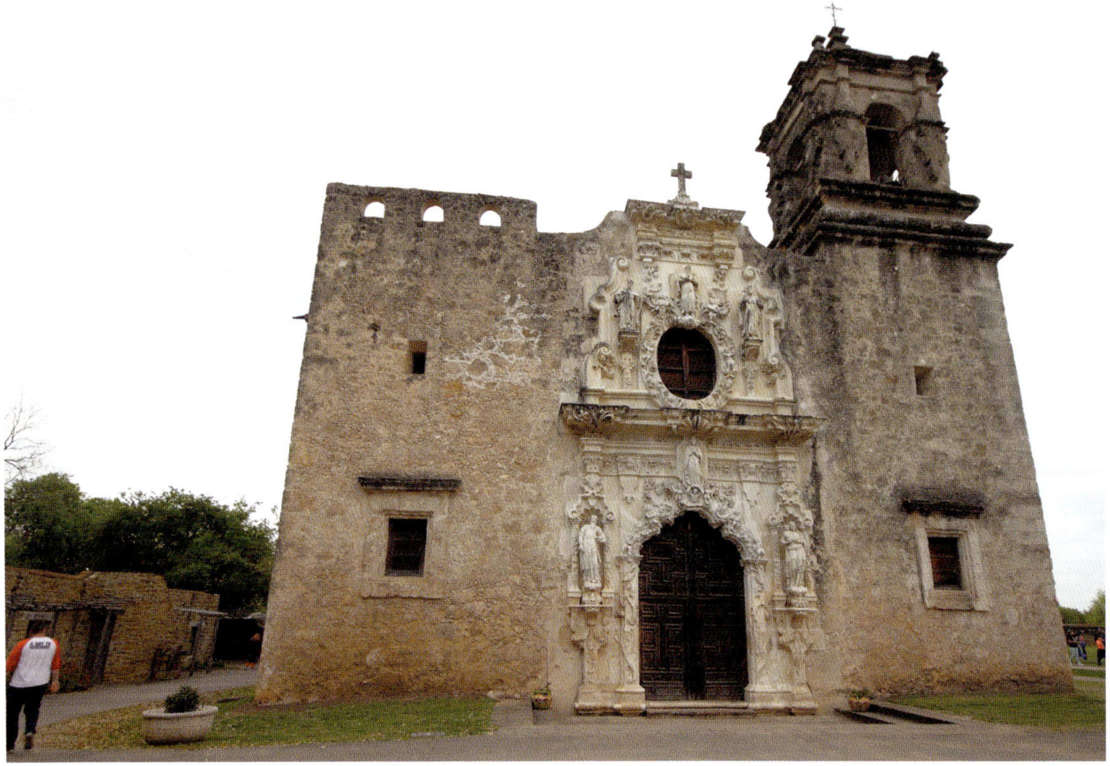

ABOVE
Mission San José,
built in 1768

RIGHT
Mission San José projected digital display, reflecting original designs and colors from the Mission as it was painted in the 1700s. 2019. Philip Prasek.

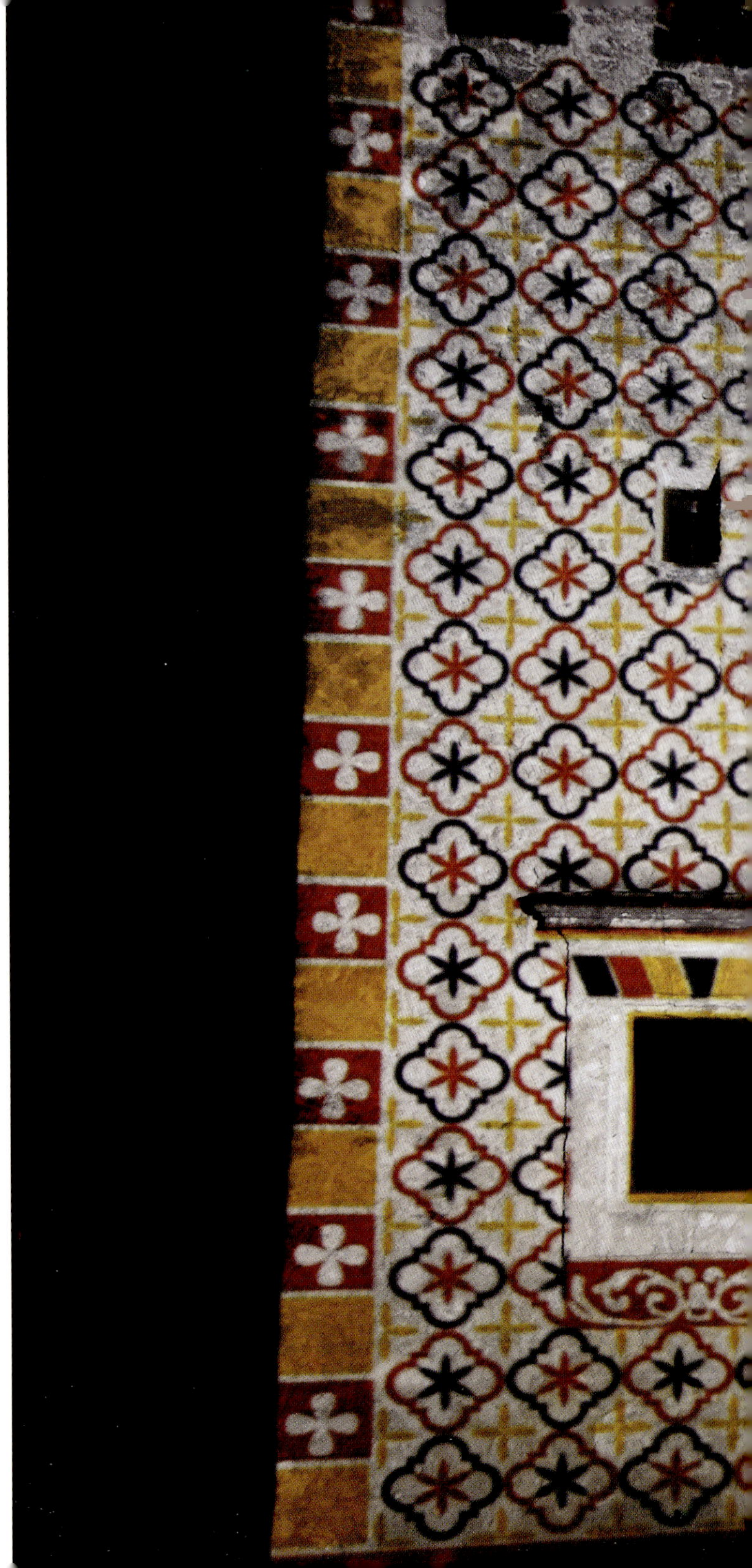

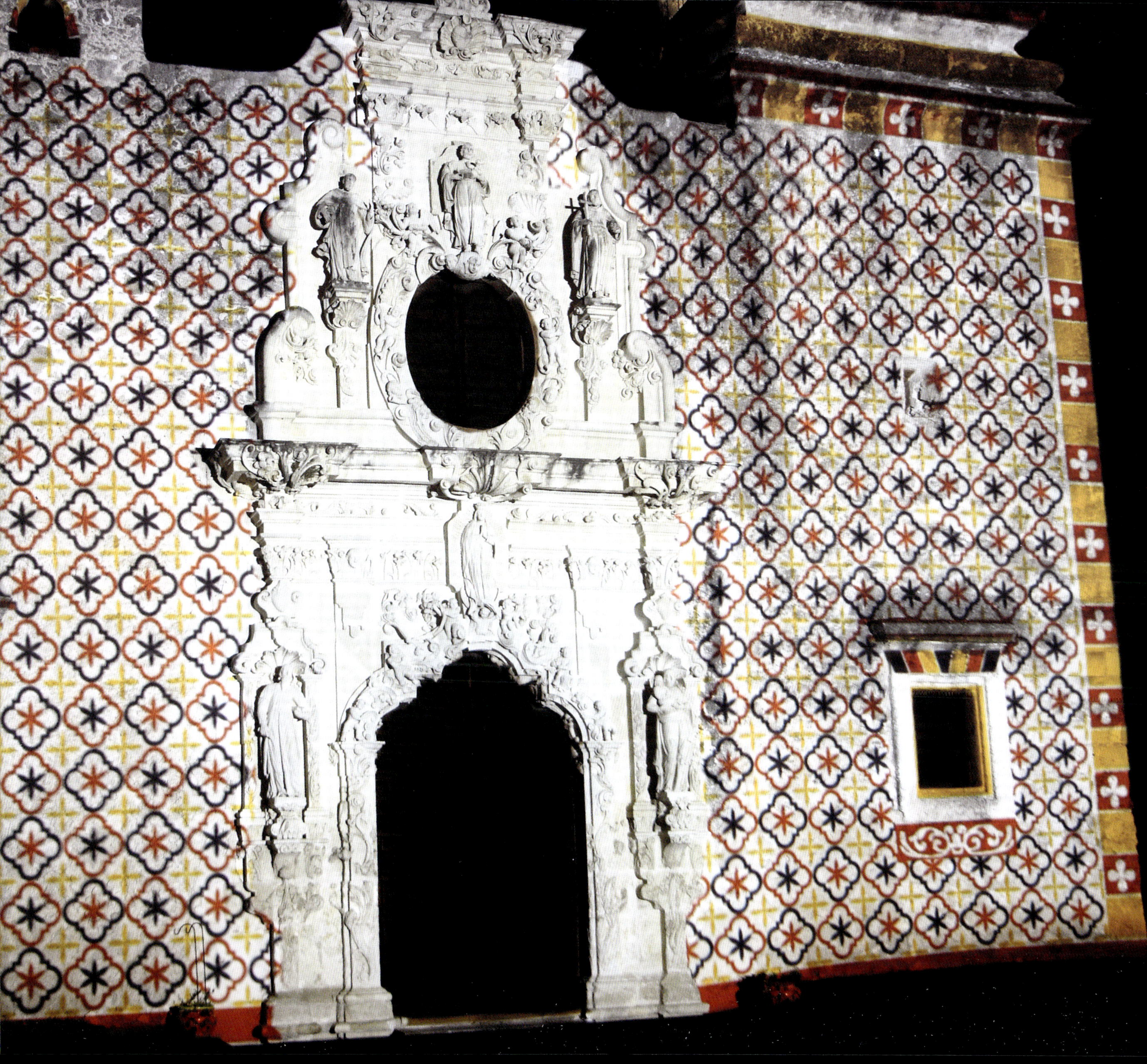

BELOW
San Fernando Cathedral lit at night. Main Plaza, 115 N. Main Avenue.

ABOVE
The Saga, 2014. Xavier de Richemont. *The Saga* is a multimedia telling of our history projected onto the walls of San Fernando Cathedral at night. Viewers sit on folding chairs or public benches, entranced by the spectacle.

OPPOSITE PAGE
The Saga, 2014. Xavier de Richemont (visiting artist from France). Light display at San Fernando Cathedral, Main Plaza. A 7,000-square-foot projected video painting combines digital art with projection mapping, choreographed music, and narrative storytelling.

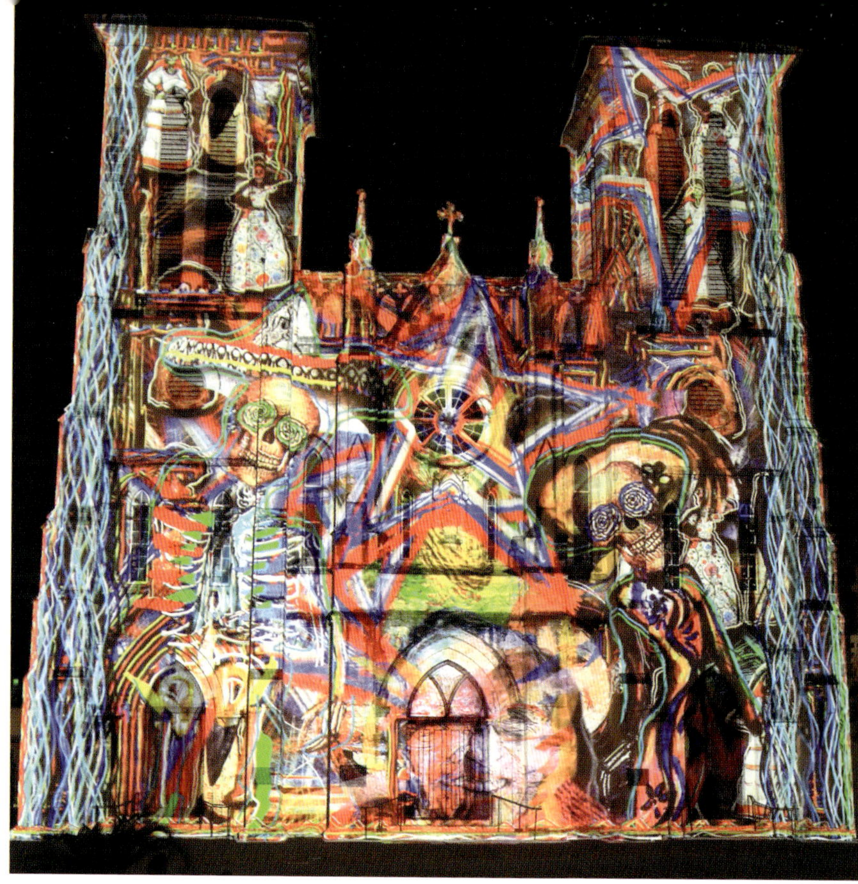

San Fernando Cathedral, the city's sweetheart since 1738 for weddings, baptisms, and the rituals of our lives, now also serves as storyteller, draped in the colors of a moving art design by de Richemont. Appropriately dressed in her history, she proudly sings the saga of our multicolored past and present.

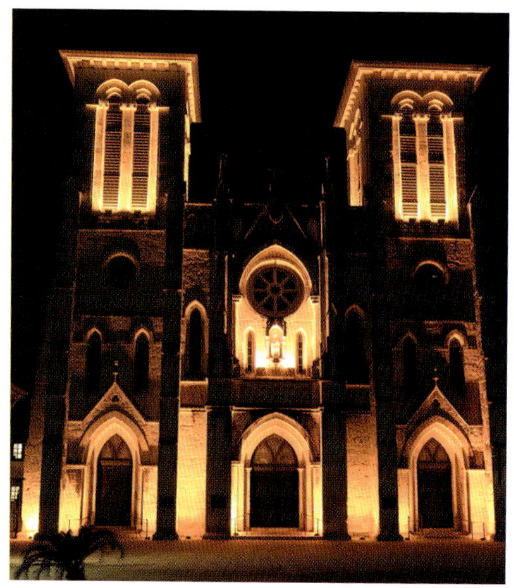

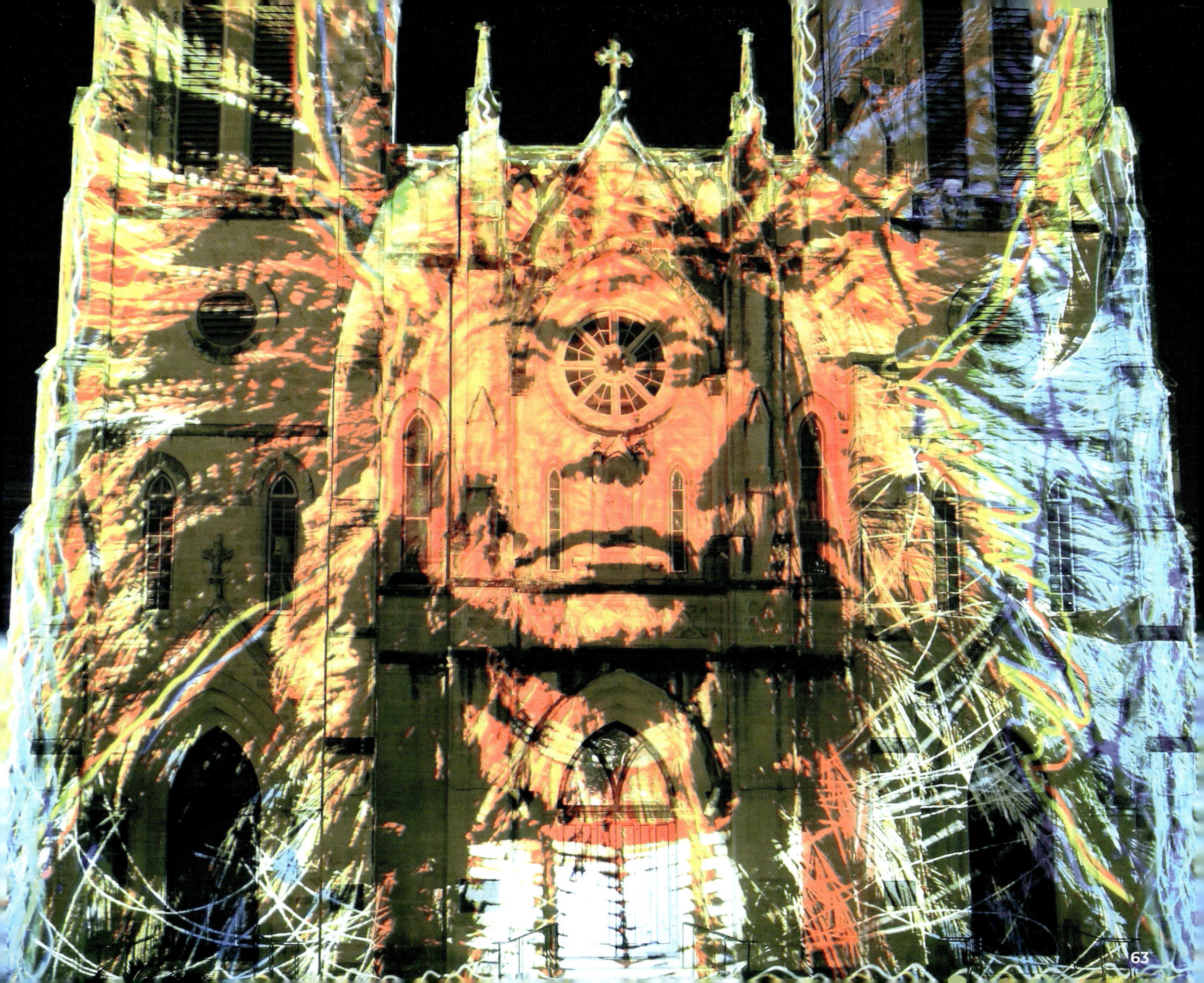

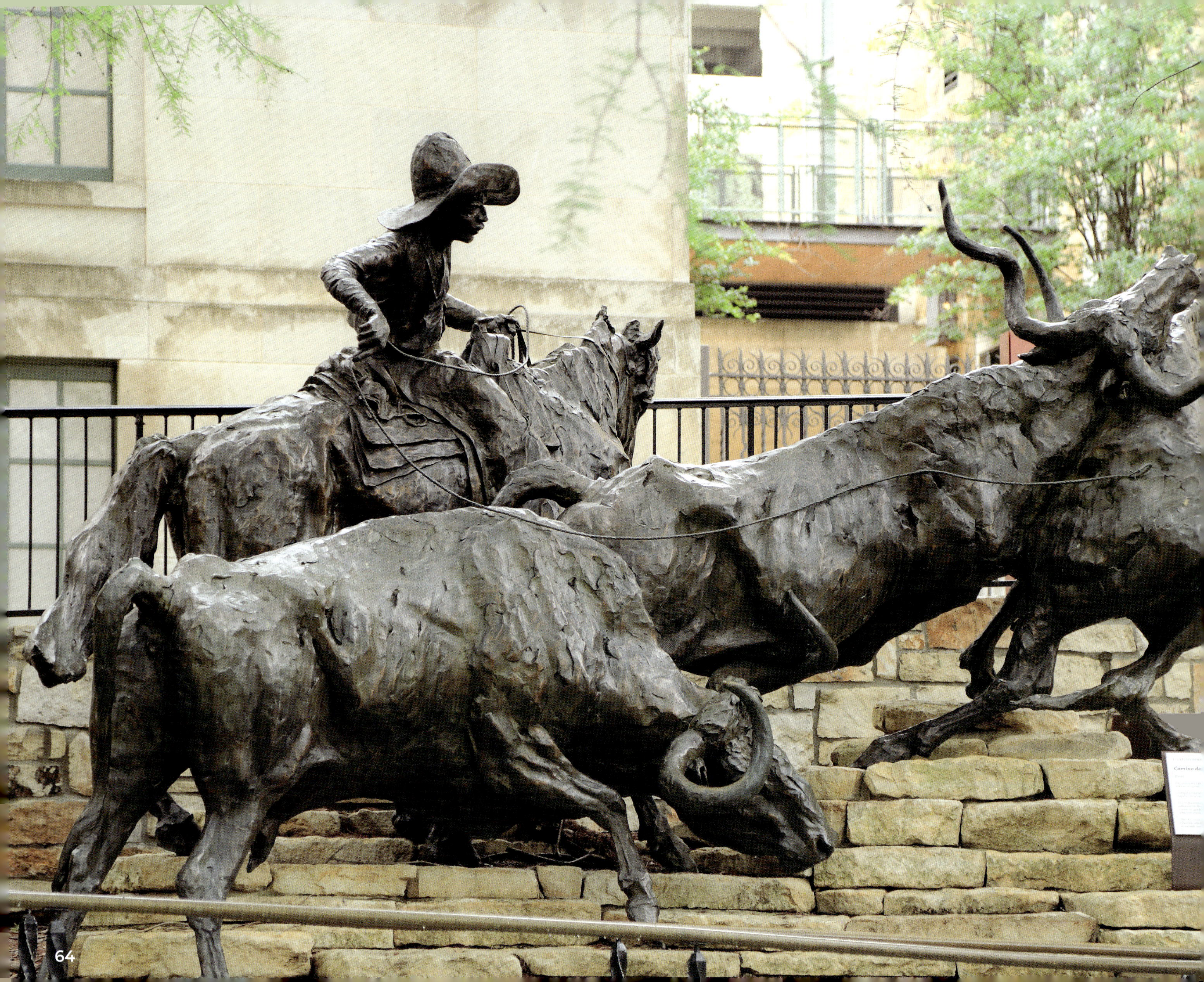

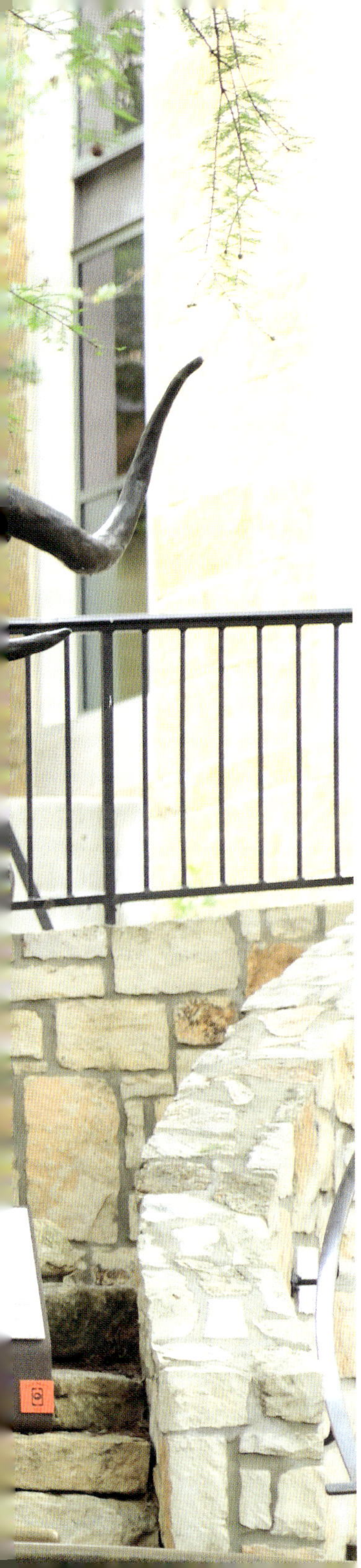

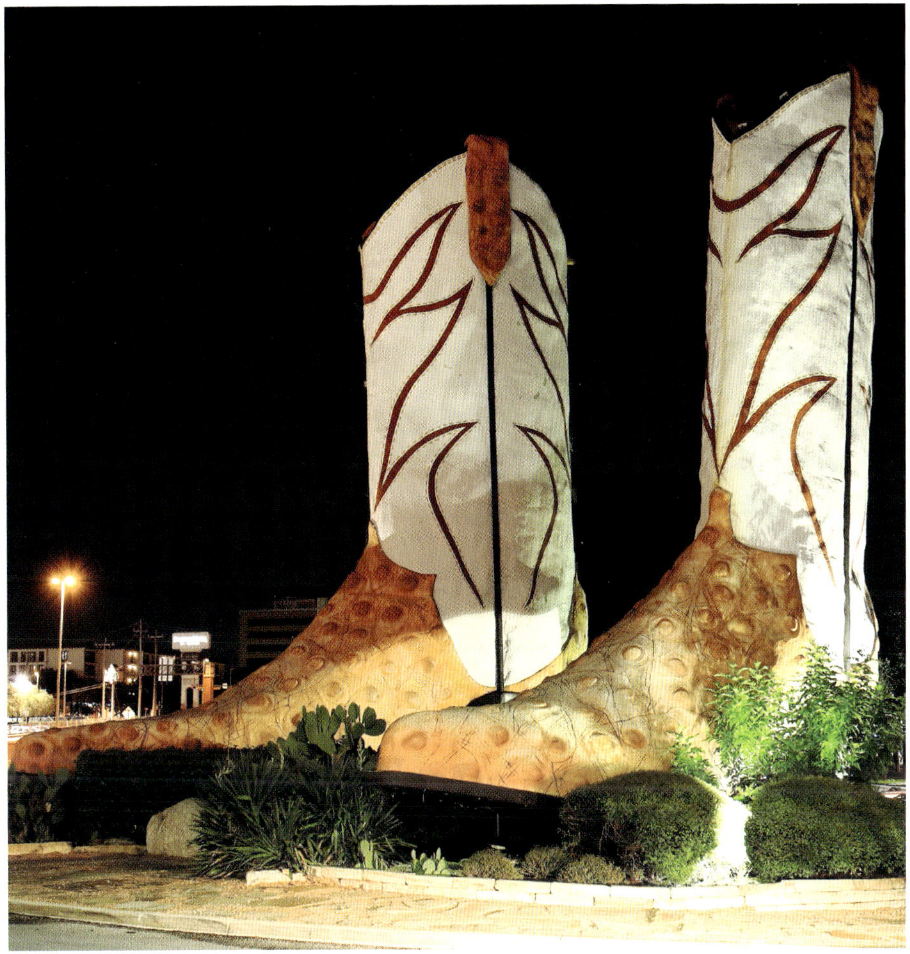

OPPOSITE PAGE
Camino de Gálvez, 2014. T. D. Kelsey. Depiction of the early *vaqueros* (cowboys) of this area, who introduced such terms as rodeo, lasso, pinto, mesteño (mustang), ranch, and hundreds of other Spanish and Indian words into the English language via a well-established cowboy culture. River Walk next to Briscoe Western Museum.

THIS PAGE
Cowboy Boots, 1979. Bob "Daddy-O" Wade. North Star Mall.

Here vaqueros bounded through *mezquital* and *montes*,
hard-drove longhorns on their *pintos* and *mesteños*,
built a culture that would shape this country's cowboy legend,
fed the nation with their cattle drives and campfire stories
that years later would inspire artists, writers, singers
to capture sweat and spirit
frozen in bronze movement or in leather boots
suspended in one moment, echoes ringing forever.

LEFT
William Travis, 2018.
Diana Kersey. San Pedro Creek bridge at Travis Street. Col. Travis was the commanding officer at the 1836 battle of the Alamo.

RIGHT
Davy Crockett, 2019.
George W. Lundeen.
Alamo grounds

OPPOSITE PAGE
Spirit of Sacrifice Alamo Cenotaph, 1936.
Pompeo Coppini.
The cenotaph was built in memory of the Texian defenders of the Alamo, at Alamo Plaza, which is also the site of an eighteenth-century cemetery where more than 1,300 of the city's Indian, Mestizo, Black, and Spanish citizens were buried.

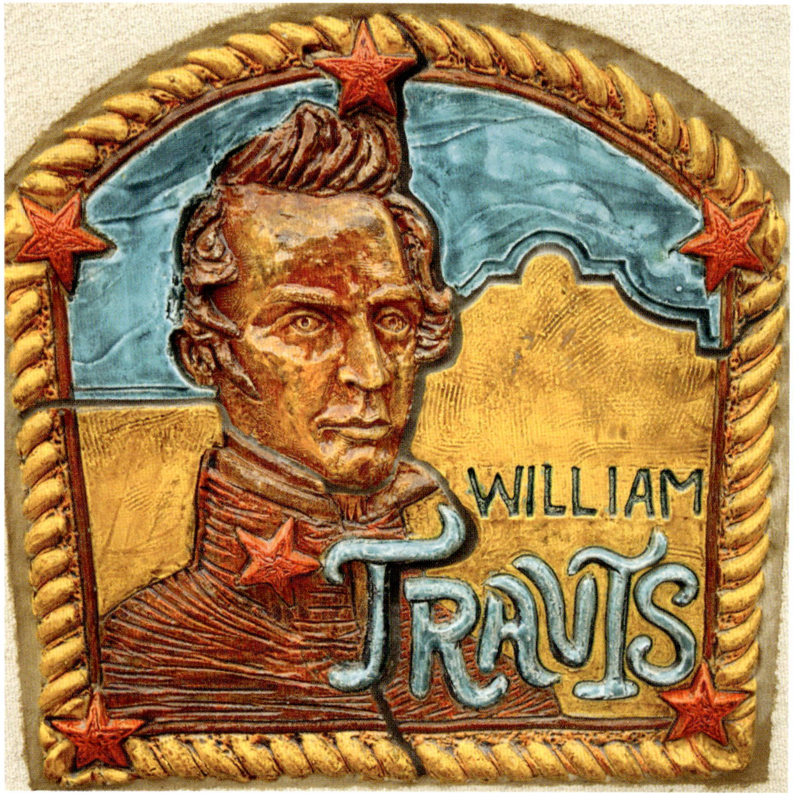

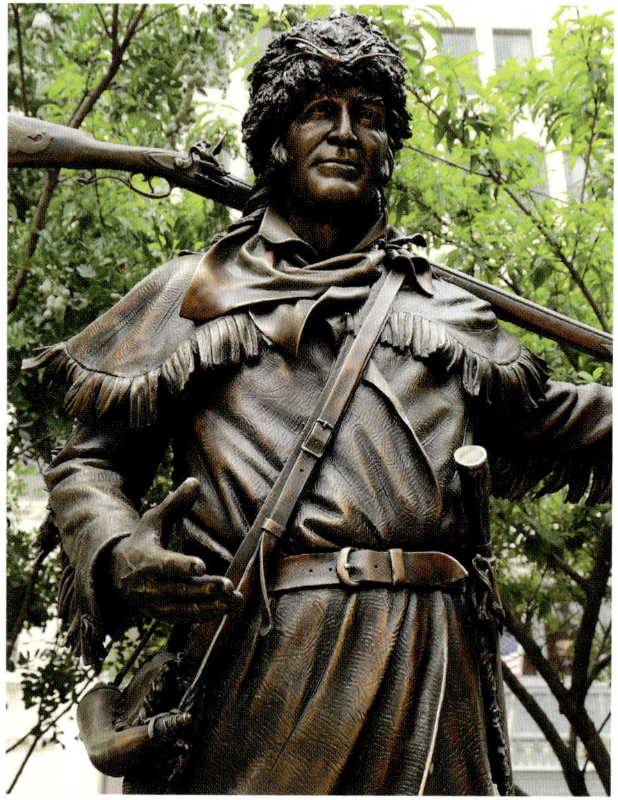

A hundred years after the missions were built,
the English speakers came from Kentucky, Tennessee, Louisiana,
hungry for a new start, eager for new land, new opportunities.
They immigrated to this place, became citizens of Mexico.

But conflict would ensue. The Republic of Mexico to which they came
elected a Black president, outlawed slavery in 1829.
The new Texian immigrants, from a region steeped in slavery,
brought enslaved Africans and wanted to bring more.
Soon, the Texians were in full rebellion, declared independence,
assembled an army, made their stand at a century-old mission,
San Antonio de Valero, a place the locals called el Alamo.

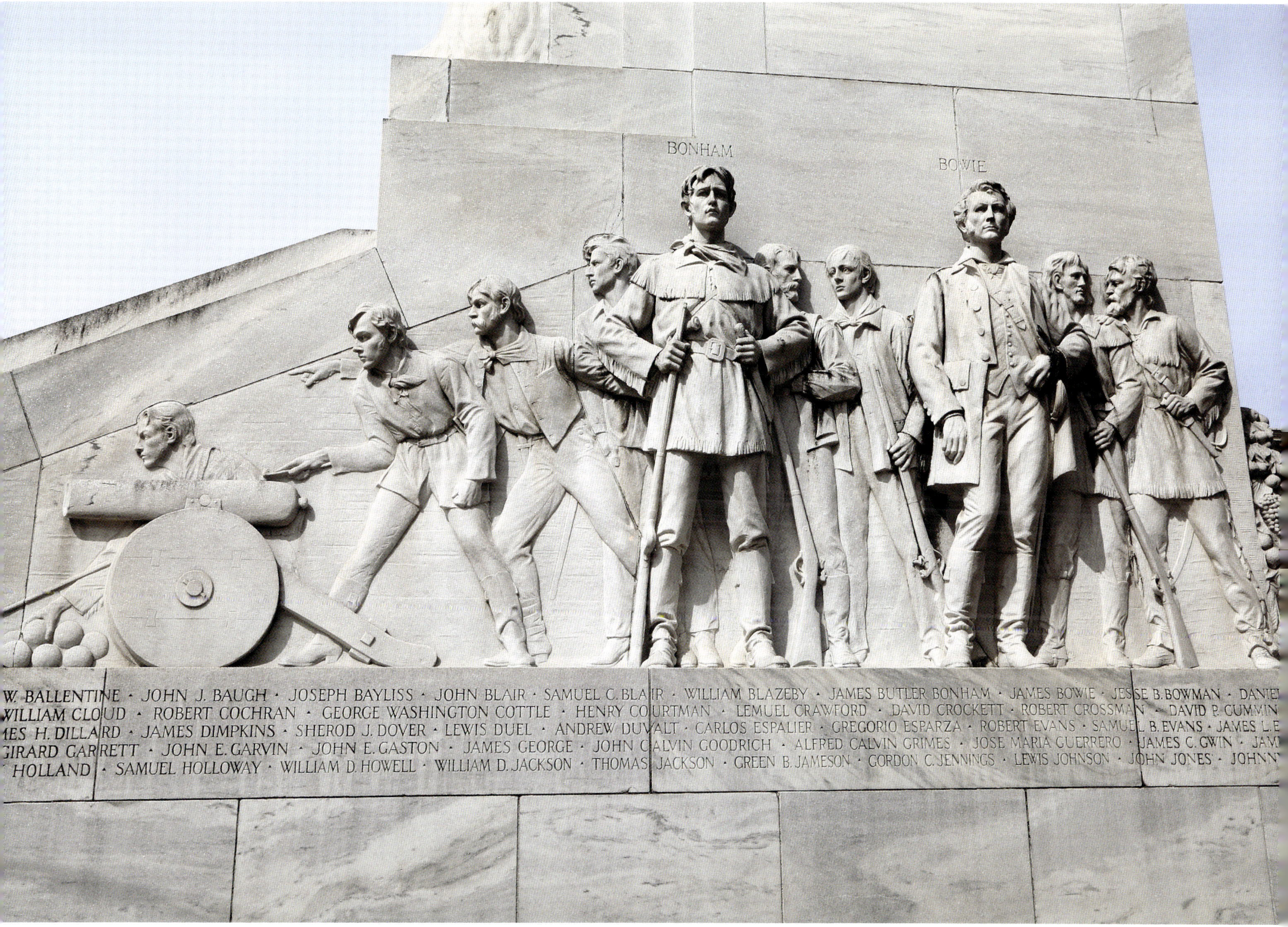
BONHAM
BOWIE
W. BALLENTINE · JOHN J. BAUGH · JOSEPH BAYLISS · JOHN BLAIR · SAMUEL C. BLAIR · WILLIAM BLAZEBY · JAMES BUTLER BONHAM · JAMES BOWIE · JESSE B. BOWMAN ·
WILLIAM CLOUD · ROBERT COCHRAN · GEORGE WASHINGTON COTTLE · HENRY COURTMAN · LEMUEL CRAWFORD · DAVID CROCKETT · ROBERT CROSSMAN · DAVID P. CUMMINGS
H. DILLARD · JAMES DIMPKINS · SHEROD J. DOVER · LEWIS DUEL · ANDREW DUVALT · CARLOS ESPALIER · GREGORIO ESPARZA · ROBERT EVANS · SAMUEL B. EVANS ·
GIRARD GARRETT · JOHN E. GARVIN · JOHN E. GASTON · JAMES GEORGE · JOHN CALVIN GOODRICH · ALFRED CALVIN GRIMES · JOSE MARIA GUERRERO · JAMES C. GWIN ·
HOLLAND · SAMUEL HOLLOWAY · WILLIAM D. HOWELL · WILLIAM D. JACKSON · THOMAS JACKSON · GREEN B. JAMESON · GORDON C. JENNINGS · LEWIS JOHNSON · JOHN JONES ·

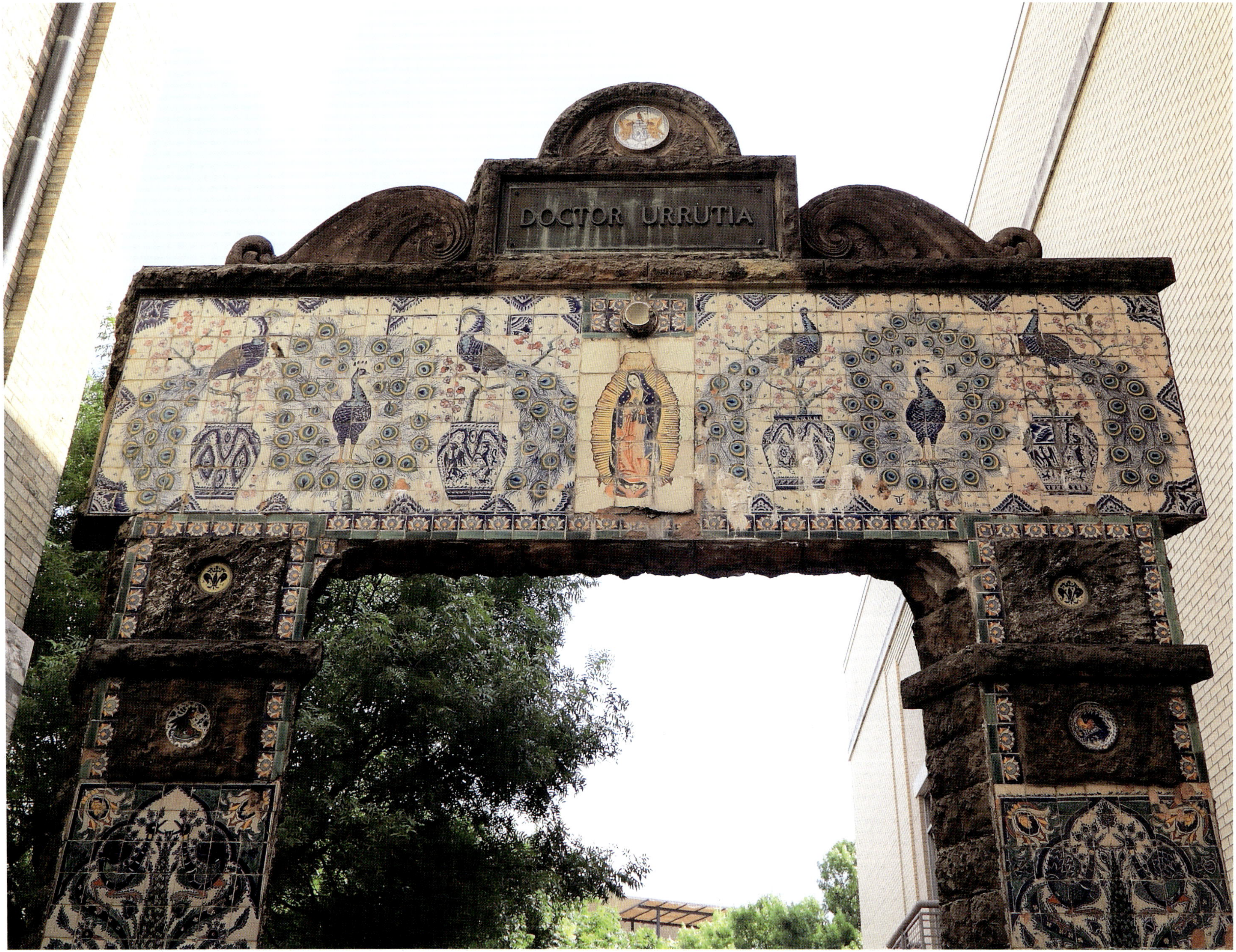
DOCTOR URRUTIA

Flags would change again, in rapid succession,
from Kingdom of New Spain and Republic of Mexico
to Republic of Texas, United States,
Confederate States, United States again.

Other wars followed
and other cries for peace,
while the people kept coming
to settle by this river,
to weep, to sing,
to build, to blend.

OPPOSITE PAGE
The Gate to Miraflores, 1930.
Dionicio Rodríguez.
San Antonio Museum of Art.

THIS PAGE
Hill 881 South: Vietnam War Memorial, 1986.
Austin Deuel.
Jefferson and East Martin Streets.

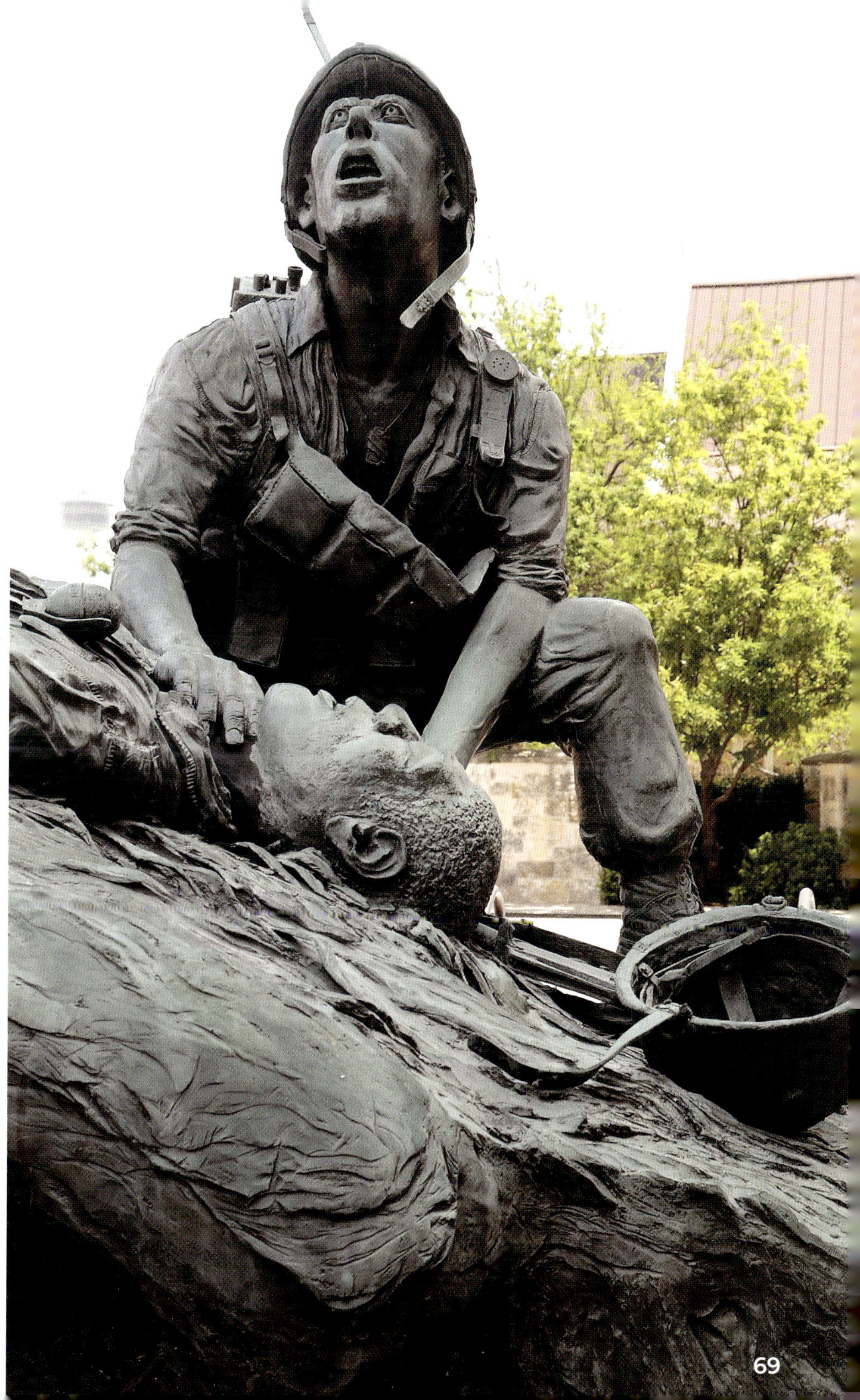

Night Watch: Korean War Memorial, 1994. Jonas Perkins. Jefferson and East Martin Streets.

OPPOSITE PAGE
Justitia Walls, 2009. George Schroeder. Bexar County Courthouse Complex.

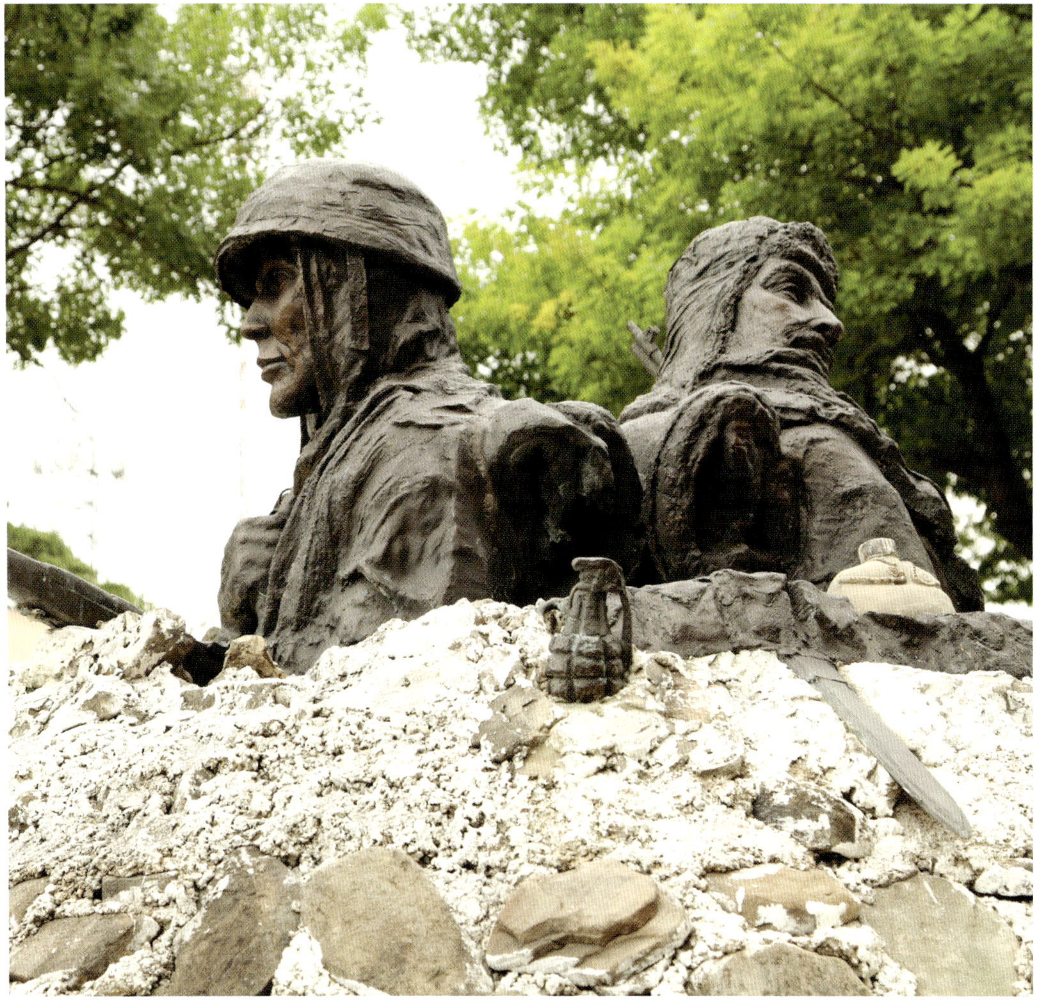

This is a place where warriors rested
by the Yanaguana River, or at the Presidio,
or returning from world wars, Korea, Vietnam,
Persian Gulf, and other conflicts,
knowing they would be welcome here
in Military City, USA.

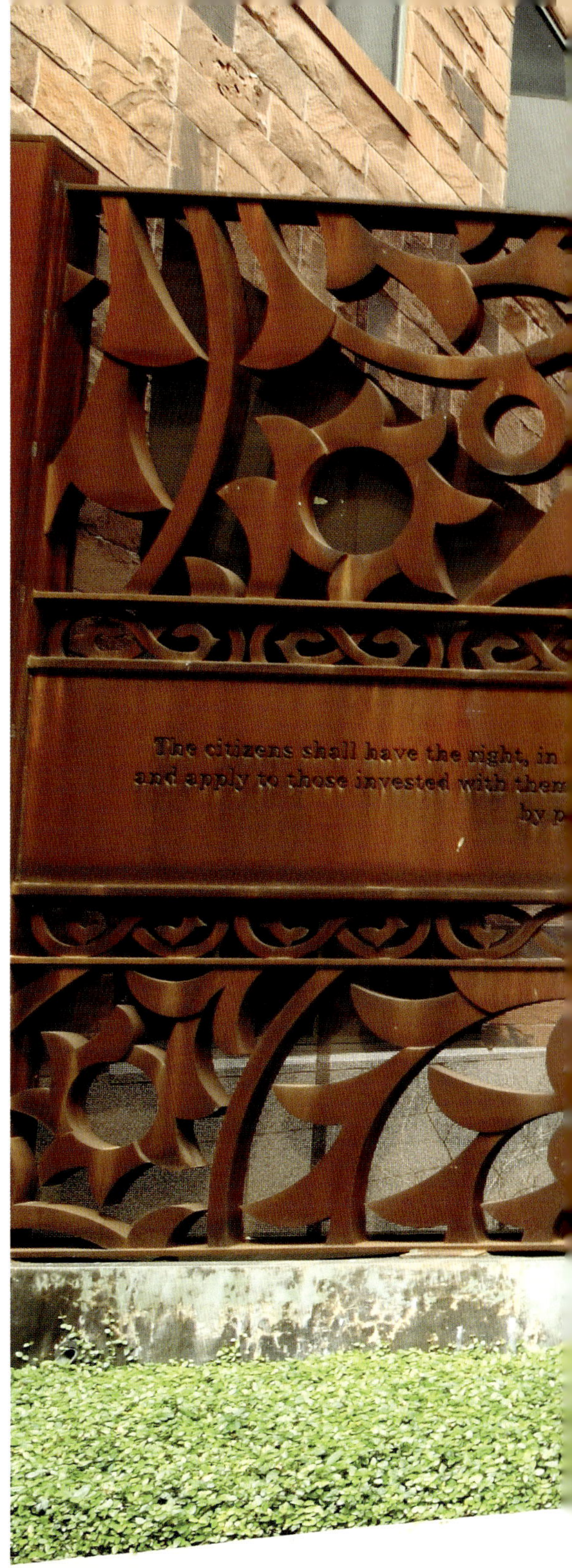

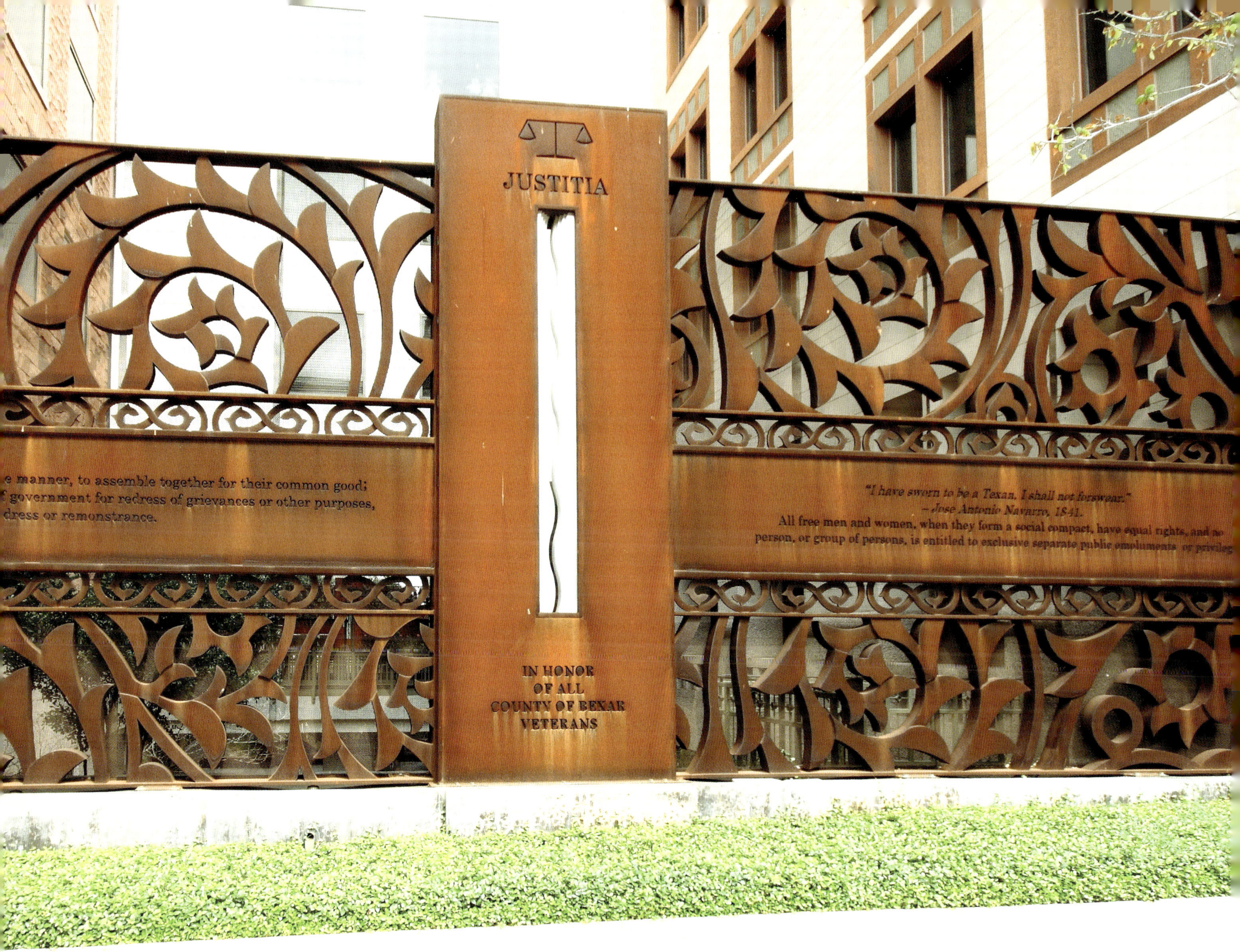
JUSTITIA
e manner, to assemble together for their common good;
government for redress of grievances or other purposes,
dress or remonstrance.
"I have sworn to be a Texan. I shall not forswear."
– Jose Antonio Navarro, 1841.
All free men and women, when they form a social compact, have equal rights, and no
person, or group of persons, is entitled to exclusive separate public emoluments or privileg
IN HONOR
OF ALL
COUNTY OF BEXAR
VETERANS

Untitled, 2017. Clinton Bopp (Los Angeles). Aerosol painting. Hoefgen Avenue and Carolina Street.

OPPOSITE PAGE *And Yet We Bloom*, 2020. Kat Cadena. E. Houston and Navarro Streets.

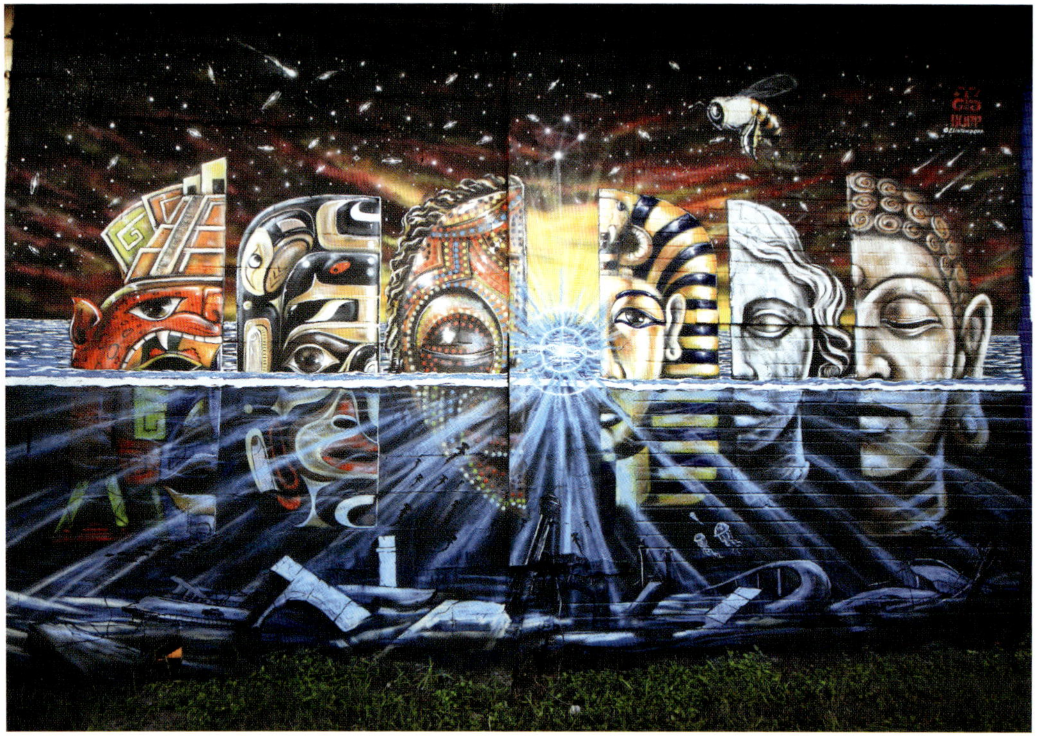

To this city came many peoples—
First Nations, Spanish explorers, Mexican soldiers from Guerrero,
Franciscan priests, Canary Islanders, Anglo-Americans, African Americans,
Germans, Czechs, and Poles, Syrians, Greeks, Latin Americans,
the Irish, the Chinese, the Africans, and Vietnamese, Indian, Iranian,
Karen, Pakistani, Bhutanese, Afghan. And more.

We met. We touched.
We blended into one city,
one grand chorus of many voices.

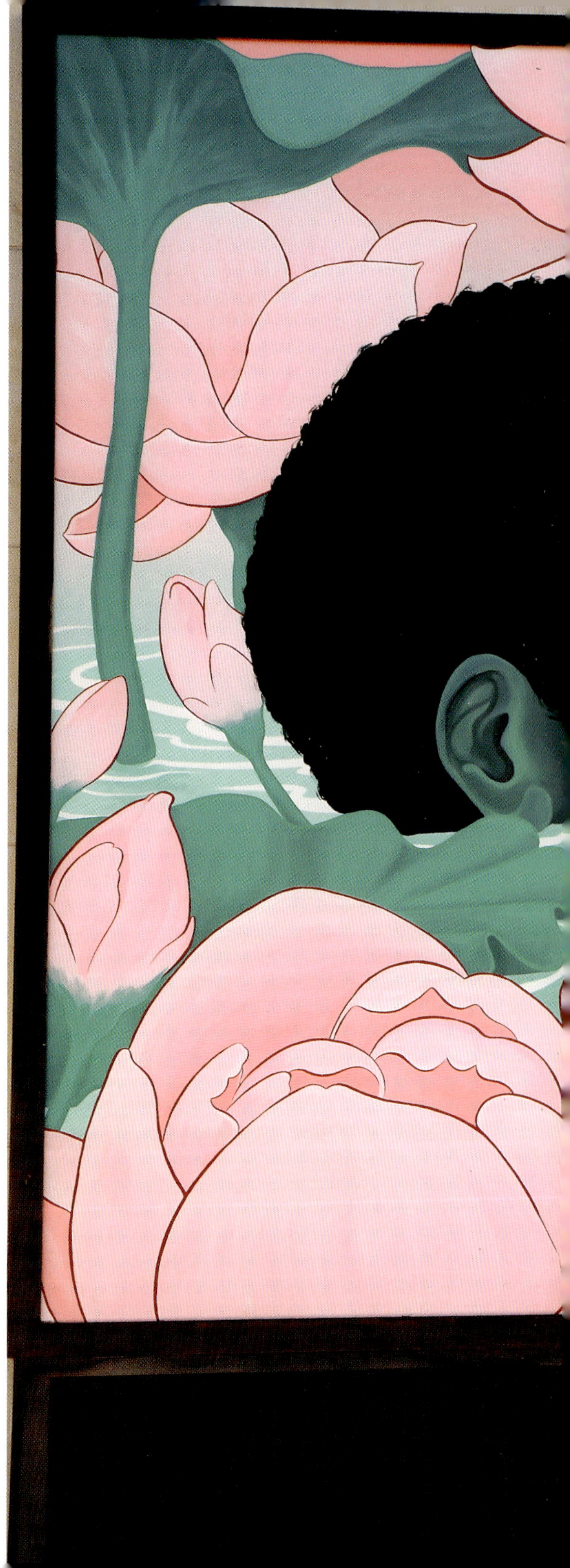

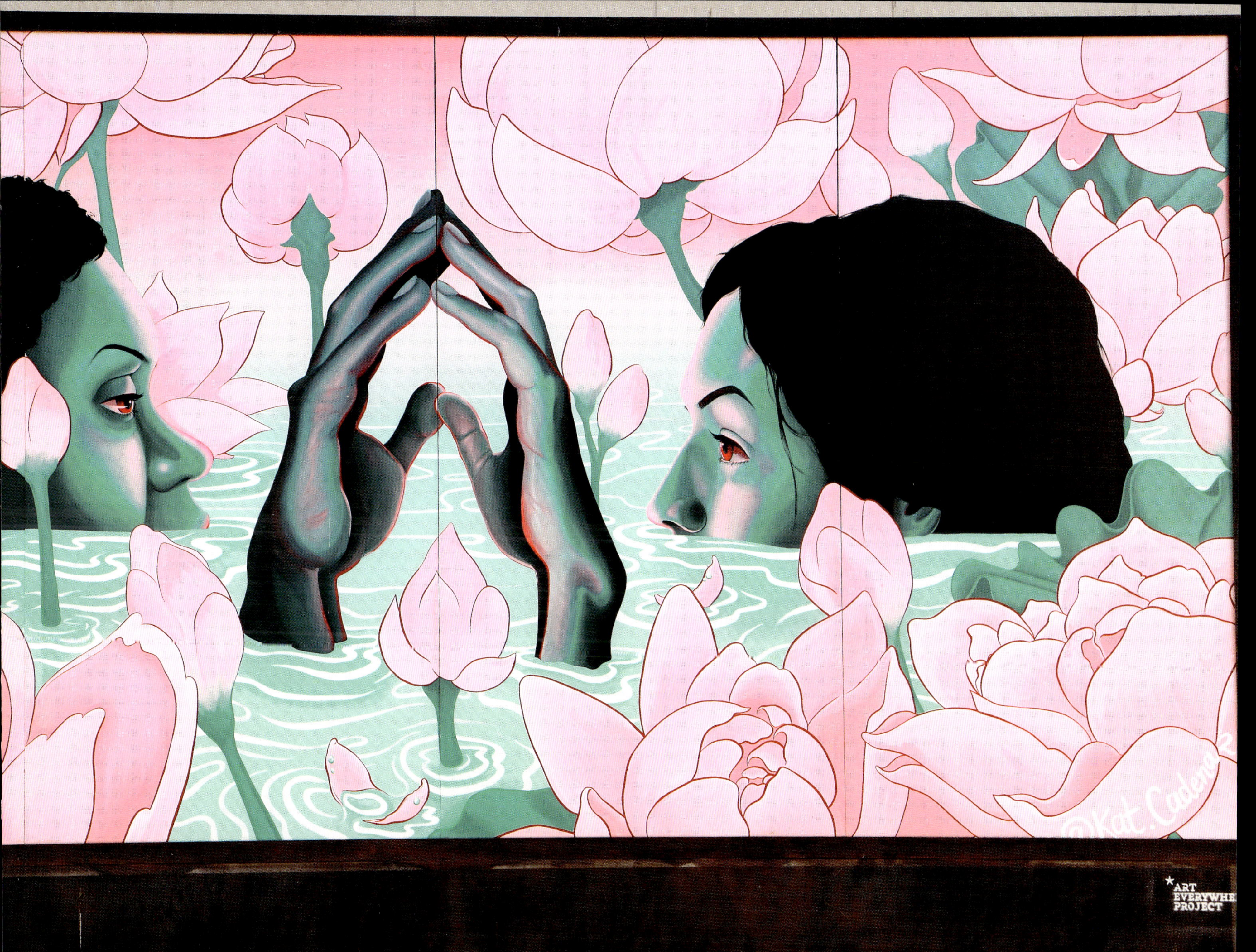
@Kat.Cadena
ART
EVERYWHE
PROJECT

Confluence of Civilizations in the Americas, 1968. Carlos Mérida. Henry B. González Convention Center.

OPPOSITE PAGE *Rain from the Heavens*, 2018. Muñoz and Scobee Planetarium. San Pedro Creek Culture Park.

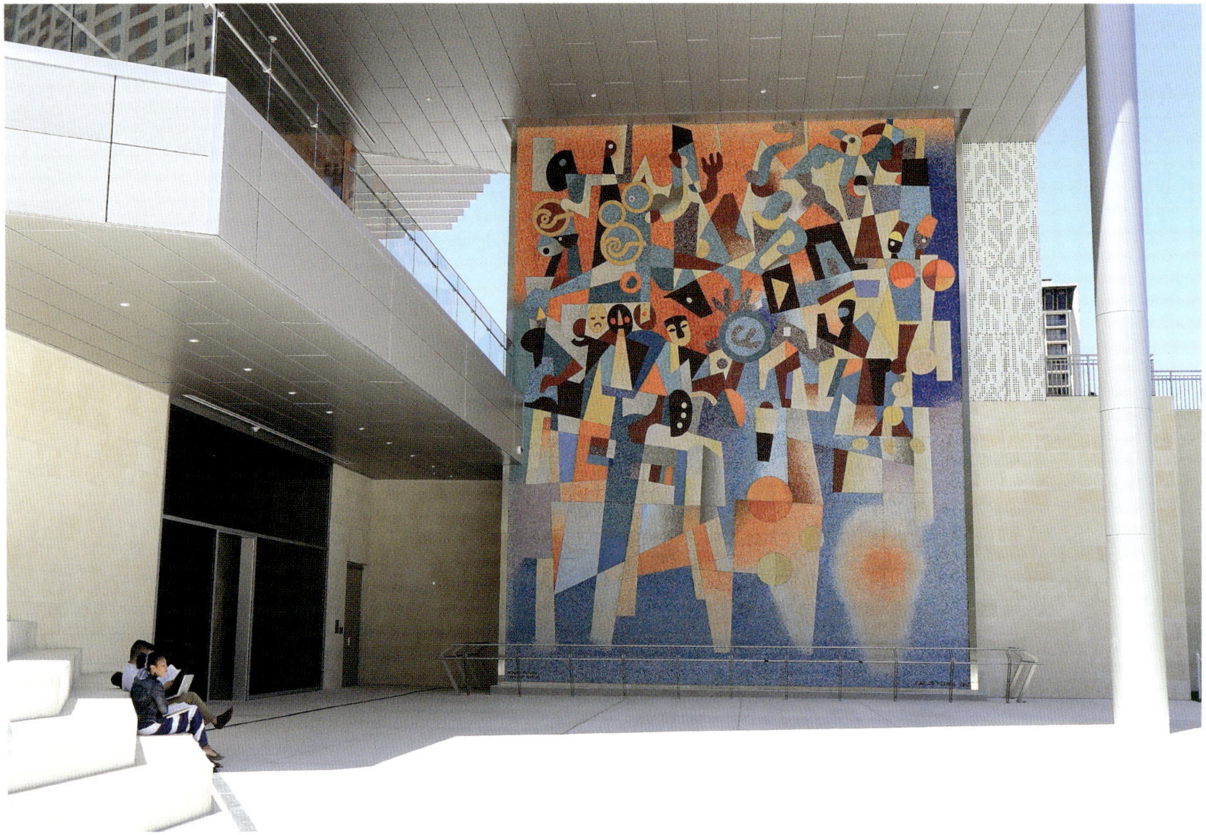

We came from different worlds
that each came from different worlds
that in turn came from different worlds
that connected us to everyone.
La raza cósmica, a constellation of hearts
made of stardust, in a world of colors.

The stars in the sky may have gazed down from different positions
on that night when the worlds of the Americas
and the worlds of Europe, Africa, Asia met
and mingled,

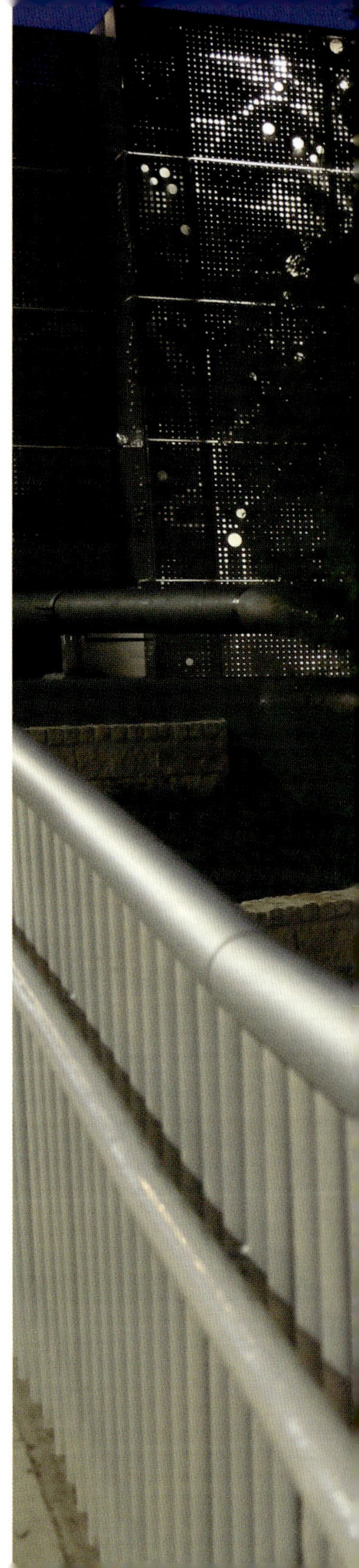

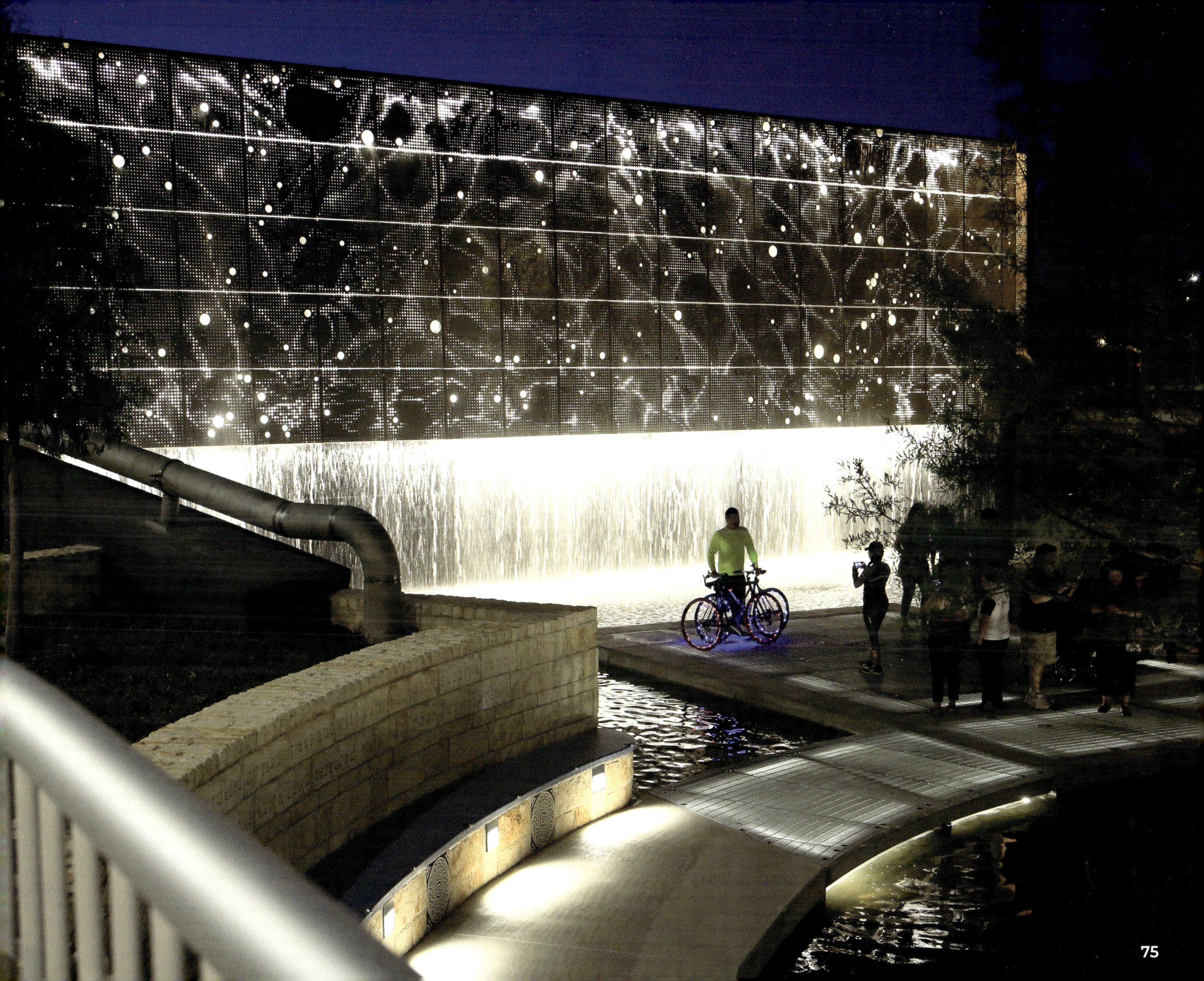

LEFT
Windows to Our Heritage, 2018.
David Blancas and Oscar Alvarado.
WHMT.

RIGHT
Windows to Our Heritage, 2018.
David Blancas and Oscar Alvarado.
WHMT, US 90 and Roosevelt Avenue.

OPPOSITE PAGE
TOP
Where I End & You Begin, 2017.
Jason E. González Martínez. WHMT, Mission Parkway and SW Military Drive.

BOTTOM
Jason E. González Martínez, 2018

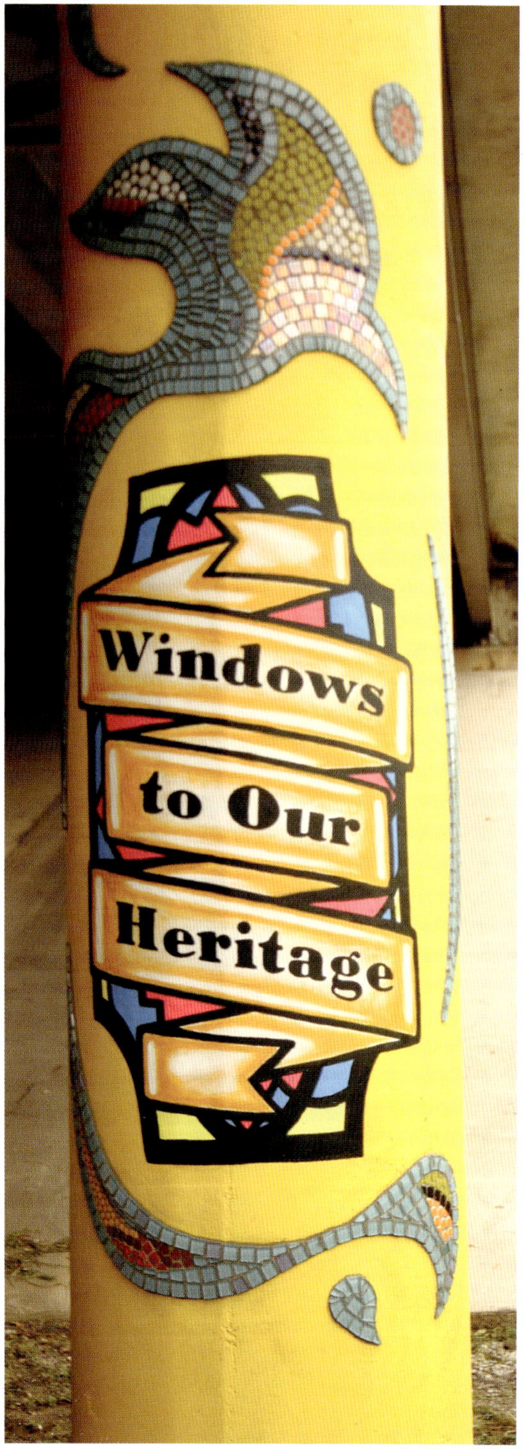

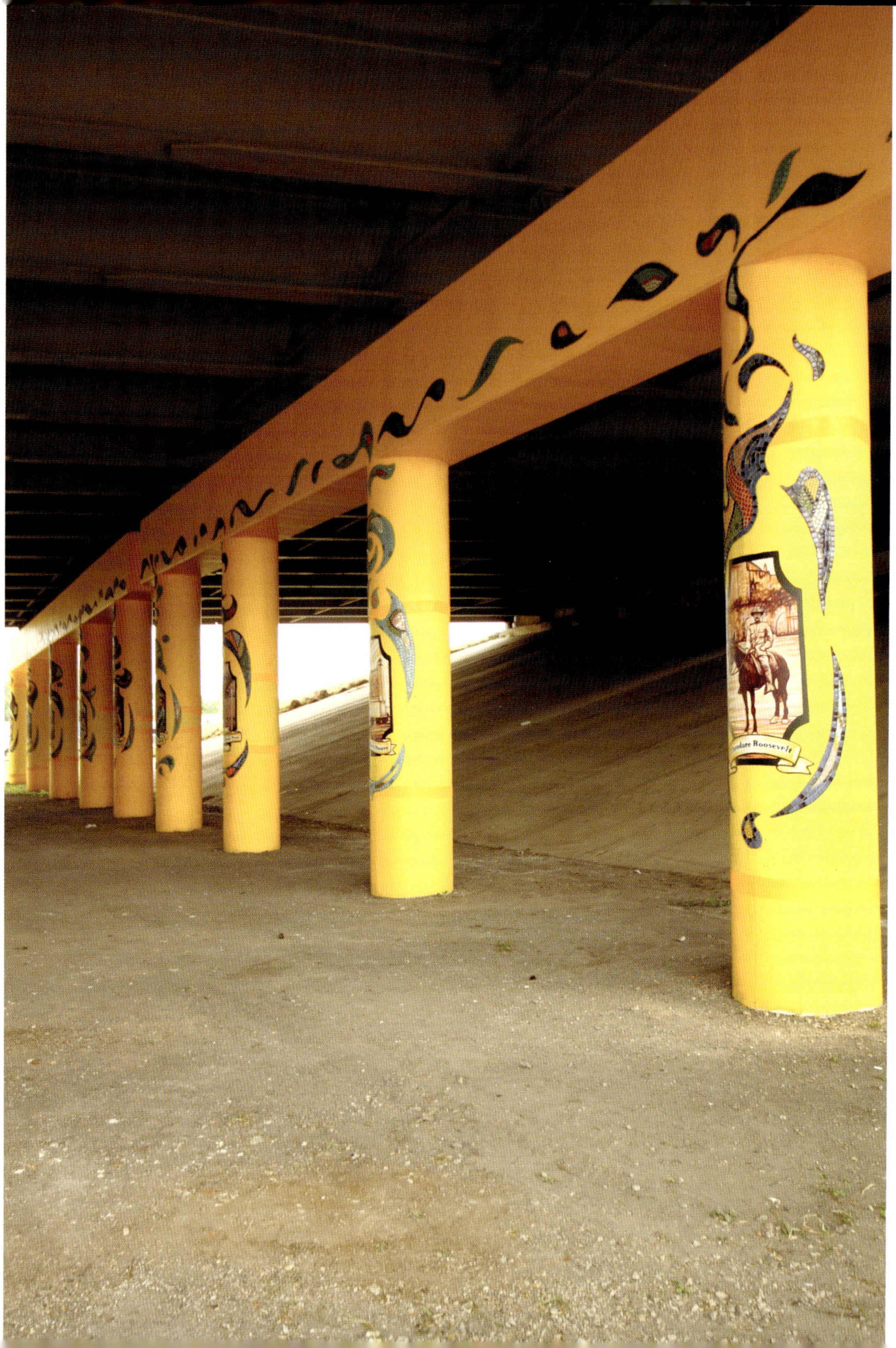

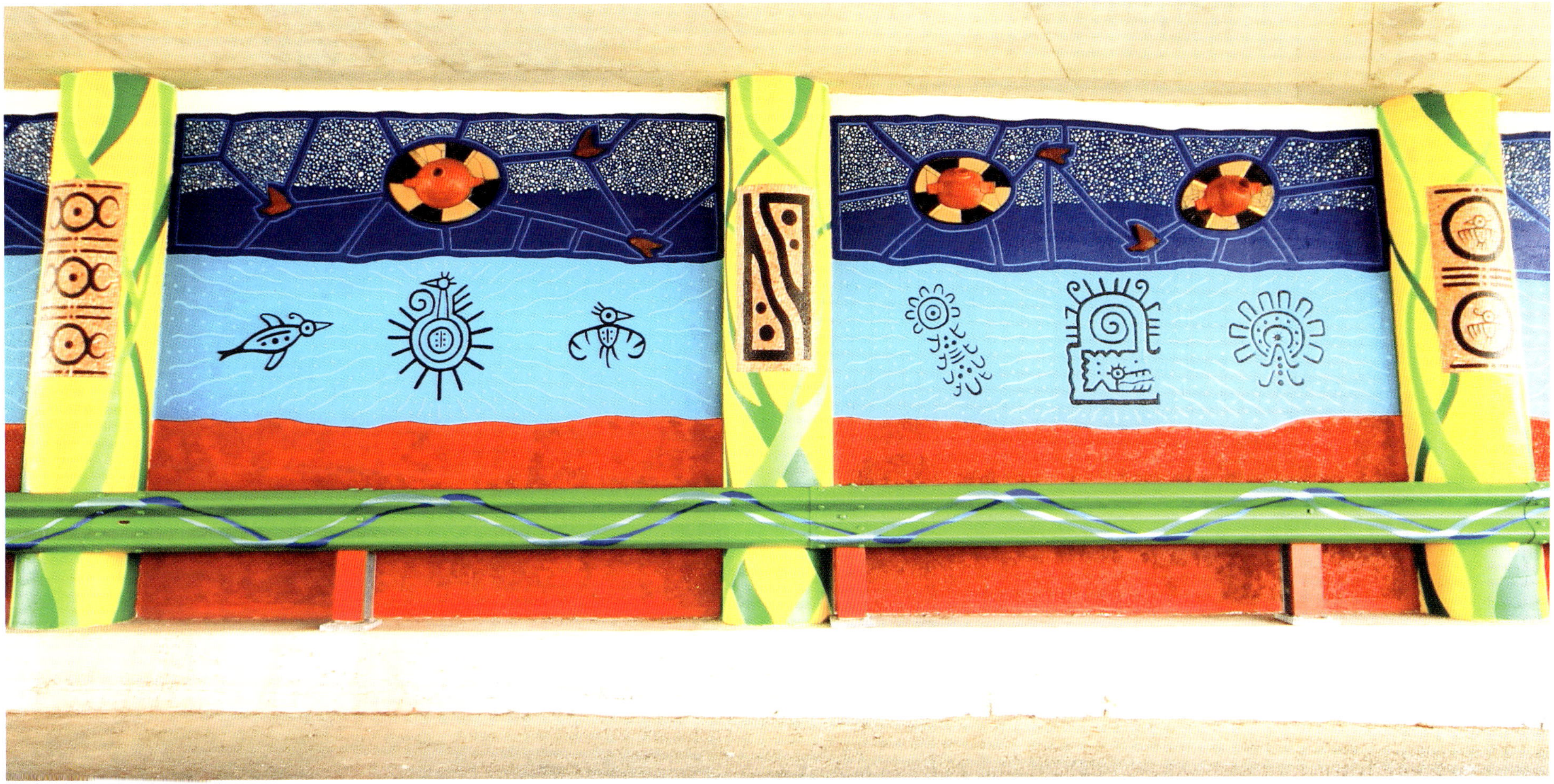

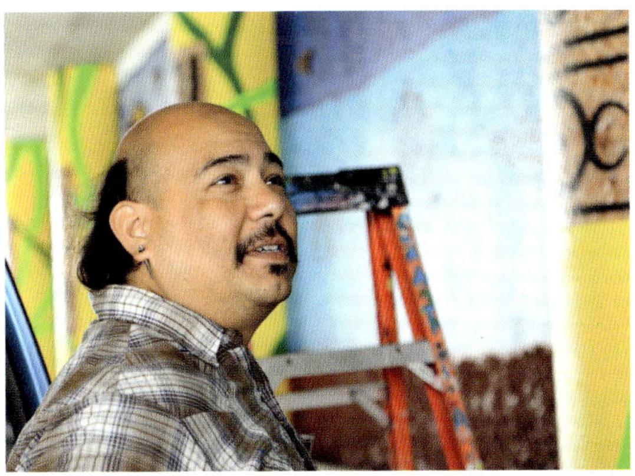

but three hundred years later, this city of the five missions still shines with
the spirit of that interchange between Indigenous, missionaries, colonizers
that, in UNESCO's words, created "fundamental . . . change
in the cultures and values of those involved and
a mestizaje that illustrates the loyalty to shared values
that go beyond the mission rule."[1]
And even the pathways leading there are now decorated in art
that sings our history proudly,

pathways decorated with the seed of our lives,
the heart of the pecan,
the sustenance of our centuries
along this World Heritage Mural Trail.

Windows to Our Heritage, 2018, Oscar Alvarado and David Blancas. WHMT, Presa Street at US 90.

OPPOSITE PAGE
TOP
Villamain Murals, 2017. Albert Garza et al. WHMT, Villamain Road.

BOTTOM LEFT
Summer, 2017. Joe De La Cruz. WHMT, Villamain Road.

BOTTOM RIGHT
Artist Cristina Sosa Noriega and City Arts & Culture staff member James LaFlore, WHMT

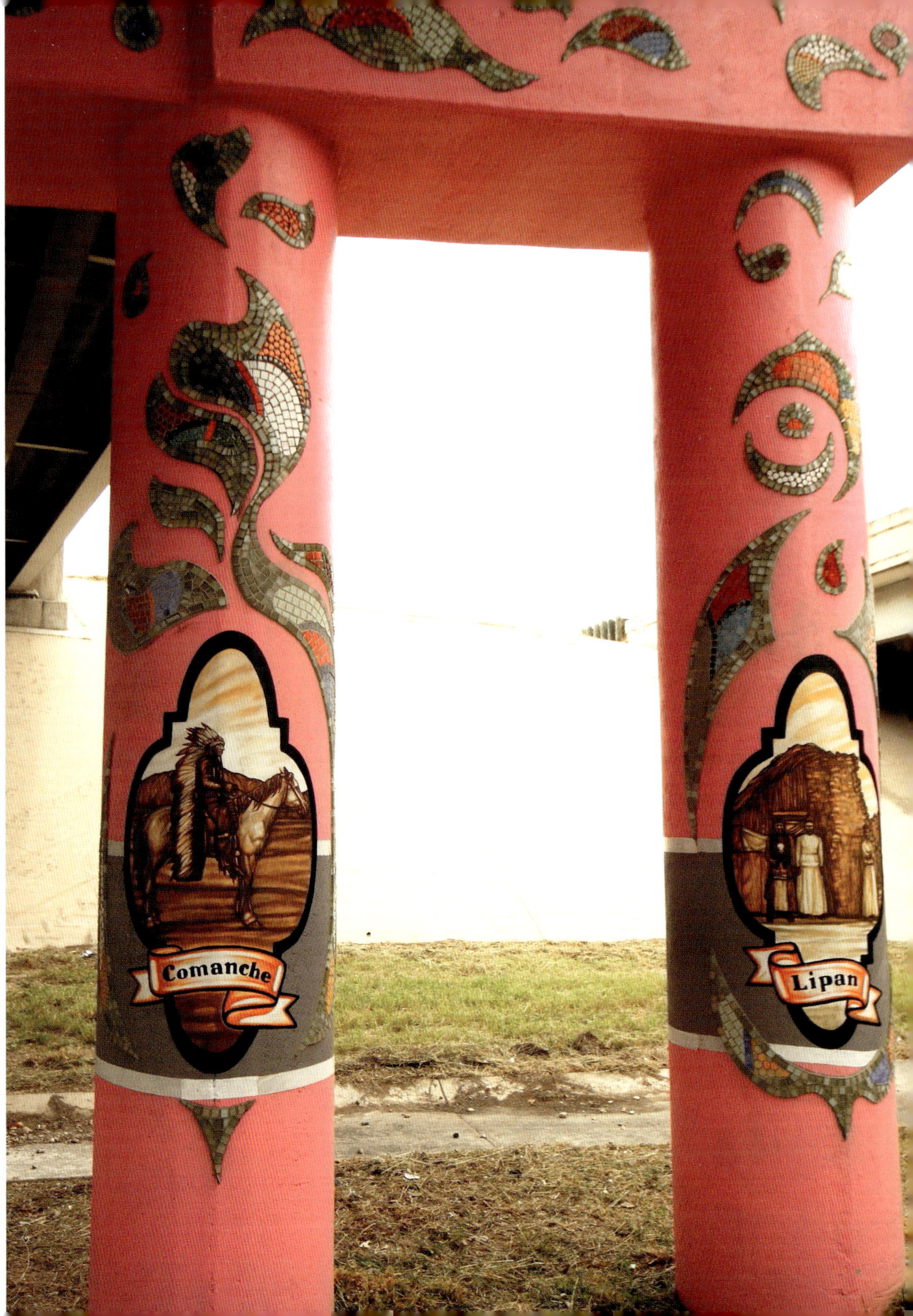

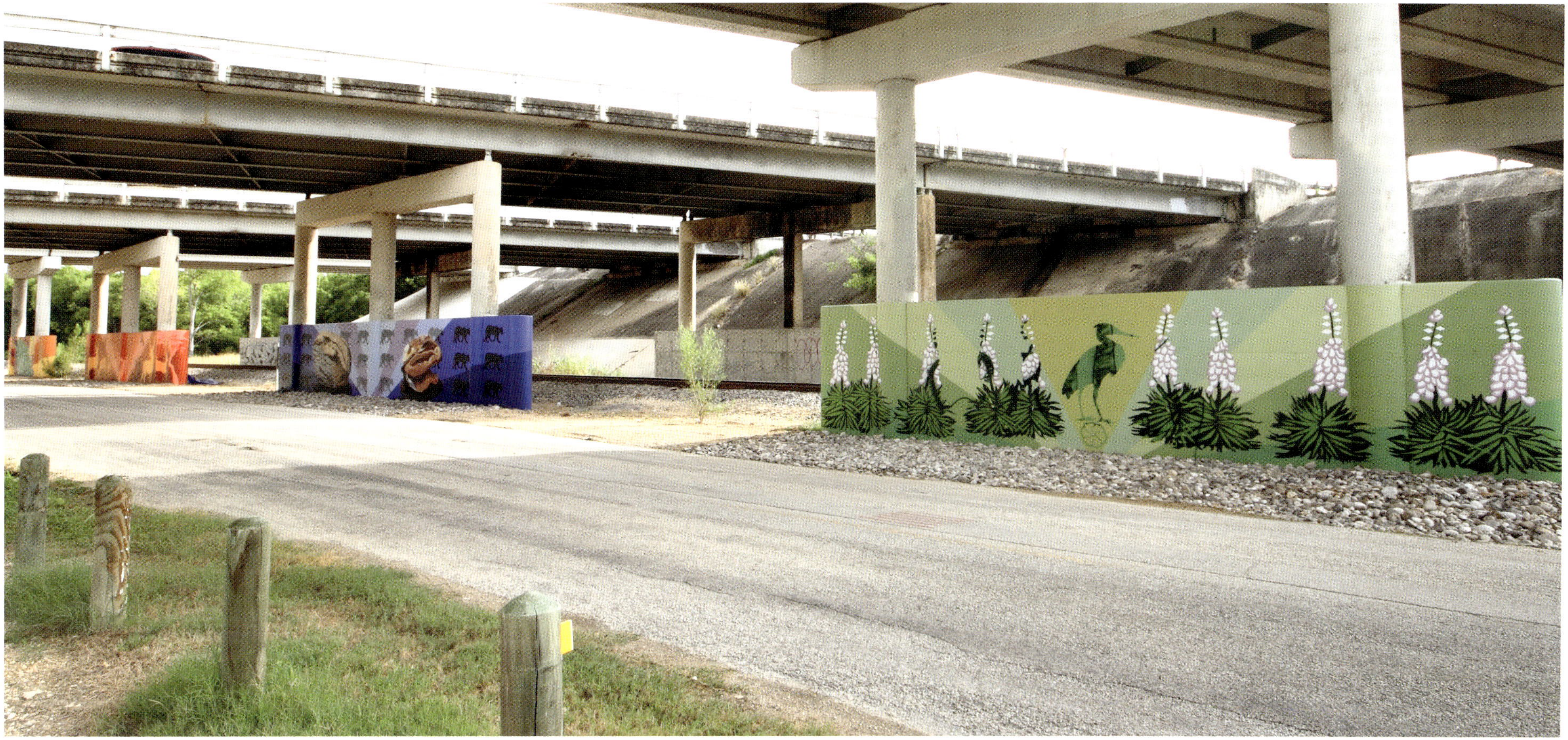

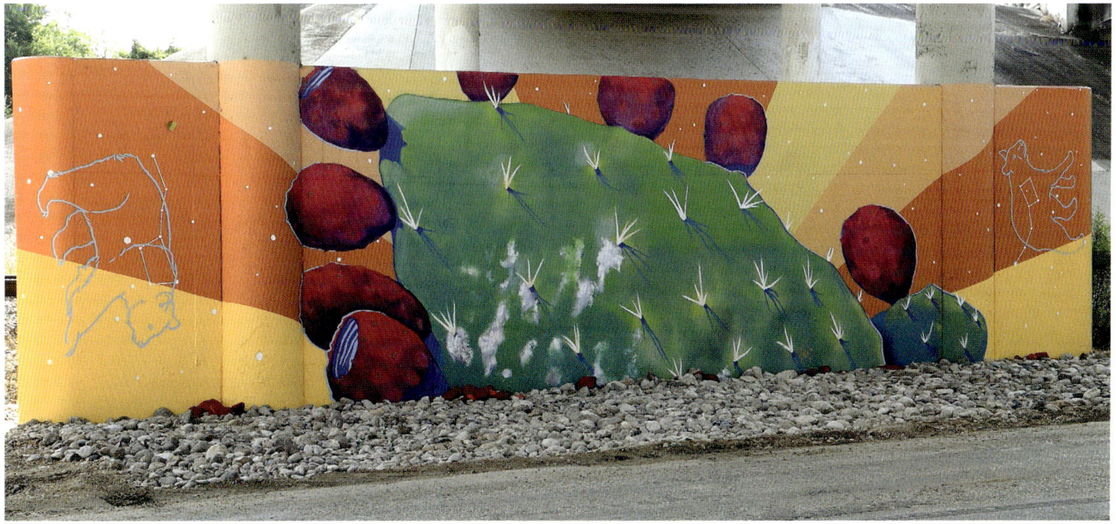

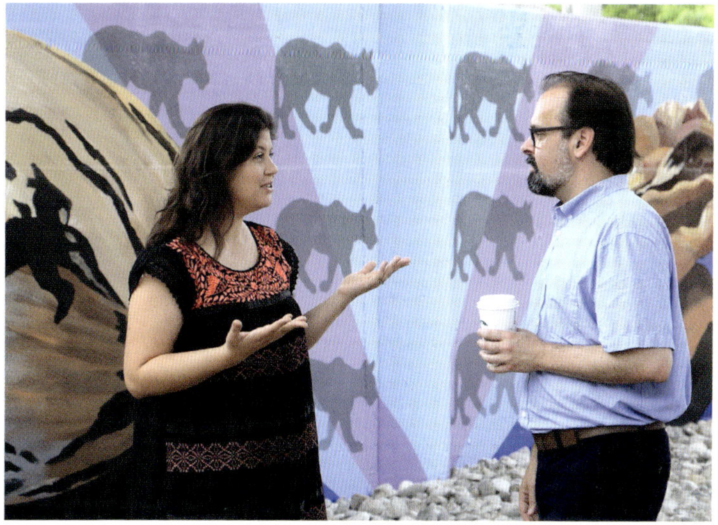

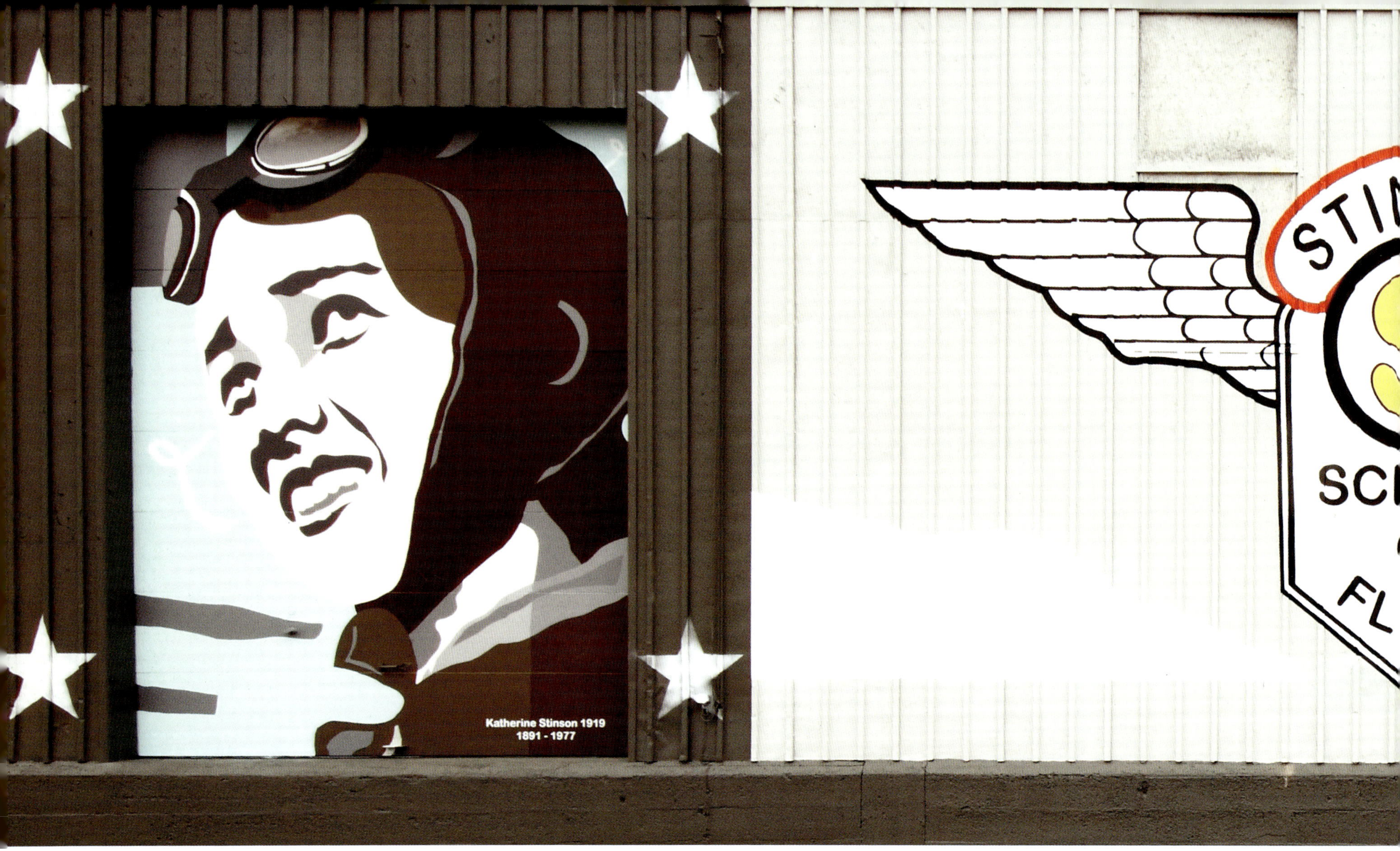

Murals down this trail and throughout our town
engrave on our minds the reminders
that despite all the limits others imagine for us,
we can still fly.

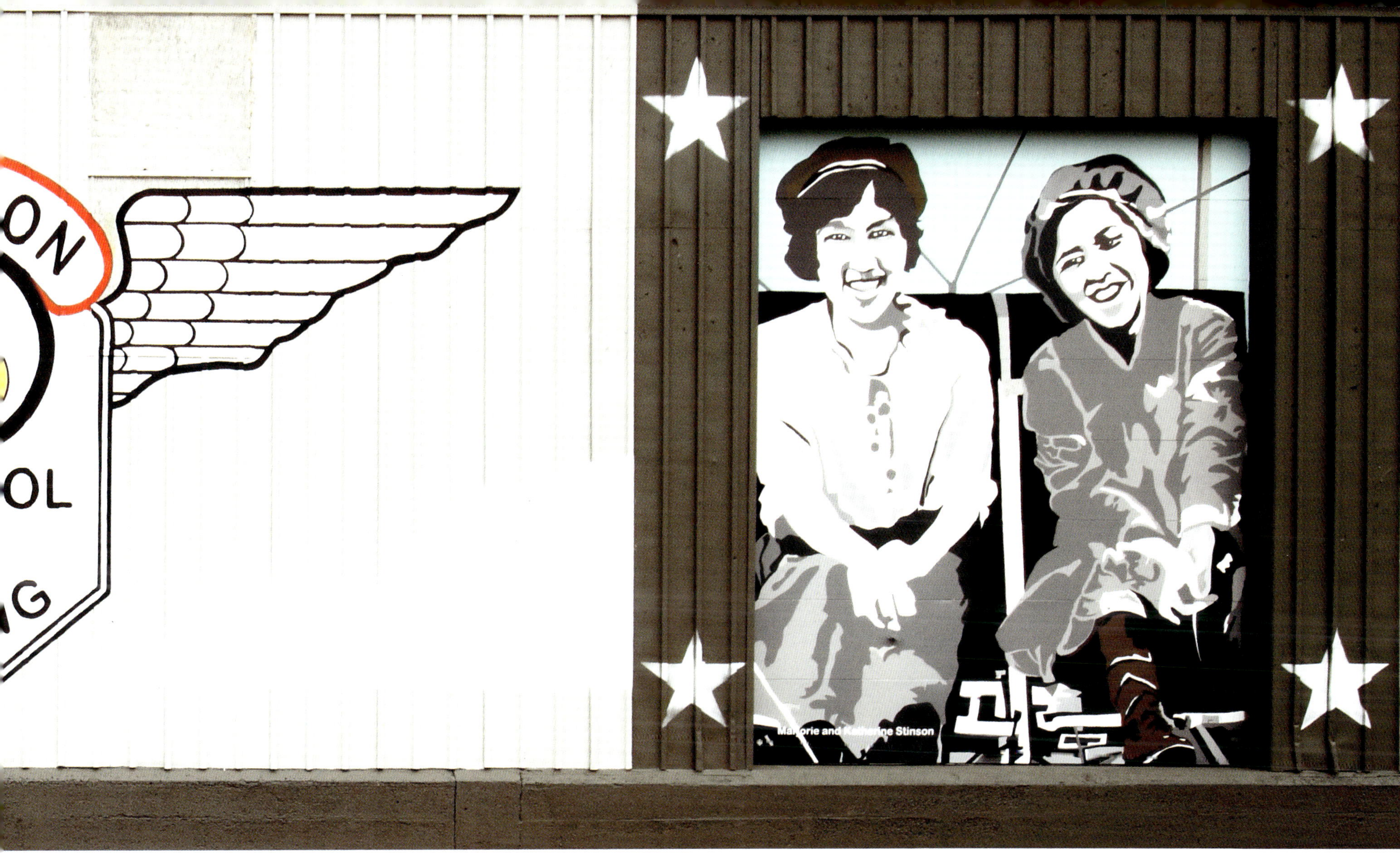

Pioneers of the Sky, the Stinson School of Flying, 2017. Andy Benavides, Joe De La Cruz, Chris Montoya, and José Comse. This Stinson Airport mural recognizes the history of women aviators such as Marjorie and Katherine Stinson, for whom the South Side's airport is named.

Texas Musical Legends, 2005. Gary V. Lett et al. Sunset Station.

OPPOSITE PAGE *La Música de San Anto*, 2009. David Blancas. 1303 W. Commerce Street.

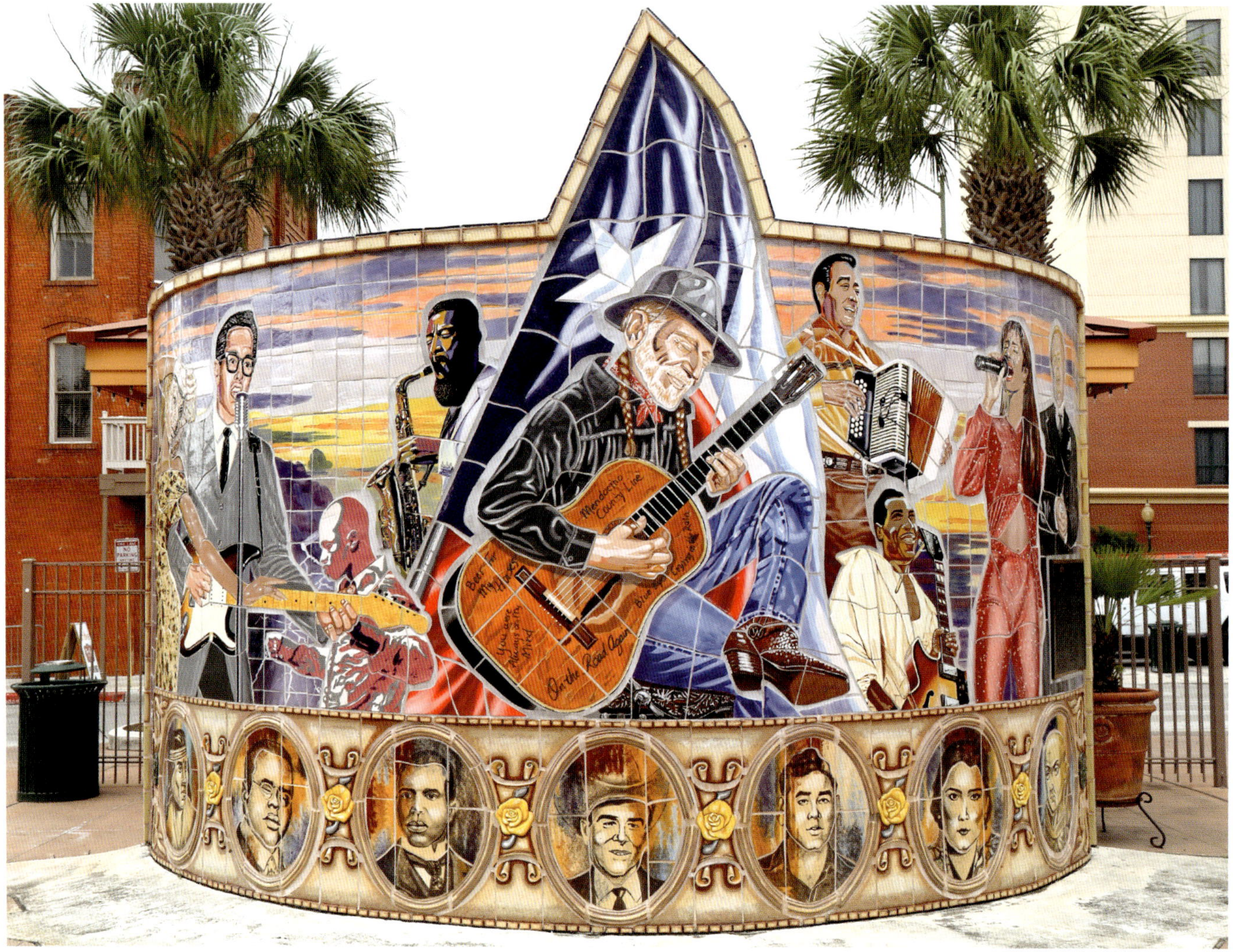

Our music, too, is a mix
of all who ever felt the melody here
in the drumming beats of its earth
in the trickling flow of its rivers
in the song of its many peoples.
We celebrate them on our walls
and in our souls,

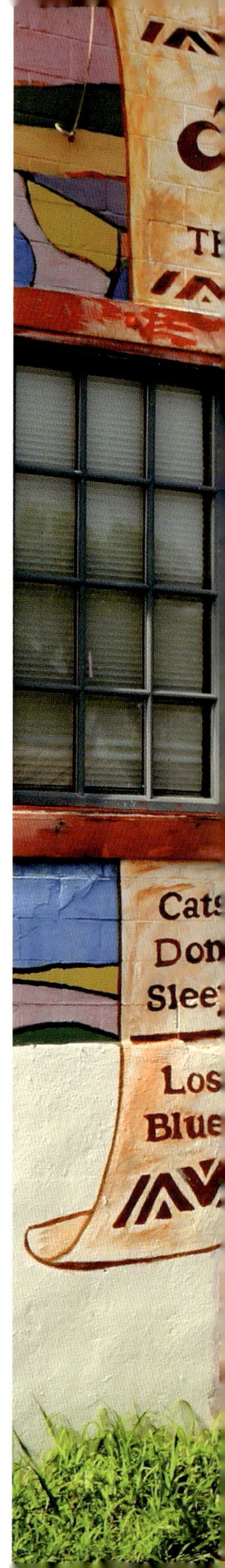

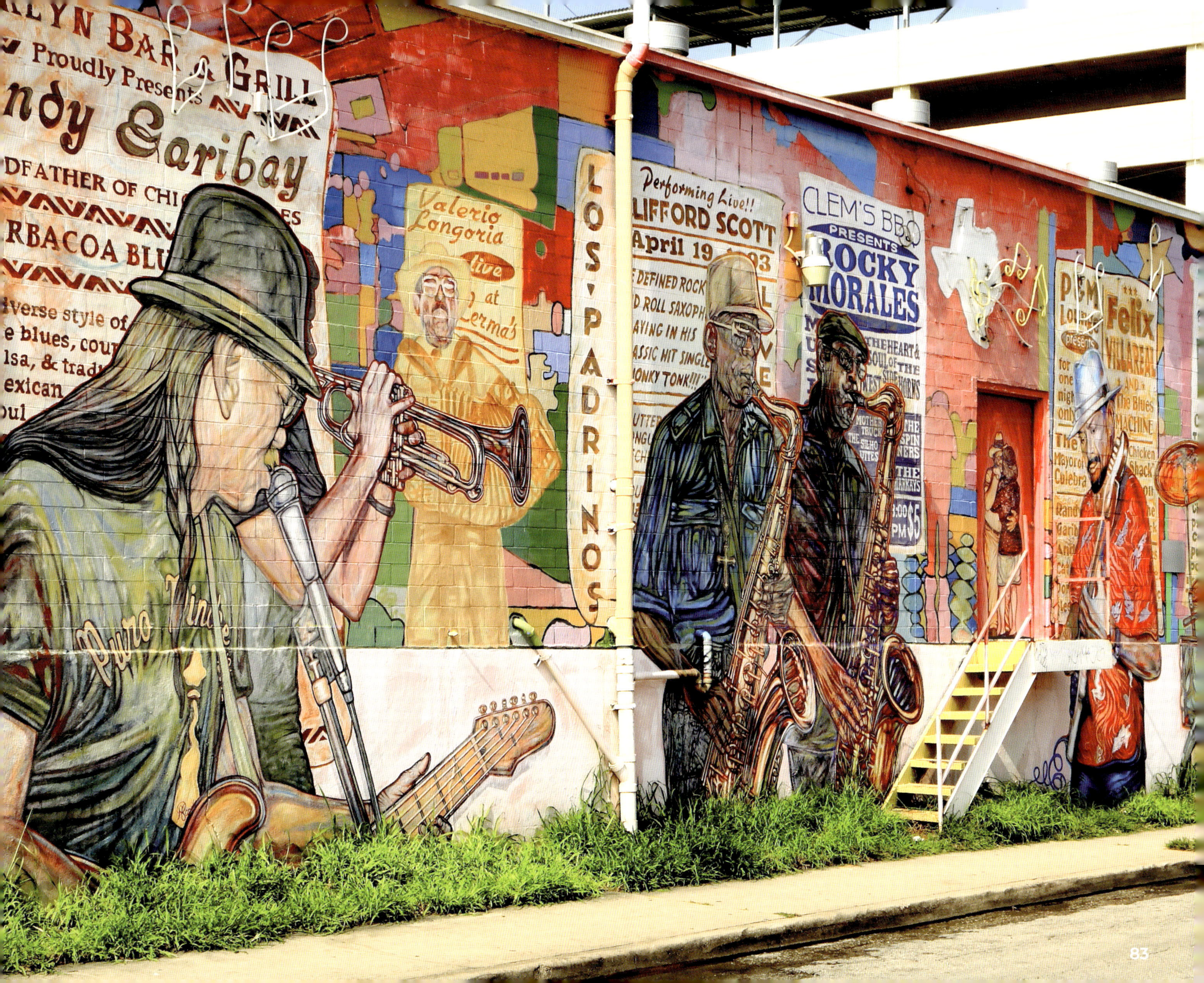
Proudly Presents
Valerio Longoria
live at Lerma's
LOS PADRINOS
Performing Live!!
April 19
CLEM'S BBQ
PRESENTS
ROCKY MORALES
Felix
VILLAREAL
AND
The Blues
MACHINE

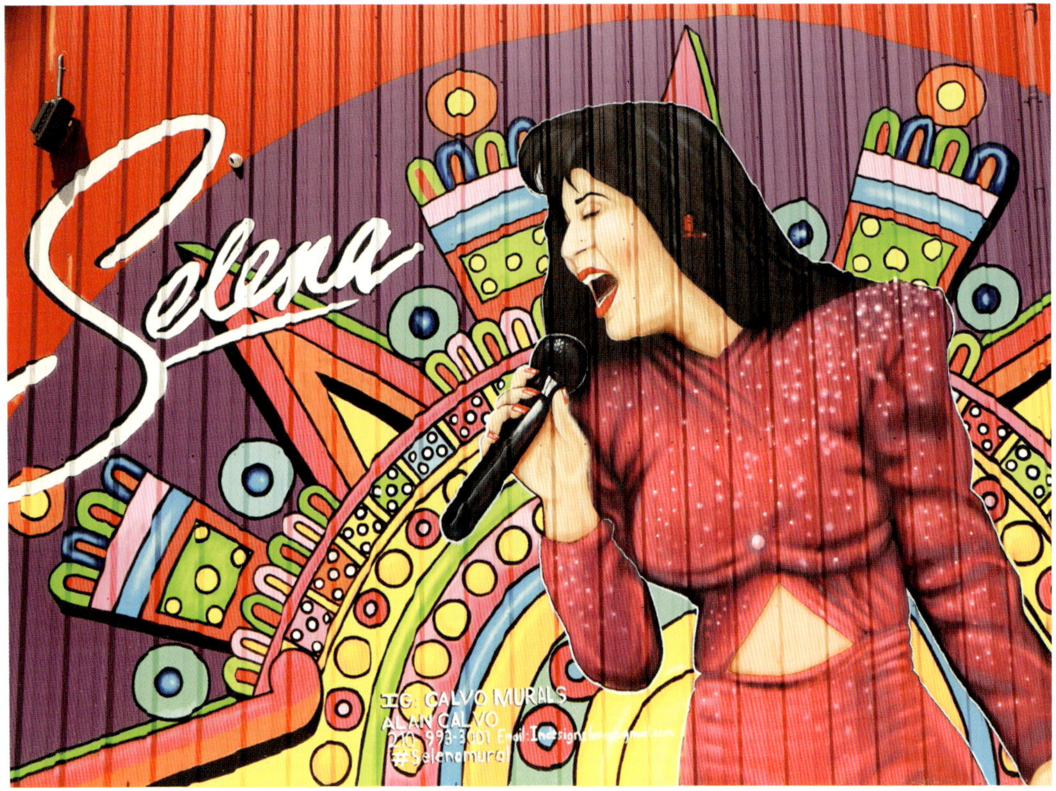

Selena, 2020.
Alan Calvo. Alamo Candy Company, Hildebrand and Capitol Avenues.

OPPOSITE PAGE
Untitled, 2018.
Paul Garson, N. St. Mary's Street.

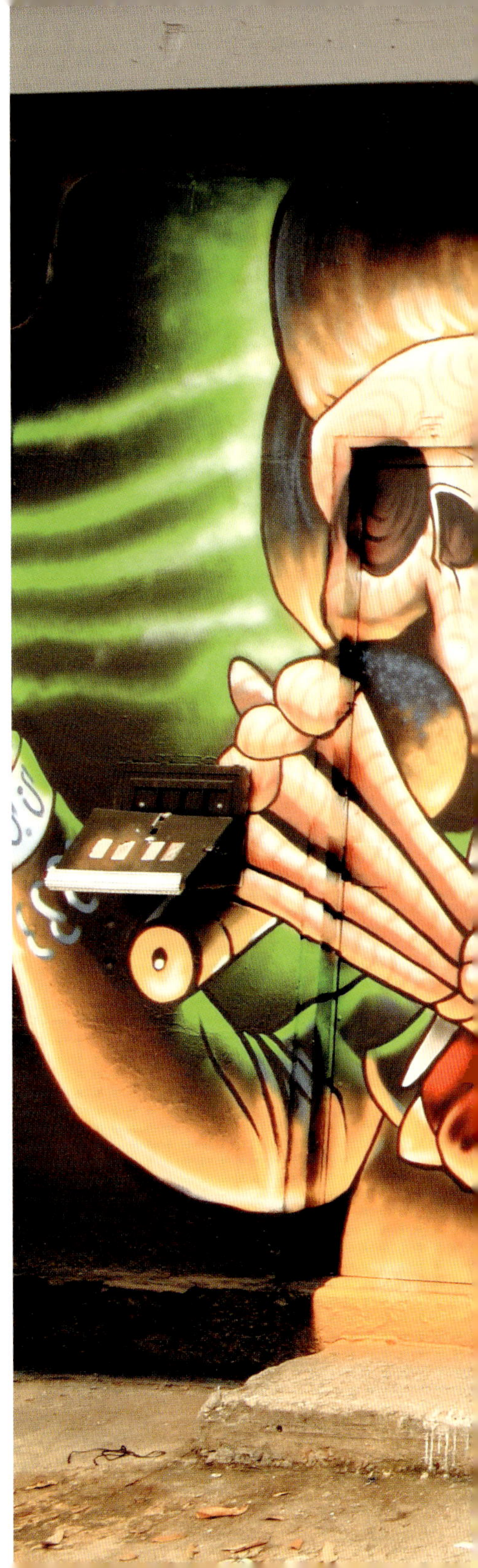

remembered forever, *como la flor*[2] that blooms from our dreams, twirling, dancing, singing to the rhythm of life.

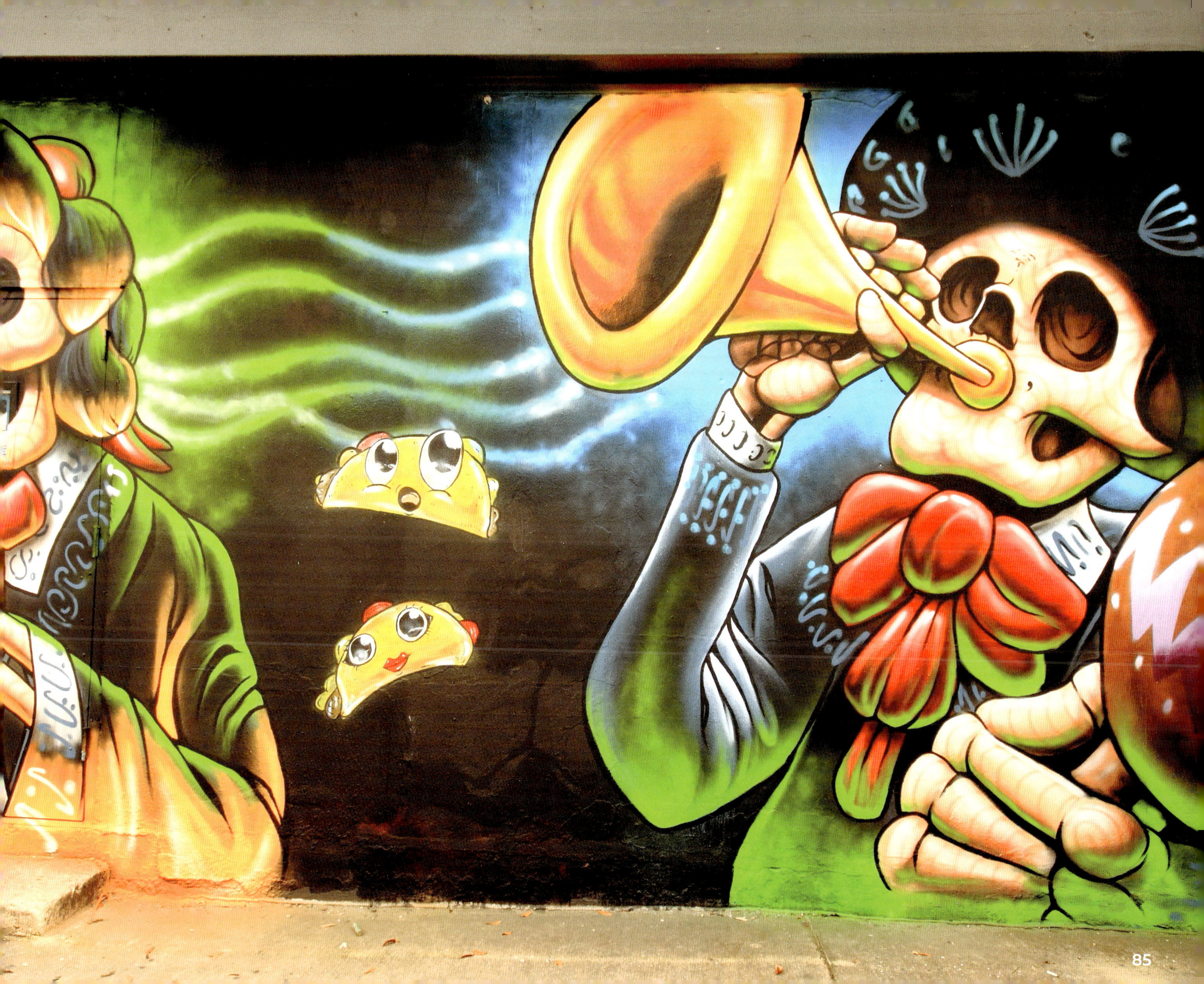

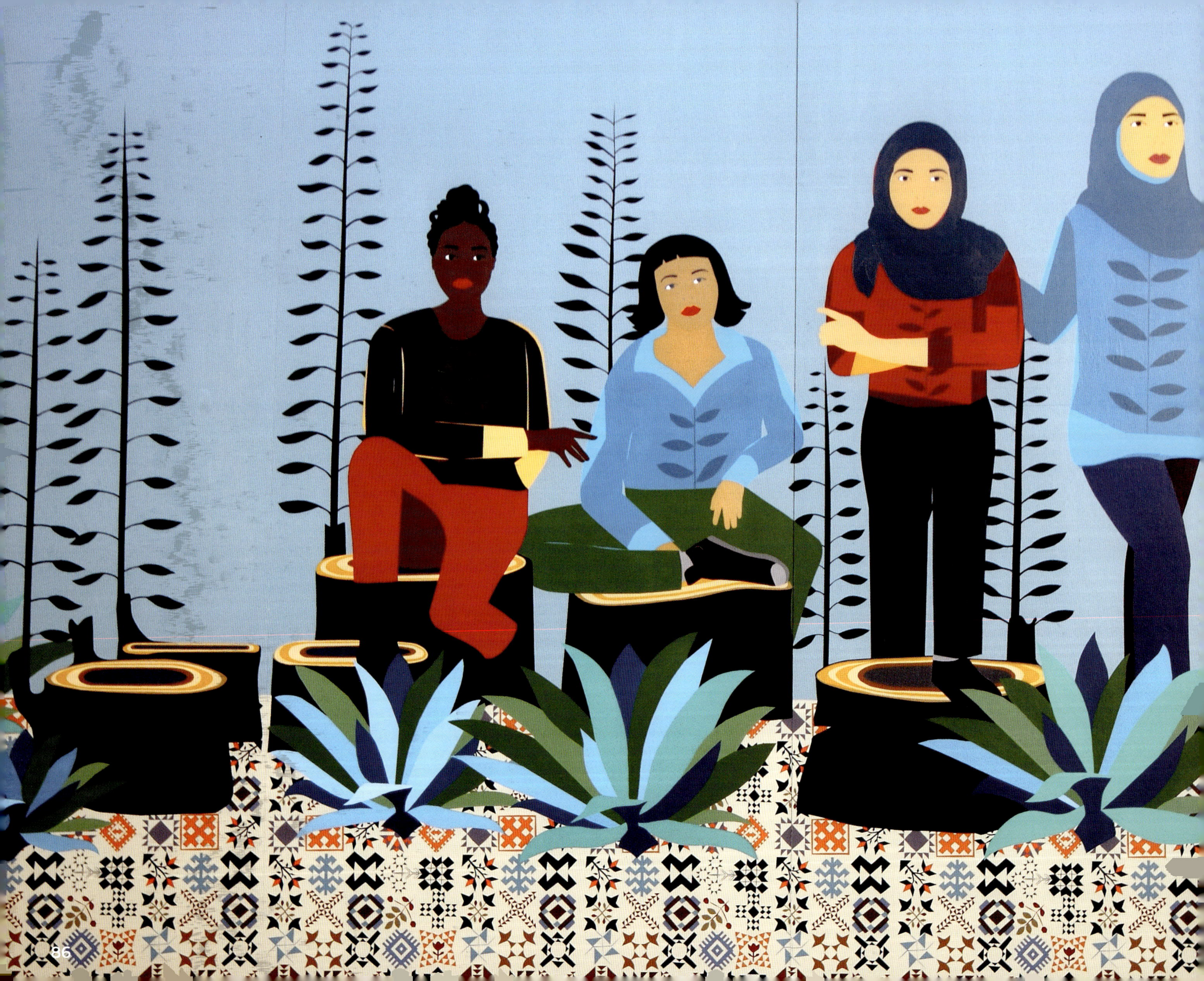

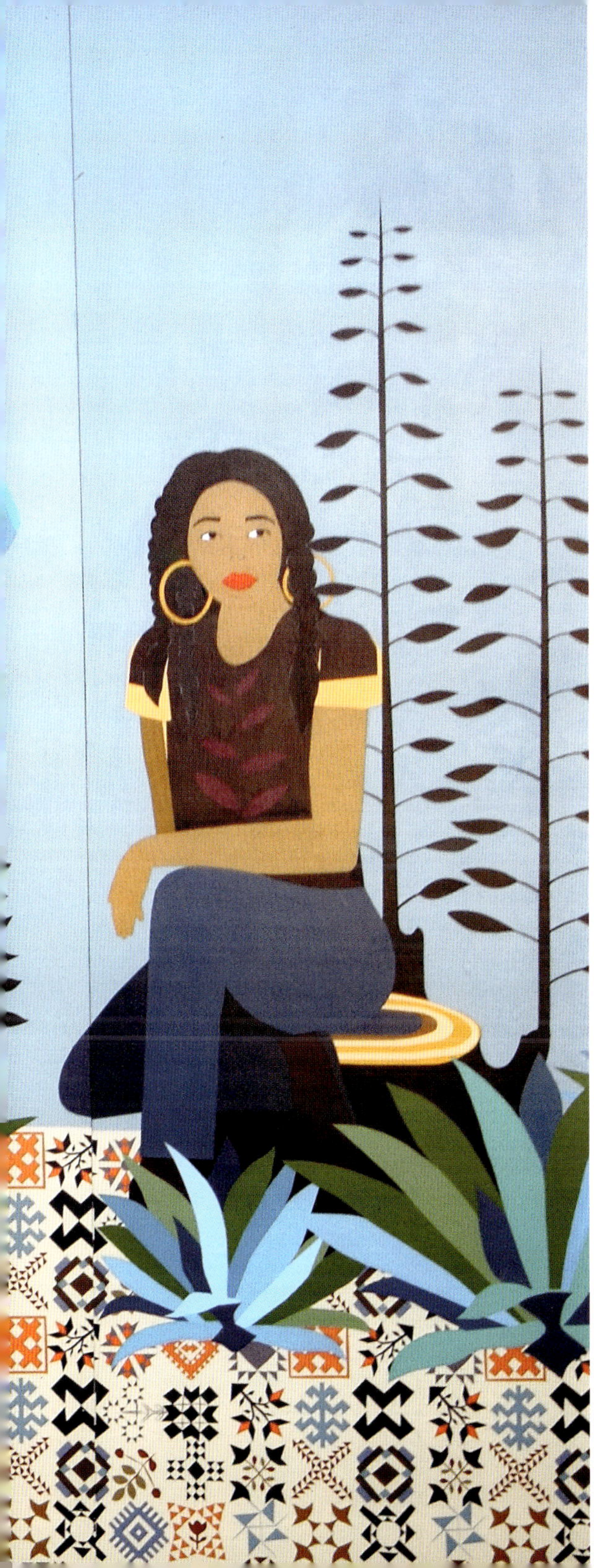

We, the people of this city, are interwoven
like a tapestry of immigrants,
each lending the beauty of their hue,
and the power of their life song
to this flow of people
moving, pulsing, making this home.

Interwoven, 2018.
Jennifer Khoshbin.
Navarro and East
Houston Streets.

NOTES

1. According to UNESCO's World Heritage website, "The missions' farmlands, cattle grounds, granaries, kilns, and water distribution systems can be seen as a demonstration of the exceptionally inventive interchange that occurred between Indigenous peoples, missionaries, and colonizers that contributed to a fundamental and permanent change in the cultures and values of all involved. . . . The enclosed layout of each mission complex and their proximity to each other, the widespread sharing of knowledge and skills among their inhabitants, and the early adoption of a common language and religion resulted in a people and culture with an identity neither wholly Indigenous nor wholly Spanish that has proven exceptionally persistent and pervasive."

2. The phrase *como la flor* translates as "like a flower" but also refers to one of the lines of "Como La Flor," a song sung by deceased music idol Selena, one that is often used to describe her life. When Selena died, dozens of red roses were left outside the site of her murder.

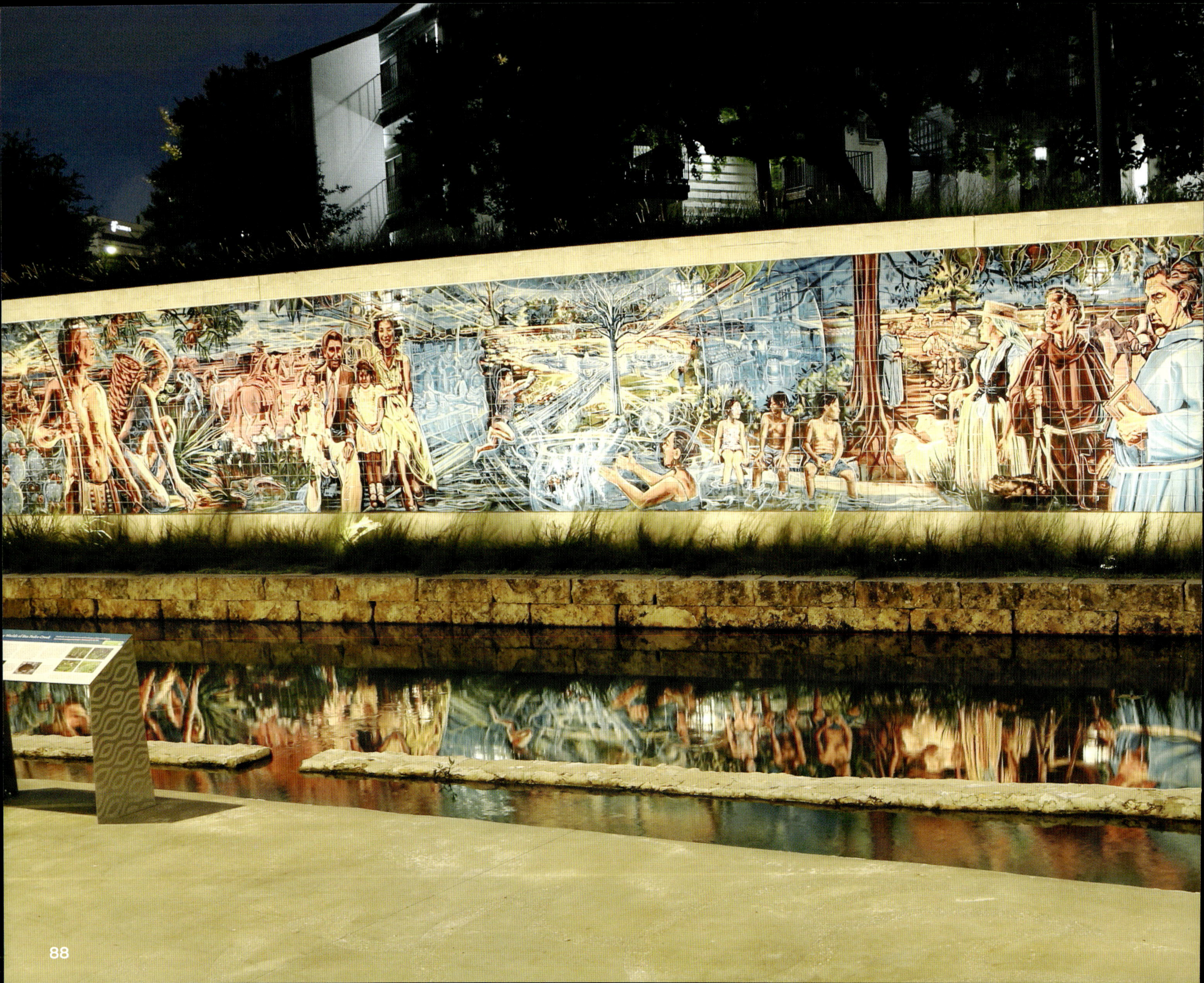

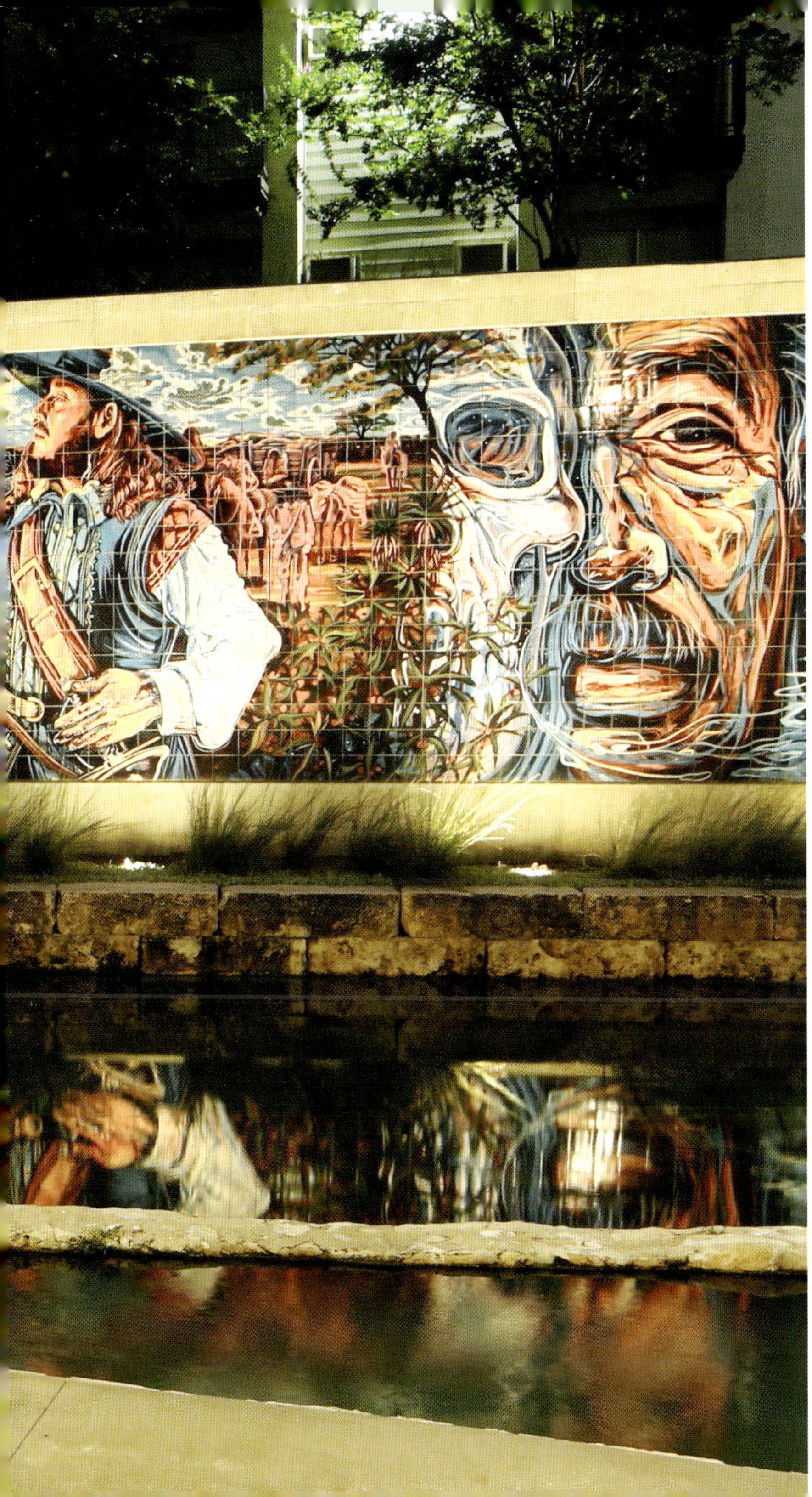

III. LIFEBLOOD OF THE CITY

OUR WATERWAYS

San Antonio is a young Yanaguana woman
all spirit, strength, and spark,
her skin a cinnamon summer, an autumn pecan,
her eyes steady stars in October's dark sky

arms graceful as weeping willow branches
she unravels her hair
that long dark wave of a river
winding, winding, right through our hearts
pouring clear through our dreams . . .

De Todos Caminos, Somos Uno, 2018. Adriana García. San Pedro Creek Culture Park.

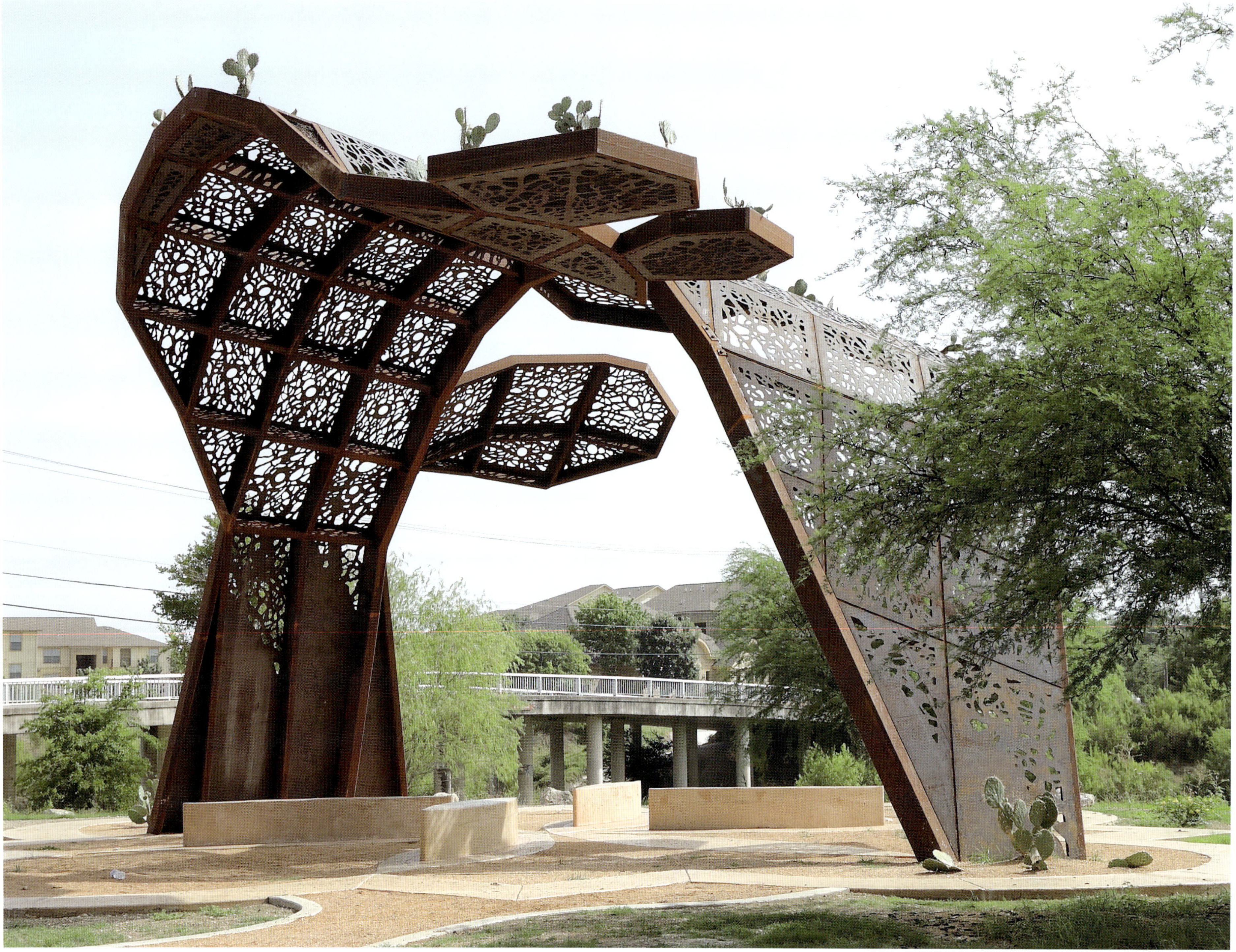

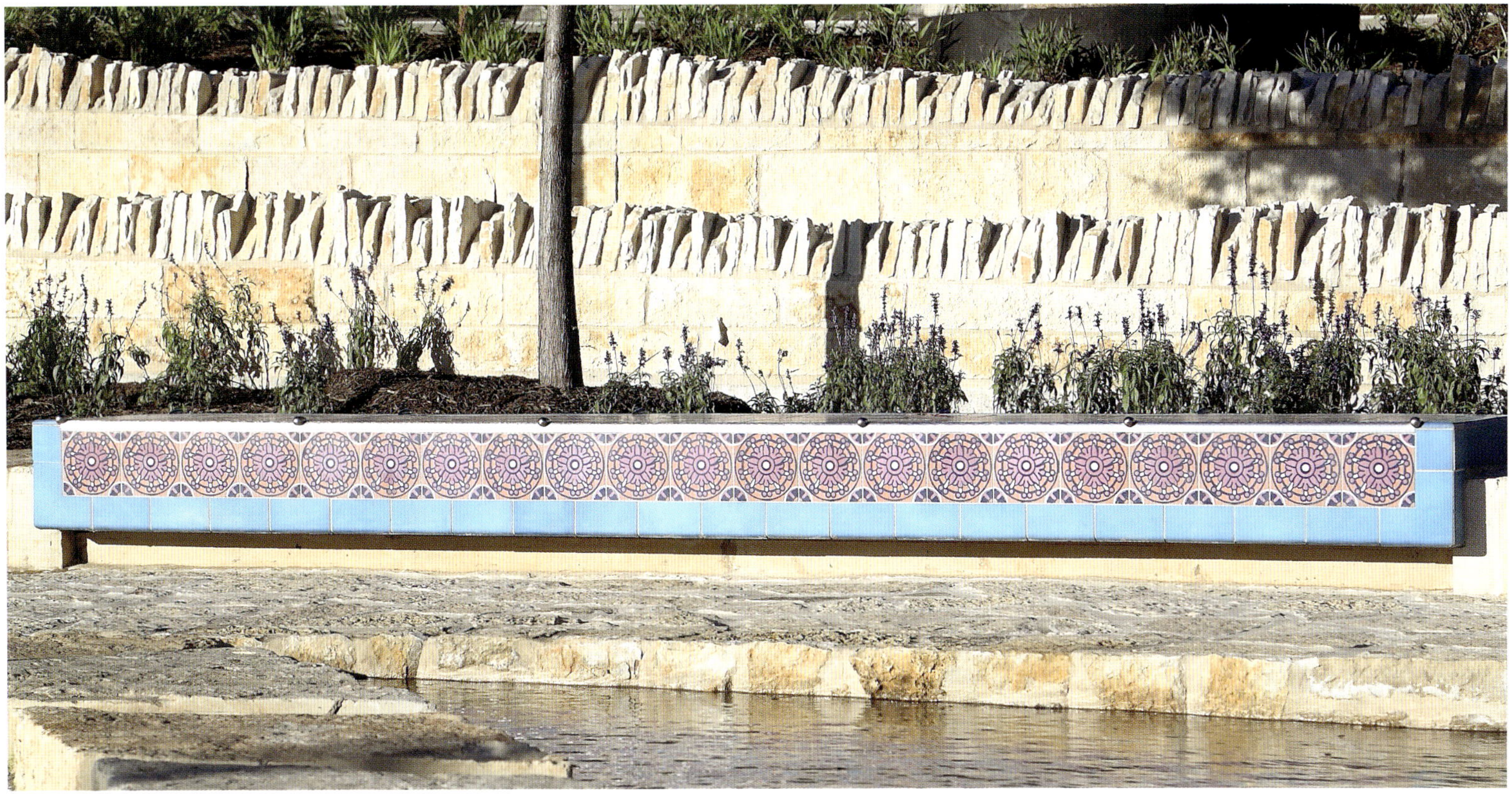

OPPOSITE PAGE
CoCobijos, 2017. Mel Chin. Mission County Park.

THIS PAGE
TOP
Tile Bench, 2018. Michael Menchaca. San Pedro Creek Culture Park.

BOTTOM
Maverick Tile Mural, 2013. Fernando Ramos and Ethel Harris. 1930. River Walk at 4th Street.

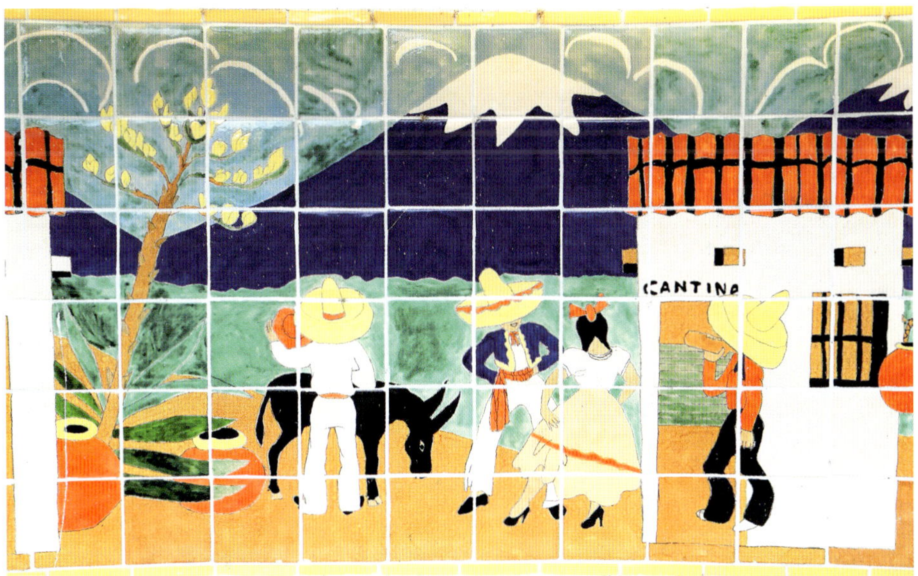

in ancient rhythms of her native tongue
unconquered tunes twirled like mesquite bark
gnarled like the centuries of river oak
a melody trickling cool as river water . . .[1]

It's the water, the water,
that essence of life
that drew us here once. And always.
And Still.

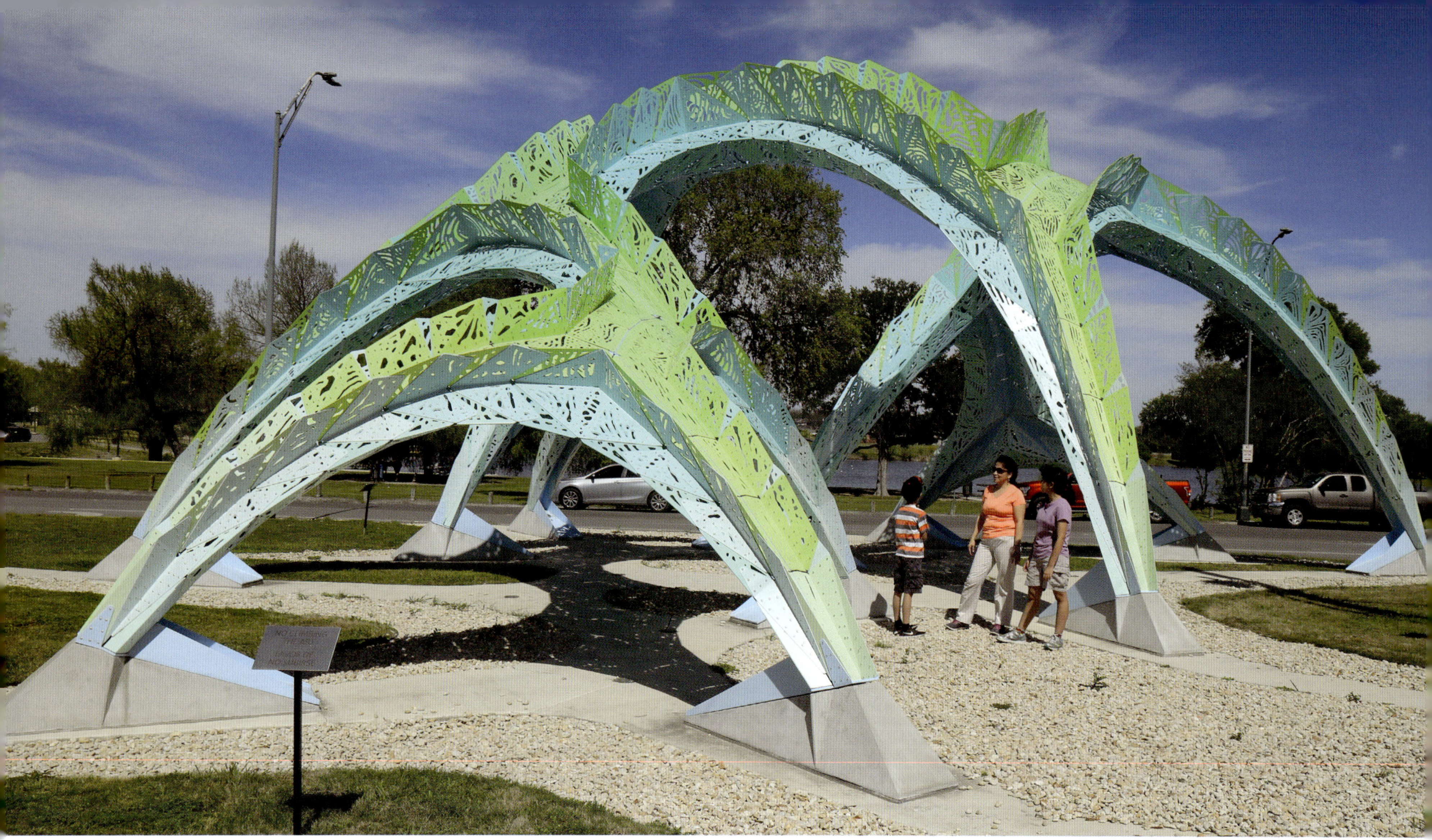

Curving into its *cálido* colors
mirrored against its own marbled movement . . .
making soft melodies ring from the leaves, from tender voices
of children who play here between the centuries
rippling in and out of laughter . . .
reflecting the very rhythm   of you.[2]

Spineway, 2015.
Mark Fornes.
Woodlawn Lake.

OPPOSITE PAGE
Running with the Moon, 2018.
Brad Oldham and Christy Coltrin.
Greenline Park.

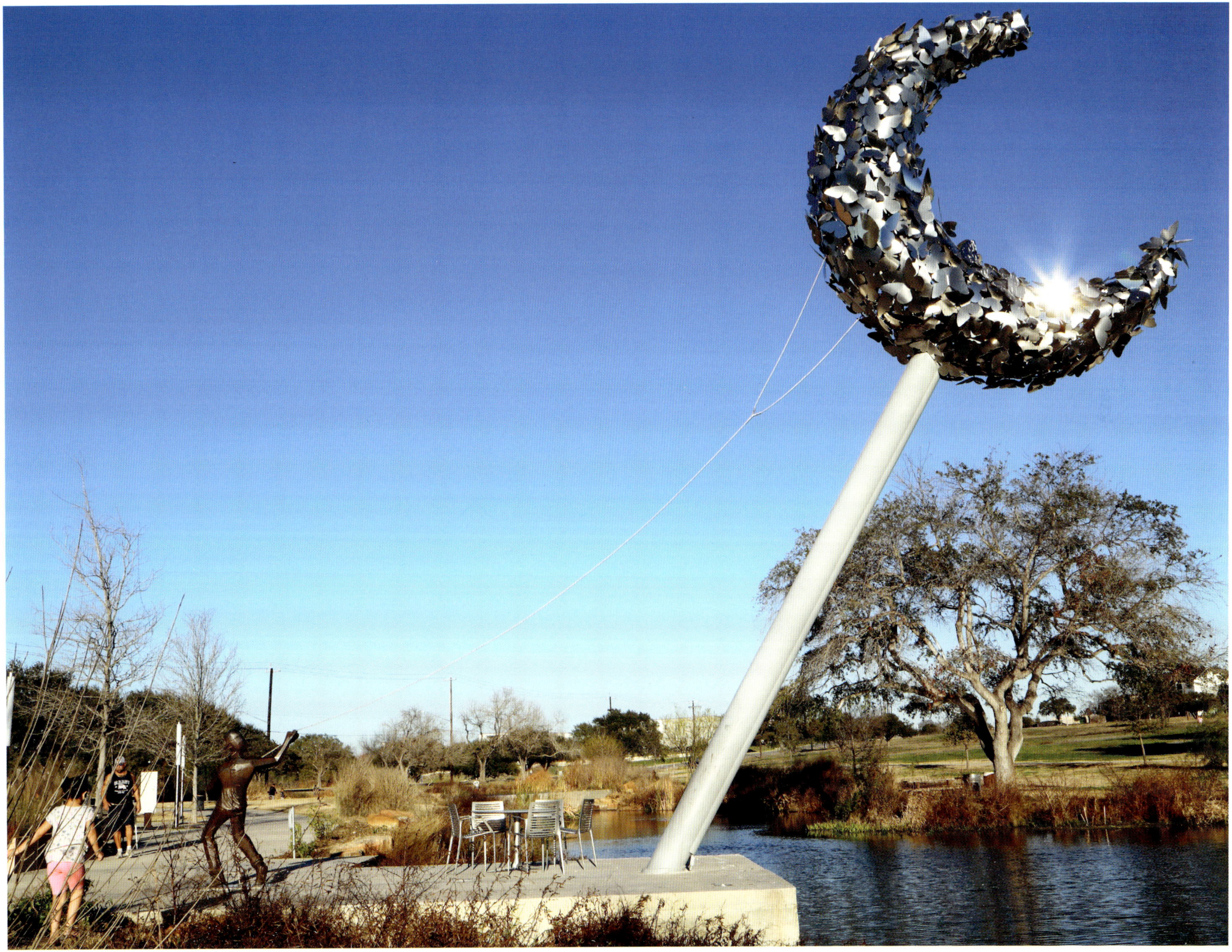

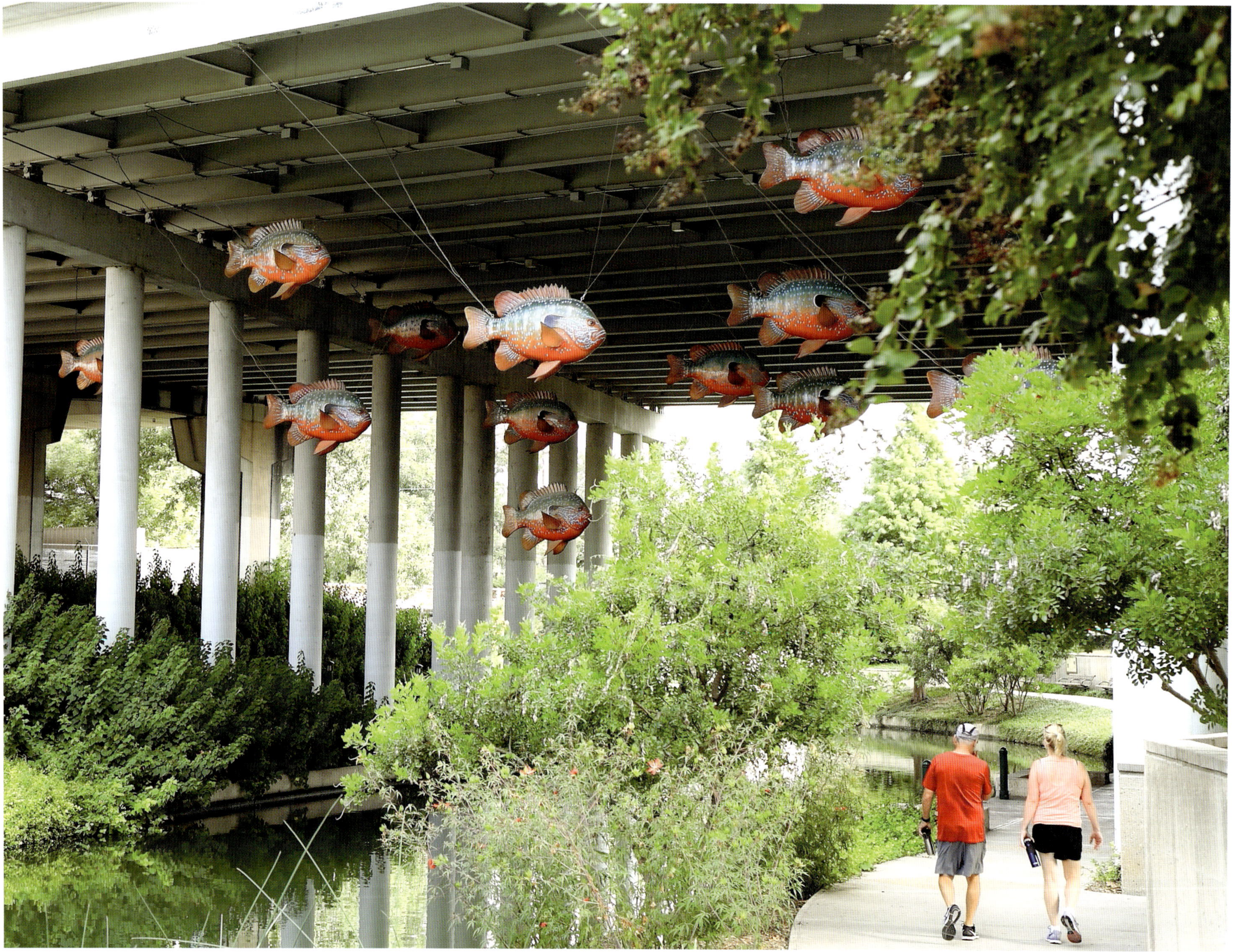

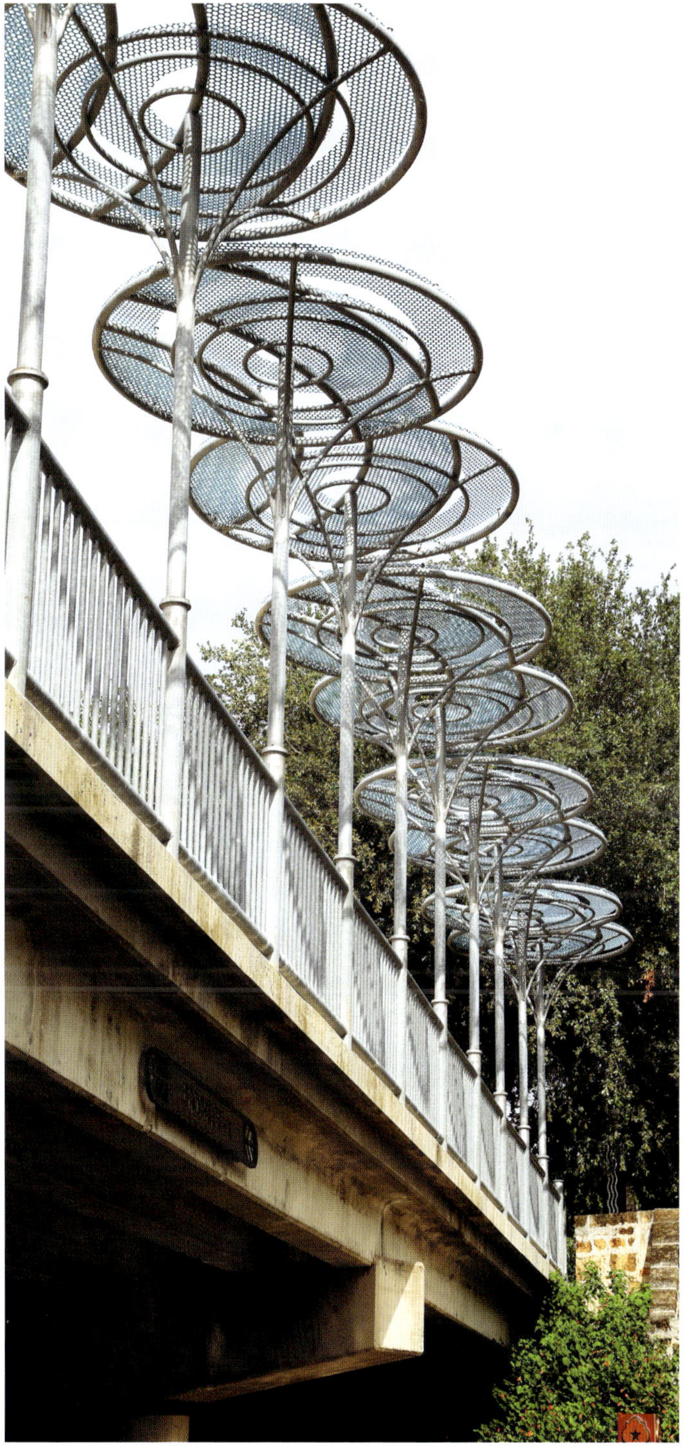

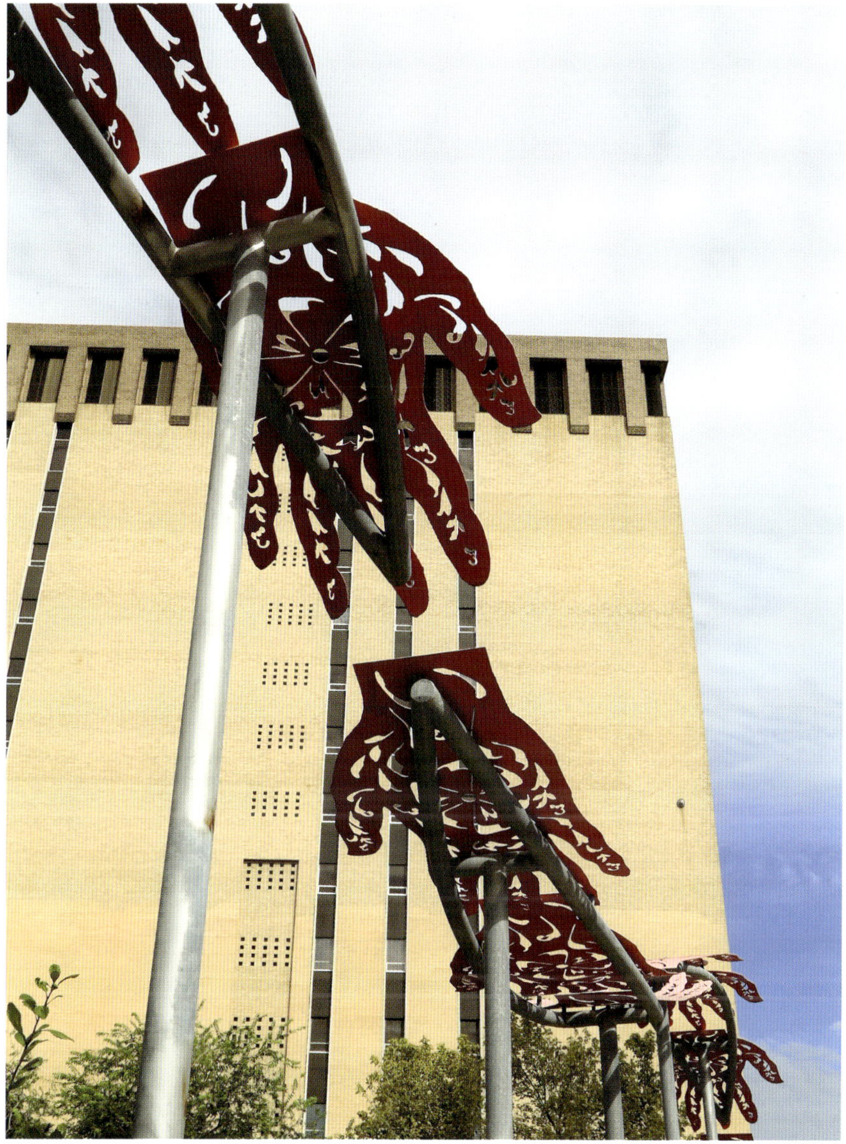

OPPOSITE PAGE
F.I.S.H., 2017. Donald Lipsky. River Walk near Camden Street bridge.

THIS PAGE
LEFT
Bridge of Rippling Shadows, 2012. Rolando Briseño. River Walk at Brooklyn Street bridge.

RIGHT
Bridge of Encounters, 2012. Rolando Briseño. McCullough Street bridge.

Installments of art are on this river's bridges, inside its caverns,
built into the benches,
floating above its currents,
fish flying through the air.

Palapa, 2009. Carlos Cortés. River Walk near Newell Street bridge. Cortés follows the style of his granduncle, Dionicio Rodríguez, whose 1930s work at Miraflores and Brackenridge Park has become an iconic San Antonio aesthetic.

OPPOSITE PAGE *Concrete Trellis*, 2002. Carlos Cortés. River Walk next to Tobin Performing Arts Center.

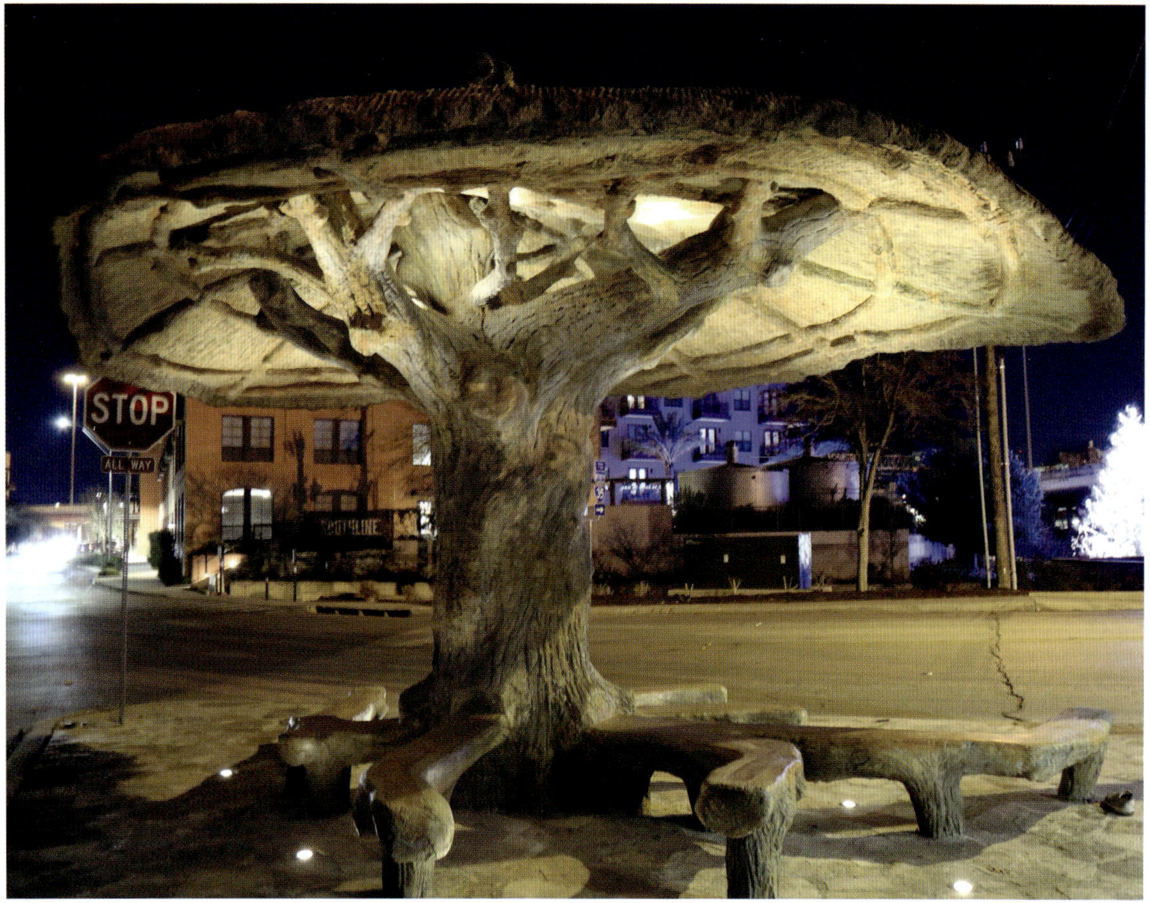

There is *trabajo rústico* here,
art in faux bois, speaking in
the voice of trees,
a San Antonio style for
the last hundred years.
It sings a legacy continued,
an arbor of carved branches
that carry us on
a footpath through time.

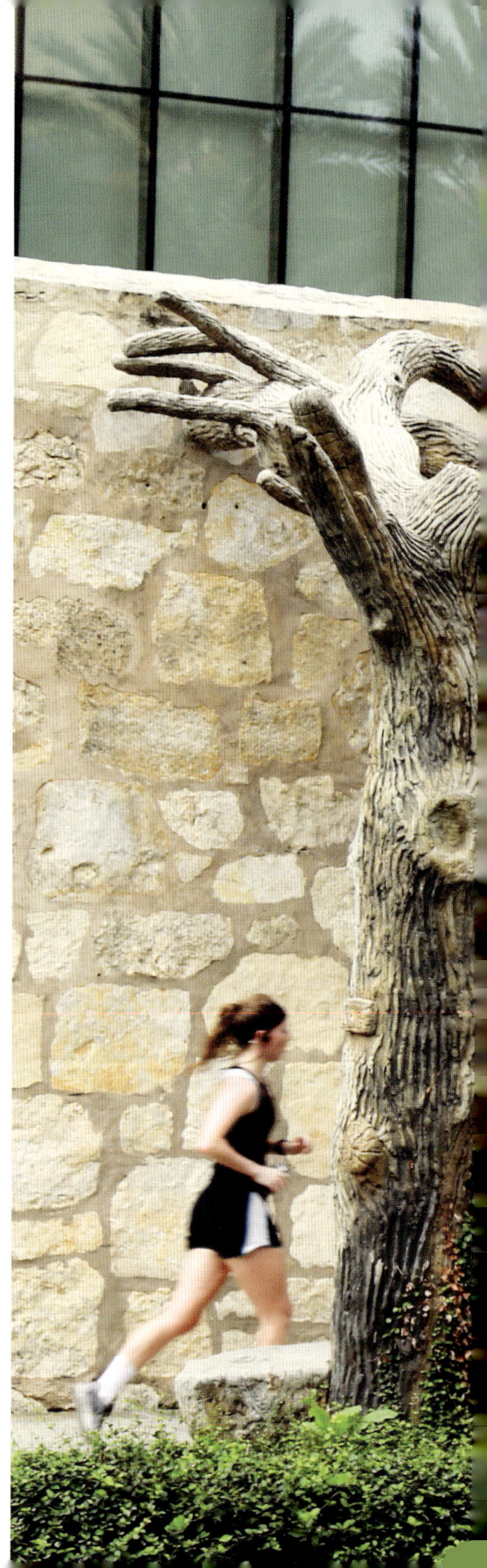

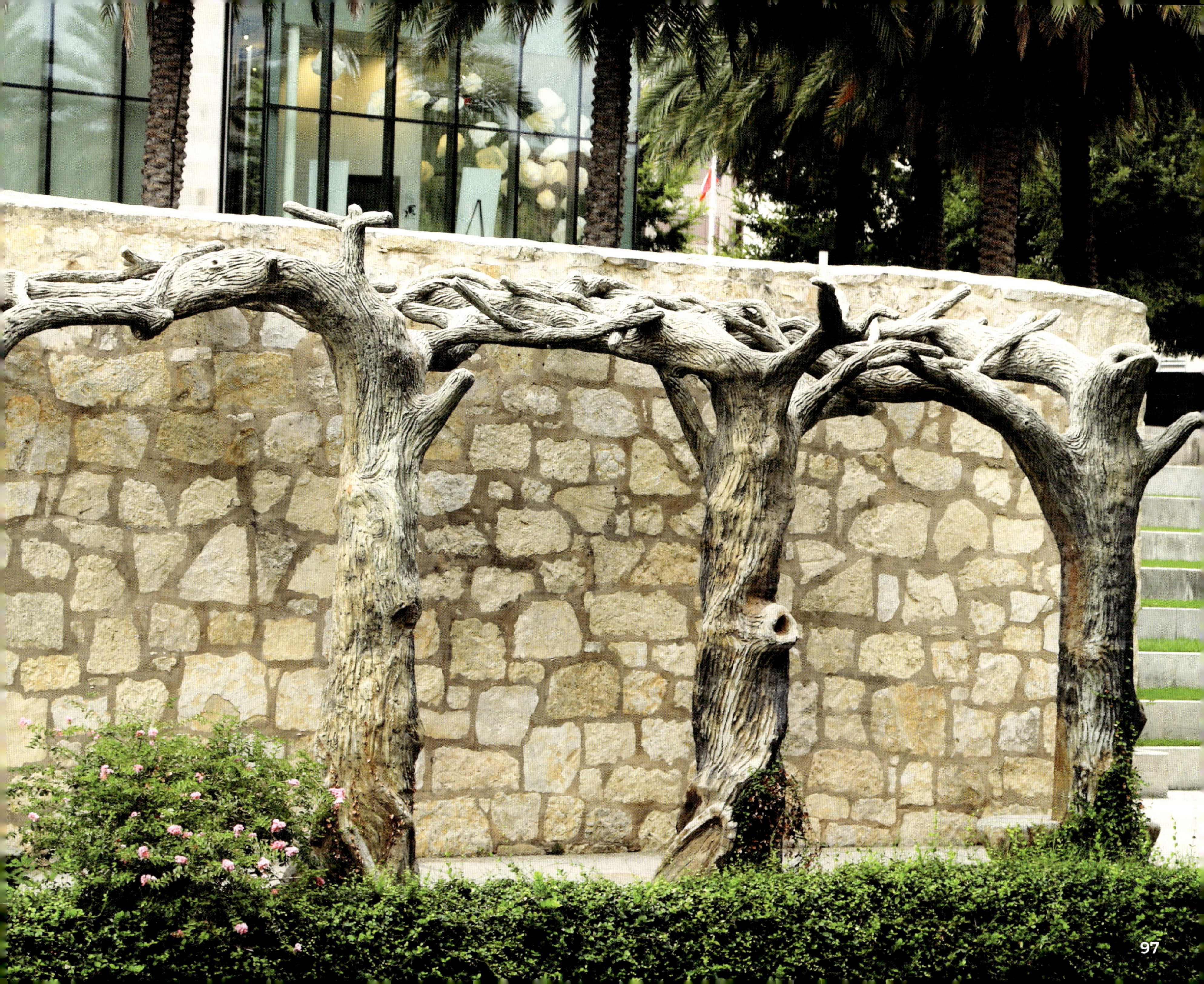

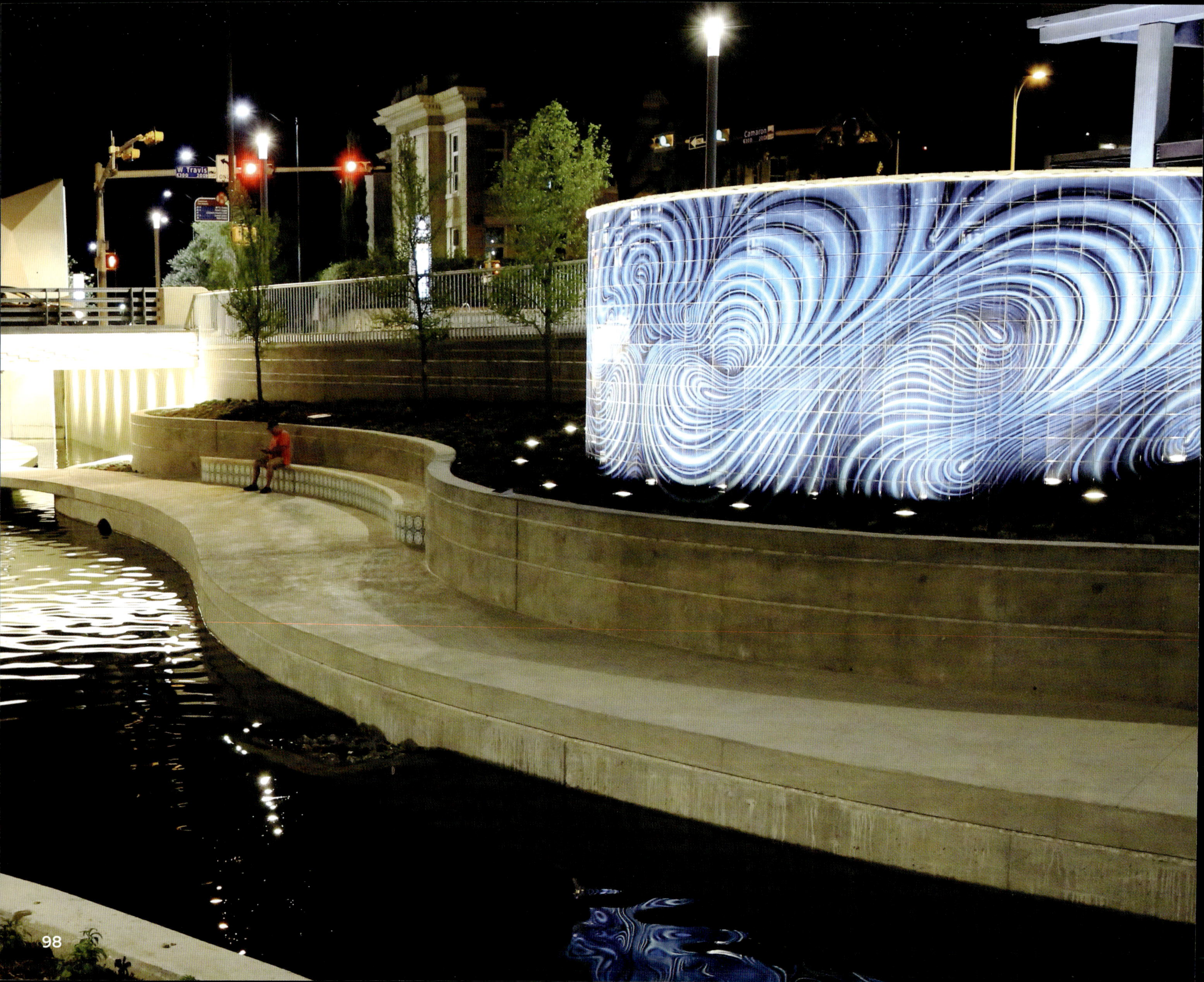
W Travis
Camaron

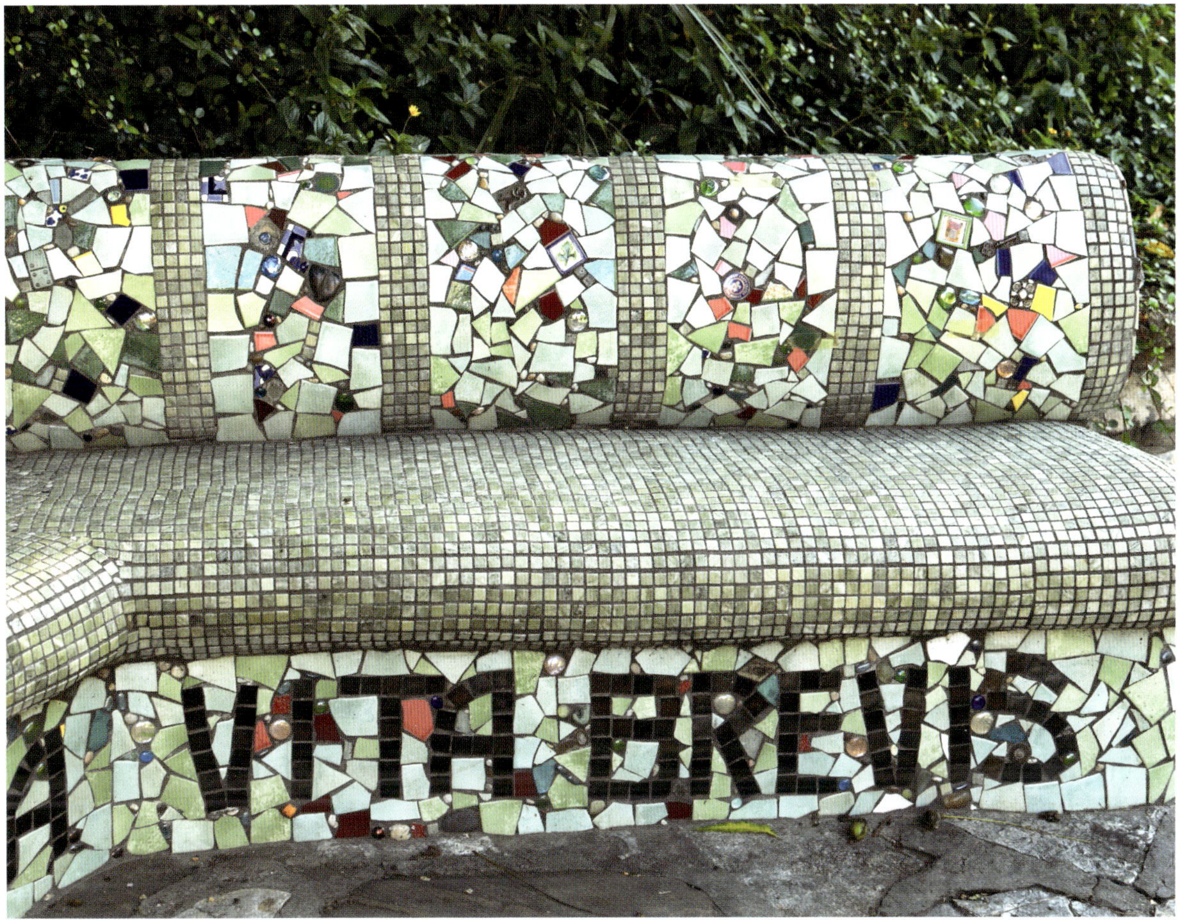

Bernard's Bench, 2009. Twyla Arthur. River Walk near Southwest School of Art.

OPPOSITE PAGE
Aqua, 2018. Alex Rubio. San Pedro Creek Culture Park.

We amble along the river walk.
We gather for concerts and banquets.
We bike and jog.
We float in the barges for leisurely tours,
or a commute to work.

We meet someone special here, or fish in its stream.
We draw out inspiration, vision, spirit, food, ánimo, love.
Holy Water, our city's lifeblood.

NOTES

1. These verses excerpted from the poem "San Antonio is a Young Yanaguana Woman," published in *This River Here* (San Antonio, TX: Wings Press, 2014).

2. These lines excerpted from the poem "River Music," published in *This River Here* (San Antonio, TX: Wings Press, 2014).

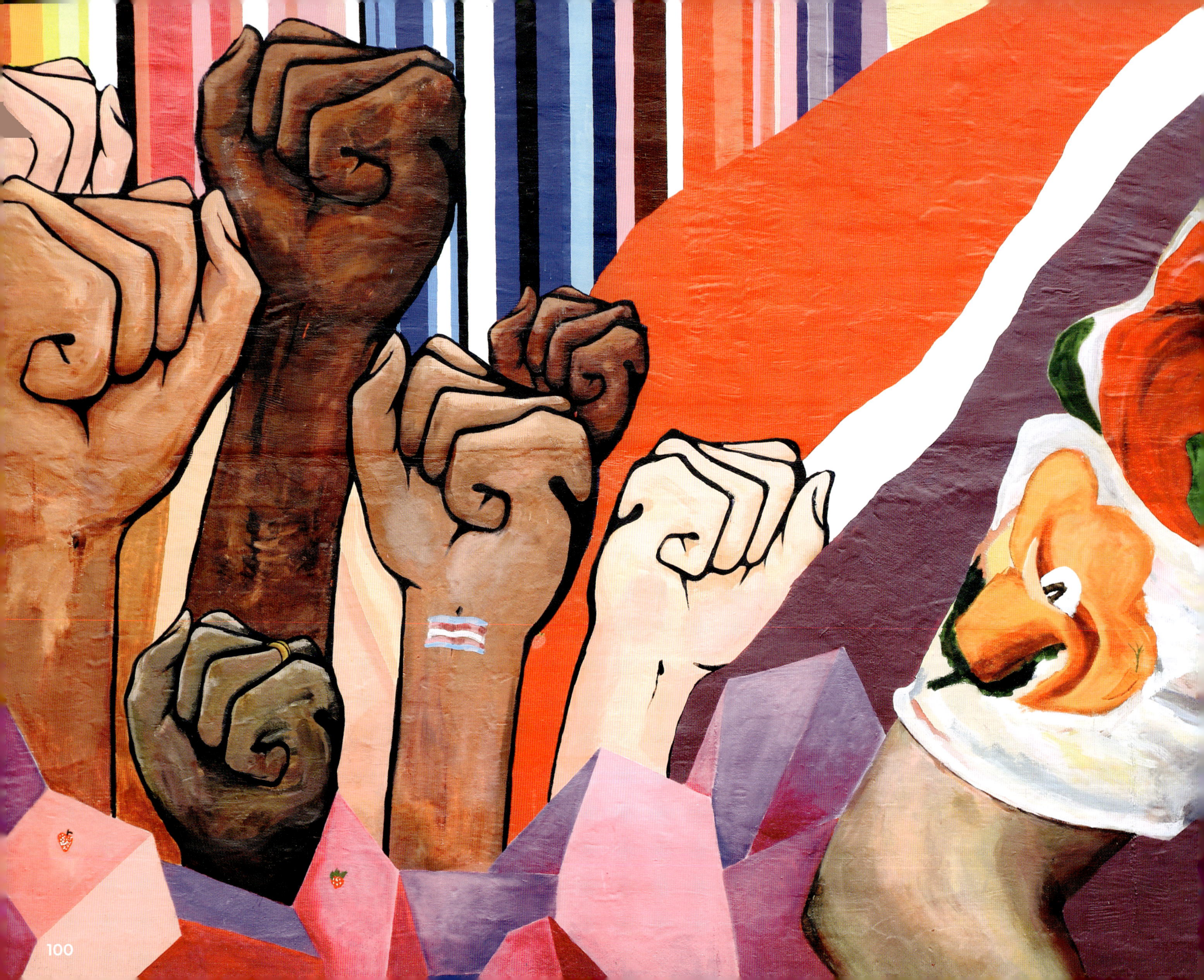

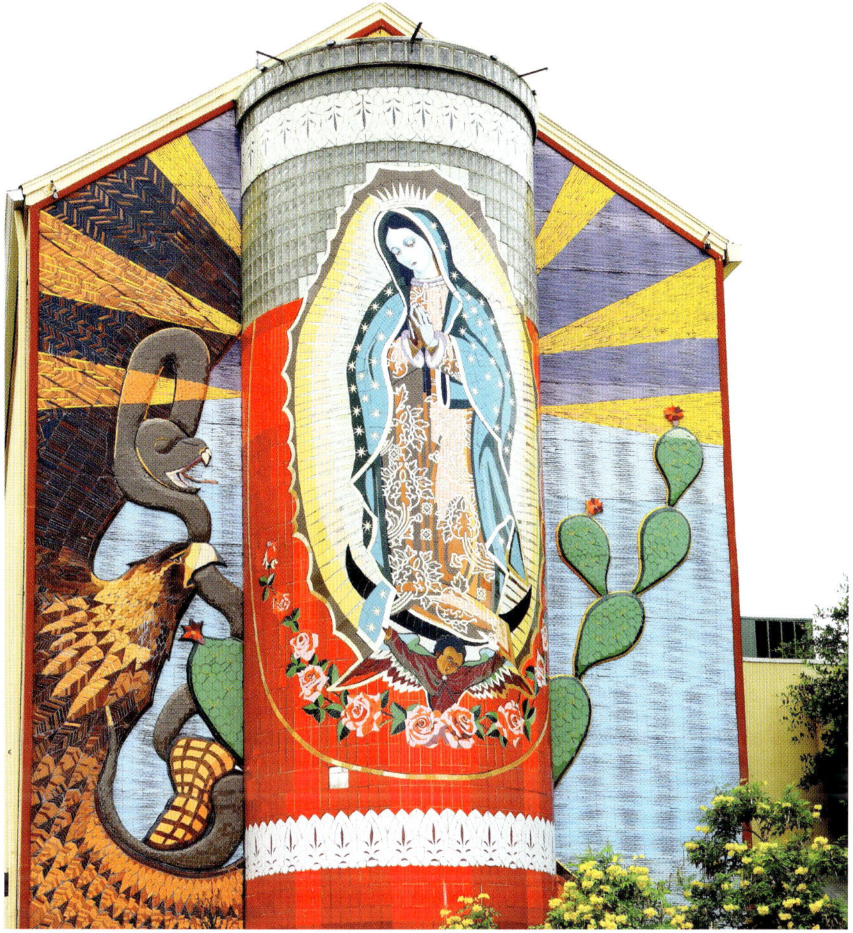

OPPOSITE PAGE
Detail of the mural *Presente*, 2018. Ana Hernández, Rhys Munro, and Rudy Herrera. 1700 block of S. Laredo Street.

THIS PAGE
La Veladora of Our Lady of Guadalupe, 2003. Jesse Treviño. A three-dimensional ceramic tile votive candle, Treviño's tribute to the votives found in many West Side homes features the Virgin of Guadalupe, a brown and pregnant woman blending clothing and symbolism of Catholic and Aztec beliefs. She appeared to Juan Diego, an Indian, in 1531 and preserved the rights (and lives) of Indigenous peoples in a theological debate over whether the Indian had a soul or could be used as property. Behind the candle is the Mexican eagle with a snake in its beak, the guiding inspiration for the Aztecs to trek south from their homeland of Aztlan to Mexico City, ca. 1064 CE. The eagle appears on the Mexican flag. Guadalupe Cultural Arts Center.

IV. EL CORAZÓN DEL WEST SIDE

HEART, ART & MURALISMO

The West Side Barrio's home altars light seven-day candles,
lay around them flowers of *esperanza*, tin *milagro* wings,
a rainbow of colors in the fringed sarape dresser scarf,
and hopes that each fragile flicker could bring a miracle.
These votive flames soft-speak the power
of things too real . . . too strong . . . too deep
to be simply
seen.

(Last sentence excerpted from "Fragile Flames"[1])

LEFT
Adelita, 1980. Velia Casiano with Robert Rendón, Raymond Méndez, Ramón Rodríguez, and Ernesto "Neto" Mendoza. One of 125 murals painted on the Cassiano Homes by students under the direction of the Community Cultural Arts Organization. This mural is paying homage to the Adelitas, women guerrilla fighters in the Mexican Revolution. Hidalgo Street.

RIGHT
Zapata, 1982. Steven Adame et al. Emiliano Zapata, Pancho Villa, and many figures of the Mexican Revolution became iconic figures in the Mexican American civil rights movement.

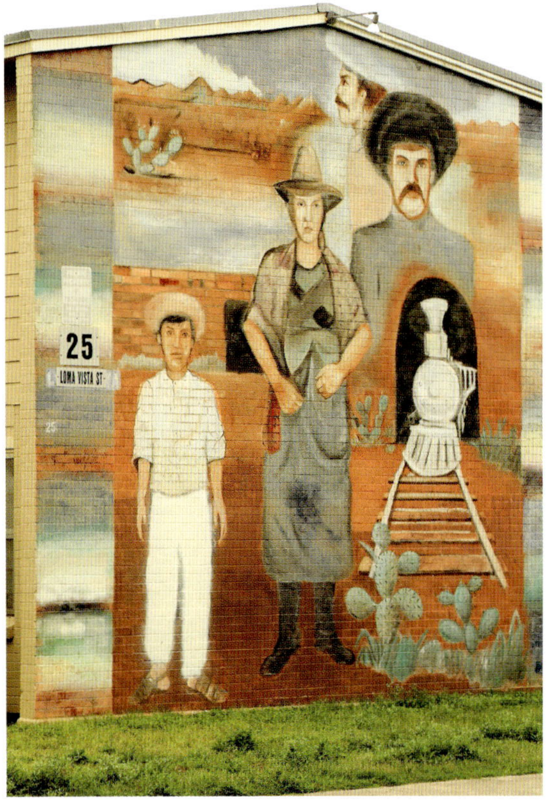

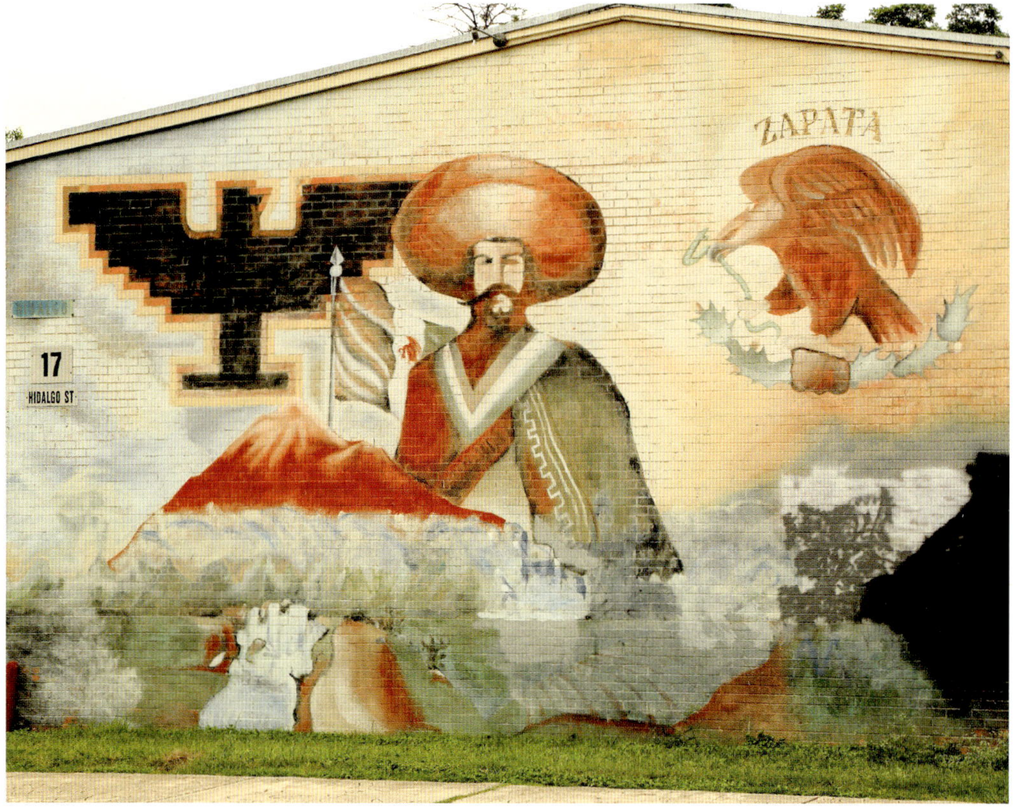

Where did this love of community art begin,
this joy of painted murals blooming open to the public eye?
Muralismo, you had your start in Mexico's nineteen teens,
a Revolución of color and political honesty,
you shook the Catrinas to their bony core.
Cholos, Pachucos, later Chicanos, and then
Rio de Janeiro, Paris, Athens, Mumbai, Melbourne, Tokyo
drew on your philosophy—
Art is too large to be contained,
too free to be
restricted.
For Art, like Hope,
should be open to all.

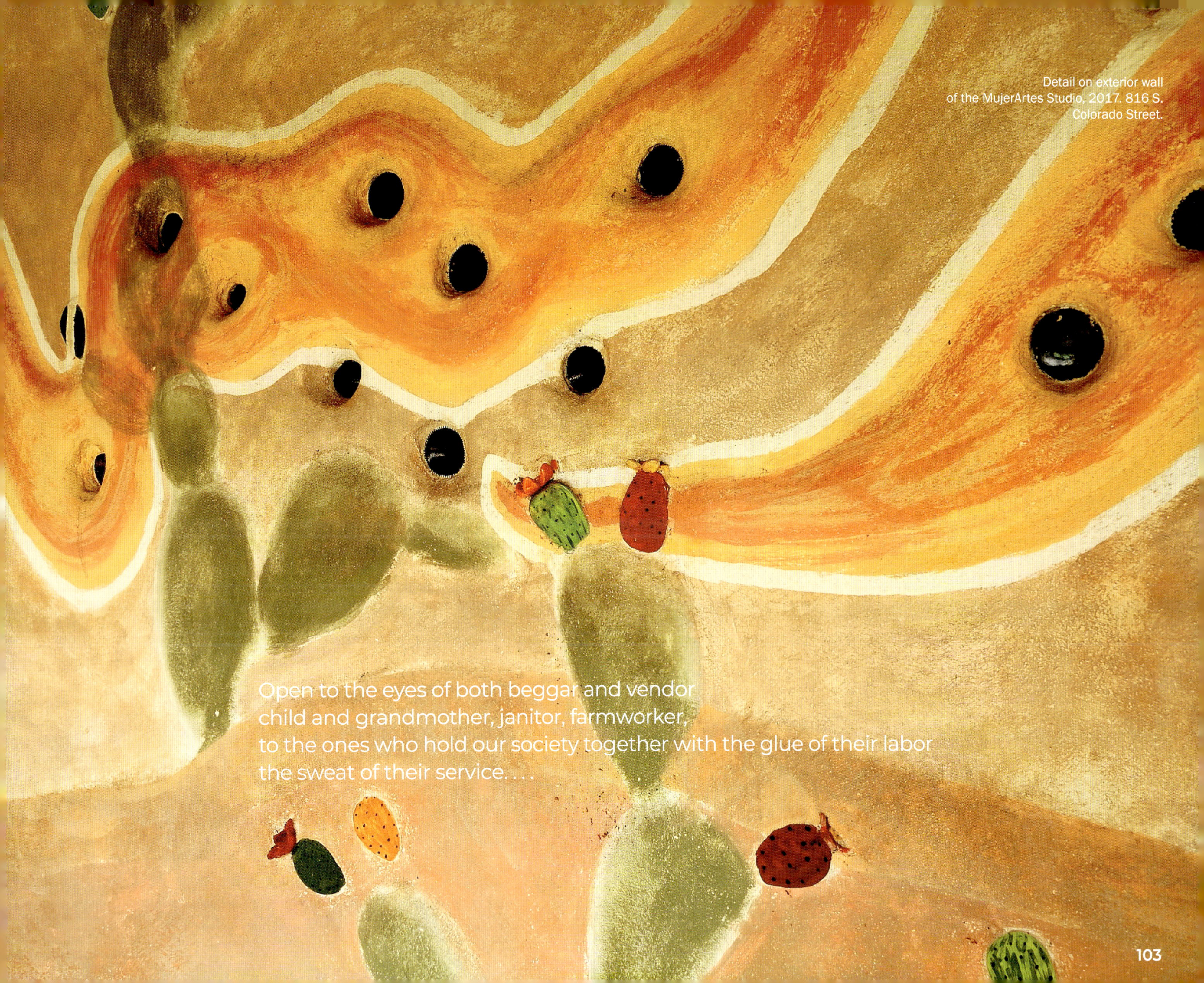

Detail on exterior wall of the MujerArtes Studio, 2017. 816 S. Colorado Street.

Open to the eyes of both beggar and vendor
child and grandmother, janitor, farmworker,
to the ones who hold our society together with the glue of their labor
the sweat of their service. . . .

TOP LEFT
Mayahuil, Nuestra Señora de los Remedios, 2017. MujerArtes Studio.

TOP RIGHT
MujerArtes Adobe Studio, 2017. 816 S. Colorado Street.

BOTTOM LEFT
Opening ceremony, September 2017. *At front, standing*, are MujerArtes Colectiva Members Rosa Vega, Adriana Netro, Teri Borrego, Patricia de la Garza, Arlene Martínez, Ana Uviedo, Olga Martínez, Hilda Ruiz, Ana Martínez, Gina Sambrano, and Graciela Sánchez. In the audience are art lovers, family members, and scholars, including Dr. Tomás Ybarra-Frausto, native of San Antonio's West Side and author of the first research on rasquachismo, a Chicano style of barrio art.

BOTTOM RIGHT
Painters at the MujerArtes Colectiva Adobe Studio

OPPOSITE PAGE
Justicia, 2018.
Ernesto Cuevas Jr.
1422 Buena Vista Street.

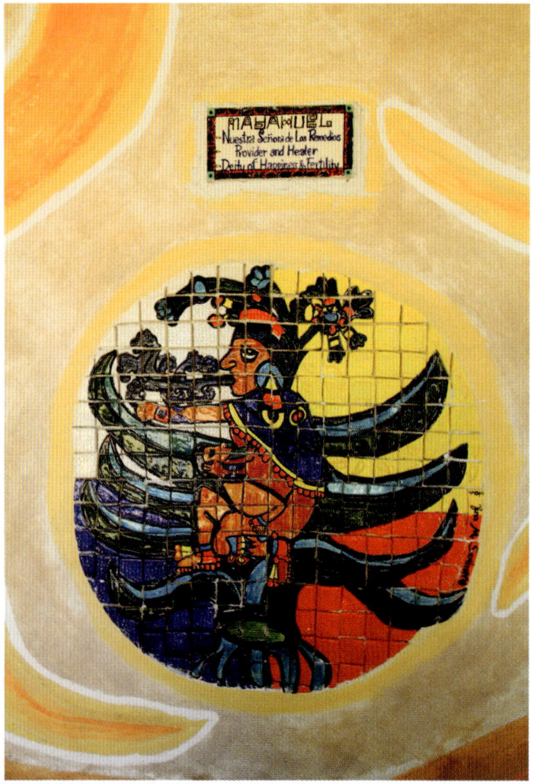

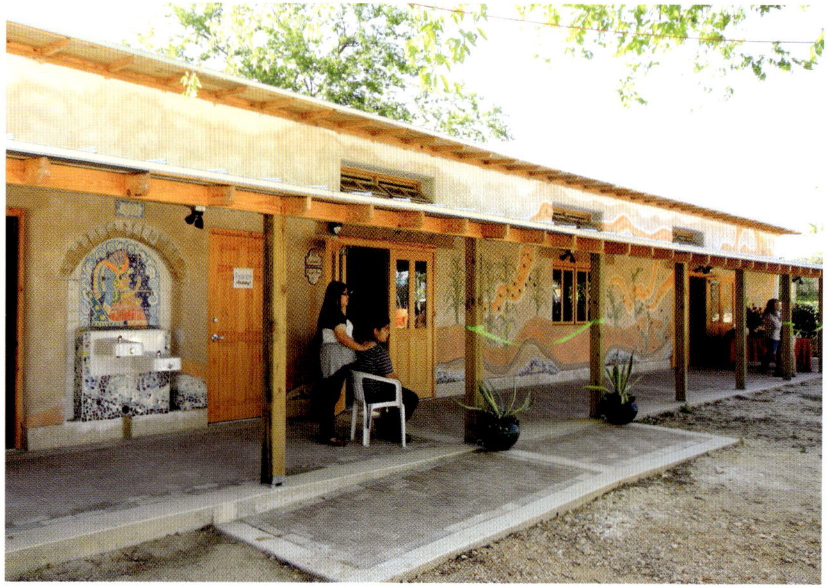

West Side, you have always been this city's corazón,
the heart of its culture, giving seed to its arts
that spread everywhere, enchant us all.

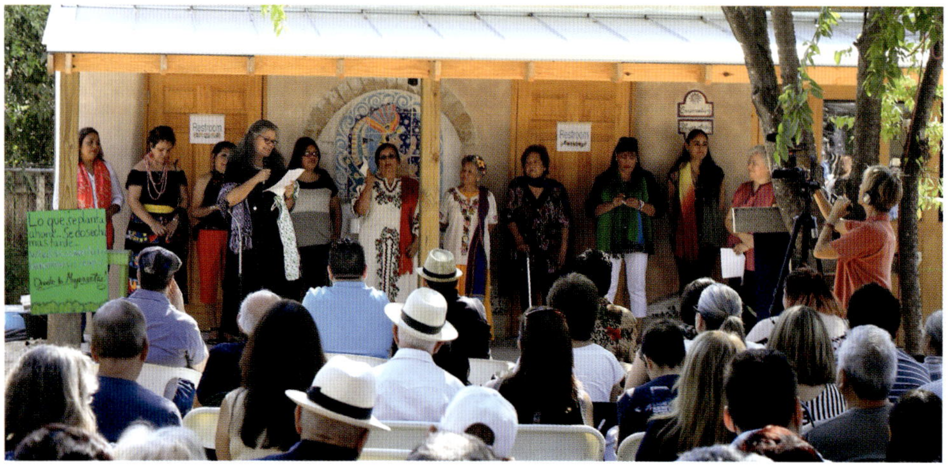

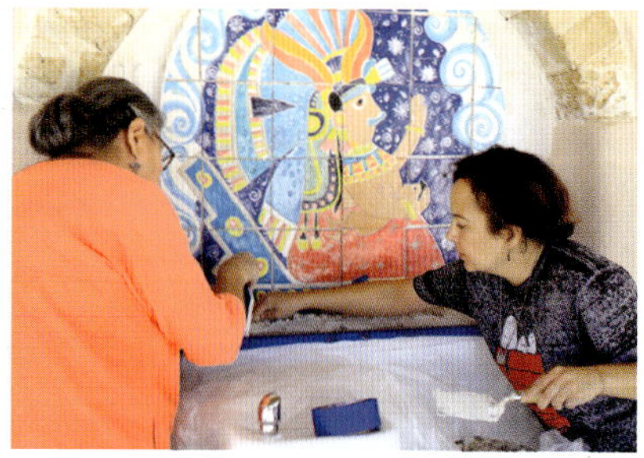

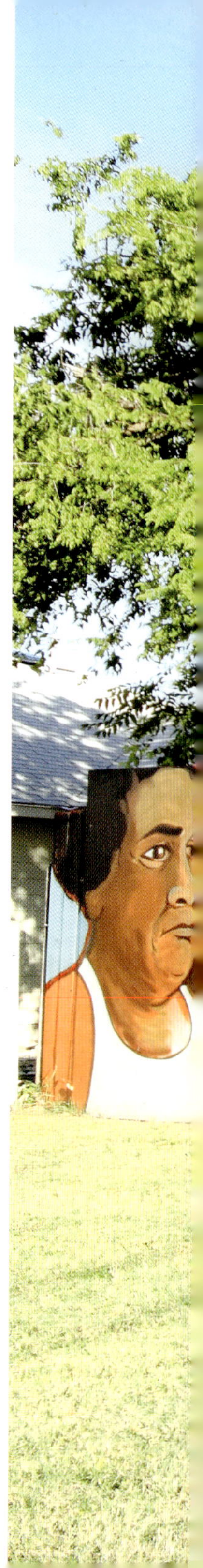

Your Murals decry injustice,
enshrine our Heroes, our Sheroes,
our cultural wealth,

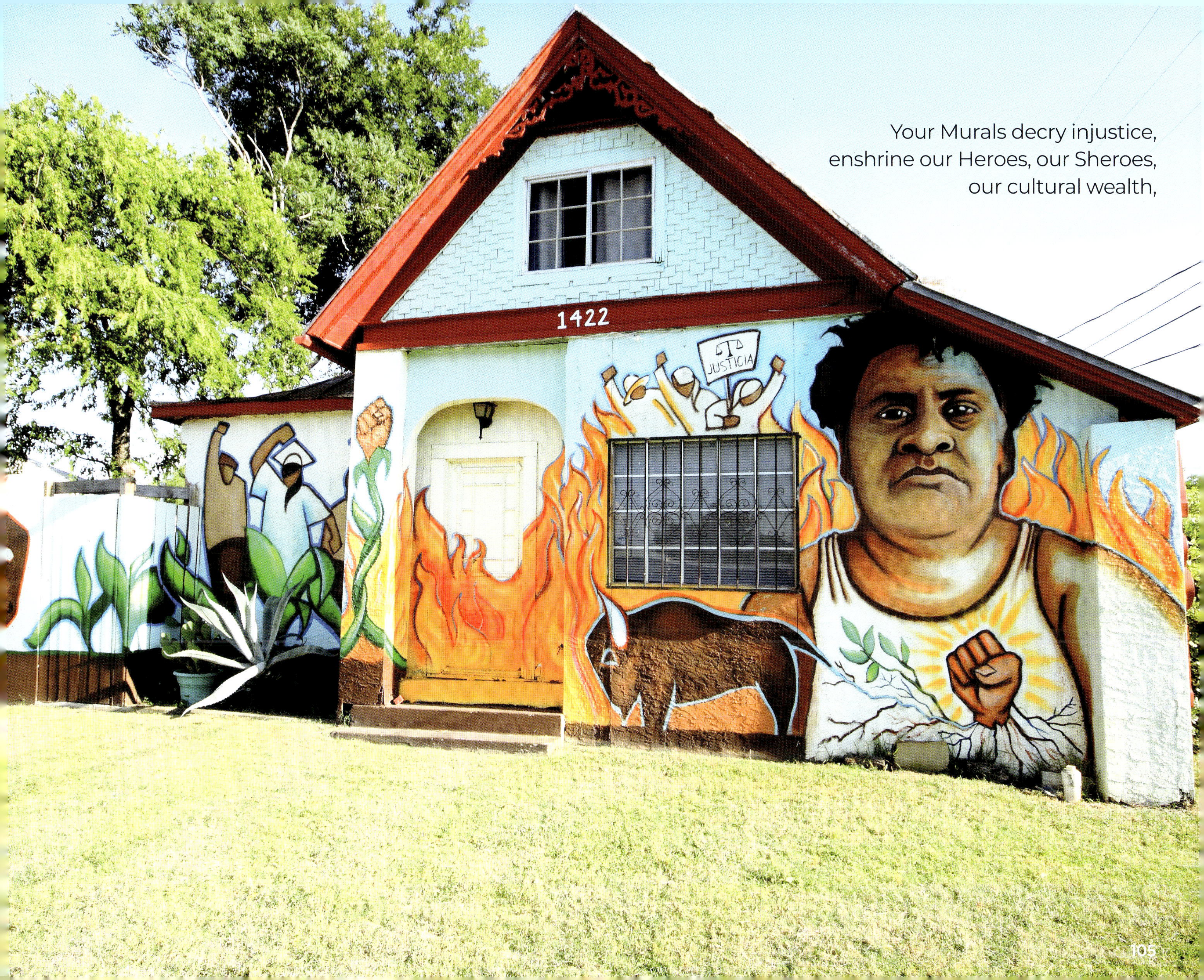

and maneuver our bilingual, bicultural identity.

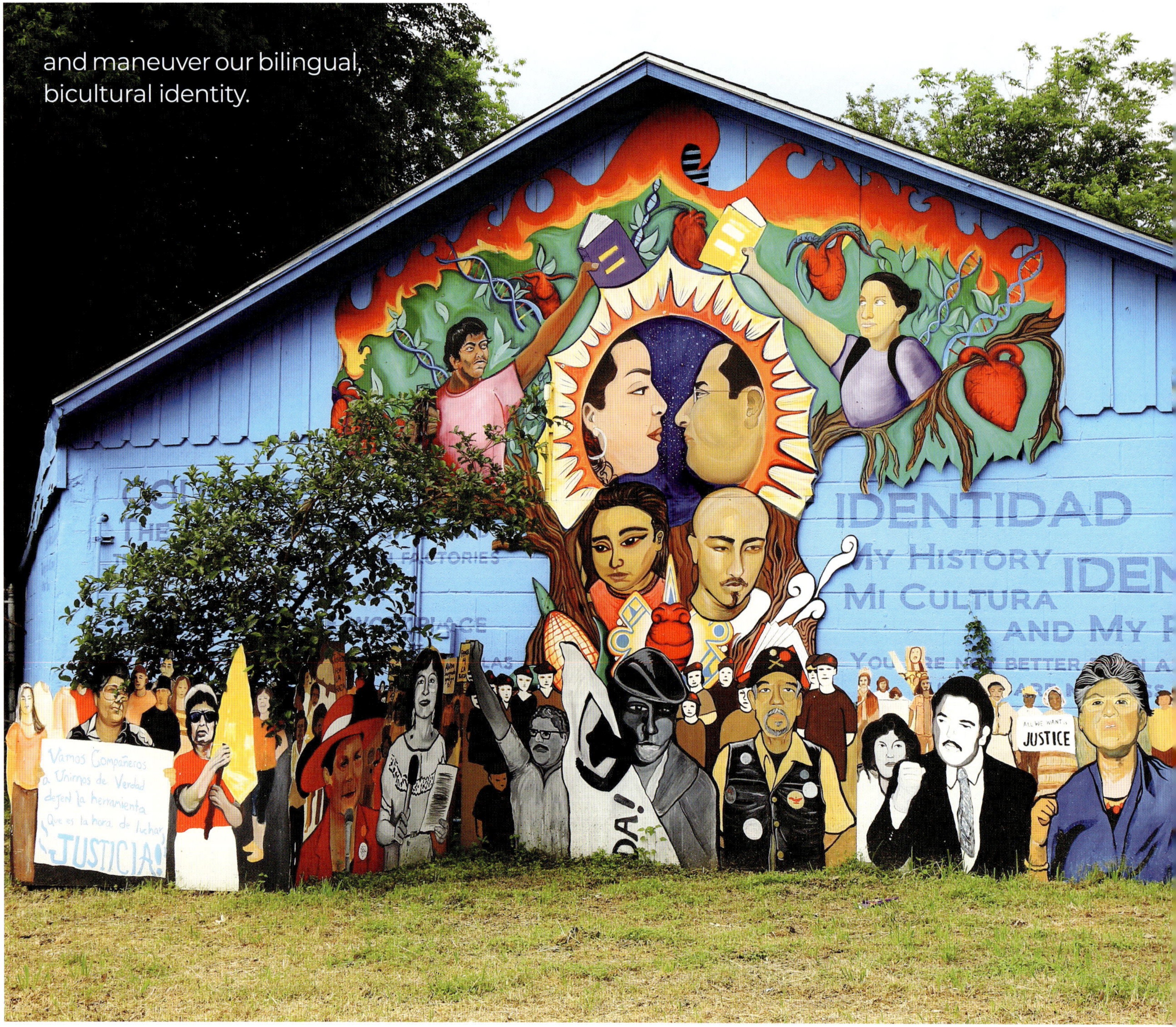

Taking It Back, 2012. Esmeralda Baltazar and Ernesto Cuevas. 710 New Laredo Highway.

OPPOSITE PAGE TOP *Entre Todas las Mujeres*, 2020. Adriana García and Ana Hernández. Segment of mural portraying Vanessa Guillén's sister, Lupe Guillén, saying to the press, "This is not a moment; it's a movement." The mural title translates to "amongst all women," referencing the biblical "Blessed art thou amongst all women." It speaks to the anger at the sexual harassment and murder of twenty-year-old soldier Vanessa Guillén, an action that sparked a MeToo movement protesting harassment and violence against women in the military. Chicho Boys' Fruit Market, 1631 S. Laredo Street.

BOTTOM *Entre Todas las Mujeres*, 2020. Adriana García and Ana Hernández. Segment of mural portraying Vanessa Guillén.

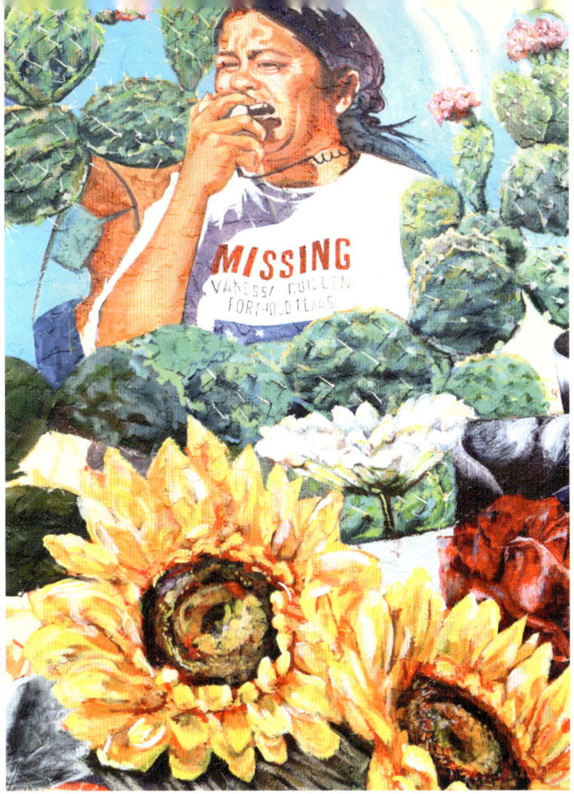

They protest the death of those taken needlessly,
and even the cactus thorns cry out our pain
till our raised fists are decorated with the war medals of stigmata.

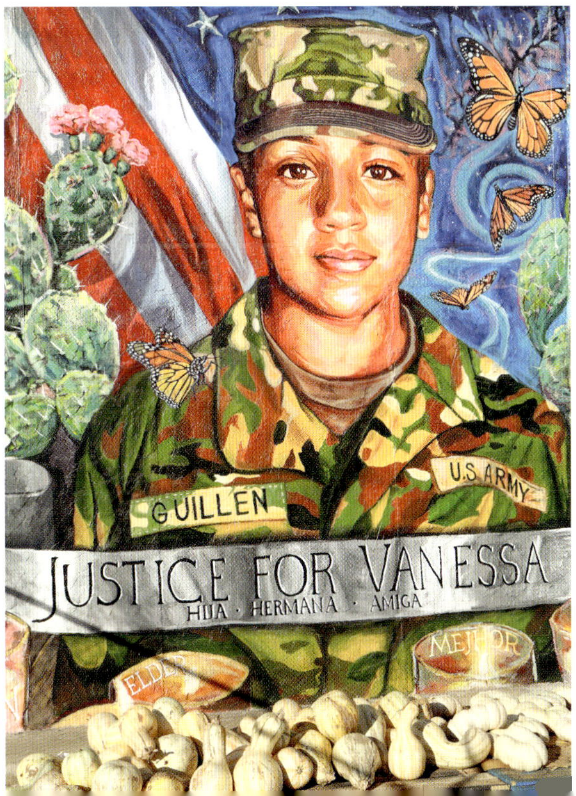

For neither hammer nor saw, fire nor earth
can erase me or dismember me.
I am whole. I am part of you.

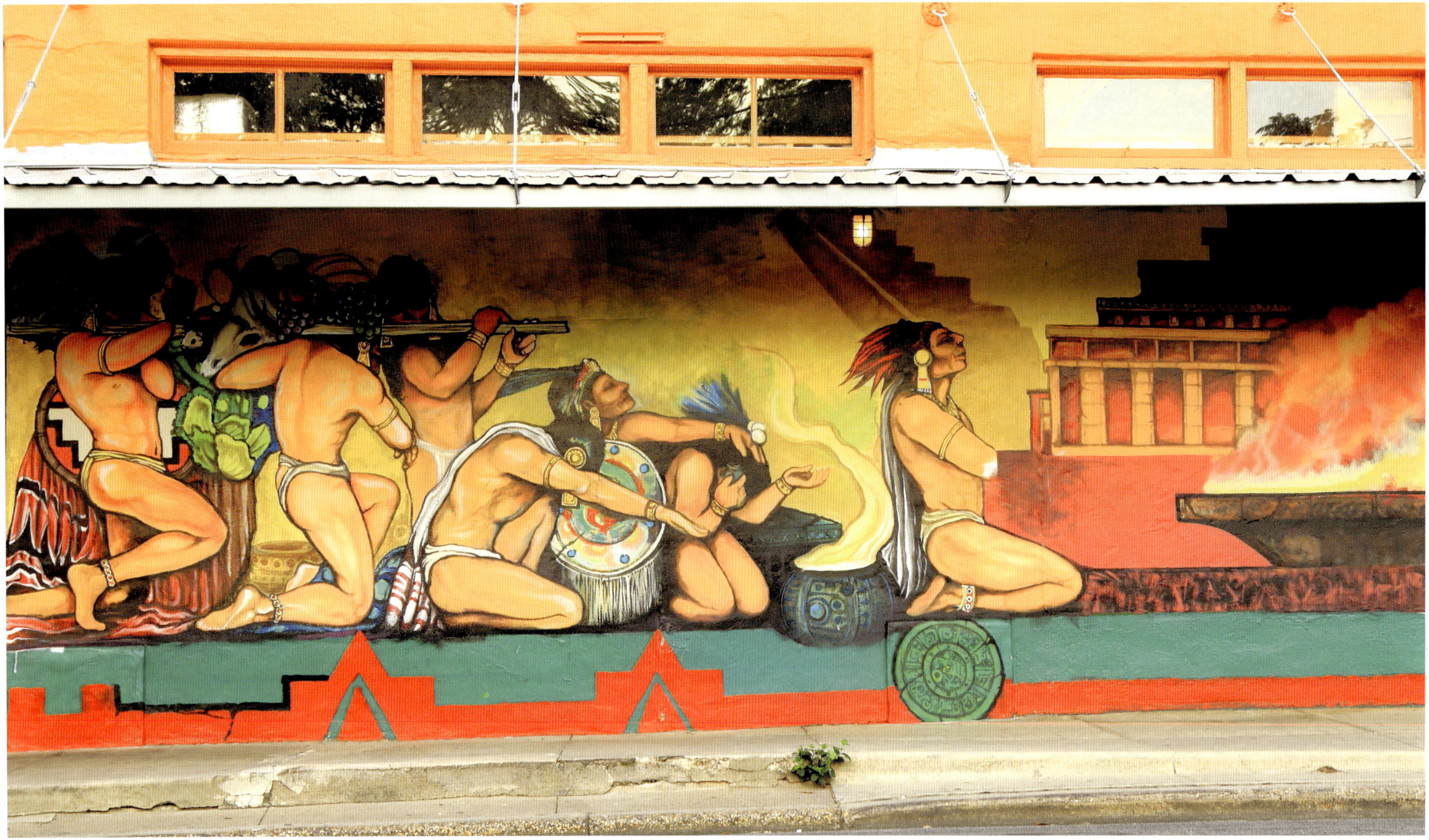

They speak our history, our dreams, our values.

Untitled, year unknown.
Ricardo M. Pérez.
Taco Haven Restaurant.
1032 S. Presa Street.

OPPOSITE PAGE
Tradición y Cultura,
2001. Alex Rubio. N.
Guadalupe Street.

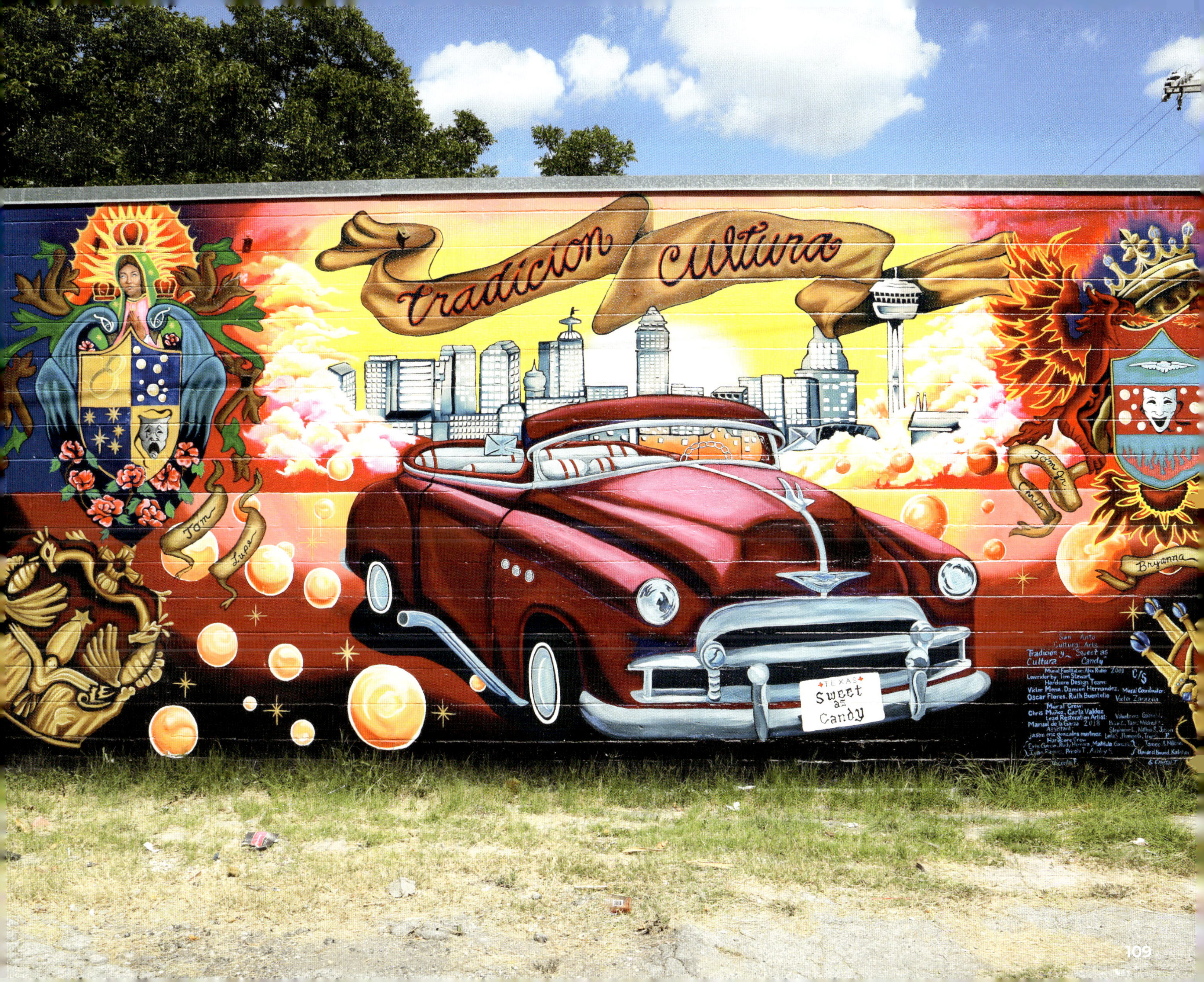
Tradicion
Cultura
Tom
Lupe
Tom Jr.
Bryanna
TEXAS
Sweet as Candy
San Anto Cultural Arts
Tradición y Cultura
"Sweet as Candy"
Mural Facilitator: Alex Rubio 2001
Lowrider by: Tom Stewart
Hardcore Design Team:
Victor Mena, Damien Hernandez, Oscar Flores, Ruth Buentello
Mural Coordinator: Victor Zarazúa
C/S
Mural Crew:
Chris Muñoz, Carla Valdez
Lead Restoration Artist:
Marisol de la Garza 2018
Assistant:
jason eric gonzales martinez
Hardcore Crew

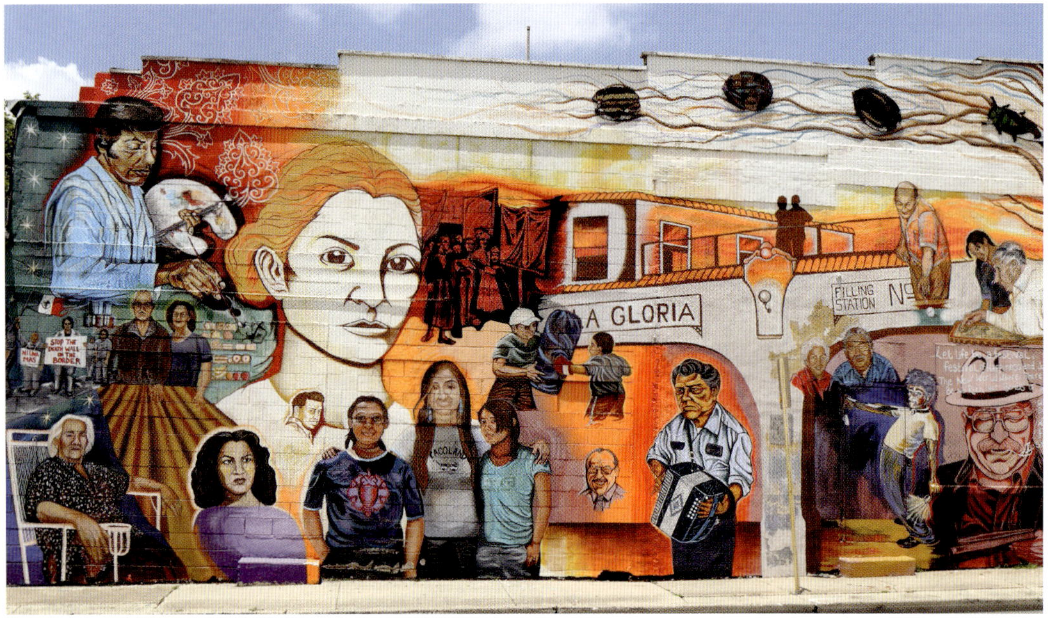

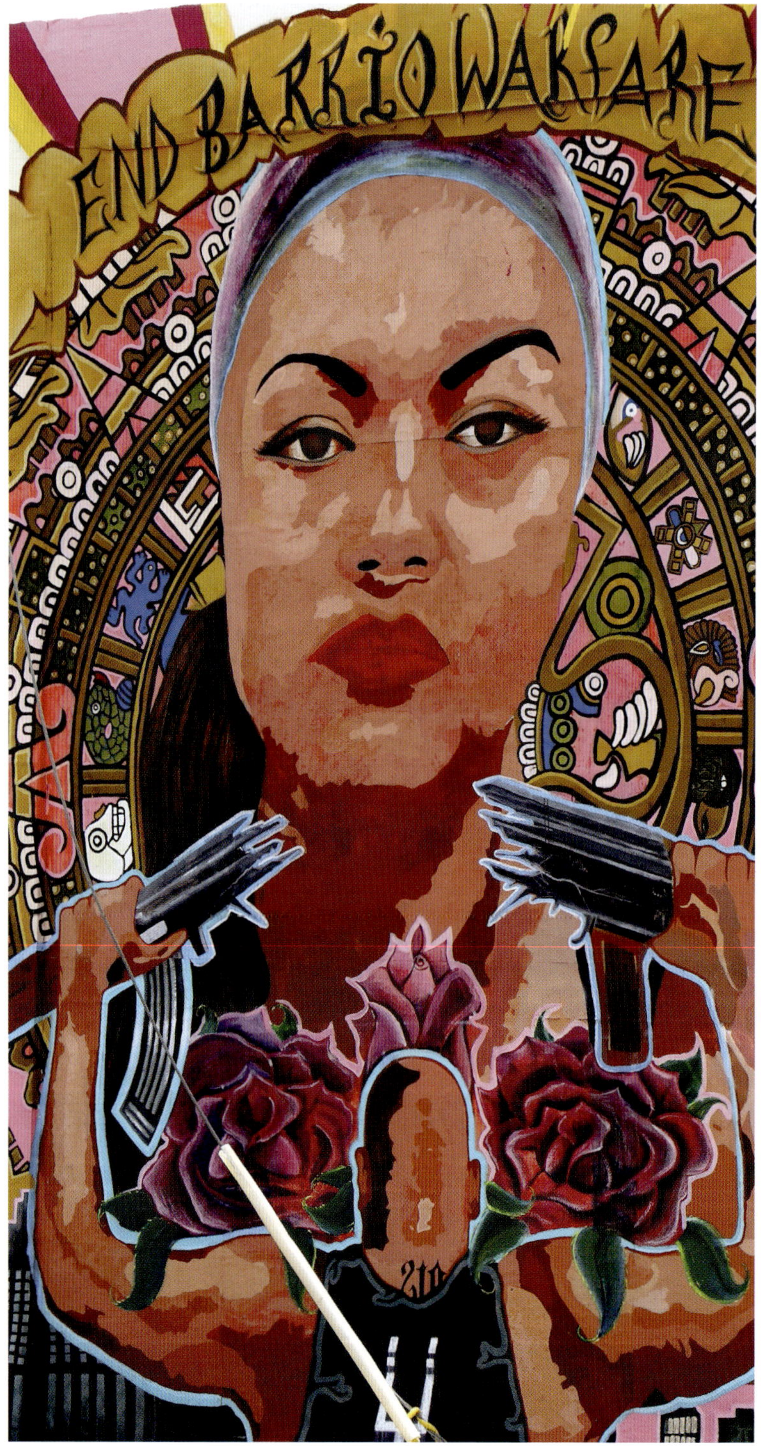

For decades, murals blossomed from the walls
of laundromats, *yerberías*, and project housing.[2]
They flowered hungrily from the hands of artists
like César Martínez, Mel Casas, and Rudy Treviño,
from groups like *Con Safos* and *Los Quemados*
in the '60s, '70s, and from students in the CCAO
from '78 to '93.[3] Terry Ybañez painted *Corazones
de la Comunidad*—with sheroes like Lydia Mendoza,
Emma Tenayuca & María Berriozabal, on a Kwik Wash
in 1992. More murals sprouted in '93, bloomed in the hands
of Manuel Castillo, Cruz Ortiz, Juan Miguel Ramos,
and the many students of San Anto Cultural Arts
who've now become masters and teachers—
like Adriana García, Alex Rubio, Vincent Valdez,

all rallying artists young and old
who long to join in,
creating more murals each year.
They proclaim an *Herencia* of Courage and *Verdad*.
They show us what it means
to be a leader.

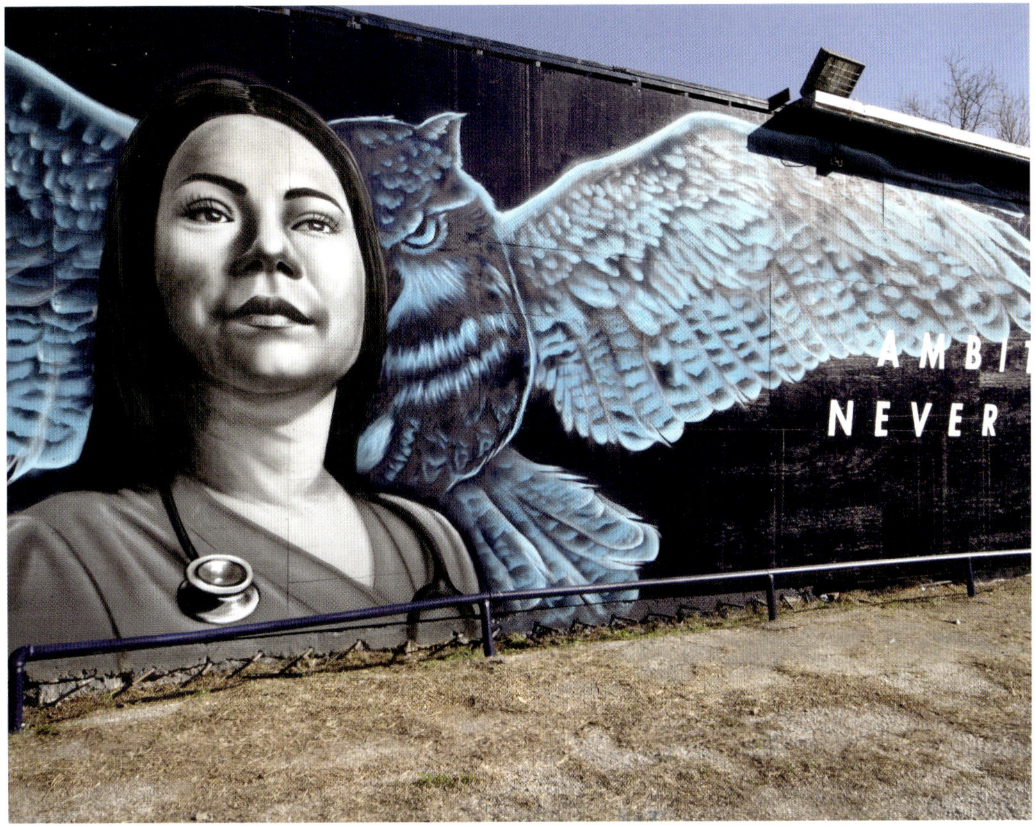

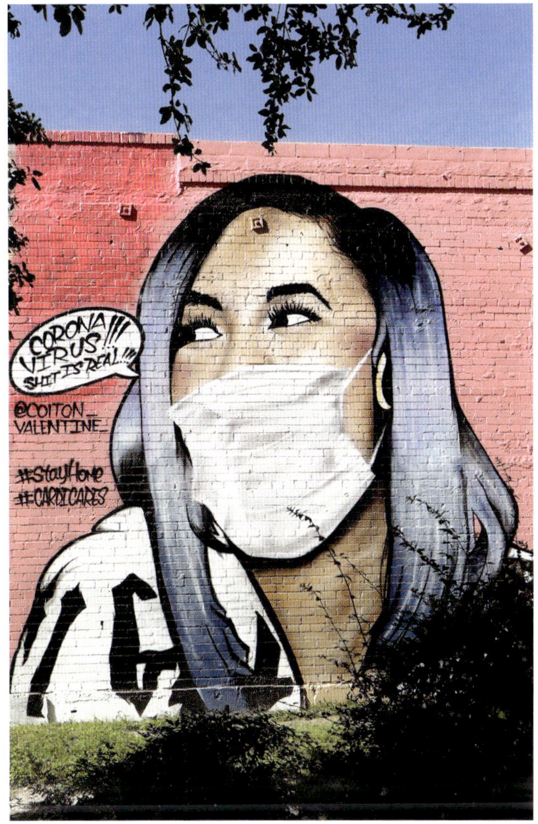

OPPOSITE PAGE
LEFT
Leaders in the Community, 2006. Valerie Aranda. 1204 Buena Vista Street.

RIGHT
End Barrio Warfare, 2010. John Montes. Brazos and S. Laredo Streets.

THIS PAGE
TOP LEFT
Ambition Never Rests, 2020. Los Otros. Zarzamora Street and Southcross Boulevard.

TOP RIGHT
Corona Virus!!!, 2020. Colton Valentine. San Pedro Avenue and W. Cypress Street.

BOTTOM
Enough Is Enough, 2020. Colton Valentine. San Pedro and West Cypress.

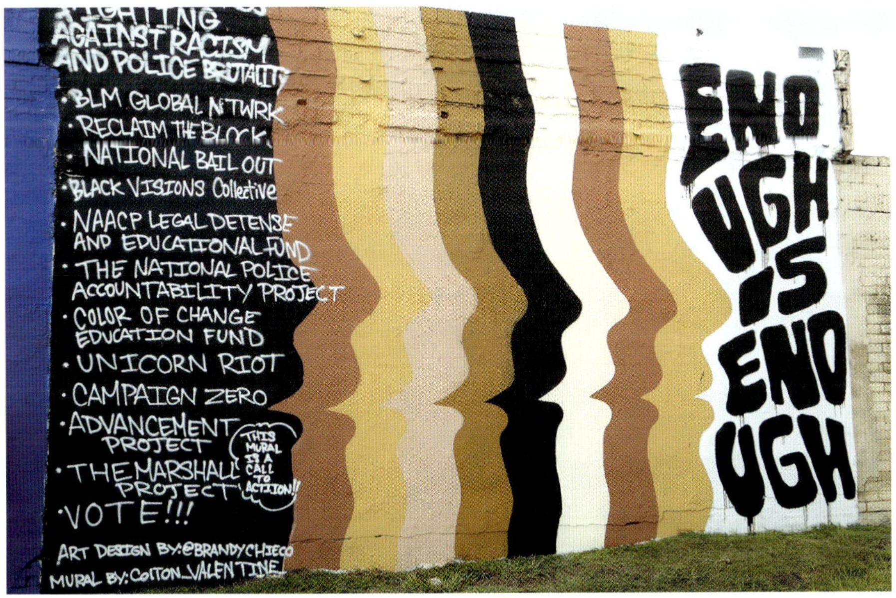

The Murals are our free billboards,
they give us the news in bold letters.
They are our shot of ánimo, our reminder
of what we stand for, what we want.
They are our invitation to the conversation.
They allow the public to be a part of what's going on,
what's happening.

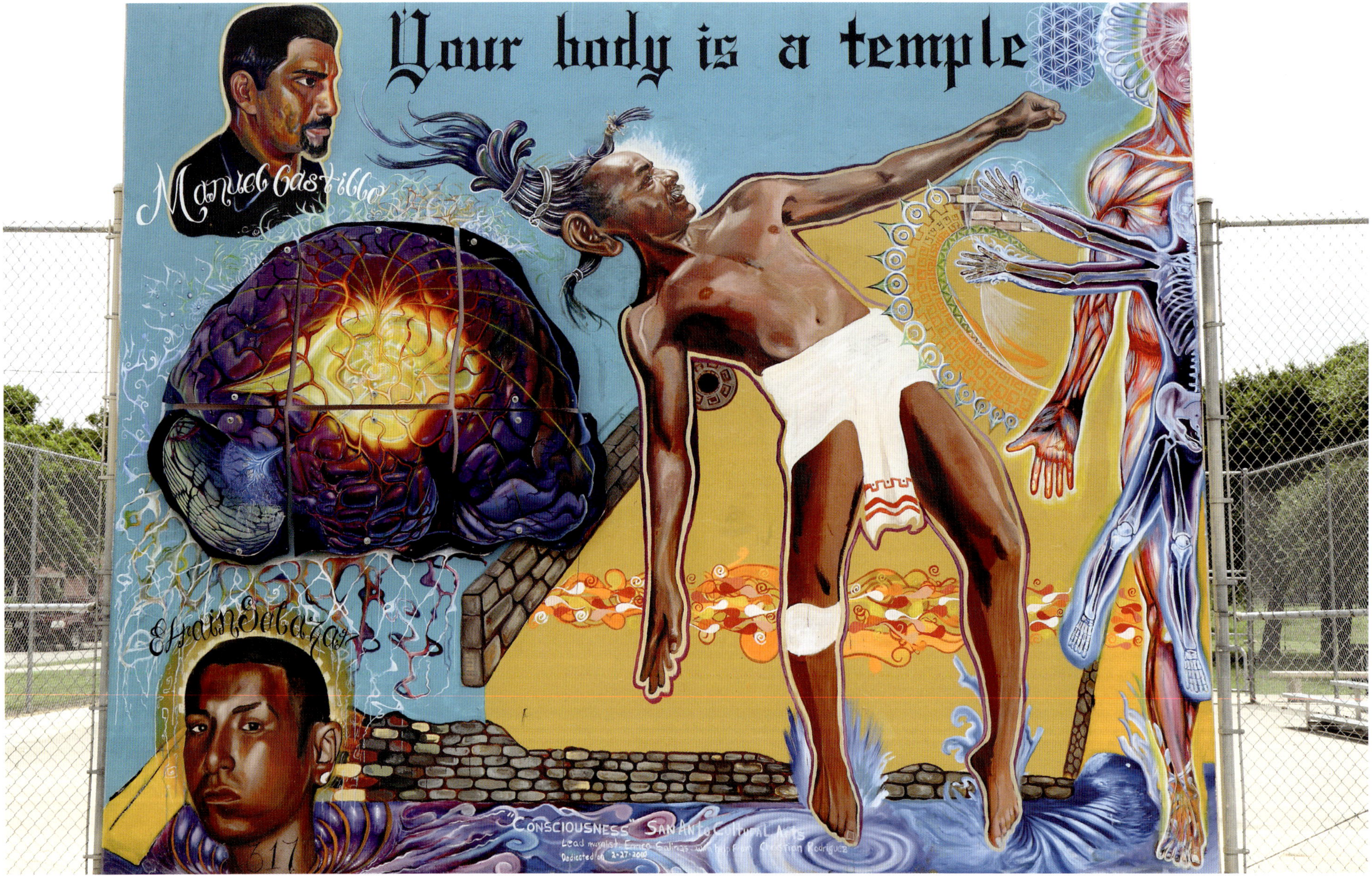

Consciousness, 2010 (first panel).
Enrico "Caso" Salinas and Christian
Rodríguez. 1400 S. Zarzamora.

OPPOSITE PAGE
Untitled, 2017. Alice Taylor.

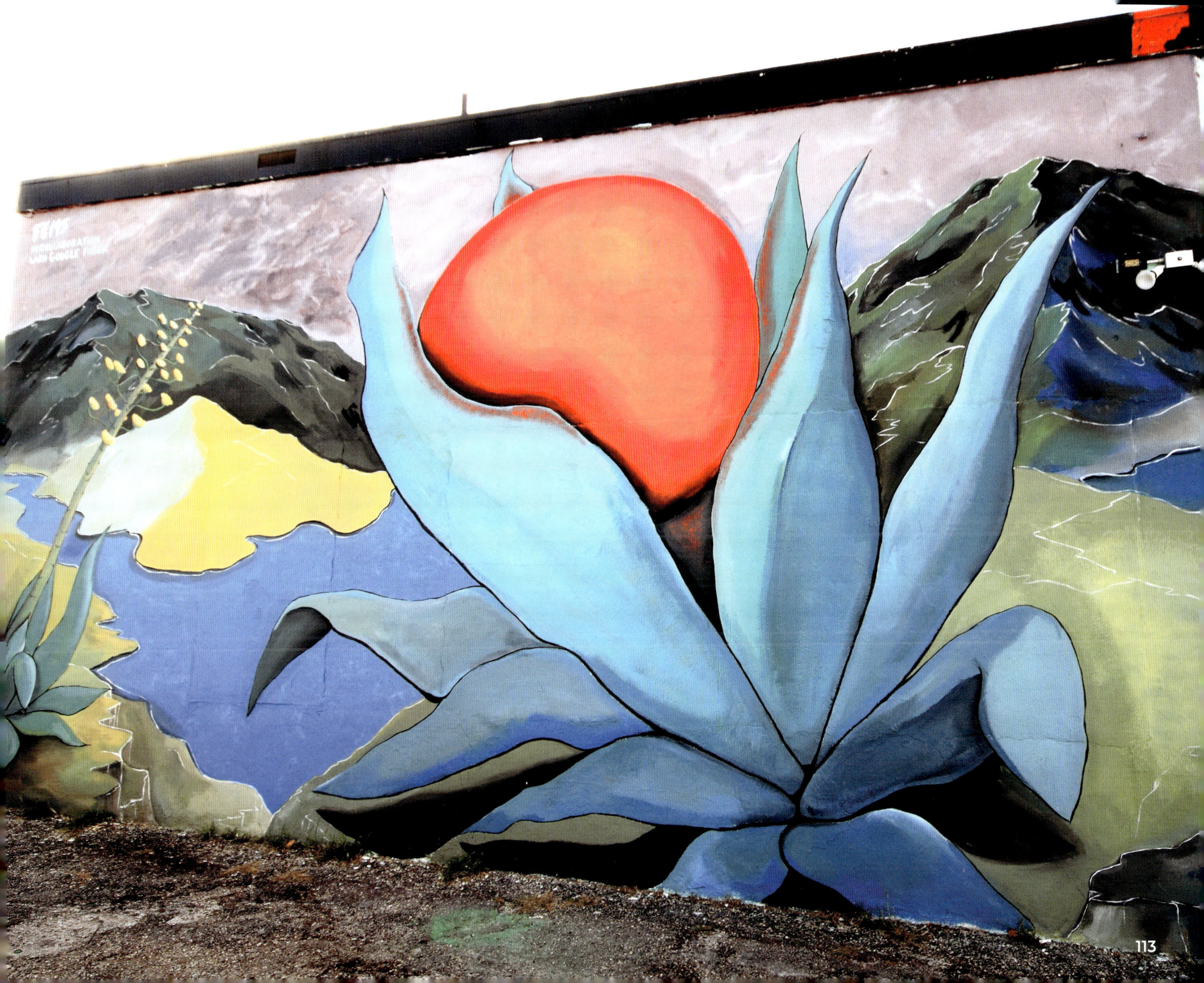

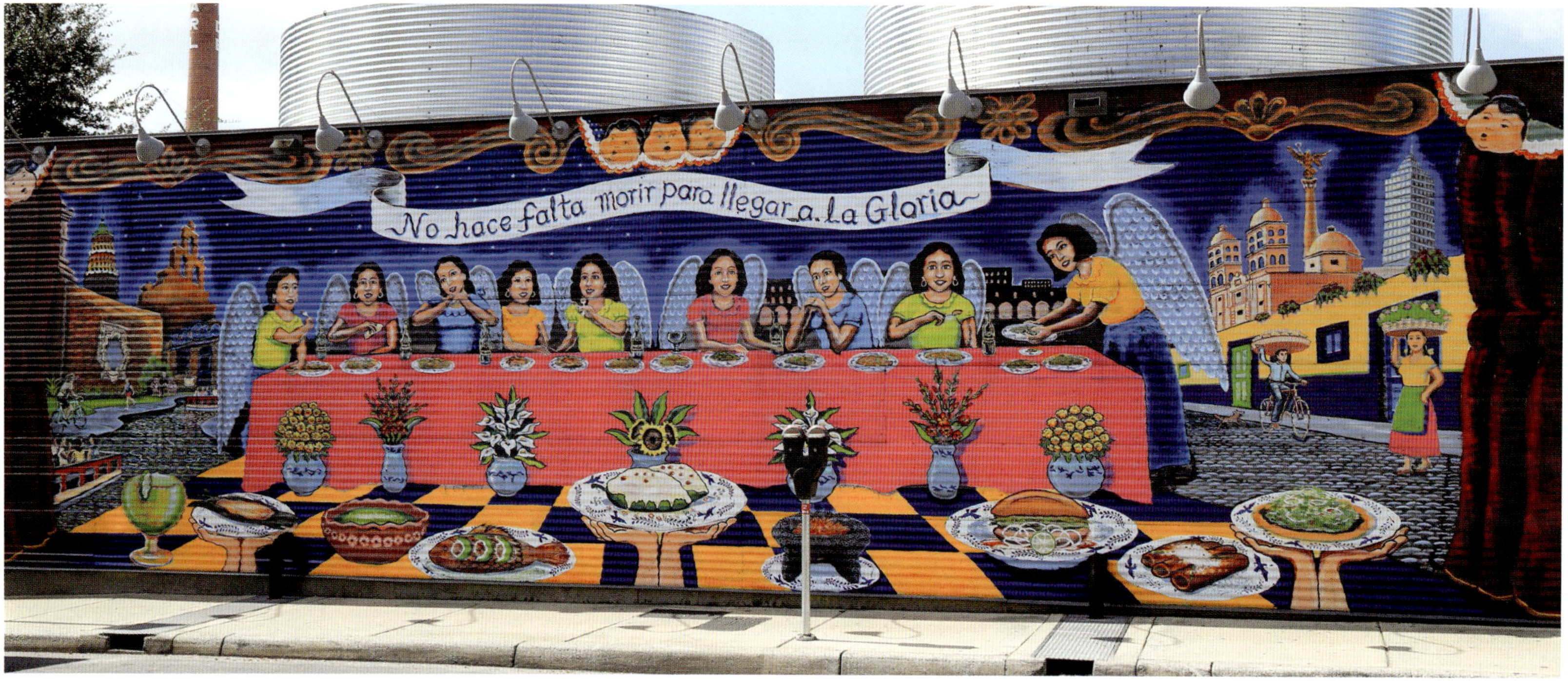

TOP
No hace falta morir para llegar a la Gloria, 2010. Claudio Aquillo. La Gloria Restaurant, at the Pearl. Translated: "You don't have to die to reach Paradise."

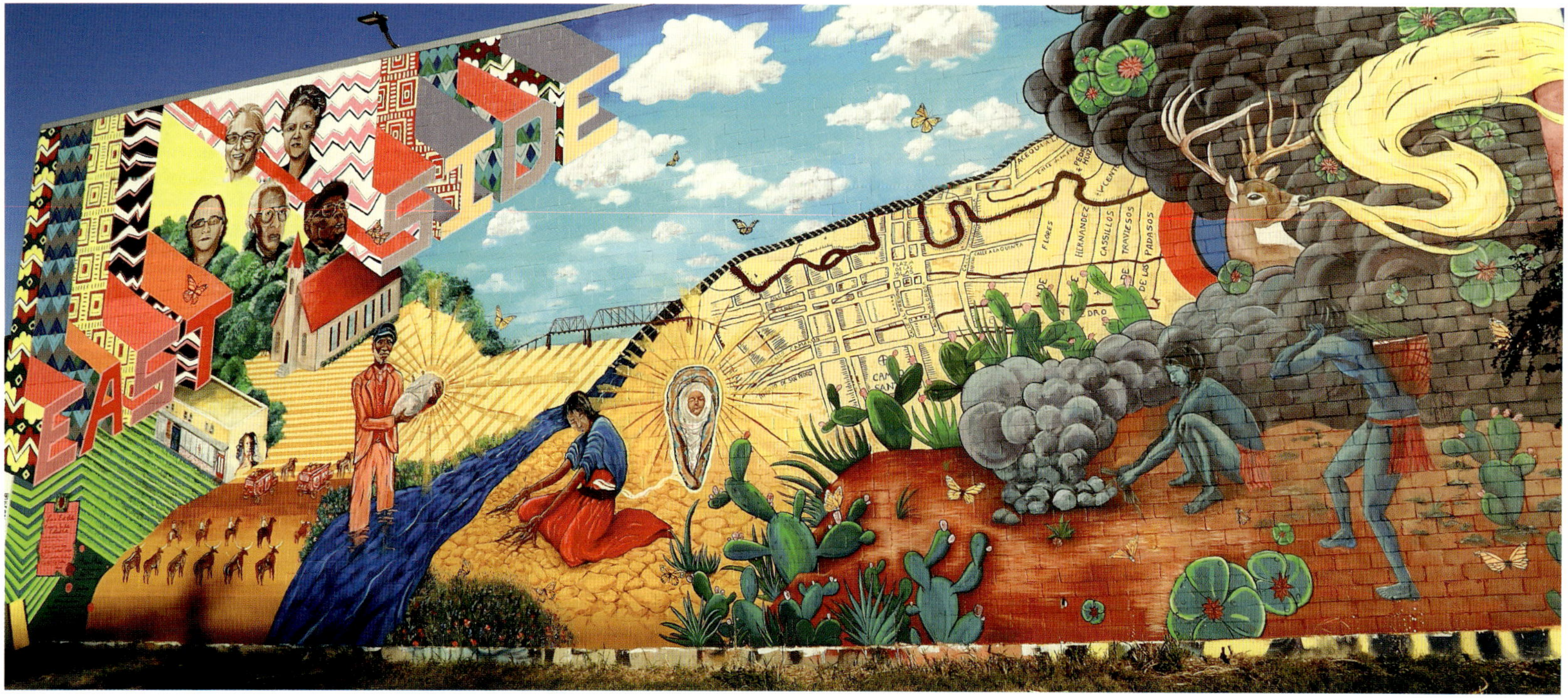

BOTTOM
Love Is East Side, 2019. Rudy "Cholotears" Herrera. Commerce Street.

OPPOSITE PAGE
Spirit of a Leader. David Blancas. 3514 Martin Luther King Drive.

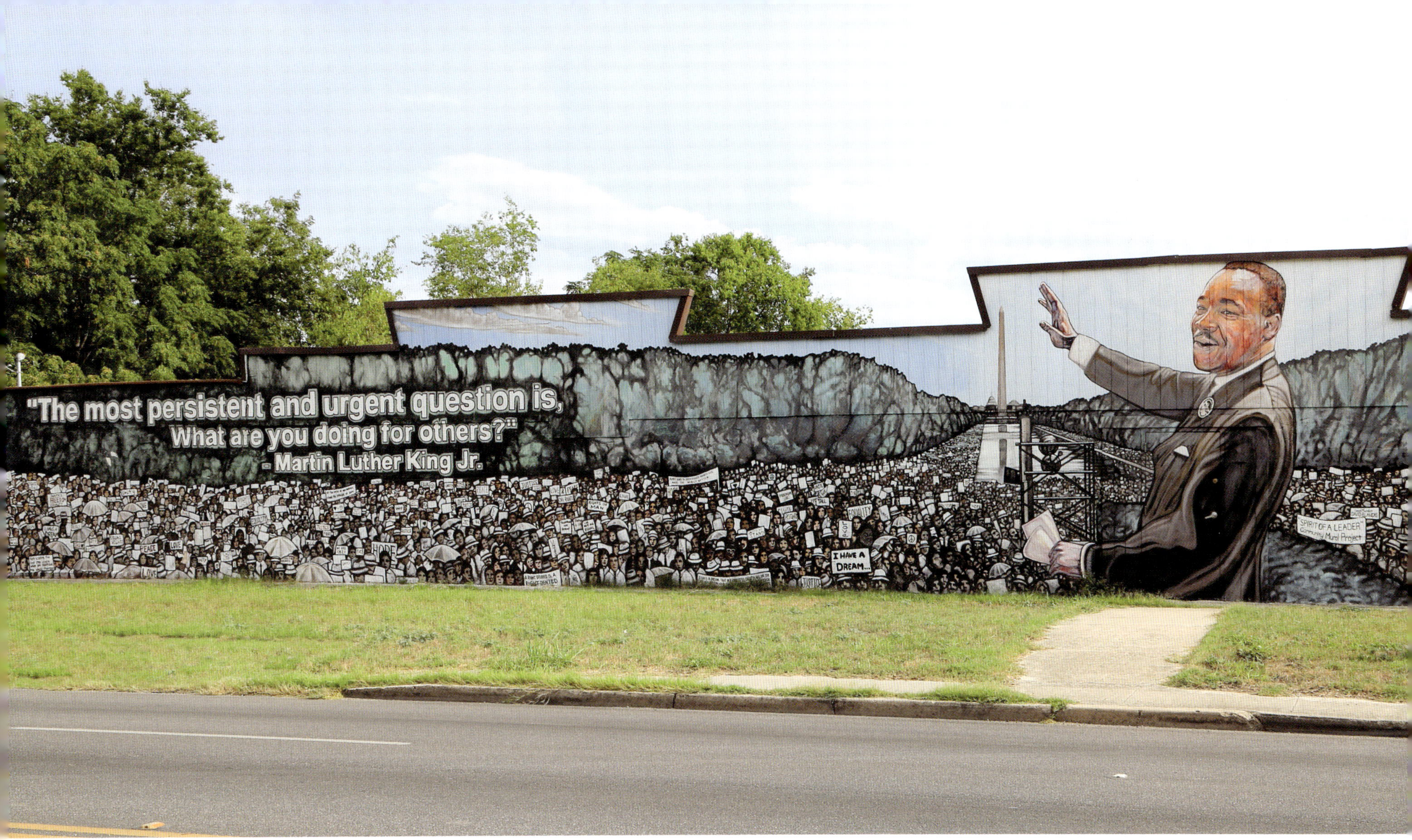

Like the entrancing notes of good music,
or the aroma from a family supper table,
it spreads everywhere.
And the murals go East Side, South Side, downtown,
blending, like everything good does.

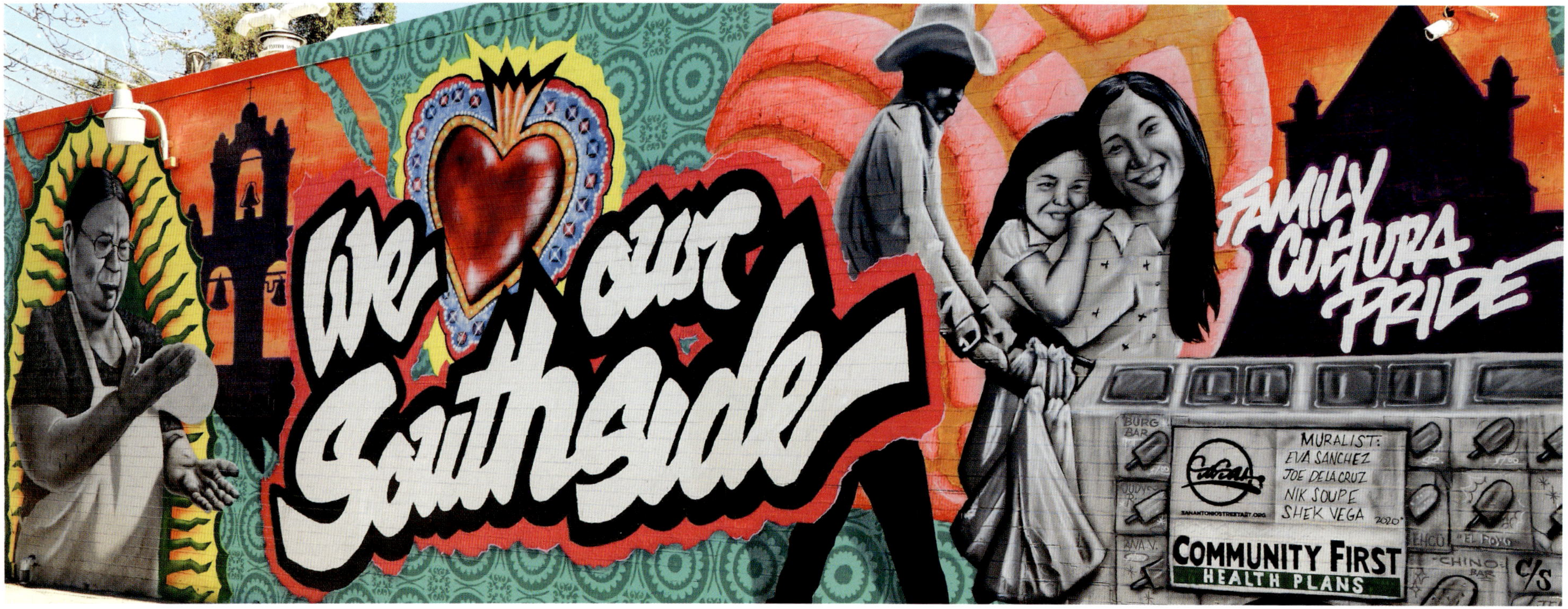

The gleeful mix of languages on our tongues
celebrates our bicultural borderland experience

and the toasty aroma of corn tortillas in the air
reminds us that for more than seven thousand years
here, warm hands have patted their task with love,
with a sense of history, with purpose.

Pedazos de arte,
pedacitos del corazón,
They remind us
how to survive.

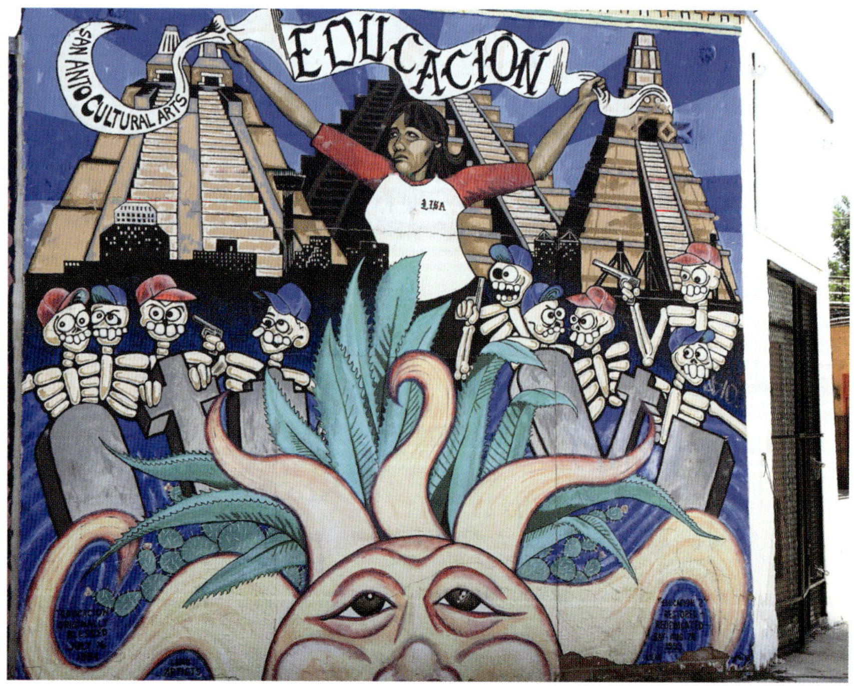

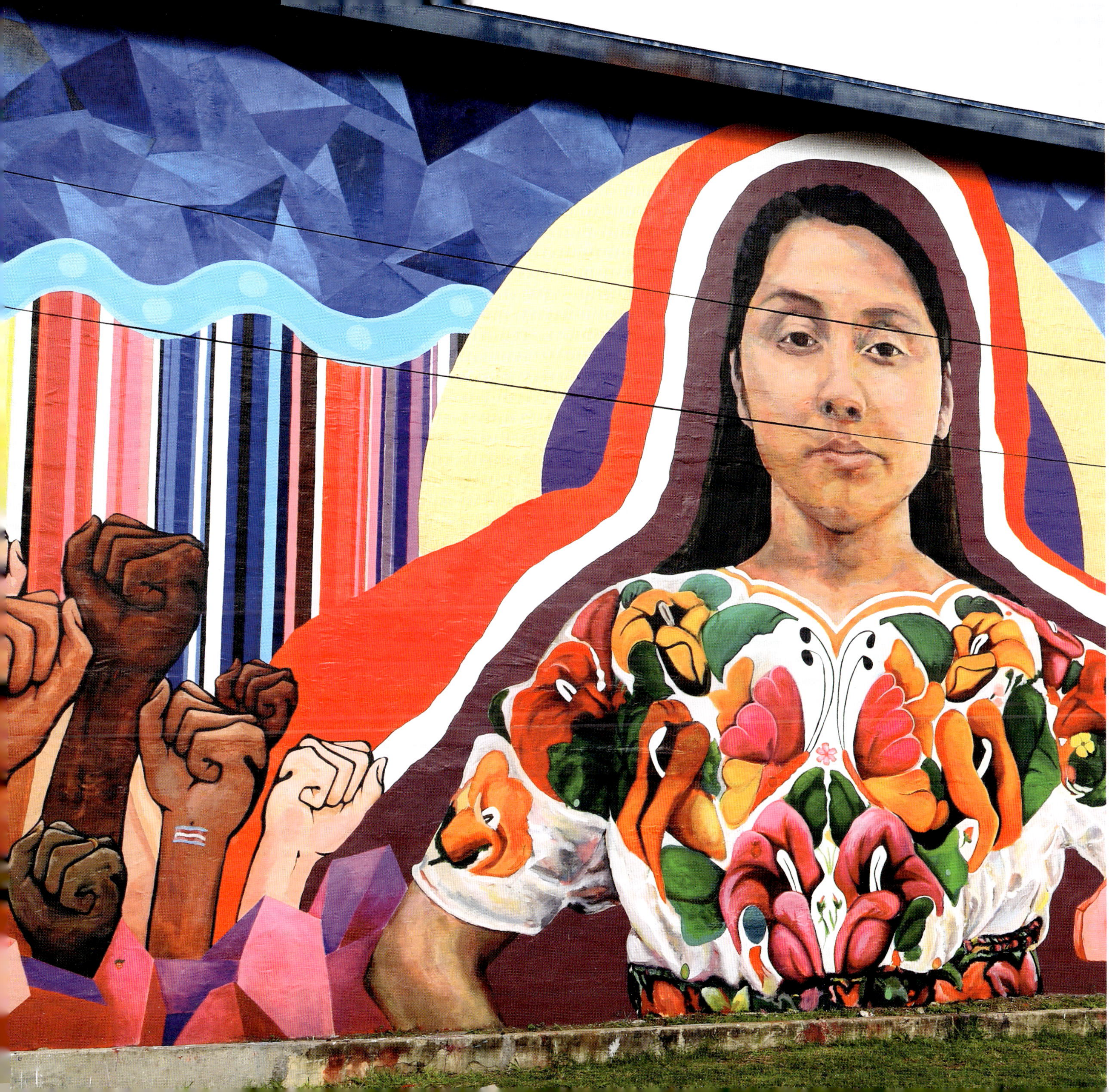

OPPOSITE PAGE
TOP
We Love Our South Side, 2020. Los Otros. S. Zarzamora St. and Southcross Boulevard.

BOTTOM
Educación, 1994. Cruz Ortiz and Juan Ramos. The celebration of bilingualism evident in our city's murals and events shouldn't be surprising (see *SA Is Amor*, page 36). For almost fifty years, state law forbade people to speak Spanish on school grounds, and many children dropped out to avoid harassment. But today's murals not only joyfully mix English with Spanish, they promote education and the power of biliteracy. 2121 Guadalupe Street.

THIS PAGE
Presente, 2018. Ana Hernández, Rhys Munro, and Rudy Herrera. 1700 block S. Laredo.

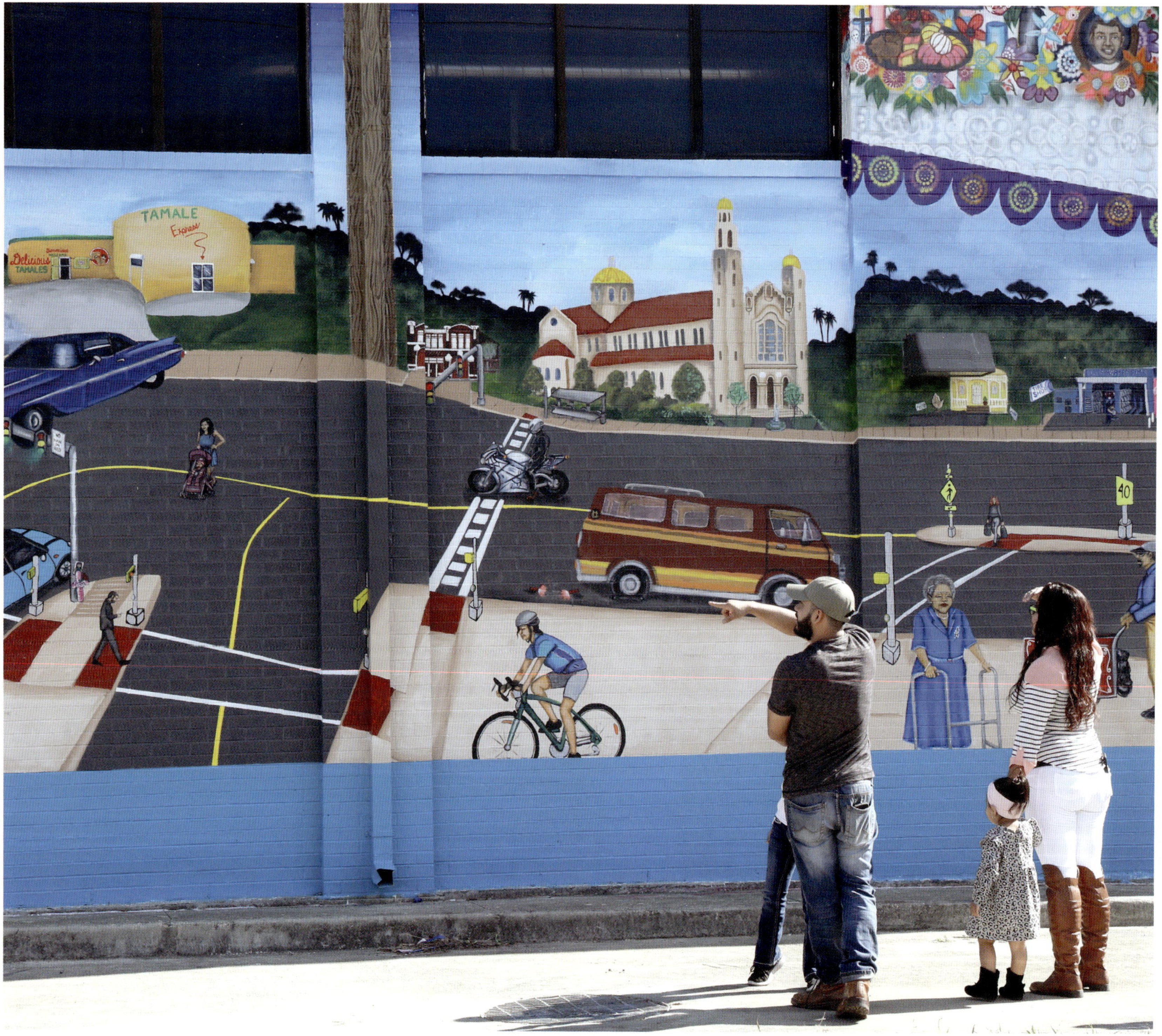

Life on Culebra Road, 2019. Crystal Tamez. Fire Station, 26 Culebra Road.

OPPOSITE PAGE *Aguas Onduladas* (Rippling Waters), 2018. RDG Dahlquist Art Studio. Three stainless-steel waves along a serpentine sidewalk to Elmendorf Park are engraved with excerpts from two poems by Carmen Tafolla. Elmendorf Lake Park at Commerce Street.

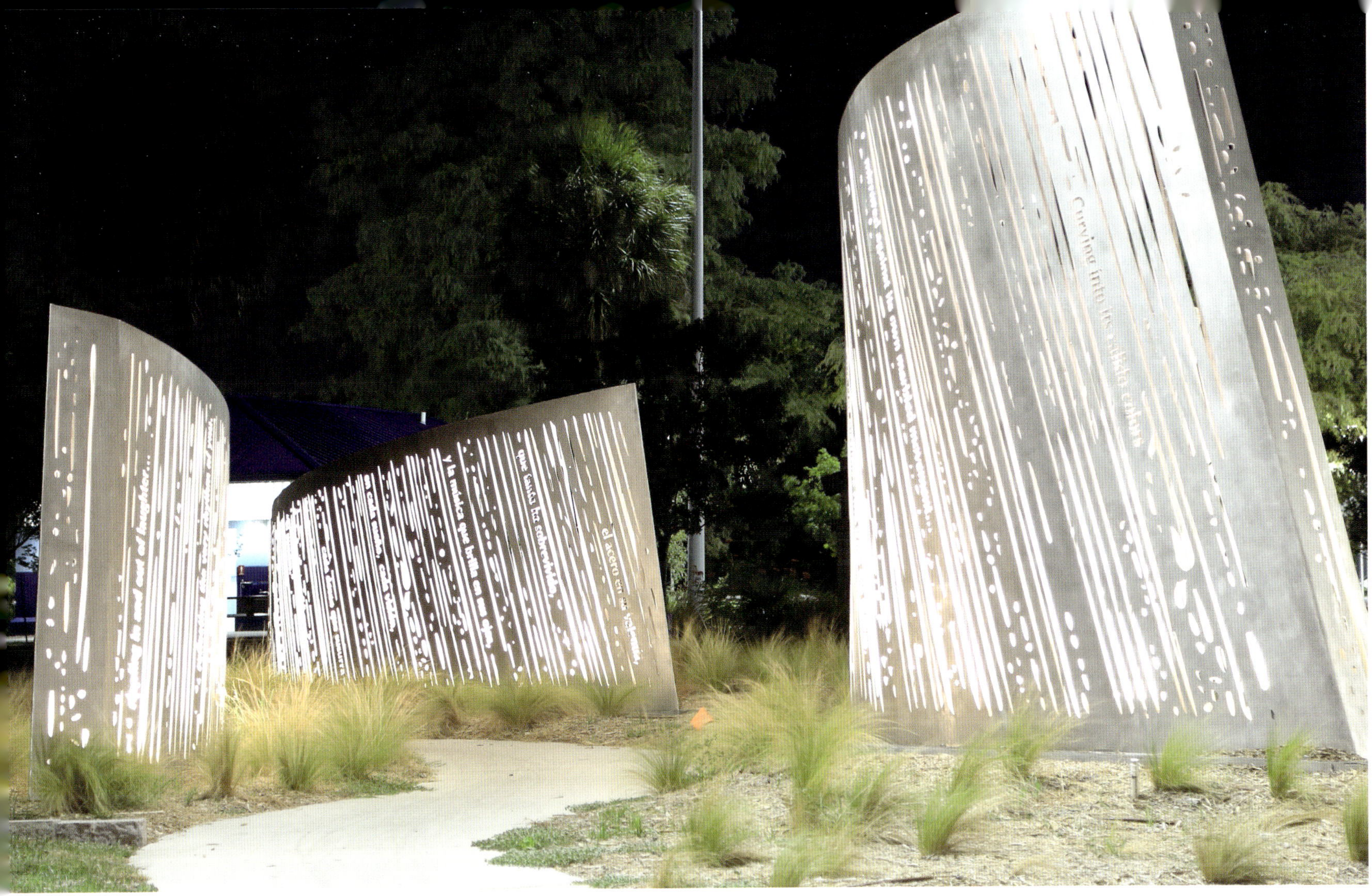

Translation:
Let not my people
forget the gold hidden
in their cinnamon skin

that has withstood
so much for so long,

the steel in their
courage that has
survived so many
struggles,

and the music
shining from their
eyes in each dream,
each vision,

each desire that
whispers to them,
Yes, you can.

Excerpt from the poem "Que no se le olvide a mi pueblo," inscribed on the sculpture *Aguas Onduladas*.

Que no se le olvide a mi pueblo
el oro en su piel canela,
que tanto ha aguantado,
el acero en su valentía,
que tanta lucha ha sobrevivido,
y la música que brilla en sus ojos,
en cada sueño, cada visión,
cada deseo que susurra,
Sí puedes.

NOTES

1. Excerpted from the poem "Fragile Flames" from *This River Here* by Carmen Tafolla (San Antonio, TX: Wings Press, 2014).

2. While murals were popularized during the Mexican Revolution, a renewed wave of murals appeared on the West Side of San Antonio with the Chicano movement of the '60s and '70s, gaining momentum with organized groups of funded artists in the '80s and '90s and significant city funding starting in 2011.

3. CCAO: Founded in 1979 by Anastacio Torres, Juan Hernández, and others, and active in creating community murals on the West Side and more until 1993, this nonprofit involved more than 1,800 high school and middle school students in the many murals they created. They painted more than 125 murals at Cassiano Homes, and more in other areas, including schools, senior centers, parks, and housing developments.

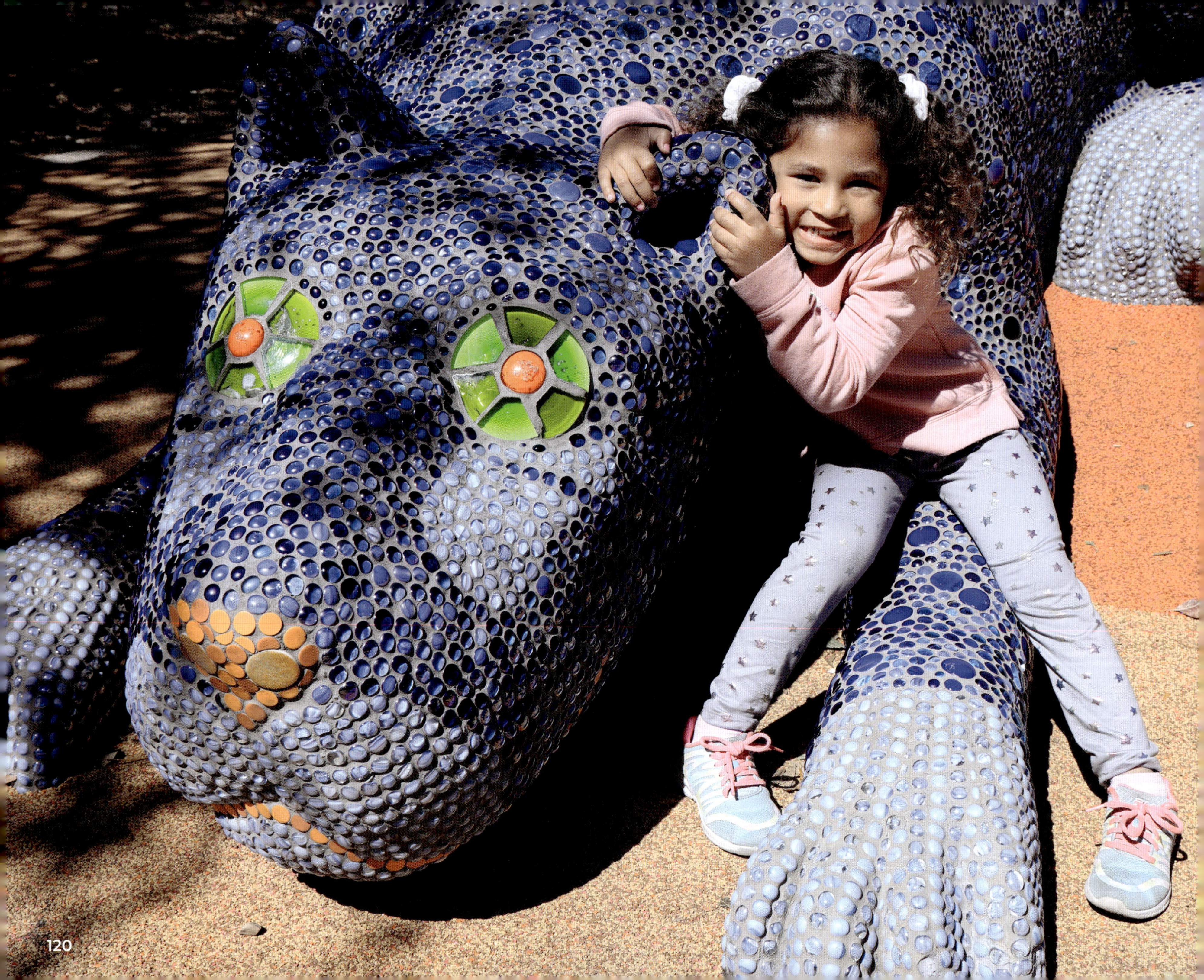

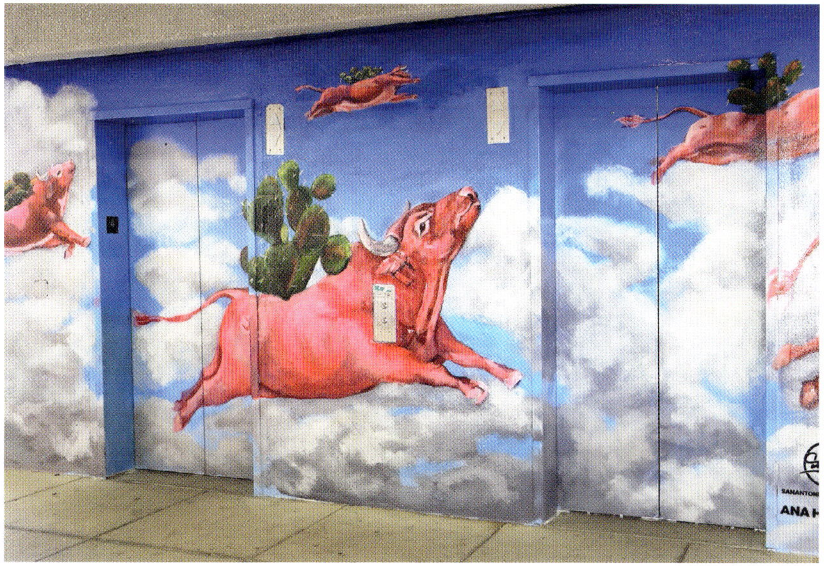

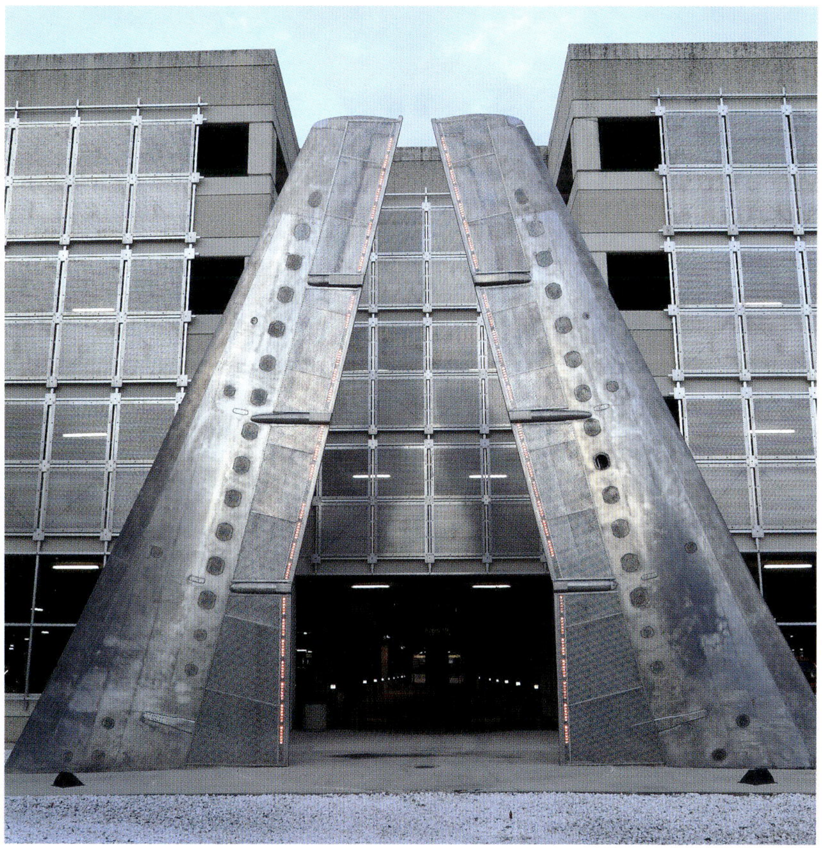

V. ROOTS THAT SPREAD OUTWARD

PARKS, HIGHWAYS, ELEVATORS & MORE

We fill our lives with art in every available space
and every available moment
from the elevator doors in an airport parking garage
that carry our dreams of pan dulce or flying bulls
to the public planters painted as vegetable cans
that take us back to Gramma's kitchen.

OPPOSITE PAGE
PanterAzul, 2015. Oscar Alvarado. Mosaic tile and cement. A central part of the city's origin story, the blue panther symbolizes the power of the water that gave birth to the Yanaguana River (now known as the San Antonio River) and provided life to the peoples living here. Hemisfair Park, Yanaguana Garden.

THIS PAGE
TOP
Untitled, 2019. Ana Hernández. San Antonio International Airport parking-garage elevator.

BOTTOM
Day Star Archway, 1999. Bill Fitzgibbons. San Antonio International Airport.

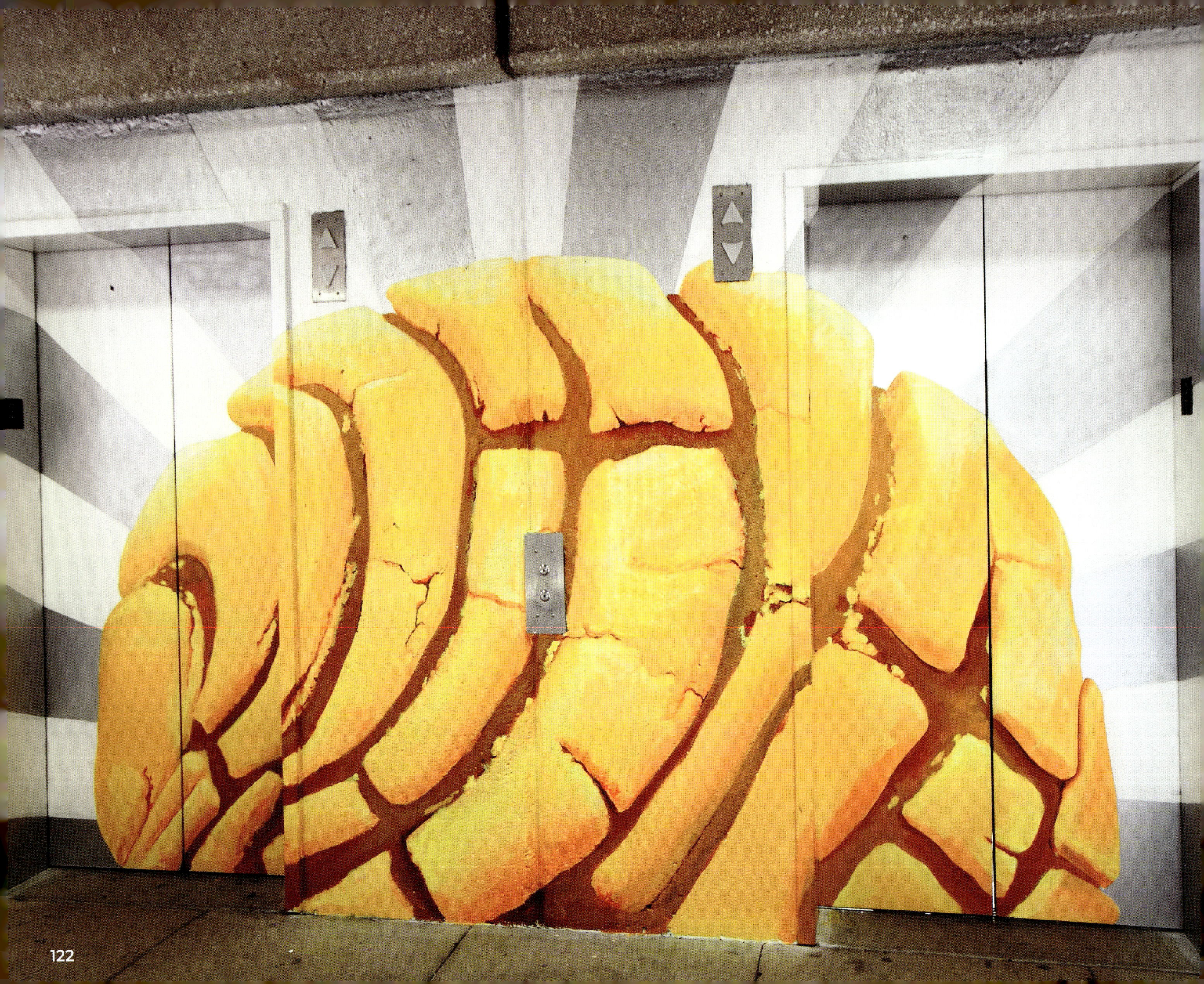

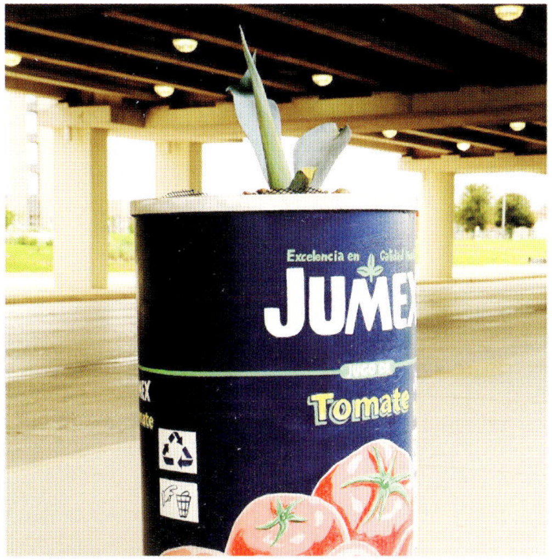

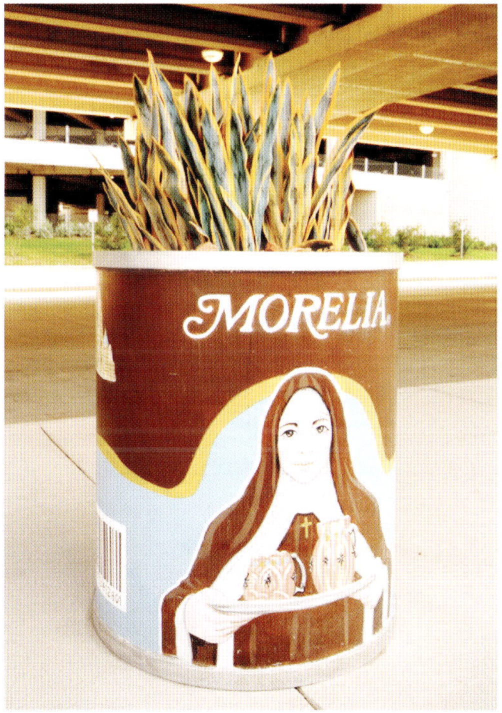

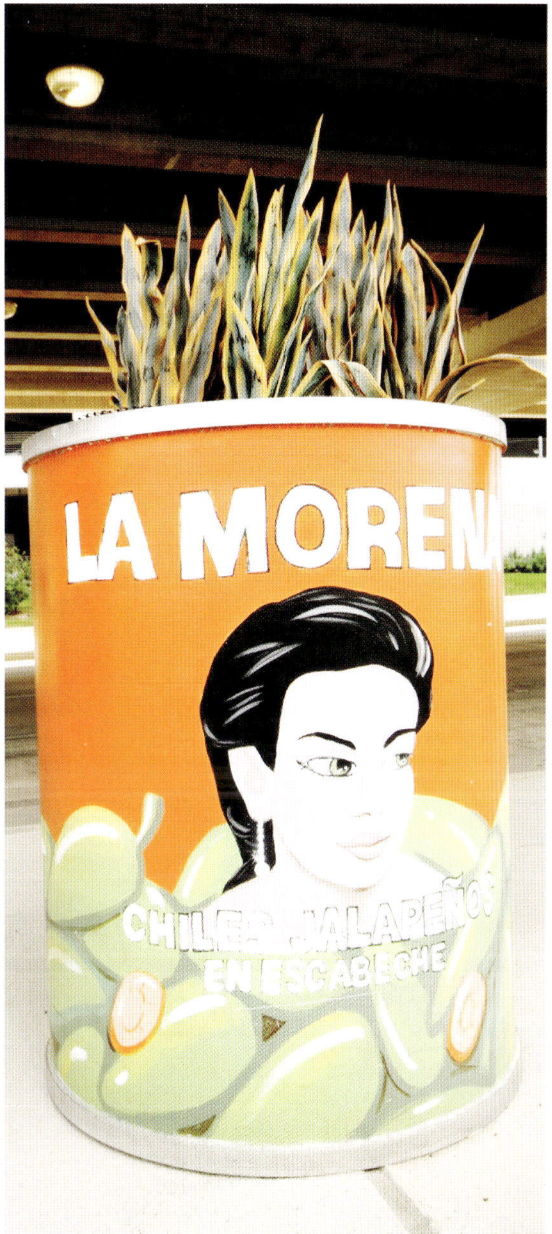

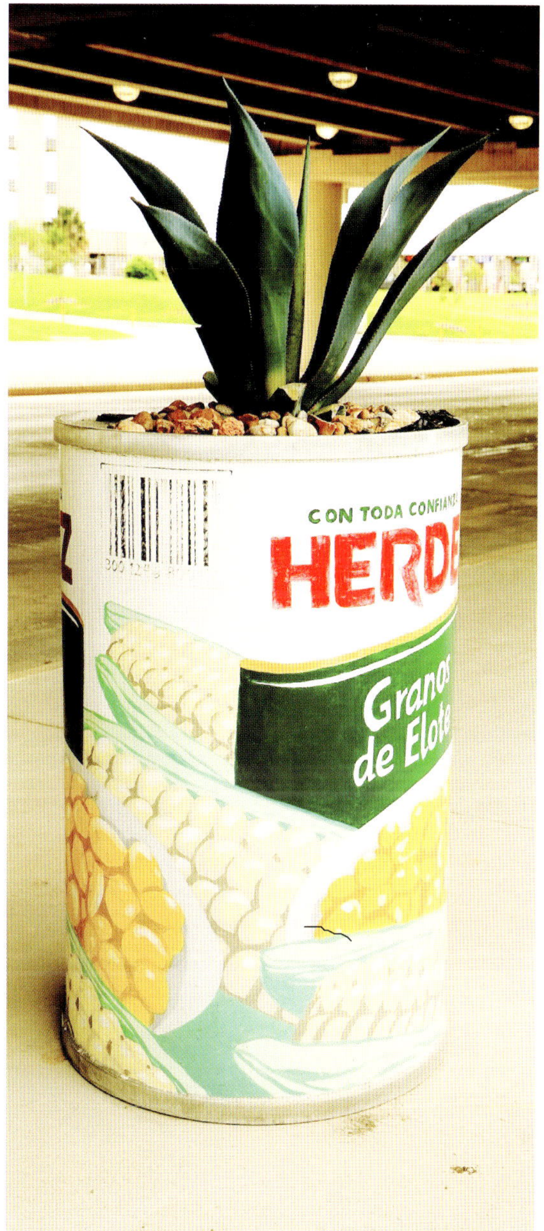

OPPOSITE PAGE
Pan Dulce, 2019,
Eva Sánchez.
San Antonio
International Airport
parking-
garage elevator.

THIS PAGE
A Call for All Seasons,
2005. Alejandro Díaz.
Planters at
San Antonio International
Airport take the shape
of traditional barrio food
cans.

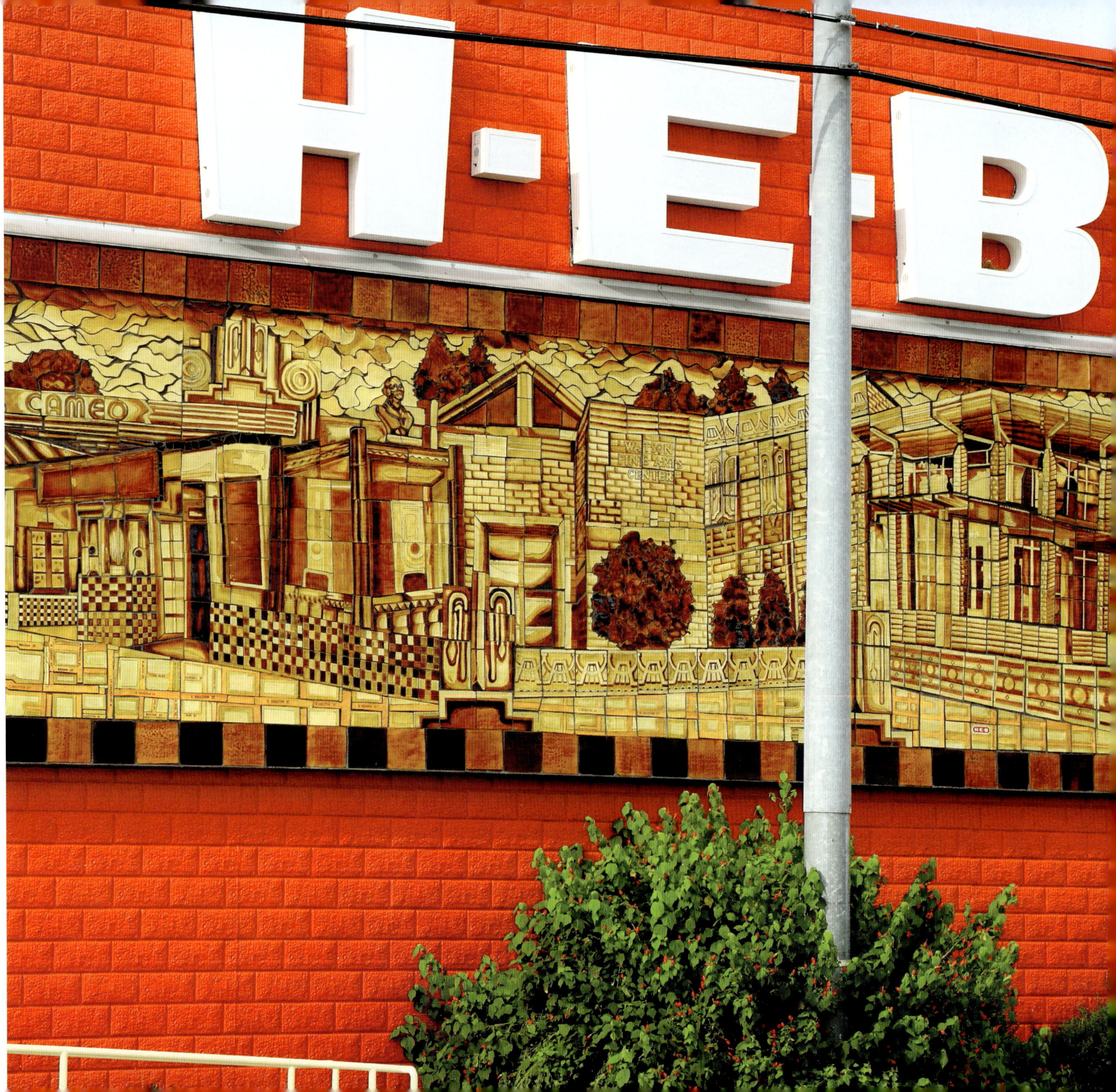

Neighborhood Landmarks, 2012. Alex Rubio and MOSAIC students. Honoring the legacy of the Cameo Theater and other neighborhood landmarks, including the Carver Cultural Center, Watson Fine Arts Center, Carver Academy, and the Ella Austin Community Center, the handmade tile work is mounted on the wall of the HEB grocery store. Tiles were created on-site at the HEB grocery store, and shoppers were invited to help cut them. 415 New Braunfels Street.

OPPOSITE PAGE
TOP LEFT
Tool Yard, 2003. Riley Robinson. Northeast Service Center, 10303 Tool Yard.

BOTTOM LEFT
PLAYhouse, 2015. Karen Mahaffy. A salt-box-style structure designed to evoke the tiny houses destroyed to clear the site for Hemisfair Park. Yanaguana Garden.

RIGHT
Reflect, 2018. Stuart Allen. Mosaic Bench, Oscar Alvarado. Hemisfair Park, Yanaguana Garden.

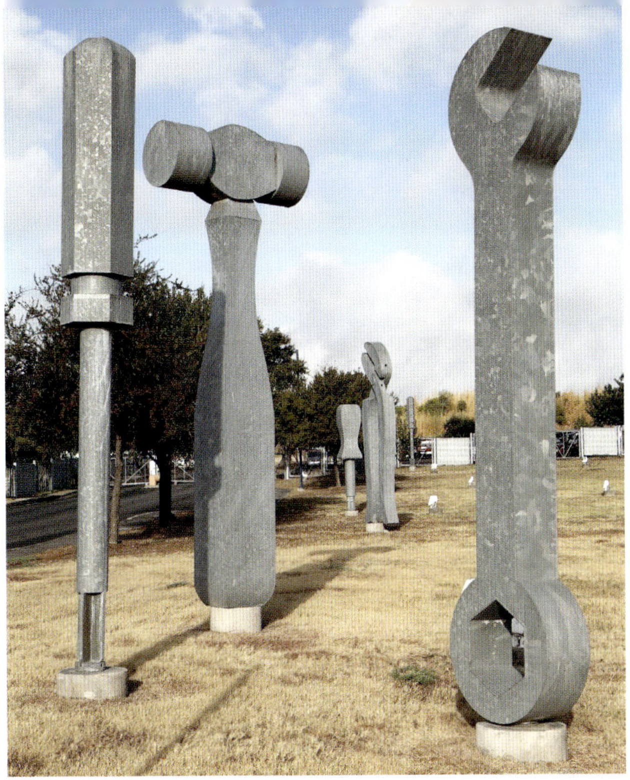

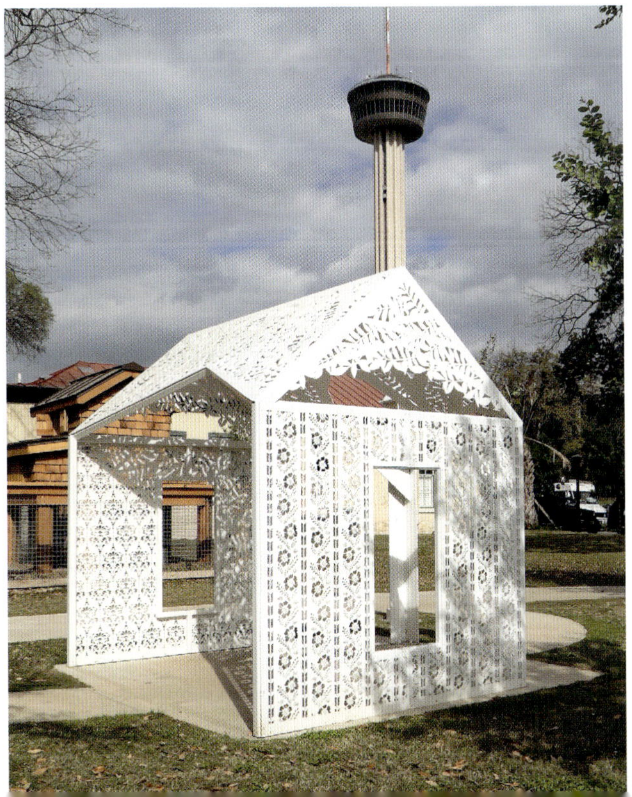

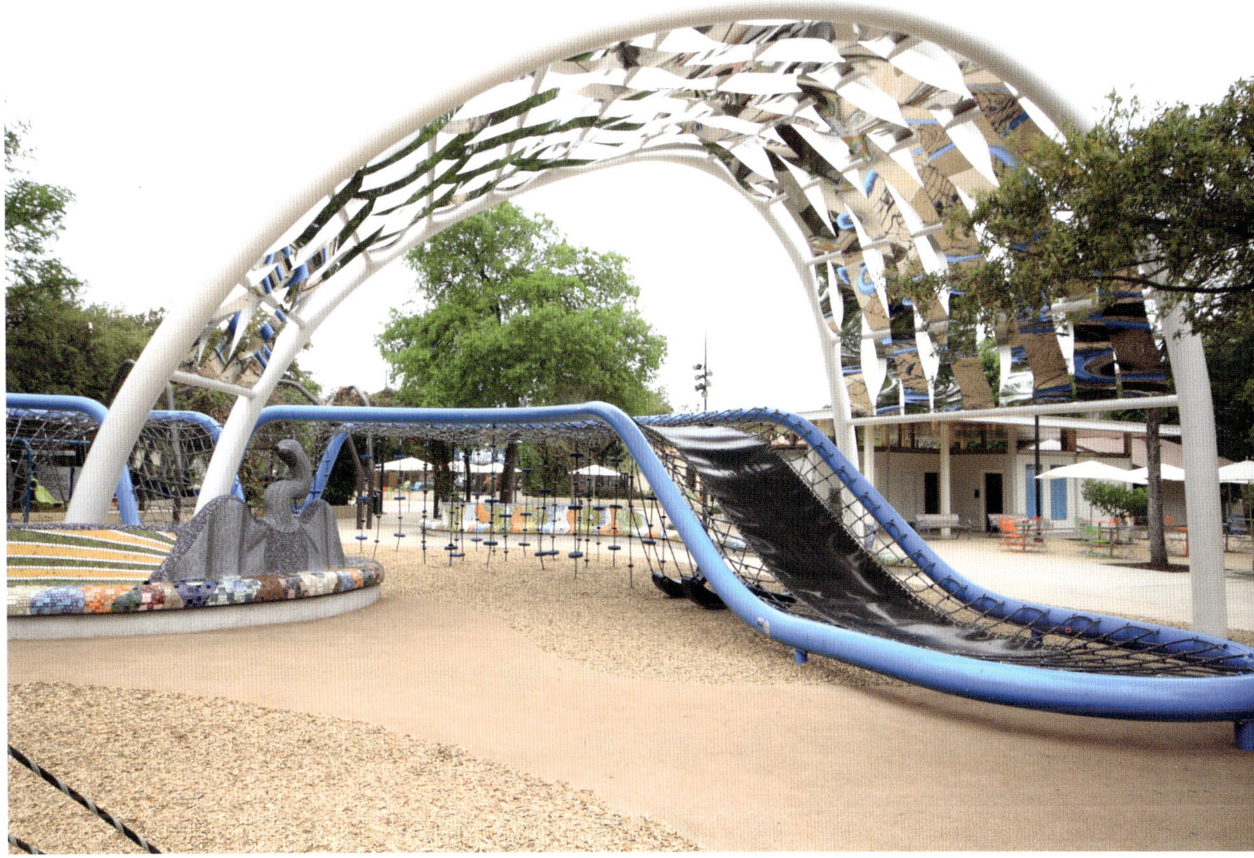

From bridges to parks to grocery stores,
art reflects our memories, and our everyday tools.

Art reflects our fantasies, and our paths through life
and we dream, play, revel in it.

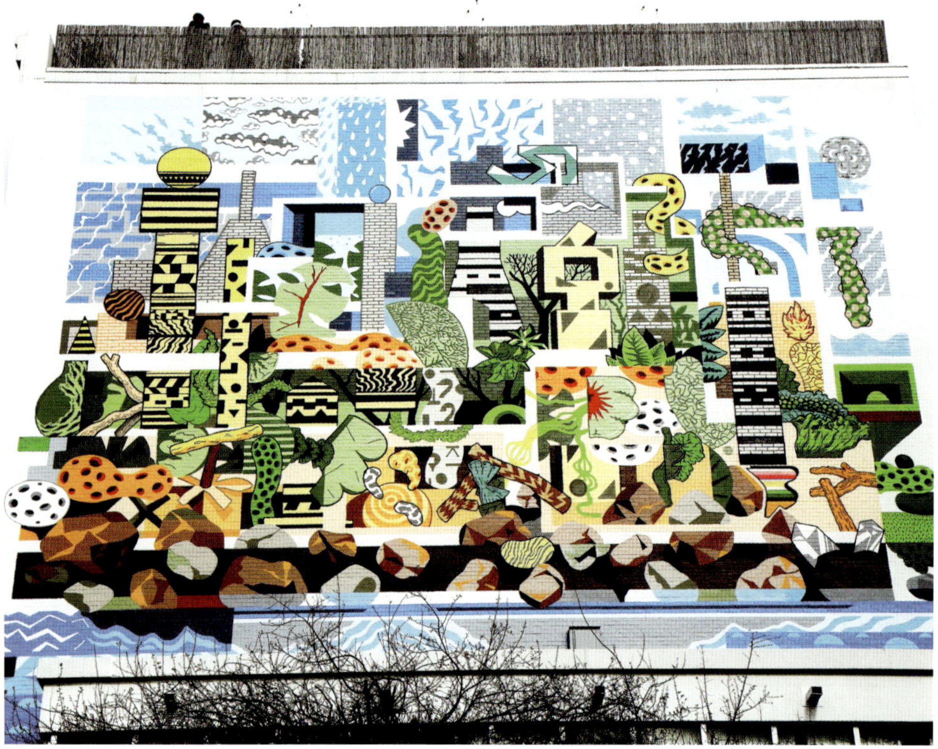

TOP LEFT
Untitled, 2014.
Basko Vazko (Chile).
Luminaria. El
Tropicano Hotel, 110
Lexington Avenue.

BOTTOM LEFT
Marketplace, 2018.
Andrei Rentería
and students.
San Antonio Zoo.

RIGHT
CommUNITY, 2019.
Ruben Sánchez.
The 68 Apartments,
Hemisfair Park.

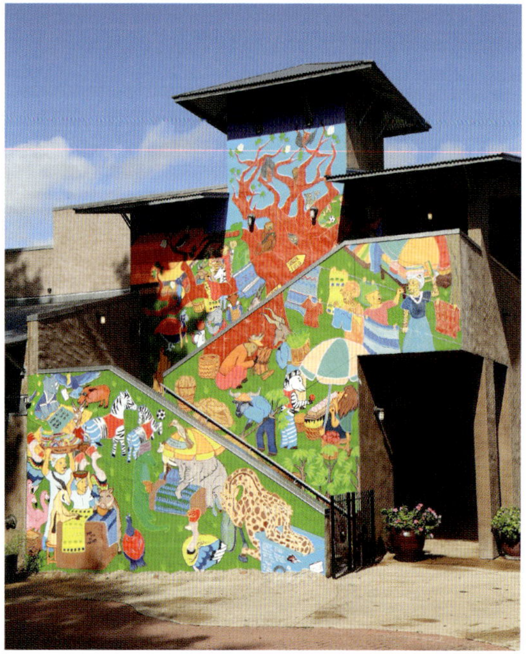

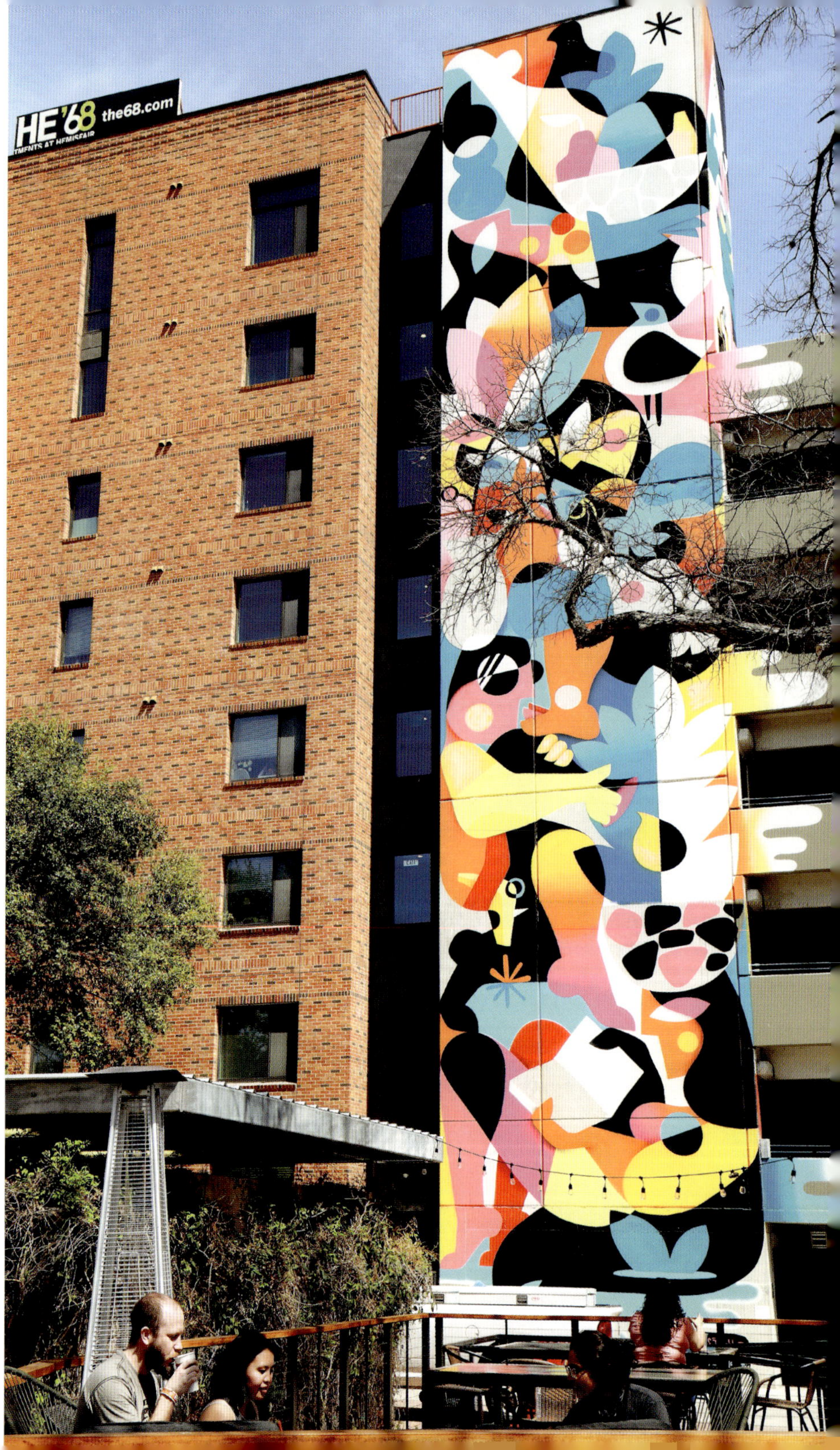

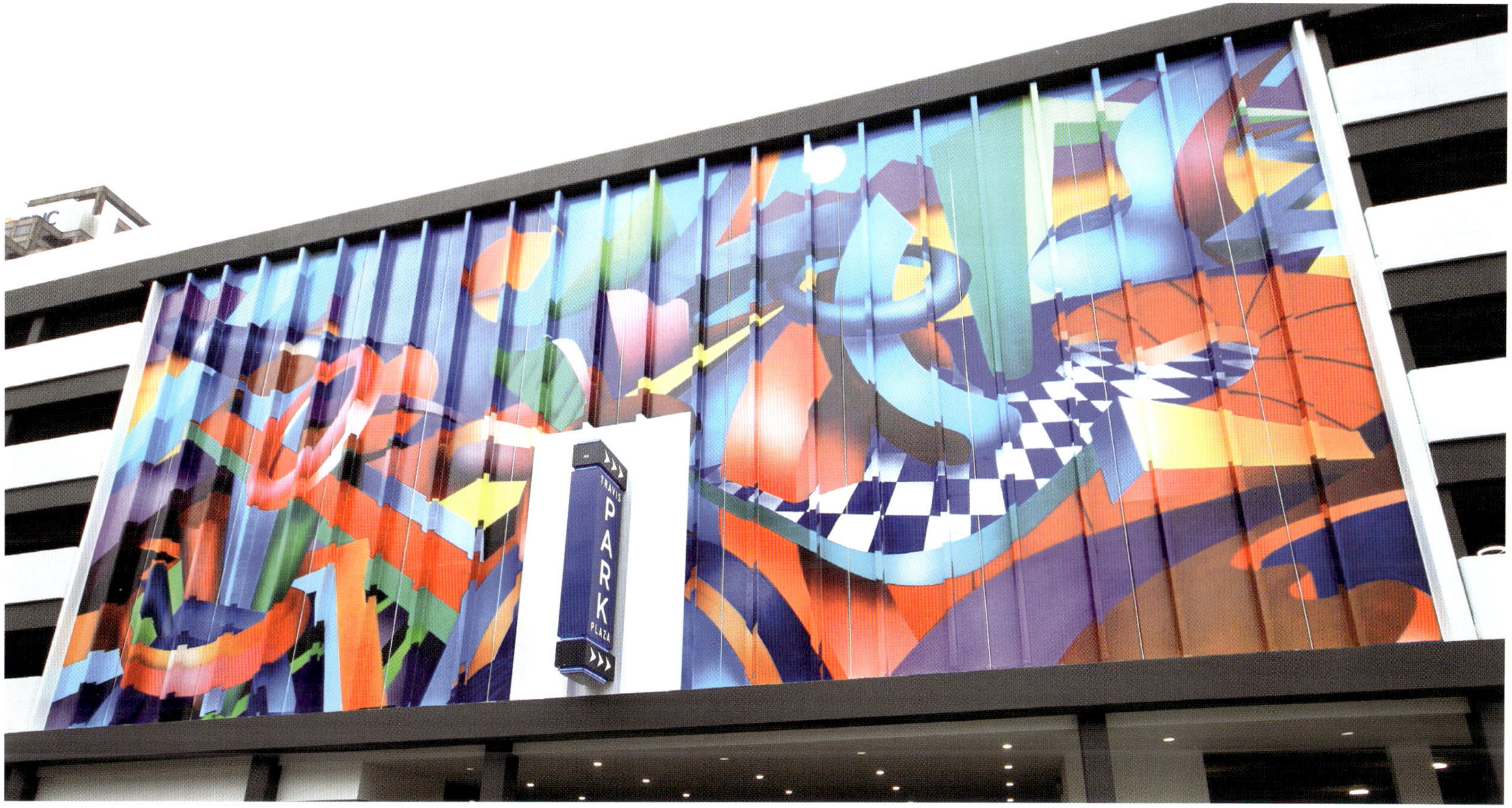

TOP
Never Completely Revealed, Never Completely Obscured, 2021. Centro San Antonio's Art Everywhere Project. Mark and Henry Hogenson. Travis Street Garage.

BOTTOM
Dare to Be Powerful, 2014. Jane Madrigal. Westfall Bridge at 100 block of S. Hackberry Street.

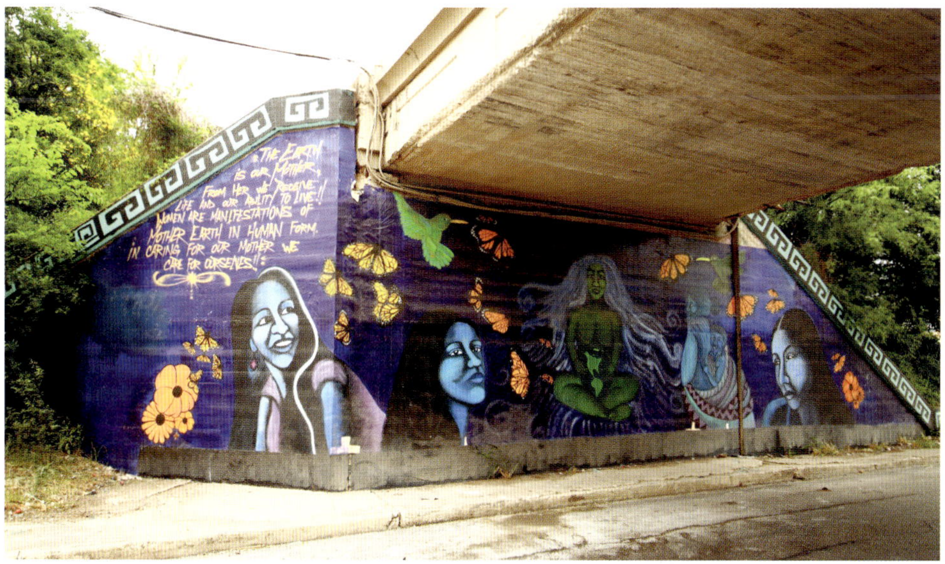

The broad arm of public art here reaches
into unexpected areas
and pours itself elegantly
onto all surfaces.

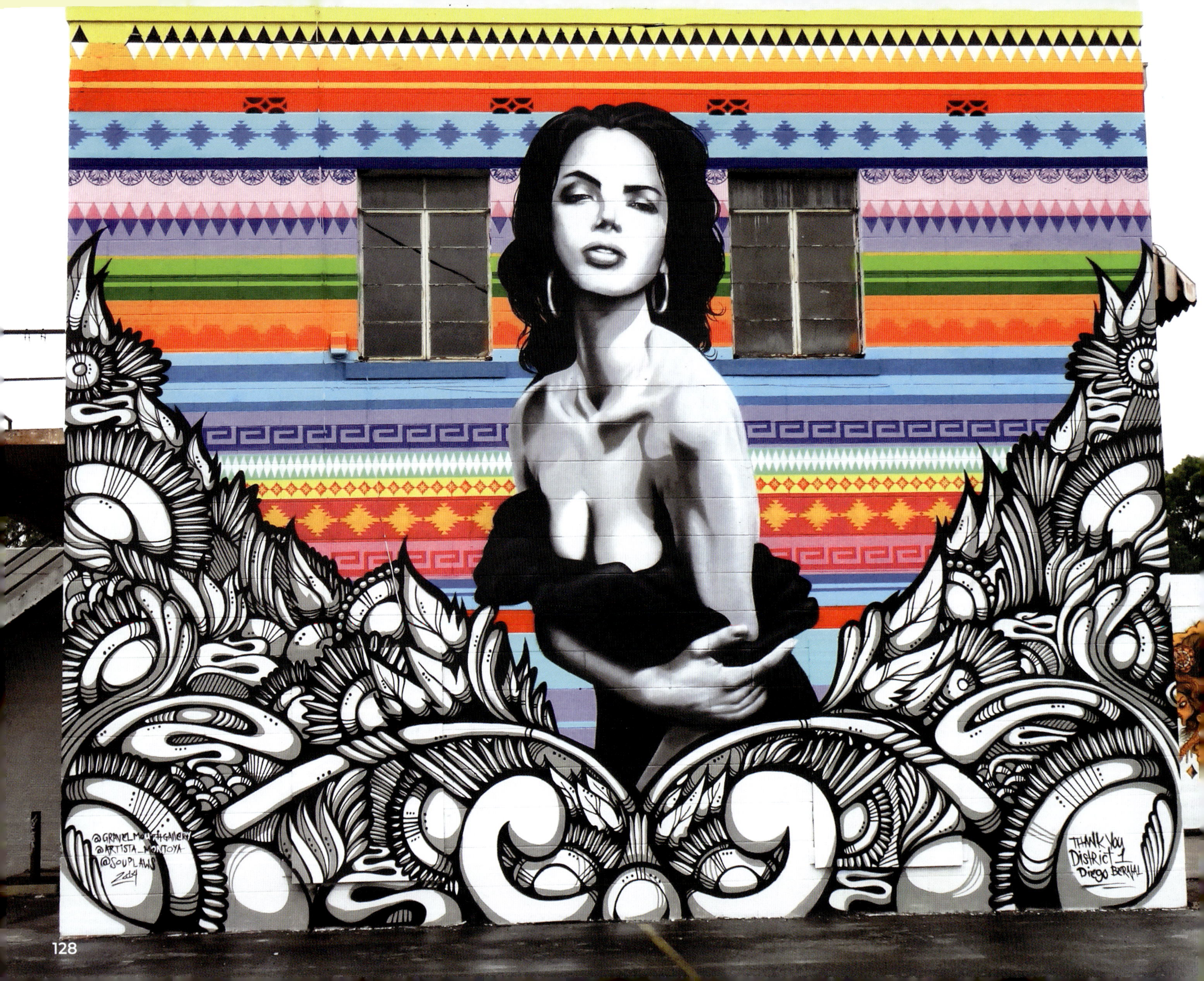
@ARTISTA_MONTOYA
@SOUPLAWS
2014
THANK YOU
DISTRICT 1
DIEGO BERNAL

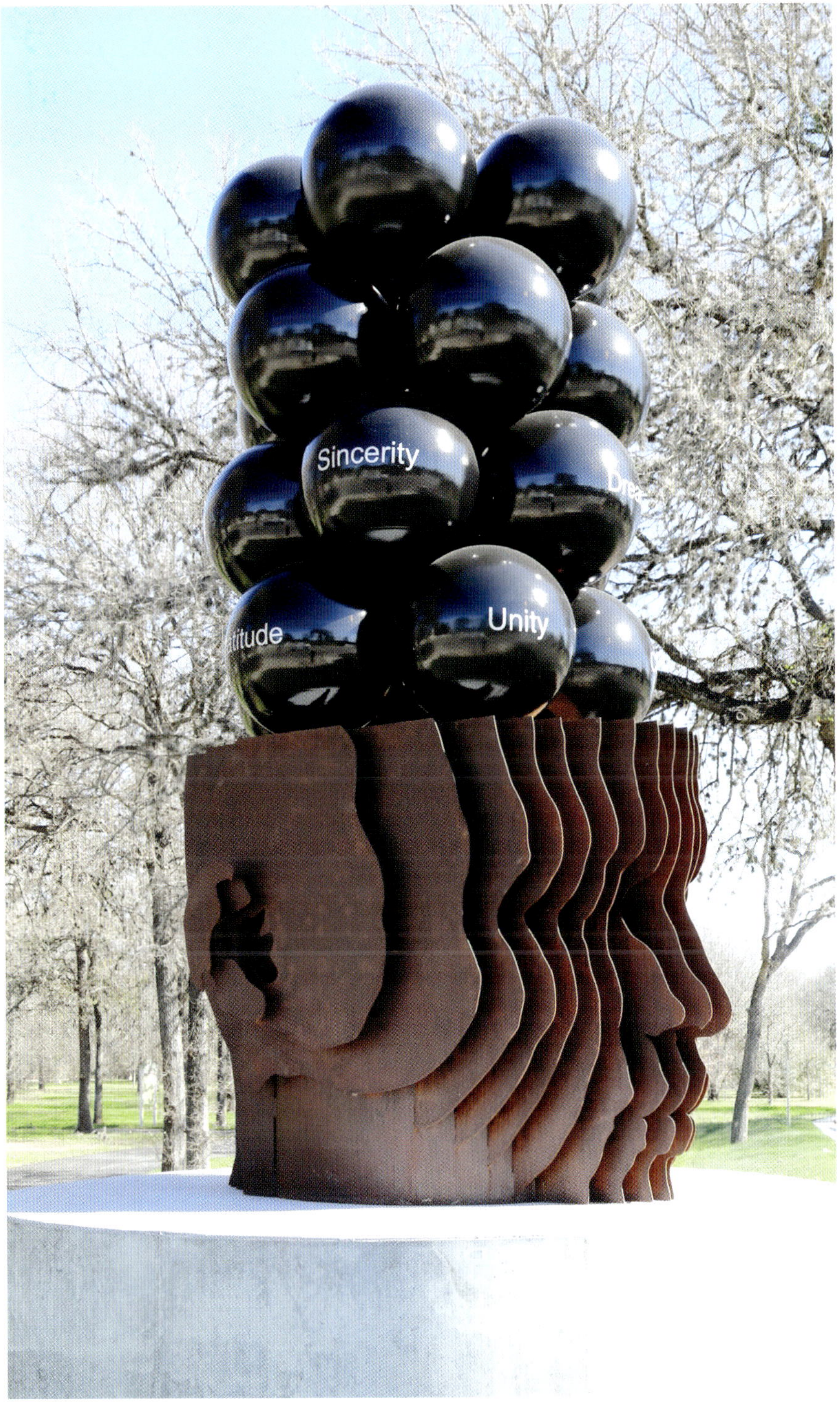

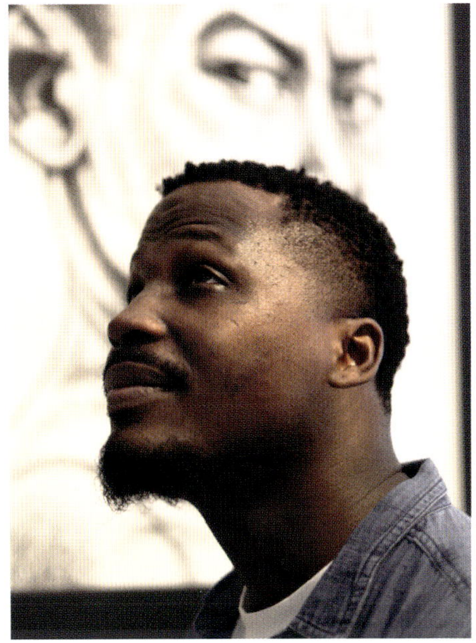

OPPOSITE PAGE
Untitled, 2014. Chris Montoya and "Shek." North St. Mary's and Navarro Streets.

THIS PAGE
LEFT
Spheres of Reflection, 2022. Kaldric Dow. MLK Park.

RIGHT
Kaldric Dow, 2022

Art dreams of a world where Black Lives Matter
Where beauty and value rest royally
on the shoulders of each human life
Where Dreams of Unity become Reality
and where three hundred thousand people
Unite to march in Brave Brotherhood, Resilient Sisterhood
Bold Change a vision within reach
at the touch of our fingertips
in every interaction, with people of every experience.

TOP LEFT
Touch, 2020. Suzy González. E. Houston and Navarro Streets.

BOTTOM LEFT
Go Spurs Go, 2016. Los Otros. Travis Park.

RIGHT
Modern Tribe, 2016. Luis López. Metropolitan Methodist Hospital.

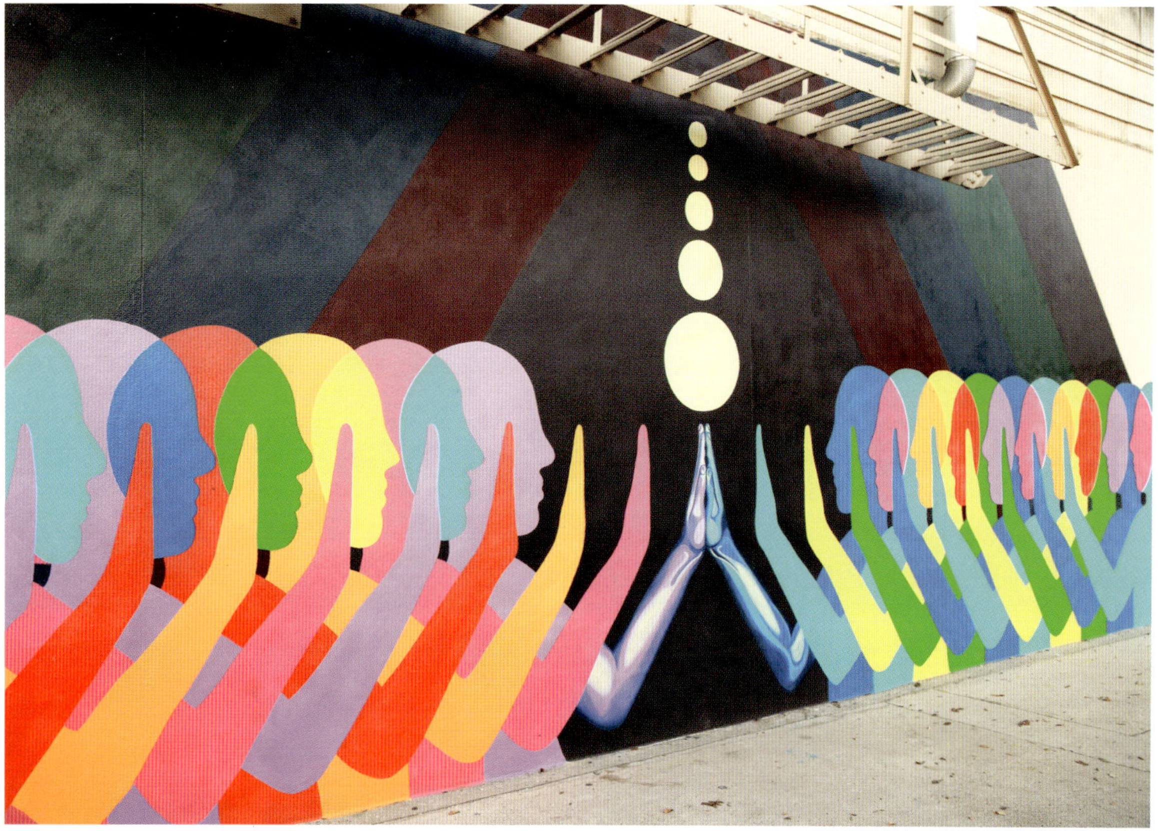

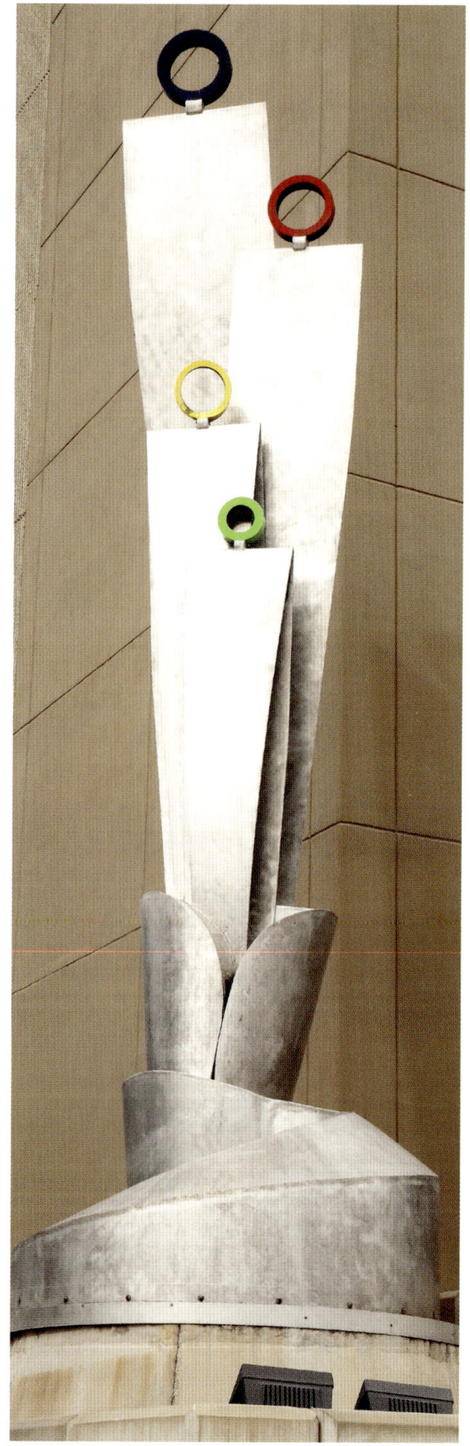

Art explores the deepest hungers of our soul and the crises of our globe, as humans long to once again touch, amid a pandemic quarantine, or dream of cheering on their favorite team.

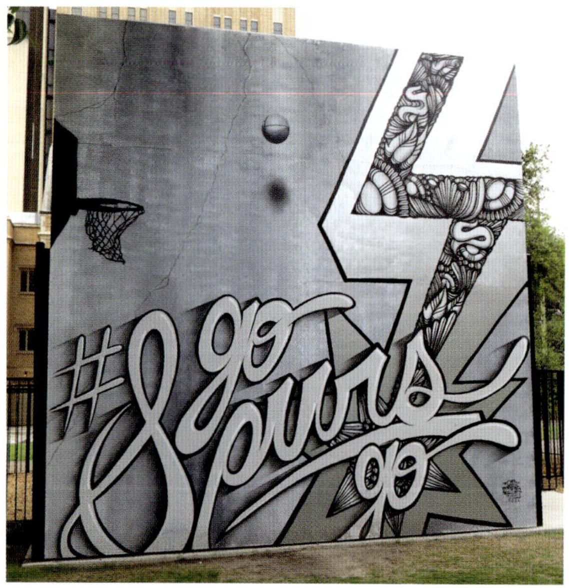

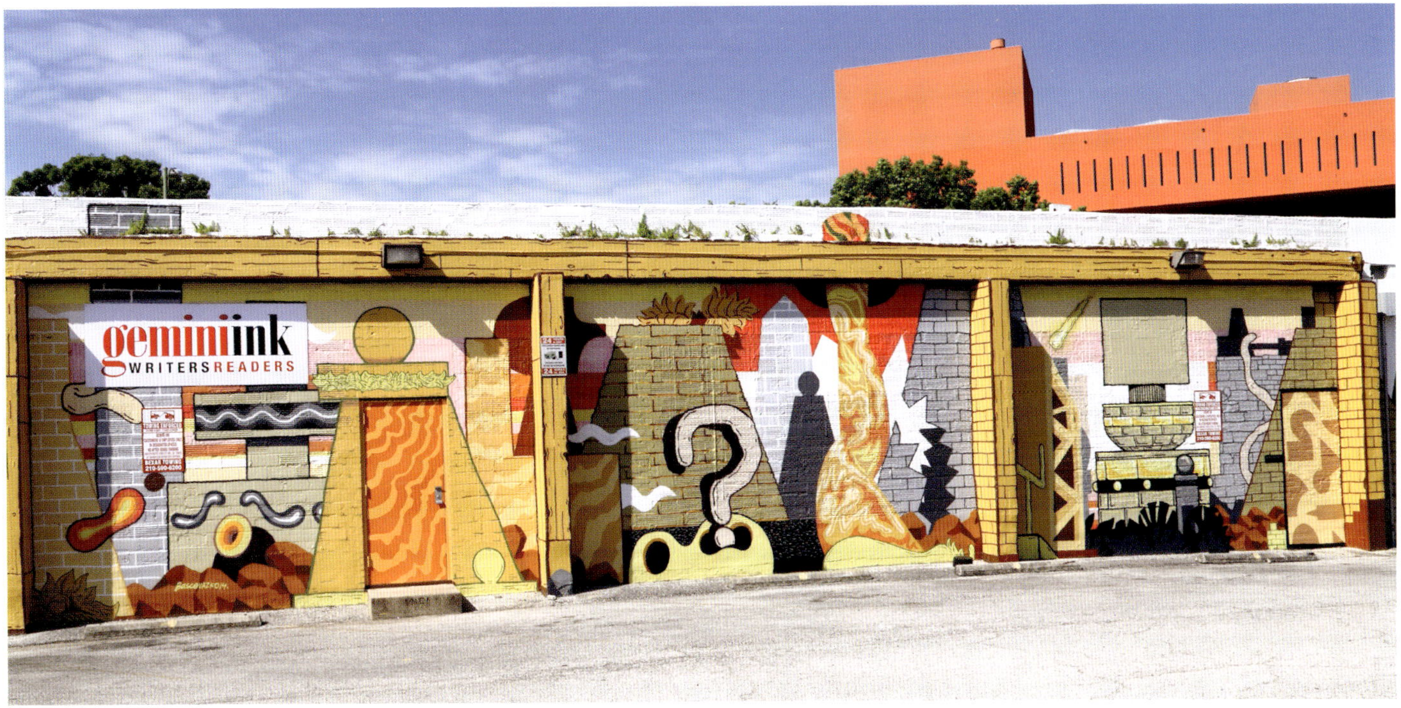

TOP
Gemini Ink, 2014. Basko Vasko. Gemini Ink Office, 1111 Navarro Street.

BOTTOM LEFT
La Peregrina, 2020. Regina Moya. Mennonite Church, 1443 S. St. Mary's Street. A community library / art piece sprouts from an old school bus. Portraying the images of migrants but adorned with the hairstyles and clothing of those who helped paint, this piece involved fifty students from three continents who helped paint the bus. The title translates as "She who is on a pilgrimage."

BOTTOM RIGHT
Riverwalk Panels, 2020. George Schroeder. Metal panels upgrade the trash storage area on River Walk near the Briscoe Western Art Museum.

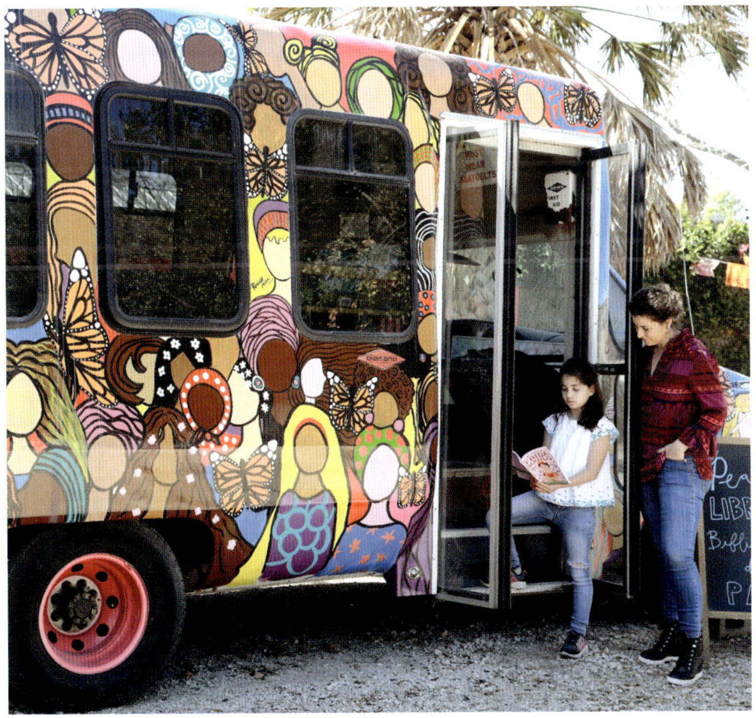

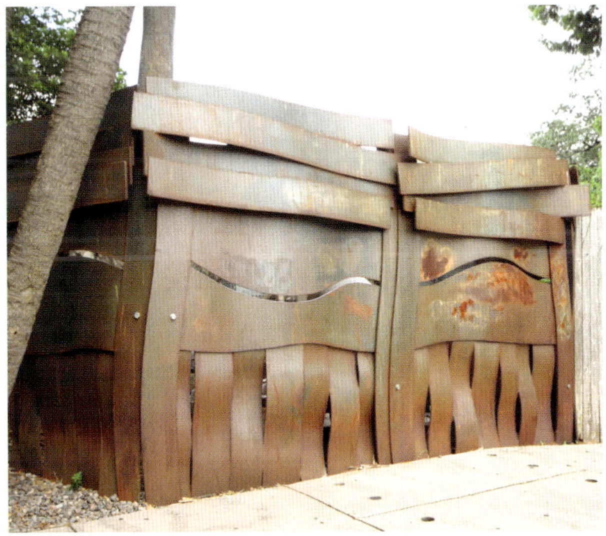

Even the back door
adorns itself with art.
The free library bus flowers
in artistic flight.
And the trash cans
receive the artist's touch,
transform into
Riverwalk Panels.

TOP LEFT
Cycles of Color, 2018.
Luis López. Dewey Street Apartments.

BOTTOM LEFT
Sonny's Airplane Parts, 1997. Nancy Rubins. Ruby City Art Museum.

RIGHT
The Simple Parameters of Extreme Gravitation, 2019. Danville Chadbourne. Temporary exhibit.

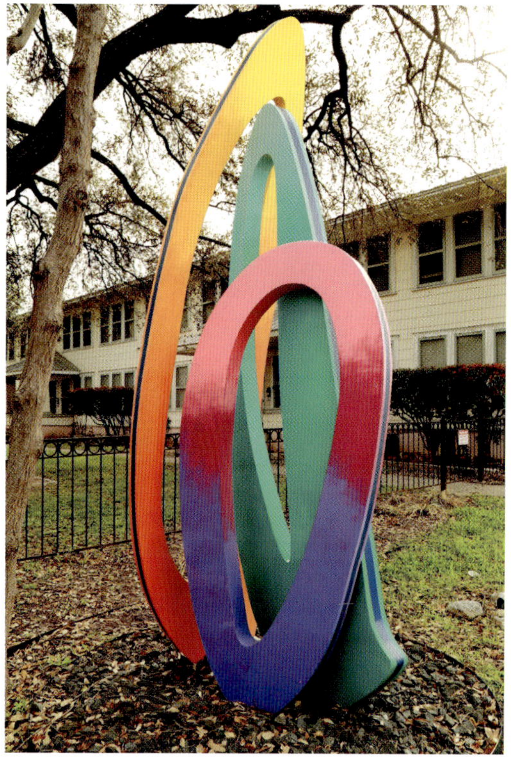

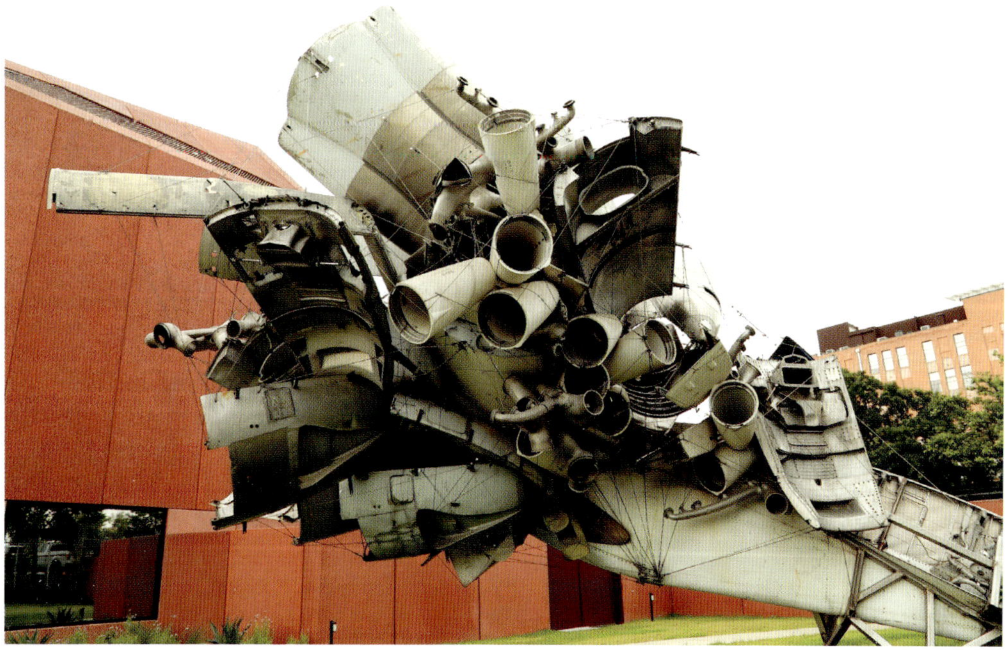

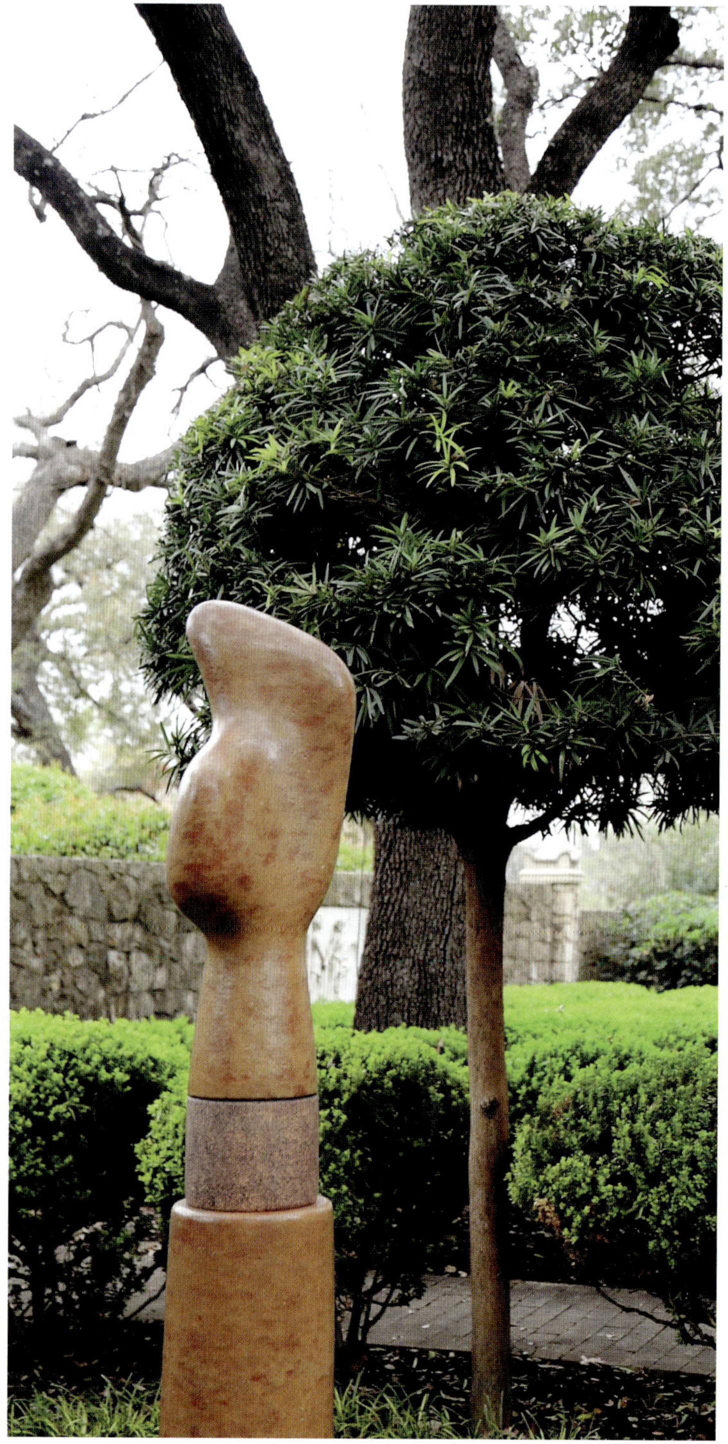

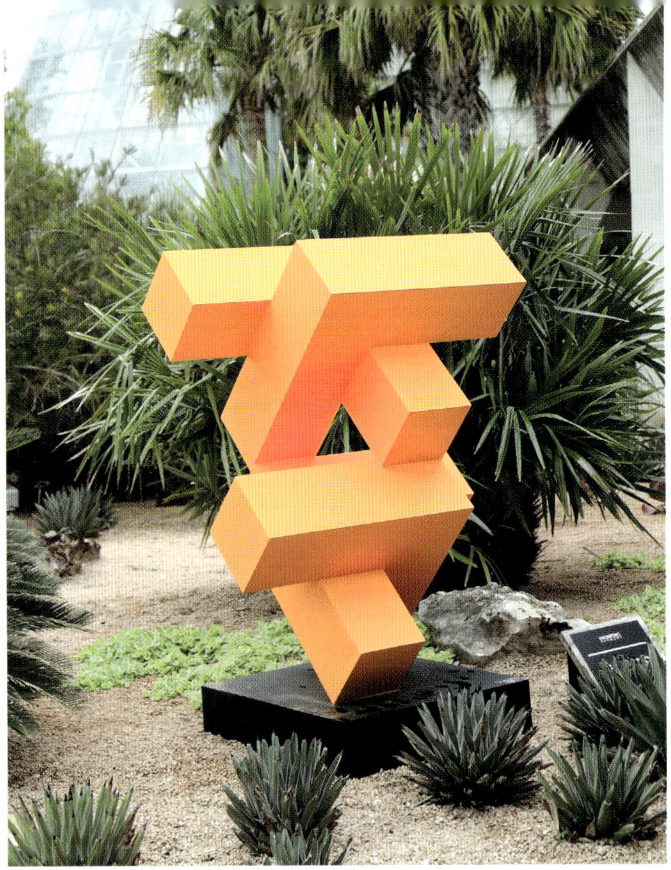

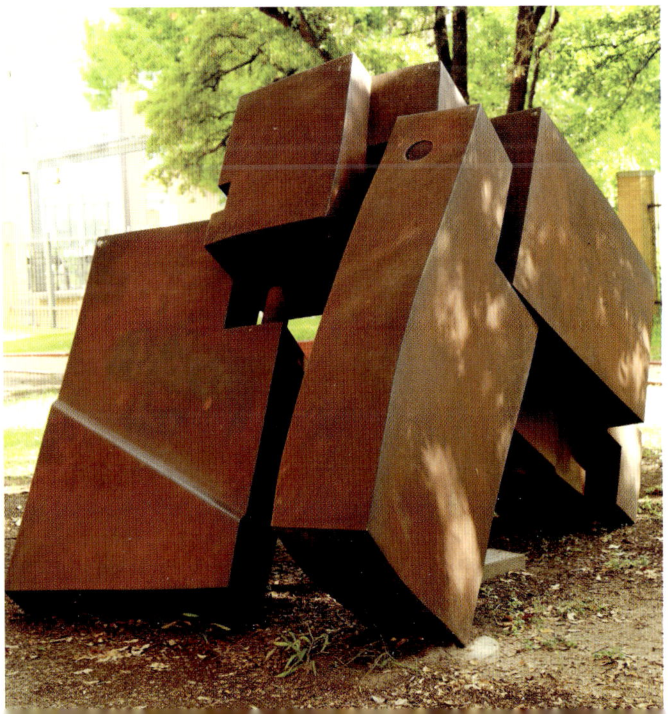

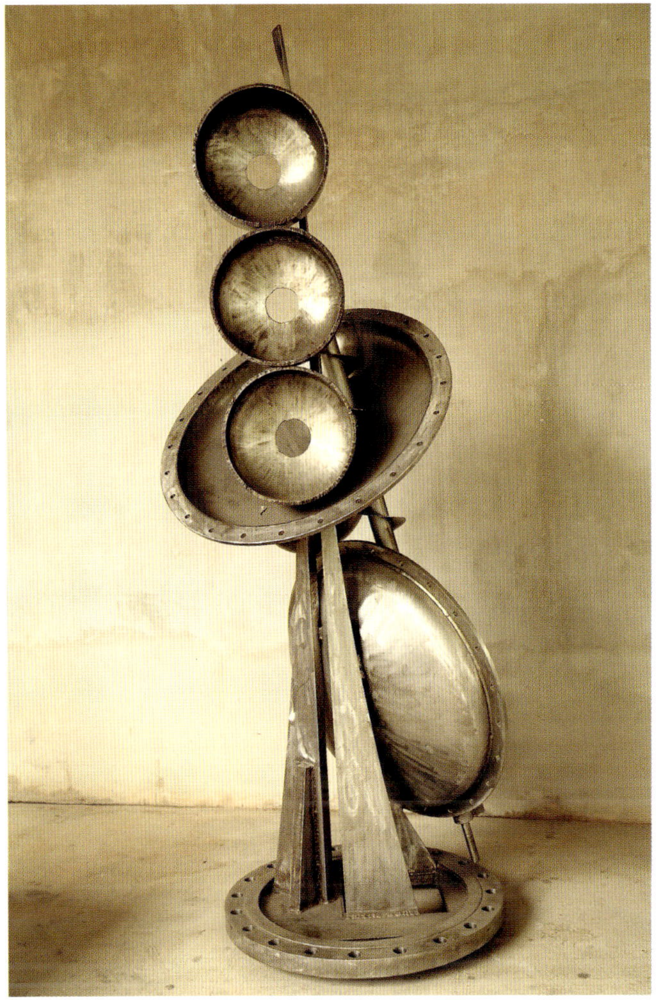

TOP LEFT
Geometric Harmony Yellow, 2019. Alejandro "Otto" Martín. San Antonio Botanical Garden.

BOTTOM LEFT
Colorado Tripod, 1976. David L. Deming. San Antonio Museum of Art. Purchased by Ms. Patricia Graves, Mr. and Mrs. Alonzo Gates, Mr. Kenneth M. Graves, and Mrs. Sam Maddux.

RIGHT
Discoveries, 2011. George Tobolowsky. San Antonio Botanical Garden.

Our artists visualize, intuit, transform, force the mind to bend into new perceptions, transcend into more holistic understandings, be they built of airplane parts or origami, rocks, blocks, or the human form. They record the past, see the present, help us build the future.

LEFT
Sotol Duet, 2015.
Jon Isherwood.
Panther Springs Park.

RIGHT
Victoria, 1991–2000,
cast 2007. Philip
Grausman. McNay Art
Museum. Museum
purchase with Russell
Hill Rogers Fund
for the Arts.

OPPOSITE PAGE
Ascent, 1970.
Alexander Liberman.
Painted steel. McNay
Art Museum. Museum
purchase with the
Russell Hill Rogers
Fund for the Arts.

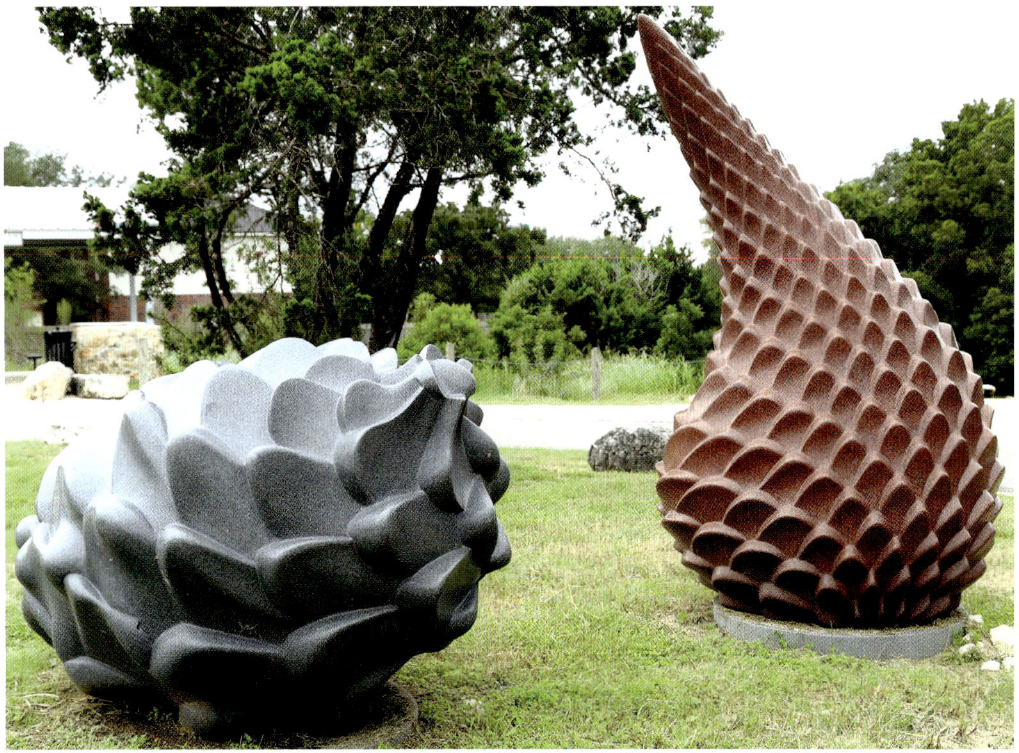

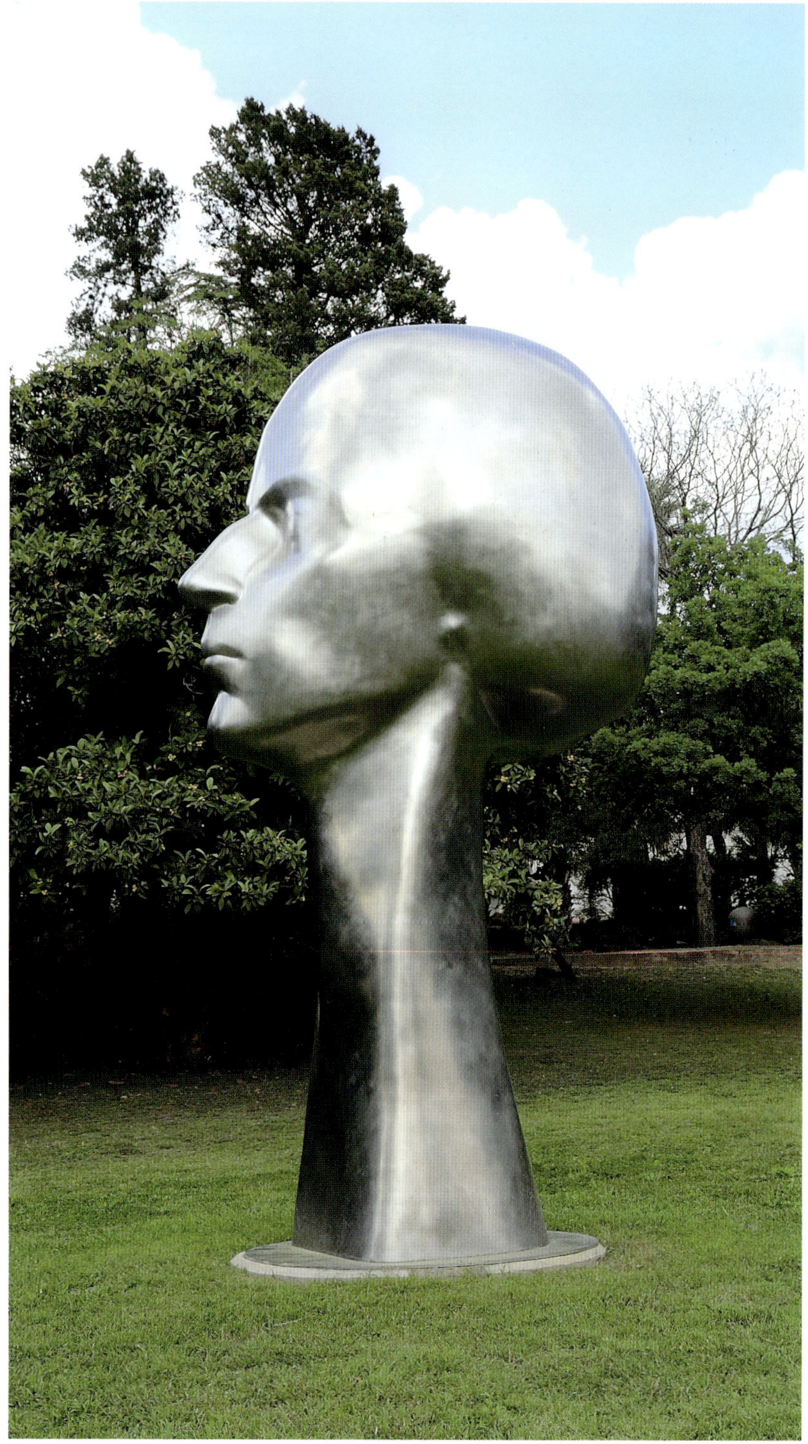

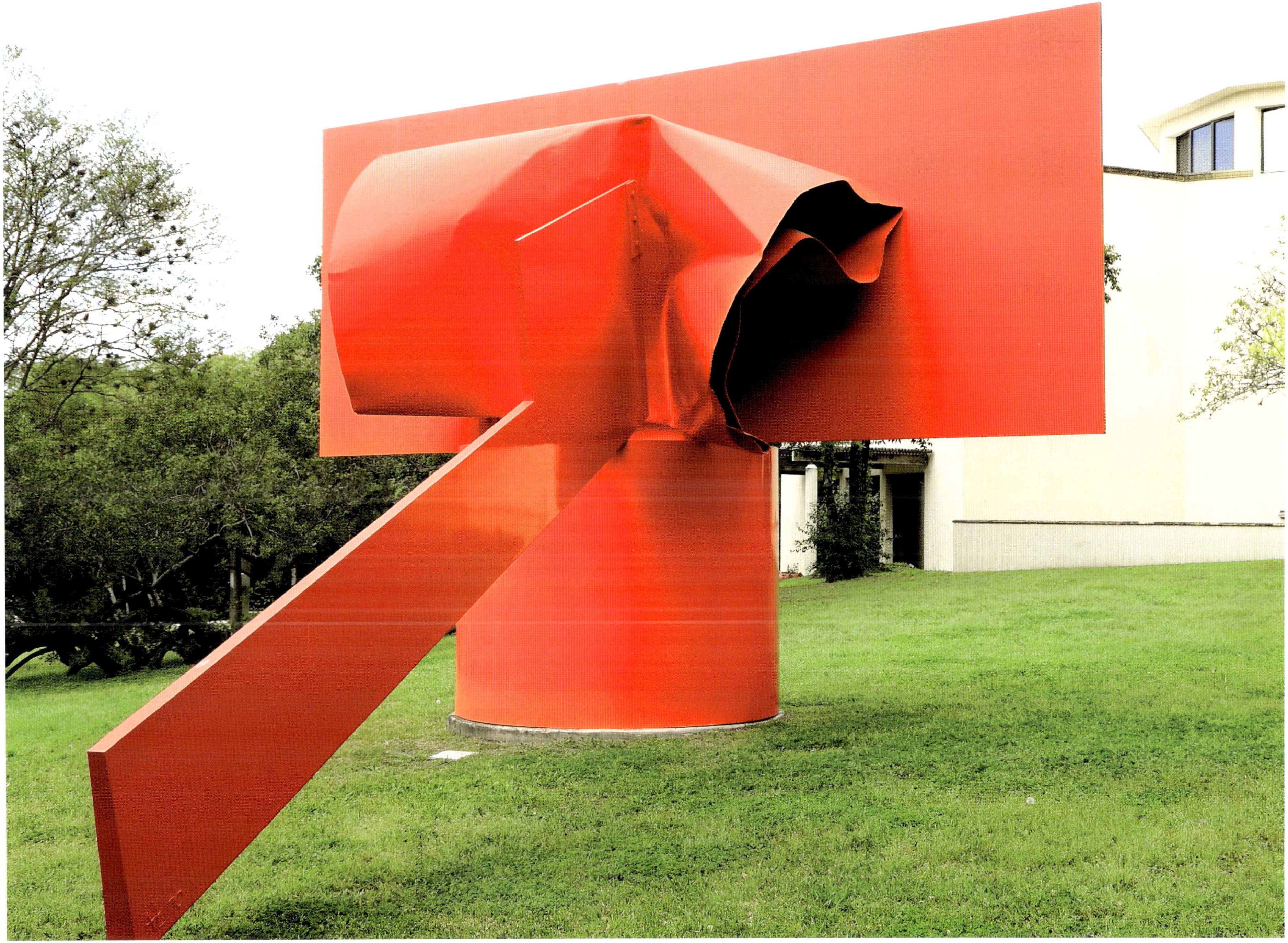

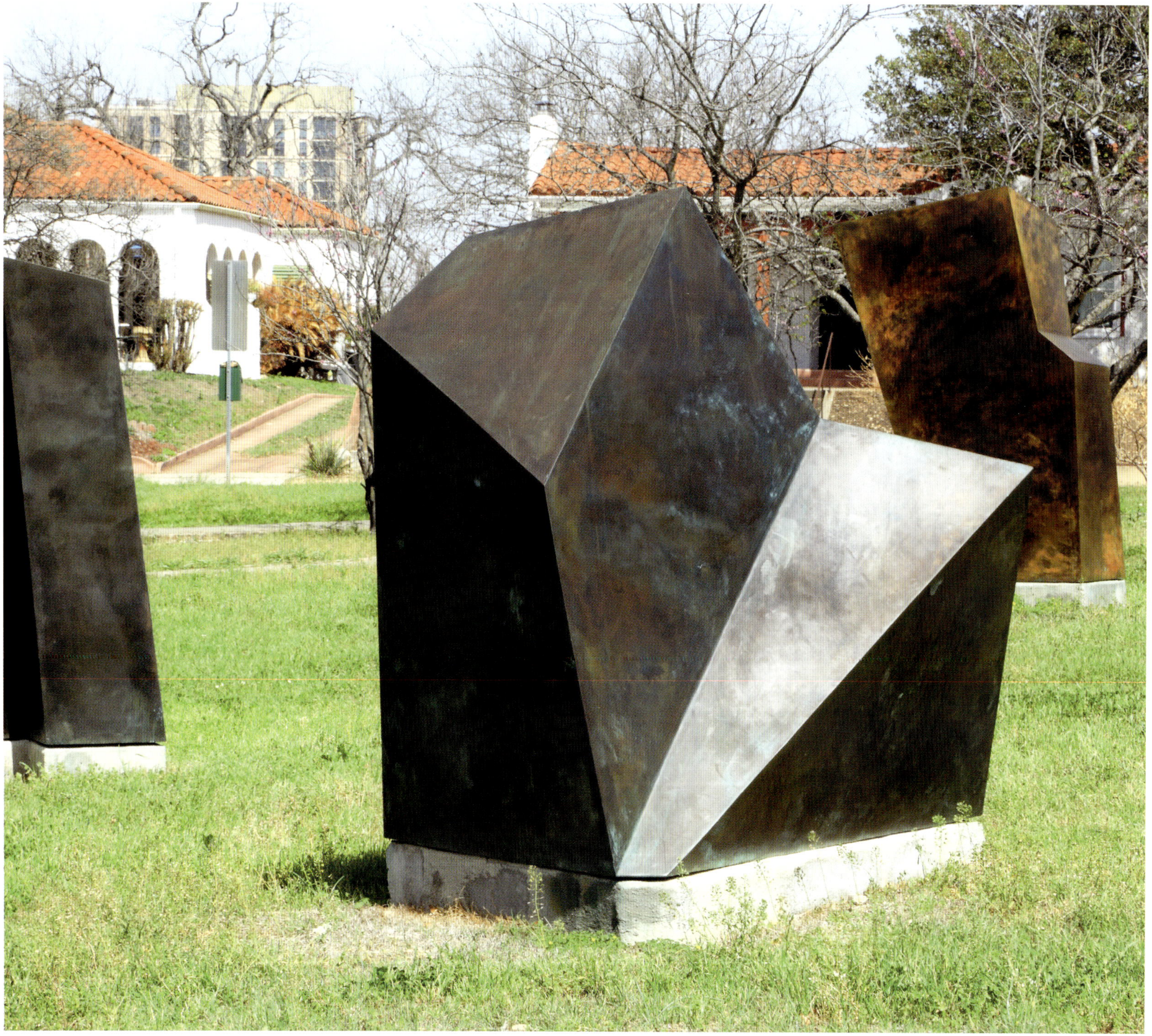

Constant Series—Question, Sorrow & Trial, 1976. Catherine Lee. N. New Braunfels Avenue and Parland Place.

OPPOSITE PAGE *Botanical Piece* and *Blooming Stars*. From the series Origami in the Garden 2020. Kevin Box. San Antonio Botanical Garden.

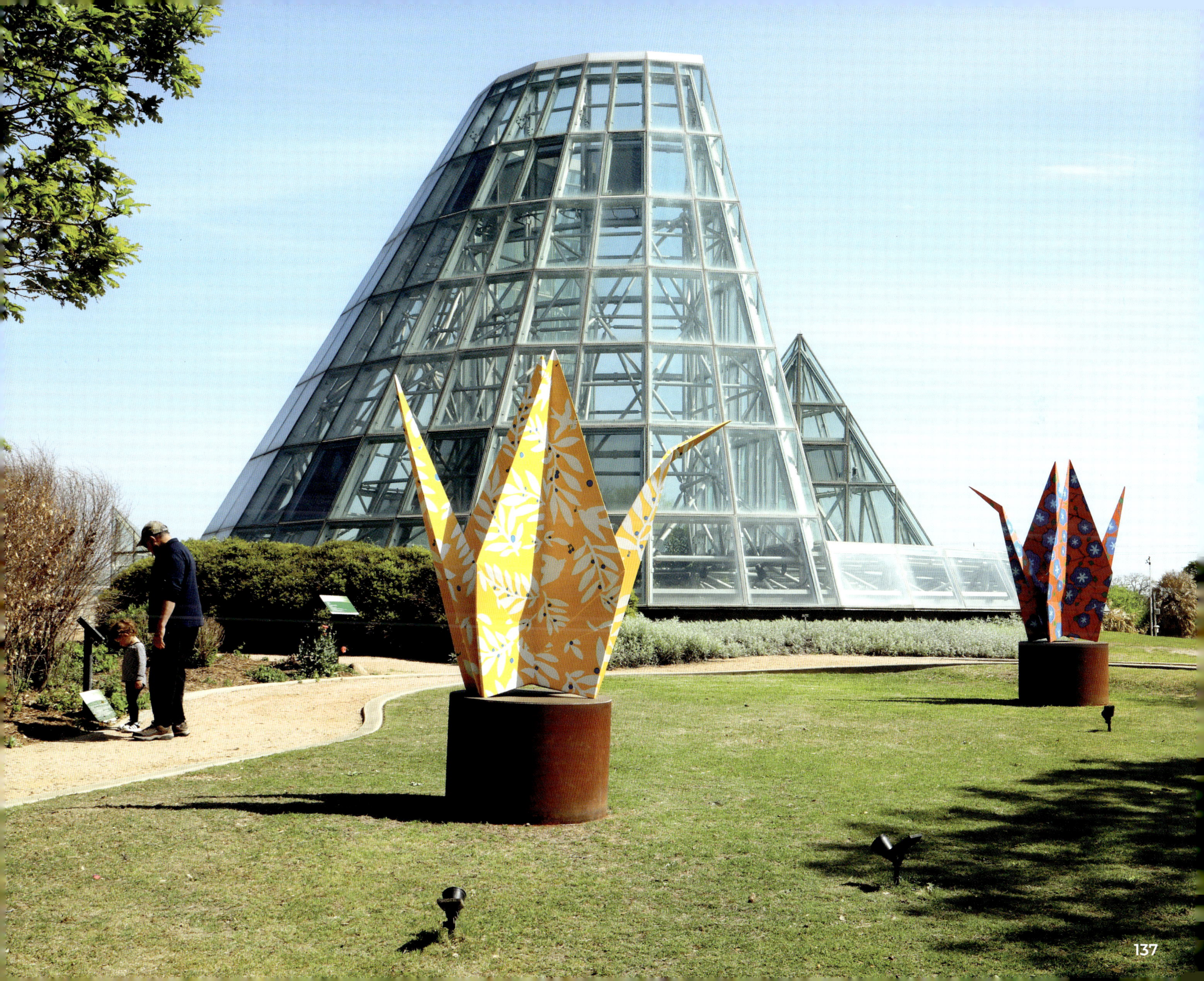

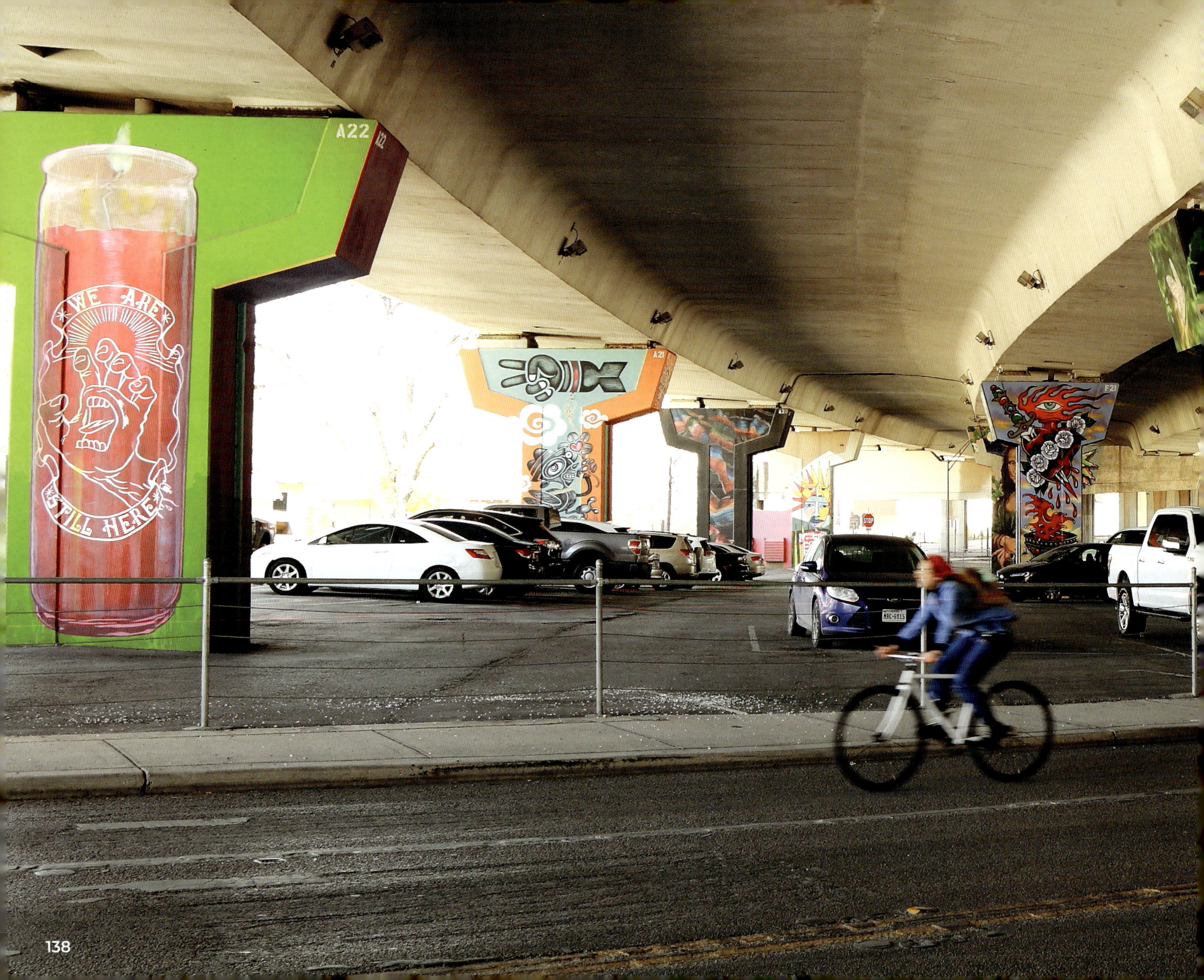
A22
WE ARE
STILL HERE
A21
F21

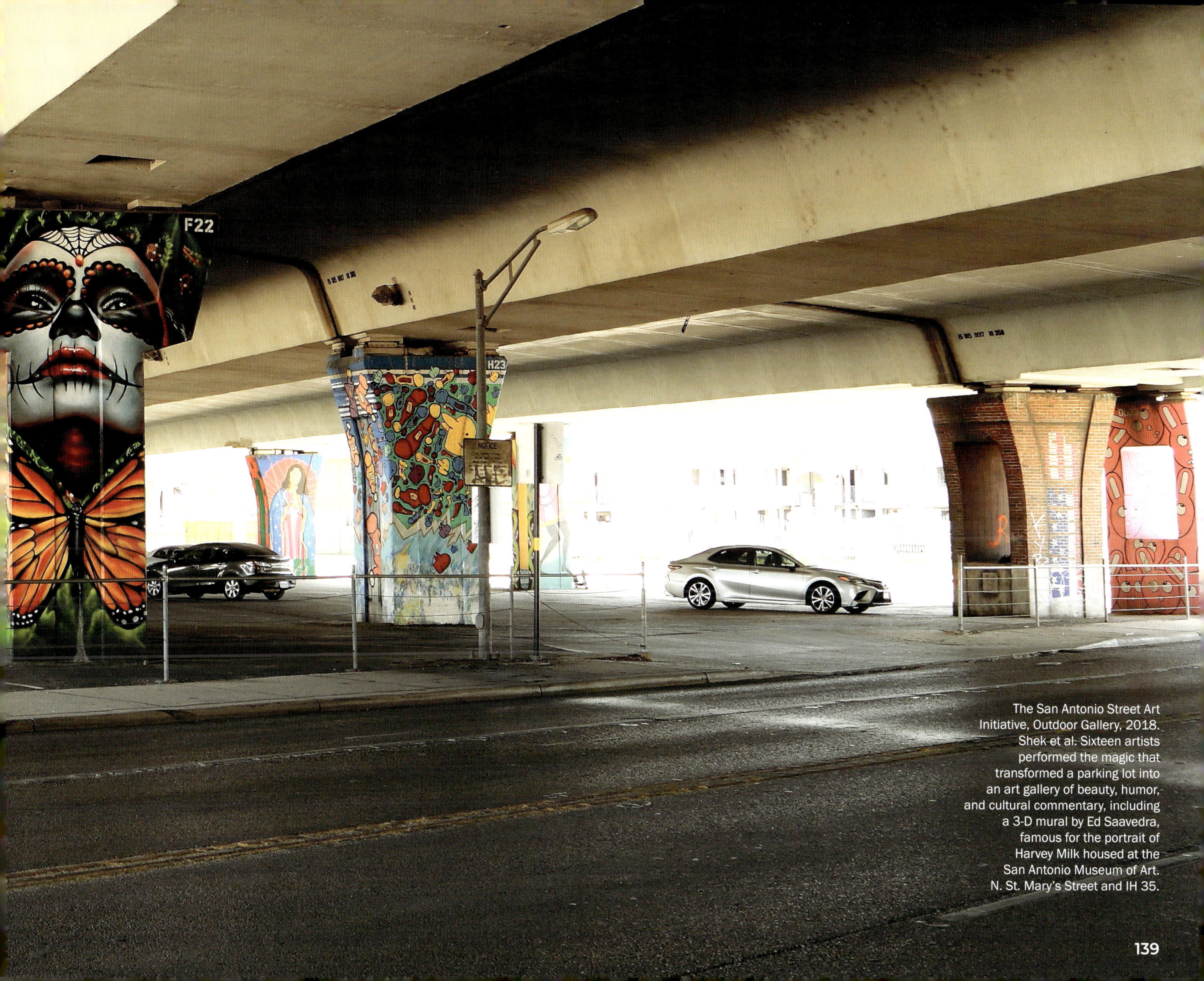

The San Antonio Street Art Initiative, Outdoor Gallery, 2018. Shek et al. Sixteen artists performed the magic that transformed a parking lot into an art gallery of beauty, humor, and cultural commentary, including a 3-D mural by Ed Saavedra, famous for the portrait of Harvey Milk housed at the San Antonio Museum of Art. N. St. Mary's Street and IH 35.

Untitled, 2020. Paul Garson. Essex Street.

OPPOSITE PAGE
TOP
Untitled, 2016. Iker Muro. N. St. Mary's and Navarro Streets.

CENTER LEFT
Paul Garson (San Antonio), 2017

CENTER RIGHT
Iker Muro (Spain), 2016

BOTTOM
Untitled, 2019. Aline Herrera (Mexico).

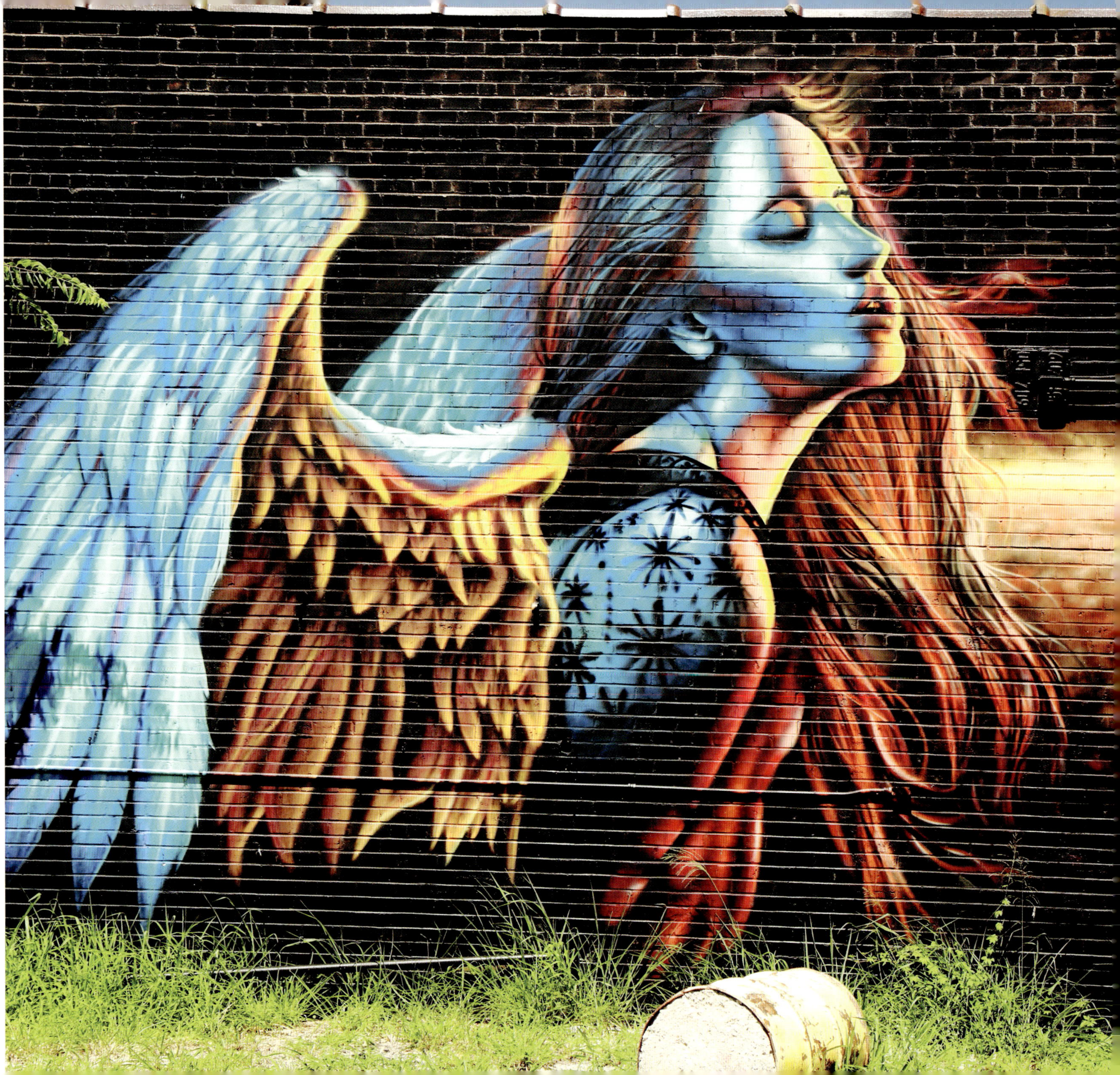

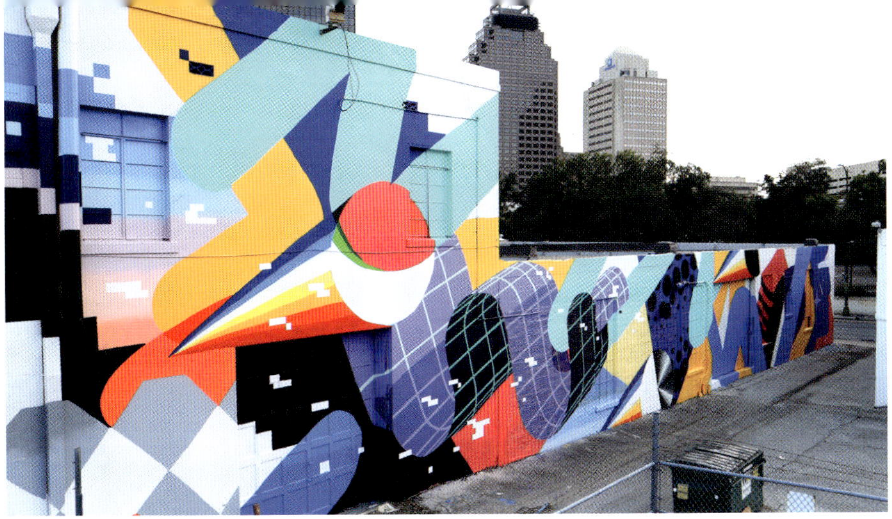

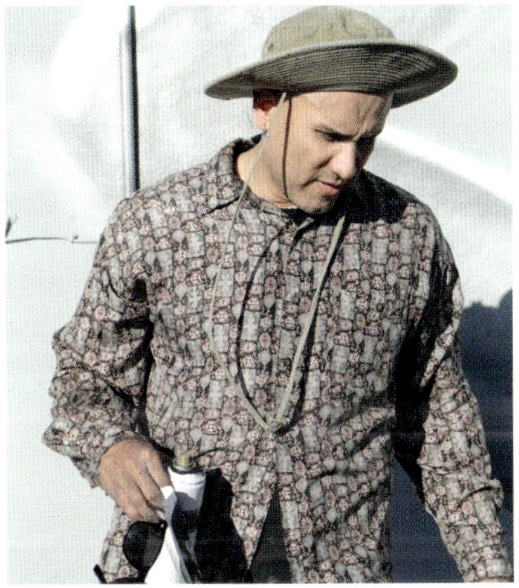

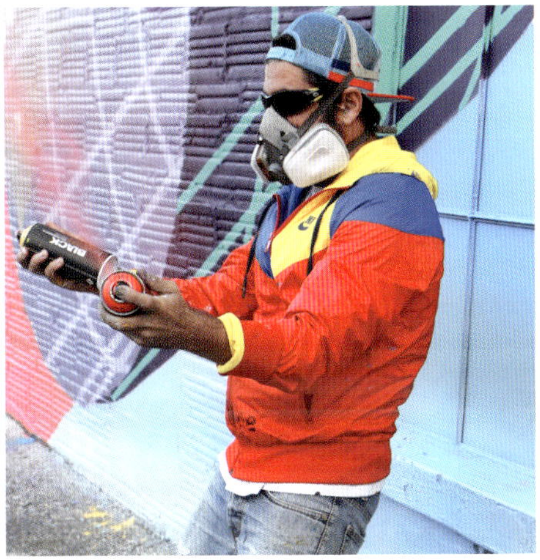

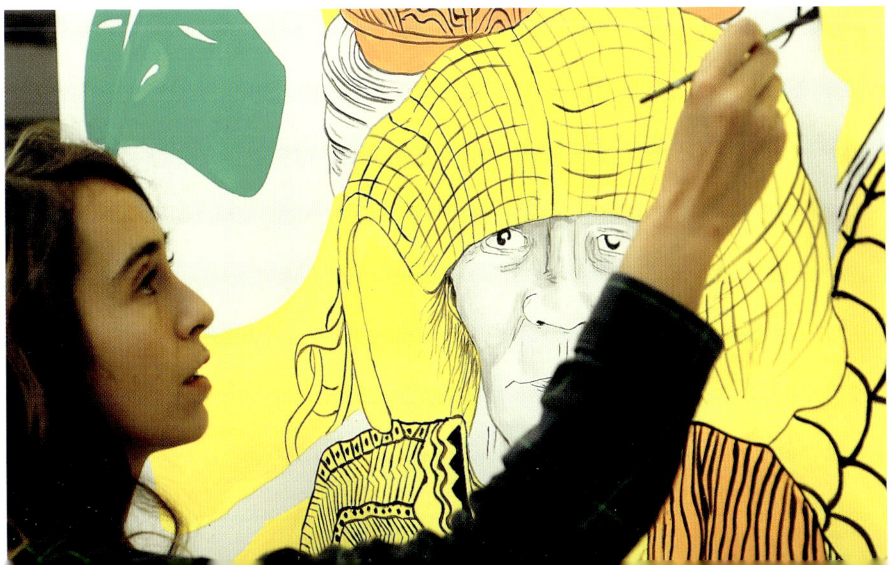

VI. EL BAILE DEL MOMENTO

CELEBRATING THE MOMENT IN STREET ART, FESTIVALS & INSTALLATIONS

They come from near and far.
They bring their visions here
to San Antonio
flying in from Africa, Spain, and New Zealand,
Belgium, Mexico City, and France.
From across town or across the world
they come to speak their spirit
and join in this cultural song
of artistic joy.

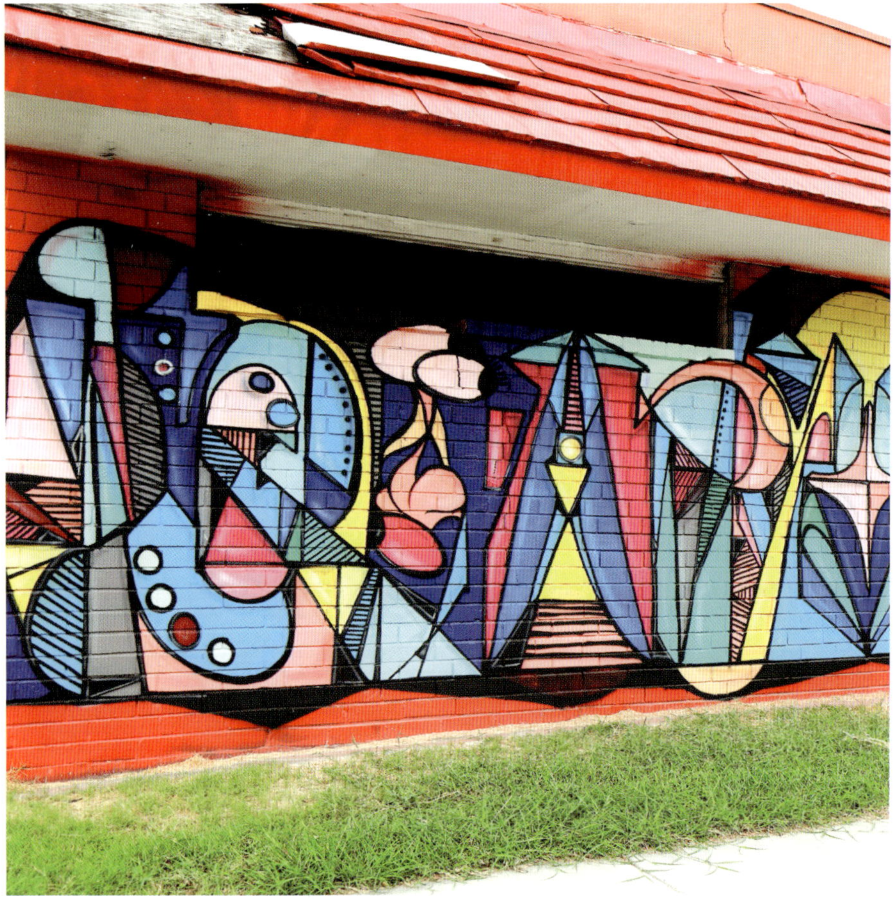

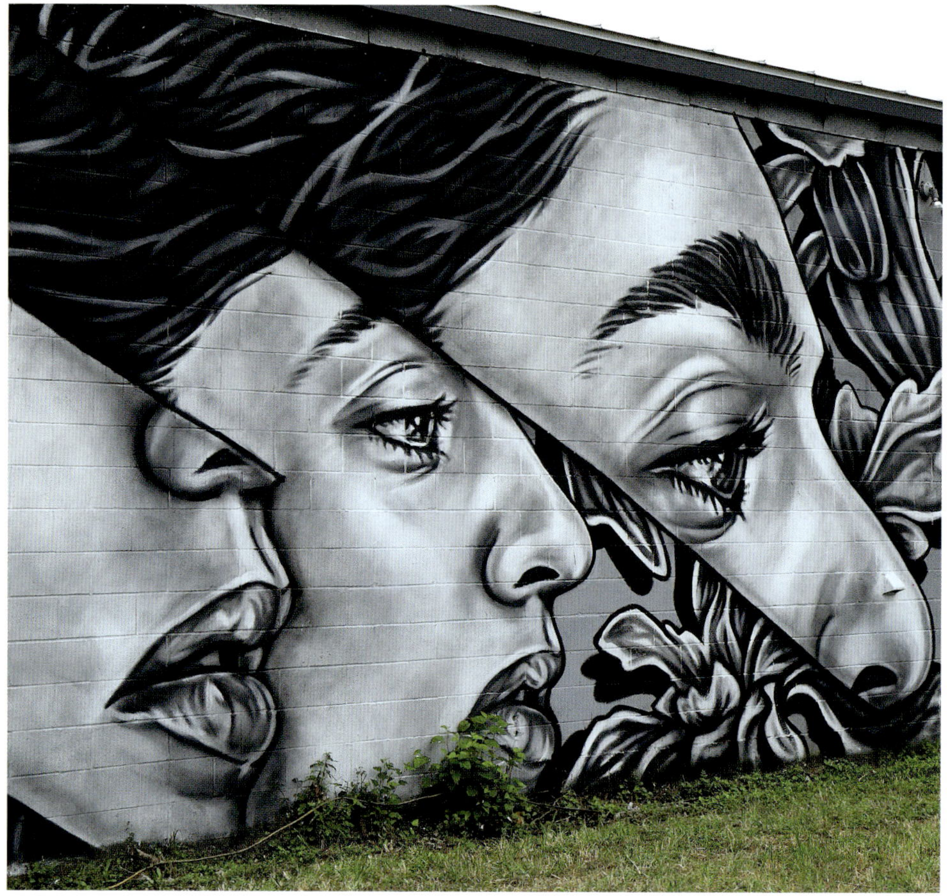

With spray paint cans and paintbrushes, spunk
and recycled debris, soldering guns and river wood,
they come to the low-rider parades
and the chalk-on-sidewalk masterpieces.
They come
for the art of it.

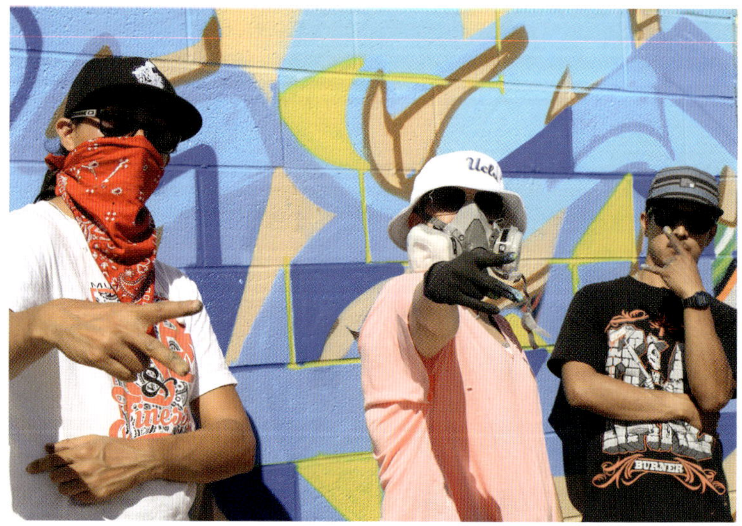

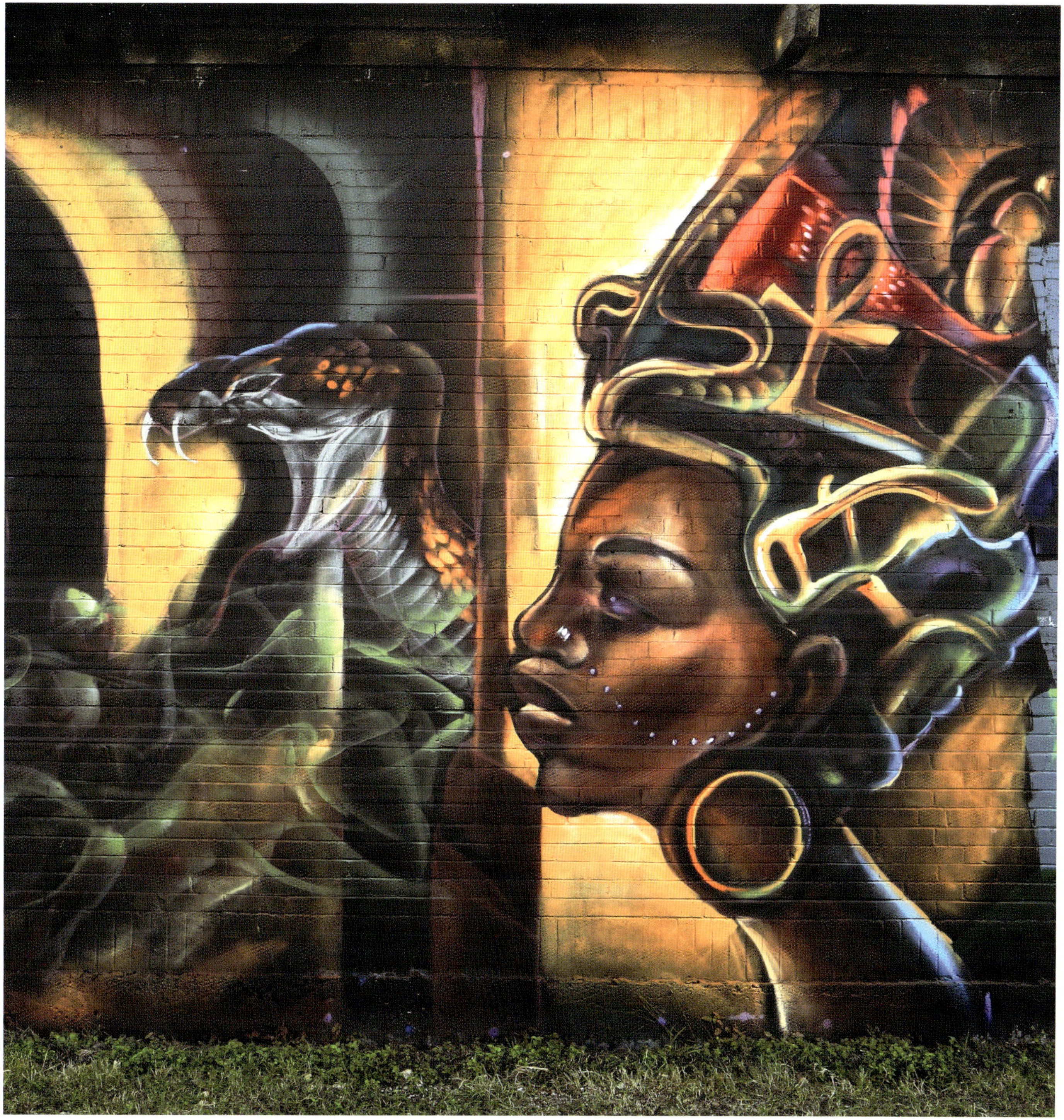

OPPOSITE PAGE
TOP LEFT
P.G.6.2020, 2020. Victor "Supher" Zarazua. Hackberry Street.

TOP RIGHT
Untitled, 2019. Paola Delfin (Mexico). N. St. Mary's Street.

BOTTOM RIGHT
Daniel "Dot One" Ariñega and crew, 2017

THIS PAGE
LEFT
Untitled, 2017. Alex Arzu. Hoefgen Avenue and E. Carolina Street.

BELOW
Alex Arzu (Houston)

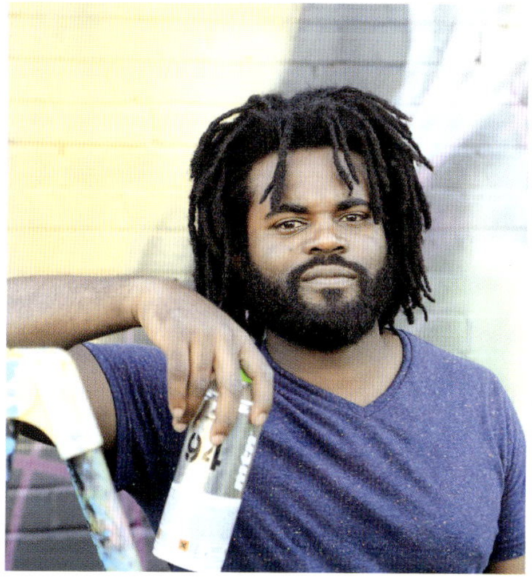

TOP
Dask.N8G, 2017. "Dask" (Corpus Christi). 1300 block of Hoefgen Avenue.

BOTTOM
Cease. MZK, 2017. "Cease" (Houston). 1300 block of Hoefgen Avenue.

OPPOSITE PAGE
Llama, 2017. "Delete." 1300 block of Hoefgen Street.

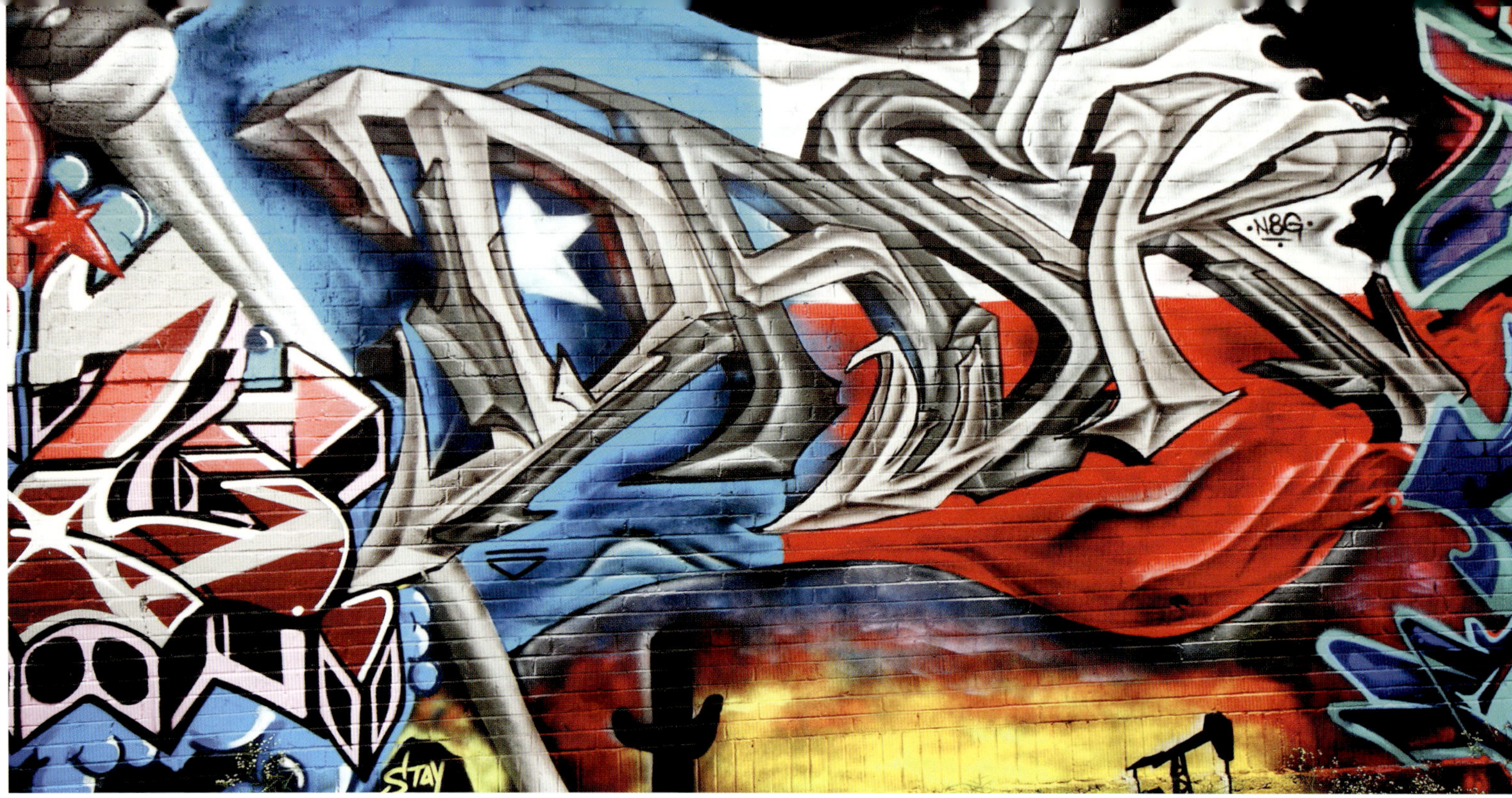

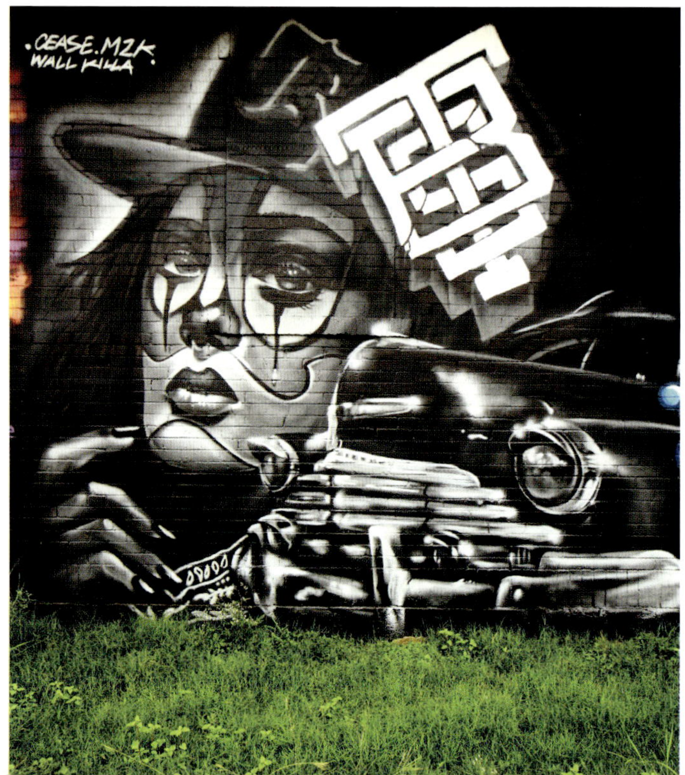

Street artists announce their sense of place, their personal energy
in unexpected conversations with an unknown public
signed in their own invented "handles" like "Cease," "Storm," "Risk."
Outside conventional bounds
On untethered canvas
Writing on walls as did the Texan Indians ten thousand years ago
in the magic of HERE
with careful, intricate panache
for an infinite audience
in the infinity of a moment or a millennium.

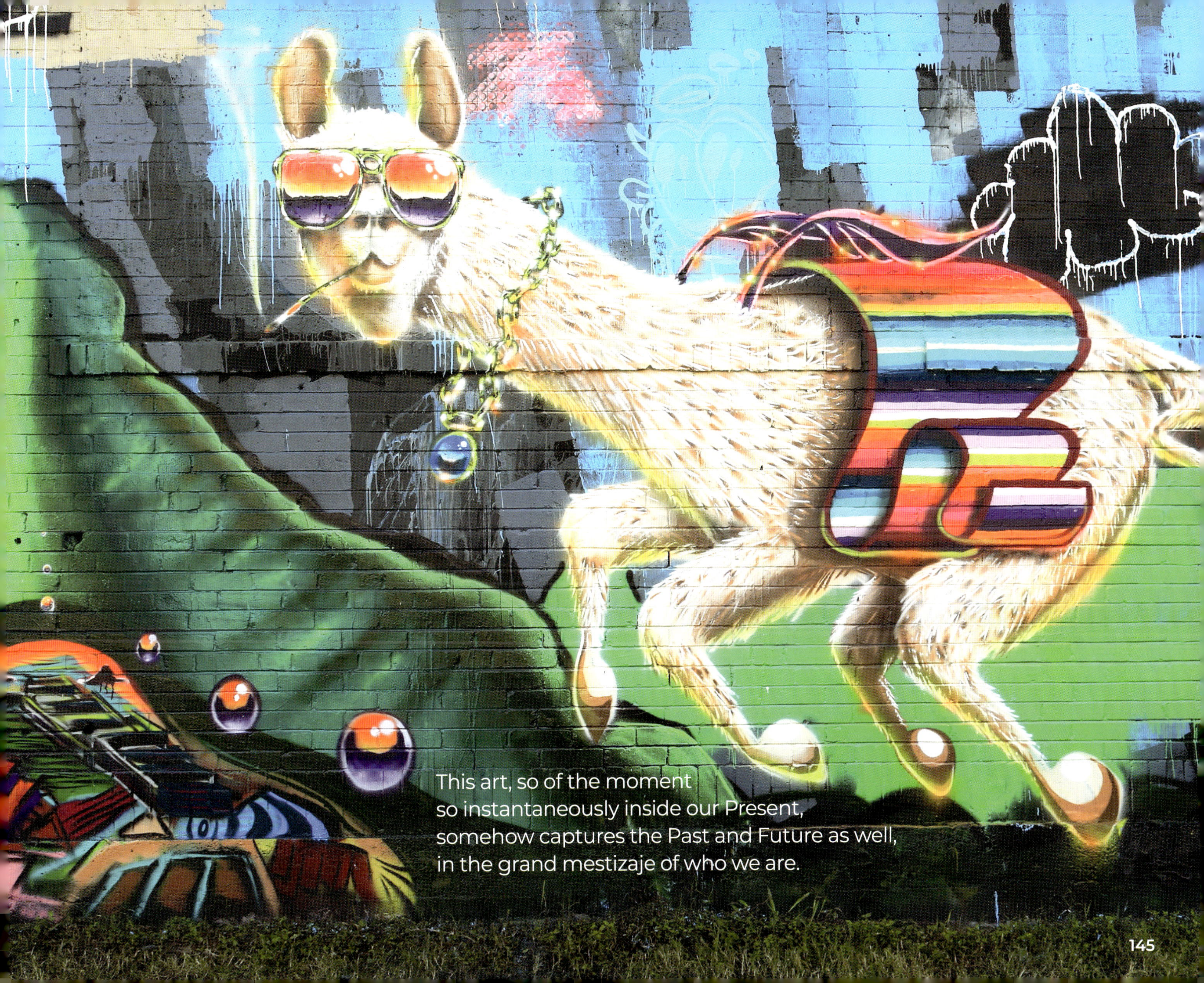

This art, so of the moment
so instantaneously inside our Present,
somehow captures the Past and Future as well,
in the grand mestizaje of who we are.

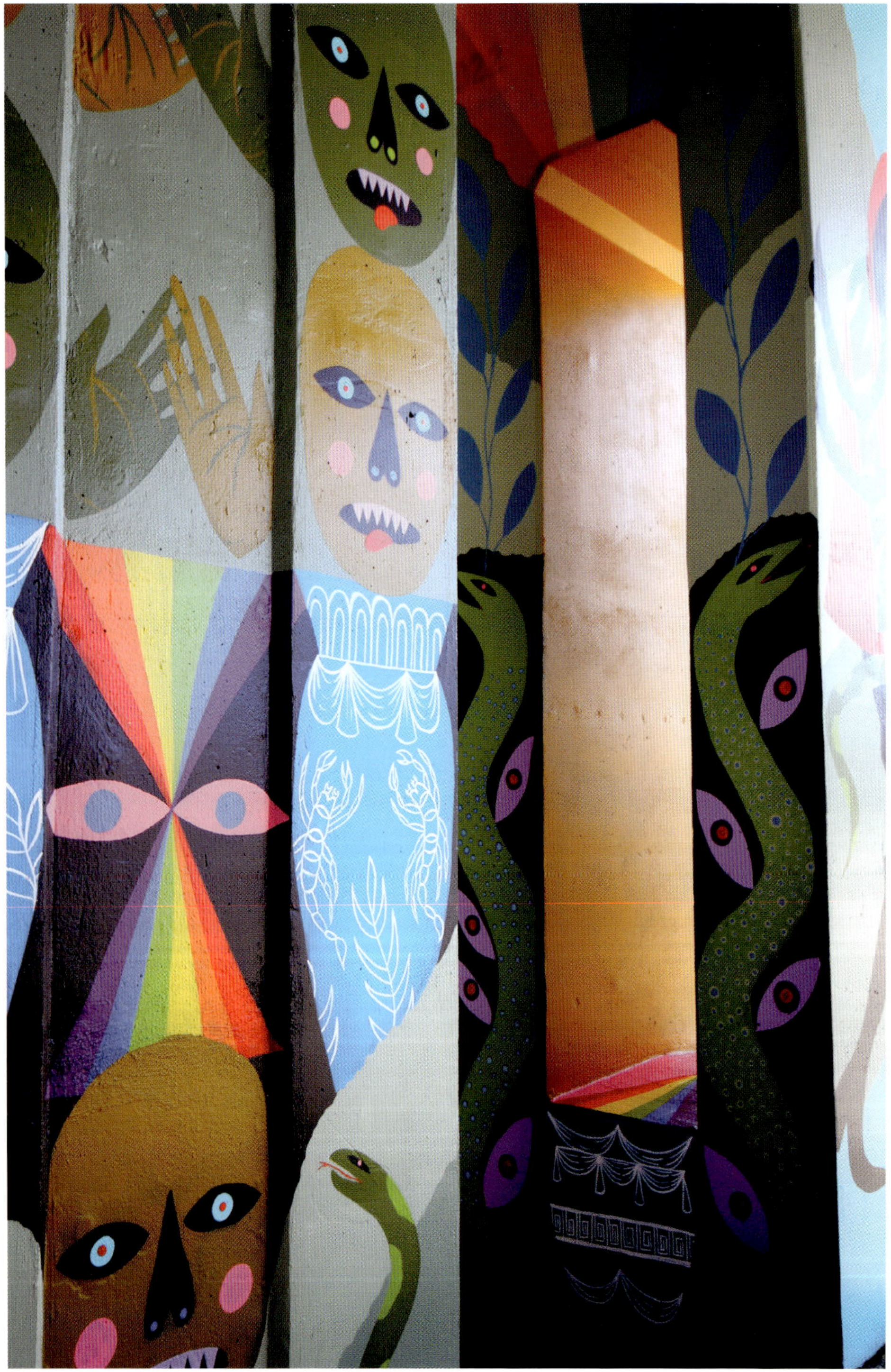

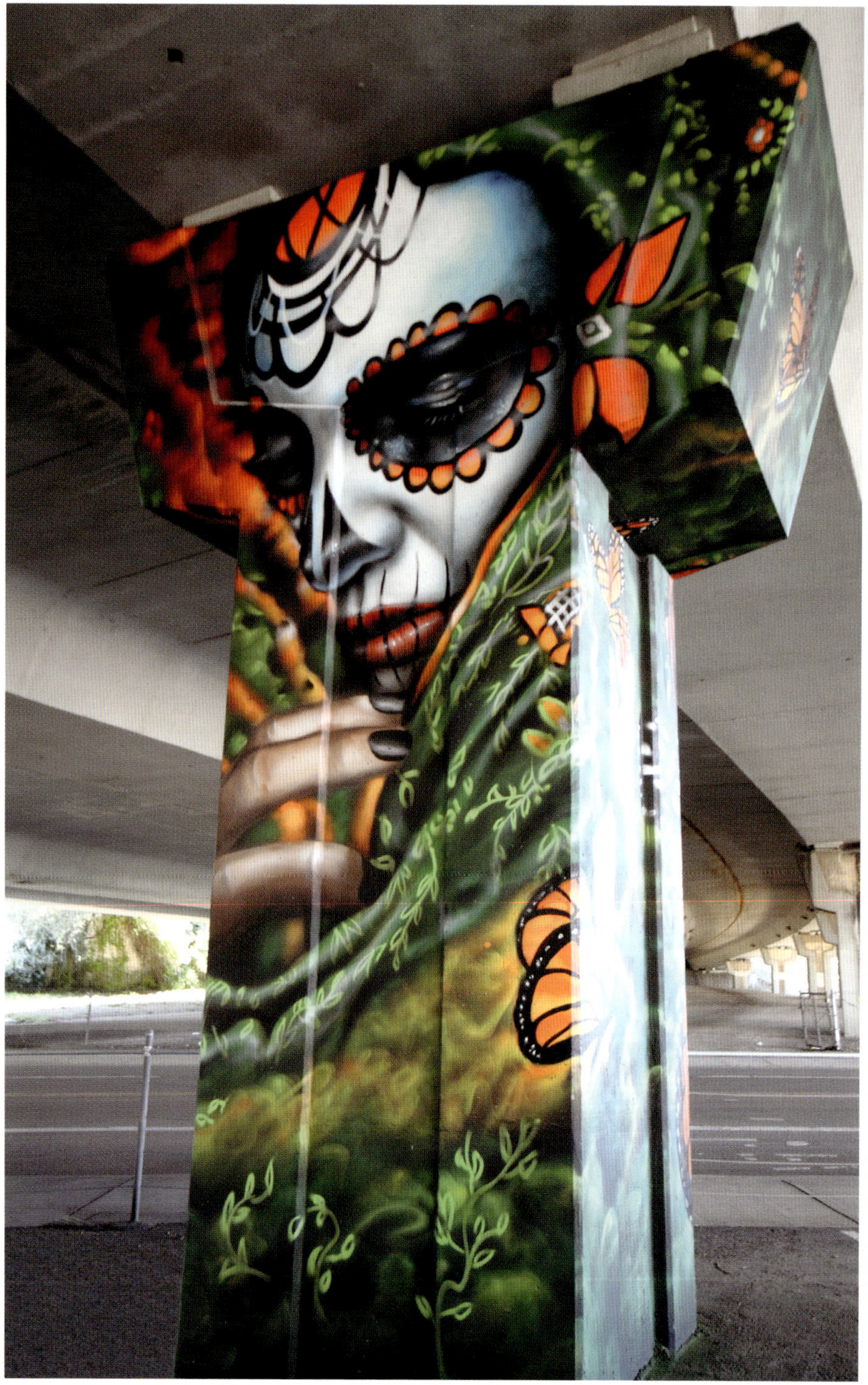

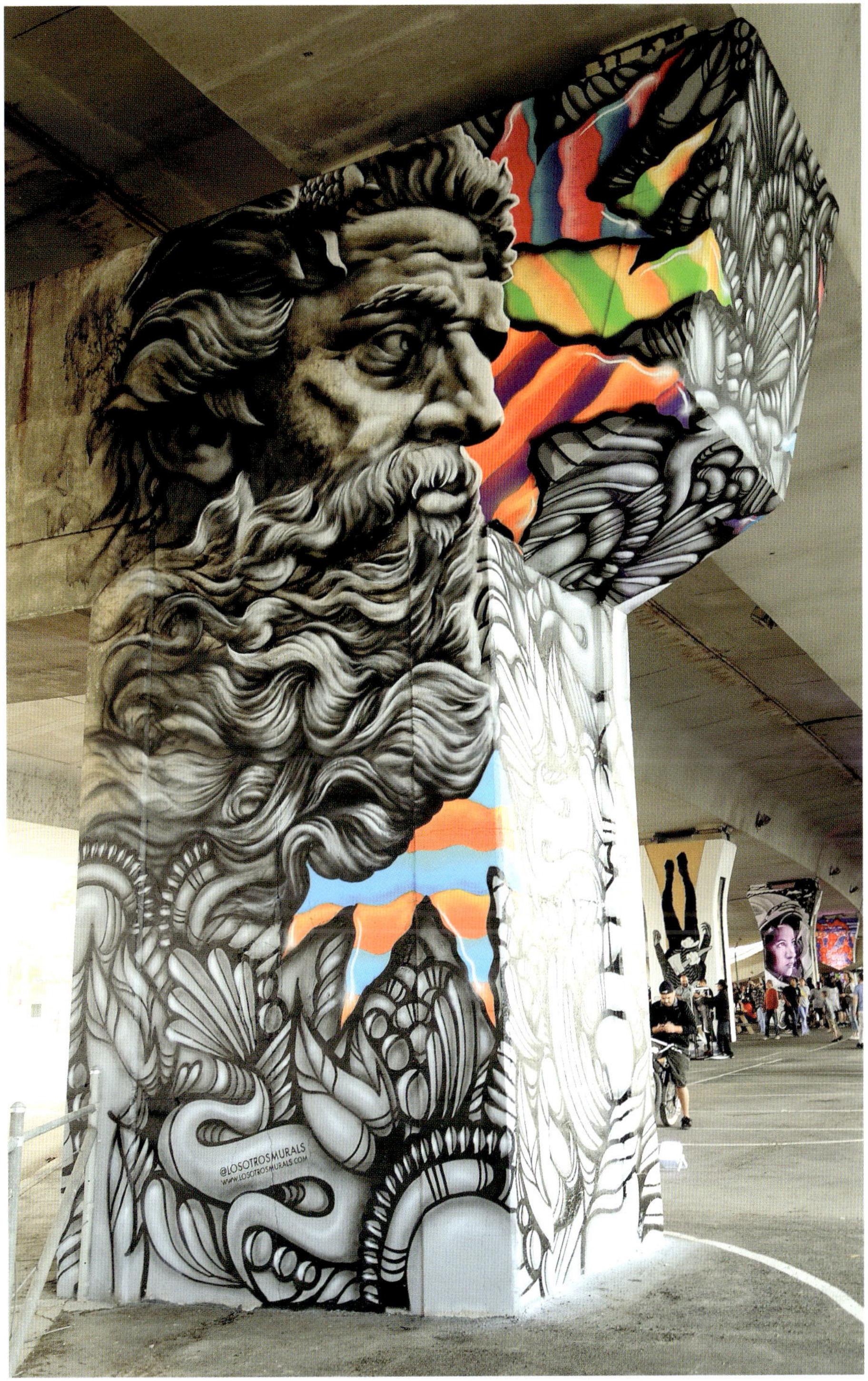

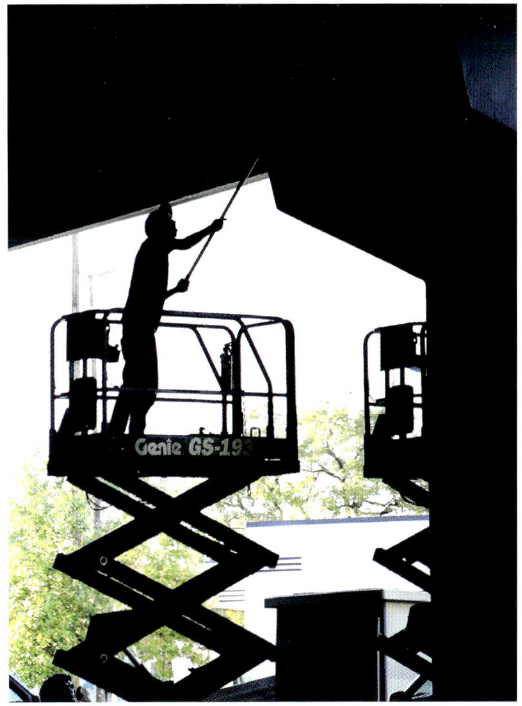

OPPOSITE PAGE
LEFT
Angela Fox, 2018.
San Antonio Street
Art Initiative.

RIGHT
Paul Garson, 2018.
San Antonio Street
Art Initiative.

THIS PAGE
LEFT
Untitled, 2018. Los
Otros. San Antonio
Street Art Initiative.

RIGHT
Shek at work on the
San Antonio Street Art
Initiative, 2018

SAN ANTONIO STREET ART INITIATIVE

The Strength of Street Art:
Constantly replaced
and replenished,
renewed, resurrected.
The Fate of a Short Shelf Life:
To be consumed hungrily,
and to feed the growth of new buds,
more hunger, more banquets
of the soul.

CENTER and RIGHT
Untitled, 2018. Mike "Comp" Arguello. Each of the four sides of this column represents a different phase in this young Latina's life and dreams. San Antonio Street Art Initiative.

BELOW
Mike "Comp" Arguello, 2018. San Antonio Street Art Initiative.

OPPOSITE PAGE
TOP LEFT
Untitled, 2018, Suzy González. San Antonio Street Art Initiative.

TOP RIGHT
Untitled, 2018. Scotch! San Antonio Street Art Initiative.

BOTTOM LEFT
Untitled, 2018. Eva Sánchez. San Antonio Street Art Initiative.

BOTTOM CENTER
Untitled, 2018. Andy Benavides. San Antonio Street Art Initiative.

BOTTOM RIGHT
Untitled, 2018. Robert Tatum. San Antonio Street Art Initiative.

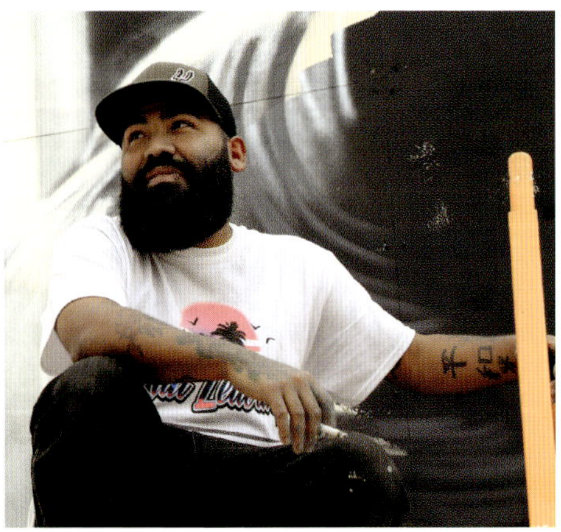

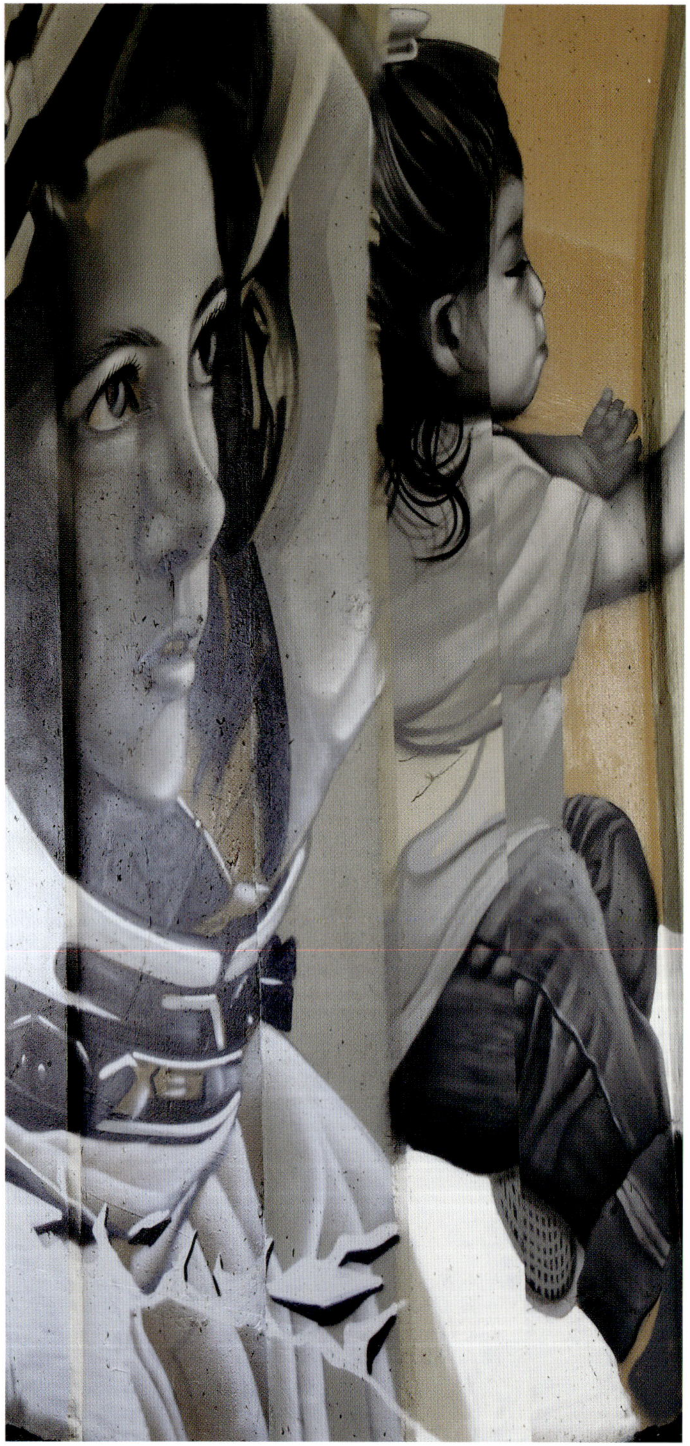

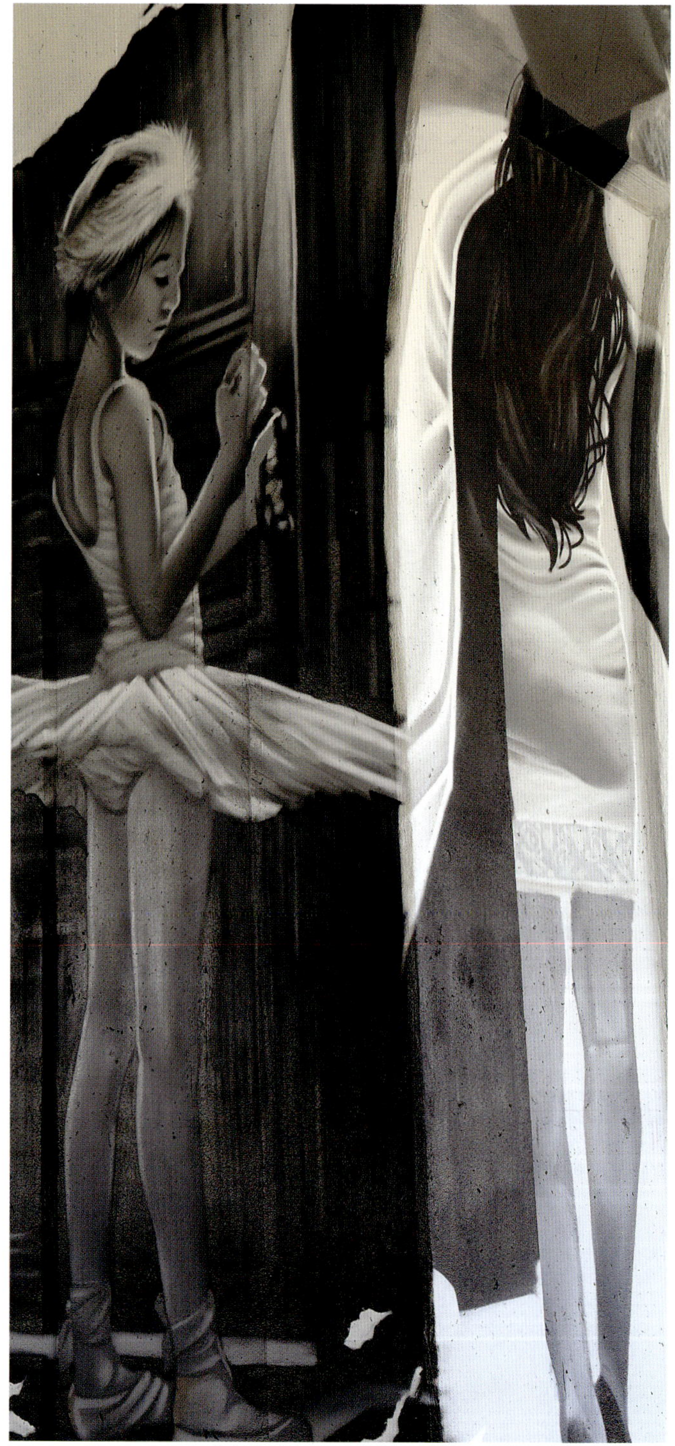

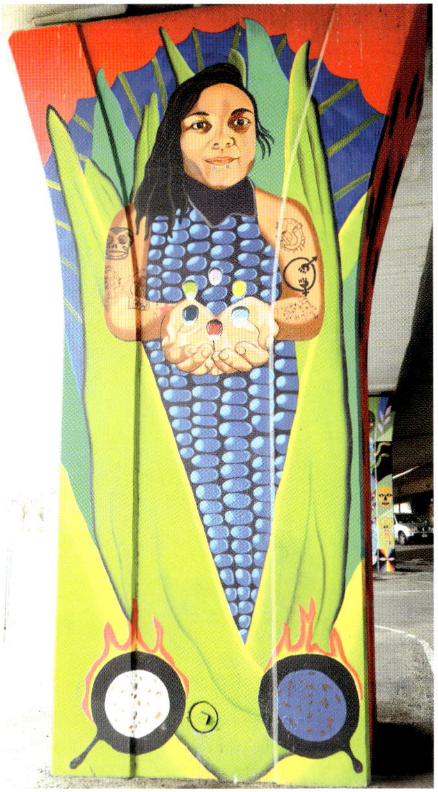

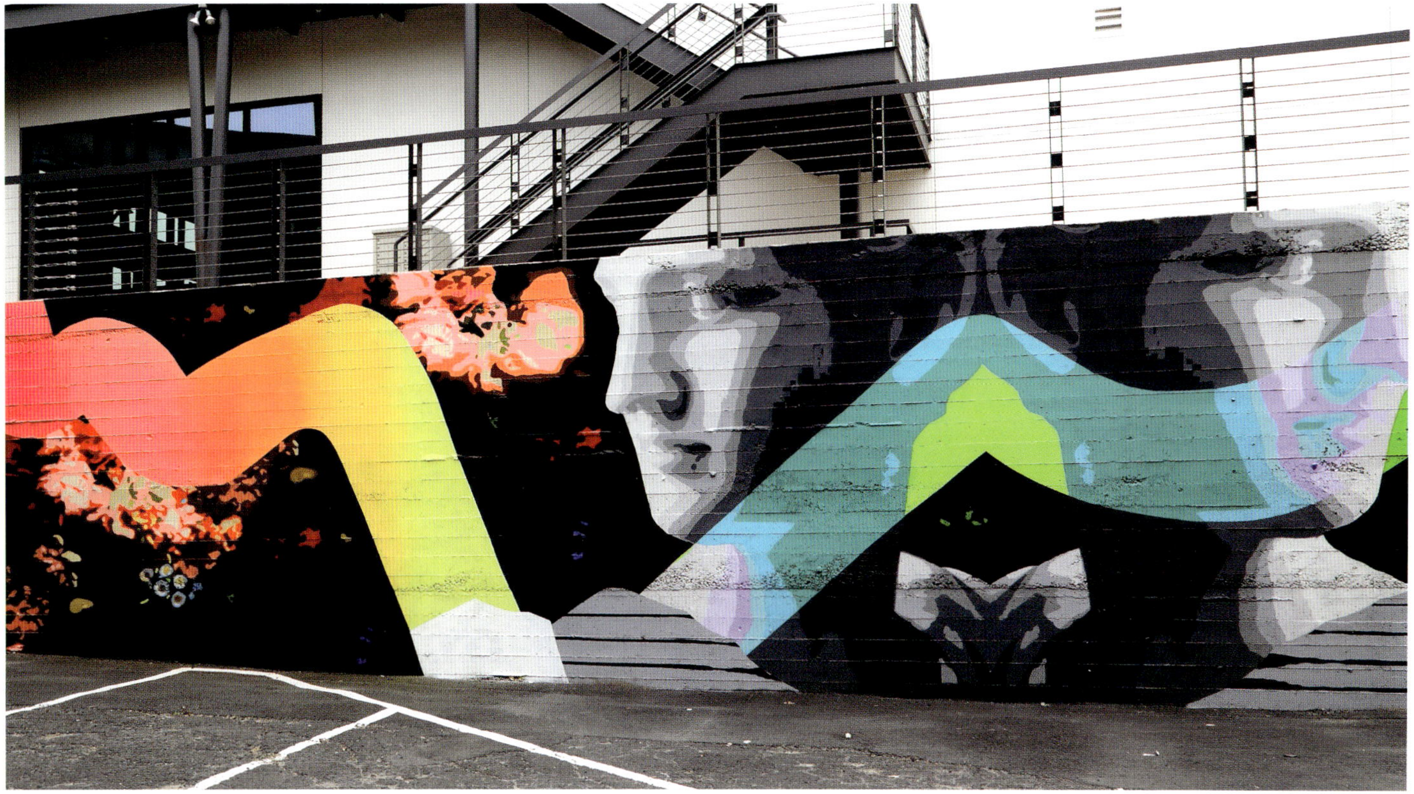

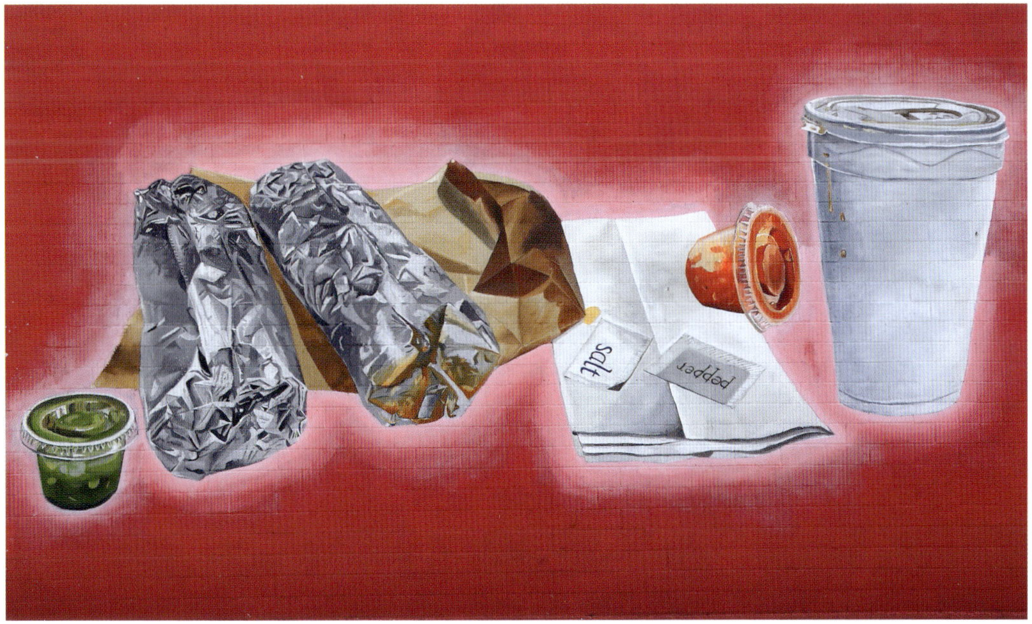
salt
pepper

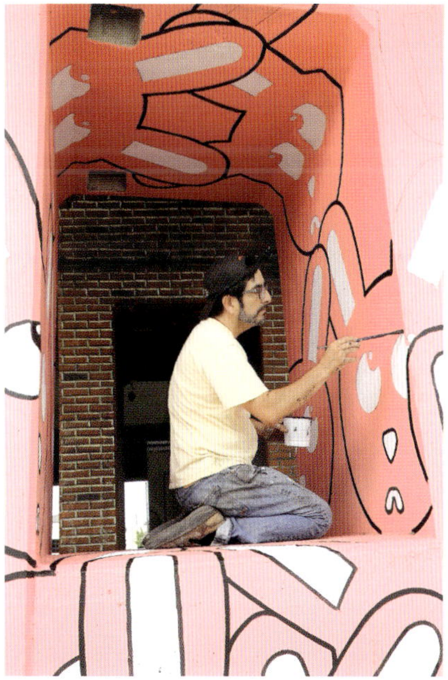

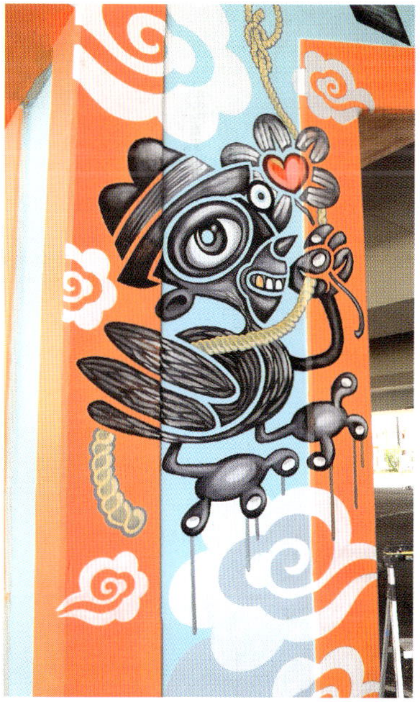

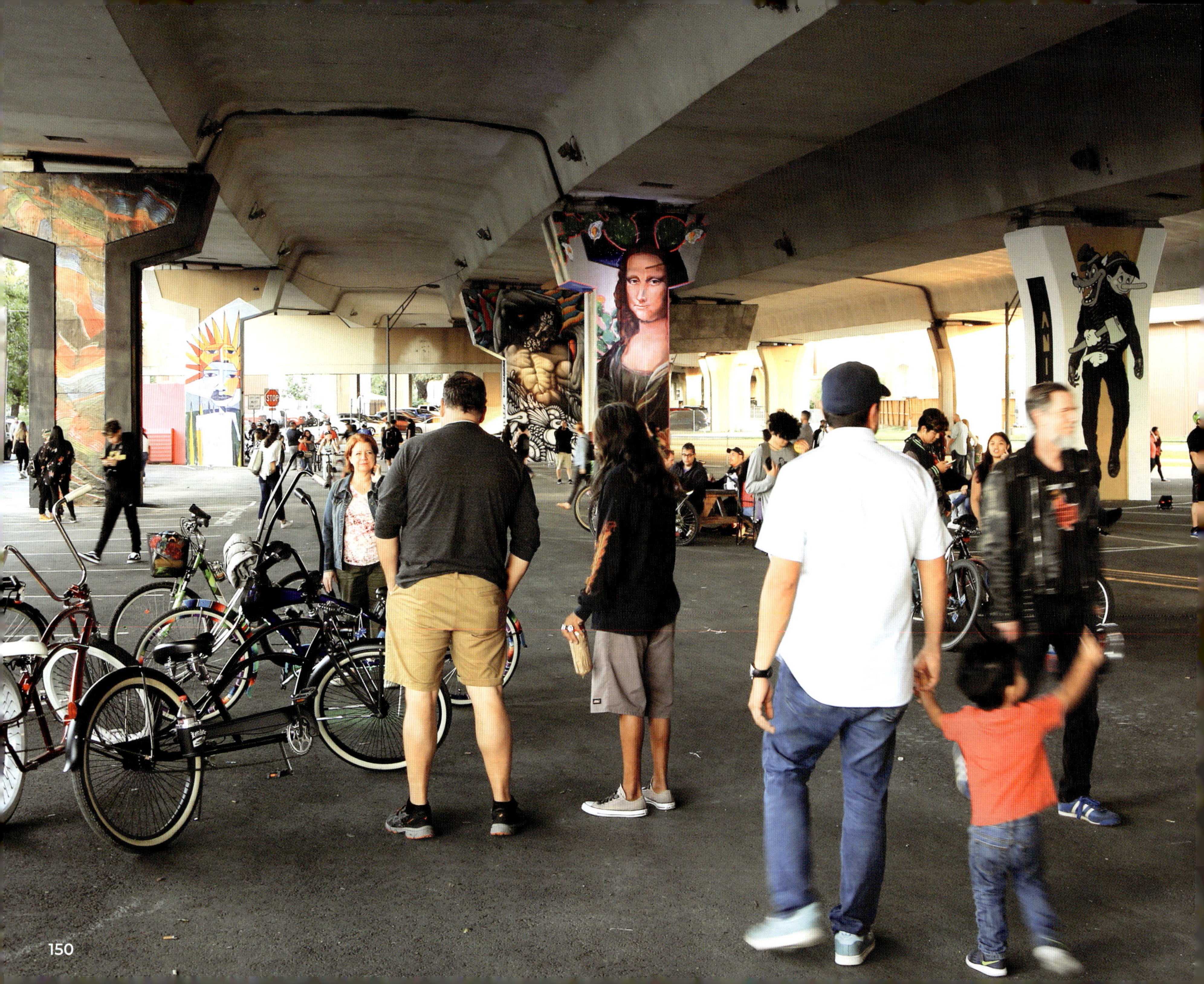

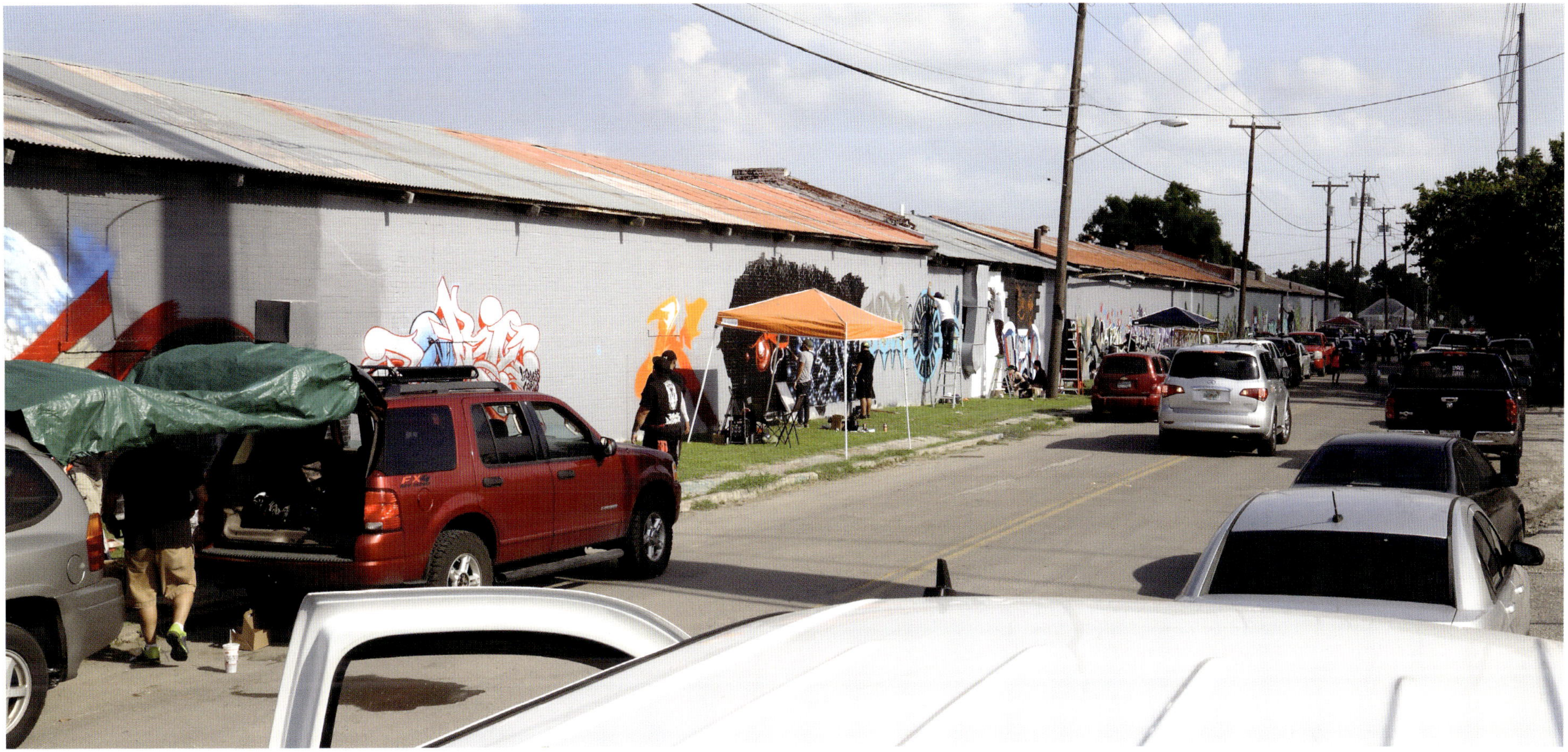

OPPOSITE PAGE
The San Antonio Street Art Gallery under the IH 35 overpass at N. St. Mary's Street. San Antonio Street Art Initiative.

THIS PAGE
Graffiti Meet-Up, 2016. Hoefgen Avenue and Carolina Street.

GRAFFITI ARTISTS MEET-UP

Artists appear from everywhere,
They fill our soul
and decorate our hearts.
Artistas del Pueblo making Arte del Pueblo
for us, with us, and about us.

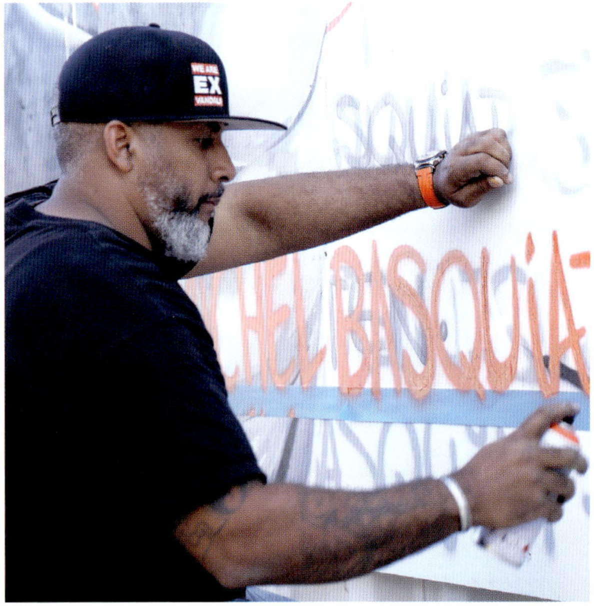

TOP LEFT
Untitled, 2019. Albertus Joseph (Queens, New York). Essex Modern City Art Project.

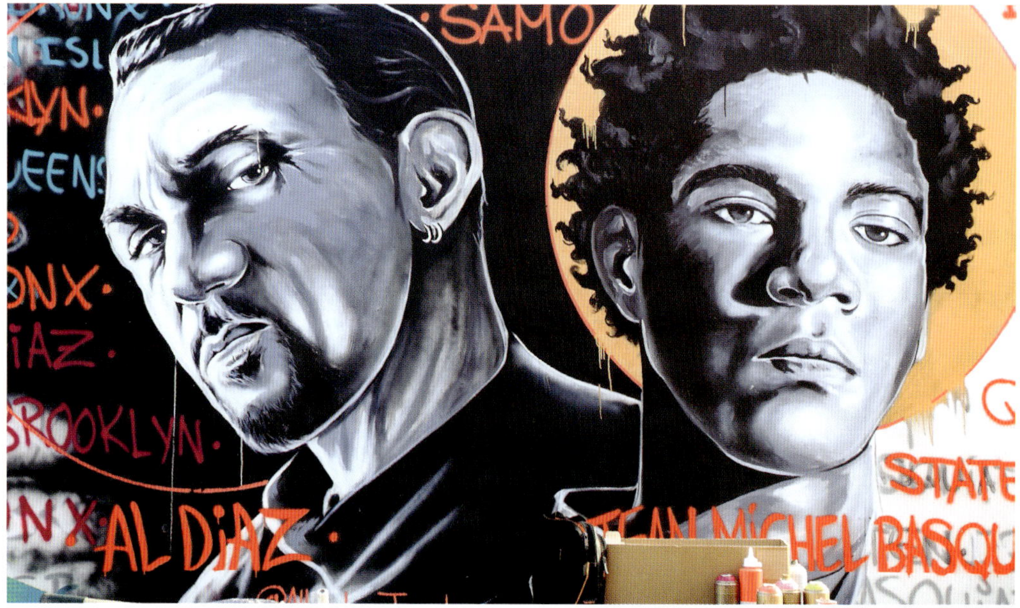

TOP RIGHT
Untitled, 2019. Albertus Joseph (Queens, New York). Essex Modern City Art Project.

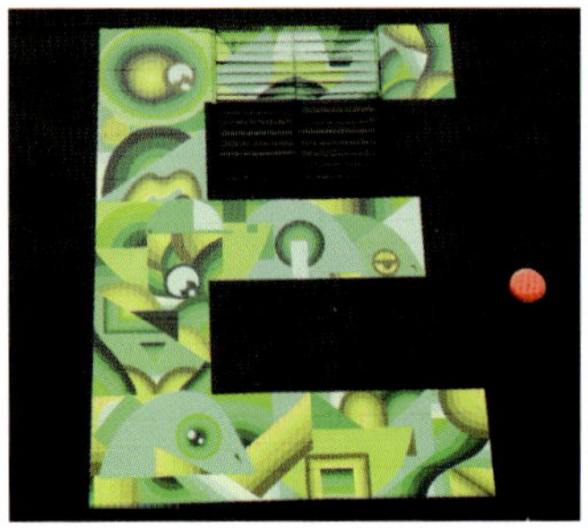
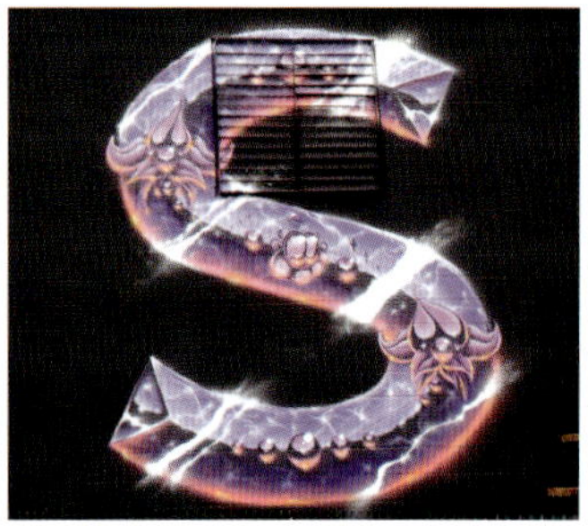
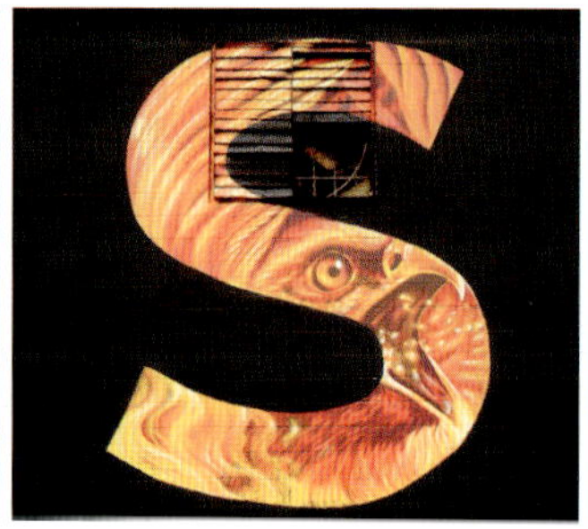
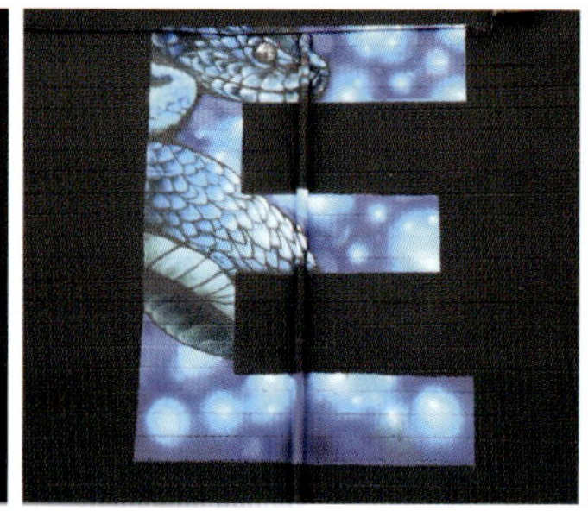
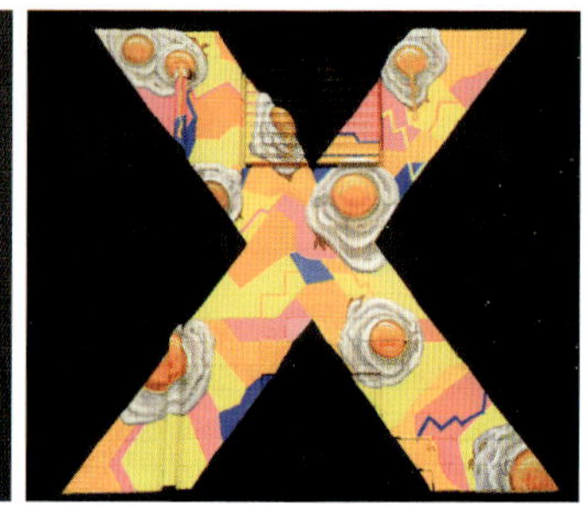

CENTER FROM LEFT TO RIGHT
Untitled, 2019. "Risk." Essex Modern City Art Project.

Untitled, 2019. "Delete." Essex Modern City Art Project.

Untitled, 2019. Paul Garson. Essex Modern City Art Project.

Untitled, 2019. "Warnuts." Essex Modern City Art Project.

Untitled, 2019. Ana Hernández. Essex Modern City Art Project.

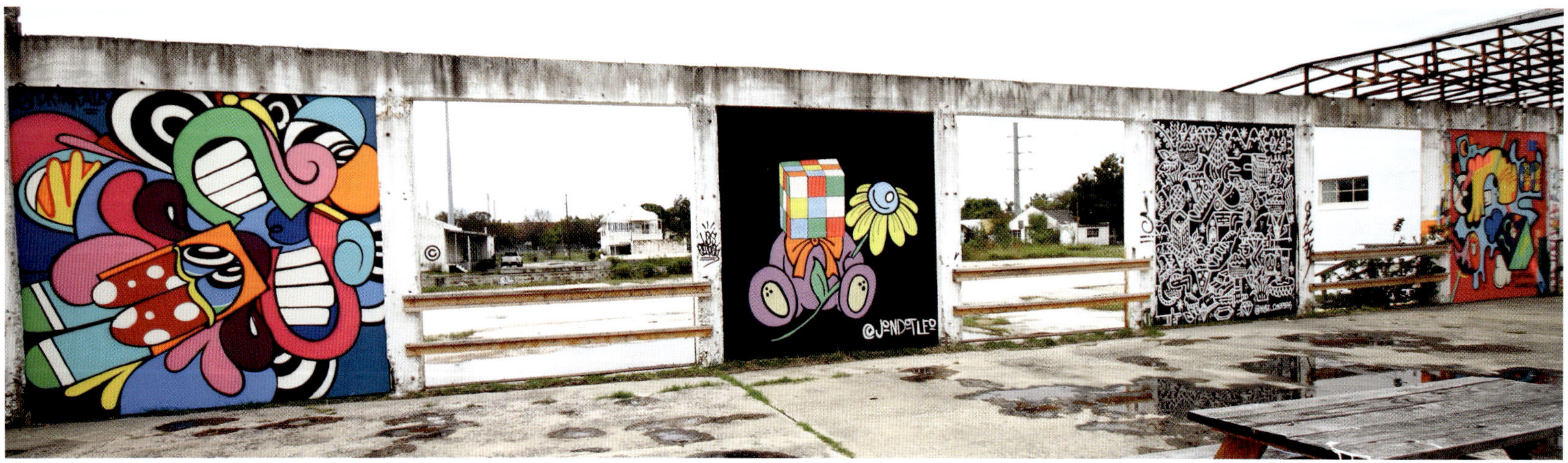

BOTTOM
Essex Modern City Art Project, 2018–19.

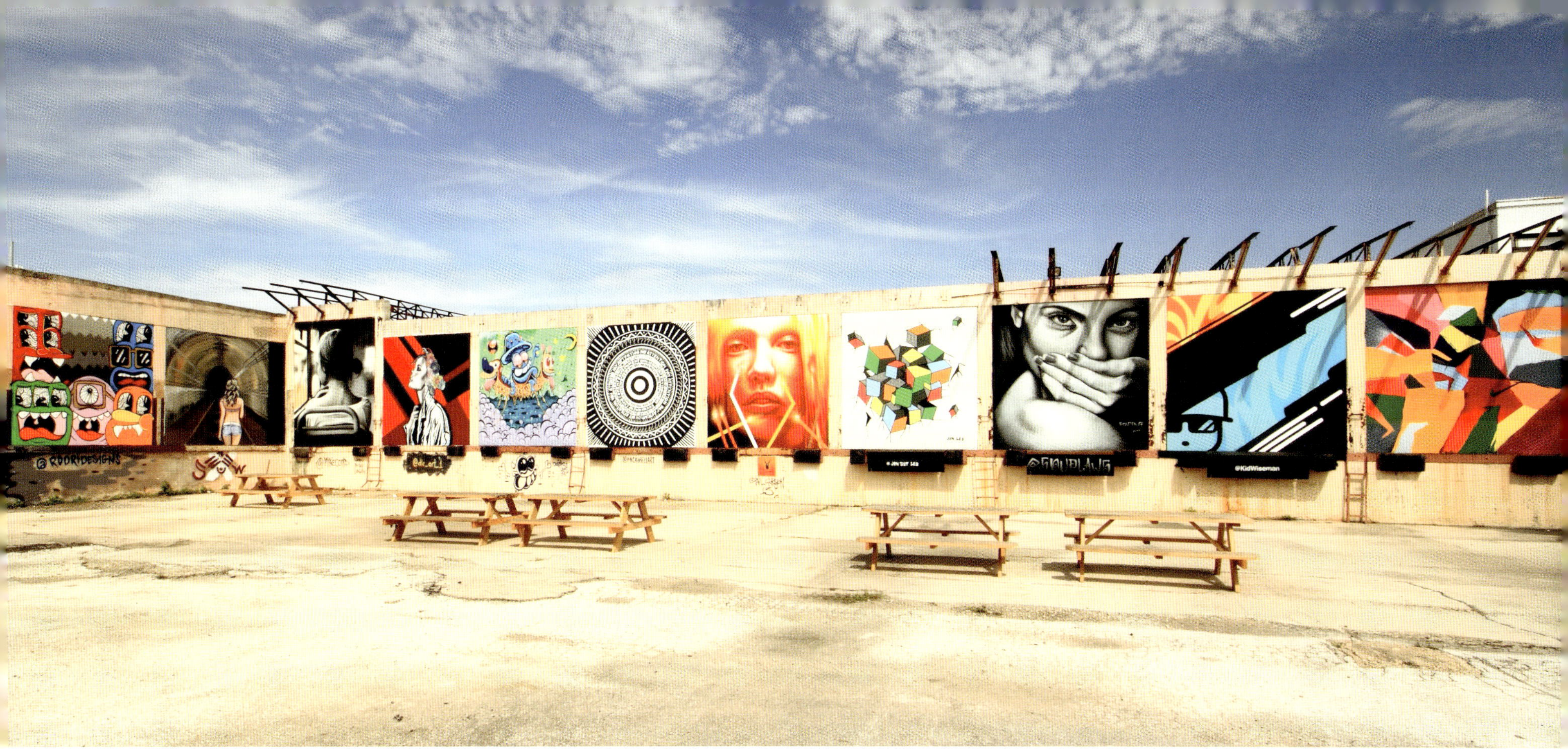

Essex Modern City Art Project (EMCAP), Jorge Miguel et al., 2018–19. Essex and S. Cherry Streets.

ESSEX, A MOVING MOSAIC OF MURALS & MOMENTS

What happens when an architect turns over a property of old cement foundations to the hands and minds of artists? What happens when they collect their works in a moving, changing, interacting mosaic of murals? What happens when Art is in the moment, and open to all?
ESSEX!

LEFT
Untitled, 2019.
Samina. Essex and
S. Cherry Streets.

RIGHT
I'll Forever Wish,
2018. WRDSMTH.
Essex City Modern
Art Project.
Essex and
S. Cherry Streets.

OPPOSITE PAGE
Untitled, 2018.
Cassidy Fritts.
Essex and
S. Cherry Streets.

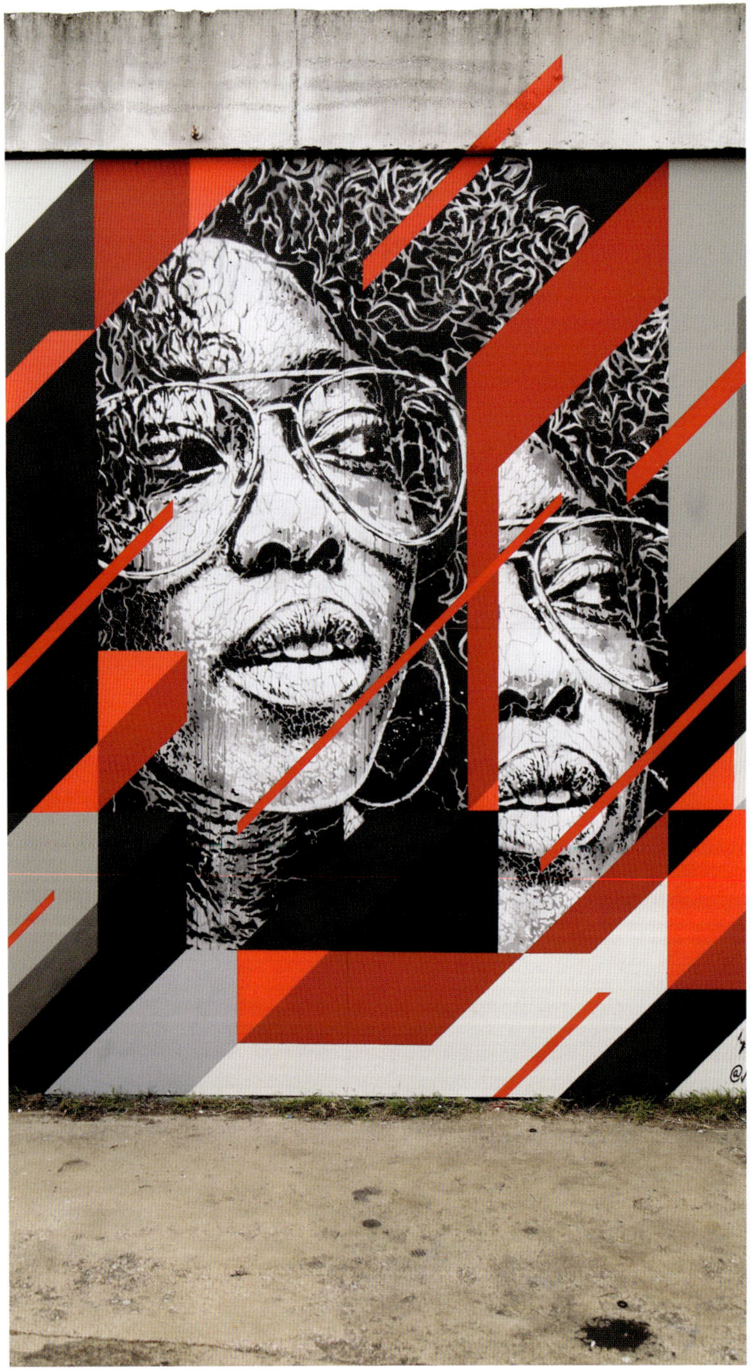

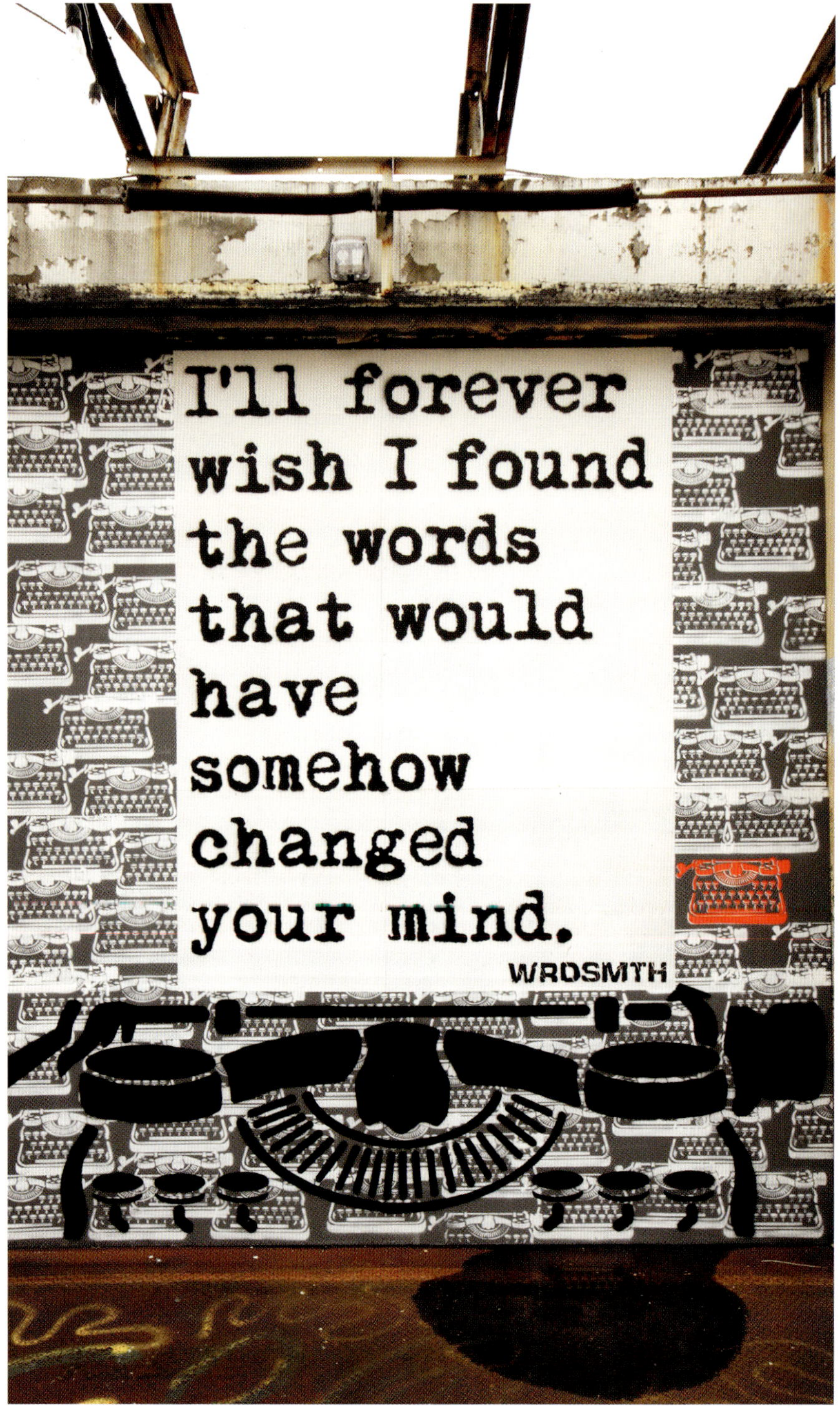

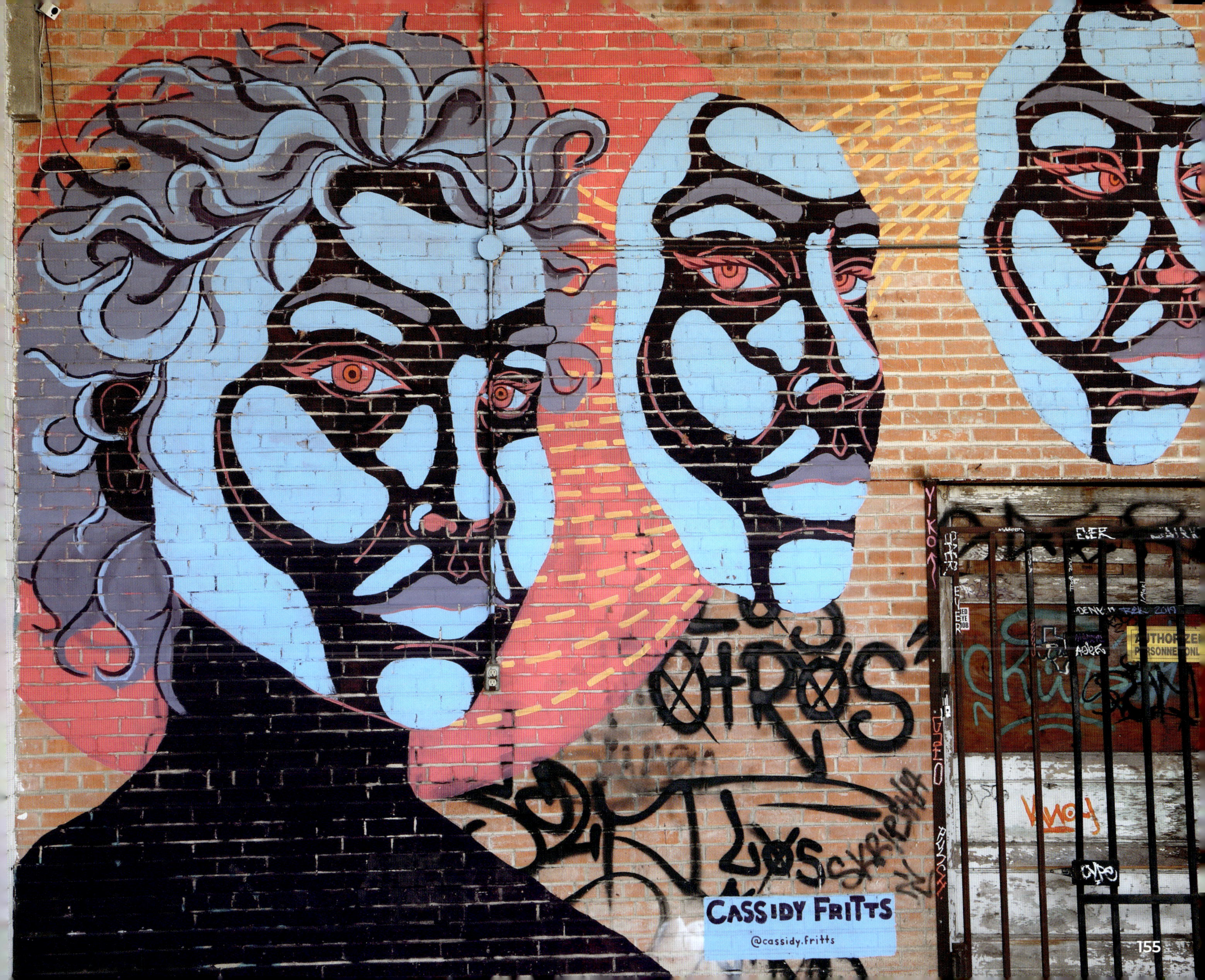
LOS OTROS
CASSIDY FRITTS
@cassidy.fritts

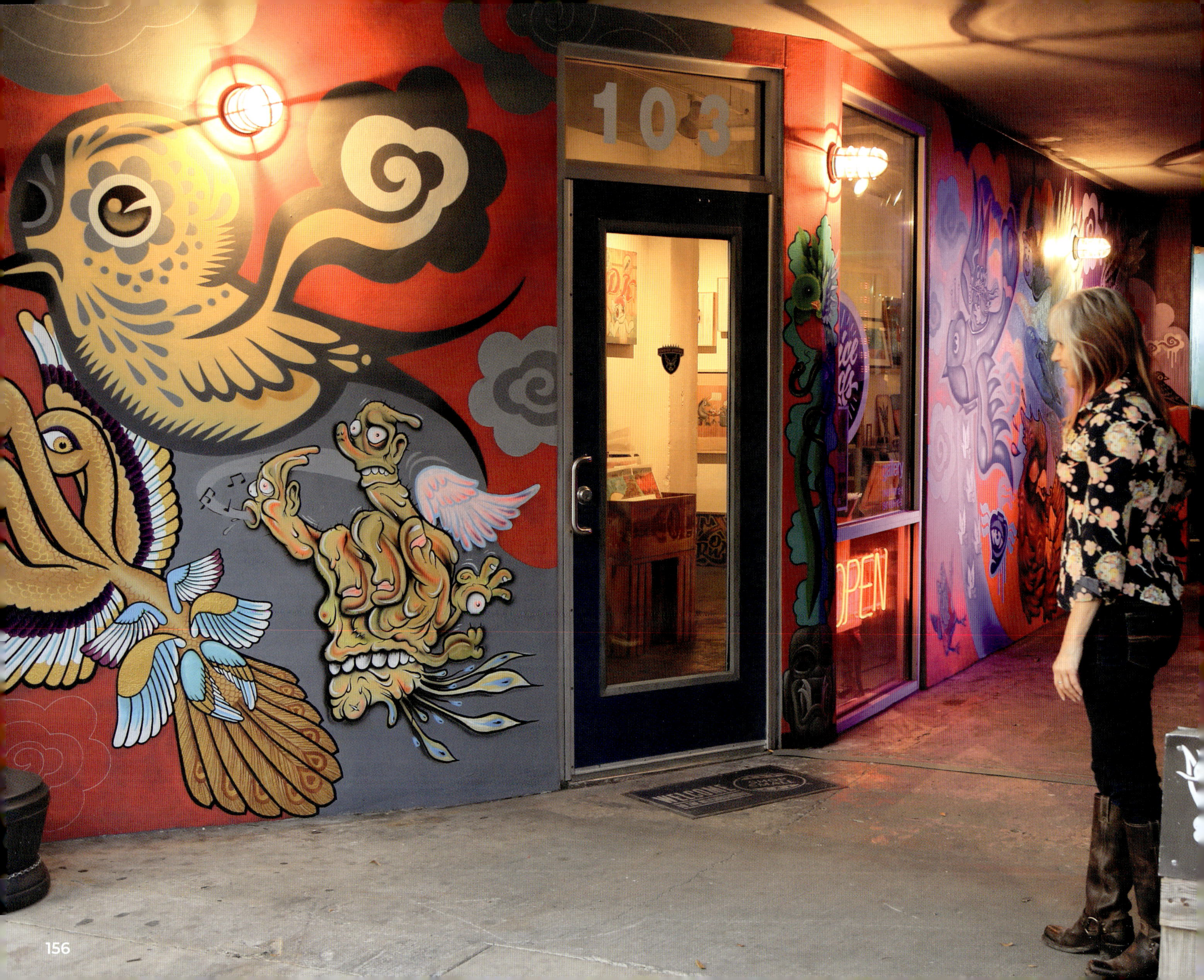
103
OPEN

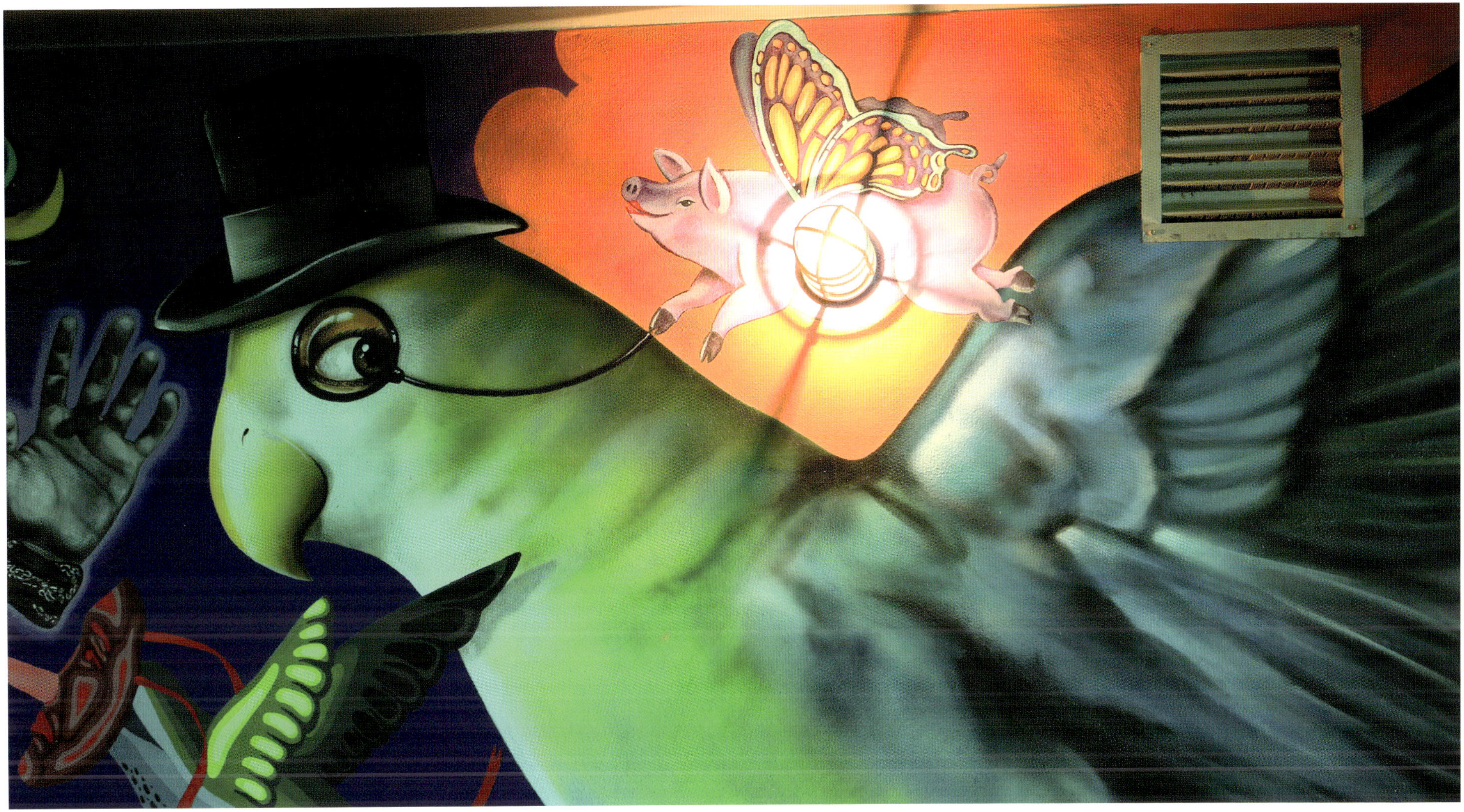

OPPOSITE PAGE
Birds of a Feather, 2018. Robert Tatum et al. Blue Star Arts Complex.

THIS PAGE
Birds of a Feather, 2018. Paul Garson and Carole Martelle. Blue Star Arts Complex.

BIRDS OF A FEATHER

paint together
at the Blue Star Arts Complex.

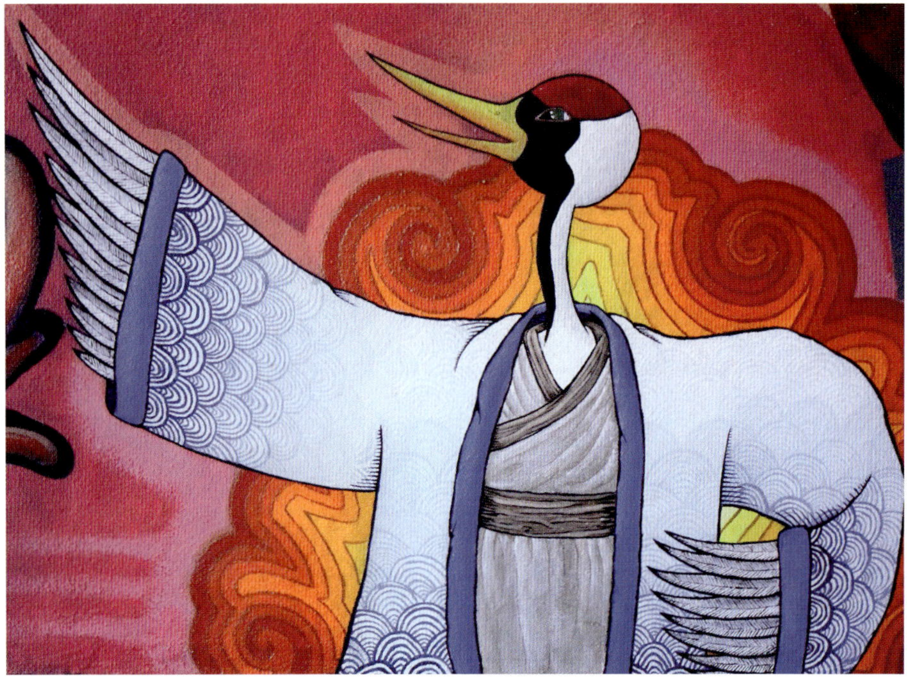

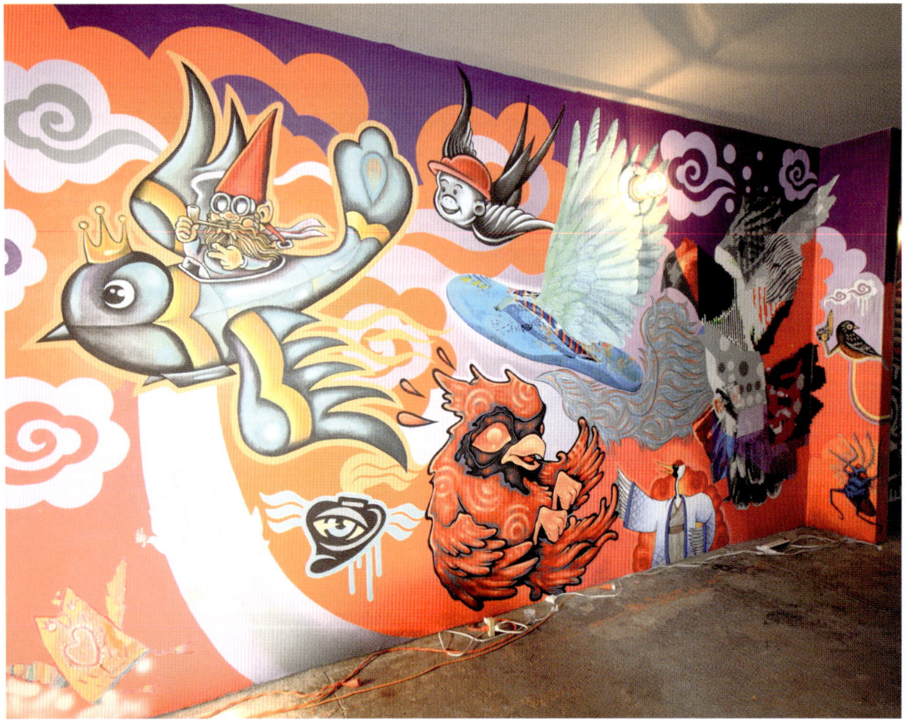

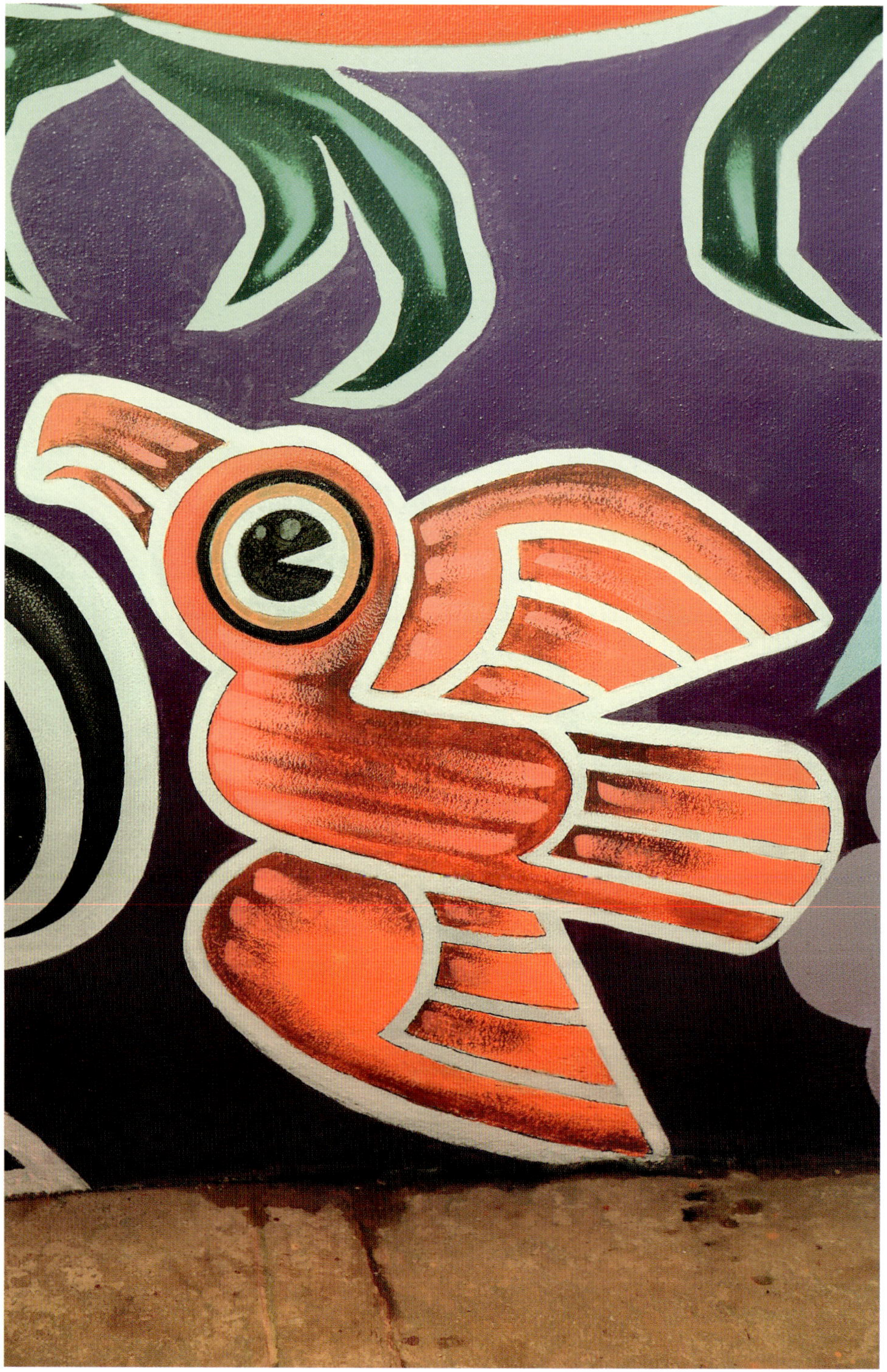

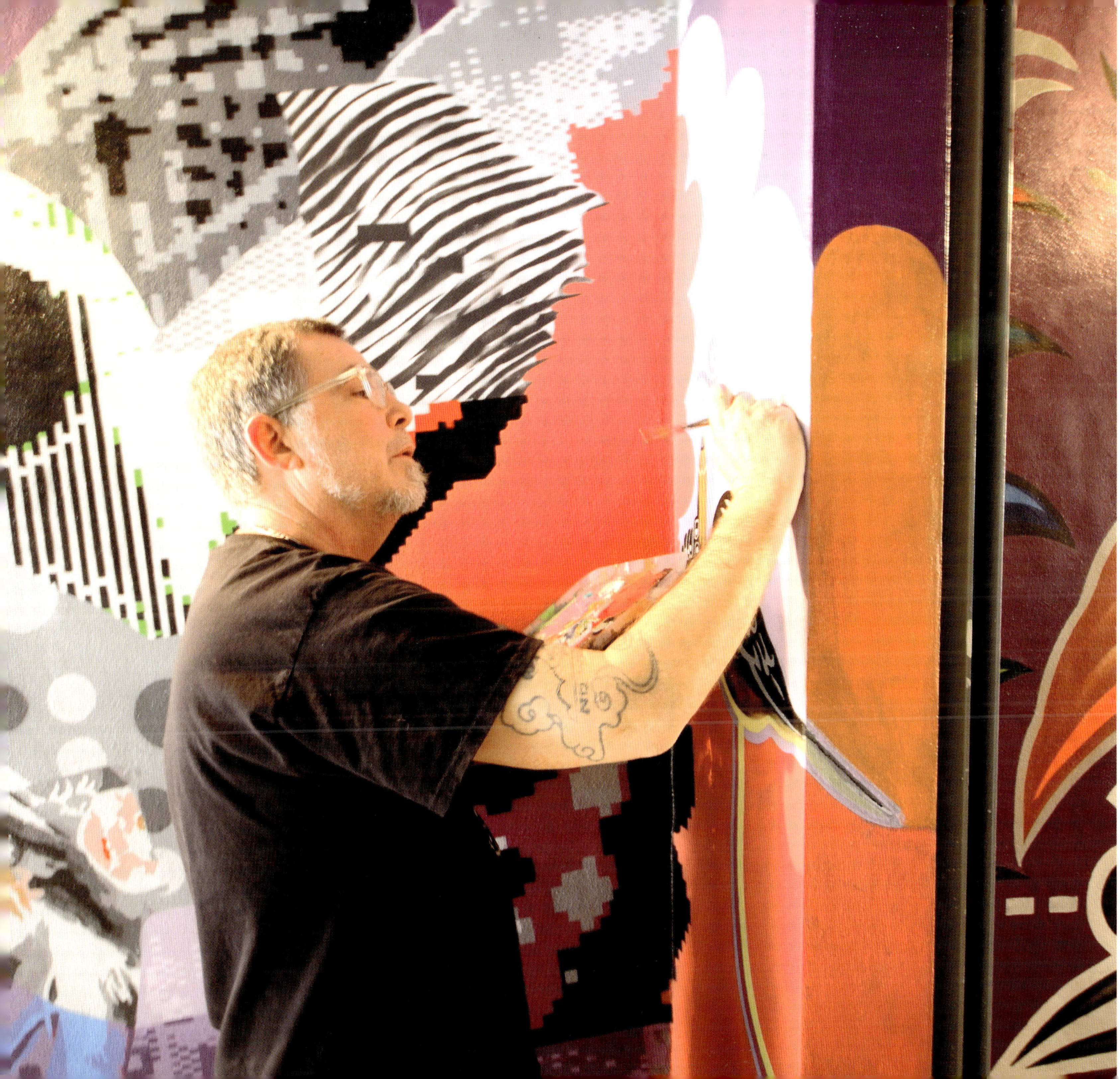

OPPOSITE PAGE
TOP LEFT
Birds of a Feather, 2018. Courtney Davis. Blue Star Arts Complex.

BOTTOM LEFT
Birds of a Feather, 2018. Robert Tatum et al. Blue Star Arts Complex.

RIGHT
Birds of a Feather, 2018. Robert Tatum. Blue Star Arts Complex.

THIS PAGE
Robert Tatum, working on *Birds of a Feather* at Blue Star Arts Complex

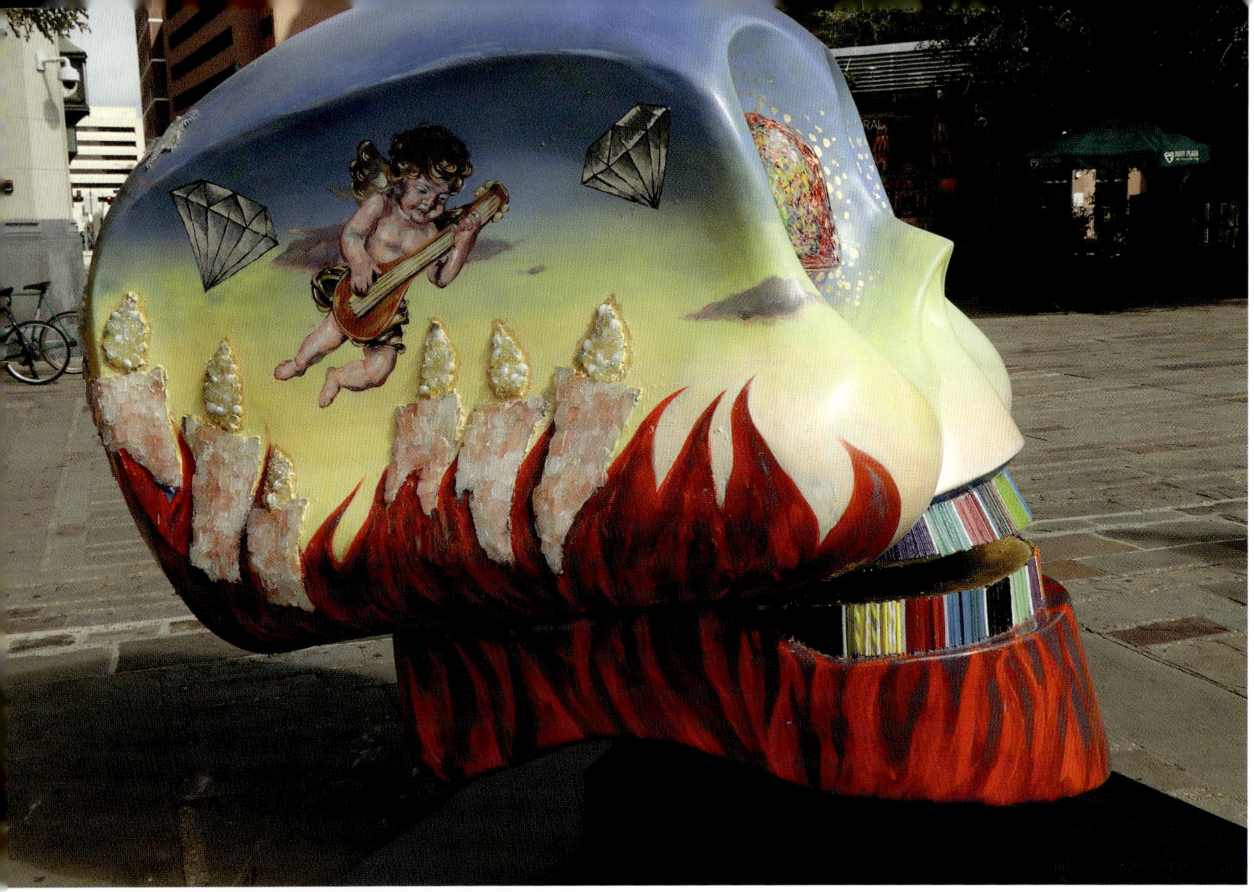

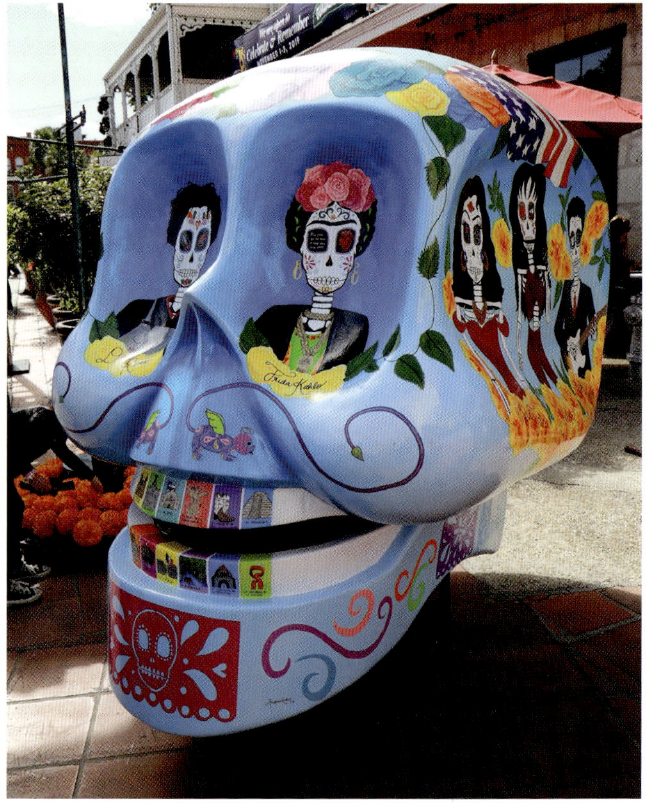

FESTIVALS & TEMPORARY INSTALLMENTS

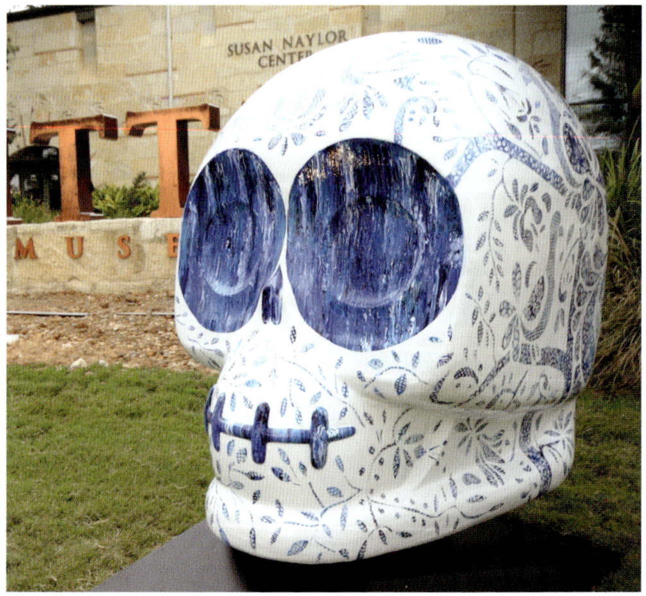

We are a city that loves the fiesta of life.
Good news or bad, we celebrate our way through.
Canta y No Llores, and life is for alegría.
So whether it's Fiesta or Luminaria or Día de los Muertos,
grab your hats and open your eyes—the Fiestas of Art are
everywhere, flickering in and out of our lives like butterflies
like hope
like joy.

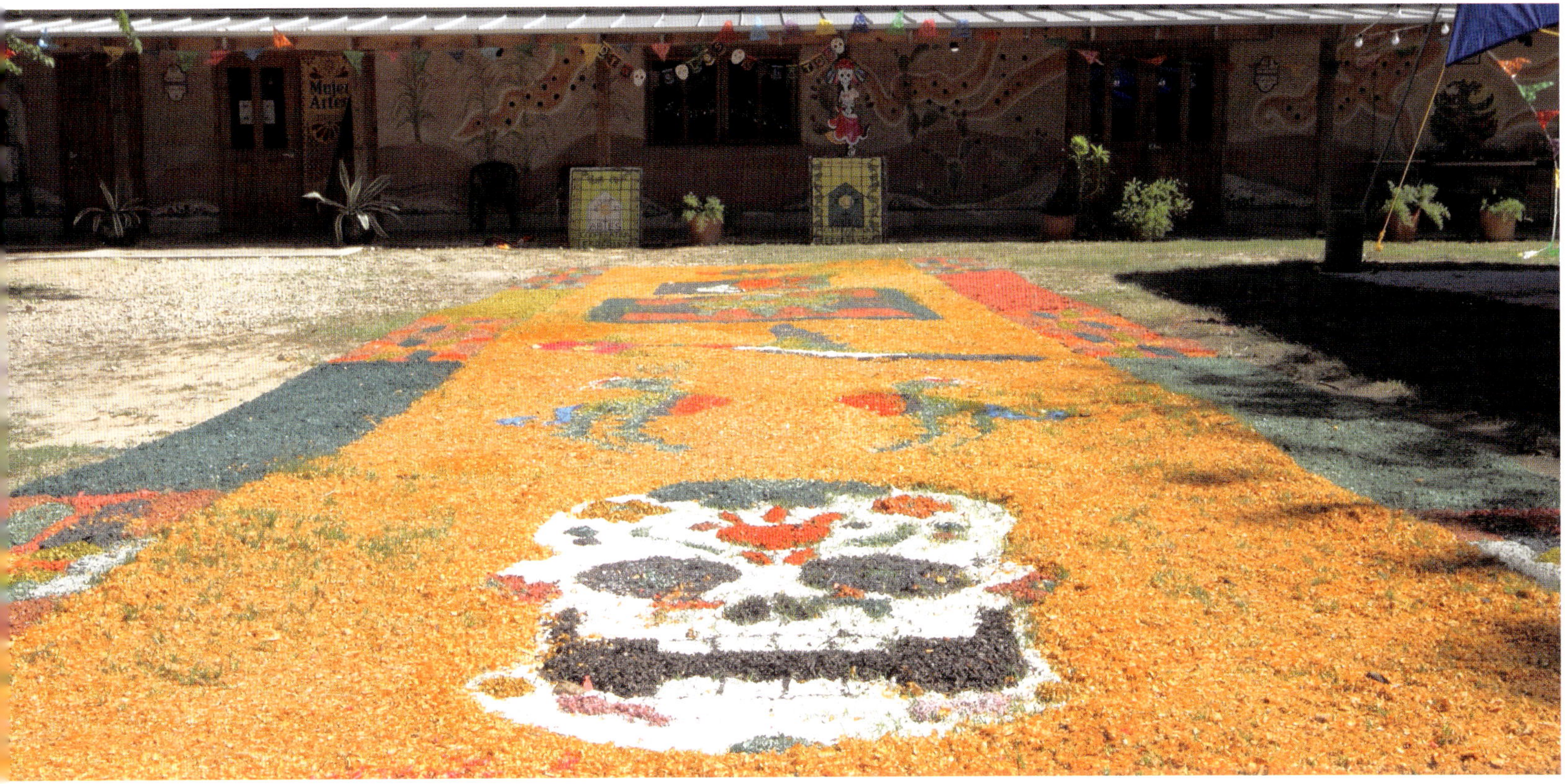

OPPOSITE PAGE
TOP LEFT
The Ascencion of Souls, 2019. Gini García.

TOP RIGHT
Untitled, 2019. Andrea Rotter. Day of the Dead Festival 2019.

BOTTOM RIGHT
Untitled, 2019. Jo Teruggi. Day of the Dead Festival.

THIS PAGE
TOP
Todos Somos Esperanza, 2018. (Translation: "We Are All Hope.") A Day of the Dead altar of flowers. MujerArtes Adobe Studio.

BOTTOM LEFT
Untitled, 2019. Le Yad. Day of the Dead Festival.

BOTTOM RIGHT
Mexico Punky, 2019. Paper King. Day of the Dead Festival

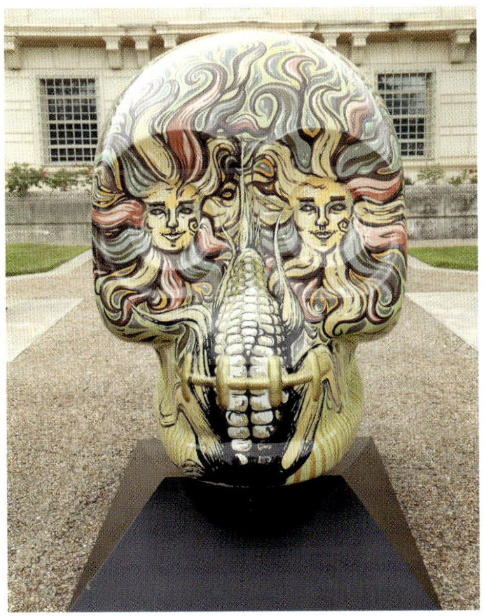

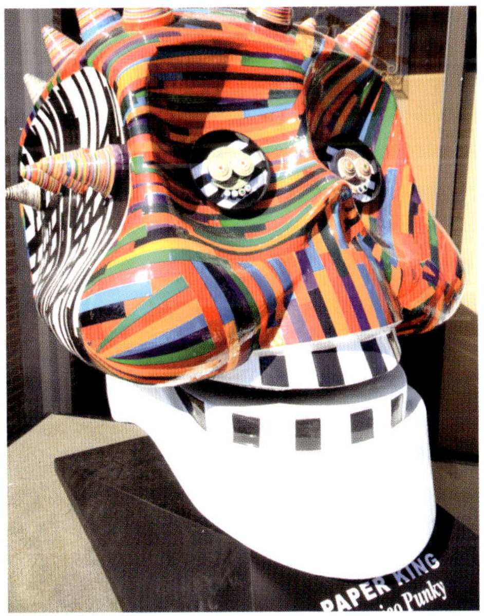

THE DAY OF THE DEAD / DÍA DE LOS MUERTOS

Today the Dead come to life, laughing
The Living dress like dead, paint their bones
And Everyone celebrates the beauty of life
through painted skulls and installations of *altares*.

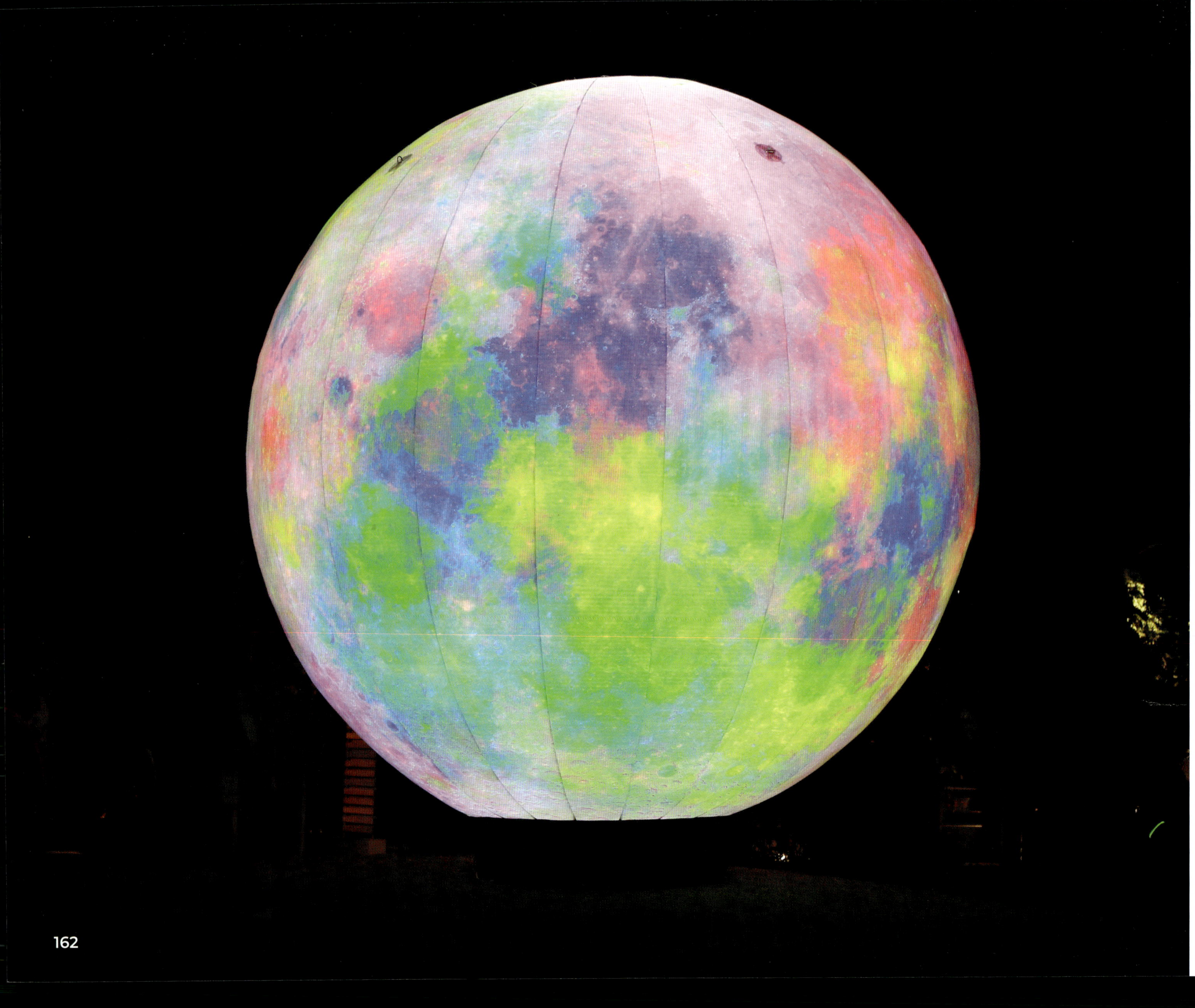

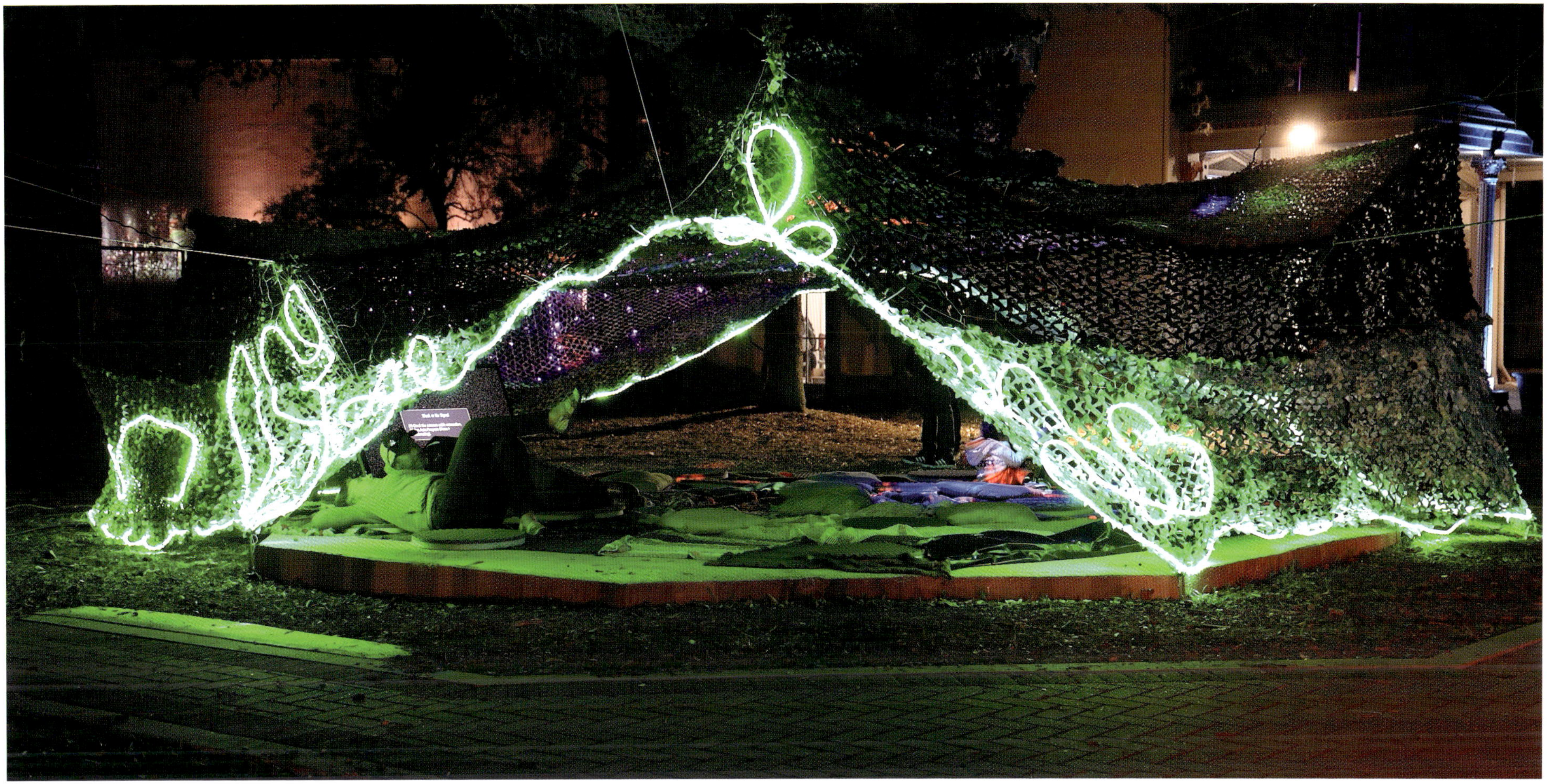

OPPOSITE PAGE
Mission Moon Glow, 2019. Tom Turner and Carol Cunningham Turner. Radiant sculptural and audio playscape. Luminaria 2019.

THIS PAGE
Asopomora, 2019. Olaniyi "AKIRASH" Akindia (Nigeria.) Textile technology art. Luminaria 2019.

LUMINARIA

A night of *luminarias*, tiny candles inside paper bags along our path,
our guiding lanterns to blaze new pathways, this yearly festival
of arts, innovation, and celebration honors our artists and their work.
A braid of light-strewn dancers from Urban-15 dances through the crowd,[1]
performers share from stages on the city streets,
and everywhere—art, light shows, art, exhibits, art, moving digital murals,
art—always a part of the San Antonio Spirit.

TOP
Untitled, 2017.
Gera Lozano.
Luminaria 2017.
Hemisfair Park.

BOTTOM LEFT
Neon Drive, 2016.
Iker Muro (Spain).
Nelson Street bridge.

BOTTOM LEFT
Don't Let Go, 2017.
Ruth Buentello.
Luminaria.

OPPOSITE PAGE
TOP
Powder, 2016.
Daniel Eime (Portugal).
Luminaria. Burnet
at Cherry Streets.

BOTTOM
Iluminados, 2016.
Ramón and Christian
Cárdenas ("Los Dos").
Luminaria. Hays
Street bridge.

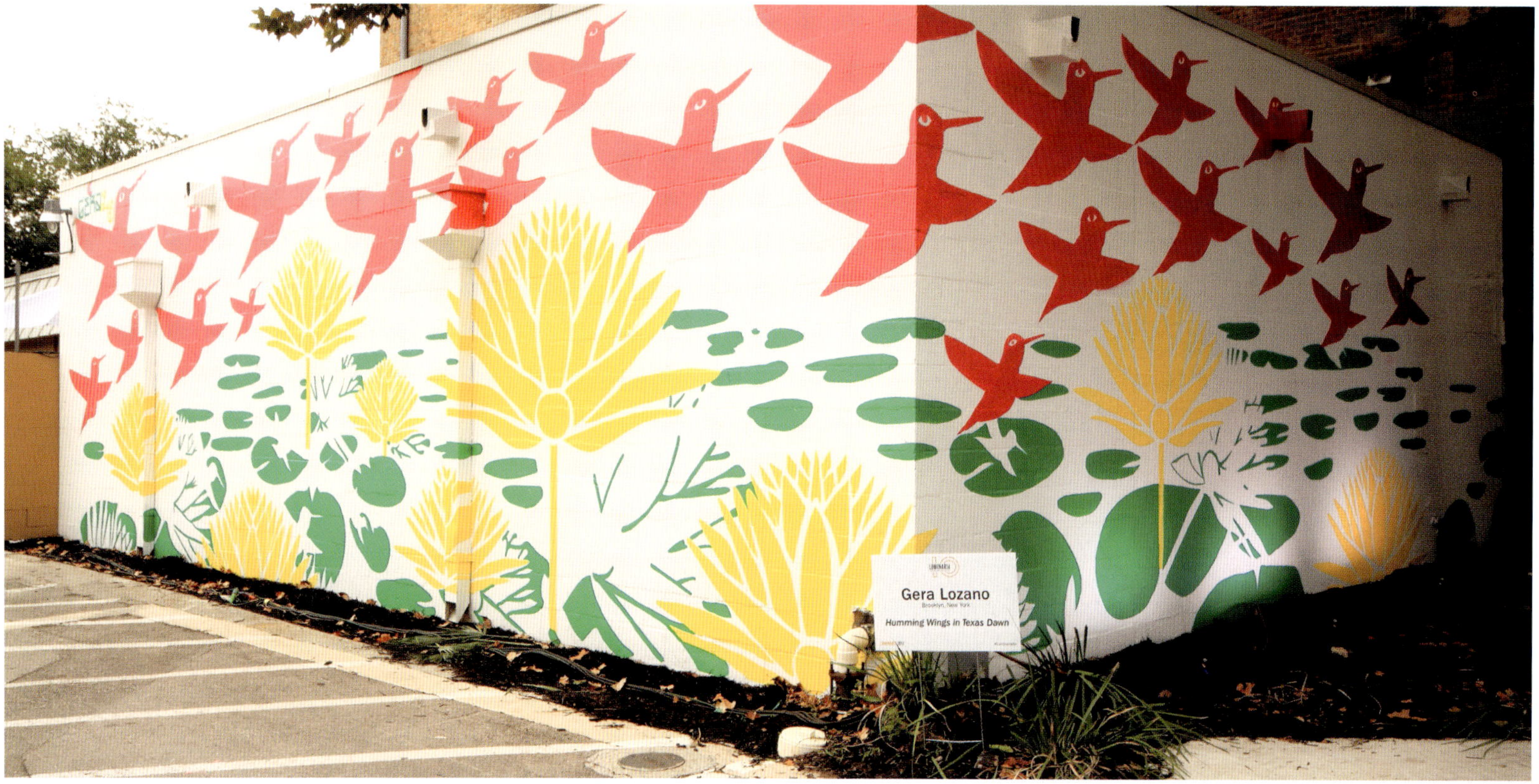

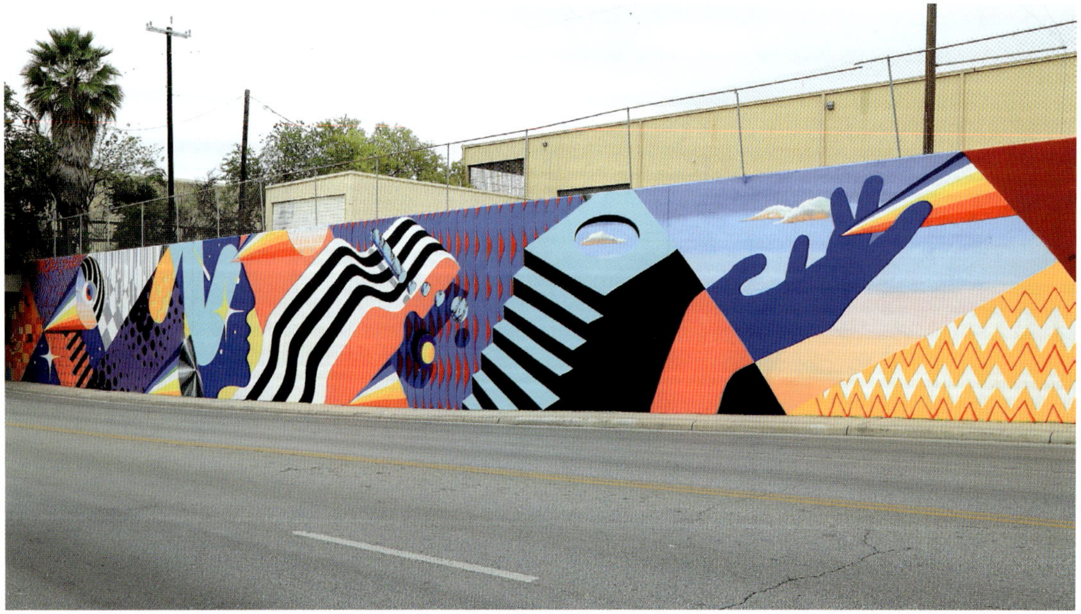

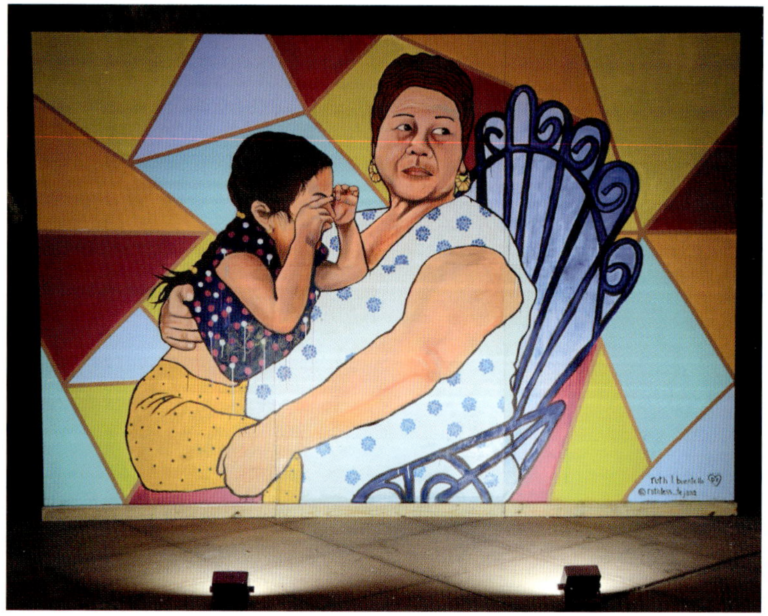

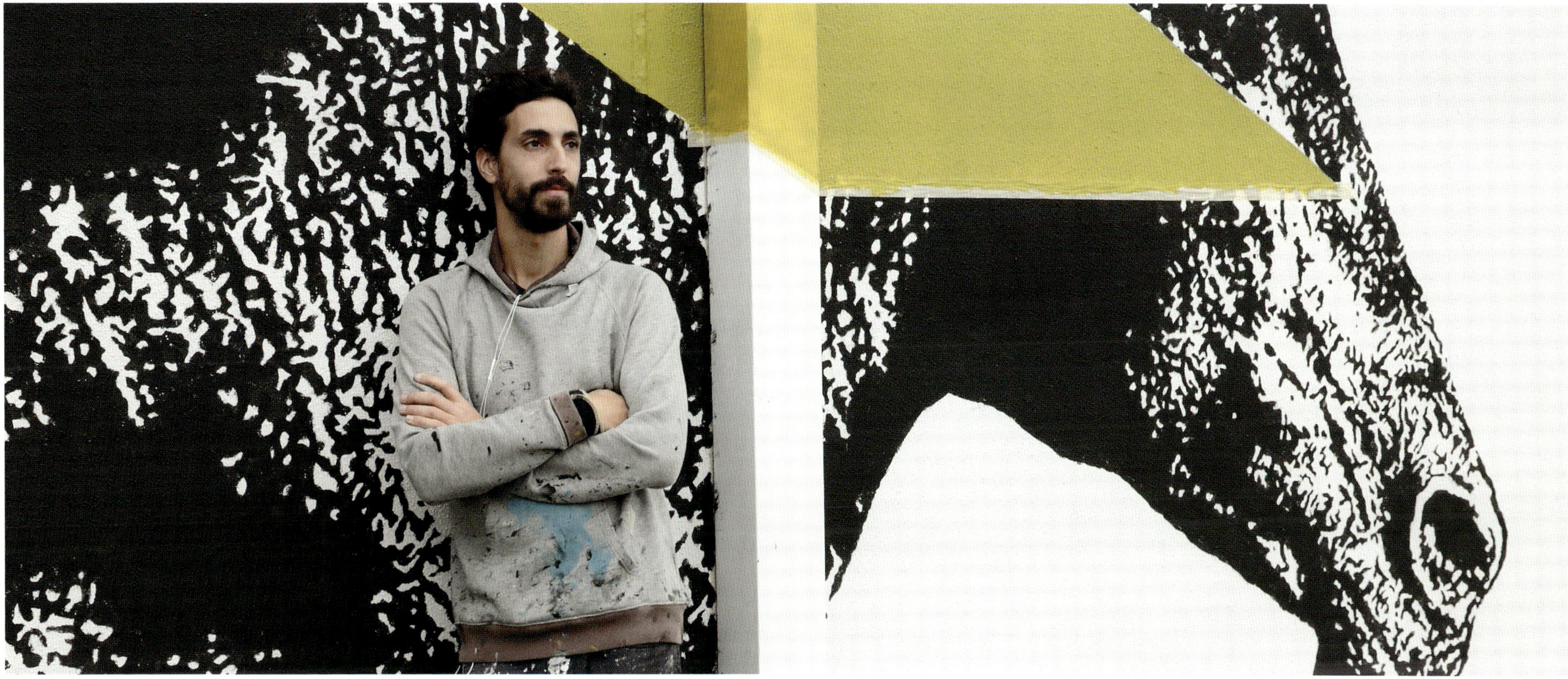

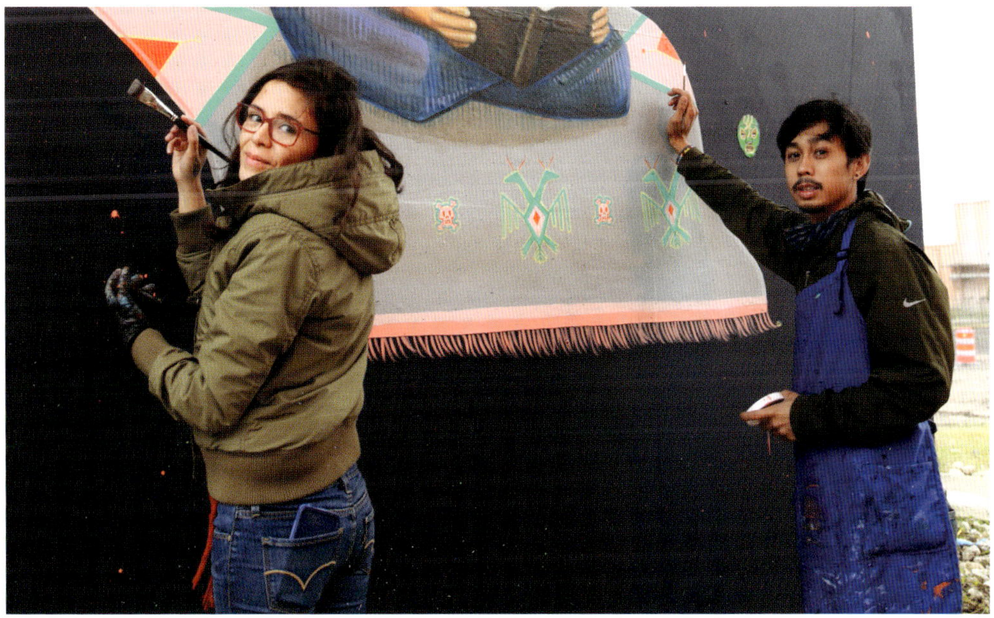

The street artist leaves an instant documentation
of the world in which we live,
clamors for social justice, reminds us
what we are and what we need.

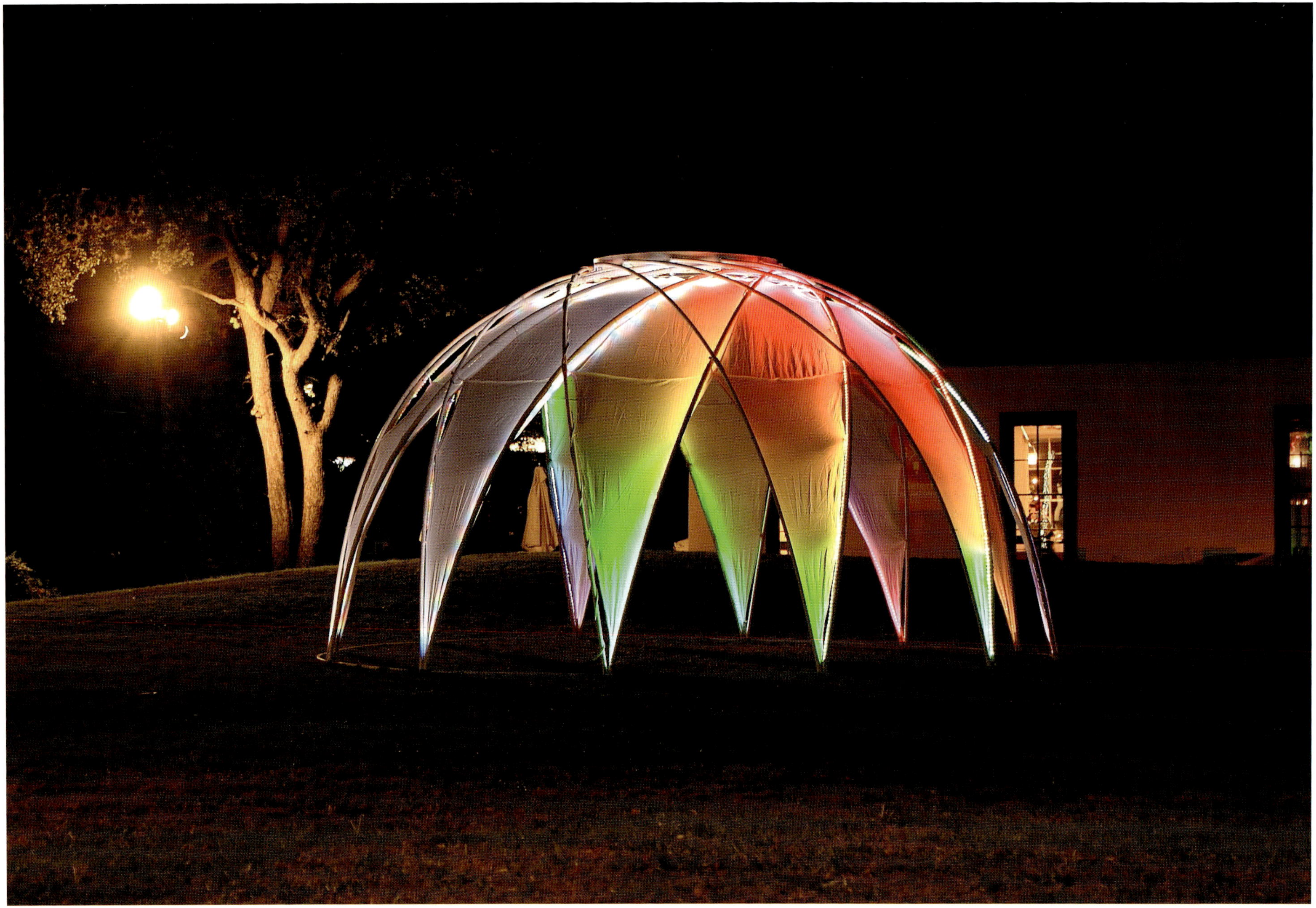

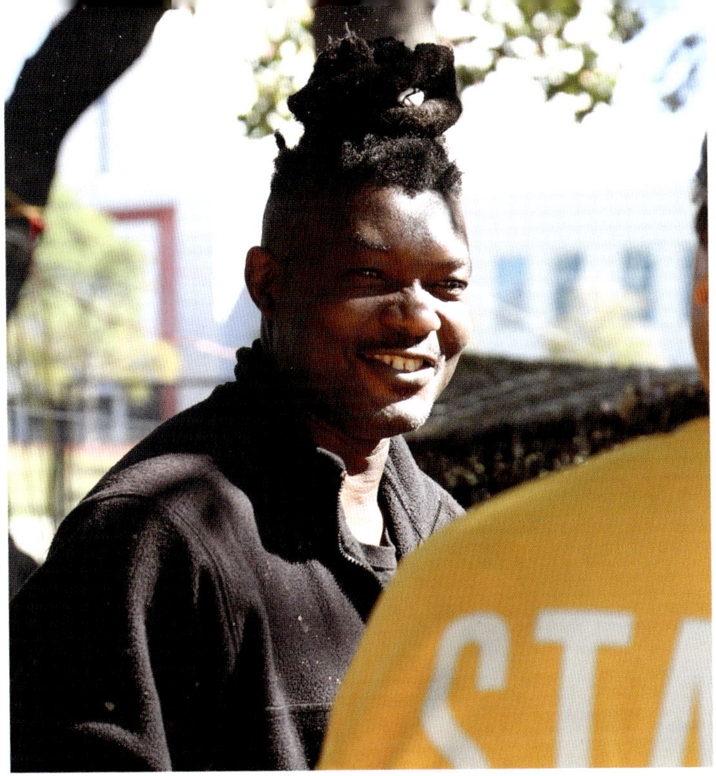

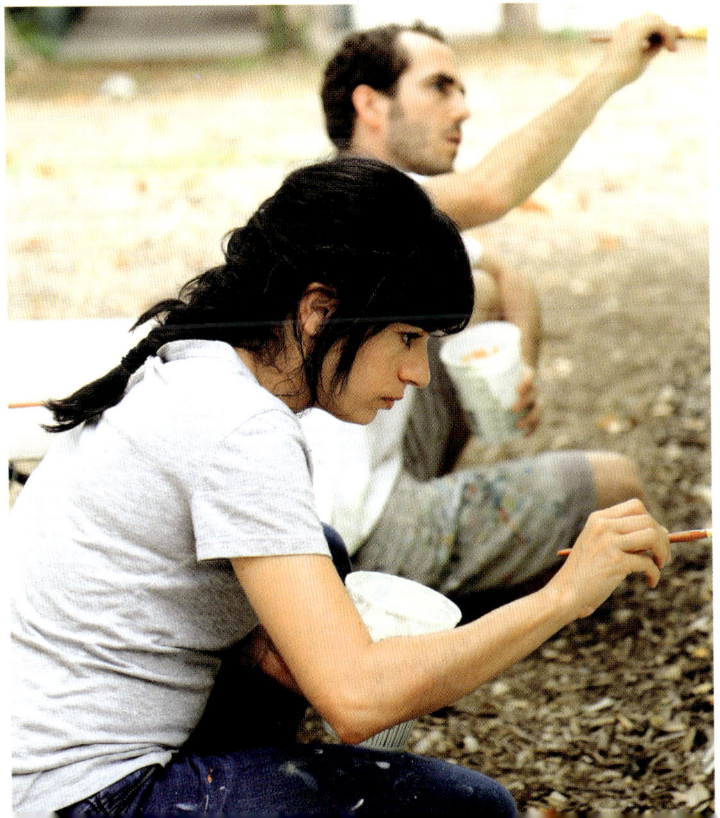

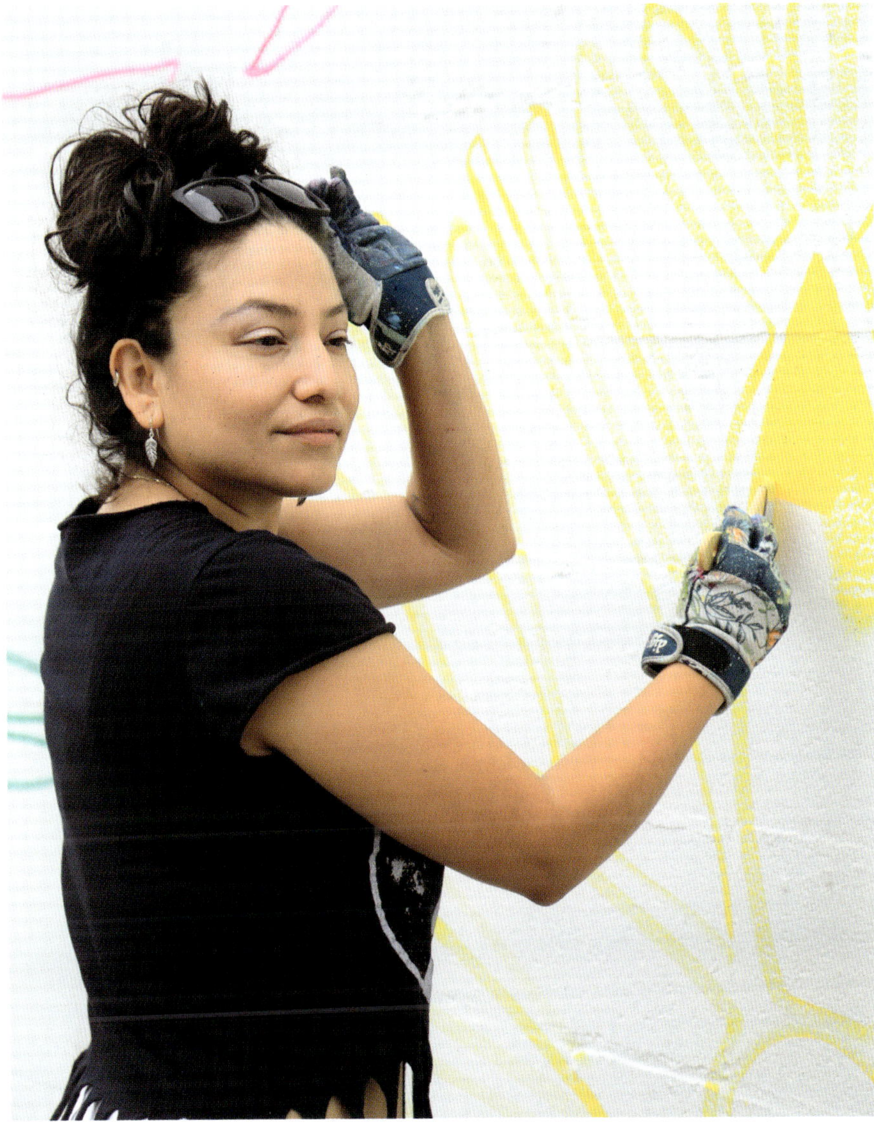

OPPOSITE PAGE
del Mar a Luz. James Eastman. Luminaria 2018.

THIS PAGE
TOP LEFT
Olaniyi, 2019. "AKIRASH" Akindiya (Nigeria). Luminaria.

BOTTOM LEFT
María López and Javier de Riba ("Reskate") (Barcelona, Spain). Luminaria 2017.

RIGHT
Gera Lozano (Brooklyn, New York). Luminaria 2017.

Luminaria is San Antonio's way of honoring the artists in our world.

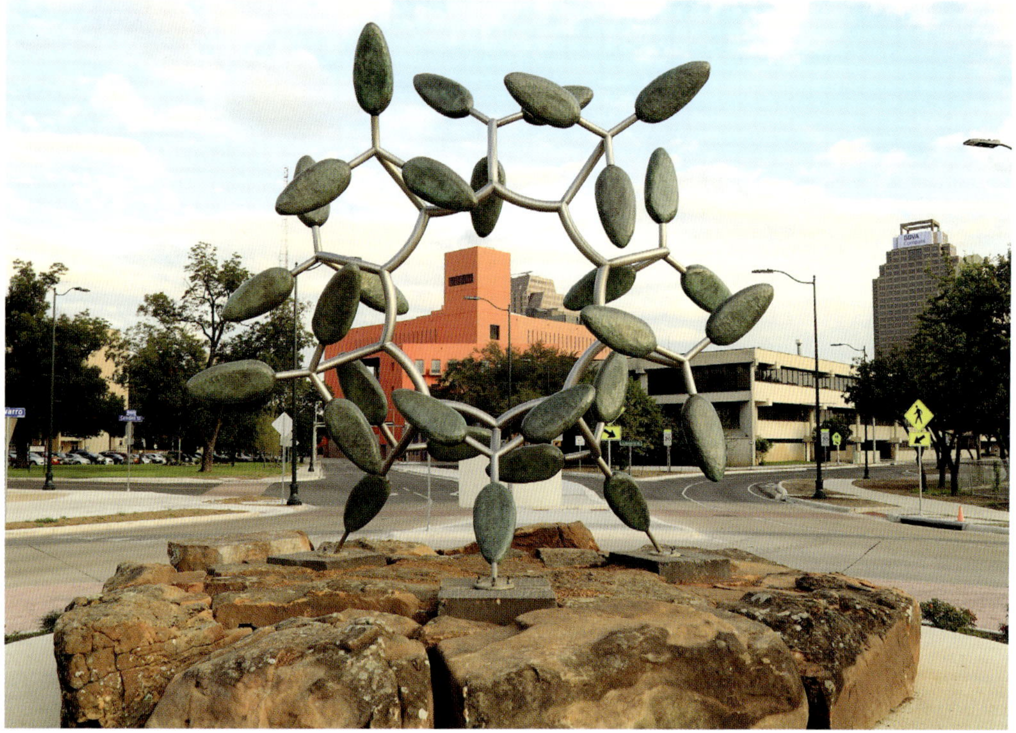

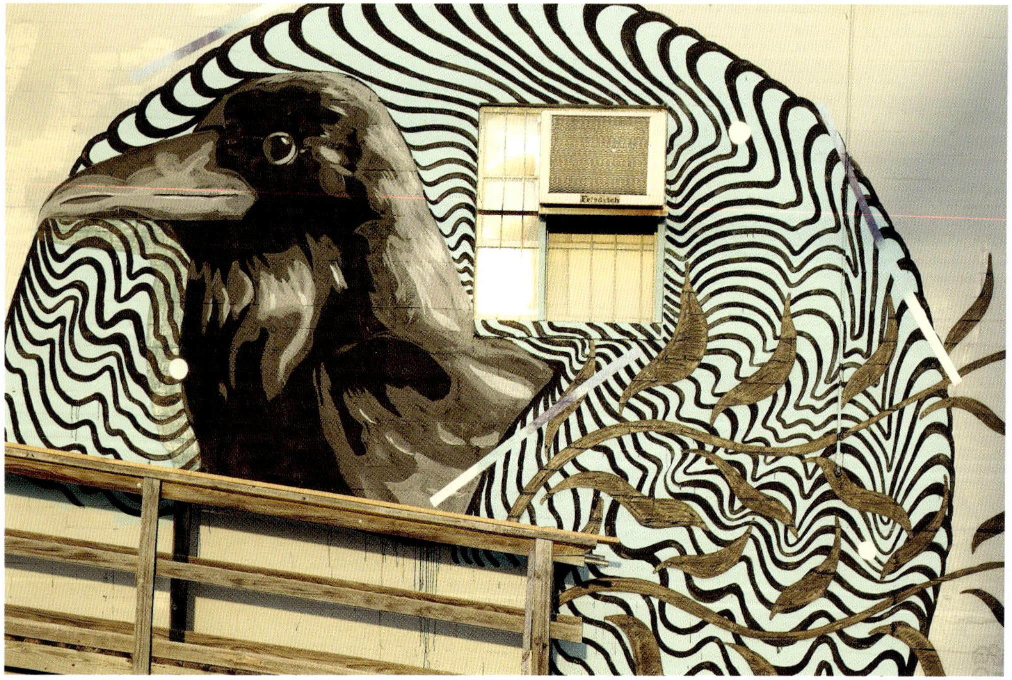

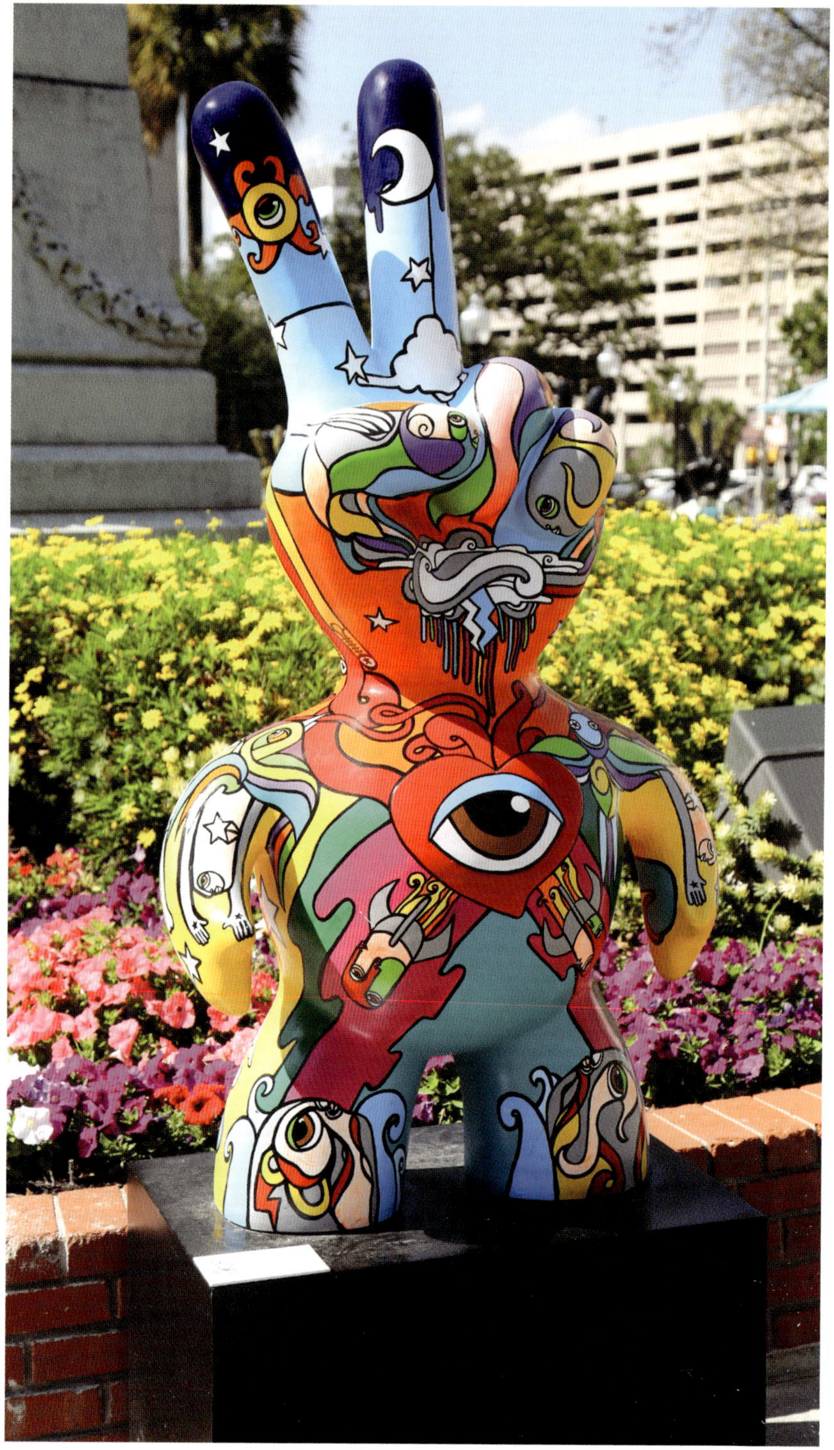

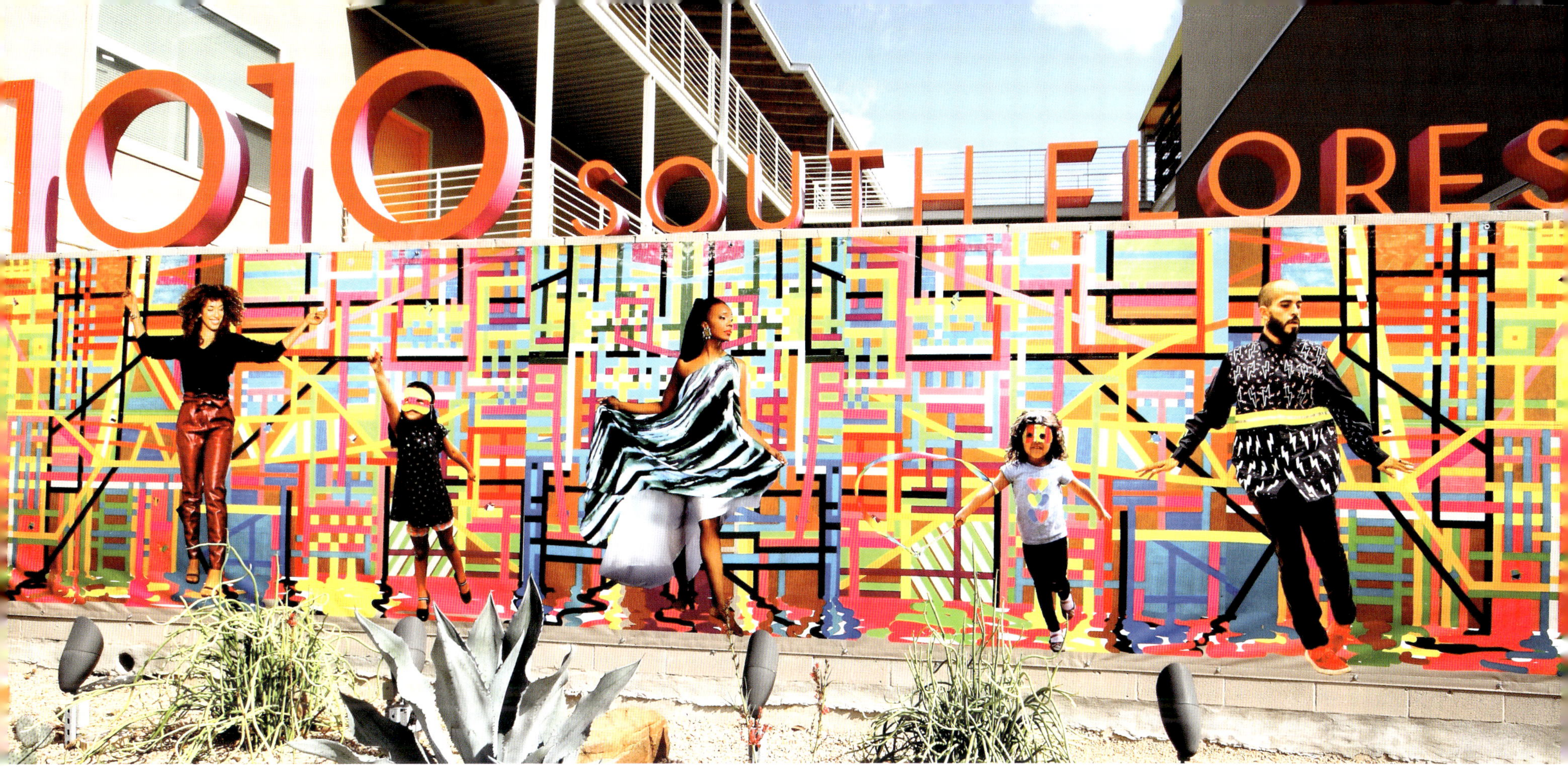

OPPOSITE PAGE
TOP LEFT
Three and Ten Flowers, 2018. James Surls. Traffic circle at Main Avenue and San Pedro Avenue.

BOTTOM LEFT
Untitled, 2017. Sabek and Tarrago.

RIGHT
Untitled, 2015. Mano Factura Arte Regio Visiting Art Exhibit from Monterrey, Mexico. Travis Park.

THIS PAGE
Untitled, 2020. Raúl González. 1010 South Flores. Printed vinyl banner.

ART ON THE GO

Images of beauty and surprise capture us in worlds
of wonder
make each moment in their presence a bolt of
lightning art that appears

and disappears.

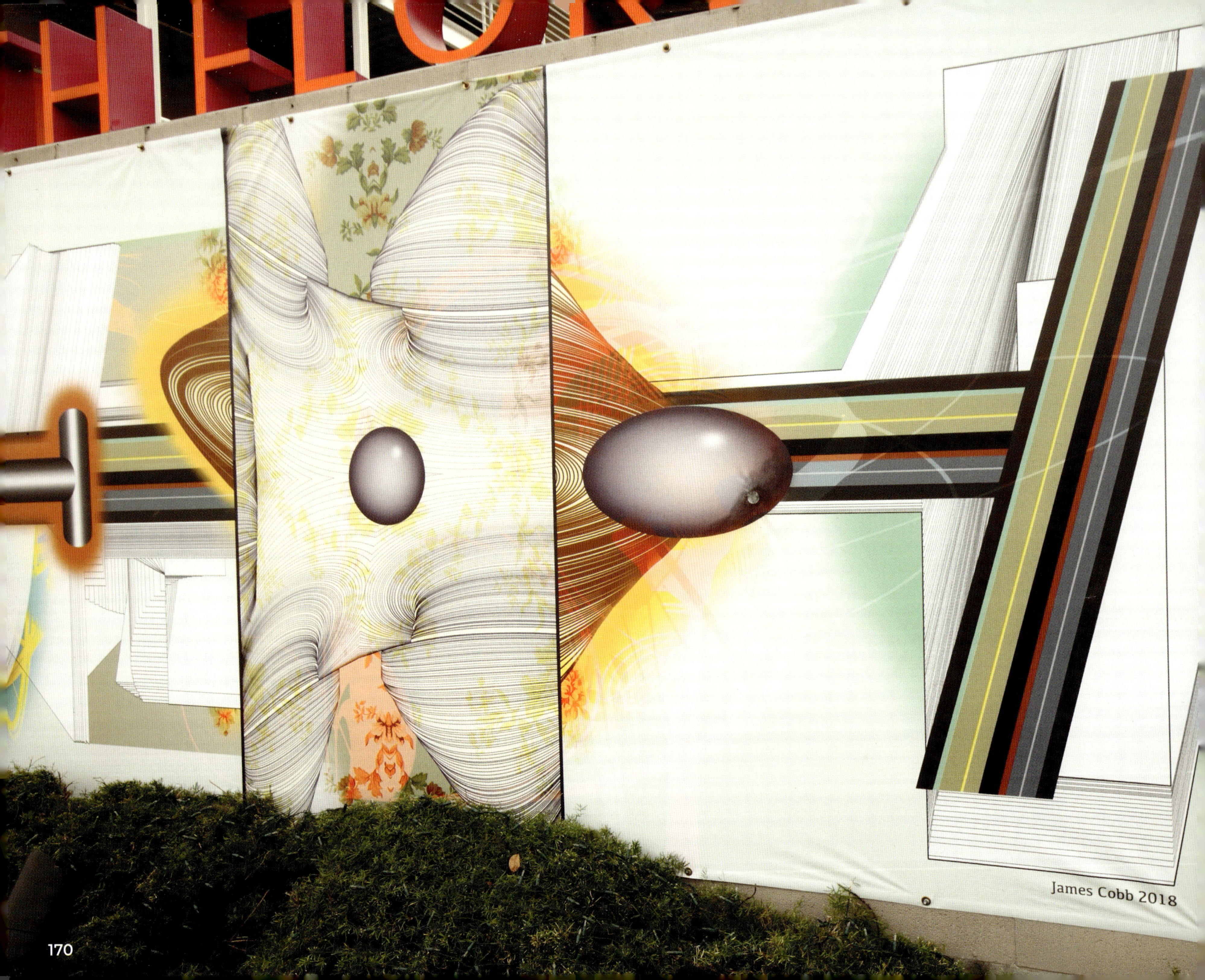
James Cobb 2018

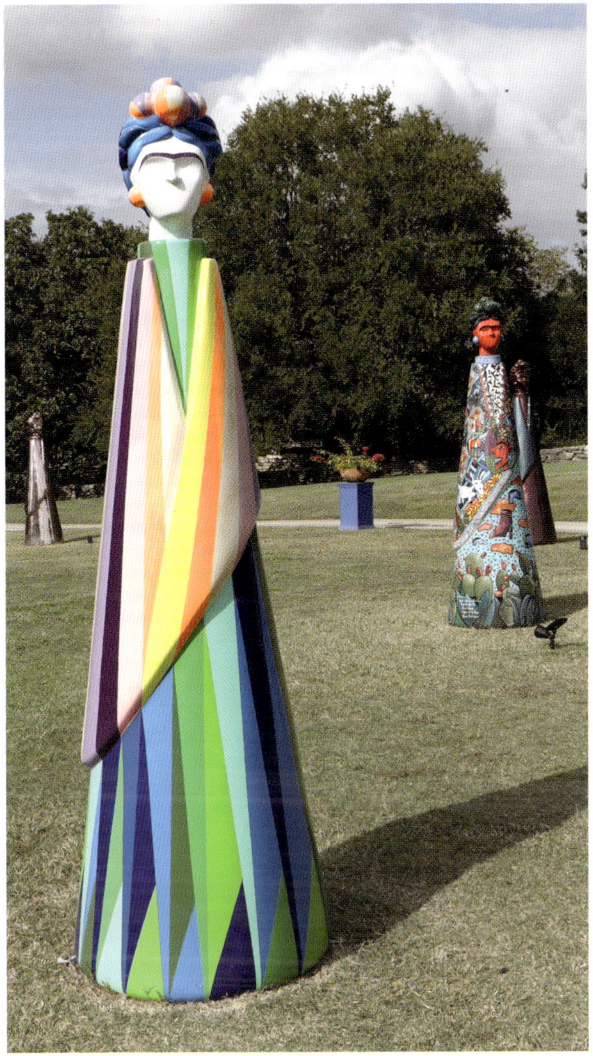

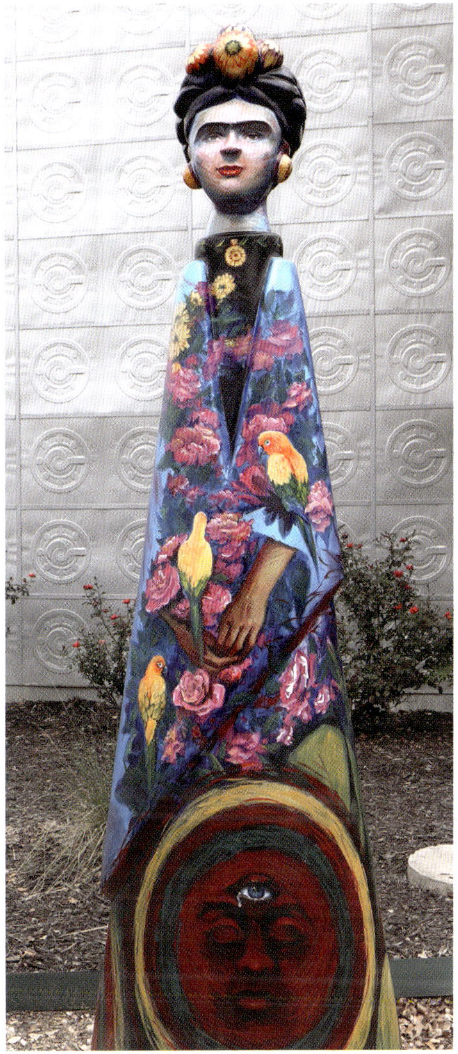

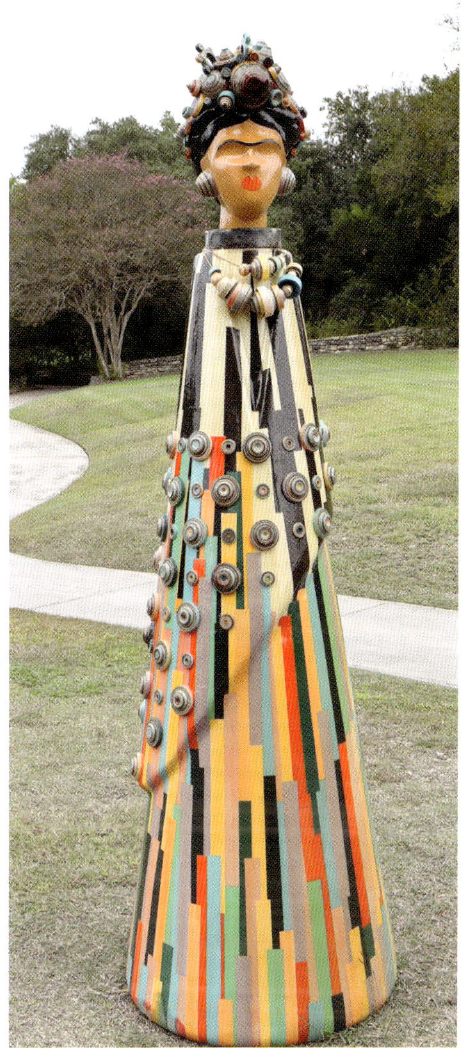

OPPOSITE PAGE
A Year of Less Thinking, 2018. James Cobb. Digital transfer onto canvas. A residential policy of regularly bringing in new creators increases art exposure at these condos. 1010 South Flores.

THIS PAGE
LEFT
Botanical Fridas, 2021. Fiberglass, resin, and acrylic paint. Leo Gabrielli, José Estéban Martinez, and Paul Zarkin (Mexico). San Antonio Botanical Garden.

CENTER
Frida Volviendo a La Vida, 2021. Robert Garza (Mexico).

RIGHT
Frida Serpentina, 2021. Jesús Rentería Franco.

The many faces of Frida also make a pilgrimage to San Antonio,
coming in from cities in Mexico and Texas, and from the hands of many artists.
They join us for the Day of the Dead and for the arrival of the Pollinators,
souls of the dead, at the Botanical Gardens and the Mexican Cultural Institute.
Almas de los muertos, coming home.

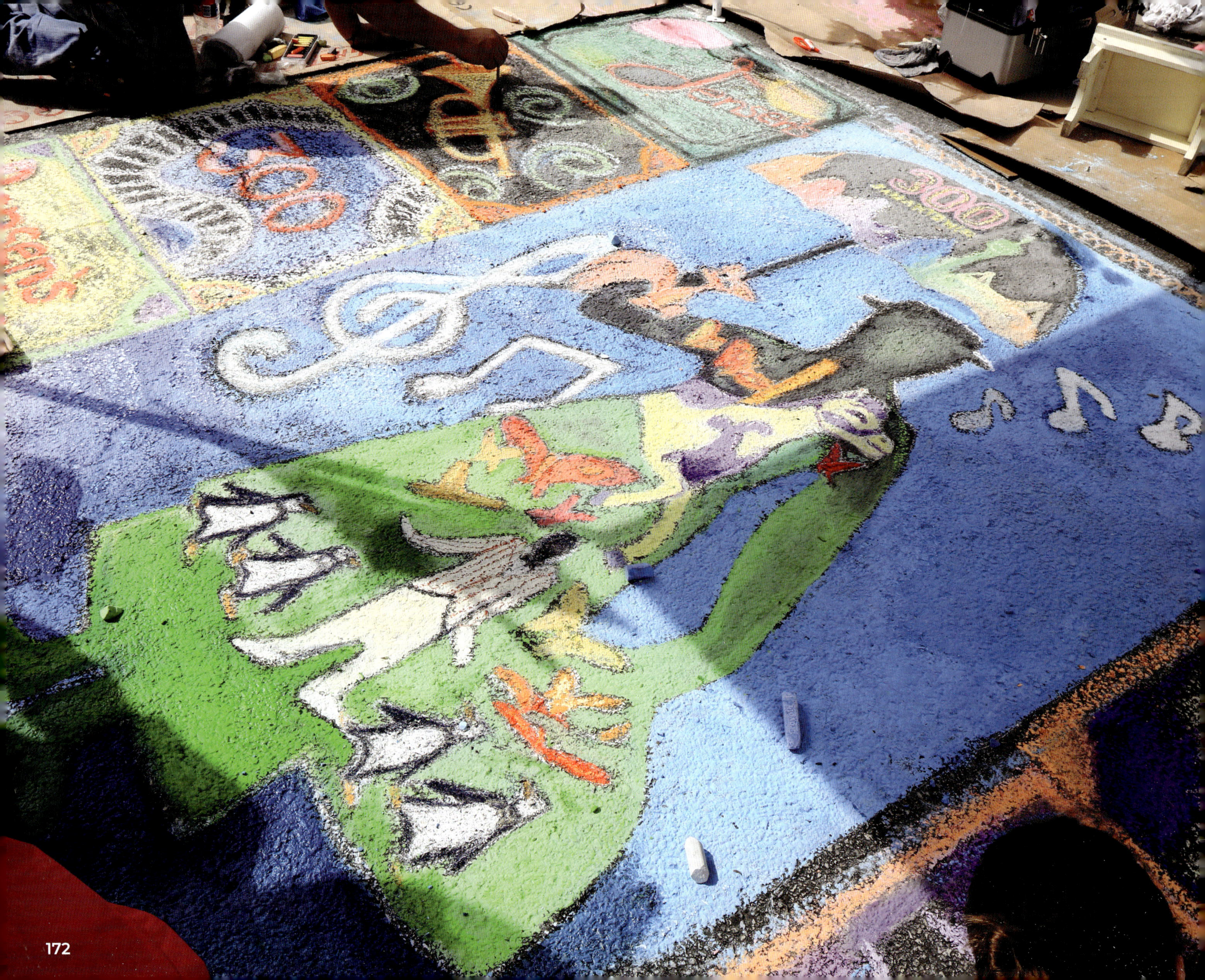
300
300

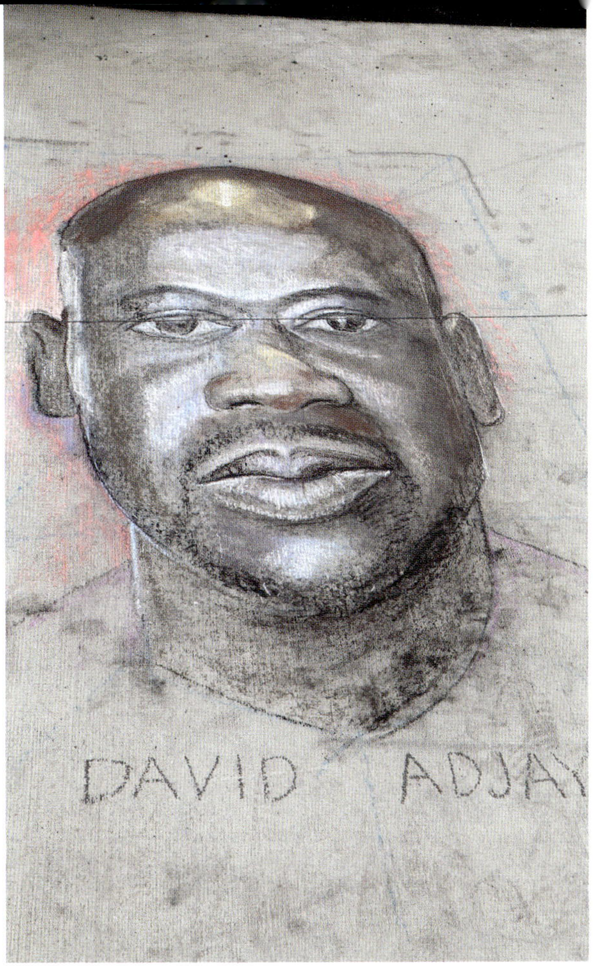

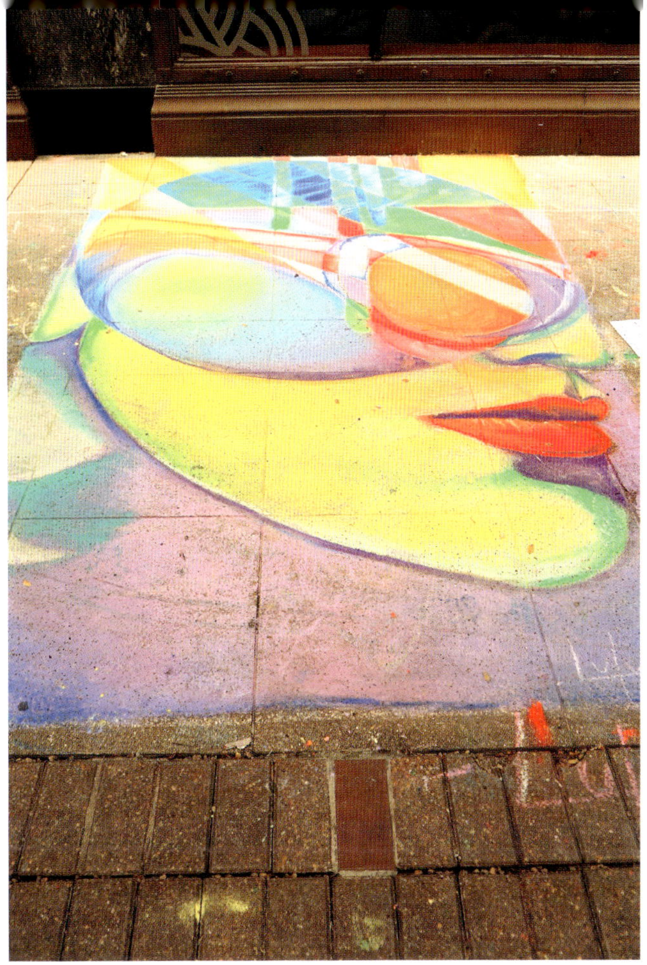
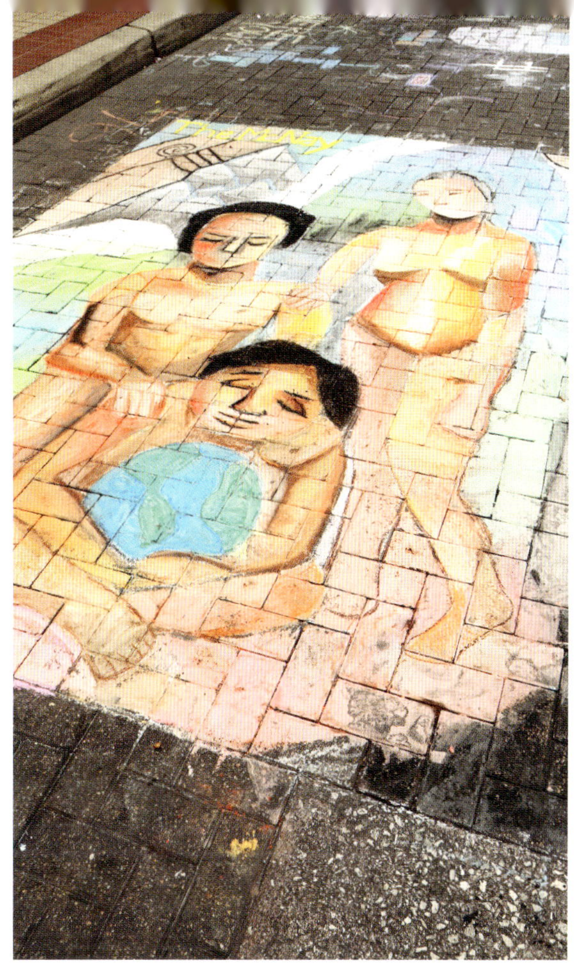

OPPOSITE PAGE
Untitled, 2018. Artist unknown.

THIS PAGE
LEFT
David Adjay, 2018.
Jeremy Teutsch.

CENTER
Untitled, 2016. Blue Star
Student Mosaic Program.
Streets of San Antonio.

RIGHT
Untitled, 2019. Thomas
Jefferson High School students
2019. Streets of San Antonio.

CHALK IT UP

High school students, codo a codo with Masters of the Arts,
pour their souls into chalk portraits of our most painful struggles,
our visions for the future, our mundane and glorious present,
then watch the sun and the rain wash away the past,
and carry us on wings of hope into another day.

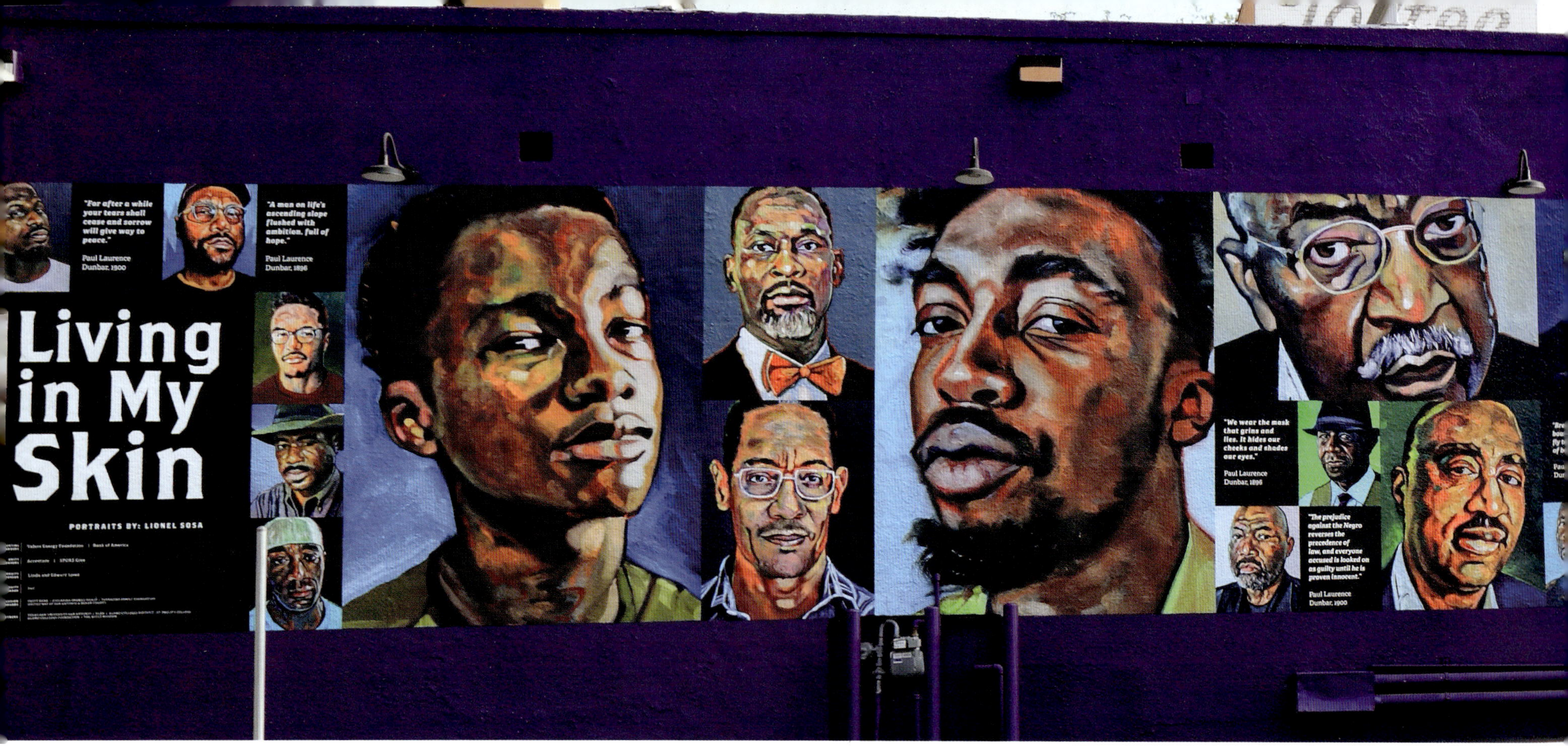
"For after a while your tears shall cease and sorrow will give way to peace."
Paul Laurence Dunbar, 1900
"A man on life's ascending slope flushed with ambition, full of hope."
Paul Laurence Dunbar, 1896
Living in My Skin
PORTRAITS BY: LIONEL SOSA
"We wear the mask that grins and lies. It hides our cheeks and shades our eyes."
Paul Laurence Dunbar, 1896
"The prejudice against the Negro reverses the precedence of law, and everyone accused is looked on as guilty until he is proven innocent."
Paul Laurence Dunbar, 1900

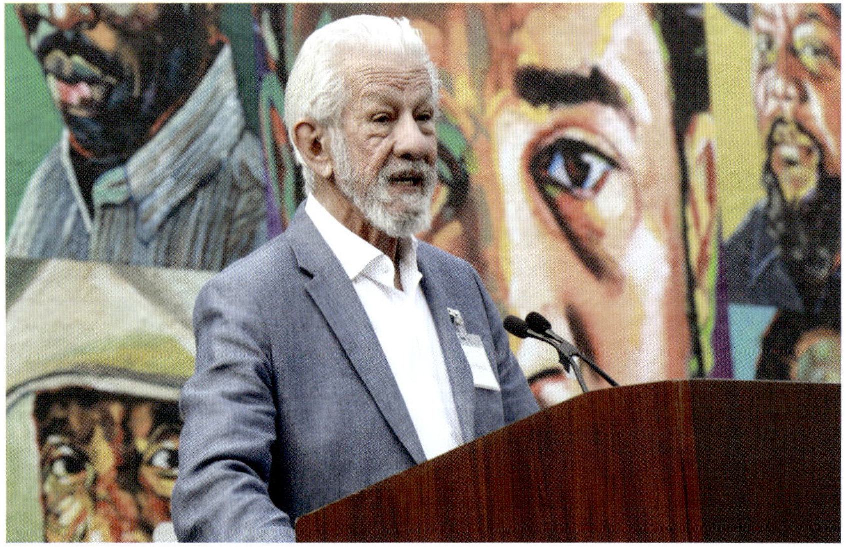

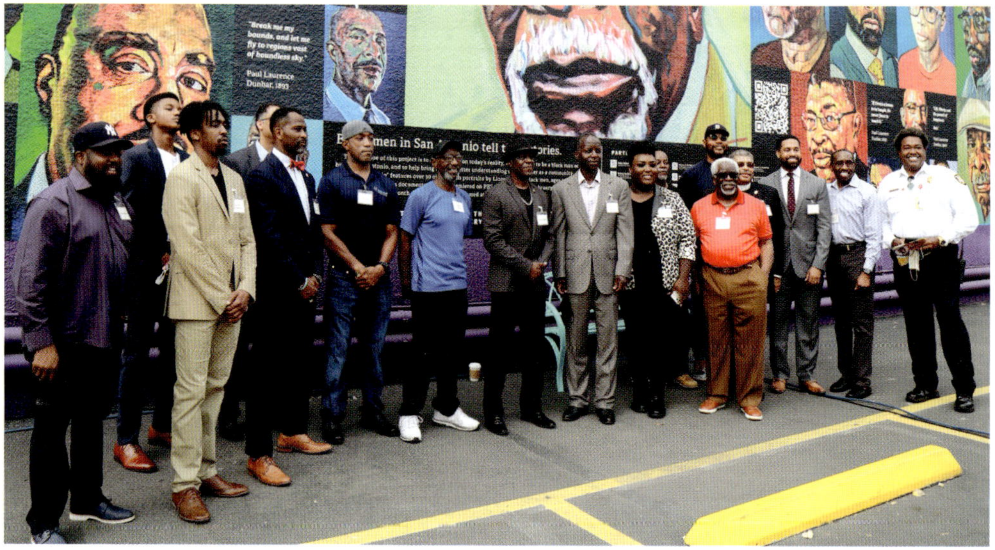
"Break me my bounds, and let me fly to regions vast of boundless sky."
Paul Laurence Dunbar, 1893

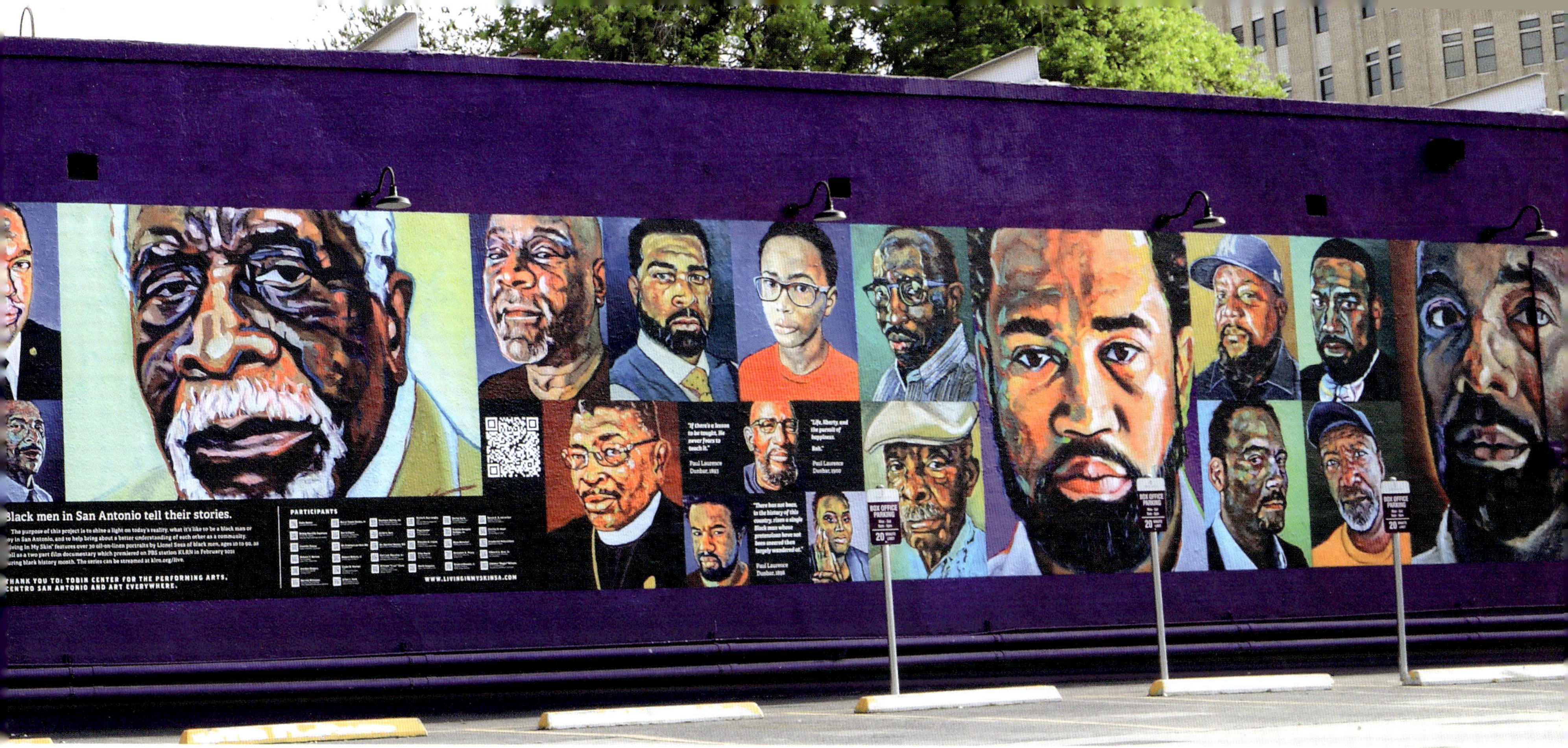

ABOVE
Living in My Skin, 2021. Lionel Sosa.
4th Street and Auditorium Circle.

OPPOSITE PAGE
BOTTOM LEFT
Artist Lionel Sosa created/painted portraits of thirty-three African American men in San Antonio through digital transfer onto vinyl. Visitors can scan a QR code on the mural to hear each of their stories. Here, Sosa is speaking at the mural's unveiling.

BOTTOM RIGHT
Living in My Skin, 2021.
Lionel Sosa. 4th Street and Auditorium Circle. Seventeen of the men portrayed in the mural attended the 2021 mural dedication.

LIVING IN MY SKIN

Our public art can mend hearts, bend minds, and, sometimes, save lives.
The daring proclamation *Living in My Skin* speaks eloquently
to the pain and metamorphosis our society is undergoing in this very moment,
confronting its own centuries of racism, its own failure to see the value and
the beauty of Black men's lives. This in-the-moment mural captures the strength
and the stories of men young and old, professional, homeless, veteran, young teen,
and affirms our vow—
we will no longer allow their lives to be endangered.

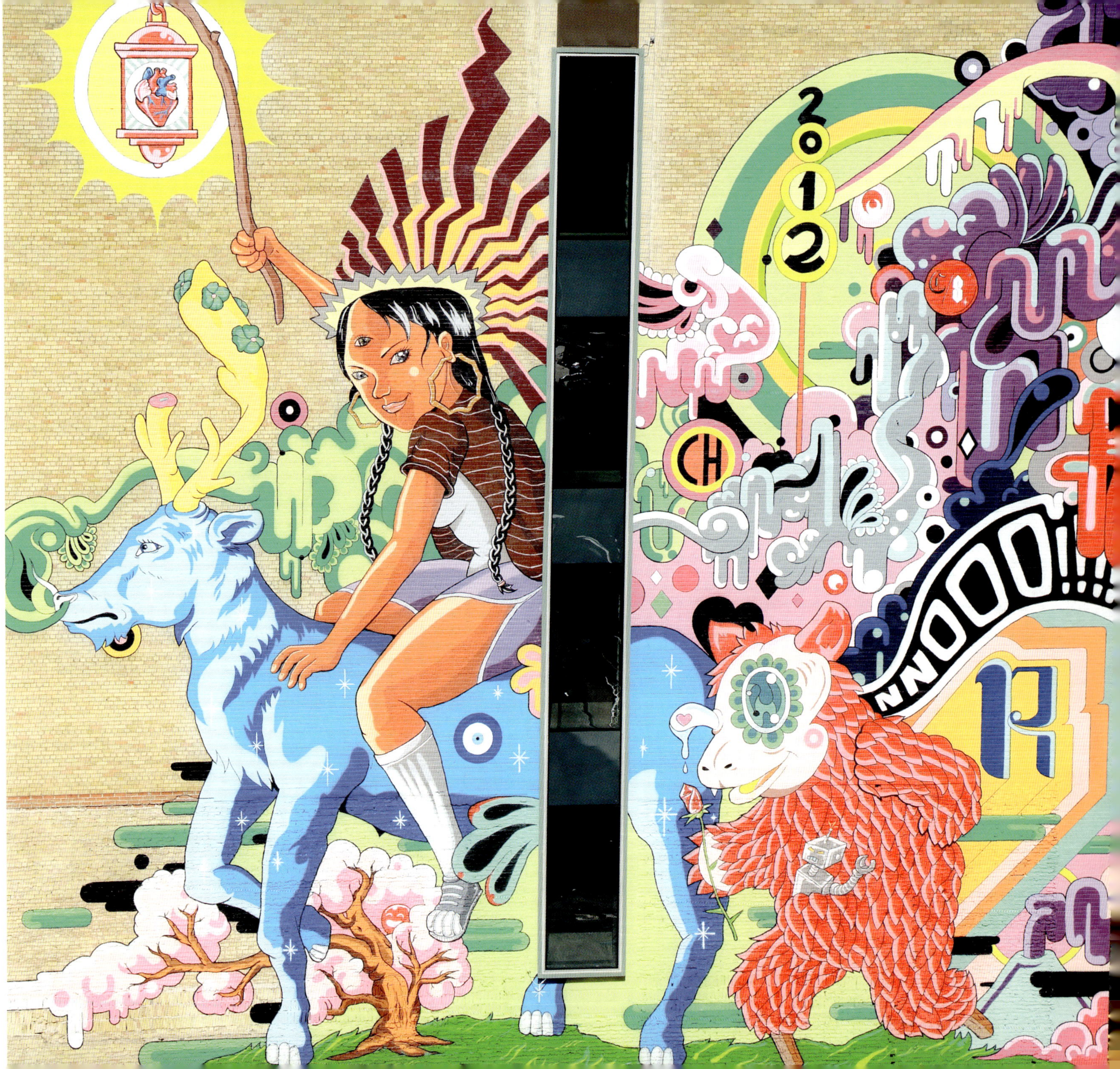

The Last Parade, 2021. Rudy Herrera. Standing 70 feet wide and 100 feet tall on the historic Kress Building, this mural honors Indigenous heritage and the courage of underground artists to leap off a cliff into the unknown. Houston Street.

OPPOSITE PAGE Artist Rudy Herrera with his wife and son, both represented symbolically in *The Last Parade* at the mural opening in 2021.

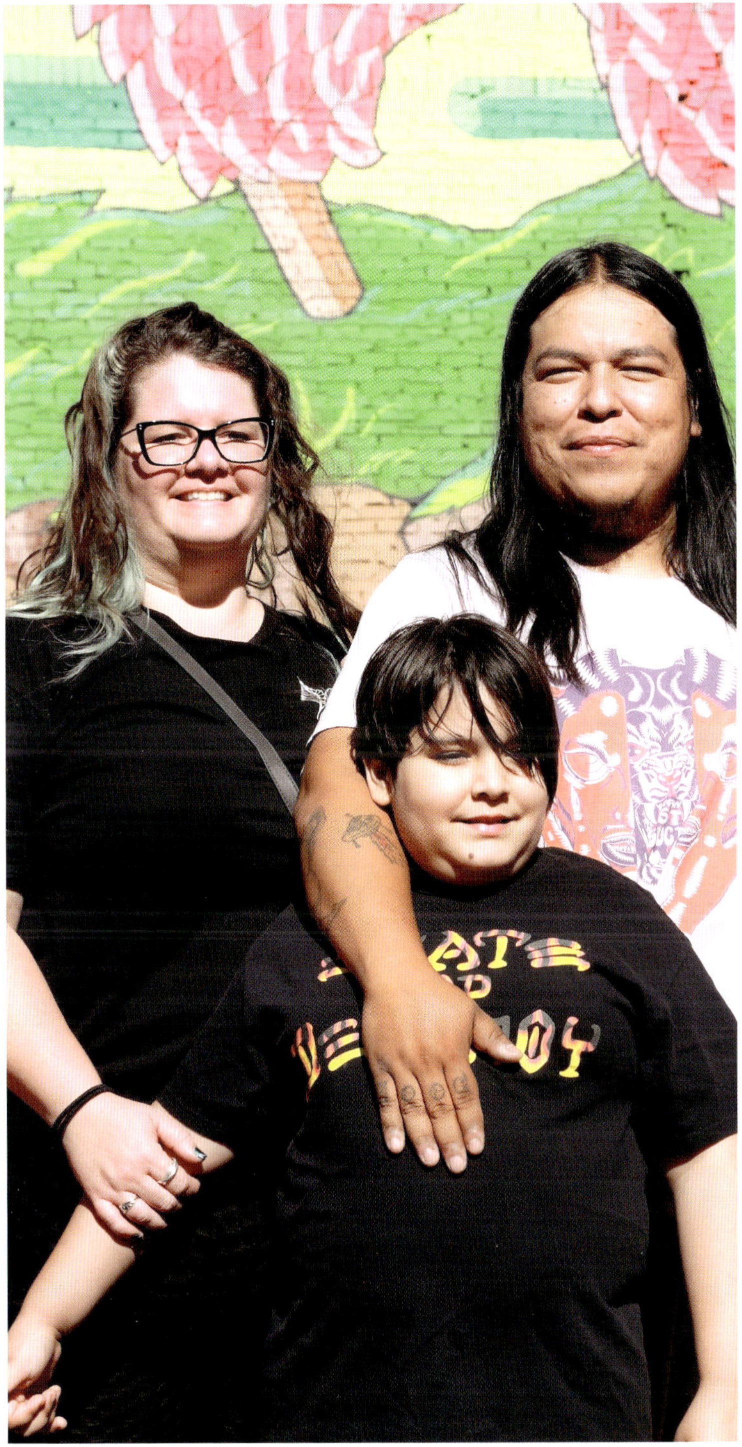

THE LAST PARADE

A rich and daring Artist's Imagination
captures that breathtaking moment
between the whispering power of our past
and the overwhelming call of the possible.
Riding the mythical blue deer of Indian ancestors,
and protected by the fuzzy, button-eyed bear
of her childhood, which, now grown,
cuddles his own Rocky Robot child,
this Chicanindia leader carries in her regalia
the mark of past, present, and future.
They approach the unknown prepared to leap,
the path ahead lit by the lantern of her heart,
their statement sealed by the eternal *Con Safos*.
They charge ahead with vision, deer leaving behind
the living, growing creations of his own breath,
which fill the air, shape-shift clouds,
and branch and root, as does the artists' work.
They approach the precipice,
leap off to new ventures, excited for the challenge,
filled with strength, hope, and
a belief in new possibilities.
This is Art.
This is Ours.

NOTE

1. *Urban-15*, established in 1974, continues to bring new and unique art forms in music, movement, and media presentations throughout the city and was asked to appear at the Inaugural Parade in Washington, DC, in 1992. Its mission is to create art that merges traditional Latino culture with modern aesthetics and technology via its presentations, educational programs, and lifelong participation in the arts.

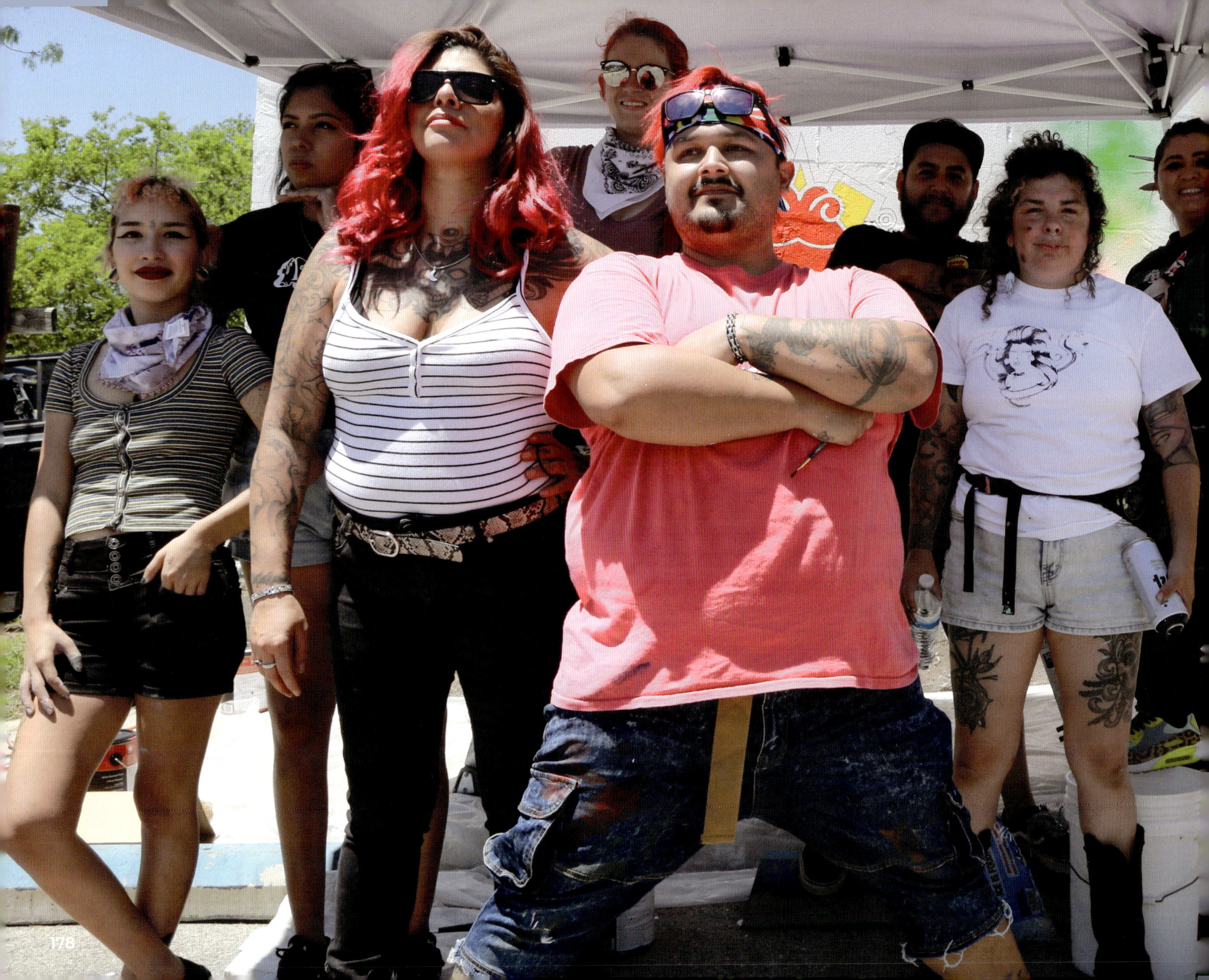

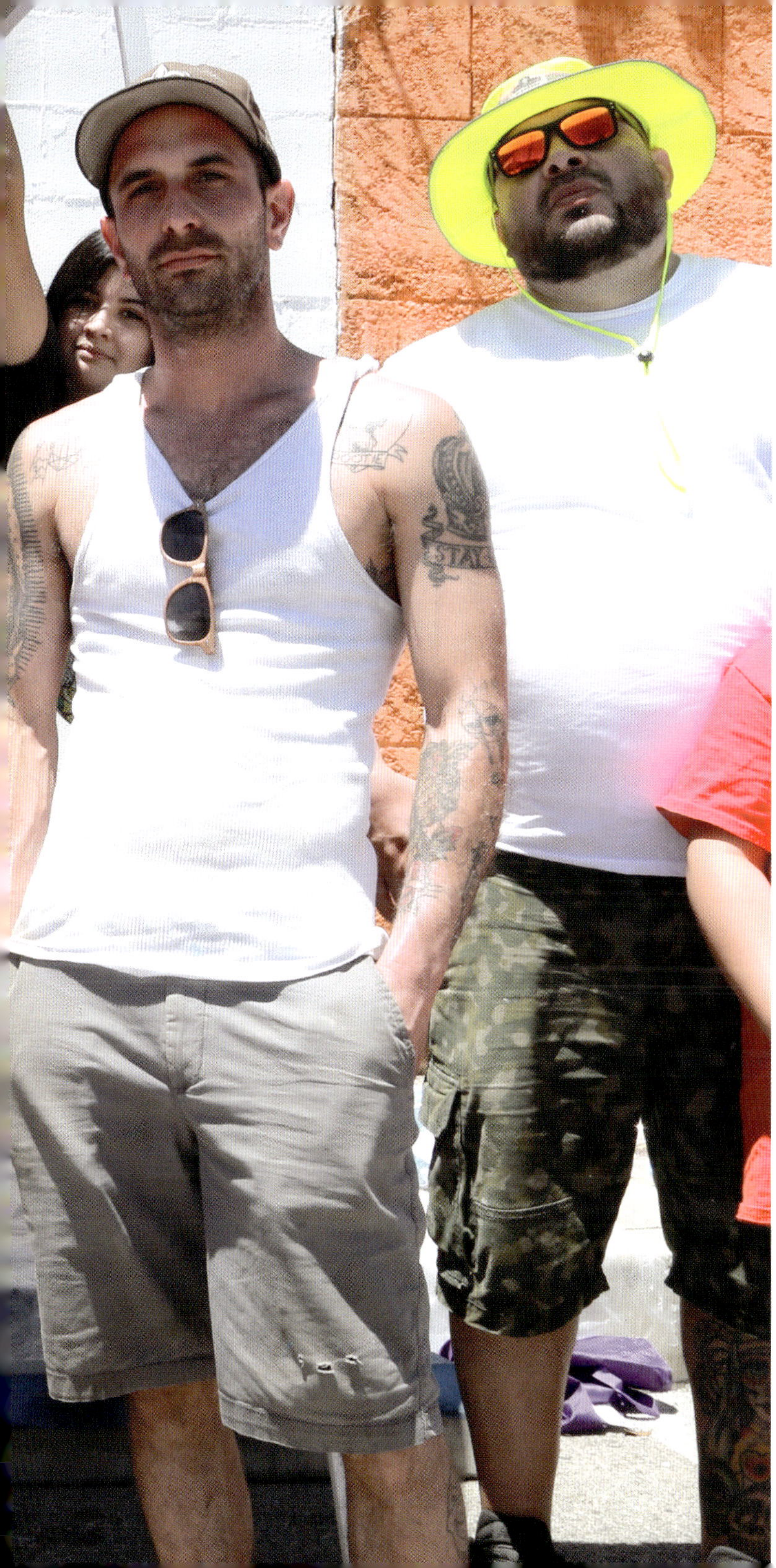

VII. IN THEIR WORDS AND IMAGES

ELEVEN ARTISTS FROM AMONG THE MANY ARTIST-SHAMANS OF SAN ANTONIO'S SPIRIT

Our artists are the shamans of San Antonio's artistic spirit. Their diversity of style and theme, genre, and life experience is impressive, and we feel honored to have every one of them in this pueblo of beauty and *cariño*.

In this section we feature eleven artists who have contributed to the San Antonio scene. While their origins, styles, and themes vary, they all reflect San Antonio; they all serve as voice to San Antonio's soul. In their words and in their artistic works, you will experience their artistic passion and their union with the San Antonio community.

Here is why they paint or sculpt, or spray or bake ceramics. Here is what San Antonio's public art means to them.

Artists gather at a San Anto Cultural Arts event, April 24, 2021. *Left to right*: "Void," Liz, "April Dawn," "Pink," "Midnite," "Relek," "Tre," "Cry," "Raine," "Rype," and "Supher."

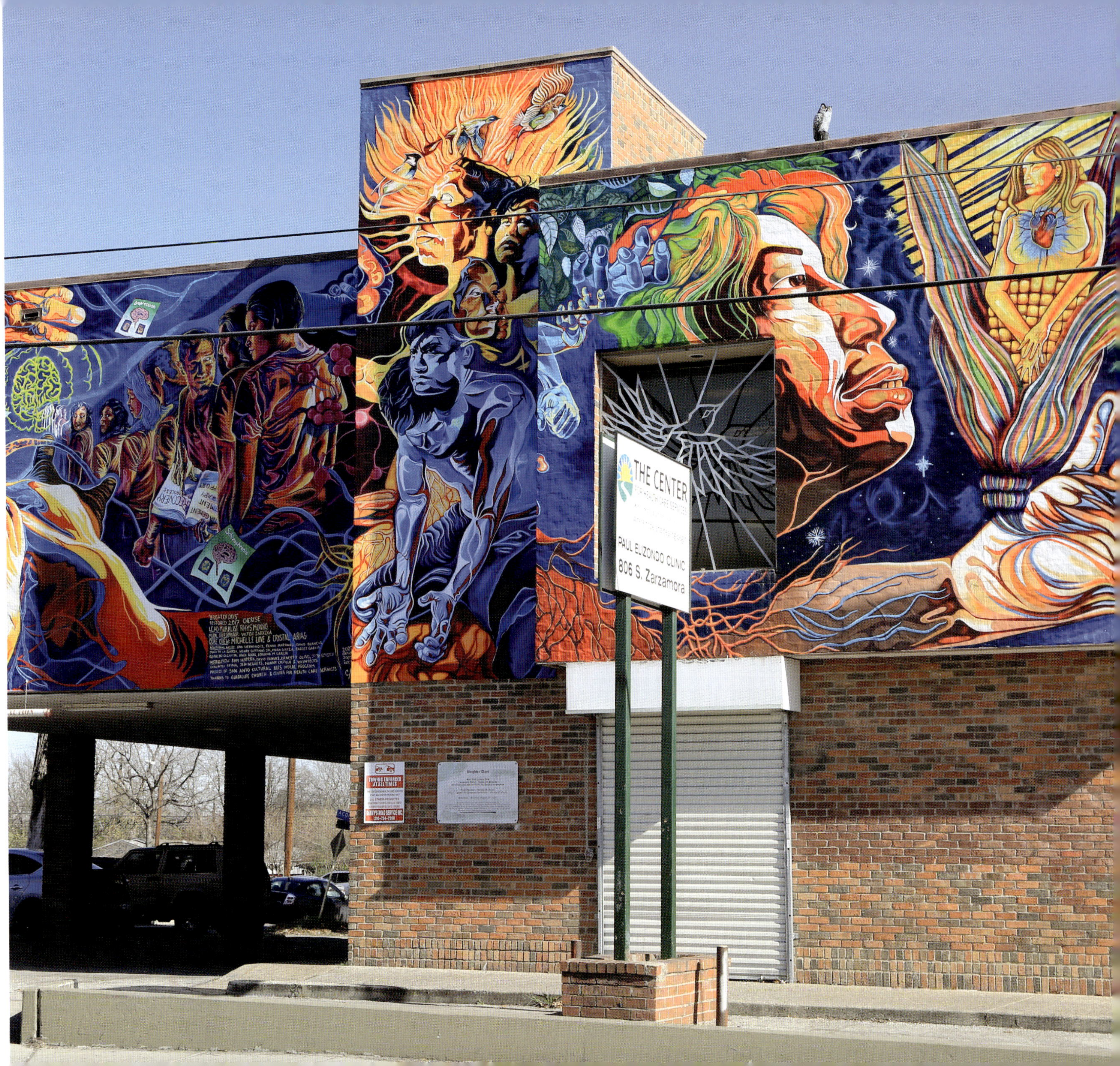

Brighter Days, 2006. 806 South Zarzamora Street.

OPPOSITE PAGE LEFT
Detail of *A Hurricane of Change Is Made of Tiny Things, Like the Beat of a Butterfly's Wings*, 2016. Adriana García's painted center section shown. 1416 East Commerce Street.

RIGHT
Adriana García, 2020

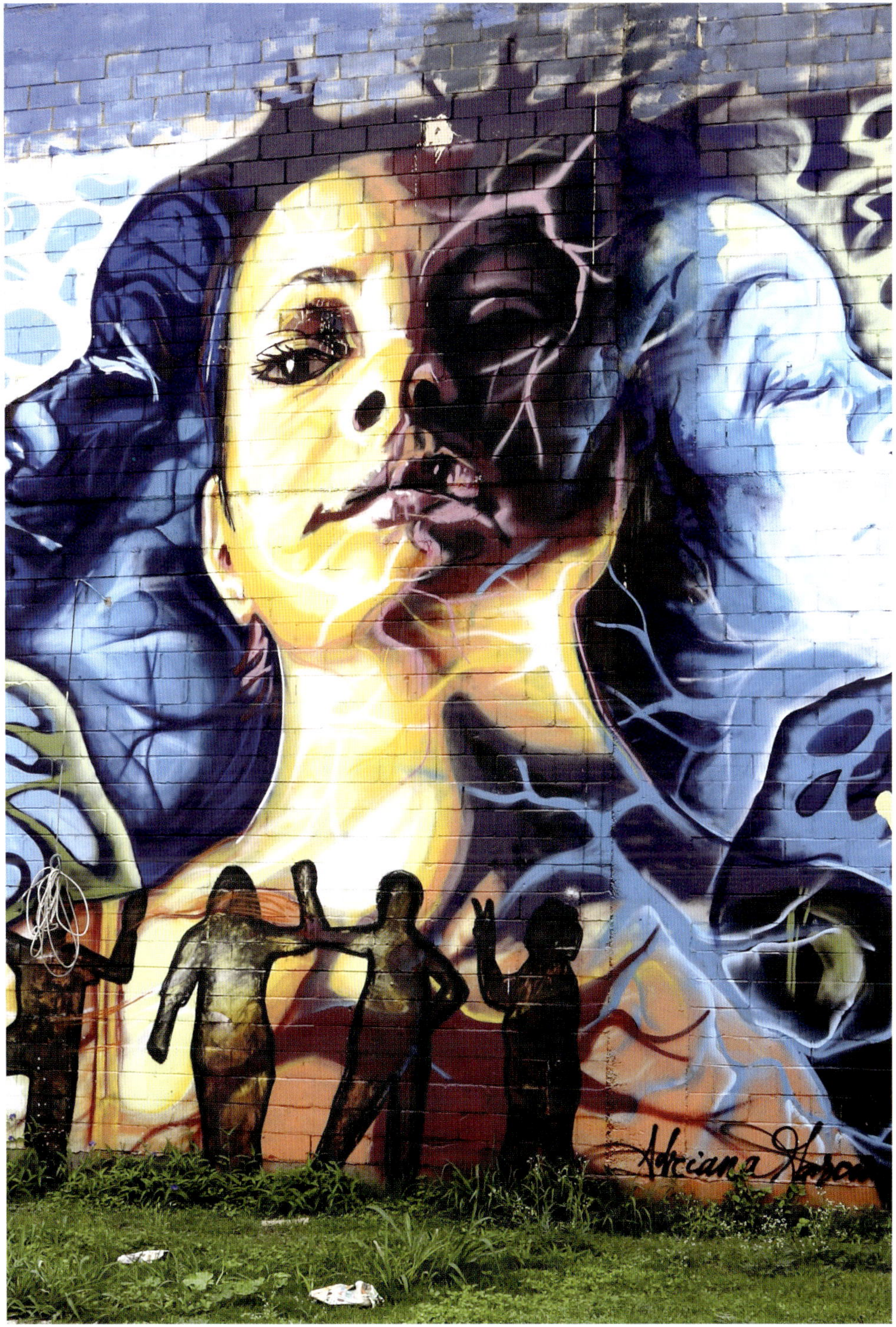

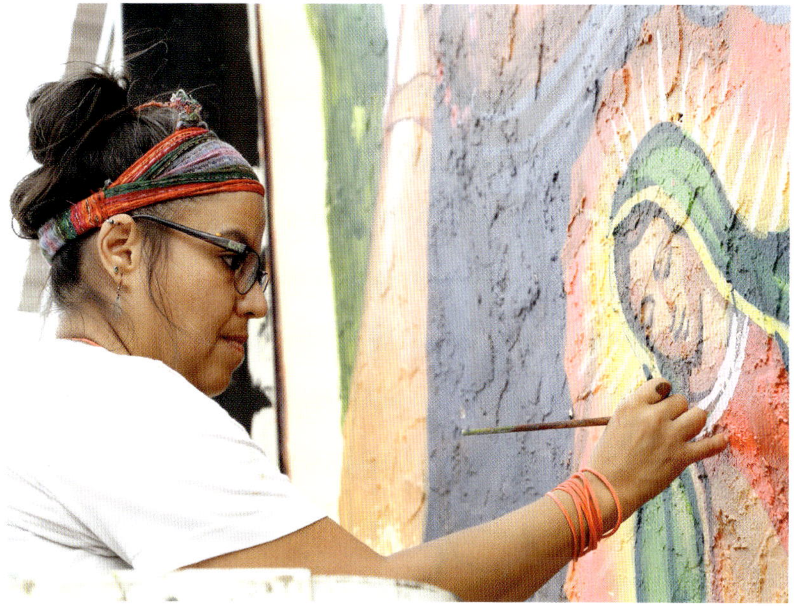

ADRIANA GARCÍA

Adriana García, raised in a family of artists and stimulated by many West Side cultural organizations, is a graduate of Carnegie Mellon School of Art. San Anto Cultural Arts invited her to take part in a collaborative mural when she was a young teen, and now she offers those same opportunities to hundreds of young artists.

García considers it essential to provide several workshops a month to youth, and to involve them in the creation of public art works plus monthlong intensive workshops in the summer. Of the need for these murals, she says, "Where was the Chicano experience in our textbooks, in our schools? Where were we even taught of our own culture, other than to tell us that we were not supposed to speak Spanish and that we would not amount to anything? I see the creation of our murals as a reappropriation of our space."

The work of this San Antonio native now graces not only her West Side landmarks but also San Pedro Creek Culture Park, the South Texas Diabetes Center, and award-winning children's books. García says, "Muralism is a vehicle for social change and for social justice. It serves also as an educational tool, teaching us how to fight for the rights of the community."

(See also the San Pedro Creek Culture Park mural on page 88.)

LEFT
Tree of Life, 2007.
Bernice B. Appelin-Williams and James Wyatt Hendricks.
Dignowity Park.

RIGHT
Bravery, 2015.
Bernice B. Appelin-Williams.
Houston Street bridge.

OPPOSITE PAGE
LEFT
Power, 2015.
Bernice B. Appelin-Williams.
Houston Street bridge.

RIGHT
Bernice B. Appelin-Williams.
Photo courtesy of Ramin Samandari.

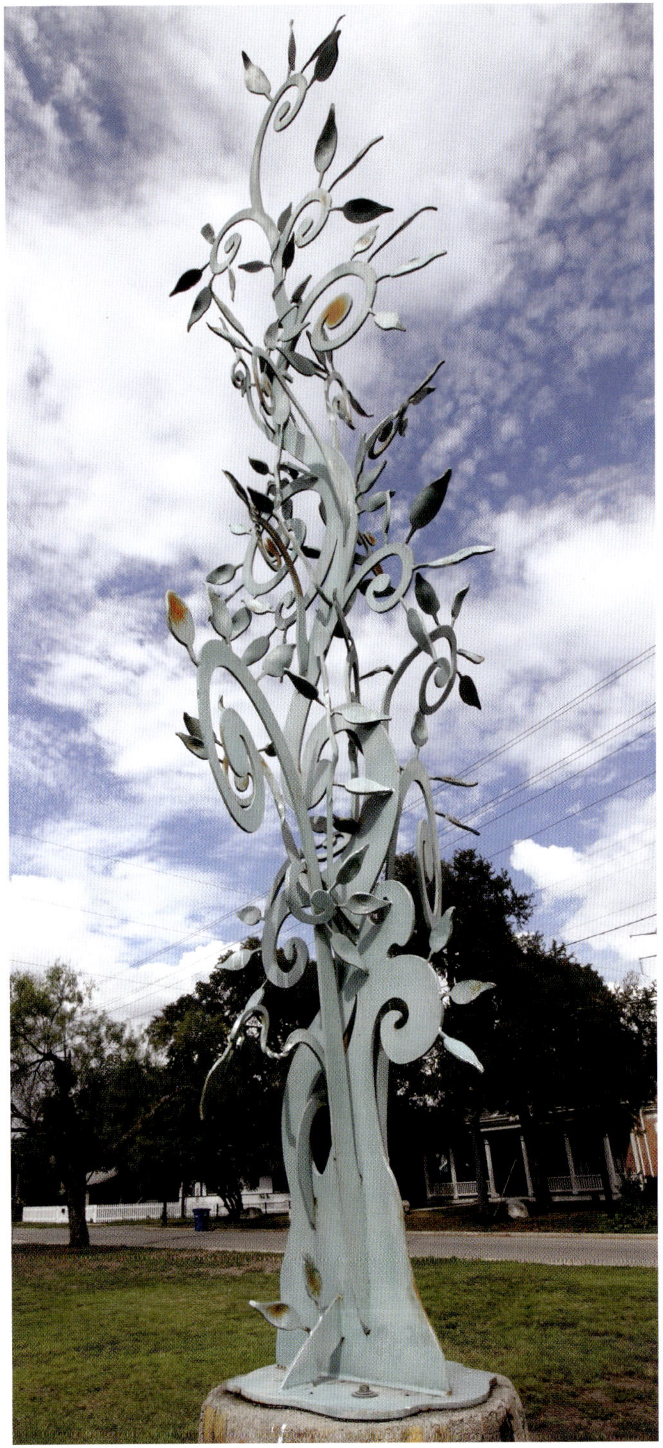

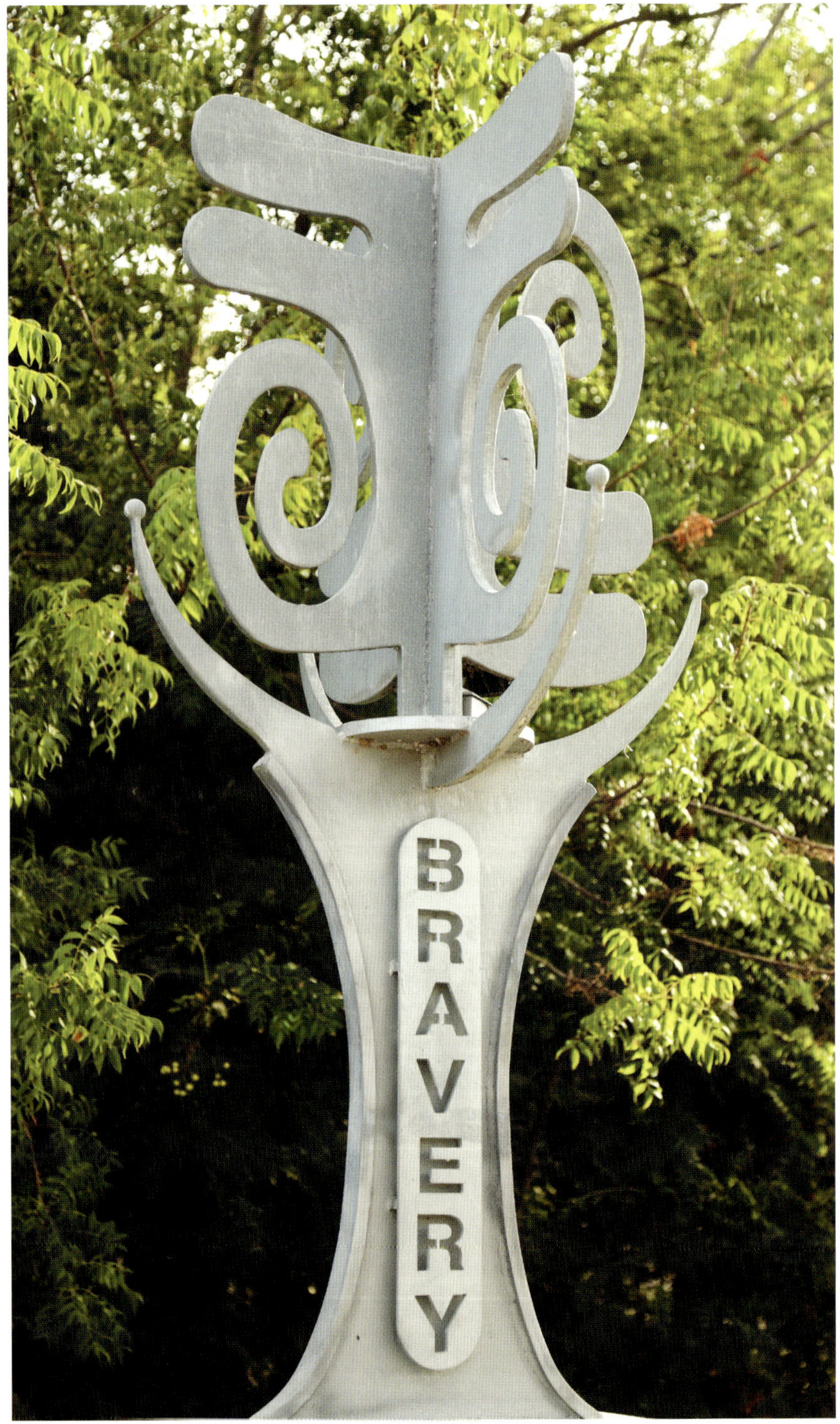

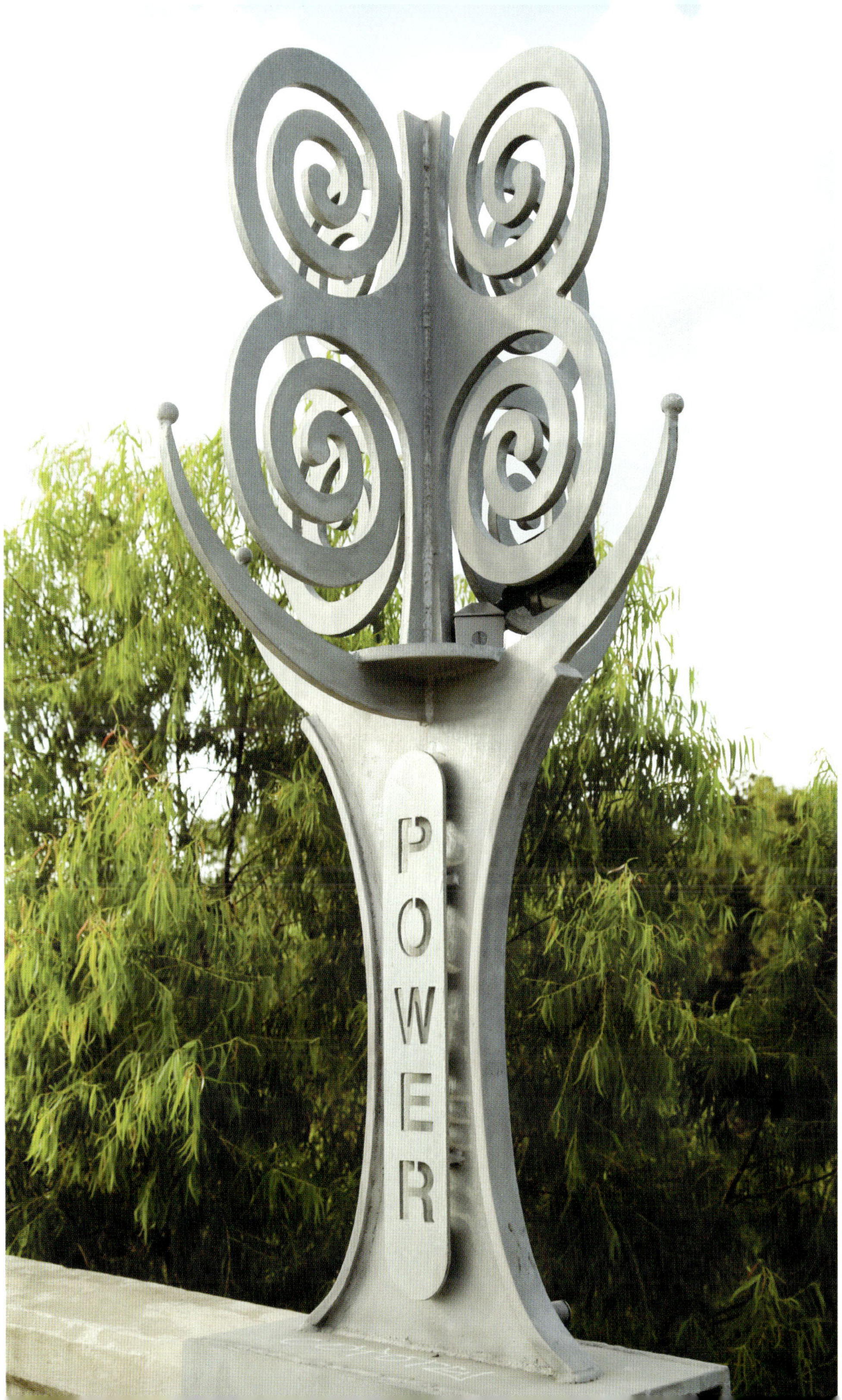

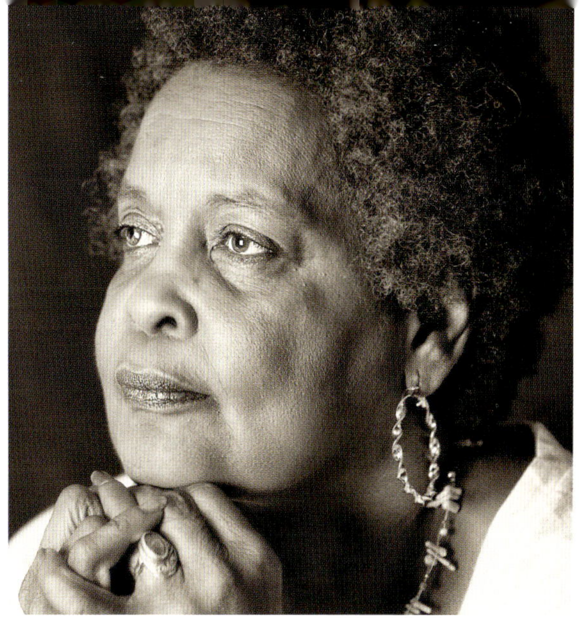

BERNICE APPELIN-WILLIAMS

Bernice Appelin-Williams reinvents the use of materials, transforming all sorts of odd objects: discarded TV screens, sewing-machine drawers, old sepia photos, and restrictive symbols of women's lives, from corsets to bizarre contemporary footwear "designed by men who don't have to wear it." From these she creates stories of life journeys, African American history, and women's oppression.

"There's power in changing the use of materials. . . . Things have multiple meanings; thus my attraction to them and to their reincarnation or repurposing," Williams says, referencing the West African term *sankofa*, which means "to move forward, we must reclaim the past." She finds expression for her message in three-dimensional sculpture, serigraphs for posters, and assemblages such as *Ant'Cha Mama*, inspired by a real woman, Nancy Green, who originally served as the model for the iconic Aunt Jemima figure.

Appelin-Williams's work is widely exhibited in San Antonio, Austin, Kenya, and other locations, but she had never entered a museum until her high school teacher introduced her to one. She saw no Black artists in museums or library books. Today her sculptures *Bravery*, *Power*, and *Faith* decorate East Houston Street, and she cocreated the sculpture *Tree of Life* with James Hendricks. Her artistic vision is still transforming, moving forward with *sankofa*, toward her next goal. "There's a monument I would love to create, and to see it placed in Washington, DC," she says. "It's a monument to Cathay Williams, the first and only female buffalo soldier, who had to hide that she was a woman."

TOP
Source of Life, 2015.
University of the
Incarnate Word.

BOTTOM RIGHT
Source of Life, 2015.
University of the Incarnate
Word.

BOTTOM LEFT
Grotto de San Antonio,
2005. Henry B. González
Convention Center.

OPPOSITE PAGE
LEFT
Witte Museum Park
parking garage, 2009

RIGHT
Cakky Brawley, 2020

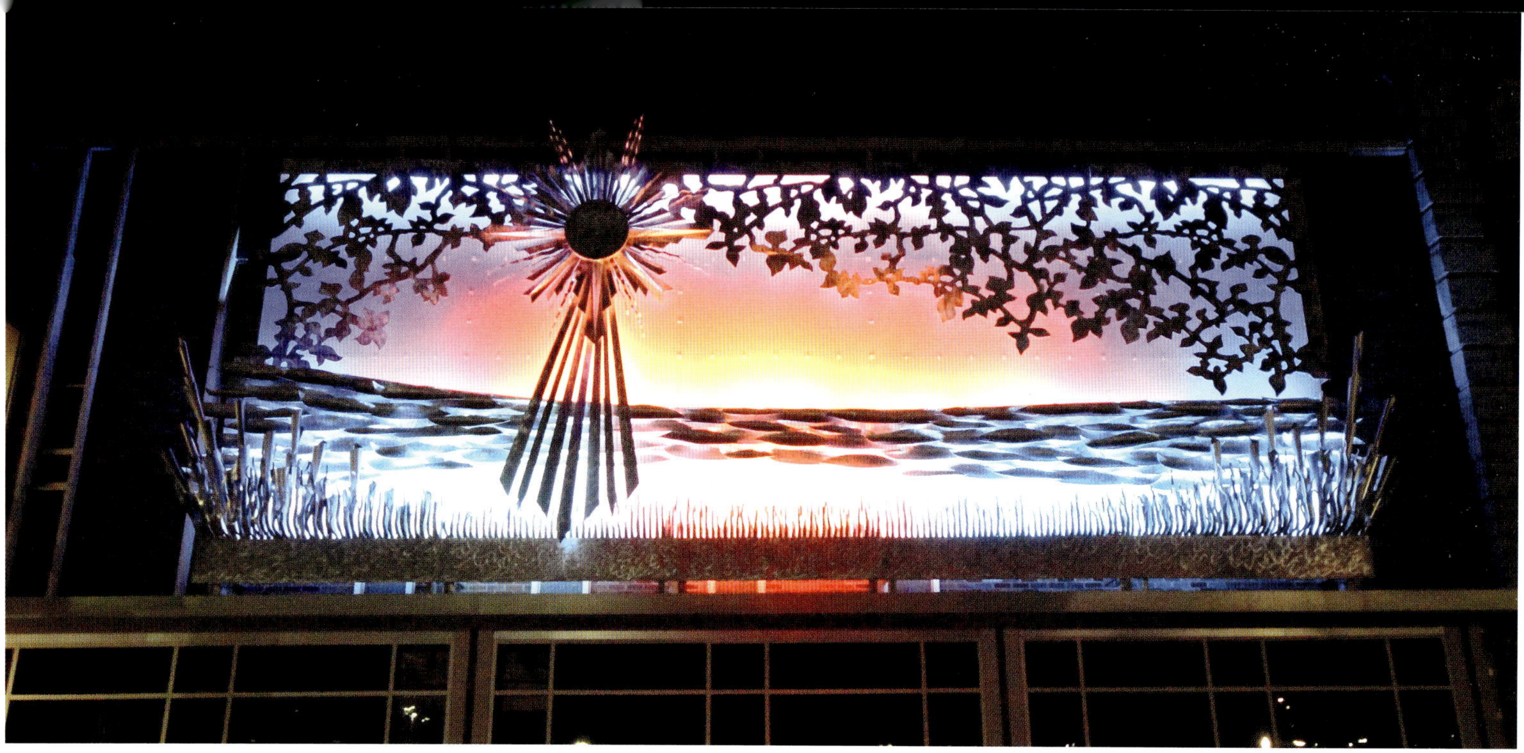

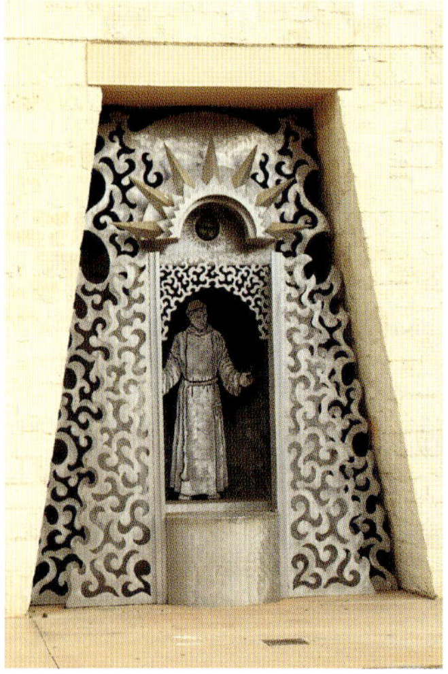

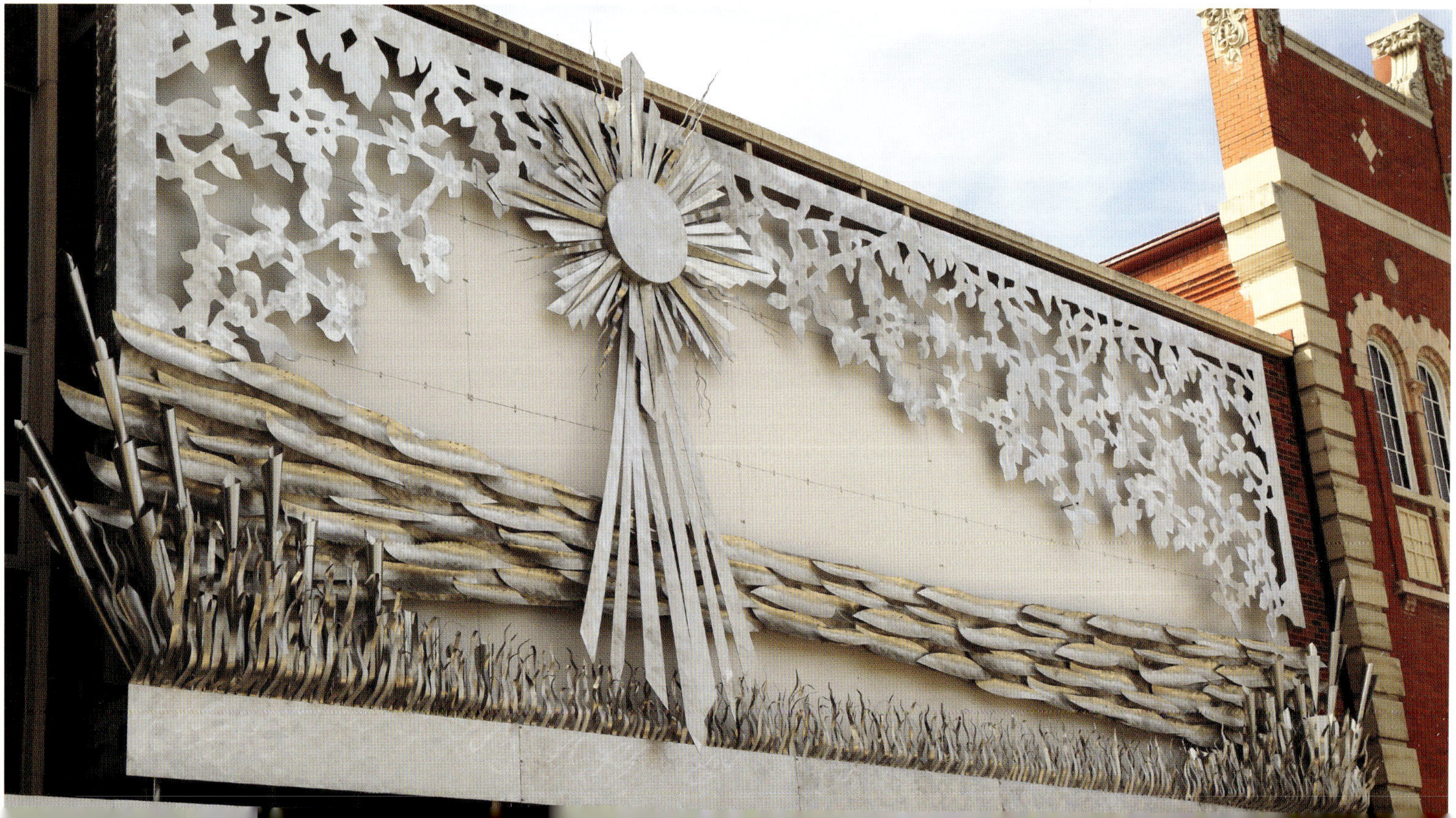

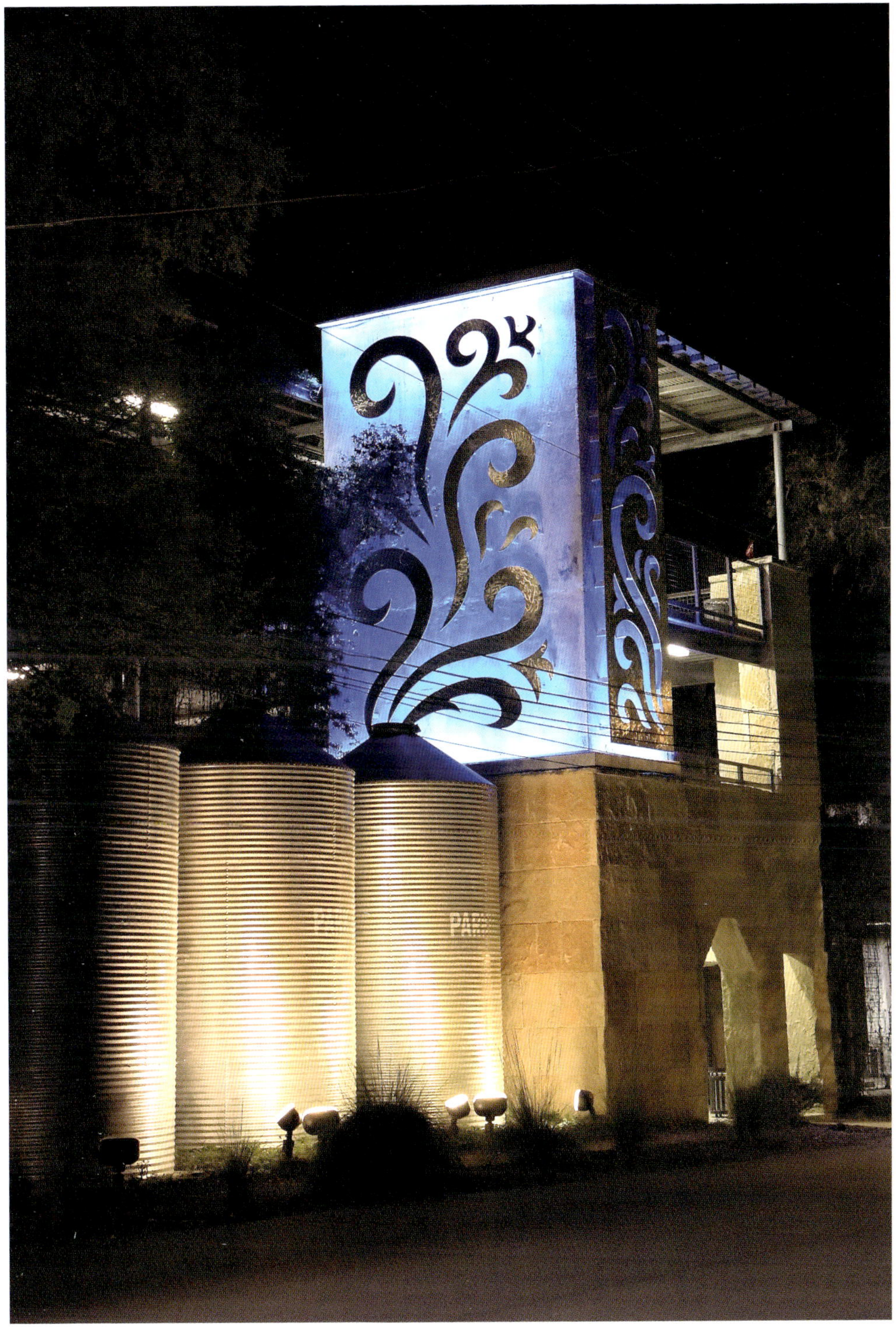

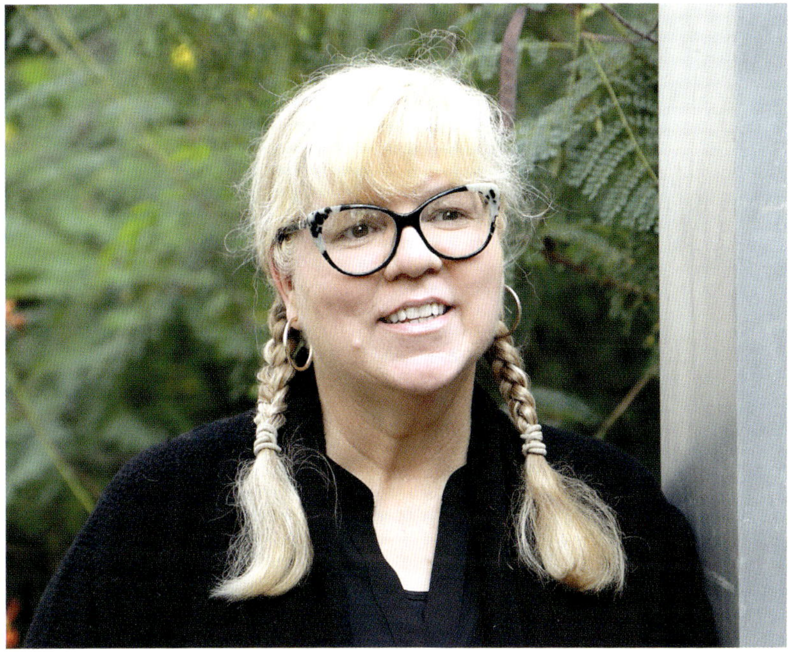

CAKKY BRAWLEY

Cakky Brawley teaches sculpture, ceramics, and 3-D design at Palo Alto College and considers her move to San Antonio in 1993 a significant turning point in her artistic development. A native of Dallas, she earned an MFA in ceramics but always was drawn to metalwork. She received her first commission from the City of San Antonio in 1998, an event she calls "a real game-changer for me." This step into public art took her work from the small scale to large-scale outdoor sculpture. She incorporates backlighting for color and silhouettes in layers, and her attraction to metal, "a more permanent . . . logical material," reminds her of the Catholic imagery of her childhood and of *milagros* and Mexican tinwork. In San Antonio "there's a warmth among the artists. There's a generosity of support, always enough to go around," she says.

Her outdoor work is visible at the Henry B. Gonzalez Convention Center, the Witte Museum, and the University of the Incarnate Word (UIW), where she was commissioned to create *The Source of Life*. "The idea of light and water, how essential they are to life," motivated her sculpture to reflect on actual water and the presence of the Blue Hole on the UIW campus, as well as on spiritual water, "with sunrise and sunset reminding us that each day we get a chance to start all over again.".

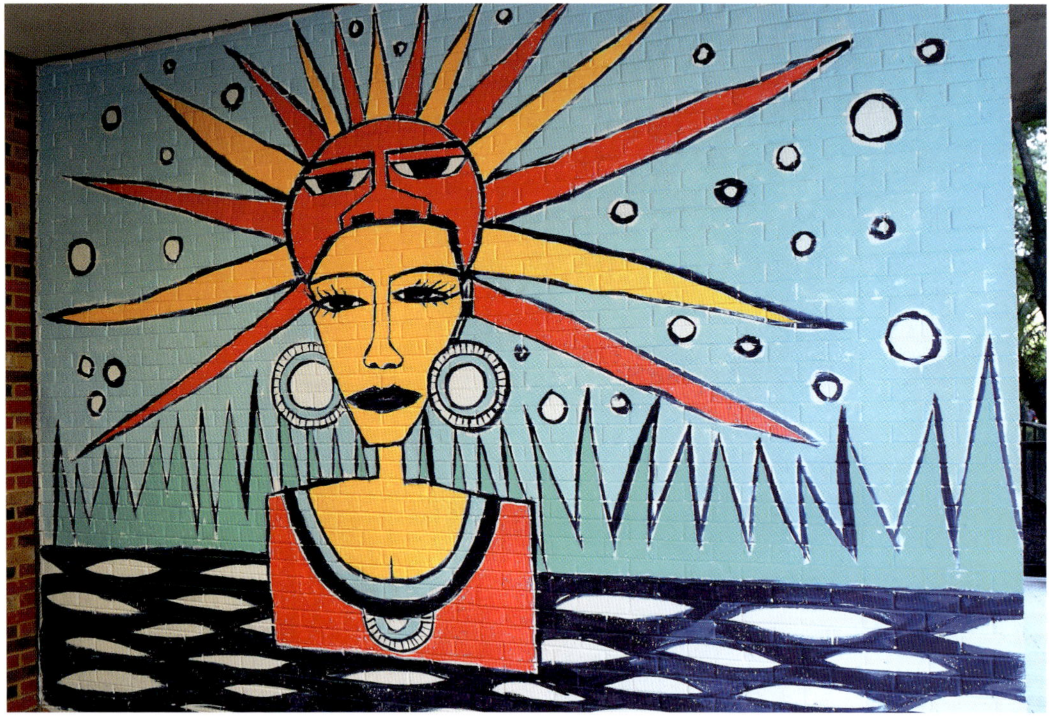

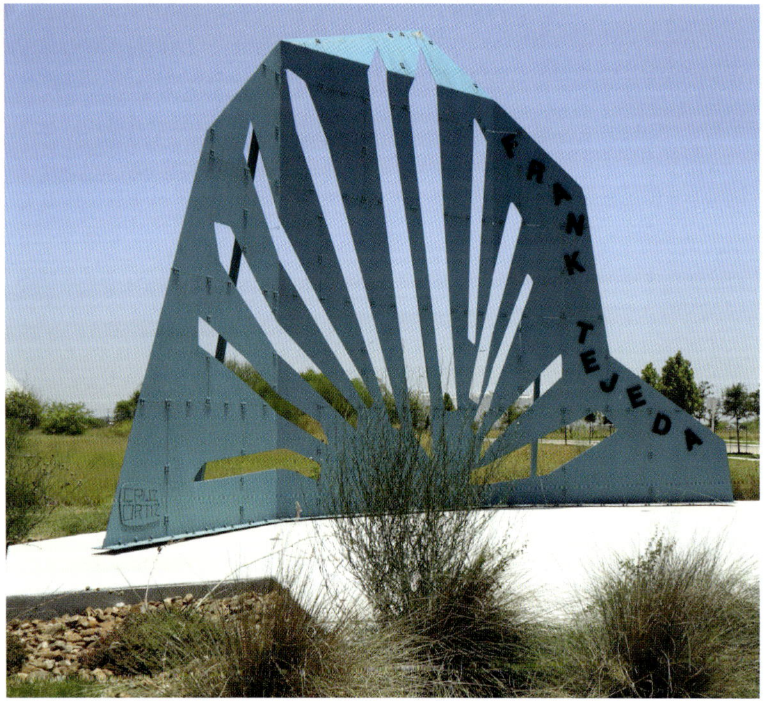

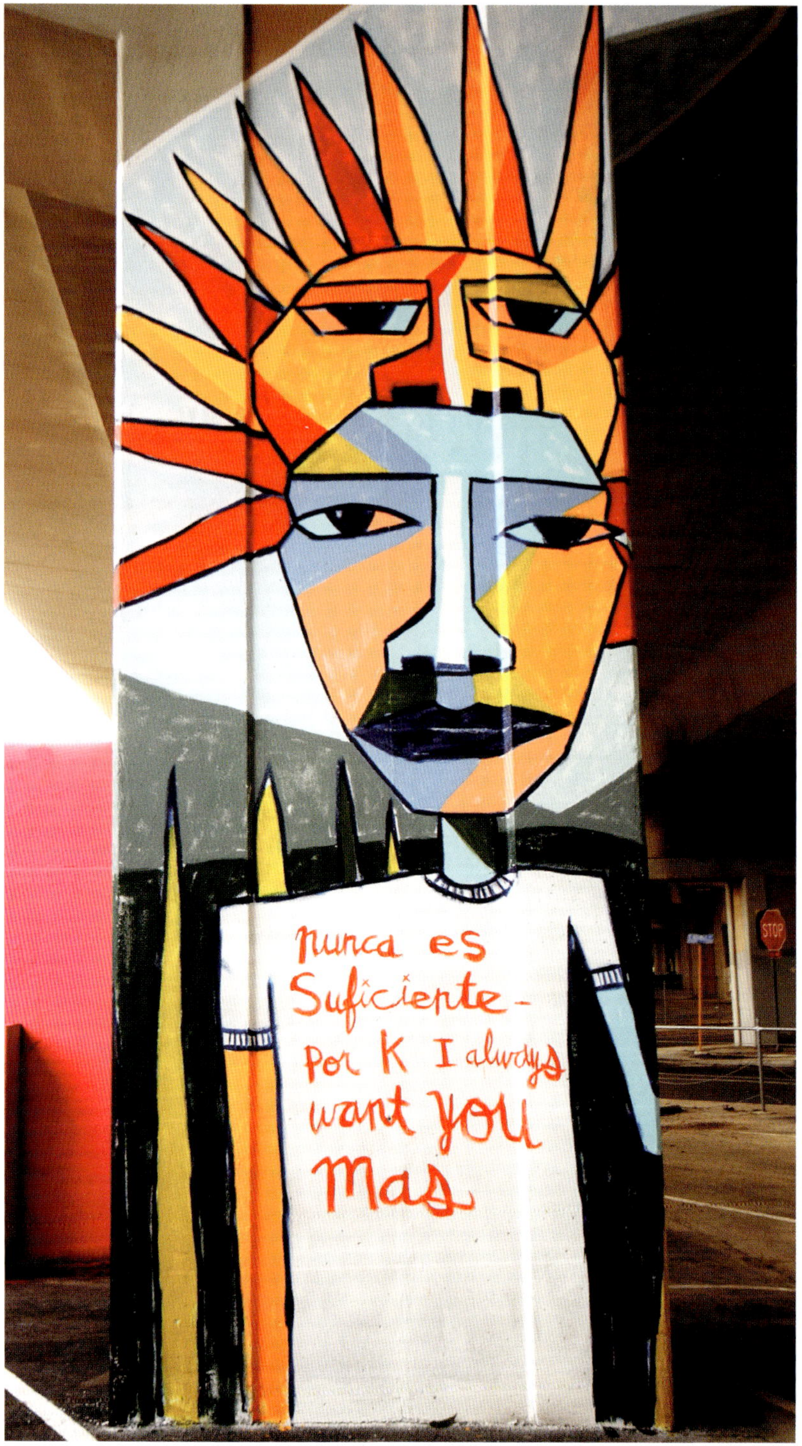

TOP LEFT
Untitled, 2019. Cruz Ortiz. The 68 Apartments, Hemisfair Park.

BOTTOM LEFT
Sun Mountain, 2019. Cruz Ortiz. City Base and Aviation Landings.

RIGHT
Por K I Always Want You Más, 2019. Cruz Ortiz. North St. Mary's Street and IH 35.

OPPOSITE PAGE
LEFT
Dream Song Tower, 2018. Cruz Ortiz. IH 35 and Zarzamora Street.

RIGHT
Cruz Ortiz, 2020

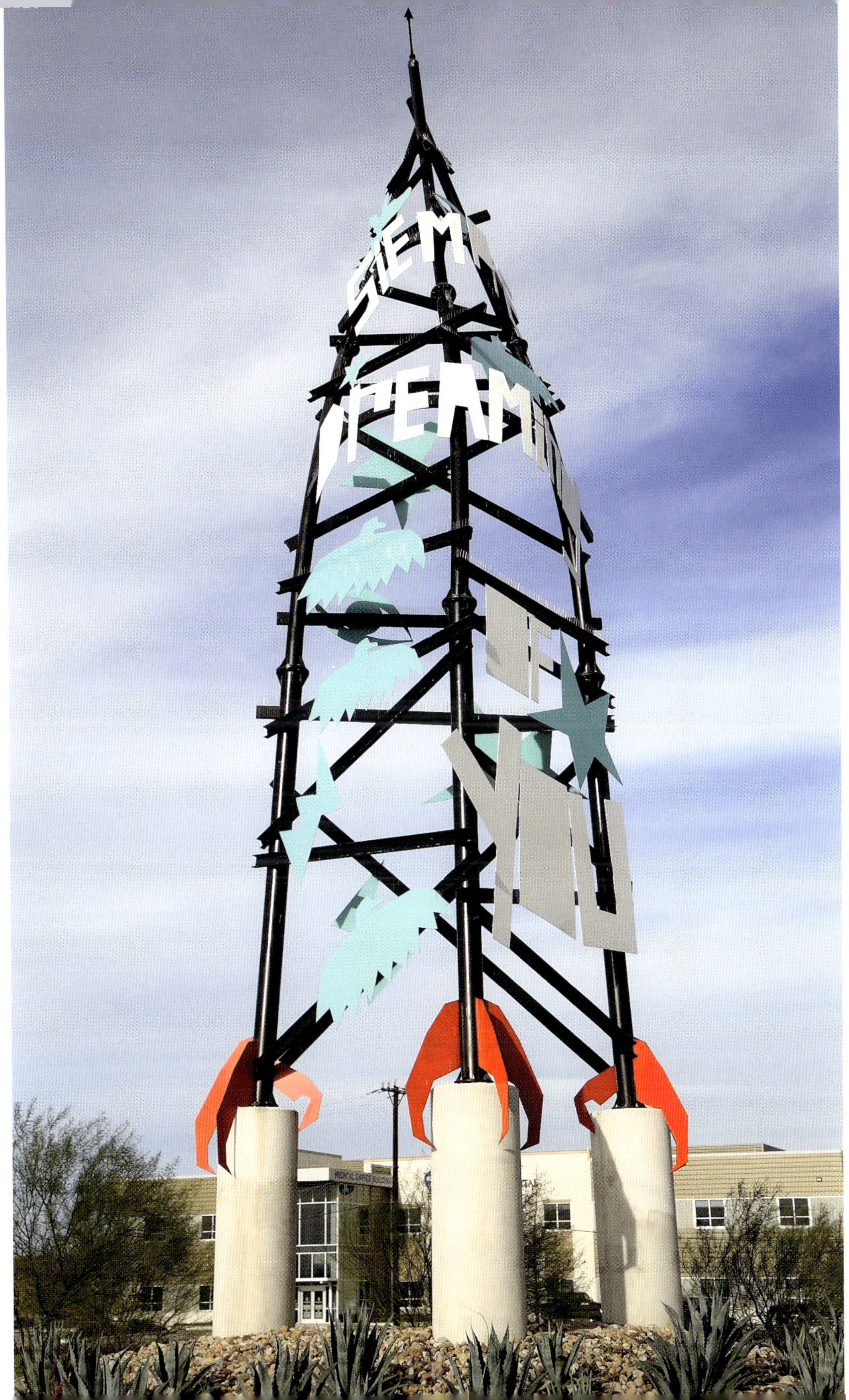

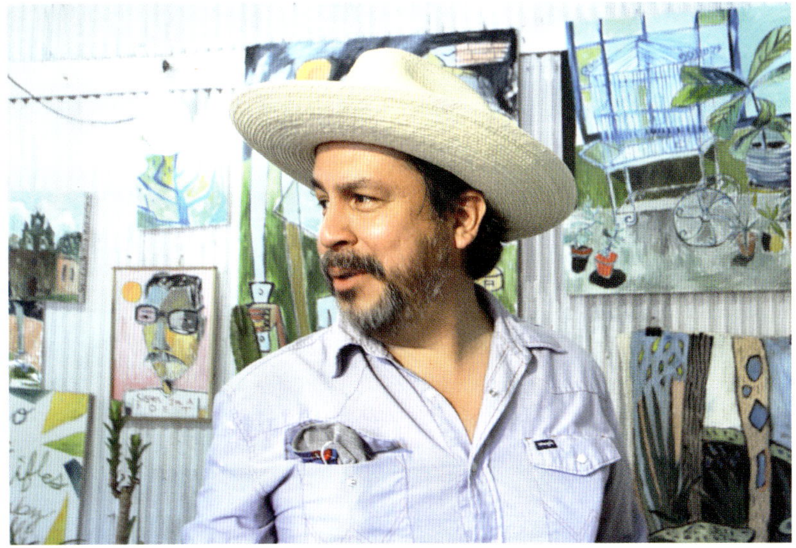

CRUZ ORTIZ

Cruz Ortiz uses multiple mediums to portray issues related to his experiences growing up in the bicultural landscape of South Texas. His work has been seen everywhere from the Louvre to the labels of Absolut vodka bottles. Ortiz examines historical sociopolitical narratives through the critical contextualization of bold graphic screen prints, figurative abstract portraiture, and dreamlike landscapes.

For fifteen years Ortiz taught a diverse range of students in public schools but now works with a great sense of urgency—in creative collaborations with cultural arts and social justice organizations—to capture moments in borderland history that colonizing forces have tried to erase from collective memory. Celebrating our Tex-Mex code-switching in titles such as *One Hundred Años* and *Por K I Always Want You Más* and inspired equally by the Mexican Cine de Oro and the space age, he sees his work as an "opportunity to come up with a new visual language based on tradition, based on native origin dialects and issues that transcend to the present."

His work has been exhibited in the Louvre in Paris, as well as in Ireland, Puerto Rico, and England and throughout the US, and has been acquired for the permanent collections of the Smithsonian National Portrait Gallery, the Arizona State University Museum of Art, the University of Texas at San Antonio Library Special Collections, Ruby City, and the San Antonio Museum of Art.

BOTTOM LEFT
Life Cycle of the Gulf Coast Toad, 2011. Diana Kersey. Mulberry Street bridge.

RIGHT
The Guardians of Five Points, 2017. Diana Kersey. Fredericksburg Road and Five Points bus stop.

OPPOSITE PAGE
TOP LEFT
Bridges of Understanding, 2018. Diana Kersey. West Martin Street bridge, San Pedro Creek.

BOTTOM LEFT
The Riparian Edge, 2020. Diana Kersey. Oxbow Office Tower, 1803 Broadway. This ceramic piece of art covers more than 650 square feet.

RIGHT
Diana Kersey, 2020

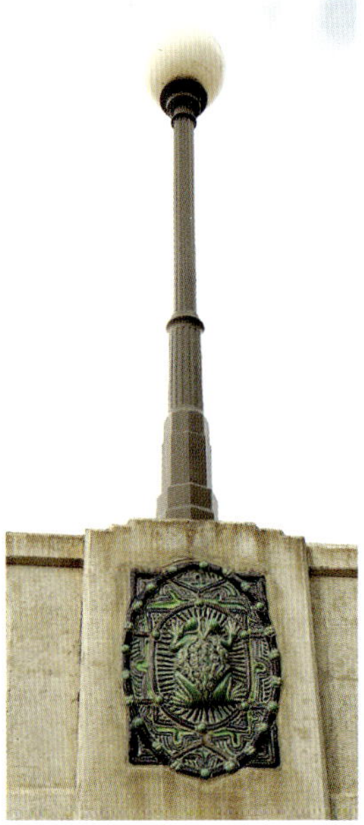

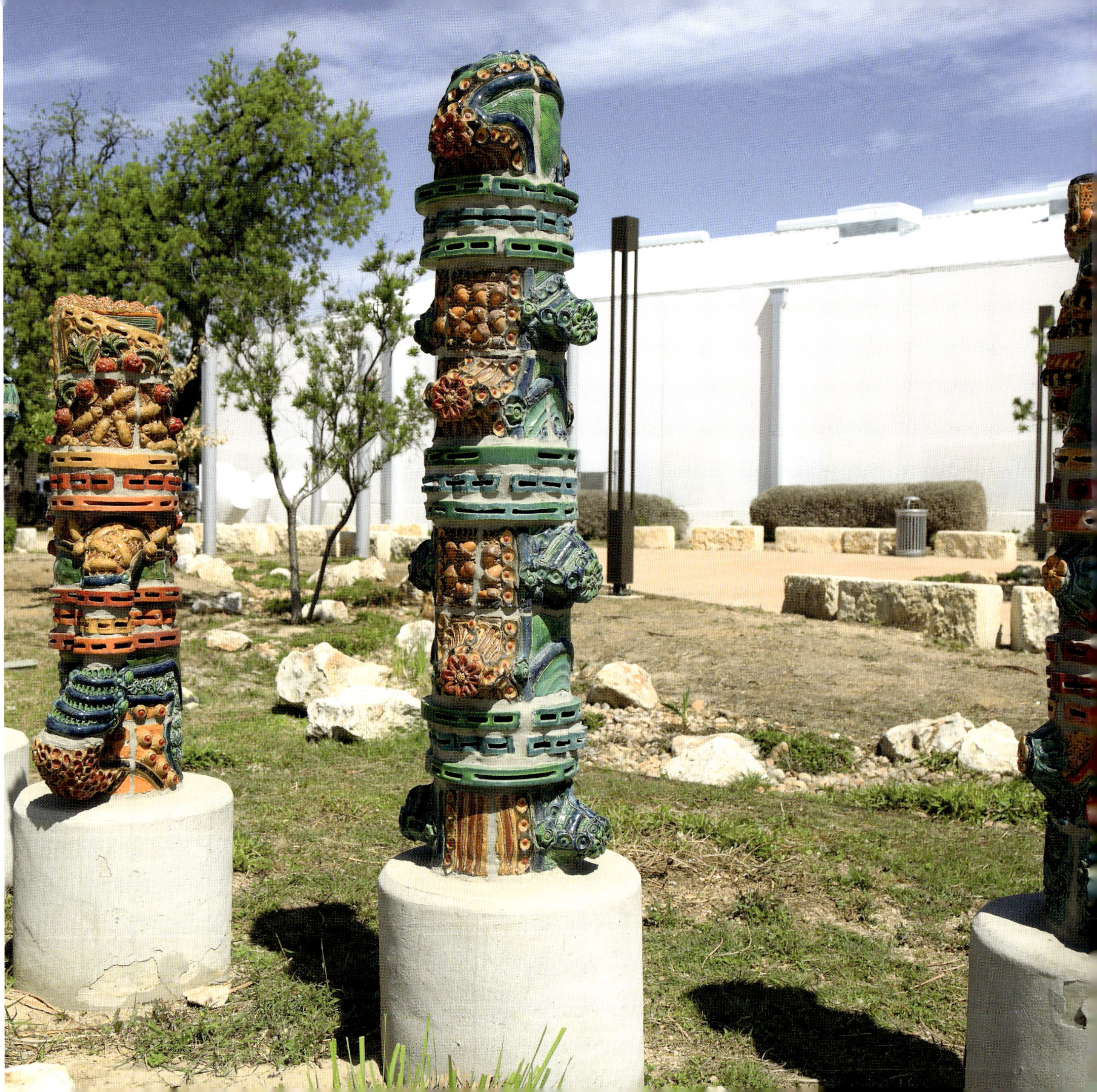

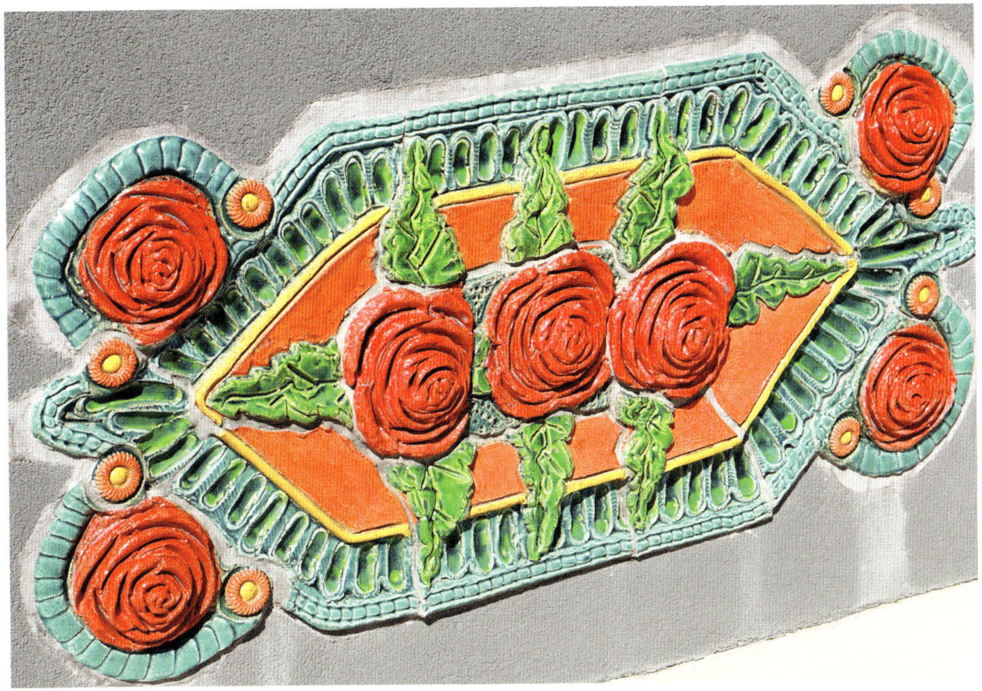

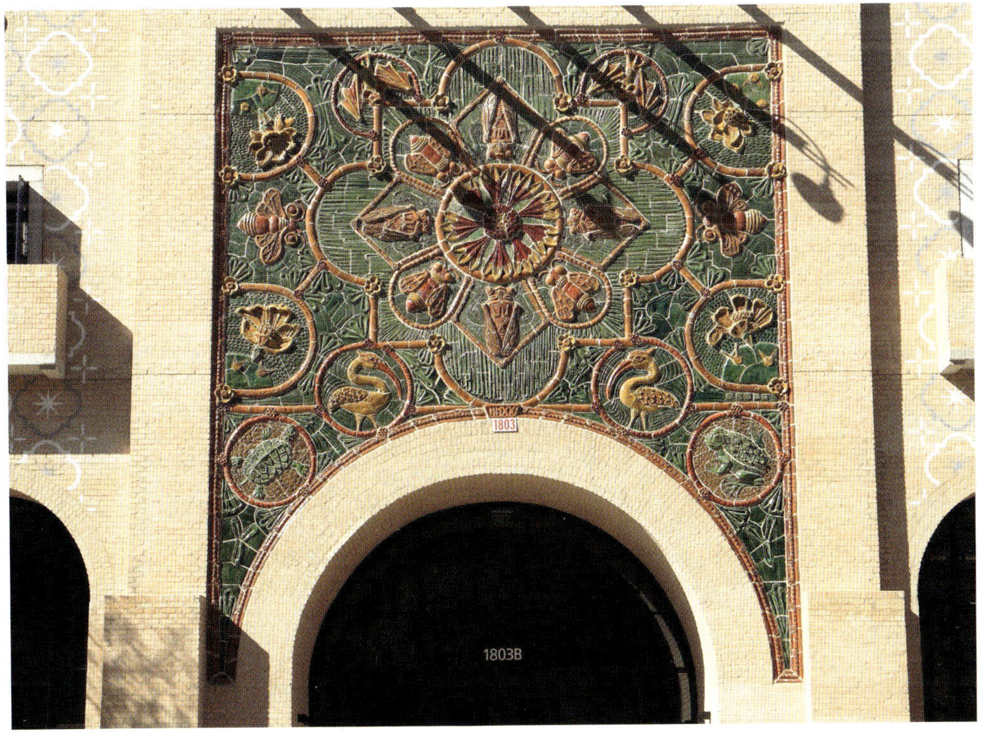

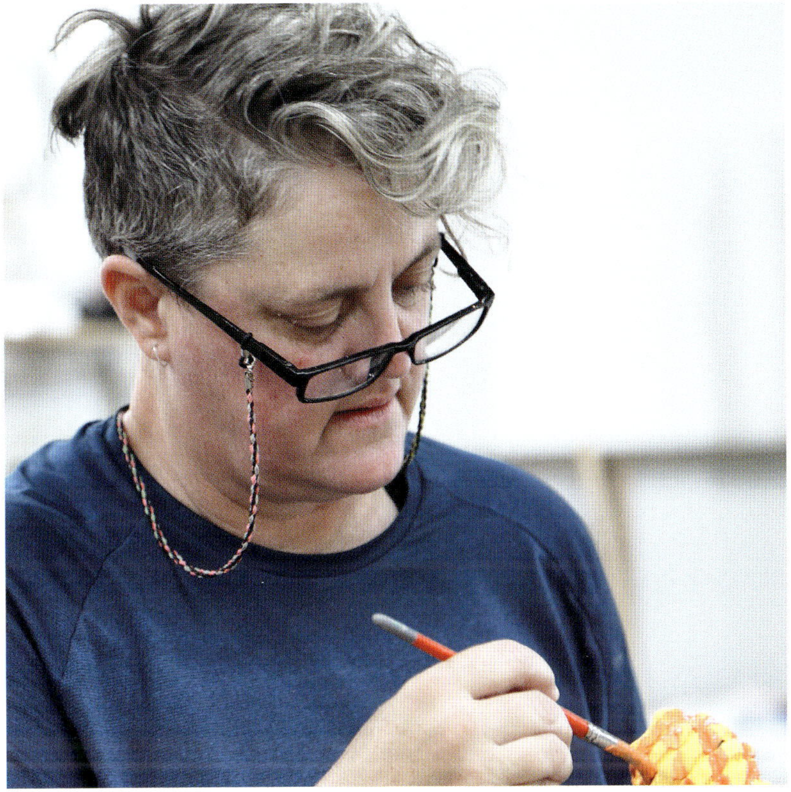

DIANA KERSEY

Artist Diana Kersey works exclusively in clay. As a child in Lubbock, her parents let her dig a mud pit in the backyard. She hit clay 13 inches down and has been creating works of clay ever since.

Her work is characterized by the muscular, textural qualities of the clay; colorful, translucent glazes; and a kiln that seems to court and preserve the beauty of nature. They also exude a profound sense of place, as in her river-green ceramic inlays of tadpoles and turtles on bridges (see page 48).

"I am always conscious that I work for an audience that will interact with my work for decades to come, and possibly, long after I am gone," she says. "Successful public art projects help to strengthen communities and lower barriers, so it must at least partially originate from within the community that surrounds it. My hope is to create work that will become an important part of the lives of the community who engages with it."

TOP
River Origins & Movements #2, 2009. River Walk near Camden Street bridge.

BOTTOM
River Origins & Movements #1, 2009. River Walk near Newell Street bridge.

OPPOSITE PAGE
LEFT
Tribute to Freedom, 2019. SW Military Drive and US Highway 90.

RIGHT
George Schroeder, 2019

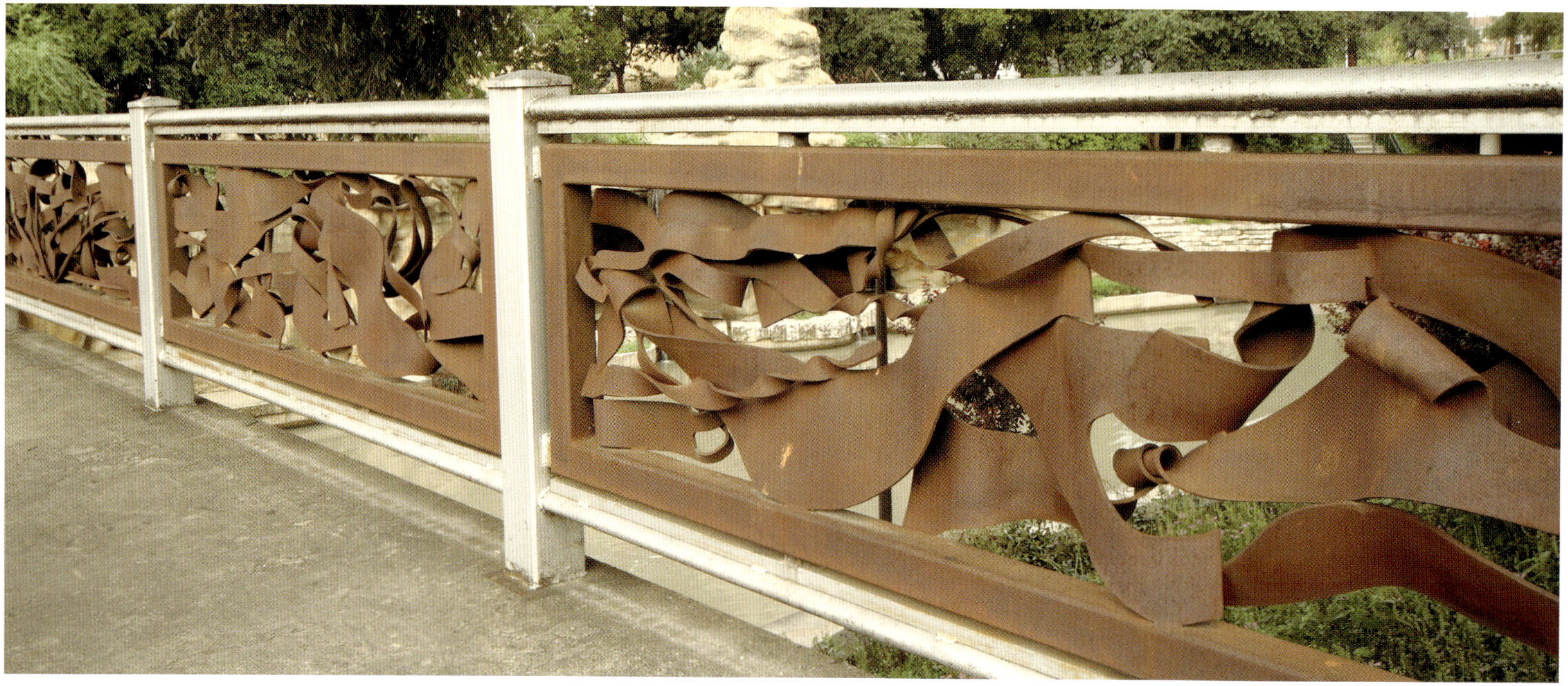

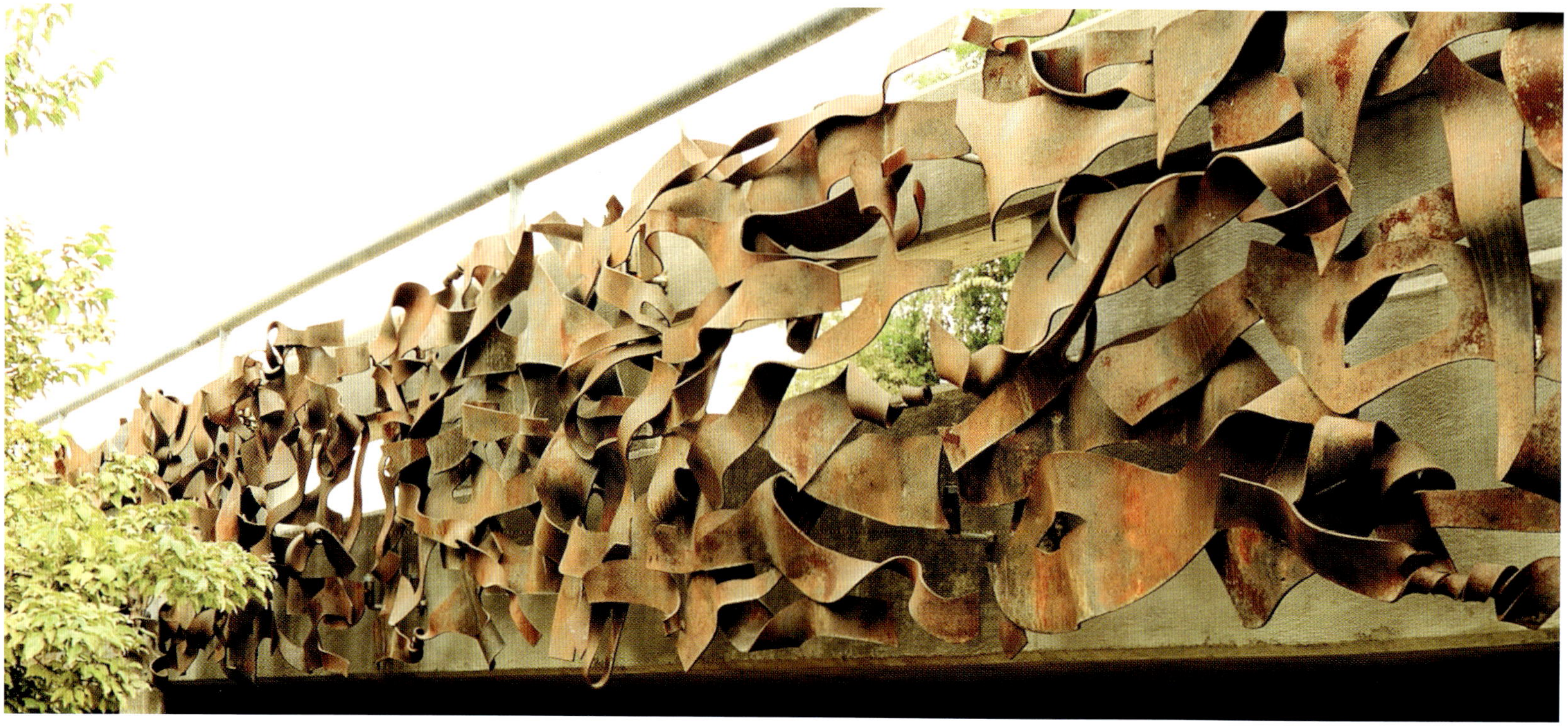

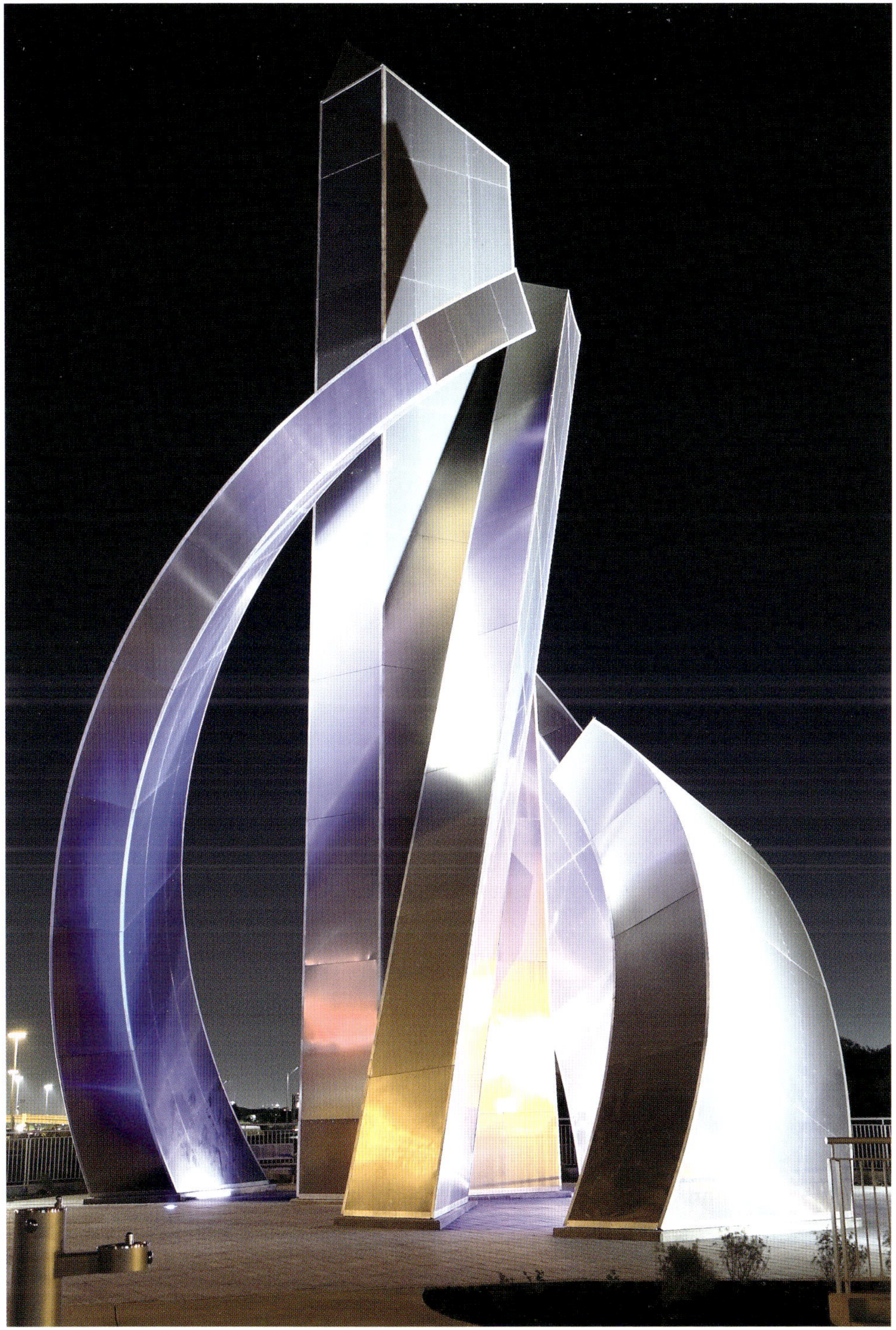

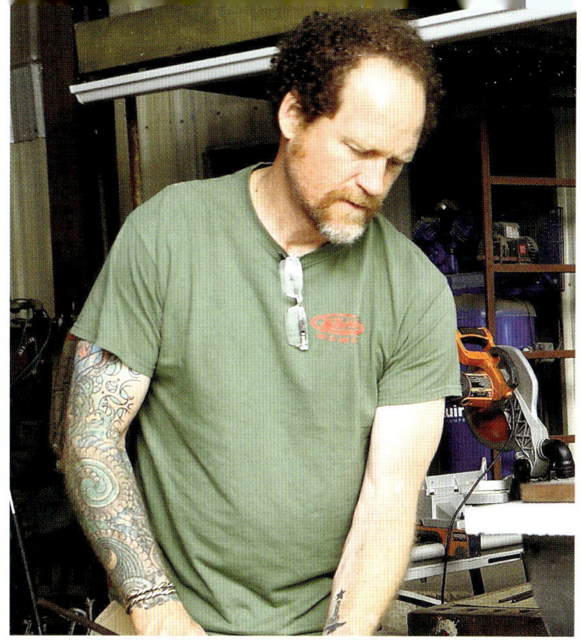

GEORGE SCHROEDER

After years of working in the corporate world and creating sculptures at night, George Schroeder decided to open a full-time studio. The founder, owner, and director of Schroeder Art Studios is a native Texan and has operated the same working studio in San Antonio for more than twenty years. His midsize to monumental sculptures and paintings and large-scale drawings enhance the beauty of hospitals, zoos, and the San Antonio River Walk.

Much of his work is done by hot-forging with airpowered hammers. "The metal is only hot for so long," he says. "You only have a moment, so you go into this hyper-accelerated decision-making—you have to be thinking about the next shape before you even do it." His *River Origins #1* and *#2* metal art pieces grace the Camden Street and Newell Street bridges over the San Antonio River Walk, suggesting abstracted animals and plants. His work is characterized by simplicity, clarity, and spatial ambiguity, he says, "baptized in fire, hammering, cutting, twisting, and water."

In 2010, Schroeder was selected to create the inaugural outdoor sculpture for the Aborg International Sculpture Park in southwestern Iceland. In 2013, University Health System commissioned him to create one of the largest shaped-metal sculptures in the US, a stand-alone sculpture designed to engage the public as they enter and exit the hospital. Of the many metal sculptures he has created, he says, "I wanted them to be timeless."

TOP
New Chapa Lion, 2000. Jesse Treviño. S. Santa Rosa and East Commerce Streets.

BOTTOM LEFT
La Feria, 1983. Jesse Treviño. Ceramic tiles. El Mercado.

BOTTOM RIGHT
Laredito Mural, 2012. Jesse Treviño. Casa Navarro State Historic Site.

OPPOSITE PAGE LEFT
Spirit of Healing, 1997. 90 feet tall, mosaic tiles. Santa Rosa Children's Hospital of San Antonio.

RIGHT
Jesse Treviño. Photo courtesy of COSA Department of Arts & Culture.

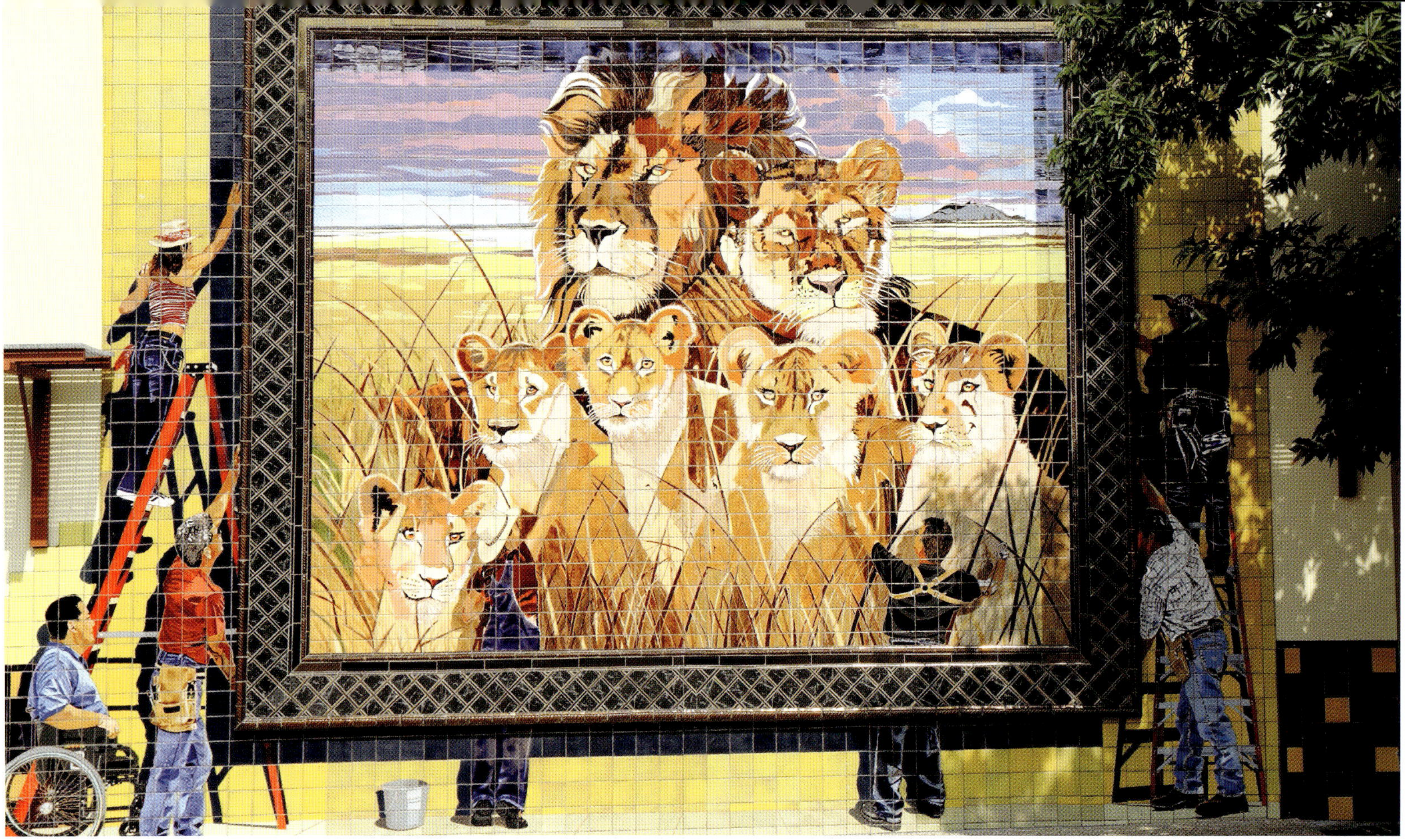

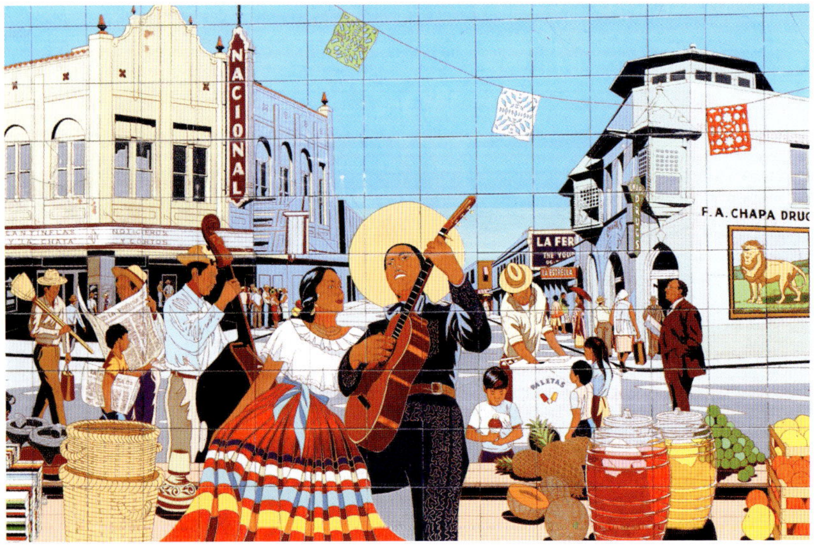

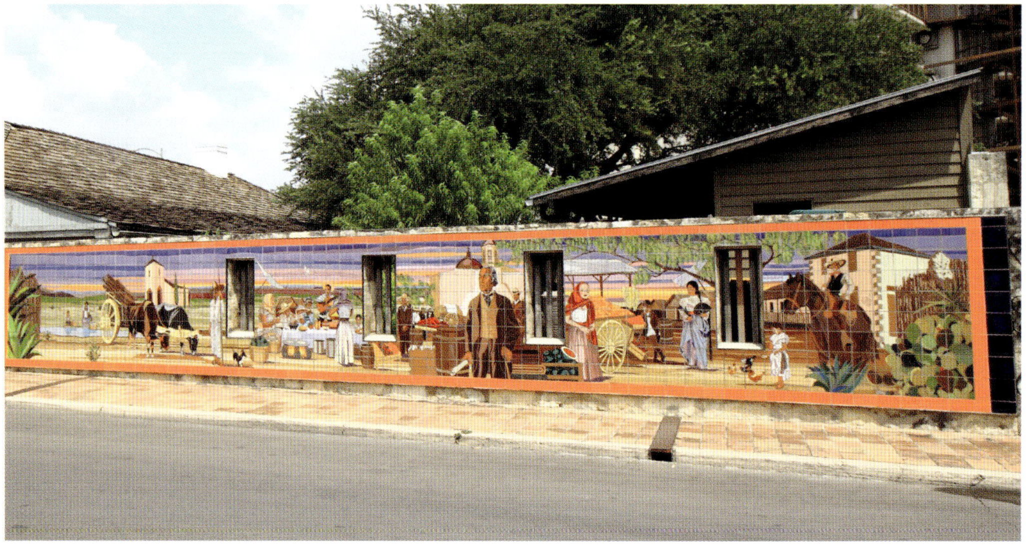

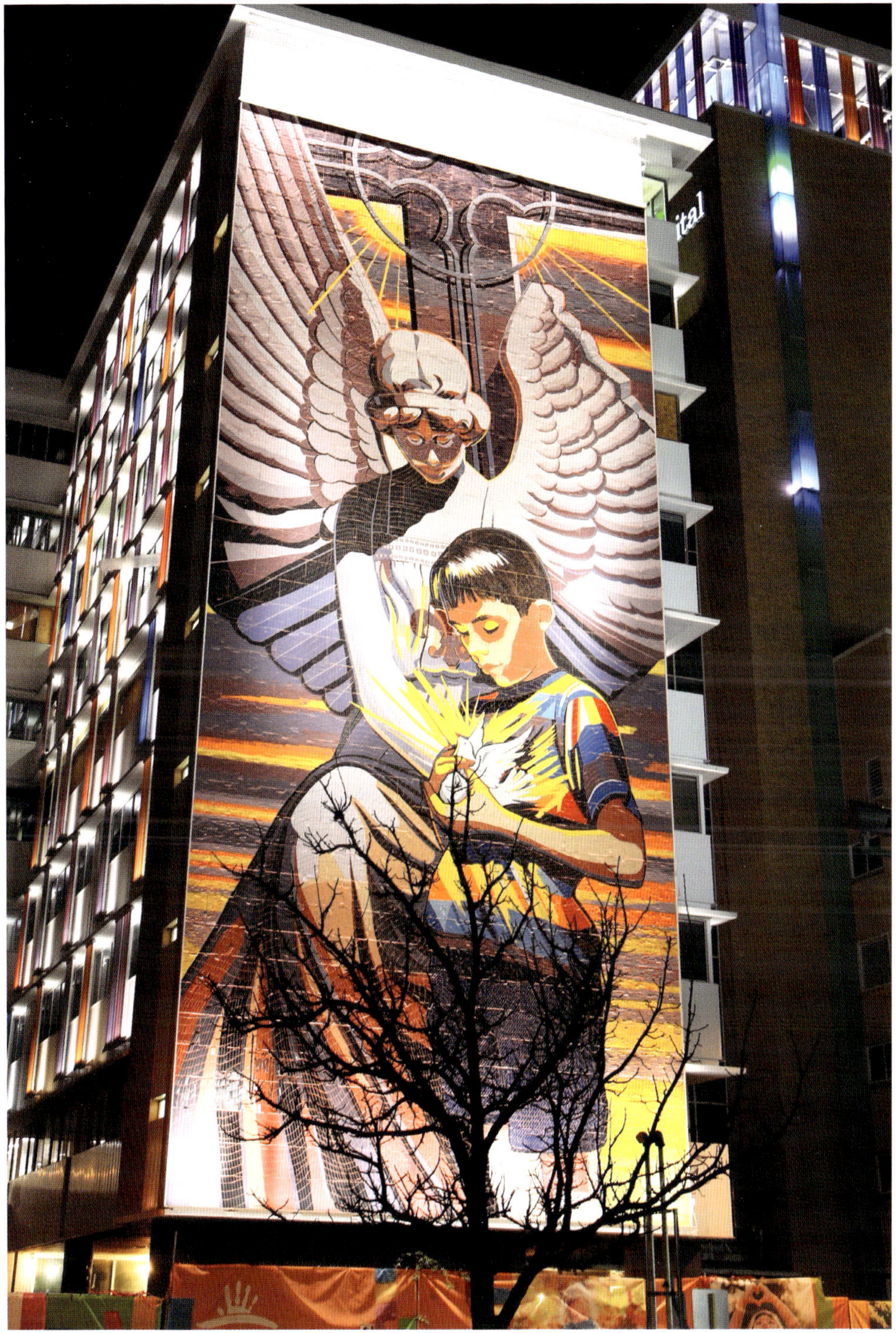

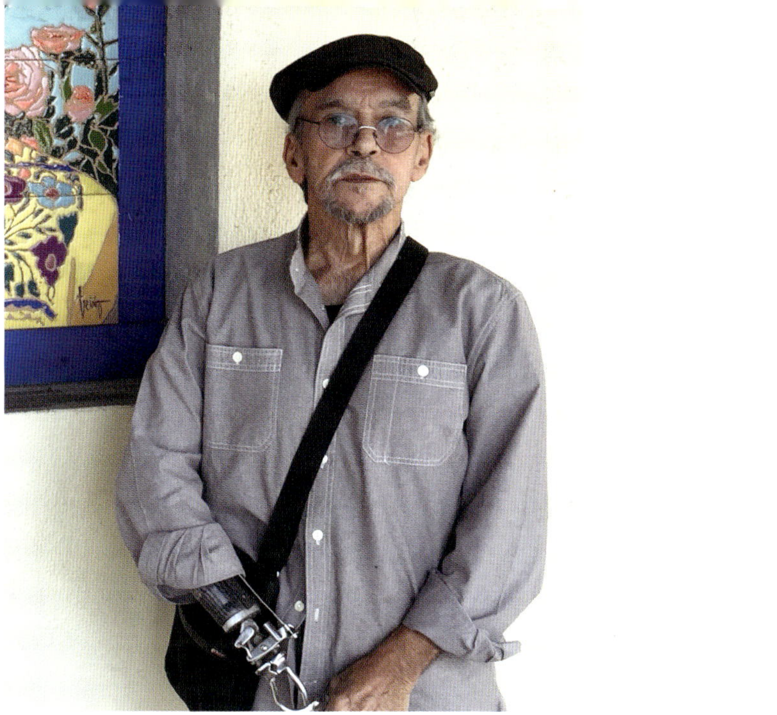

JESSE TREVIÑO

Renowned for his ability to capture in paint and tile the values, history, and power of the Mexican American experience, Jesse Treviño's works also reflect the tastes, feel, and sounds of San Antonio. No murals speak San Antonio as well as his two iconic tile masterpieces—*La Veladora*, at Avenida Guadalupe (see page 101), and *The Spirit of Healing* at the Santa Rosa Hospital downtown (shown here).

A promising young art student, he was drafted to Vietnam, where he stepped in a booby trap in the Mekong delta. Near death, he made a promise that if he recovered, he would paint the most important things in his world: his family, home, friends, and community. Treviño suffered the amputation of his right arm but retrained his nondominant arm to paint and continued *adelante*, to boldly support the rising *movimiento chicano* and the renaissance of San Antonio's *muralismo*.

Honored at the White House, and featured in a one-man show at the National Museum of American Art at the Smithsonian in Washington, DC, he humbly credits his community. Of his work, he says, "It's my gift back to my cultura, for all the gifts my culture and my gente have given me. . . . My next dream is to honor the veterans, those who gave so much. Some of us came back alive. Some didn't. But all of us offered up body and soul to do what was asked of us."

BOTTOM LEFT
Optimism Starts with You, 2020. Los Otros. COVID-19 mural.

RIGHT
Untitled, 2017. Los Otros. North St. Mary's Street.

OPPOSITE PAGE
TOP LEFT
Untitled, *2017. "Soupe" and "Shek." Houston Street.*

CENTER LEFT
Cap Canvas, 2020. Brittany Taylor and Jack Polarsky wear cap art by Los Otros.

BOTTOM LEFT
Untitled, 2017. Los Otros. FiestaStore. 2611 Broadway.

RIGHT
David "Shek" Vega and Nik Soupe ("Los Otros")

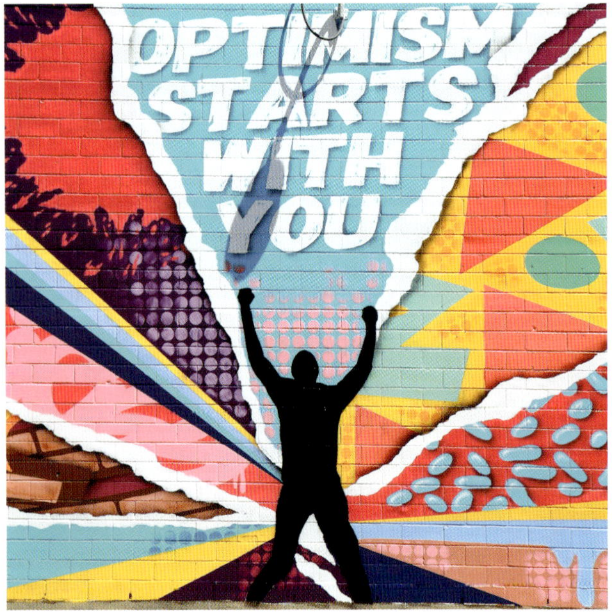

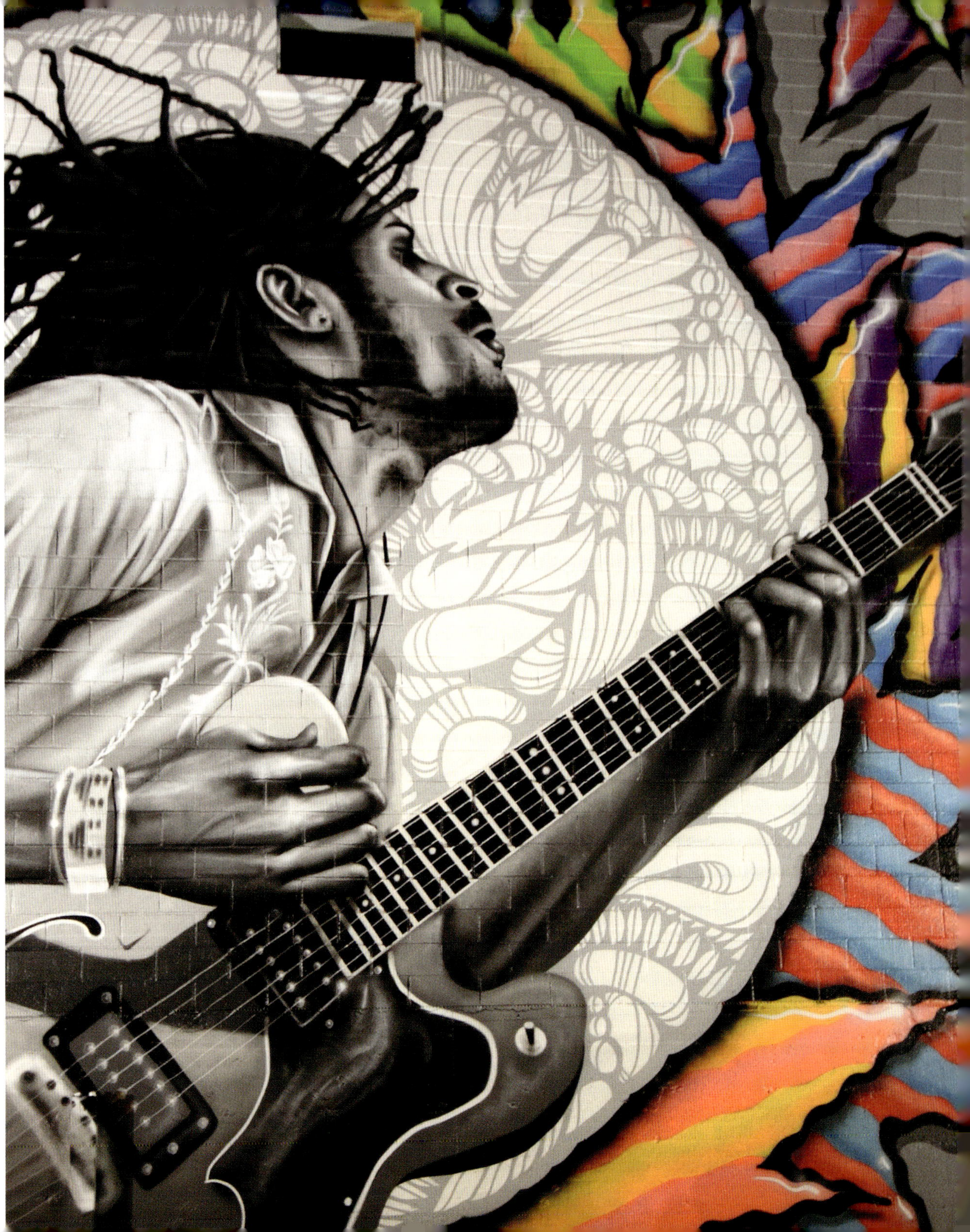

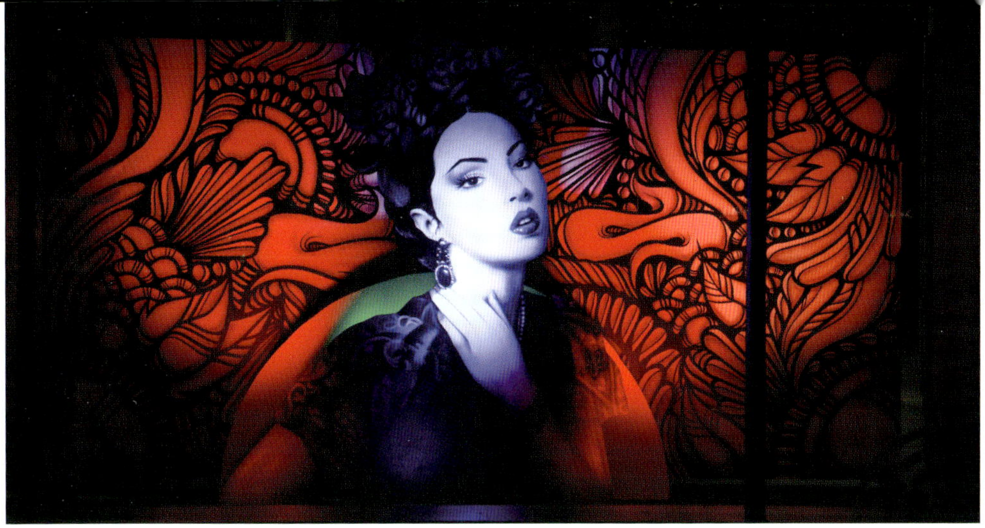

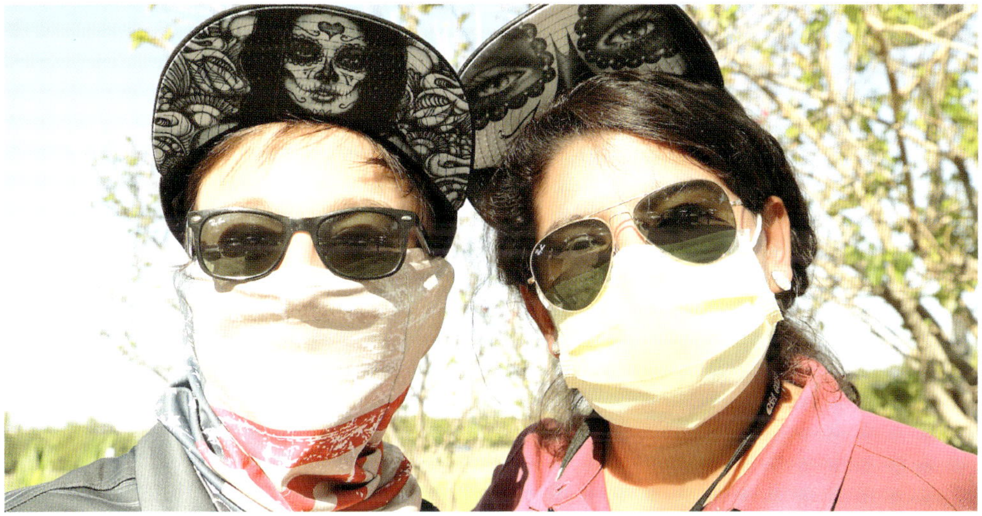

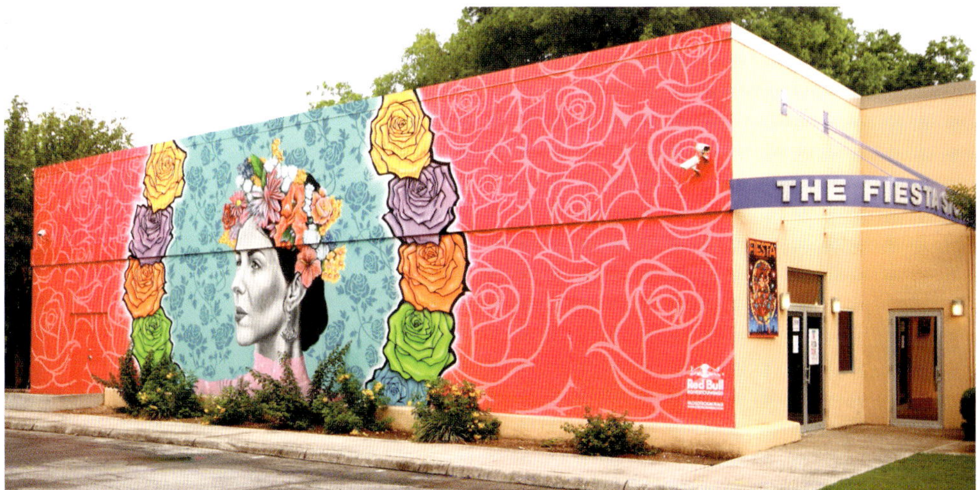

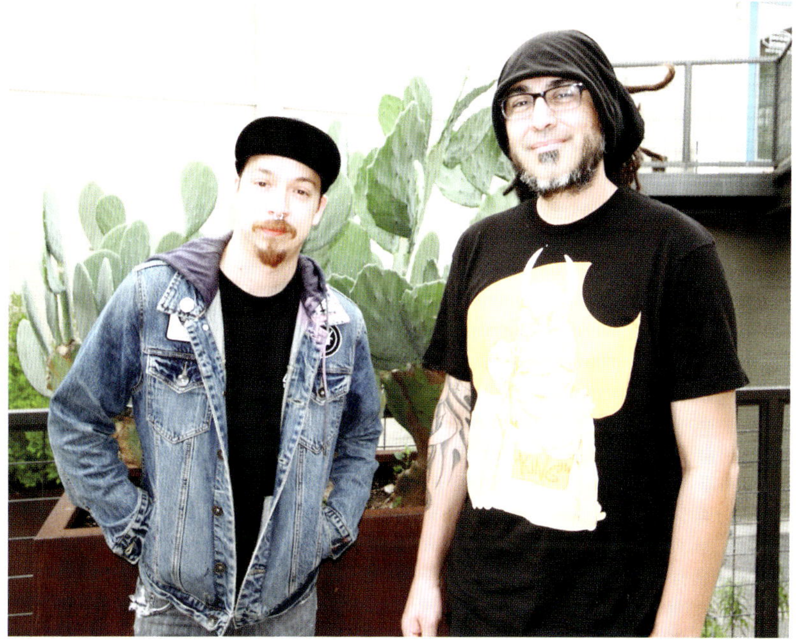

LOS OTROS (DAVID "SHEK" VEGA AND NIK SOUPE)

Los Otros (David "Shek" Vega and Nik Soupe) have left their mark all across San Antonio. Shek, creator of the first street art gallery in San Antonio, Gravelmouth, and his Los Otros partner, Nik Soupe, have painted for personal and public art projects and for a wide variety of businesses and organizations, and their themes are as diverse as the city. The duo captures the joy of fusion collaborations that blend colorful contextual patterns and design with aerosol portraiture.

"We have fought for decades to legitimize street art and are proud to now see it interwoven into the fabric of our community," says Shek. In 2019, he founded the nonprofit San Antonio Street Art Initiative, which debuted its major projects with the transformation of a parking lot under an overpass into what they dubbed the "Largest Outdoor Gallery in Texas" (pages 138–139, 146–147, and 150). Shek and Soupe continue working to not only bring artists together to paint dozens of murals, but to create their own Los Otros masterpieces as well. Shek summarizes it well: "We don't just *love* the street mural art form. We've *lived* it for most of our lives."

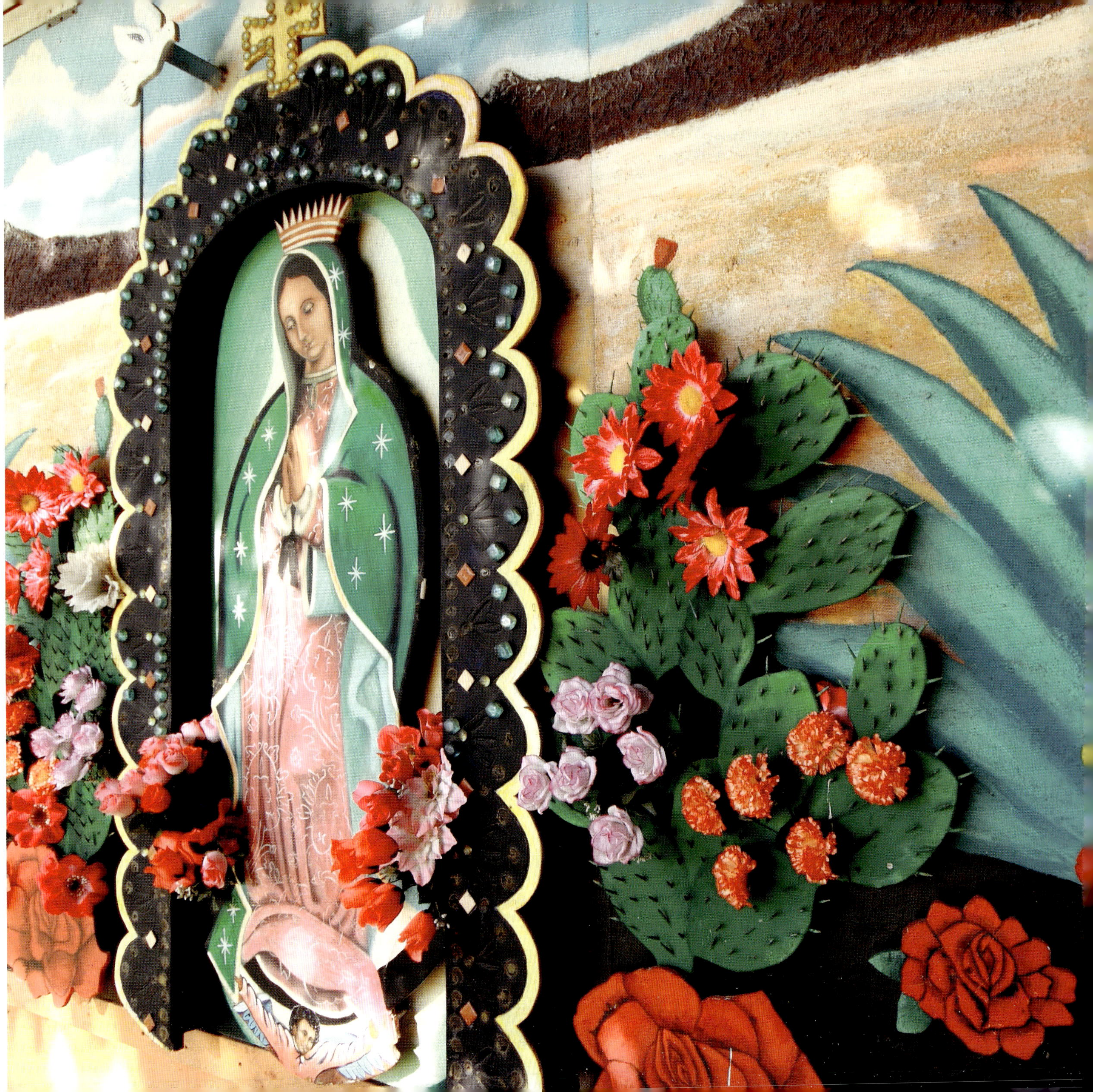

Nicho para la Virgen de Guadalupe, 2001. Mary Agnes Rodríguez and Janie Tabares-Ornelas. 1512 El Paso Street.

OPPOSITE PAGE
TOP LEFT
Para Manny, 2012. Mary Agnes Rodríguez. Front wall of San Anto Cultural Arts office, 2120 El Paso Street.

BOTTOM LEFT
Ceramic masks, 2020–21. Mary Agnes Rodríguez.

RIGHT
Mary Agnes Rodríguez, 2019. San Anto Cultural Arts.

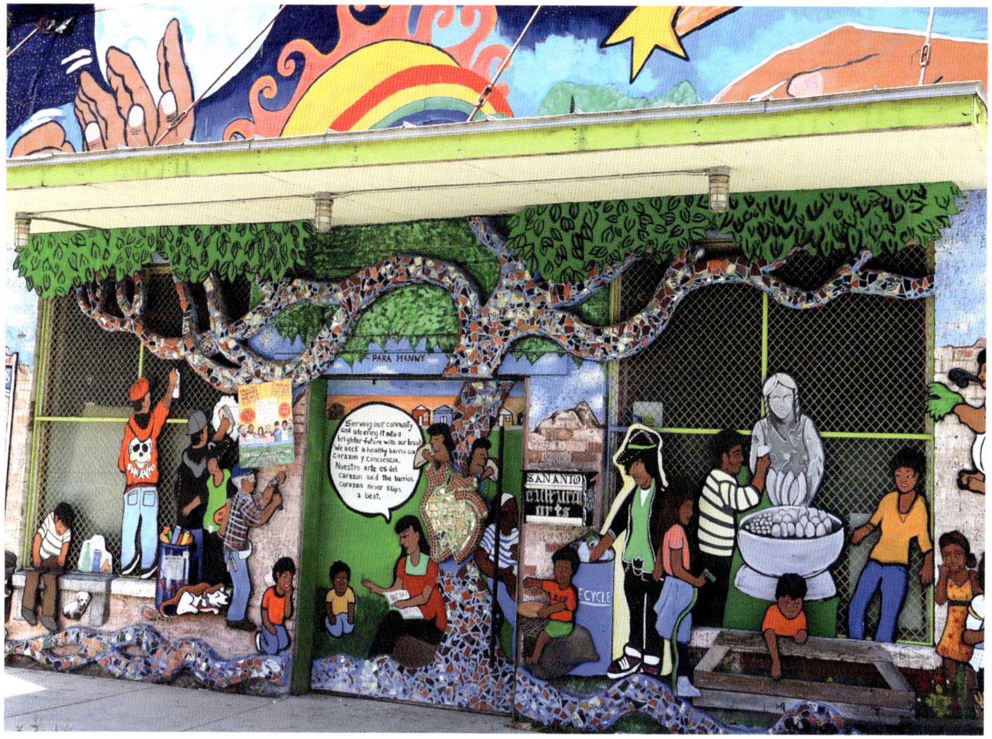

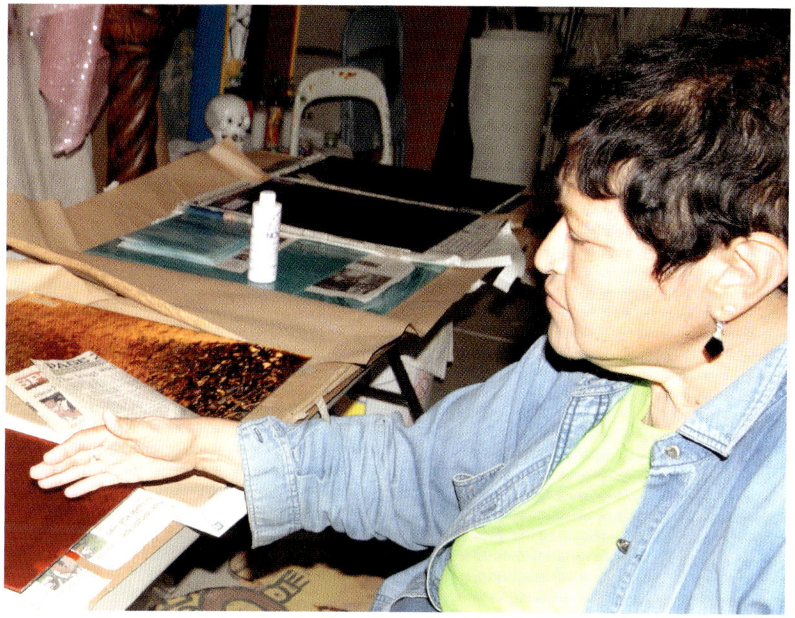

MARY AGNES RODRÍGUEZ

Born and raised in San Antonio, Mary Agnes Rodríguez is a community-based artist/muralist in the West Side and a part of the MujerArtes de Esperanza Co-op, whose themes center on women's empowerment and the telling of their stories through clay.

While Rodriguez also produces paintings and illustrations, she feels that the murals and the women's clay co-op are important because they build community with their traditions, *cultura*, ancestors, histories, and community-issues awareness and achieve this through a public art that everyone can access. "It's like a museum, but outdoors," she says. "And, especially important for our community, it's free."

Rodriguez has completed various murals whose messages empower community, youth, and women. In addition, in response to the COVID-19 pandemic, she began to create beautifully hand-painted masks, in layers of cloth and canvas for wearing and in ceramic for artistic exhibits. She has worked with numerous community art organizations, including the San Anto Cultural Arts (whose front wall she painted), the Esperanza Peace and Justice Center, and Centro Cultural Aztlan. Her goal for her artwork is that it "make an impact of some kind within my community, and that it keep our *cultura* alive for future generations." (See also *Sacred Water / Agua es Vida* on page 20).

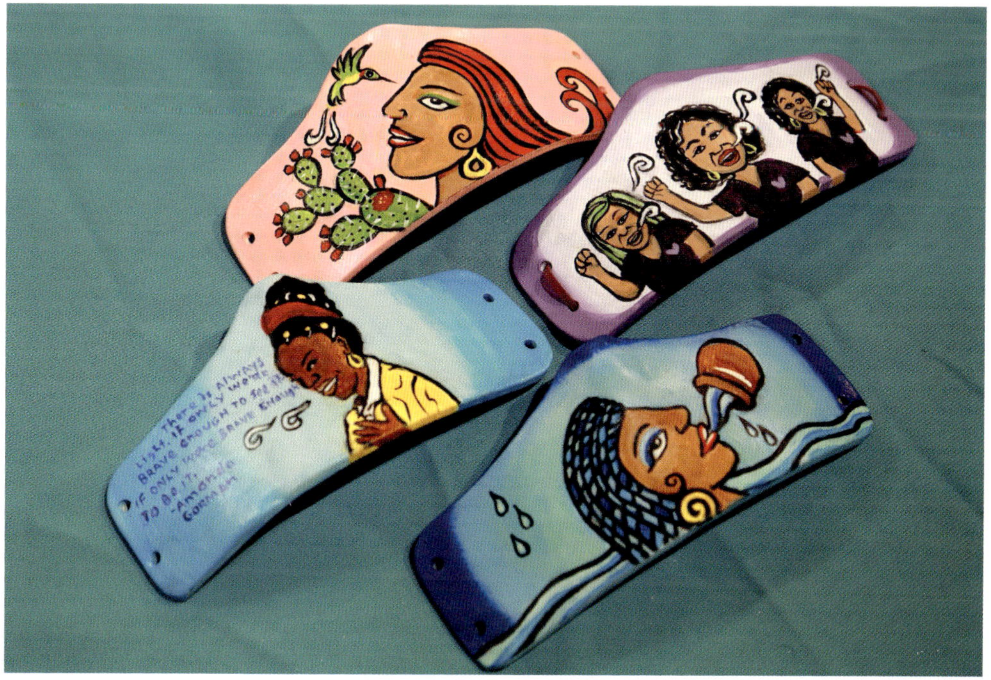

TOP LEFT
Take Me to the Moon, 2013. Oscar Alvarado. S. Zarzamora Street.

BOTTOM LEFT
Rejuvenecimiento, 2002. Oscar Alvarado. Elmendorf Park.

RIGHT
Grown in Granite, 2007. Oscar Alvarado. 1001 Roosevelt Avenue.

OPPOSITE PAGE LEFT
The Blue Hole, 2015. Oscar Alvarado. Hemisfair Park, Yanaguana Garden.

RIGHT
Oscar Alvarado at his studio

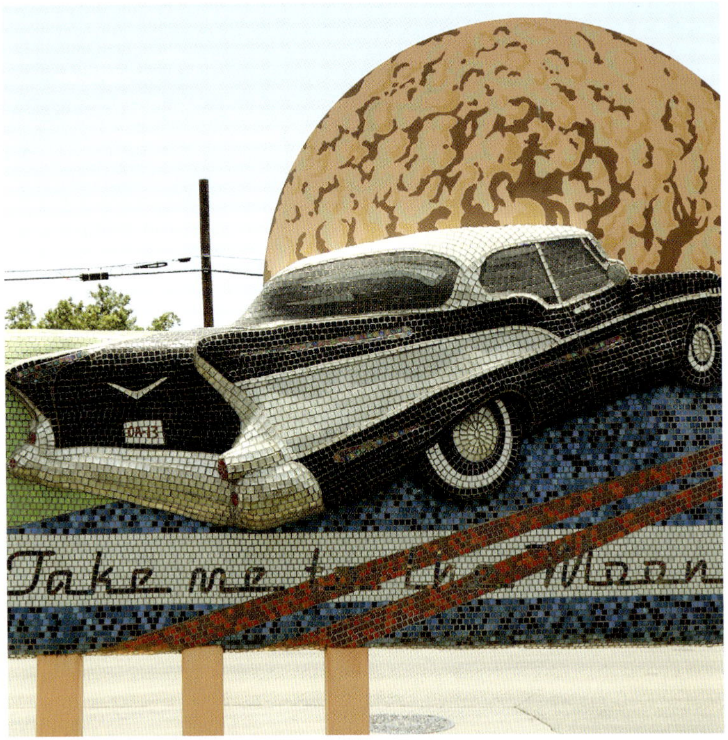

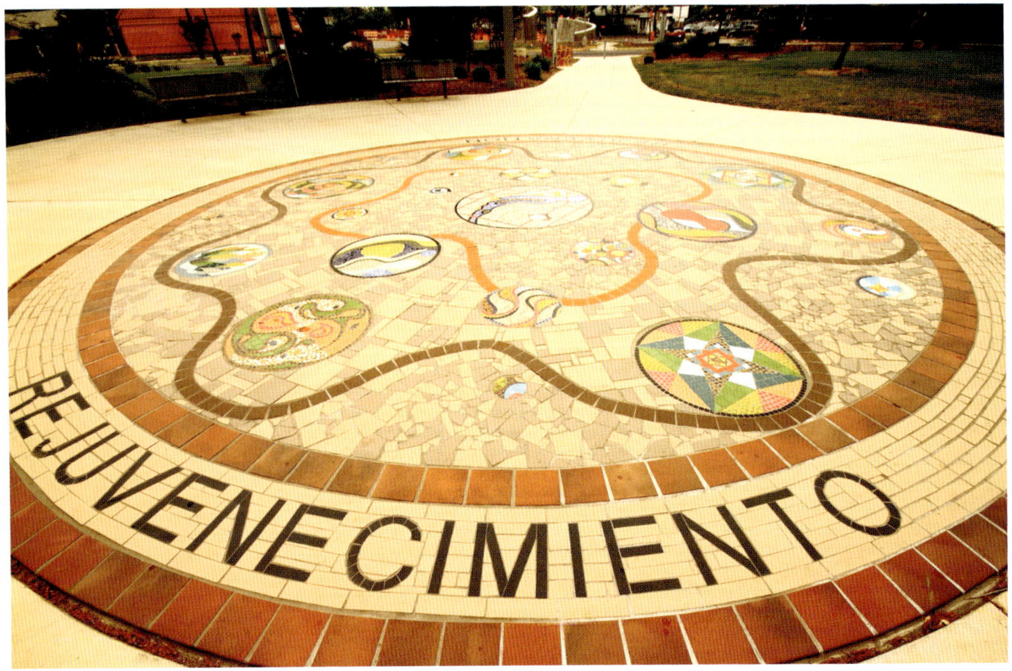

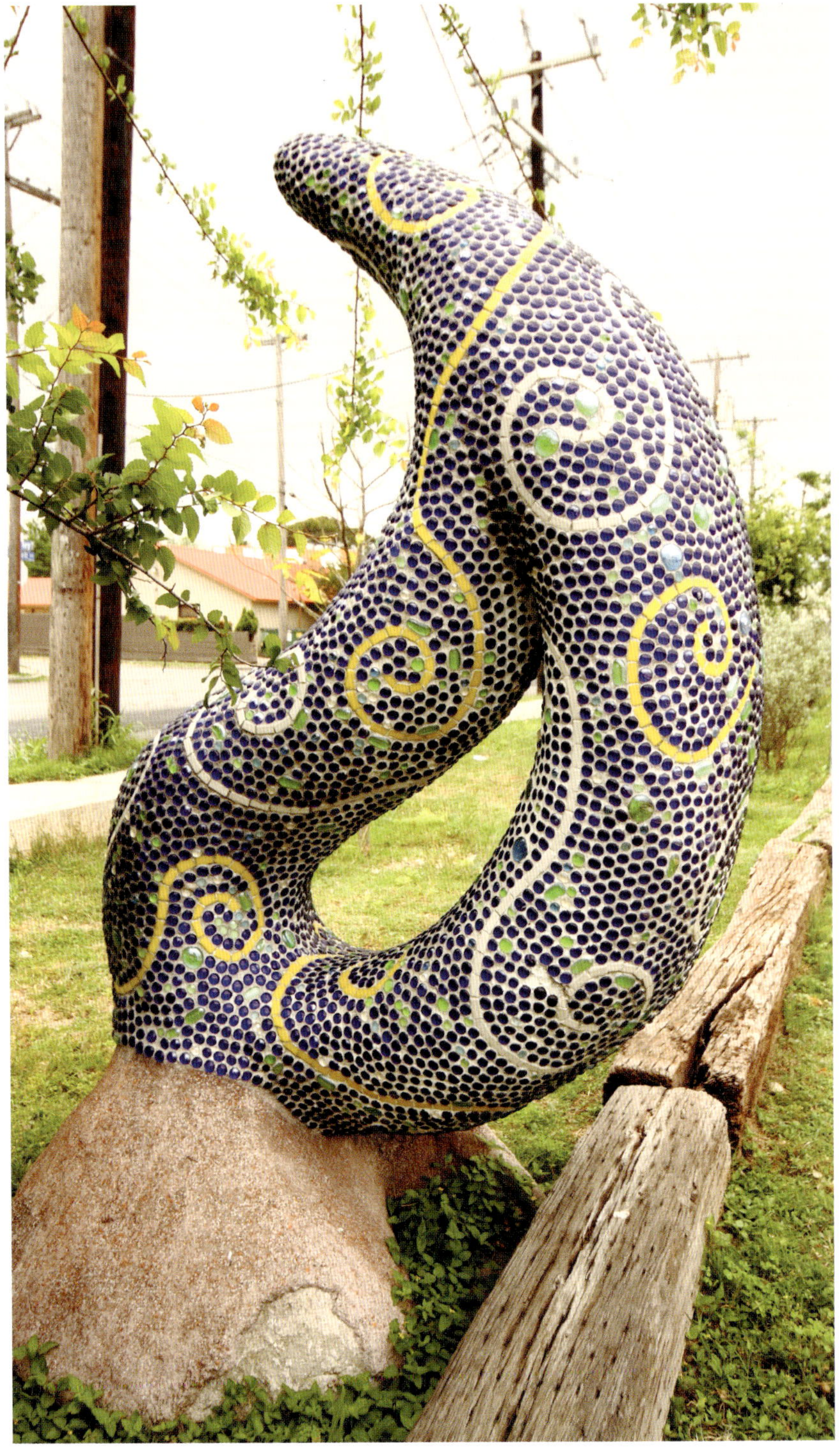

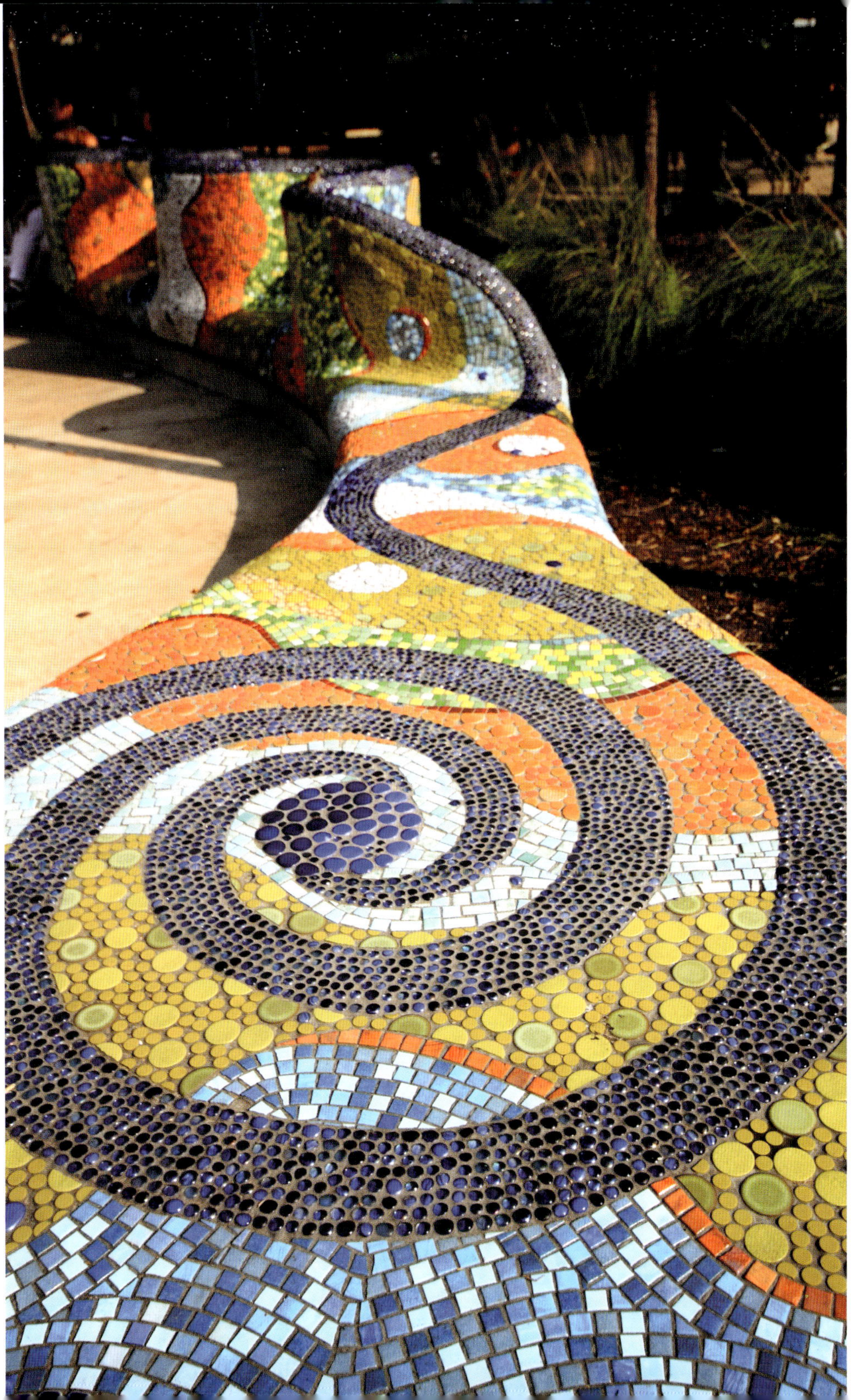

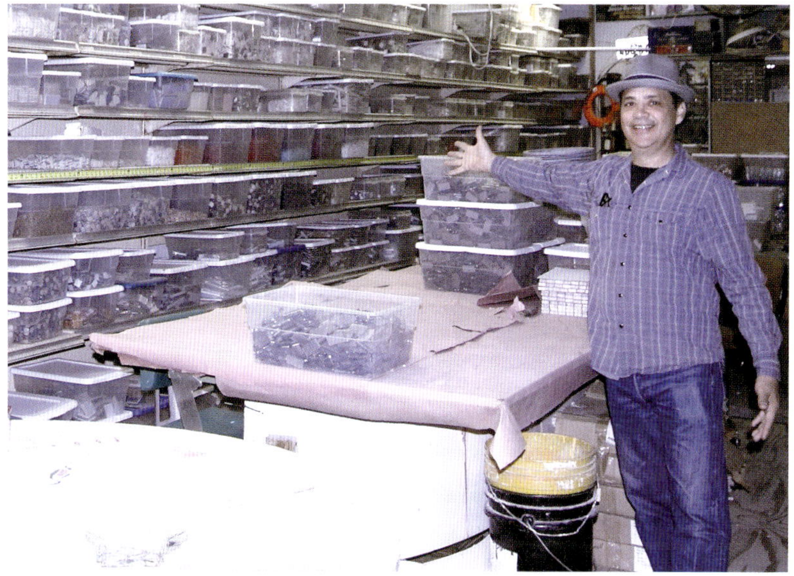

OSCAR ALVARADO

Oscar Alvarado started his mosaic art work by checking art books out of the library and "trying to reverse-engineer how they did it by staring at the images under a magnifying glass." His mosaic pieces now grace statues, benches, and walkways in city parks and shopping centers.

In Alvarado's *PanterAzul* (page 120) in Yanaguana Garden, the creation story of San Antonio takes form in a mosaic panther with a facial expression as mysterious as Mona Lisa's smile. From one angle the panther looks menacing, from another surprised, and from another, he is playfully smiling.

In Alvarado's work *Windows to Our Heritage*, part of the World Heritage Public Art Project, he embedded elegant tile pieces to frame muralist David Blancas's images of San Antonio people. The installation is just a few yards from Alvarado's studio. "I told the people on the committee, 'You gotta hire me. My studio's right here, and I'm just gonna hate going to work every day if I don't get this job.' My family has been here for 285 years. I'm a direct descendant of José Antonio Navarro. And so, I'm like, 'I have roots here, and I have proven my ability in my medium. So just give me the opportunity to decorate my part of the city.'" He has decorated not only his part of the city, but all parts of this city, and his solid tile works reflect his commitment to permanence. "I am committed to the 'thousand-year solution' of making art that is built to last."

LEFT
Pochycereus, 1984.
Sebastián. River Walk
Public Art Garden.

RIGHT
Nudo Torusado, 2014.
Sebastián. River Walk
Public Art Garden.

OPPOSITE PAGE
LEFT
Celosia Borunda, 2008.
Sebastián. River Walk
Public Art Garden.

RIGHT
Sebastián. Photo by Joel
Salcido. Courtesy of City
of San Antonio.

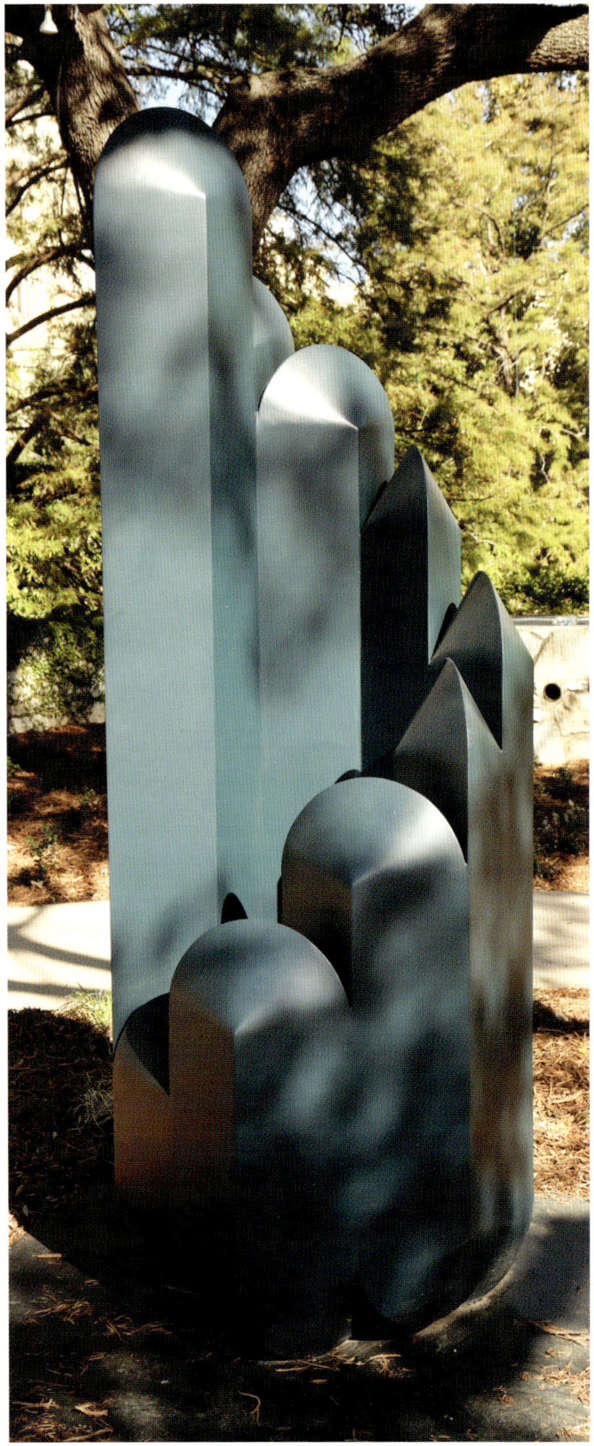

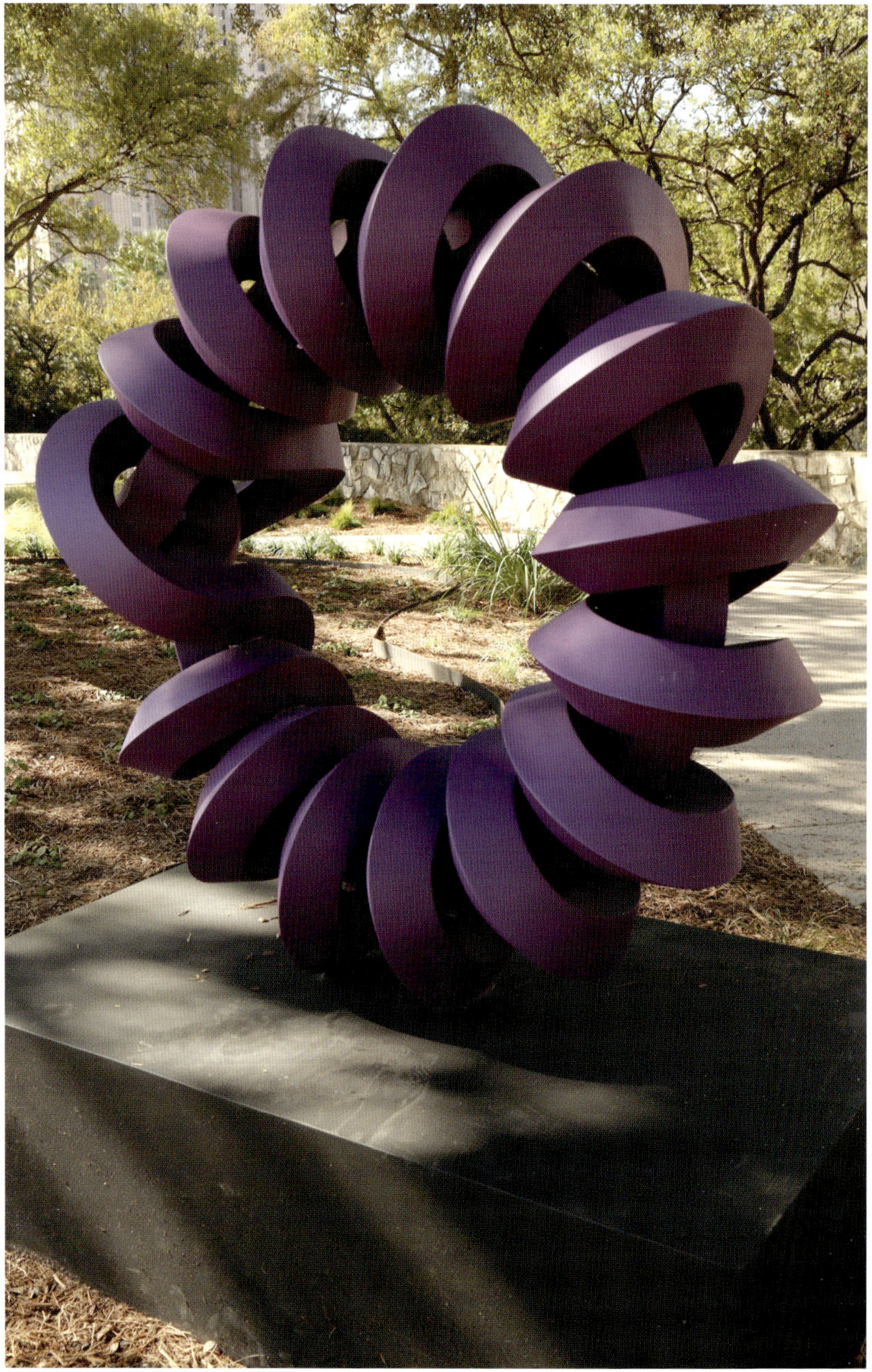

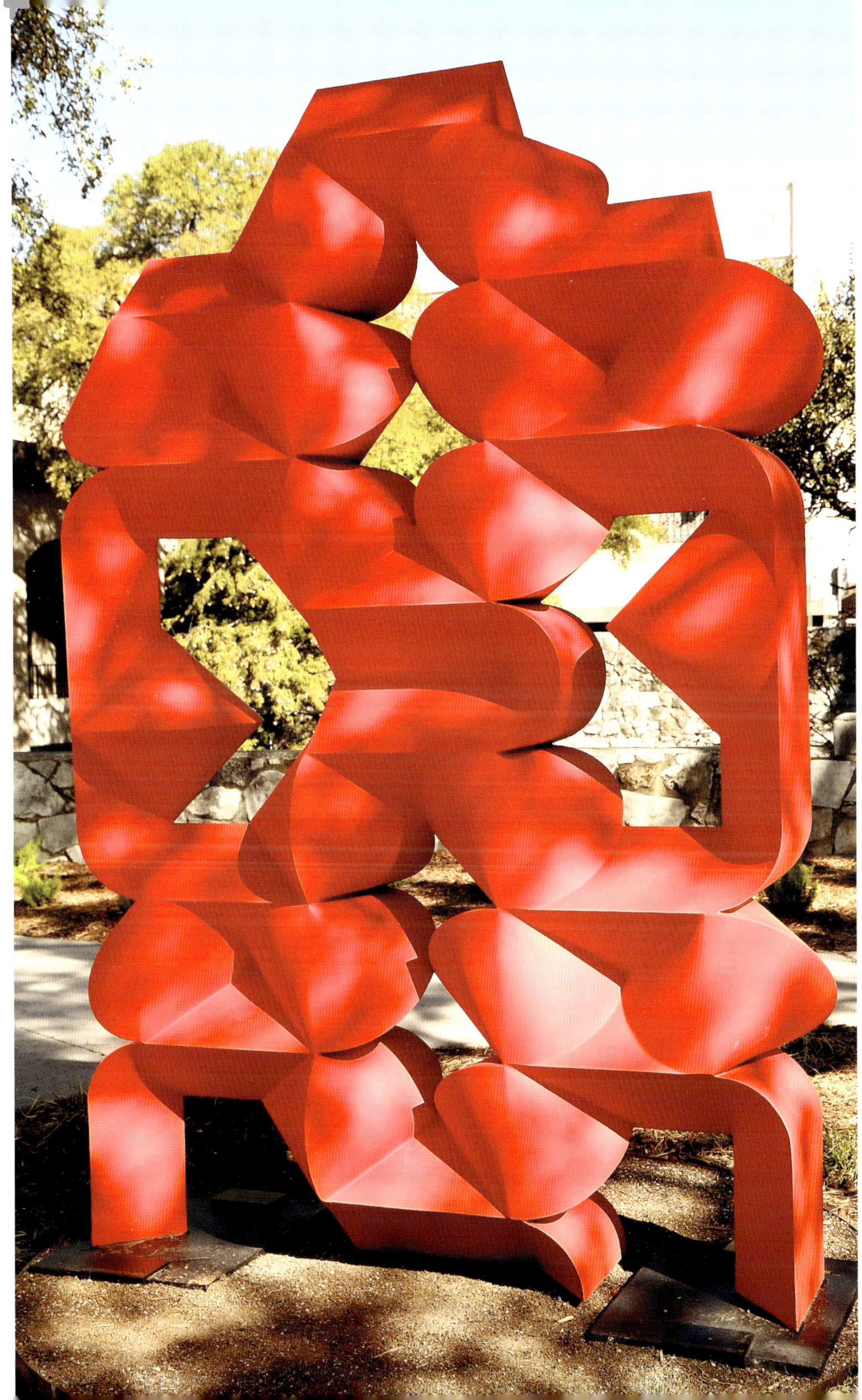

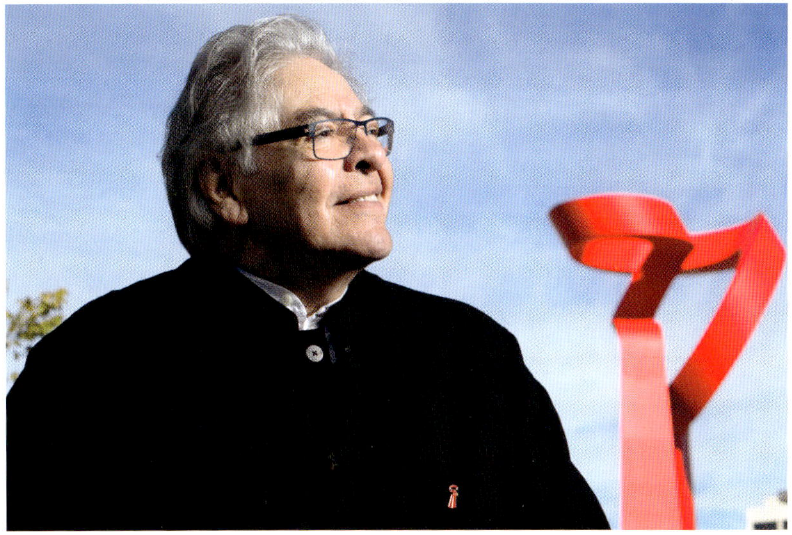

SEBASTIÁN

Sebastián has graced the spaces of his *segundo pueblo* (second city) with some of its most iconic works. His pieces marking the downtown area speak to the intertwining power of friendship: *Antorcha de la Amistad* (on this page in background and on page 32) at Losoya, Market, Alamo, and Commerce Streets in the heart of downtown, and the bold and beautiful *Door of Equality / Puerta de la Igualdad* (page 202) at the northern gateway to downtown.

Numerous Sebastián pieces sparkle across the city, but the massive *Door of Equality* holds special significance for this highly bilingual city. Side by side, the two 33-foot-tall cobalt-blue columns frame the library by day and capture the light of the city streets at night, declaring "Equality" boldly on one side, and "Igualdad" on the other.

A native of Mexico City, Sebastián affirms "el cariño tremendo a esta ciudad" (the great affection I have for this city). Upon gifting *Door of Equality* to the city, he said, "I want to donate it to San Antonio because I love San Antonio. San Antonio is my second home."

This landmark sculpture was gifted from Fundación Sebastián and Siempre to commemorate the city's rich civil and human rights history. Sebastián feels that *Door of Equality* holds a deeper meaning for the whole community and the world, as "a constant echo, a constant reminder" that we are all equal, "regardless of social stratum, race, and economic capacity."

ARTIST INDEX

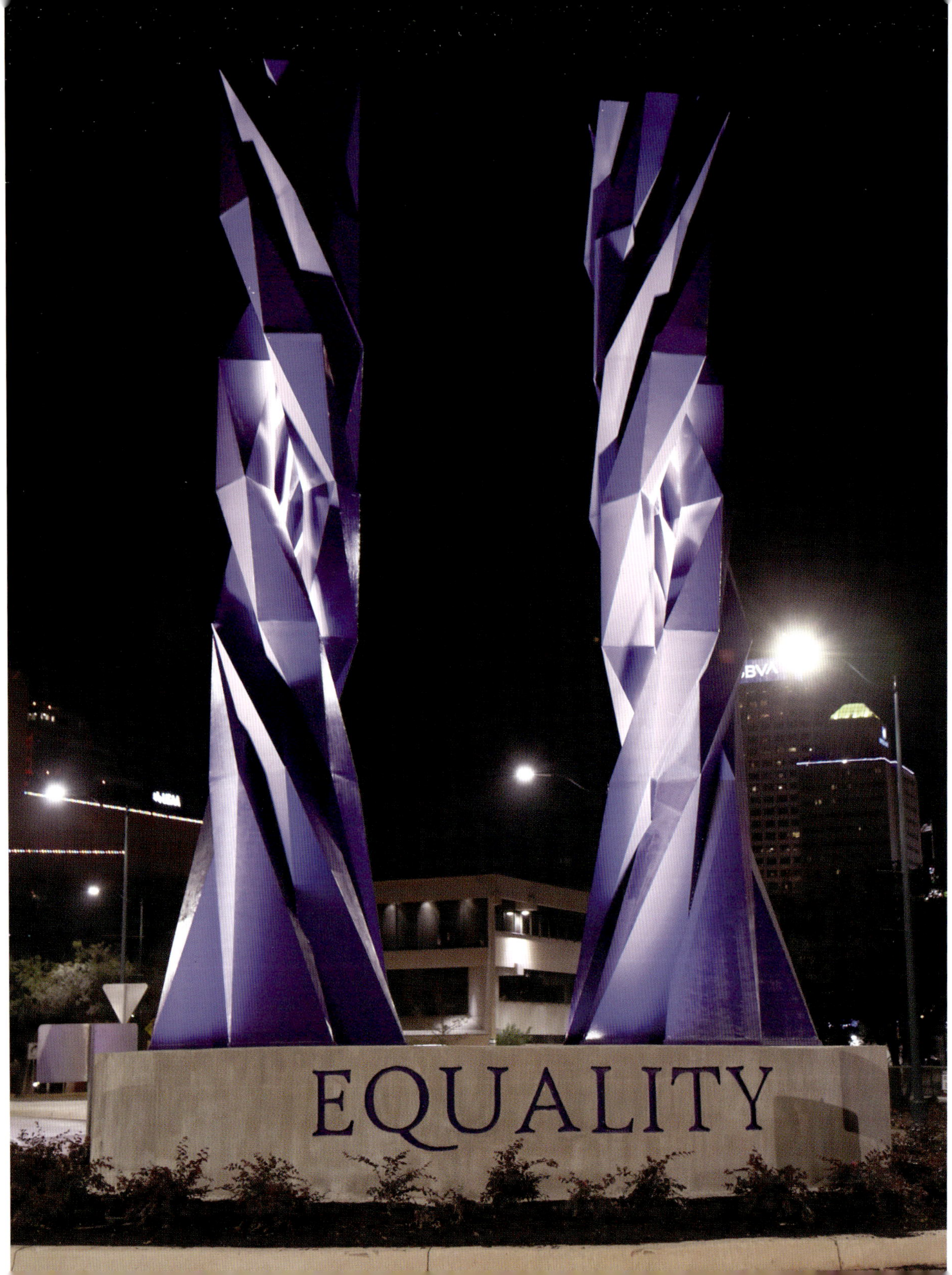

OPPOSITE PAGE
Door of Equality / La Puerta de Igualdad, 2020. Sebastián. On the side looking toward the San Antonio Public Library, "Equality" is stated boldly. On the reverse, facing from downtown northward, "Igualdad" is written in Spanish. Gifted to San Antonio by Fundación Sebastián and Siempre Mexico. San Pedro Avenue and N. Main Avenue roundabout.

NOTE

Where a nation appears within parentheses after an artist's name in the text or captions of this book, it indicates that the person noted was a visiting artist from that country, many of whom came during Luminaria or the Street Art & Graffiti events. Also, many of the murals are created in collaboration under a lead artist, and some involve students or other artists not listed. The early CCAO (Community Cultural Arts Organization), between 1979 and 1993, often involved students from Lanier High School and Rhodes Middle School, in the Cassiano Homes Art Projects, where more than 125 murals were painted, and San Anto Cultural Arts has typically involved more than 1,200 students a year since its inception in 1980. Three of the many young people who benefited from its programs are distinguished artists Adriana García, Alex Rubio, and 2015 State Visual Artist Vincent Valdez. Many who were involved in the creation of the murals in this book are not listed here, or they're unknown.

To map the location of these artworks and more, see the City of San Antonio's website map of public art: **www.getcreativesanantonio.com/Public-Art/Public-Artworks-Map**. We also suggest a leisurely tour along the River Walk, the Museum Reach, and some of San Antonio's great museums, where you could choose to spend an hour or a year.

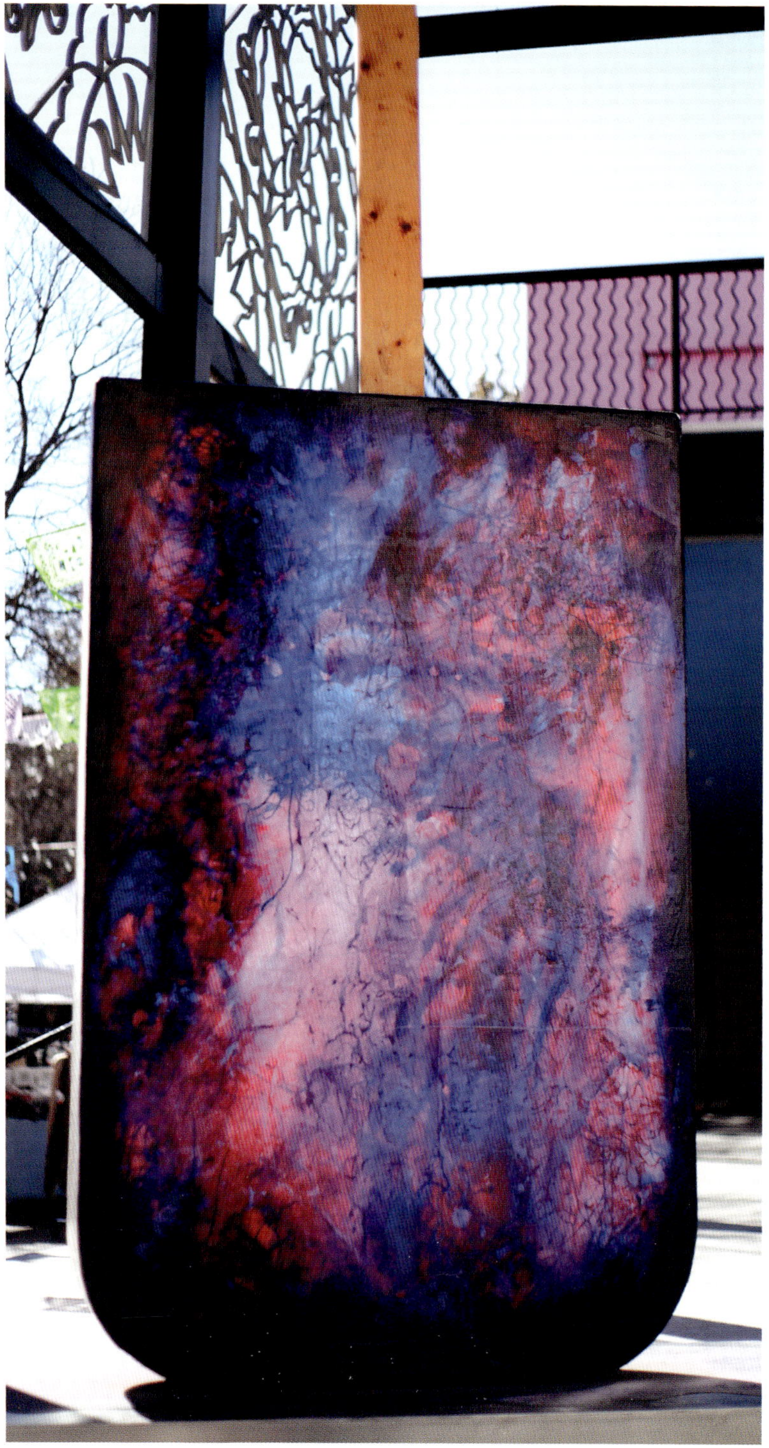

Sabor del Mercado–La Paleta, 2022. David Blancas. The flavor of Market Square is a juicy Mexican popsicle.

1. DOWNTOWN TOUR

Find these fourteen featured pieces and expect to run into some other unexpected art delights along the way. Downtown is packed with artistic treasures.

- *The Spirit of Healing*, by Jesse Treviño, at Christus Santa Rosa Children's Hospital
- San Pedro Creek Culture Park: artwork by Adriana García, Alex Rubio, and others
- *Sabor del Mercado–La Paleta*, by David Blancas, at Market Square
- Yanaguana Garden, including *PanterAzul* by Oscar Alvarado, *PLAYhouse* by Karen Mahaffy, and *My Home is Your Home* by Diana Calvillo de Chapa.
- *Citlali* (Stargazer) by Pedro Reyes, across from Riverwalk Shopping Center
- *And Yet We Bloom* by Kat Cadena on East Houston and Navarro Streets
- *The Last Parade* by Rudy "Cholotears" Herrera on Houston Street
- Tobin Center for the Performing Arts, Auditorium Circle (for sculptures by Jonas Perkins and Austin Deuel, and *Living in My Skin* interactive mural by Lionel Sosa)
- *Firstborn* sculpture at the Children's Museum on Broadway. (If you're traveling with children and want to end your day at the Children's Museum, the tree trunk chair on page 35 is inside the DoSeum's garden area. Call for info.)

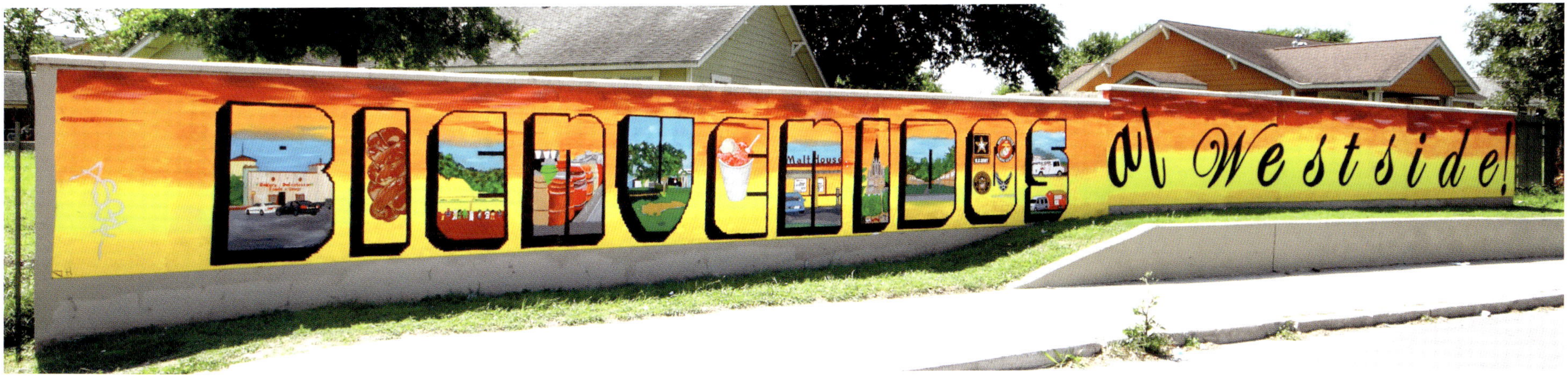

2. WEST SIDE CULTURAL ARTS TOUR

The West Side Neighborhoods have a long history of bold and richly cultural public art, many of them painted by community and students working collaboratively with distinguished masters of the arts. For more information on the San Anto Cultural Arts Mural Tours, see **www.sananto.org**.

- MujerArtes at Adobe Studio
- *Justicia* on Buena Vista Street
- *La Música de San Anto* on Colorado Street
- *You Are Not Forgotten* on Zarzamora Street
- *Velorio a la Virgen de Guadalupe*, Jesse Treviño
- *Nicho para la Virgen de Guadalupe*, Mary Agnes Rodríguez
- Elmendorf Lake Park, with *Mosaic Bench* by Oscar Alvarado and *Aguas Onduladas* by RDG Dahlquist

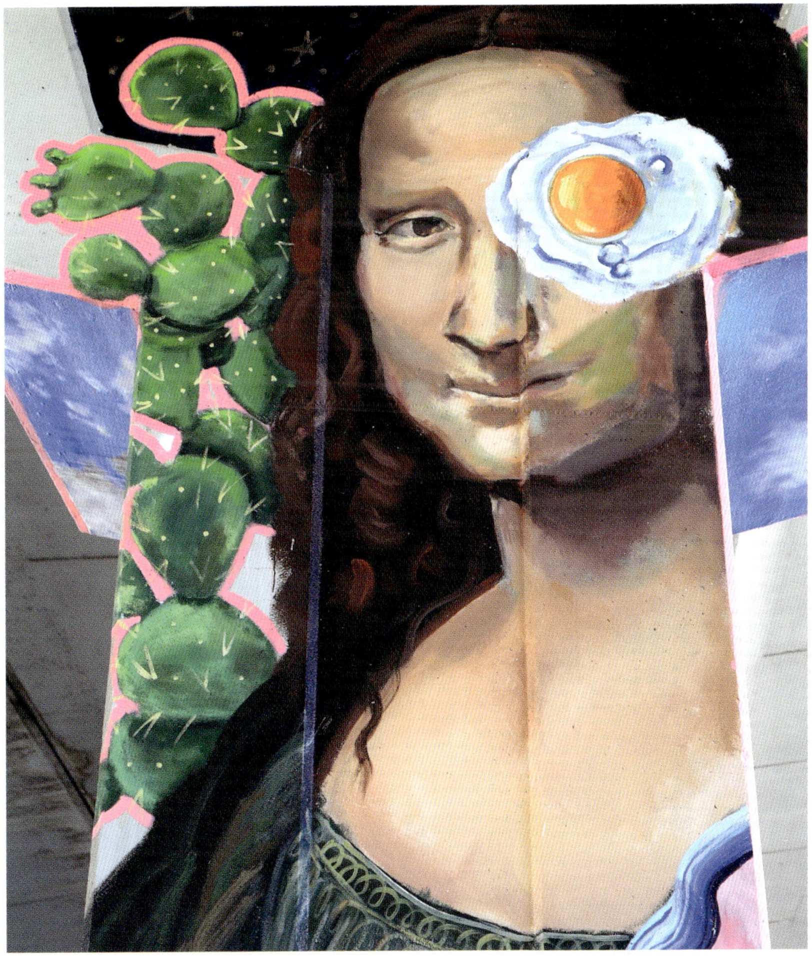

3. SAN ANTONIO STREET ART GALLERY

Sixteen artists created the largest outdoor gallery of street art along St. Mary's Street under the I-35 overpass (pages 138–139, 146–147, and 150).

TOP
Kaylee Diaz, 2018

LEFT
Ana Hernandez, 2018

GLOSSARY

agua: Water. *Aguas onduladas*—rippling water.

amor: Love

ánimo: An encouraged and encouraging spirit. An enthused mood.

aprecio: Appreciation

altares: Special altars made for seasonal or year-round remembrance of saints and the deceased, often in the home or patio and covered with candles, *milagros*, and prayer

arte: Art, as in arte del pueblo: art of the people

cadena: A chain

calavera: A skull, often sculpted in sugar to celebrate the Day of the Dead; satirical verse published in newspapers and flyers to make fun of public figures or friends

cálido: Warm

camino: A road or path

Canta y no llores, and life is for alegría: Sing and don't cry (popular phrase from the song "Cielito Lindo"), and life is for joy.

catrina: A female skeleton figure dressed in aristocratic turn-of-the-twentieth-century clothing, often used as a style for makeup, costumes, or giant puppets during Día de los Muertos. Originally created by José Guadalupe Posada and later painted and named by Diego Rivera in his murals. An iconic symbol of death, or of the Days of the Dead, it also speaks to the humor of Día de los Muertos and is a mockery of the self-important and the bourgeois or elitist.

Chicano: A term of proud self-identification for individuals in the United States of Mexican heritage, with strong ideological associations with the civil rights movements of the 1960s and 1970s. Chicana, the feminine form, often implies feminist or activist stances. "One is born a Mexican American, but one chooses to be a Chicano" — Gaspar Enríquez, artist. Also Chicanindio/Chicanindia, which emphasizes the Indigenous heritage of Chicanos, literally Chicano Indian.

cholo: A sometimes derogatory and classist term for Mexican Americans; a cultural mestizo or "half-breed," both Mexican and American. Associated with barrio culture.

cobijo: A shelter or refuge

codo a codo: Literally "elbow to elbow," side by side

corazón: Heart; for example, San Antonio de mi corazón, tu corazón es arte (San Antonio of my heart, your heart is art)

Con Safos: A term popularized during the 1940s Pachuco era, along with a Pachuco style of lettering, to protect their graffiti from being tampered with or dishonored

Día de los Muertos: Day of the Dead, a holiday celebrated on November 2, often in cemeteries, to honor deceased family members. It has transformed into a much-larger popular event with festivals, parades, and home altars. Based on Indigenous beliefs, during the Days of the Dead, the dead come back to visit loved ones.

dulce: Sweet. Pan dulce refers to Mexican pastries.

entre: Between, among

esperanza: Hope

faux bois: Artistic imitation of wood or wood grains in various media; French for "false wood." This style was popularized in San Antonio during the WPA, when Dionicio Rodríguez created many benches, park gazebos, and concrete art in this style, which is still carried on by his grandnephew, Carlos Cortez, and called *trabajo rústico* (rustic work).

herencia: Inheritance, legacy, cultural heritage

igualdad: Equality

justicia: Justice, equity

Justitia: In Roman mythology, the goddess of justice

lotería: Popular Mexican game similar to bingo that uses cards with images of characters or items, labeled in Spanish; modernized versions have been appearing; for example, Estar Guars (Star Wars).

luminarias: "Little lanterns"; group of small lights outlining a walkway or altar. Traditionally made with small brown paper bags filled with sand and a small burning candle. They have special relevance at Christmastime, representing the pathway to the manger. Often used for celebrations, it inspired the name for San Antonio's annual citywide celebration of artists, Luminaria.

máscara: A mask, often created as folk art for public celebrations and dances; may be wood, fabric, even ceramic

Mayahuel: In Aztec mythology, the female deity associated with the maguey plant, generally representing fertility and nourishment

mestizaje: A mixture of races; the term *mestizo* was originally used in Latin America and Mexico to mean a person who is half Indian and half Spanish, and it now refers to any blend of Spanish and Indian.

milagro: A miracle; also, a small religious charm representing a part of the body that is in pain or needs healing. Petitioners often pin one to a saint's altar, requesting help.

mujer: Woman; wife

muralismo: A philosophy popularized during the Mexican Revolution, emphasizing justice for all social classes and the belief that doors of opportunity should provide access for all to enjoy the benefits previously available only to the rich. By drawing large murals on public walls, art (and the education implicit in its message) could be shared with everyone regardless of their ability to afford to buy art or purchase entry to art galleries.

pachuco: Young man of Mexican heritage in the United States described as a wearer of zoot suits; active in night life, rock, and jazz. Originated in El Paso and Ciudad Juárez before becoming prominent in Los Angeles as an important part of teen Chicano culture in the 1950s. Sometimes stereotyped as gang members. Fem.: pachuca.

palapa: Outside gathering spot with a palm roof, often found in beach or tropical areas

pan dulce: Traditional Mexican pastries from *panaderías*, including a wide variety of pan de huevo, empanadas, marranitos, huesos, pan de polvo, campechanas, pan de muertos, etc., traditionally served on weekend mornings and special festivities

papel picado: Colorful paper with designs and images cut into it, used in festivities to drape from ceiling lights or veranda roofs, and to blow in the wind as decor

pedazos de arte, pedacitos del corazón: Pieces of art, tiny pieces of the heart

pueblo: Town or village, or the people of that village; often encompasses a much-broader sense of a community with common experiences and values. A people.

puerta: Door

rasquachismo: According to Dr. Tomás Ybarra-Frausto, a scholar of Chicano studies, this is a Chicano sensibility that transforms everyday objects into works of art and appreciates the beauty and practicality in the items that surround us, regardless of their monetary value. The term *rasquache* was commonly used to describe the sometimes falling-apart, jerry-rigged innovations of the poor. While many used it pejoratively, the love of rasquache art pervades the Chicano community and is evidenced in yard grottoes made from discarded cast-iron bathtubs or plastic kiddie pools, bottle cap earrings, coffee can flower pots, and curtains made from sewn-together flour sacks.

Raza Cósmica: Theory that the mixed race of people emerging in Latin America (Indigenous, European, and African) would create a new civilization focused on the shared essence of all peoples and their common destiny. Originally proposed by José Vasconcelos, Mexican secretary of education, in 1925.

rebozo: Traditional long shawl worn mostly by Mexican women for protection against the sun, chill, or dampness, and sometimes as a sling for an infant or goods; made of woven fabric (cotton, linen, wool, rayon, silk) with a pattern and fringe

rejuvenecimiento: Revitalization or modernization to recover the characteristics of youth—energy, strength, fresh ideas, exhilaration

respeto: Respect

sarape: Wool blanket created in northern Mexico during colonial times; often brightly multicolored and fringed at both ends

segundo pueblo: Second city; a second home

todo(s): All, everything, everyone

trabajo rústico: Work from rustic areas; often characterized as simple or coarse. Used by Carlos Cortez to describe his granduncle Dionisio Rodríguez's style of public art.

vaqueros: Cowboys

veladora: Votive candle in a tall glass container with a religious image, lit to ask for spiritual support or a special favor, and usually left burning at an altar for many days. Common *veladoras* (or *velas*) in the San Antonio area include Our Lady of Guadalupe (an Indian Virgin called Queen of the Americas and Protectoress of the Mexican people, and sharing many characteristics with the Aztec goddess Tonantzin), St. Jude (saint of desperate causes), St. Anthony (saint of lost things and desperate loves, and, of course, namesake for the city of San Antonio), San Martín de Porras (social justice and racial harmony), and St. Michael Archangel (law enforcement and military).

verdad: Truth

Yanaguana: Refreshing Waters, or Spirit Waters, the name given to the San Antonio River in prehistoric times by the Payaya people, whose village was in the geographical area that became Bexar County, the location of San Antonio. Also refers to the village itself and the people who lived there.

yerbería: Herbalist shop, primarily in Latino neighborhoods, that sells herbs, oils, pamphlets on herbs and health, votive candles, and other religious or spiritual items. The owners sometimes offer suggestions about herbal remedies or spiritual guidance. The term originates from the word *yerba/hierba*, Spanish for herb. Sometimes called a *botánica*.

Untitled, 2017.
Rick Havok.

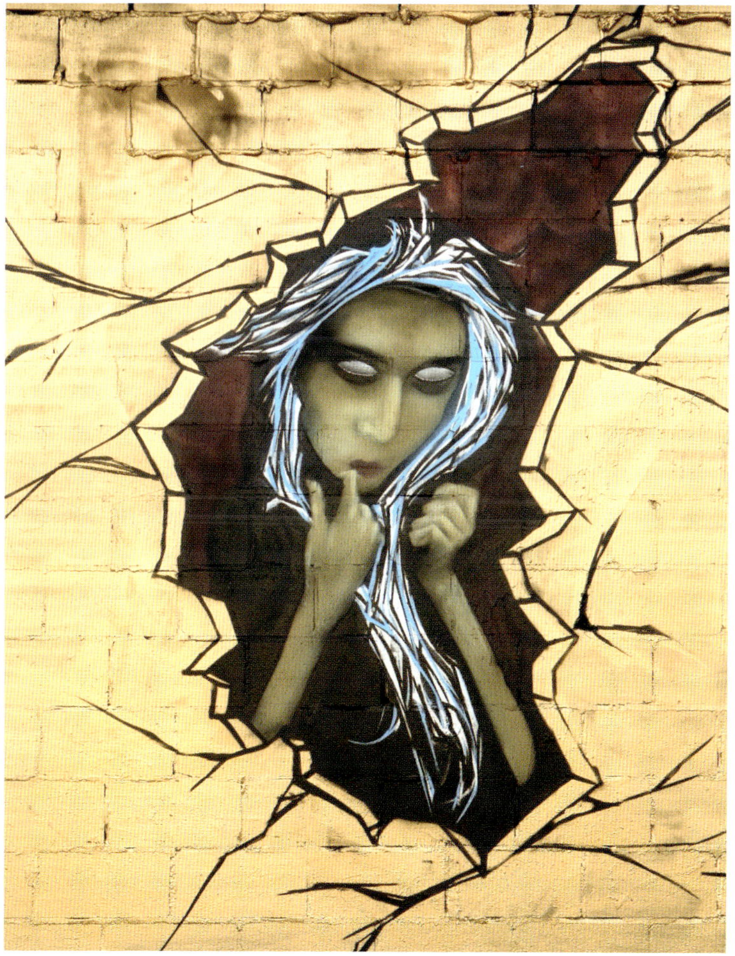

ABOUT THE AUTHORS

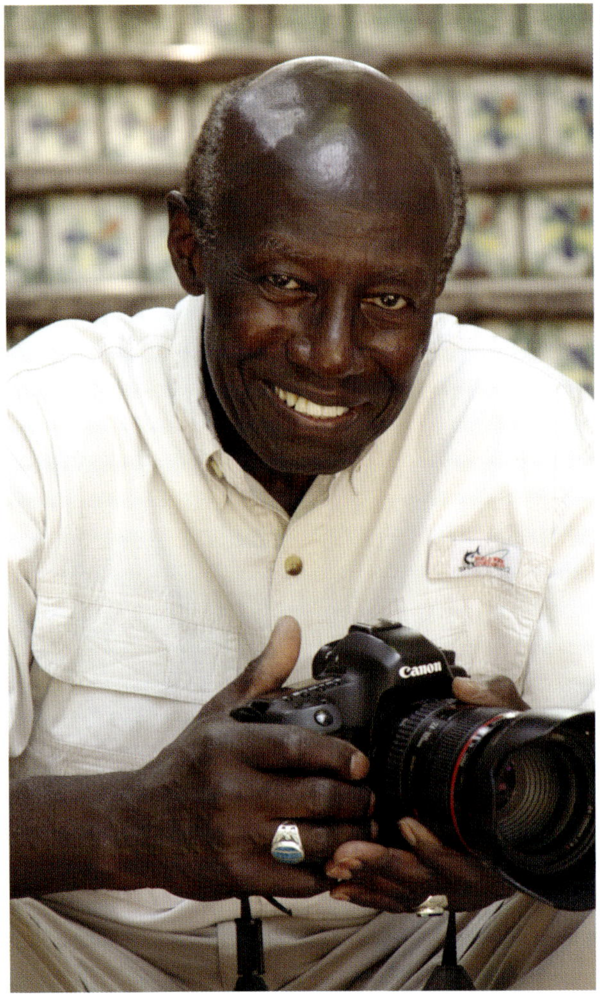

COURTESY OF LAURA NIKAS

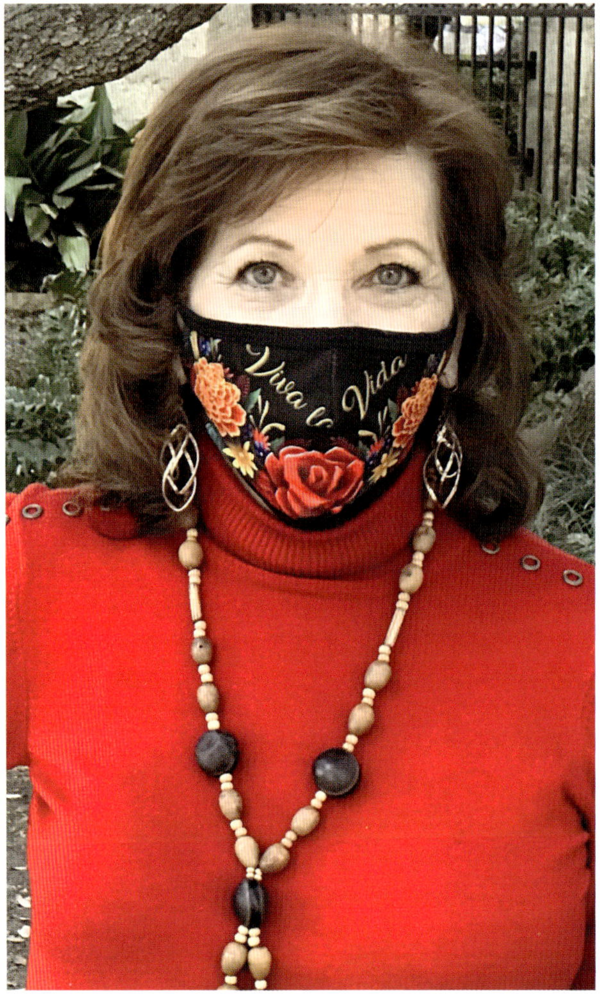

COURTESY OF JEN YAÑEZ-ALANIZ

DR. FREDERICK R. PRESTON, author of *Historic Doorways of San Antonio* (Schiffer Publishing, 2012), is a world-traveled photographer; a former vice president at the State University of New York, Stonybrook; and a volunteer golf coach for children and young teens at the First Tee at Brackenridge Park. He has photographed the landscapes of China, Vietnam, Ghana, Vienna, and Italy and has lived in San Antonio for more than seventeen years, where he volunteers for many arts organizations and for Big Brothers, Big Sisters.

DR. CARMEN TAFOLLA, State Poet Laureate of Texas (2015–16) and the first City Poet Laureate of San Antonio (2012–14), is the award-winning author of more than 30 books, including *The Holy Tortilla and a Pot of Beans*, *Rebozos*, and her latest book, a novel in verse, *Guerrera Warrior* (Penguin Books, 2023). A professor emerita of bicultural bilingual studies at the University of Texas–San Antonio and former president of the Texas Institute of Letters, Tafolla was born and raised in San Antonio, where her ancestors have lived for more than 300 years.

Untitled, 2016.
Los Dos. Luminaria.
Under Hays
Street bridge.